SECOND EDITION

Textiles and Apparel in the Global Economy

KITTY G. DICKERSON

University of Missouri-Columbia

Merrill, an imprint of
Prentice Hall
Englewood Cliffs, New Jersey
Columbus, Ohio
London   Sydney   Toronto   New Delhi
Tokyo   Singapore   Rio de Janeiro

LIBRARY OF CONGRESS
CATALOGING-IN-PUBLICATION DATA
Dickerson, Kitty G.
      Textiles and apparel in the global economy /
Kitty G. Dickerson.—2nd ed.
            p.   cm.
      Rev. ed. of: Textiles and apparel in the
international economy.
      Includes bibliographical references and
index.
      ISBN 0-02-329502-3
      1. Textile industry. 2. Clothing trade. 3.
International economic relations.   I. Dickerson,
Kitty G. Textiles and apparel in the international
economy. II. Title.
      HD9850.5.D53   1995
                                              94-19854
338.4'7677—dc20   CIP

Cover art: Mike Palumbo, Illustrated Alaskan
      Moose, Inc., 1994
Editor: Linda James Scharp
Production Editor: Mary Irvin
Photo Editor: Anne Vega
Text Designer: Susan Frankenberry
Cover Designer: Susan Frankenberry
Production Buyer: Patricia A. Tonneman
Electronic Text Management: Marilyn Wilson
      Phelps, Matthew Williams, Jane Lopez, Karen L.
      Bretz

This book was set in Zapf Calligraphic by Prentice-
Hall and was printed and bound by Book Press,
Inc., a Quebecor America Book Group Company.
The cover was printed by Phoenix Color Corp.

 © 1995 by Prentice-Hall, Inc.
A Simon & Schuster Company
Englewood Cliffs, New Jersey 07632

Earlier edition entitled *Textiles and Apparel in the
International Economy*, © 1991 by Macmillan Publishing Company.

Printed in the United States of America

10 9 8 7 6 5 4 3 2 1

ISBN: 0-02-329502-3

Prentice-Hall International (UK) Limited, *London*
Prentice-Hall of Australia Pty. Limited, *Sydney*
Prentice-Hall of Canada, Inc., *Toronto*
Prentice-Hall Hispanoamericana, S. A., *Mexico*
Prentice-Hall of India Private Limited, *New Delhi*
Prentice-Hall of Japan, Inc., *Tokyo*
Simon & Schuster Asia Pte. Ltd., *Singapore*
Editora Prentice-Hall do Brasil, Ltda., *Rio de Janeiro*

To Harman, Derek, Donya,
and to my mother, Virgie Gardner

ABOUT THE AUTHOR

Kitty G. Dickerson, Ph.D.

DR. DICKERSON is Professor and Department Chairman, Department of Textile and Apparel Management, University of Missouri–Columbia. Since the late 1970s, she has met with industry leaders, policymakers, and other scholars—at both the national and international levels—to gain insight into the complex issues associated with international trade, particularly related to the textile, apparel, and retailing industries. On numerous occasions, she has met in Geneva, Brussels, and Washington with policymakers representing various national and international organizations and most regions of the world. Additionally, she has had short-term experiences in a number of the countries and has been an invited participant to the World Economic Forum Industry Summit.

Dr. Dickerson was named a Fellow in the International Textile and Apparel Association; she has also served as president of that group.

She serves as Chairman of the Textile Economics Group of the Textile Institute, a worldwide organization of textile/apparel professionals. Dr. Dickerson was named to *Textile World's* "Top Ten Leaders" list. Her awards include the American Fiber Manufacturers Association Research Award, the Virginia Textile Award of Merit, and numerous others. She serves on the Board of Directors of Kellwood Company, a Fortune-500 firm, with both U.S. and international manufacturing and marketing operations in the apparel, textile home furnishings, and recreational camping softgoods industries. Dr. Dickerson has also had previous experience in retailing.

Additionally, Dr. Dickerson has published more than 65 articles in both scholarly and trade journals. Various academic and industry groups in the United States and in other countries have invited Dr. Dickerson to address those audiences.

PREFACE

Since publication of the first edition of this book, *Textiles and Apparel in the International Economy*, many changes have occurred to escalate globalization of the world economy and the softgoods industry. Hence, the title of this edition is changed to reflect the increased globalization that has occurred during this relatively short period of time.

World geography has changed as old alliances have fragmented and new countries have emerged. New trade relationships have emerged as trading blocs have formed in most regions of the globe. Under new production arrangements, we see products whose components and assembly represent many countries. Boundaries and barriers to trade have faded unlike any period in recent history. An era of new trade policies, with changes that are particularly significant for the softgoods industry, has begun. Communication systems have revolutionized the way in which we conduct business, facilitating global commerce with speed and efficiency unparalleled in human history.

Textiles and Apparel in the Global Economy addresses the rapidly changing global setting. The book considers globalization in terms of the implications for the softgoods industry and the players affected by these changes. In addition to providing an update on geo-political changes, formation of trade blocs, trade shifts, and the overhaul of trade policies, this edition includes a brief overview of the textile and apparel industries in major regions of the world. Discussion on the role of the textile complex in the economic development of nations and the chapter of trade theory have been expanded.

In a world of global interdependence, no industries are more broadly dispersed around the world than textiles and apparel. Just as the textile industry led the industrial revolution, textile and apparel production has been among the first sectors to be part of today's international division of labor. In a world riddled by trade problems, the textile and apparel industries have been in the forefront of significant shifts in production and trade.

The general purpose of this book is to provide an overview of the global textile and apparel industries and to consider the U.S. textile complex and the U.S. market within an international context. A primary goal is to encourage the reader to develop a global perspective as the book considers what is happening in these dynamic industries today. Virtually no aspect of the softgoods industry is unaffected by today's global activity. Additionally, I hope that readers will become increasingly sensitive to the fact that our global interdependence places on us responsibilities as global citizens as well.

For a number of years, I have followed the drama surrounding international shifts in the production and trade of textiles and apparel.

This book represents a distillation and synthesis of various perspectives based on considerable research and extensive contacts with industry and government leaders as well as other academicians at both national and international levels. Over time, these interactions have been with persons representing virtually all regions of the world. Although my views have been shaped by each of those visits and interviews, in the end, the book represents one person's judgment on what seemed appropriate for a broad, multidisciplinary look at textiles and apparel in the global economy. Reviewers helped in shaping views on relevant content.

Given the sensitive nature of textile and apparel trade, I have accepted the reality that no presentation of the material will be perceived by various interest groups as the final truth. Accepting that fact, this book is an attempt to present objectively the complex economic, political, and social dimensions of the global production and trade of textiles and apparel.

The book is not intended to be prescriptive. Since most aspects of textile and apparel trade have no one "right" answer, I have tried to avoid the pitfalls of prescribing remedies. A top priority in writing the book was to provide as much objectivity as possible. I represent no interest group. Yet, I understand the position of most interest groups and why they take the course of action they do. I have felt a responsibility to readers to attempt to present objectively the various perspectives and let readers arrive at their own conclusions on appropriate strategies or responses to global activity in these sectors. On occasion, I have identified areas of concern that may not be popular with certain interest groups, but I felt these perspectives were an important part of the total picture.

The book is intended to be used by students, individuals involved in various facets of the softgoods industry, policymakers, and others with an interest in the multiple dimensions of the textile and apparel industries in the global economy. The book is written for persons who have a basic working knowledge of textile and apparel terminology, either from professional experience or earlier studies.

In writing the first edition, my initial goal was to feature various regions of the world somewhat equally; however, by the time I had written the first three or four chapters, the enormity of my plan became all too evident. Constraints on length simply prohibited doing so to the degree I had intended. After all, entire books are written on the industry in specific countries or regions. In an effort to return to that original goal to a greater extent, this edition includes a new chapter that provides an overview of the textile complex in select regions of the world. Additionally, the overview of geographic regions has been updated and expanded. Another chapter expands on the textile complex in relation to overall development.

Emphasis is on concepts and a general understanding of the textile complex within a global perspective. Almost any approach for accomplishing this goal requires fairly extensive use of data. The reader is cautioned, however, that such an approach using data on textile and apparel production and trade has at least some inherent difficulties that go far beyond my capacity to resolve. For example, data are available in many different units (dollar value, square meter equivalents, pounds, etc.), and often it is not possible to find consistent measures. Different systems of collecting data create another problem. Data collected under one system are not directly comparable to those collected under another. Further, country groupings are not consistent among the international organizations involved in data collection and analysis. Additionally, political changes in various regions of the world—for example, the former Soviet bloc—have caused some international organizations to develop new country groupings for data analysis. Therefore, continuous data that are directly comparable over decades may not be available. Both the international and national offices that compile and use the data must live with this problem (and some of them have large staffs working on these data). Consequently, I have used data in the form in which they were available to me, but I have pointed out limitations of the measures or data at various points in the book.

And finally, I hope that the book will enhance the reader's appreciation of the vital importance of the global textile complex. The industry has shaped the economic and industrial history of the world. As the world's largest manufacturing employer, the textile complex has had a profound role in global economic development. In many instances, textile and apparel production and trade have redefined international political and social relationships. In short, no commercial sector other than agriculture has had a more significant impact on global economic, political, and social development.

A NOTE ON ORGANIZATION OF THE BOOK

Chapters are intended to be complete enough that they may be reasonably meaningful if read alone or if switched in order of study. Some subjects may be discussed more than once to make different points. As an example, the 1985, 1987, and 1990 U.S. textile bills are discussed in more than one chapter to illustrate various points such as (1) the growing power of the retailer/importer coalition and (2) the opposing efforts of various interest groups to influence policymakers.

ACKNOWLEDGMENTS

As I write these acknowledgments, I am reminded of the extent to which I am blessed by having a supportive family and many helpful colleagues. At the top of the list is my husband, Harman, who provides support, encouragement, and a great deal of tolerance when other tasks are left undone. More than that, he assumes many of those tasks. Our son, Derek, our daughter, Donya, and my mother, Virgie Gardner, have provided inspiration and support.

Many industry leaders and policymakers in the United States and abroad have provided valuable insight into the status of both the domestic and the international textile complex and an understanding of textile trade policies. Among them, Robert Shepherd, recently retired U.S. Minister-Counselor of Textiles in Geneva, played a particularly important role in opening doors to help expand my global understanding of the subject and in helping me keep up with changes at the global level. Similarly, Marcelo Raffaelli, Chairman, and Tripti Jenkins, Counselor and Assistant, of the Textiles Surveillance Body (TSB) under the General Agreement on Tariffs and Trade (GATT) in Geneva have been tremendously helpful in these efforts. I am especially grateful to Roslyn Jackson, Chief, Merchandise Trade Section in the Statistics and Information Systems Division at the GATT, who has played a particularly vital role in assisting with global data.

Dean Bea Smith has been supportive of the efforts required to complete the book and has exhibited faith and pride in its contributions. I am also indebted to the individuals in this country and abroad for the positive, reinforcing response to the first edition. These have included other educators, individuals in industry, and those in roles associated with developing and/or implementing national and international policies.

Dennis Murphy, who has provided most of the illustrations for the book, has added a delightful and vital dimension to the book. For each illustration, I have described the idea I wanted to convey and sometimes provided feeble sketches. For each, Dennis transformed my ideas into illustrations that give the message I wanted to tell, but with more creativity and wit than I could have imagined.

Three of my original reviewers still deserve special thanks for the help they provided. Their influence continues to carry through this edition. Sara Douglas, (University of Illinois), Margaret Rucker (University of California, Davis), and Linda Shelton (trade analyst at the U.S. International Trade Commission) were my "partners" in the enterprise. Each of them gave extensively of their time and expertise in reviewing the manuscript and offering helpful suggestions. All three have continued to be helpful on matters related to the book.

I am grateful to the following individuals for their review of portions of the book and/or the manuscript for the revised edition, and for their helpful comments, which were used to improve the revision:

Sanjoy Bagchi, Executive Director, International Textiles and Clothing Bureau, Geneva.

Eric Barry, President Canadian Textile Institute, Ottawa.

Sara Douglas, Associate Professor of Textiles and Apparel, University of Illinois.

Roslyn Jackson, Chief, Merchandise Trade Section in the Statistics and Information Systems Division of GATT, Geneva.

James Jacobsen, Executive Vice President, Kellwood Company, St. Louis.

Tripti Jenkins, Counselor and Assistant, Textiles Surveillance Body, GATT, Geneva.

Ron Levin, Director of the Office of Textiles and Apparel (OTEXA), International Trade Administration, U.S. Department of Commerce, Washington.

Marcelo Raffaelli, Chairman, Textiles Surveillance Body, GATT, Geneva.

Linda Shelton, Textile and Apparel Trade Analyst, Textile and Apparel Branch, Energy, Chemicals, and Textiles Division, U.S. International Trade Commission, Washington.

Robert Shepherd, U.S. Minister-Counselor of Textiles, Office of the U.S. Trade Representative, Geneva.

John Turnage, Vice President for Manufacturing and Sourcing, Kellwood Company, St. Louis.

Assistance from reviews of sections in the first edition is still significant for this revision. These individuals included Maury Bredahl, Rachel Dardis, Art Garel, Jean Hamilton, Elizabeth Jungk, Patrick McGowan, David Olson, Ernst Ott, Dennis Rudy, Robert Schooler, Robert Wallace, and Colon Washburn.

Note: The fact that the above individuals helped to review certain sections for accuracy does not imply their support of the views presented in those sections. Nor does this mean those individual have seen or support views presented elsewhere in the book.

Other reviewers, whose input was valuable: Dorothy Behling, Bowling Green State University; Rochelle Brunson, Southwest Texas State University; Jinger Eberspacher, Texas Tech University; Jana Hawley, Indiana University; Hazel O. Jackson, The Ohio State University; Linda Shelton, U.S. International Trade Commission; and LoErna Simpson, Oregon State University.

Others have contributed importantly to the book. A number of helpful anonymous reviewers chosen by the publisher provided feedback on the revision plan. Soyeon Shim, Mary Barry, and Marjorie Wall were contributing reviewers on portions of the first edition. Jana Hawley helped with computer graphics for a number of charts and other figures.

Funding from a variety of sources permitted visits with national and international policymakers and industry leaders. I am appreciative of funding support from the University of Missouri—Columbia Research Council, The University of Missouri Weldon Spring Fund, the Everett Dirksen Congressional Research Center, and the German Marshall Fund.

So many others contributed to the book in important ways that space does not permit acknowledging each individually. These include busy industry leaders, policymakers, and others who gave generously of their valuable time to share various perspectives important to the work. Similarly, many other helpful individuals provided data, illustrative materials, and other information. Of these, some of the most helpful were the staffs at the American Textile Manufacturers Institute (in particular, James Morrissey and David Link), the American Apparel Manufacturers Association, the Textiles and Apparel Branch at the U.S. International Trade Commission, the Office of Textiles and Apparel at the U.S. Department of Commerce (especially Sergio Botero), various GATT offices, the International Labour Office in Geneva, several U.N. offices, various EU Commission offices in Brussels, the office of the Coordination Committee for the Textile Industries in the European Community (COMITEXTIL) in Brussels, and Textiles Intelligence Limited in England.

Gracious hosts in many parts of the world have contributed to my education and appreciation for the cultures and perspectives of these regions. In particular, Huilan Wang, T. F. Ying, Willie Fung, Dr. Tan Chuan Cheng, Ir. H. Safioen, and Budi Danuwihardja helped me to have a better understanding of parts of Asia.

Finally, I am grateful to the Merrill staff for their valuable contributions and support. My former editor, Linda Sullivan, was a thoughtful and diligent facilitator who represented her company well to the field. From my production editor, Mary Irvin, I have appreciated sincere interest in my subject, a helpful, gracious spirit, and capable orchestration of the production of the book.

BRIEF TABLE OF CONTENTS

CONTENTS

3

The Setting—An Overview   44

4

Theoretical Perspectives   84

III

An Overview of the Global Textile and Apparel Industries   125

5

An Overview of the Global Textile Complex   126

6

The Textile Complex in Select Regions of the World   147

9

The U.S. Textile and Apparel Industries and Trade 268

V

"Managing" Textile and Apparel Trade in the Global Economy 317

10

Textile and Apparel Trade Policies 318

11

Structures for Facilitating and "Managing" Textile and Apparel Trade   375

VI

Balancing Conflicting Interests in Textile and Apparel Trade 407

12

The Interests of Industry and Labor in Textile and Apparel Trade 409

15
Policymakers and Textile/ Apparel Trade 519

VII
Conclusion 551

16
Conclusions: A Problem with No Answer 552

ACRONYMS AND ABBREVIATIONS

AAMA American Apparel Manufacturers Association

ACP African, Caribbean, and Pacific (countries)

AFMA American Fiber Manufacturers Association, Inc.

AFTA ASEAN Free Trade Area

APEC Asia Pacific Economic Cooperation Conference

ASEAN Association of Southeast Asian Nations

ATMI American Textile Manufacturers Institute

CAF Canadian Apparel Federation

CARICOM Caribbean Economic Community

CBI Caribbean Basin Initiative

CFTA Canada-U.S. Free Trade Agreement

CIS Commonwealth of Independent States

CITA Committee for the Implementation of Textile Agreements

CITT Canadian International Trade Tribunal

COMITEXTIL Coordination Committee for the Textile Industries in the European Economic Community

CTI Canadian Textile Institute

EAI Enterprise for the Americas Initiative

EC European Community (now European Union)

ECLA European Clothing Association

EEA European Economic Area

EFTA European Free Trade Association

EU European Union (formerly EC)

EURATEX European Apparel and Textile Organization

FTA Free Trade Area (or sometimes Free Trade Agreement)

GATT General Agreement on Tariffs and Trade

GSP Generalized System of Preferences

HS Harmonized System of Tariff Nomenclature

ILO International Labor Office

IMF International Monetary Fund

ITCB International Textiles and Clothing Bureau

LDC Less developed country (or lesser developed country)

LTA Long Term Arrangement Regarding International Trade in Cotton Textiles

MFA Multifiber Arrangement

MFN Most favored nation

MNC Multinational corporation

MTN Multilateral Trade Negotiations

NIC Newly industrialized country (or newly industrializing country)

NIEO New International Economic Order

NRF National Retail Federation

NTB Non-tariff barrier

OECD Organization for Economic Cooperation and Development

OTEXA Office of Textiles and Apparel (U.S. Department of Commerce)

QR Quick Response

QR Quota restraint

STA Short Term Arrangement Regarding International Trade in Cotton Textiles
TFC Textile Federation of Canada
TMB Textiles Monitoring Body
TNC Transnational corporation
UNCTAD United Nations Conference on Trade and Development

USITC United States International Trade Commission
USTR United States Trade Representative
VAT Value added tax
VER Voluntary export restraint
WTO World Trade Organization

I

Introduction

A primary goal of this book is to consider the textile and apparel industries in a global context. In Chapter 1, we consider globalization and global interdependence as realities of the world in which we function today. As we examine linkages between economies and the interconnectedness of nations, we become increasingly sensitive to the fact that a country's textile and apparel sectors are part of an international or global complex. Activities on one continent may have a profound impact on industries and workers in yet another part of the world. Moreover, all segments of the softgoods industry are affected by the global changes in textile and apparel production and trade.

In Chapter 1, we explore some of the developments that have fostered an increased interaction of the world's inhabitants. Furthermore, we consider how these changes have had an impact on the global textile complex.

In addition to providing key terms and concepts for the book, Chapter 1 describes how various disciplines help to provide insight into the complex study of textiles and apparel in the global economy. And, finally, the chapter includes a brief review of changes that have occurred in the global textile and apparel markets. This review helps to prepare the reader for the complexity of issues considered later in the book.

1

Textiles and Apparel as a Global Sector

Not long ago, globalization was a futuristic concept. Today, globalization is a reality. The interconnectedness of people and nations characterizes the modern world. Advances in communication and transportation systems provide linkages with people throughout the world to a degree unprecedented in history. Moreover, increased interaction has developed into a **global interdependence** of humans and nations. Our economic production and consumption, our national security, the quality of our environment, our health, and our general welfare have become surprisingly dependent on the world beyond our borders.

The Global Economy

Our global interdependence is clearly evident today in economics—the means by which the human family produces and distributes its wealth. We have moved to a "globalization" of the economy—in which we have shifted from self-sufficient national economies to an integrated system of worldwide production and distribution. The unit of economic analysis and policy is expanding from the national to the world economy. As we learn to think globally, we will find there is no room in our vocabulary for words such as *foreign*.

We can easily trace how we depend upon other parts of the world to provide many of the goods we consume daily, and we can think of how producers in other parts of the world are affected by our demand for their goods. Our global economic interdependence is far more complex, however, than this simple cause and effect relationship between consumer and producer. The global economy includes a web of linkages through which the actions of the actors in one system can have

Interdependence (global economic interdependence) refers to the situation in which all the world's nations are dependent on other nations for their economic well-being. Furthermore, countries are interconnected in such a way that one nation's actions affect other countries; similarly, that nation is affected by the actions of other countries.

consequences—often unexpected, unintended, and unknown—for actors in another system (Kniep, 1987). For example, a dramatic change in the stock market in one country has been shown to have a profound ripple effect on stock markets around the world; a change in currency exchange rates can cause dramatic shifts in where production takes place and how much products will cost; plant closings in one country may create jobs in other countries; and changes in consumer tastes can cause production to shift from one region of the world to another.

The United States is only one part of a much larger world—and a much larger world economy. Americans often forget that the United States represents roughly only 250 million persons in a world inhabited by more than 5.5 billion persons. Although the United States has a long history of participating in the international economy, we have become increasingly a part of the interdependent global economic system. Moreover, we are now increasingly dependent on that system. Our economy is dominated by what is happening globally.

As players in the global economy, we have unprecedented opportunities to interact with others in the human family, with whom we share a common destiny. The global economy offers challenges, too, as nations, firms, and individuals learn how to function on a larger scale and how to interact with persons of different races who may speak different languages. We see the emergence of a growing number of global companies (also called world corporations) whose executives conduct business with little regard for national boundaries. The global economy brings with it the advantages of varied products and lower relative prices due to differing costs of production in certain regions of the world. On the other hand, in countries such as the United States, firms are also discovering the increasing challenge of sharing their domestic market with producers in other countries.

A New Era Emerges

Political and economic events have changed the world in recent years at a pace that would have been unimaginable even a decade ago. Borders and barriers have been eliminated to bring the people of the world together as never before. The fall of the Iron Curtain freed the spirits of millions who had been isolated and bound by communism. Old economic and political systems were scrapped, with new ones launched on a painful road to change. Geographic boundaries were redrawn. New countries asserted their independence, expanding the number of nations recognized by the World Bank to about 200 (up from about 170 in only 4 years).

The European Community became a single market known as the European Union. North America became a single market. Asian countries formed cooperative trade agreements. Regional trade groupings began to form around the world. At the global level, we witnessed the most dramatic overhaul of world trade policies (including those affecting the softgoods industry) in recent history.

New trade liaisons have formed. Economic power through trade has replaced military power. Old barriers are fading. Globally, we are redrawing the lines of who buys what from whom and where. Technologies of a postindustrial era not only facilitate global business but also sometimes drive it.

Now, more than ever, companies, governments, and individuals must think globally. The removal of borders and barriers represents opportunities—but only for those willing to become informed, to think in global terms, and to take the risk to participate.

A GLOBAL PERSPECTIVE ON TEXTILES AND APPAREL

Not long ago, textile and apparel industries around the world constituted many independent sectors and independent markets. In many ways, today's textile and apparel industries are one global sector—with one global market. Although individual countries have their own textile and apparel industries, the complex production and marketing chain that produces and sells textile and apparel products is unquestionably an international business. Countries no longer operate these industries in isolation, but, rather, textile and apparel production and marketing activities are among the most dynamic in global commerce.

Not only does the textile complex serve the basic needs of humans around the world by providing clothing and other basic textile needs, but the textile and apparel industries also play a powerful role in sustaining life around the globe by employing masses of the world's peoples. Together, textile and apparel production is the *largest source of industrial employment in the world*, providing jobs for millions of persons. These industries play a particularly vital role in employing masses of persons who have few other job alternatives—both in the **developing countries** and generally in the **developed countries** as well.

As a vital sector in nearly every country of the world, textile and apparel production is dispersed around the globe. This global industry has both manufacturing operations and marketing centers throughout the world. National boundaries no longer confine production, and globalization has given birth to creative production options.

 EVIDENCE OF GROWING GLOBAL INTERDEPENDENCE

- Of all profits earned by the 500 companies in Standard & Poor's index in 1993, a staggering 45 percent now flows from operations in other countries (Raghavan, 1993).
- In 1990, over 7 million U.S. jobs resulted from merchandise exports. Additionally, workers in export industries generally earn above-average wages ("A New Way," 1990).
- In 1990, merchandise exports accounted for almost 90 percent of real GNP growth in the United States ("U.S. Trade Facts," 1991).
- The 23 largest U.S. banks derive about half their total earnings overseas (Council on International Educational Exchange, 1988).

FIGURE 1–1
Today's textile and apparel industry is an interconnected global production and distribution network.

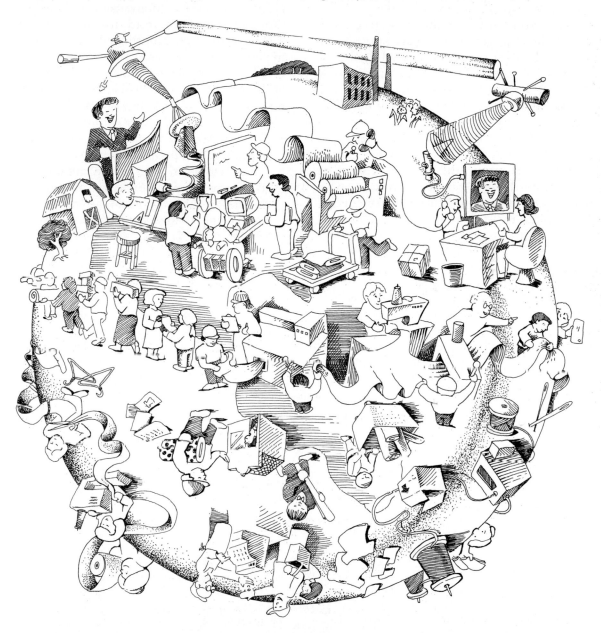

Source: Illustration by Dennis Murphy, based in part on a *Leviworld* graphic, adapted with permission by Levi Strauss & Co.

Often, production processes are interlinked on a worldwide scale. The resulting global production systems have made it increasingly difficult to identify products as either "foreign" or "domestic." Now, many of our products are **global products**—those which are the result of manufacturing operations in several different countries, as suggested in Figure 1–2. As an example, a Korean company may ship fabric made of Japanese fiber to the United States, where it is cut. Bundles of cut garments then may be sent to a sewing plant in Jamaica, which might be a joint venture between a Hong Kong corporation and a Jamaican corporation. After the garments are assembled, they are re-exported back to the U.S. market.

Virtually every nation in the world has at least a rudimentary textile and/or apparel industry to serve its domestic market, to provide employment, and to earn foreign exchange through exporting. Today, approximately 200 nations produce for the international textile/apparel market. Production occurs under an almost unbelievable range of conditions. Examples of the range of contrasts are

- From the sophisticated cities in the world to mud huts in poor developing countries
- From factories in quiet rural communities to refugee camps on the edges of some of the most troubled spots on the earth
- From highly trained textile scientists to child laborers who toil for long, grueling hours

FIGURE 1–2
A globalized textile and apparel sector produces "global products."

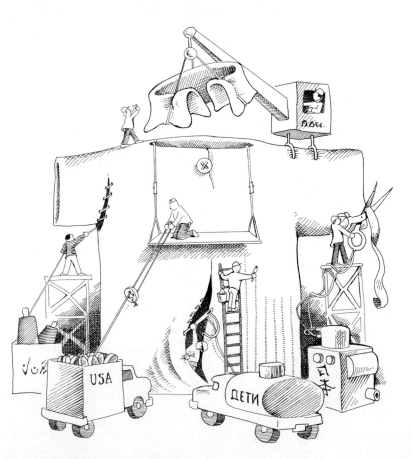

Source: Illustration by Dennis Murphy.

FIGURE 1–3
These Salvadorian refugees seeking asylum in Honduras learn to become self-supporting through textile and apparel-related work at a refugee camp.

Source: Photo by M. Vanappelghem, courtesy of United Nations High Commissioner for Refugees [UNHCR], Geneva.

- From state-of-the-art equipment to looms hand-fashioned from scrap, weathered wood
- From complex chemical fibers to cotton picked by hand and hauled by oxen
- From production of high-fashion garments in designer salons to assembly of clothing in makeshift alley shops in the slums of the poorest, most underdeveloped countries
- By polymer chemists to workers in their first industrial jobs
- By workers in lab coats, saris, veils, jeans, and tribal dress

Figures 1–3 to 1–6 depict the contrasting circumstances under which textile and apparel products are made.

The U.S. Textile and Apparel Industries Within the Global Economy

International trade (the exchange of goods and services among nations) has always influenced to some degree the U.S. textile and apparel industry. However, the U.S. industry focused on its domestic market in the past. Moreover, a limited number of other countries directed their textile and apparel products to U.S. markets. More recently, however, the proliferation and increased proficiency of textile and apparel producer nations around the world have changed dramatically the environment in which U.S. textile and apparel

FIGURE 1–4
A weaver inspects cloth as it is woven on state-of-the-art water jet weaving machines. The vehicle at left, called a "Prontow," is an example of a sophisticated computer-operated materials handling unit employed to reduce labor input.

Source: Photo courtesy of Burlington Industries, Inc.

FIGURE 1–5
This young Indian boy is preparing yarn for home weaving, using a spinning wheel he has devised from a bicycle wheel.

Source: Photo by Pittet, courtesy of International Labour Office (ILO), Geneva.

FIGURE 1–6

This young woman is threading the reed at a textile mill in England.

Source: Photo by J. Maillard, courtesy of International Labour Office, Geneva.

manufacturers—and all those individuals affiliated with the industry—must function. In short, *the globalization of production and marketing in textiles and apparel is the single most important phenomenon to reshape the softgoods industry in this century.*

Changes in global production in textiles and apparel and the resultant changes in the international market require that we now focus on the **world view**. We can no longer think of a purely domestic industry—or a domestic market. Virtually all aspects of the production and distribution of textile and apparel products in the United States have been affected profoundly by increased global activity in this sector. The same may be said for those firms and industry employees within nearly all nations who are now manufacturing and distributing textile and apparel products.

The U.S. textile and apparel industries now function as part of a **global economy**. U.S. manufacturers are part of this global economy, and even if they choose not to participate actively in international trade, they are affected nevertheless by activities in the world market. Manufacturers are competing for many of the same markets sought by producers in nearly 200 other countries. Industry workers are part of the worldwide sector and compete for jobs, often without knowing it, with workers from other countries around the world.

Similarly, retailers of textile and apparel products are affected by the proliferation of goods in a shrinking world—a world that seems smaller because of advanced communication and transportation linkages. Many merchandisers must also assume a global view as they scout the far corners of the globe for the selection of merchandise they deem appropriate for their stores. Choices have expanded for retailers—as an increasing number of the textile- and apparel-producing countries compete for their orders. As consumers choose from merchandise produced throughout the world, they, too, are part of this international economy.

To participate meaningfully in almost any aspect of the textile and apparel industry, individuals and companies must come to view themselves as part of a global community and as players in an international market. Participants in the textile and apparel sector no longer have a choice. To engage meaningfully, even at the domestic level, we must understand the broad scope and some of the complexities of the international market. Increasingly, textile and apparel industry leaders must have a global perspective—along with global skills—to function effectively in this competitive sector.

Reasons for the Shifts to a Global Perspective for Textiles and Apparel

Developments in the latter half of the twentieth century have thrust all of us who are involved in various aspects of the textile and apparel industry—from the largest, most powerful firms to the most unassuming con-

ARE WE PREPARED FOR GLOBAL PARTICIPATION?

If we are to participate effectively in an increasingly interdependent world, we must possess certain basic competencies. By and large, Americans are lacking in these competencies. In international contexts, U.S. citizens have been criticized for a lack of understanding of international events and our limited sensitivity to activities in the rest of the world. Examples of our shortfall in global competencies are the following:

- In a Gallup survey of adult geographic knowledge and skills in the United States and eight other countries, U.S. adults ranked seventh.
- In the same study, young American adults (age eighteen to twenty-four) knew the least about geography of any age group surveyed in any country.
- Another study found that Americans watching major television news programs under-

stood the major points of only one-third of the stories about events outside the United States (National Governors' Association, 1989).

- In an eight-nation survey on international current events, U.S. citizens scored seventh, followed only by Mexicans (In the Know, 1994).

Various U.S. leaders have begun to address our lack of global competencies (NGA, 1989). The American educational system must accept some of the responsibility for these shortcomings in global knowledge and skills. The NGA Task Force on International Education noted: "In educating students, the languages, cultures, values, traditions, and even the location of other nations are often ignored" (p.4). Unfortunately, in the past many economics courses and textbooks have focused on the U.S. economy as if it were a closed system, functioning in isolation from the

sumer—into a global arena. Among the most influential developments causing this change are

1. *Economic growth.* During periods of sustained global economic growth, such as that since World War II, trade between countries has tended to increase. Although fluctuations have occurred during this period, it has been a time of relative prosperity for many parts of the world. Trade is affected by changes in economic growth because (a) in periods of economic growth, consumers in many countries have had the means to purchase products from various parts of the world; (b) companies have been willing to add capacity to serve foreign markets when they believed sustained demand would occur; and (c) in general, fewer restrictions have been applied to imports when the economy has been

booming (for political reasons, textile products are often an exception to this point).

2. *The movement of many newly developing countries toward varying stages of economic development.* In recent decades, many of the developing countries have made concerted efforts to improve their economic status, and, more recently, this has involved export of manufactured products (apparel, for example) rather than commodities such as agricultural products and minerals. Textile and apparel production often has been a first industry for these countries as they have moved toward economic and industrial development. Apparel production in particular has been an attractive first industry. The amount of labor involved in manufacturing garments, the availability of low-cost labor, and the limited technology and capital requirements for

apparel production make this industry a natural first choice for these emerging countries.

3. *Increased global communication.* Communication technologies such as satellite transmissions and fiber optics have reduced the time and distance demands of international trade. These technologies have not only thrust us into the global era, but they also represent perhaps the most significant single dimension for exponential leaps ahead in this postindustrial era. Kobia, an executive with AT&T, noted: "Today, information is equivalent to the raw materials of the industrial age. The trade routes of the New World are made of hair-thin glass fibers. The cargo (information) moves across those routes as tiny pulses of light. The machines that process, switch, and transport cargo, like trading ships in the past, are today's critical assets" (Kabala, 1992, p. 42).

Advances in communication technologies mean that importers (individuals or companies who bring merchandise into a country) and exporters (individuals or firms who ship products to other countries) can conduct international business more quickly than ever before with individuals in various parts of the world. Prompt communication is particularly important for areas of the textile and apparel industry in which the timeliness of fashion is critical.

Several softgoods companies are using these advanced technologies in various ways in manufacturing, merchandising, marketing, and sales. Among these, Levi Strauss & Co.'s LeviWorld™ Network is a communication system that sends and receives information from LS&CO offices and locations around the globe. The system permits worldwide videoconferencing and electronically sending new patterns and fabric designs to LS&CO facilities around the world. The company's Levi-link electronic services system, which is connected with retail customers to replenish inventories quickly, is now connected to global retailers. J.C. Penney uses a form of videoconferencing to send sample informa-

tion to buying offices, headquarters, and offshore contractors rather than having to send a sample garment. Mast Industries, the design and purchasing arm of The Limited, Inc., provides videoconferencing for the company's buyers to view fashion lines in Hong Kong, Paris, Milan, or distant regions of the United States. The videoconferencing saves time and expensive buying trips. Wal-Mart Stores uses a variety of state-of-the-art communication technologies to facilitate its vast buying and distribution programs.

Additionally, the worldwide spread of electronic media has played a powerful role in stimulating demand in other parts of the world. As consumers around the world observe the lifestyles and the new fashion trends in other countries, markets become increasingly globalized.

4. *Easy access to most parts of the world through improved transportation systems.* The unprecedented ability to transport people and goods throughout the world has altered dramatically the world economy. As a result of improvements in global transportation systems, retail buyers can travel to any country in the world with relative ease to find products for their stores. Similarly, manufacturers may travel to various countries to promote the sale of their products in other countries or to establish production facilities in those areas. Improved transportation systems also make it possible for merchandise to be moved thousands of miles for sale in other countries. Because most textile and apparel products are relatively lightweight, these products are more easily and more economically transported than many products.

Transportation advances permit us to travel farther and faster than a decade or two ago. These advances, along with those in communications, have created a global community not even dreamed of when the United Nations was born. Transportation improvements have led to a shrinking world; Figure

FIGURE 1–7
"Global Shrinkage" resulting
from advances in transportation.

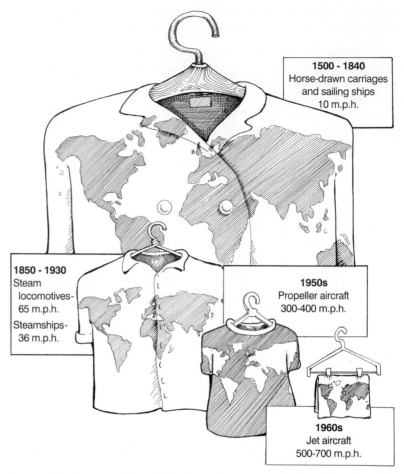

1500 - 1840
Horse-drawn carriages
and sailing ships
10 m.p.h.

1850 - 1930
Steam
 locomotives-
65 m.p.h.

Steamships-
36 m.p.h.

1950s
Propeller aircraft
300-400 m.p.h.

1960s
Jet aircraft
500-700 m.p.h.

Source: Illustration by Dennis Murphy. Information based on Dicken, 1992;
McHale, 1969.

1–7 depicts this concept to help us remember it in relation to the softgoods industry.

5. ***Institutional arrangements on the part of business and government.*** Various institutional innovations have made it possible for individuals and businesses in various countries to participate with moderate ease in international trade. These institutional arrangements facilitate both the exchange of goods and services and the transfer of payment for those goods and services. An important example is the development of basic rules and guidelines to establish order in international trade. Other examples of these arrangements include transfer of payments from one country to another rather than reliance on barter, conversion of payments from one country's currency to that of another, and procedures for clearing shipments from one country into another (port authorities, shipping visas, and so on).

To illustrate these institutional arrangements, consider that a U.S. retailer has purchased garments made in India. Among the arrangements that make this trade possible are the following: the existing rules for orderly trade between the two countries; the mechanisms for transferring payment from the U.S. retailer's bank to an Indian bank, with an accompanying conversion from U.S. dollars to Indian rupees; and finally, U.S. Customs Service operations that process the shipments of Indian garments so they may enter the country and be received by the retailer who ordered the merchandise.

In recent years, a combination of these five developments enhanced global trade. That is, the international economic climate fostered increased global production and distribution while improved communication and transportation systems, along with improved institutional arrangements, helped to facilitate this expansion.

Key Terms and Concepts

An understanding of several key terms and concepts is necessary to establish a common vocabulary to approach the study of textiles and apparel in the global economy. In the following chapters, important terms are printed in boldface when they are first introduced and explained and are then combined with their definitions in the Glossary at the end of each chapter.

Although new terms and concepts will be introduced in the manner described throughout the book, clarification of a few basic terms necessary for further discussion may be helpful here.

- The **textile complex**, as shown in Figure 1–8, refers to the industry chain from fiber, to fabric, through end uses of apparel, home furnishings, and industrial products.
- The term **textile sector** has two common interpretations—which at times can be confusing. (1) Often the term is used in a comprehensive sense (synonymous with *textile complex*) to include all aspects of textile and apparel production from the fiber stage to completed end-use products. Typically, trade officials use the term in this manner and even shorten it to *textiles* in references

to the comprehensive sector. In this usage, trade sources might say, "Textiles poses special problems in world trade." (Often this form suggests difficulty with grammar if one is unfamiliar with this usage!) (2) The term is also used for the portion of the industry that produces "textiles" in a more limited sense, that is, the segment that manufactures fibers, yarns, fabrics, and select finished products. Except for certain knitwear, use of the term in this manner usually does not include apparel. Generally, in this book, the term *textile sector* will be used in the latter manner. An exception will be in discussions related to trade policies, in which the working language—e.g., "textile policies"—includes policies for the entire complex.
- References to the **textile industry** may also have the same double meaning mentioned earlier. However, this term more commonly refers to the fiber-to-fabric segment of the industry in the more narrow sense.
- References to the **apparel industry** are less confusing. This term applies only to the industry segment involved in the manufacture of garments and certain accessories.
- The **sewn products industry** includes all stages of apparel production and, in addition, includes a number of other sewn product categories such as interior furnishings items (such as draperies and linens), luggage, awnings, and sewn toys.
- The terms **softgoods chain** and **softgoods industry** are the most comprehensive given here. Each of these terms includes the manufacture of textile or apparel products from the fiber stage through completion of end-use products and, in addition, includes the retailing or other distribution phases associated with making the products available to the consumer.
- **Upstream activities** refer to those processes in the early stages of the manufacturing/distribution chain. These include specialized suppliers of the inputs

FIGURE 1–8
The textile complex.

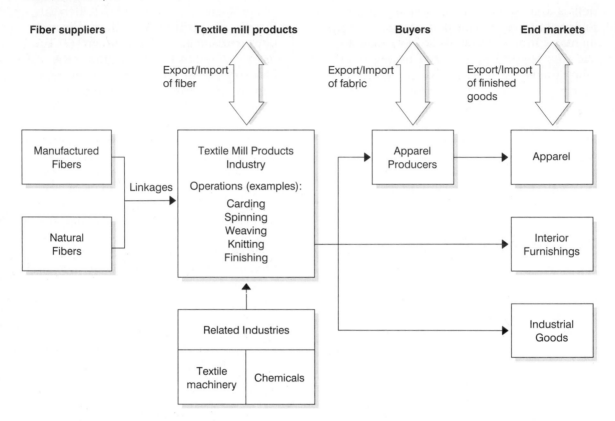

From The Global Textile Industry (p. 9) by B. Toyne, J. Arpan, A. Barnett, D. Ricks, and T. Shimp, 1984, London: George Allen & Unwin. Copyright 1984 by Unwin Hyman. Adapted with permission.)

for production—for example, fibers, textile machinery, and dyestuffs.

- **Downstream activities** refer to those processes further along in the manufacturing/distribution chain. These include the wholesale and retail trade, as examples.
- **Intermediate inputs,** for our purposes, are the textile components used in producing finished or more nearly finished goods. These include the fibers, yarns, and fabrics sold to producers at the next stage of the production chain.
- **International activities** (production, trade, marketing, etc.) are those that occur in interaction with others outside the home

base country. Although the terms *international* and *global* are used interchangeably, many sources consider *international* to be more limited (*inter-* means *between*). Although international activities involve interaction related to other countries, these may be fewer in number and may be limited, for example, to a firm's own regional trading bloc. Some interpretations consider international firms to be those that operate entirely from a home base.

- **Global activities** are generally considered to be much more encompassing than "international" ones in terms of geographic spread (if we think of *inter-* as *between,* *global* might be considered *among*). Global activities are likely to include countries beyond the firm's own regional trading bloc and may be worldwide. *Global* may also reflect a different way of thinking in which there is not a "headquarters mentality" that may exist in an international firm.

- **Global products** are those that are the result of manufacturing, and sometimes marketing, operations in several different countries.
- **Microeconomics** is the study of individual behavior in the economy and of the components of the larger economy. Thus, a microperspective refers to a focus on the individual units—for example, the consumer, an individual nation, or a specific sector treated as a single unit participating in the economy.[1]
- **Macroeconomics** is the study of aggregate economic behavior, that is, of the economy as a whole. Thus, a macroperspective refers to a focus on the aggregate or the whole, such as the global impact of a particular trade policy on all countries involved in textile and apparel trade. Schiller (1983) compares macroeconomics to looking at a completed puzzle; microeconomics focuses on each of the pieces.
- The terms **developed** and **developing countries** are common means of describing and classifying nations according to their levels of economic and industrial development. **Developed countries** are the more industrially advanced and prosperous countries in which a higher level of living is common. **Developing countries** are limited in their economic progress and may have little or no industrial development; these

are typically the poorer countries. A third group of countries, the **newly industrialized countries (NICs)**, are former developing countries that have progressed to more advanced levels of economic and industrial development; the NICs have become proficient exporters of manufactured goods. Country groupings will be discussed in greater detail in a later chapter.

- **Imports** are intermediate and final goods and services purchased from other countries.
- **Exports** are intermediate and final goods and services produced within the home country and sold to other nations.

AN INTERDISCIPLINARY PERSPECTIVE

A study of textiles and apparel in the international economy draws upon the contributions of a number of academic disciplines to understand the issues involved. That is, the insight provided by various disciplines provides an interdisciplinary perspective. Relevant disciplines include economics, geography, history, sociology, political science, anthropology, and certain functional business fields such as marketing, management, and finance. A fundamental grasp of some of the theories and concepts from these disciplines can help in understanding the complexities of global textile trade. Several relevant theories will be presented later, but at this point, a brief review of the contributions of these fields may be helpful:

- *Economics* provides theory that explains why nations exchange goods and services with one another, and some of the analytic techniques provide ways of determining the impact of trade and trade policies.
- *Geography* provides helpful perspectives on the location and type of the world's resources and their availability for use by

---

[1]Although a microeconomic perspective may commonly focus on an individual, a household, or a firm as an appropriate unit of analysis, in international trade, an individual nation or a specific sector might be treated as a single unit (Salvatore, 1987).

individuals or industries. For example, the study of the distribution of the world's population is particularly relevant to the global textile sector as an employer.

- *History* permits us to review the past in systematic ways to better understand the present. As an example, an awareness of the historical development of the textile industry as a leader in a number of global industrial movements may give us a greater appreciation of this sector. Or, in a more specific example, an understanding of early textile trade policies helps us to understand current policy.

- *Sociology* provides theories of development and social change that may help us understand issues of social stratification, the distribution of power, and international relations. An awareness of these changing international forces is relevant to the study of the production and trade shifts for the textile complex within a global economy.

- *Political science* provides an objective study of governmental institutions and processes and how these may determine the business environment in various countries and at the global level. As an example, a political science perspective is helpful in analyzing the influence of special interest groups on the development and implementation of textile trade policies.

- *Anthropology* aids in understanding and appreciating the differences in cultural environments in various parts of the world. Sensitivity to cultural differences is vital to functioning effectively in the global economy.

- *Business areas* help us to understand the specific applications needed to operationalize global production and distribution of textile and apparel products. For example, a study of international marketing provides expertise to promote products differently from one country to another.

A BRIEF REVIEW OF CHANGES IN GLOBAL TEXTILE AND APPAREL MARKETS

Since the early development of a domestic industry, U.S. textile producers have considered foreign competition a threat. The degree of concern has vacillated from time to time. In the twentieth century, however, U.S. textile and apparel manufacturers experienced remarkably little *serious* competition from producers in other nations until the 1950s. Manufacturers had the luxury of directing their products toward a receptive, and nearly captive, domestic market. Because of the vast size of the U.S. market, the country's textile and apparel manufacturers found ready markets for the products they made. The industry enjoyed relative prosperity, and most companies saw little reason to become involved in international activities or to be concerned about a global perspective.

In the 1950s and 1960s, however, significant changes affected the global environment for the textile and apparel sector. In contrast to earlier years when a relatively limited number of countries manufactured textile and apparel products for world markets, several nations—particularly those in Southeast Asia—became proficient producers. Many of these countries developed their textile and apparel industries as primary export sectors for economic development. That is, these countries directed their resources and efforts to building textile and/or apparel industries that could produce goods to sell to other parts of the world. Payments received for those products contributed importantly to the economic advancement of those countries. By the 1950s, U.S. textile and apparel manufacturers began to feel the impact of increased international activity in the sector.

In the last two decades, the number of producers for world markets has increased greatly, with nearly every nation competing for market share. Although the number of new producers for world markets has escalated, the industry remains a top employer in the developed countries. In both the United States and the European Union, for example, the textile complex employs nearly one of every ten manufacturing workers, (COMI-TEXTIL, 1992b; U.S. Department of Commerce, *U.S. Industrial Outlook*, various years). Consequently, as developing countries gain an increasing share of the world market, the industrialized countries face major adjustment problems as they attempt to maintain employment of large work forces dependent upon this sector.

In recent years, the growth in the number of textile- and apparel-producing nations around the globe has changed dramatically the climate for producers everywhere. Excessive production capacity has fostered intense competition. Because of the greatly increased competition among nations for market share, world trade in textiles has become sensitive and volatile. Many political and social issues accompany the economic concerns as developing countries and industrialized nations attempt to resolve the excessive production capacity. Determining who can export textile and apparel products to whom and who will import these products from whom, and to what extent, engenders the following concerns, as depicted in Figure 1–9:

- *Economic concerns* Which nation's economy should gain at another's expense? To what extent can U.S. policymakers justify trade policies or other legislation to shield the large domestic textile and apparel industry from the impact of increasing imports? To what extent do the developed countries have an obligation to assist developing nations in their economic growth? These questions are further complicated by the need to balance sectoral interests; for example, if textile and apparel imports are

FIGURE 1–9
Many economic, political, and social concerns are involved in resolving issues related to producing textile and apparel products for global markets.

restricted, will foreign governments retaliate in ways that affect other sectors, such as agriculture?

- *Political concerns* How will opening or restricting the markets of the developed countries to textile and apparel imports affect broad political relationships with the exporting countries? How can the political pressure of a particular sector be coordinated with concerns for political goodwill with other nations? Does some other political agenda determine the volume of imports to be accepted from a country or region? As an example, the U.S. government has supported programs to develop apparel production in Latin America in an effort to reduce civil unrest and to increase political stability.
- *Social concerns* As a global industry that employs in production jobs persons with few gainful employment alternatives, which nation's workers in which sector should lose at the expense of others?

Should workers in France or the United States give up their jobs so that individuals in the Philippines or Nepal can be employed? If so, to which jobs should the displaced workers turn? Alternative jobs for both these groups of workers may be limited. Consequently, global textile and apparel production and trade involve complex global social concerns as well as those within specific countries.

From any perspective, textile trade has become a difficult segment of global commerce. National economies, international political relationships, and workers' lives depend upon policymakers' ability to resolve the problems caused by excessive production capacity within a limited global textile market.

The U.S. textile and apparel industries have experienced increasing competition in the international marketplace for more than three decades—longer than most other U.S. industries that are now facing similar competition. In this sense, the trade problems of the textile and apparel industries have been forerunners of similar difficulties that followed for other sectors. Just as they fostered economic development historically, textile and apparel producers are in the front line of today's changes in the global economy.

ORGANIZATION OF THE BOOK

This book provides a global focus, at both the micro- and macrolevels, of the textile and apparel industries. Special attention is given to the U.S. sectors within the context of the international economy.

Chapter 2 provides a historical perspective on the development of both the global and the U.S. textile and apparel industries. Special attention is given to the role of the industry as a leader in industrial movements. A brief history of broad global trade developments is fol-

lowed by an overview of the special trade problems that emerged for the textile and apparel sectors.

Chapter 3 provides an overview of the global environment in which textile/apparel production and trade occur. Attention is given to groupings of nations since these divisions are of special significance in the study of textiles and apparel in the global economy. Economic, political, and cultural systems are considered as important environmental factors affecting production and trade. Chapter 4 builds, to some extent, on concepts in the prior chapter and provides a brief review of theory relevant to global trade in textiles and apparel. Variations of trade theories and development theories are presented.

Chapter 5, 6, and 7 focus on the textile and apparel industries from a global perspective. Chapter 5 provides an overview of the global textile complex and considers the stages of industry development in relation to a country's or region's overall development. Chapter 6 reviews the textile complex in select regions of the world, particularly in relation to the restructuring of the industry that is occurring on a global basis. Chapter 7 focuses on global patterns of textile and apparel activities (production, employment, consumption, and trade) with particular attention given to major global shifts for these activities.

Chapters 8 and 9 focus on the U.S. textile and apparel sectors. First, Chapter 8 gives an overview of the textile complex and covers common areas affecting both textiles and apparel. Chapter 9 gives a separate overview of the U.S. textile and apparel industries, with special emphasis on issues that influence each sector's ability to compete in the global economy.

Chapter 10 covers textile and apparel trade policies, both at the global and U.S. levels. The U.S. position is given within the broader context of global policy development and implementation. In addition, the chapter provides an overview of the evolution of the Multifiber Arrangement, the unique trade agreement for global textile trade. Chapter 11 presents an overview of the major global and U.S. structures for facilitating or "managing" textile and apparel trade. The goal of this chapter is to help the reader understand how the trade policies are operationalized through key organizations or other structures.

Chapters 12, 13, 14, and 15 focus on textiles and apparel in the international economy from the perspectives of key groups of players. These chapters are intended to provide insight into the conflicting interests of various groups that have a great deal at stake in textile and apparel trade. Chapter 12 presents the interests of industry and labor in textile and apparel trade; Chapter 13 covers the interests of retailers and importers; Chapter 14 considers the interests of consumers; and Chapter 15 focuses on the dilemma of textile trade for policymakers.

Chapter 16 provides a review of the difficulties associated with attempting to resolve international textile and apparel trade problems. The chapter is intended to encourage reflection on the content of the book and to help the reader understand the need to acquire a global perspective in dealing with all aspects of the softgoods industry.

resents the largest source of industrial employment in the world. Production processes are linked on a global scale, often resulting in *global products*. The globalization of textiles and apparel production has not been without its problems, however. As growing numbers of nations entered these sectors as a means of fostering economic development, an overcapacity of production occurred in an international market where demand was increasing slowly. As a result, competition in the global textile and apparel market is intense. Consequently, many economic, political, and social concerns are inherent in efforts to resolve the problems associated with excess global production capacity.

Expanded worldwide textile and apparel production, along with accompanying trade shifts, represent the most important changes affecting the global complex today. Similarly, the textile complex within many countries is affected by these global changes. Without question, all aspects of the U.S. softgoods industry are affected by the globalization that has occurred. Given the growing international dimensions of the textile complex, in order to participate meaningfully in any aspect of the U.S. industry, individuals and firms must have an understanding of the broader global context in which we now operate.

SUMMARY

Advanced communication and transportation systems have led to increased interaction of the world's inhabitants. The resulting interdependence has led to a global economy characterized by a web of linkages through which actions of the players in one system can have consequences for those in another system.

As an important part of an increasingly globalized economy, textile and apparel production is dispersed around the world. Together, textile and apparel production rep-

SUGGESTED READINGS

Borrus, A., Zeller, W., & Holstein, W. (1990, May 14). The stateless corporation. *Business Week*, pp. 98-106.
A review of the increased growth of world corporations that function with little regard for national boundaries.

Boulding, K. (1985). *The world as a total system.* Beverly Hills: SAGE.
An examination of several systems of which the total world system is composed.

Dicken, P. (1992). *Global shift*. New York: Guilford Press.
This book focuses on the internationalization of economic activity.

Forney, J., & Rabolt, N. (1991). *Global perspectives modules for textiles and clothing: Curricular and research applications*. Monument, CO: Association of College Professors of Textiles and Clothing.
A resource book for encompassing a global perspective in textile and apparel curricula and research. Organized in modules with extensive accompanying citations.

Global Perspectives in Education, Inc. (1987). *The United States prepares for its future: Global perspectives in education*. Report of the Study Commission on Global Education. New York.
A study and recommendations on global education needs for the United States.

National Governors' Association. (1989). *America in transition—The international frontier*. Washington, DC: Author.
A review of America's growing need for international competencies to participate fully in an increasingly interdependent global economy.

Ohmae, K. (1990). *The borderless world*. New York: Harper Business.
A management consultant's view of a borderless world that has already emerged in the financial and industrial spheres.

Toyne, B., Arpan, J., Barnett, A., Ricks, D., & Shimp, T. (1984). *The global textile industry*. London: George Allen & Unwin.
A study of the global textile industry and factors affecting its competitiveness.

United Nations. (1990). *Global outlook 2000*. New York: Author.
United Nations writers look back at the past 30 years and forward to 2000 and predict changes related to economic, social, and environmental issues.

II

An Overview: History, the Global Setting, Theory

The chapters in Part II are intended to set the broader stage for the study of textiles and apparel in the global economy. These chapters are designed to prepare us to view our study within the broader context of history, within the various dimensions of an international setting, and within a theoretical context.

Chapter 2 provides a historical perspective on the development of both the global and the U.S. textile and apparel industries. Special attention is given to the role of the industry as a leader in industrial movements. A brief history of broad global trade developments provides the backdrop for our study of textile and apparel trade. Subsequently, we shall consider an overview of the special trade problems that emerged for the textile and apparel sectors.

Chapter 3 provides an overview of the global environment in which textile/apparel production and trade occur. Attention is given to groupings of nations, since these divisions are of special significance in the study of textiles and apparel in the global economy. Economic, political, and cultural systems are considered important environmental factors affecting production and trade.

Chapter 4 builds, to some extent, on concepts in the prior chapter and provides a brief review of theory relevant to global trade in textiles and apparel. Select economic (trade) theories and development theories are presented to provide a framework for considering the shifts in production and trade for textiles and apparel in the global economy.

2

Historical Perspective

INTRODUCTION

Textile production, from the production of fiber through subsequent steps, represents one industry common to all countries in the global economy. Textile manufacturing, one of the oldest industrial sectors in the world, has contributed in important ways to the development of economies and the resulting living standards of inhabitants in regions scattered around the globe. A study of the development and the geographic shifts of the textile sector as it has moved through time and around the globe provides insight into the economic and social condition of the occupants of continents and countries at a given time.

Textile production became one of the earliest large-scale economic activities that led the industrialization process centuries ago. Similarly, certain segments of the industry continue to play a key role in the initial industrialization process of most countries. This role has resulted because (1) the industry serves a basic need of nearly all humans and usually provides for some or all of domestic demand, and (2) different aspects of the industry's production have been adaptable to a wide range of available resources. For example, when capital and technology are available, more technologically advanced textile production occurs. On the other hand, when a country has neither of these, certain segments of production (for example, small-scale textile production or apparel assembly) often thrive because of other abundant resources such as labor.

Both as a leader and a sustainer of economic and industrial activity, the textile sector has contributed in important ways to serving the needs of the world's peoples. In many respects, the emergence of the textile industry and its role in economic development are themes often replayed in country after country. The early development and the socioeconomic impact of the textile industry in England and the United States are repeated today, in somewhat different forms, in many poor, developing countries. This almost universal reliance on the textile sector for economic and industrial advancement accounts for many of the complexities found in today's global textile market.

In this chapter, we will consider (1) a historical perspective on the development of the textile and apparel industries; (2) the development of global trade; and (3) a brief review on how textiles and apparel became difficult areas of trade.

THE ROLE OF THE TEXTILE SECTOR IN HISTORIC GLOBAL INDUSTRIAL MOVEMENTS

The Textile Sector as a Leader

The textile sector played a lead role in the development and evolution of worldwide economic and industrial history. In this role as an industrial leader, developments in the textile industry shaped economic and social thought. Many of these developments occurred first in England and later spread in similar form to the United States and to other countries. Some of the ways in which the textile industry was a leader are

- Textile production led the **Industrial Revolution** when it became the first sector to shift from the use of skilled hand labor to production based on hand-powered machines and later steam power.
- The textile sector's early use of technical inventions positioned the industry to become the first to build factories to apply the new developments on a large scale. This means that the industry was among the first to transform England and later the United States from an economy based on farming and household industries to one using factories and mills.

- The establishment of factories to produce textiles led to the development of mill towns in rural areas of England and later the United States.
- Development of textile production into a factory system created the jobs that led to participation of the first generations of both English and American women in widespread employment for wages outside the home.
- Poor working conditions in the textile mills, and later the garment factories, led to the first industrial reforms. Workers' protests against excessive work demands and poor working conditions led to policies to protect workers from abuse by their employers.

Some of these developments for textiles not only had an impact on other sectors of industry that came later, but they also profoundly shaped the socioeconomic environment of many nations. Although other contributions could be given, these represent significant examples of the ways in which the textile industry left its imprint on economic and industrial history. A brief overview of these developments provides a useful historical backdrop against which we will consider the present status of the global industry. An awareness of the leadership of the textile industry in these areas helps to provide a special appreciation of the importance of this sector in global social and economic evolution. This historical perspective, as portrayed in Figure 2–1, is particularly useful because a number of recent industry developments in various locations of the world parallel certain aspects of the industry at earlier stages in the United States, Great Britain, and other developed countries.

Textiles as a Leader in the Industrial Revolution in England

Until 1750, most English families lived on farms or in small villages, and family members produced virtually everything they

FIGURE 2–1
The textile sector as a leader in historic industrial movements.

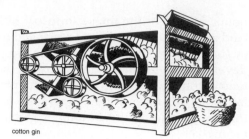

cotton gin

Use of machines for production
(Industrial Revolution)

Development of factories

Migration from farms,
development of mill towns

Widescale employment of
women outside the home

Worker protests leading
to industrial reform

needed. Ordinary people lived simple lives and required little from outside the family or the village. Poverty was common. Up to this time, methods of production had changed slowly.

Although scientific investigations and inventions had occurred in the 1600s, these were not focused on machines or other processes related to production. Although wealth was present, money was not invested generally in inventions related to science or production. The movement we now call the Industrial Revolution began to occur in the mid-1700s when, for the first time, both science and capital were used to solve the problems of production. Although both science and **capital** had been available before, they had not been applied *together* to solve practical problems (Crawford, 1959; Ellsworth & Leith, 1984).

As the English became interested in new products and new conveniences, **capitalists** saw an opportunity to make profits by bringing science and capital together to produce new goods. Around 1690, for example, textile production was stimulated by cotton cloth from India, which appealed to fashionable persons because of its lightness, cleanliness, and brightness. Demand grew as others saw these fabrics. Although production of cotton fabrics (*fustians*, a blend of cotton and linen) had begun in England as a cottage industry in about 1600, it was viewed as a *household* activity, as the earlier woolen industry had been. Until the colorful hand-loomed Indian cottons grew in popularity and were banned by Parliament, growth of domestic textile production was slow. Consequently, this political action, which cut off Indian textiles, was instigated so the British could develop their own industry, produce their own fabrics, and keep the profits at home (Ellsworth & Leith, 1984).

Elimination of competition quickly expanded England's cotton cloth production. At first, the cloth was made by domestic workers who were supplied raw materials by "manufacturers" or entrepreneurs. Once the Indian textiles were no longer an option, the purchase of English cloth grew rapidly because, in addition to domestic use, the cloth was valued in the slave trade. Producers could not keep up with the demand. Seeing an opportunity, early capitalists encouraged inventors to develop machines to produce the goods. Manufacturers began to offer prizes for a machine that would increase production and improve the profitability for British producers.

Gradually textile production became more sophisticated and played a prominent role in broader industrialization efforts. The textile industry led the Industrial Revolution with the development of a series of interrelated mechanical inventions. As each development solved a pressing industrial need, it created an imbalance within the industry that necessitated other inventions. In 1733, John Kay developed the mechanical flying shuttle, which permitted a single worker to weave fabric wider than the length of a person's arm. Prior to Kay's invention, if wide fabrics were woven, two workers were required to move the shuttle back and forth to insert the weft thread. Kay's flying shuttle expanded weaving output greatly, making it more difficult than ever for spinners to support the demand for yarn. Up to that time, a weaver required five or six spinners to supply yarn for the weaving, but Kay's improved loom had made it impossible for spinners to meet the demand.

Three important inventions revolutionized spinning between 1764 and 1779. These were Hargreaves's spinning jenny, Arkwright's water frame, and Crompton's mule. The jenny produced yarns of fine quality that were too weak to be used for the warp, whereas the water frame produced stronger yarns of lesser quality. Crompton's invention combined the principles of the jenny and the water frame to produce strong, fine-quality yarns. The mule was soon fit with three to four hundred spindles, permitting it to replace that many spinners. At that point, spinning potential would have surpassed availability of raw material had it not been for the 1793 invention of the cotton gin by the American Eli Whitney (Crawford, 1959).

The Industrial Revolution altered profoundly the notion about how goods could be produced, and the textile industry led the way in this revolution. As the new industrial developments began to spread abroad, these production changes provided the groundwork for the transformation of the Western world into a true international economy (Ellsworth & Leith, 1984).

Marszal (1985), a Polish industrial geographer with a special interest in the textile industry, reinforced the view that the British textile industry was a forerunner of similar industrial developments in other countries and other sectors. Textile production also led the Industrial Revolution on the European continent years later, with France having the distinction of being the next European country to develop its textile industry (Strida, 1985).

Development of the Factory System

New spinning machines led to the development of the factory system because the machines were so large that cottages could not hold them. Further, the machines were so heavy that mechanical power was needed to run them. Because the inventions were operated most economically by water, factories clustered where water power (and later steam) was available. Arkwright became the first industrial capitalist, establishing a large number of textile factories during the 1800s employing 150 to 600 workers (many of whom were children), outmoding England's cottage industry (Addy, 1976; Crawford, 1959). These early mills are generally regarded as the first modern factories. Other industries such as iron and steel soon copied the factory model developed in the textile industry.

As noted in the earlier example, one invention for textile production often created an imbalance in other areas. Whereas yarn was scarce earlier, weavers later found they could not keep up with the over-abundance of yarn being produced in the spinning mills. To fill this need, Cartwright developed a power loom in 1795; however, handloom weavers—concerned about job security—blocked its use in the industry and prevented its widespread adoption until about 1810. Although the use of power looms in factory settings had the potential for operating on a more widespread basis, Mantoux (1927) noted that large numbers of handlooms continued to be operated until late in the nineteenth century.

Early Developments in the United States

Although early industrialization began in England, a review of the earliest developments of the textile industry in the United States will be helpful at this point—particularly since the remainder of our historical industry perspective in this chapter will focus primarily on the U.S. industry. The industry in many other countries followed at least some aspects of this pattern of development. Although the U.S. industry developed after the English system had been in operation for a long time, once the first machines for textile production came into use in the United States, the new nation followed quickly in the British path of establishing factories.

Although the influence of the Industrial Revolution spread much later to the textile industry in the United States, compared to Europe, colonists had long valued textile production. As early as 1645, the Massachusetts Bay Colony encouraged newcomers to bring as many sheep from England as they could. Families from the textile-producing areas of England and other parts of Europe settled in the Colonies and applied their knowledge and skills to fledgling textile production

THE ENGLISH TEXTILE FACTORIES

Although English textile mills led the way in establishing the factory system, working conditions were shameful. According to Addy (1976), men hated not only the new textile machines but also the factories. They disliked the long hours and the rigid rules. "The domestic worker saw little difference between the mill and going to prison or to an army barracks. Hence the early manufacturers found it difficult to obtain labour" (Addy, 1976, p. 30).

Gradually the factories attracted workers from the poorest areas seeking more opportunities and better earnings. Women and children were considered excellent prospects for the industry because their nimble fingers and natural dexterity made them suitable for joining broken threads on the mule or water frame. In addition, child labor was cheap—about one-third the cost of adult labor, plus food and lodging (Taylor, 1912).

An easy way to obtain child laborers was through the town poorhouses. Overseers of the poor were authorized to board out pauper children and pay a bonus for each one that survived. Addy cites accounts of 50 to 100 pauper children being shipped to the textile mills, where conditions were disgraceful:

- "Their working day was often from sixteen to eighteen hours and some worked twenty-four hours per day, and accidents were frequent when the exhausted children had to continue working" (p. 31).
- "The conditions of the factory buildings were a hazard to health. Rooms were low, with narrow windows that were nearly always closed, to economise on space. The carding rooms had an atmosphere heavily laden with fluff, making it probable that eventually lung diseases would develop in the operative" (p. 32).
- "Those who survived the stresses and strains of the factory system were stunted, deformed and mutilated as well as ignorant and corrupt. They had received little education and little technical training, only sufficient to enable them to perform a routine process, and therefore unable to take up any other employment, which made them virtually factory slaves. Adult workers were not treated so badly as the apprentices and free children but in turn adults suffered from long hours, overcrowded mills, objectionable foremen and employers. The basic cause of the trouble was the uncontrolled power of the capitalist, whose responsibility was confined to the payment of wages for work done and nothing else" (p. 33).

efforts. Colonists were eager to become proficient at producing their own fabrics so they might clothe themselves and reduce their dependence on England. British authorities believed, however, that a major role of the Colonies was that of absorbing products from the mother country; as a result they tried to block the development of a textile industry in the Colonies and prohibited trading with any other nations. The British wanted the Colonies to remain dependent and, in addi-

tion, they wanted the profits that accompanied the sale of goods.

In 1705, Lord Cornbury expressed the concern that English officials could foresee in the dangers of letting the Colonies achieve self-sufficiency in textile production: "If once they see they can clothe themselves, not only comfortably, but handsomely too, without the help of England, they, who are already not very fond of submitting to government, would soon think of putting in execution designs they had long harbourd [sic] in their breasts" (de Llosa, 1984, p. 8; original source unknown).

George Washington envisioned the potential of the domestic textile industry:

> Many articles, in wool, flax, cotton, and hemp may be fabricated at home with great advantage. If the quantity should be encreased [sic] to tenfold its present amount (as it easily could be), I apprehend the whole might in a short time be manufactured especially by the introduction of machines for multiplying the effects of labour in diminishing the number of hands employed upon it. (de Llosa, 1984, p. 8; original source unknown)

In the early years after independence from England, the United States was buffeted by changes in the international economy, and the new nation groped to establish a secure economic independence. Textiles continued to be an important product area to the new country, and Thomas Jefferson noted in 1786 that homespun cotton produced by the four southernmost states was "as well manufactured as the calicoes of Europe" (de Llosa, 1984, p. 8; original source unknown).

During these same transition years, Philadelphian Tench Coxe, who was a delegate to the Continental Congress and later became Assistant Secretary of the U.S. Treasury, "emptied his pockets" to secure some of the English textile inventions such as the spinning jenny. In addition to securing new technology to develop the domestic industry, the new nation imposed measures to keep out foreign products. In an ironic twist from earlier regulations imposed by England on the colonists, the first Congress in 1789 imposed its own **tariff** of three cents a pound to protect American cotton production, estimated at a million pounds annually.

Although 1793 had been a time of two milestone textile developments in the United States—Whitney's cotton gin and Samuel Slater's cotton mill (the first successful cotton mill in America, which Slater had constructed

from memory)—the new nation lagged behind England in the industrialization process in the early 1800s. British industry, and textiles in particular, had been developing new technology for decades. In the early nineteenth century, the United States adapted (or stole) technology developed in Britain and also began to develop its own inventions.

The War of 1812 exerted new demands on the fledgling U.S. textile industry to provide cloth and blankets for soldiers. In addition, **embargoes** on foreign products added to the scarcity of textile goods. Leading what was perhaps the first formal textile lobby, Eleuthère Irénée DuPont led a committee to Congress to plead the case of 27 cotton manufacturers and 14 wool producers. DuPont's committee sought "the interference and protection of our own Government to nurse and foster their infant manufactories for a few years," because they found they were "incapable of entering upon the competition with even a hope of success" against "superior advantages, public and private capital, illfounded prejudices of a part of their own fellow citizens, and a powerful foreign Government." The committee's appeal indicated the manufacturers' wishes that their efforts "would highly conduce to our national safety and independence, our Army and Navy clothes by our own industry" (de Llosa, 1984, p. 10; original source unknown). As we will see in later chapters, this argument for protecting the domestic industry for national security purposes surfaced in more recent years.

The U.S. textile industry experienced impressive growth between 1812 and 1816, with 170 mills reported by the end of the war. Poulson (1981) noted that a major issue in studies of early American industrialization is the extent to which the growth of these industries can be attributed to **protective tariffs**. Poulson speculates that embargoes were more influential than tariffs in fostering industry growth. Although restrictions on foreign products aided the development of the industry, technology was also important. Adoption of the power loom contributed greatly to the success of the industry during this period. Although 170 textile mills existed by 1816, only 5 percent of all textile manufactures came from factories. Nevertheless, the early textile mills led the young country into the Industrial Revolution and indelibly altered the structure of manufacturing from that time on.

The Shift from Farms to Mill Towns

As it had in England earlier, textile production became an industrial enterprise that affected the development of the new country as a whole. Workers migrated from the farms, and small villages developed where the factories emerged. Young men and women attracted to the textile mills, shoe factories, and a few other budding industries were part of a mass social movement that in the early to middle decades of the nineteenth century transformed New England from a rural, agrarian society into an urban, industrial society. The textile industry's influence in restructuring the socioeconomic character of New England is but one example of the social implications of the industry and its evolution, both in the United States and in many areas of the world.

Employment of Women Outside the Home

In addition to leading the industrialization of production and the development of factories and mill towns, the textile industry contributed to another historic global industrial movement—the widescale employment of women outside the home.

After Samuel Slater build a spinning machine in the late 1700s, his factory was the first to be established in the United States. The first spinning mills were modeled after the English factory system, which employed whole families. Child labor was common, and many critics opposed this form of industrialism. Figure 2–2 shows children employed in the mills.

Most early U.S. industry leaders wanted to avoid duplicating the horrors of the English factory system as they moved toward industrialization. A group led by Francis Cabot Lowell argued that it was possible to develop manufacturing without the accompanying human degradation typical of the factory system in England. The resulting "Waltham system" introduced both the first modern factory

---

    EXPANSION OF A MILL TOWN

In the 1830s, Lowell, Massachusetts, home of the Merrimack Manufacturing Company (a large textile firm), experienced growth unmatched in America. As Dunwell (1978) noted:

> The city bloomed more quickly than its most optimistic promoters could have imagined. Mills and boarding houses multiplied along the canals. Farmers' daughters poured into the city and took their places at the machines. This seemingly magical growth astonished all observers. John Greenleaf Whittier, who resided briefly in Lowell, called it "a city springing up, like the enchanted palaces of the Arabian tales, as it were in a single night—stretching far and wide its chaos of brick masonry and painted shingles" and he felt himself "thrust forward into a new century." Lowell seemed the prelude to a "millennium of steam engines and cotton mills" [Whittier, 1845, p. 9], and Whittier, though impressed, was troubled by the prospect [p. 40].

FIGURE 2-2

Although many critics opposed the practice, use of child labor—adopted in the early days of the industry—continued well into the 19th century. (Photo by Lewis W. Hine, courtesy of U.S. Library of Congress.)

in America as well as a new labor system different from the English factory system. The textile factory established in Waltham, Massachusetts, on the Charles River, was a fully integrated mill (with spinning and weaving under one roof) in which, for the first time, all machinery was power driven.

Designers of the "Waltham system" deemed that *adult females* would be the production workers in factories built on this model, rather than employing whole families. This decision may have been partly due to the fact that the equipment at Waltham was too complicated to be operated by children. Moreover, if mills were to reduce the use of child labor, another source of low-cost labor was required (child

laborers continued to be used in other jobs in the factories, however). Male leaders conceived the mills and the factory towns and directed the activities of workers. These same industry men "created a paternalistic system that employed and controlled the young women drawn into the mills from the surrounding countryside" (Dublin, 1981, p. 2). These young women came to be known as "the factory girls" (a label still used in many areas in the latter part of the twentieth century).

Industrialists convinced rural families that their daughters would be provided a safe life of "culture" in the mill villages. This assurance was particularly critical because of the need to overcome the vice-ridden reputation of the

English factories. Mill owners built boarding houses and dormitories and staffed them with matrons who supervised the young women's behavior and church attendance. In efforts to attract workers, mill towns were promoted as centers of moral and cultural development for young women.

The Waltham factory system flourished even more in Lowell, Massachusetts, than it had in Waltham. Factories accompanied by dormitories spread throughout New England, and young women continued to leave the farms for the new alternative employment. Often the workers sent all or part of their meager earnings (in the late 1830s, about $1.75 per week after they paid their board) home to their families. Typically the factory women arose at 4:30 in the morning and worked until 7:00 at night, with two half-hour meal breaks. Some factory visitors observed that the factory women seemed more like the victims than the beneficiaries of their industrious labor (Lerner, 1969).

Early Stages of Industrial Reform

Eventually the production demands of mill owners exceeded the willingness of workers to respond. As a result, the textile industry experienced another new form of industrial change—worker revolt. The textile industry was once again the forerunner in the earliest stages of a broad industrial reform that eventually spread to most other industrial sectors.

Female workers tolerated the long workdays because they were accustomed to dawn-to-dusk schedules on the family farms before they entered the factories. However, owners of the newer factories refined their power systems in ways that permitted a steady increase in the pace of work required of women in the mills. As stockholders demanded greater profits, employers increased the workload of each mill hand. For example, the average number of spindles per worker increased by about 64 percent in the eight major textile firms in Lowell. In addition to increased production demands and in some cases longer workdays, wages were reduced twice during the early 1830s (Dunwell, 1978; Foner, 1977).

In acts of great courage, contrary to social conventions of the day, female factory workers rallied in protest to the excessive work demands, the pay cuts, and other grievances. In 1834 and 1836, the workers took to the streets and paraded in protest of their treatment. During this time, they formed the Factory Girls' Association, which had 2,500 members by 1836[1] (Wertheimer, 1977). By 1845, the factory women became more militant and organized another early union of female factory workers, the Female Labor Reform Associations. A petition bearing over 2,000 signatures was presented to the Massachusetts legislature to shorten the length of the working day (Dunwell, 1978). By 1853, the workday was shortened to eleven hours. Thus, the courage of the female textile workers thrust the industry into another historic industrial movement—labor reform.

In addition to the significance of the Lowell protests in labor reform movements, the mill women's courageous efforts were also of broader historical importance. The Lowell factory workers organized one of the first large-scale protest efforts of women to assert their rights. At the same time that other early feminist leaders were pressing for full citizenship for women, the militant factory workers pressed for the justice due them. The mill women were outspoken about the excessive demands made on them in the factories— efforts that permitted the mill owners to live in luxury. The factory women were aware of the need to organize to assert their right to

---

[1]According to Wertheimer (1977), the first women's union was not in the New England mills, but rather in New York City. In 1824, the United Tailoresses formed their own union and demanded higher wages.

THE REALITY OF FACTORY LIFE

The "factory girls" found the conditions in the mills to be oppressive and quite unlike what they had expected from the promotional efforts that had lured them to the mill towns. This first-hand report denotes the hardship:

> The time we are required to labor is altogether too long. It is more than our constitutions can bear. If any one doubts it, let them come into our mills of a summer's day, at four or five o'clock, in the after-noon, and see the drooping, weary persons moving about, as though their legs were hardly able to support their bodies. . . . I have been an overseer myself, and many times have I had girls faint in the morning, in consequence of the air being so impure in the mill. This is quite a common thing. Especially when girls have worked in the factory for consider-able length of time. We commence as soon—and work as long as we can see almost the year round, and for nearly half the year we work by lamp light, at both ends of the day lighting up both morning and evening. And, besides this, from November till March our time is from twenty minutes to half an hour too slow. So you see instead of getting out of the factory at half past seven o'clock in the evening, it is really eight. (by "R," from Voice of Industry, March 26, 1847)

justice and in this role also became pioneers in the movement for women's rights.

Shaping the Economic and Industrial Future

Although the textile industry assumed many roles of leadership in economic and industrial development both for the world and the United States, not all of these developments generate a feeling of pride. However, few persons dispute the *significance* of this industry in shaping the economic and industrial future of the world and the nation. Technological changes in textile production led to a complete revolution of industry, and the transfer of the new industrial techniques from one country to another provided the groundwork for an international economy.

EARLY DEVELOPMENT OF THE APPAREL INDUSTRY

The U.S. apparel industry did not begin to develop, at least to a significant degree, for nearly a century after textile production was industrialized. The textile industry was instrumental, however, in fostering apparel production outside the home. First, the widespread availability of good quality cloth encouraged improved garment making over the earlier crude, homemade clothing methods. Many persons aspired to better quality, more attractive clothing. Second, the industrial movement led by textiles caused shifts to employment outside the home, from farms to mill towns—creating a more hectic lifestyle than had been experienced before. Many persons became preoccupied with business and were ready for easily obtained clothing.

Tailors filled an important role in the transition from home-produced clothing to mass-produced clothing. Adapting their custom tailoring approaches, tailors began to produce a selection of completed garments available for customers to consider. Later, the earliest known clothing "manufactory" was established in Philadelphia to produce uniforms for the War of 1812 (Kidwell & Christman, 1974). The sewing for this early "mass production" operation and those that followed was done by women in their homes, for which they were paid a piecework rate. All of the sewing was done by hand for most of this period.

The development of the sewing machine advanced garment production because manufacturers discovered the extent to which output could be increased. As demand for ready-made clothing increased in the latter half of the 1800s, the massive immigration of Europeans to the United States provided the necessary labor to run the growing industry. As in the textile industry, garment workers were treated poorly, often working in sweatshop conditions. Courageous workers eventually resisted the abuse and exploitation. Protests led to one of the earliest known collective bargaining efforts and, eventually, to the establishment of the International Ladies' Garment Workers' Union (ILGWU). In addition to providing the groundwork for the type of collective bargaining common today, the ILGWU achieved a number of welfare and educational advancements on behalf of workers.

The apparel industry continued to grow, eventually passing the textile industry as a major U.S. industrial employer. Many of the characteristics of the early industry still describe the present-day sector: The industry requires a great deal of **labor**—that is, it is a **labor-intensive industry**; labor is a major cost in producing the end product, particularly compared to other industries; the industry is easy to enter, requiring only limited capital and technical knowledge; the sewing machine is still the basic piece of equipment; this basic production equipment is fairly easily mastered; and the industry is quite fragmented—that is, it is composed of a large number of small manufacturing establishments. These characteristics also explain why the apparel industry is often the first entered today by many developing countries.

TRANSITIONAL YEARS FOR INTERNATIONAL TRADE

A brief review of the major changes in international trade will provide a helpful setting for understanding the global development of the textile industry and the changing environments in which textile/apparel **trade** took place. We shall consider briefly the period between the early development of the textile industry and the latter part of the twentieth century—in which the pace of global textile/apparel trade quickened.

The Seventeenth and Eighteenth Centuries

The Era of Mercantilism

Early developments in the textile industry took place during the seventeenth and eighteenth centuries in an era of **mercantilism**. This economic philosophy relied on the belief that a country's wealth was dependent upon its holdings of treasure, usually gold (by means of stockpiling). **Exports** were expected to exceed **imports** as a means of increasing wealth. This was an era of close regulation and control of foreign and domestic business as the colonial powers (particularly England, France, and Spain) attempted to monopolize trade by restricting manufacturing in the colonies. In fact, one grievance that led to the American Revolution was the British restriction on colonial manufacturing.

In this period, enterprising British business leaders successfully transferred industrial production techniques from textiles and iron to a broader range of industry. British capital, labor, and expertise were applied to provide these same production advances on the European continent.

The Emergence of Capitalism

As the middle class—which included merchants and manufacturers—became more numerous and more prosperous, mercantilism began to restrict business leaders' opportunities for economic expansion and growth. As the merchant/industrialist class became more powerful politically and economically, it successfully pressed for reducing the restric-

REGULATION OF TEXTILE TRADE UNDER MERCANTILISM—AN EXAMPLE

The British government went to great lengths to promote exports of *finished products* rather than *raw materials*. It was believed that keeping raw materials at home made them abundant and cheap for use in production of finished goods, which were more profitable to export. The government enacted a number of measures to prohibit the export of raw materials and semifabricated goods. One of the most severe measures was in textiles, as Ellsworth and Leith (1984) related:

> The English woolen textile industry, accounting in 1700 for half the country's exports, was thus

favored; we find sheep, wool, woolen yarn, and worsted, as well as fuller's earth (used in cleaning wool) all on the list of prohibited exports. Enforcement of the law was Draconian in its severity; for the first offense the transgressor was to have his left hand cut off; the second offense carried the death penalty. (p. 21)

In addition, strict measures applied to importing finished goods into England. Most products carried prohibitively high tariffs. Because of the importance of the textile industry, importing finished woolen and silk fabricated goods was prohibited, whereas incentives existed for imports of textile raw materials.

---

tions of mercantilism. Many of the capitalists wanted to broaden their markets, and the best way of doing that was through freer trade. The decline of mercantilism and the movement toward more economic freedom—and thus, the emergence of **capitalism**—were reinforced by the thinking of Adam Smith.

Smith (1930, originally published in 1776) advocated a policy of *laissez faire*, or a let-alone approach for the functioning of business. Smith believed all benefited by the greatest possible freedom of enterprise and as few regulations as possible. The liberal political and economic thinking of Smith and some of his contemporaries was important in reducing the influence of mercantilism and in promoting individual thought and action. Smith's thinking provided the intellectual groundwork for specialization of production within nations. Smith, who has been called the "father of **free trade**," believed that the specialization and increased interdependence among nations would lead to greater benefits for *all* countries involved.

The Nineteenth Century

Foreign Expansion

With the elimination of mercantilism during the 1800s, British and other European business leaders began investing in foreign countries. This international investment expanded the markets for lending countries' export industries and provided to the borrowing countries the capital for economic growth. Free of mercantilist restrictions, international trade grew rapidly. Rough estimates indicate that the value of international trade doubled between 1830 and 1850. Then, in the next 30 years, the value of world trade increased by three or four times what it had been (Ellsworth & Leith, 1984). Foreign trade became a primary economic activity rather than an unimportant adjunct to domestic activity.

A Time of Important Changes in the United States

The nineteenth century brought tremendous economic change to the United States, and by the end of the century, the young nation was the major industrial power in the world, dominating international markets. This was a boom period for the textile industry, as the New England textile mills developed and prospered. The U.S. cotton industry was a relatively minor industry at the beginning of the nineteenth century, but it emerged as the country's leading manufacturing industry prior to the Civil War. Poulson (1981) provides a number of possible explanations for the growth: (1) population growth, (2) westward expansion, (3) increased per capita income, (4) introduction of the power loom, (5) reduced transportation costs, and (6) of particular significance was **import substitution**. Poulson noted that between 1820 and 1830, domestic producers' contribution to the U.S. market went from 30 to 80 percent. Import substitution appeared to have been encouraged by the high tariffs levied on imported textiles in 1816, 1824, and 1828, thus providing protection to U.S. producers.

Migration of Labor

In focusing again on the international perspective for this era, migration of labor was another major development that accompanied the foreign investment mentioned earlier. Between 1820 and 1930, 62 million people (mostly from Europe) migrated; about three-fifths of these relocated in the United States (Ellsworth & Leith, 1984). Ellsworth and Leith (1984) noted that for the most part both labor and capital moved from areas where they were abundant to geographic areas where they were scarce and dear. In the latter half of this period, immigrants became an important labor source in both the New England textile mills and later the garment factories in New York and other areas of the northeast United States.

The Early Twentieth Century

Development of an International Economy

The period between the Napoleonic Wars and World War I (1814–1914) were particularly sig-

nificant to the development of an international economy in a number of ways. Government regulation of trade was replaced by *regulation by market forces*. Specialization among nations developed, and as Ellsworth and Leith (1984) put it: "A large and constantly growing volume of international trade linked the various regions of the world into a smoothly functioning, integrated economy of global scope" (p. 281). A sense of *international economic interdependence* developed during this time. The volume of world trade grew more rapidly than world output, and this boom era provided an opportunity for a greater number of nations to participate in the gains from trade and, as a result, helped the newer entrants move toward economic growth. Also significant during this period was the development of an **international monetary system** based on the gold standard; this facilitated world trade and provided greater stability to this trade.

Economic Nationalism Builds

By the late 1800s and early 1900s, the positive spirit of global integration and economic interdependence that had fostered international trade suffered from growing threats of **economic nationalism** from the major world powers. Ellsworth and Leith (1984) have referred to this as a period of "colony grabbing" in which most of the major powers, excluding the Americas, extended their empires into foreign territories. These authors speculated that economic growth fostered the claiming of new lands as sources of raw materials. Economic growth required new sources of raw materials because traditional sources were inadequate.

Emergence of Protectionism

The emerging nationalism in the latter part of the nineteenth century provided at least a predisposition toward protecting markets from imports by imposing tariffs, quotas, or other restrictions (that is, **protectionism**).

Ellsworth and Leith (1984) noted that the United States was one of the first countries to disrupt the positive flow in international trade by launching increased tariffs on foreign products. Other countries responded by imposing similar trade restrictions. Consequently, international trade was already greatly hampered, even before World War I, and the war itself further divided nations.

The economic environment of the early twentieth century was quite different from that of the nineteenth century and, as a result, international trade declined. The two world wars and the Great Depression altered seriously the international cooperation and interdependence that blossomed earlier. Nations imposed trade restrictions and **devalued** their **currencies** to bolster trade positions. Nationalistic economic policies slowed both trade and migration of people. Devalued currencies buy less abroad and encourage consumption of domestically produced goods.

U.S. trade declined sharply during the Great Depression but grew rapidly after each world war. Industrial exports reflected the increasing importance of industry in the American economy. The foreign market exerted a major influence on U.S. industrial growth in the twentieth century in contrast to the importance of the domestic market in the nineteenth century.

The United States as a Leader in World Trade

The United States began to occupy an increasingly important position in world trade in the early 1900s. The young country had already passed Great Britain as the world's leading manufacturing power and in this era became the major exporter and the principal international investor. As the United States assumed this dominant global position, Ellsworth and Leith (1984) emphasized the importance of this role: "As the world's outstanding manufacturing power, its largest creditor, and one of its two largest traders, the economic health

and the economic policies of the United States were of the greatest significance to the suppliers, customers, and debtors of that world" (p. 461). This meant that economic changes in the United States "could easily disrupt economic life in most of the rest of the world" (p. 461). Similarly, the economic importance of the United States permitted the country to have a positive influence on other countries. In this role, the country's leadership also imposed serious responsibilities in its relationships with the rest of the world.

Poulson (1981) noted that in absolute terms international trade in the United States grew rapidly in the twentieth century. In the years after World War II, the expansion of trade fueled a tremendous surge of economic growth and was the basis for the United States' global economic leadership between 1945 and 1960. As U.S. trade expanded, it closed the distance that separated the U.S. from other cultures—and competition.

The Mid-Twentieth Century

Trade Became More Volatile

Although trade grew more rapidly as the U.S. economy matured, trade also became more volatile. Increased trade brought growing concerns about "protecting" domestic markets. Remembering the devastating effects of the Smoot–Hawley Tariff Act[2] of 1930, which had hampered world trade tremendously

---

[2]The Smoot–Hawley Tariff Act of 1930 enacted severe measures to restrict imports and stimulate domestic employment. Although more than 1,000 American economists signed a petition urging President Hoover to veto the bill and 36 countries threatened to retaliate, the president signed the bill into law. Under the Smoot–Hawley provisions, the average import duty in the United States was 59 percent by 1932, a record high. By 1932, 60 countries retaliated by imposing their own high tariffs. The Smoot—Hawley Act had a devastating effect on global trade, causing the worldwide economic depression to worsen. By 1932, U.S. imports were only 31 percent of the 1929 level; exports dropped even more dramatically (Salvatore, 1987).

(and many believed it had triggered the Great Depression), government leaders looked for other solutions. Leaders in major trading countries initiated two efforts in the early years after the war, which had important stabilizing effects on the global trading climate. These were

- **Establishment of the International Monetary Fund (IMF).** In 1944, representatives of the Allied governments met in Bretton Woods, New Hampshire, and established the rules by which exchange rates between currencies would be determined. Up to that time, home governments had been able to manipulate to some extent the value of their currencies. A country could lower the value of its currency in relation to other currencies and slash the price of its exports. In doing so, its exports became more attractive to other countries to buy; however, this created a bias in trade. The Bretton Woods conference established the **gold-exchange standard** (as opposed to the **gold standard**), which initiated a system of fixed exchange rates and ended the practice of manipulating currencies. Under this system, the dollar (which had replaced the British pound as the world's major currency) was convertible—for official monetary purposes—into gold at a fixed price.
- **Establishment of the General Agreement on Tariffs and Trade (GATT).** The GATT was established in 1947 and became the second pillar of the postwar economy. GATT's goal was to promote unrestricted trade, particularly the reduction of tariffs. Although efforts to reduce tariffs had occurred earlier, the GATT represented a comprehensive approach. A founding principle of GATT was its "most favored nation" provision, which meant that if a country gives a trade advantage to one country, it should give the same advantage to every other country with whom it trades. This concept means that every

country has an equal opportunity in trade with a particular country. (Textile trade has provisions that permit countries to violate this principle. This controversial point will be discussed later in the book.)

The GATT was a positive influence on international trade during an era in which trade expanded rapidly. As world trade grew, so did GATT membership. Originally established by 23 member countries, which were the major industrial powers, GATT was at times considered a "rich man's club" (because membership consisted of the more prosperous nations). Nearly 120 countries are now members. Furthermore, about two-thirds of those members are developing countries—an important point to remember for later discussions on textile trade policies.

The United States prospered in world trade during the first 25 years of GATT's existence. As one of the few major industrial economies not damaged by World War II, the United States was in an advantageous position to export. U.S. technological innovations during this era added to the strong exporting activity. As a result, the U.S. economy prospered.

The Late Twentieth Century

Development of Floating Exchange Rates

By the late 1950s, the dollars flowing out of the United States through loans, grants, military expenses, and private investment exceeded foreign demand for U.S. goods. By 1958, the U.S. dollars abroad exceeded the value of the nation's gold reserves. During the 1960s, government spending expanded even more—especially to finance the Vietnam War and the social welfare programs promoting the "Great Society." Unwilling to raise taxes to cover high levels of spending, the U.S. government began to print more dollars—a step that fostered inflation and encouraged foreign governments to obtain the gold available to them as part of the Bretton Woods plan. Half the U.S. gold reserves were gone by 1969.

The large U.S. balance of payments deficits and the sharply reduced U.S. gold reserves caused widespread concern that the dollar would be devalued. This led to a speculative flow of funds to other currencies—especially to the German mark, the Japanese yen, and the Swiss franc—which had a further destabilizing effect on the Bretton Woods fixed exchange rate system. This led to the demise of the Bretton Woods system of converting dollars into gold.

In 1971, President Richard Nixon ended the Bretton Woods system—a step that did, in fact, cause a devaluation of the dollar. By 1973, the prices of most currencies were "floating"—like the prices of commodities such as sugar or coffee, with their value going up or down according to supply and demand. Although the devaluation of the dollar fostered trade (goods were less expensive) and the trade balance improved for a time, global markets became far less stable than had been true under the Bretton Woods system. The resulting **floating exchange rate** system introduced an element of unpredictability into foreign trade. Trading nations had to accept the fact that favorable or unfavorable shifts in exchange rates would affect conditions of trade.

Growing Difficulties in Textile Trade

Within the larger picture for the 1970s, as total U.S. imports increased significantly, this was a period in which the textile/apparel sectors felt keenly the impact of imports. Although a great deal of the growth in total imports (particularly in discussions that consider the *value* of imports) was accounted for by increased prices for petroleum products, the 1970s were the decade of highest growth up to that time for textile imports. Poulson (1981) noted that at the time of his writing most of the acceleration in trade had been prices rather than

quantities of traded goods, particularly for imports. Although prices for petroleum products greatly influenced these calculations, the same observation holds for textile products. (In fact, this is a controversial point in calculating the extent to which textile imports have penetrated U.S. markets. At issue is whether to report import growth in prices or quantities; the extent of apparent import growth varies according to the measure used.)

DEVELOPMENT OF TEXTILES AND APPAREL AS A DIFFICULT AND SENSITIVE SECTOR IN THE GLOBAL ECONOMY

By the 1960s both the textile and apparel industries in most industrialized countries felt the impact of increased imports from the low-wage developing countries. Although the relative economic well-being of apparel and textiles as separate industry segments in the developed countries varies from one time to another, the two segments have experienced many similar problems in maintaining international competitiveness in the last two decades.

Problems experienced by the U.S. textile and apparel sectors in this era began to receive special attention because of certain characteristics of the industries, particularly the large numbers of persons employed. We should keep in mind, however, that the textile and apparel industries in most of the other developed countries were undergoing similar difficulties. Moreover, several other mature industries (e.g., iron and steel, shipbuilding, shoes) in the developed countries experienced many of the same problems.

A Leader in Trade Problems

Although other sectors had similar difficulties, in some ways the problems for the textile and apparel industries may have been more acute. Many economists have debated the claim, however, that problems associated with textile and apparel trade are unique. Nevertheless, problems related to international competitiveness of the developed countries' textile and apparel industries have been forerunners to similar problems for other sectors. In this sense, this sector was *once again in a lead position in a major international and national industrial (and trade) dilemma*, albeit a role the sector would not have chosen to occupy. (Similarly, as we shall learn later in the book, the sector has been a leader in securing policy measures as a means of attempting to protect domestic markets.)

Changes in the U.S. Textile and Apparel Industries

Job losses in the *textile* segment of the industry have been common for all developed countries, particularly since 1973, when a recession severely affected this and many other industries. Employment in this segment of the U.S. industry has declined since World War II, when the industry boasted a peak employment of 1.3 million workers in 1945. In 1993, the U.S. textile segment employed around 649,400 persons[3] (U.S. Department of Commerce, *U.S. Industrial Outlook*, various years). Despite employment declines, textile *production* increased during this period.

Although the size of the U.S. *apparel* work force increased in the 1950s to a peak of 1.4 million persons, it has declined to approximately 939,000 persons. The number of apparel establishments declined substantially, losing, for example, nearly one per day between 1970 and 1976.

---

[3]This employment figure includes both the textile mill products segment and the manufactured fiber segment of the industry.

The Impact of Imports

The surge of textile and apparel imports into U.S. and other developed country markets was surely disruptive. No market can absorb massive quantities of imports in a particular sector without affecting severely the domestic producers in those industries. The textile/apparel sectors in the industrialized countries were unable to offset the influx of imports with a comparable increase in exports, although some segments of the industry were at times quite competitive in exporting. Thus, the trade imbalances were often seen as responsible for the unemployment, decline in establishments, and drop in earnings experienced by both segments of the industry at times in recent decades. The growth of imports cannot be blamed as the sole reason for the problems that occurred in the industry, however, because many of these would have happened without imports. Significant increases in imports no doubt aggravated and accelerated many problems. At the same time, imports may have encouraged improvements in the domestic industries as manufacturers attempted to remain competitive.

Changes in the Global Market

The increasing competition in world textile and apparel markets cannot be minimized. In any sector of global trade, a dramatic increase in the number of producers for the market will intensify competition. In the case of the textile and apparel sector, many newly developing countries began producing for the same world markets that had many fewer producers only a short time ago. The combination of rebuilding textile sectors in the developed countries after World War II and the entry of many producing nations accounted for a sevenfold increase in international textile trade between 1945 and 1975 (Ford, 1986). And, to further complicate the problem, the world

FIGURE 2–3
Even as recently as the 1960s, the number of countries producing textile (and apparel) goods for the world market was relatively limited.

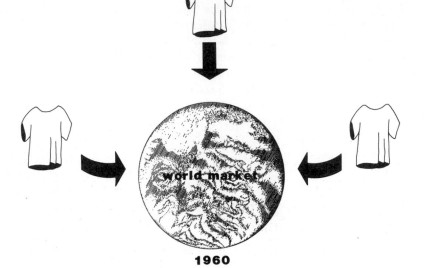

TEXTILE-PRODUCING COUNTRIES
(a limited number)

1960

market grew minimally during these latter years when many new producer nations entered the picture. Figures 2–3 and 2–4 illustrate the change; the numbers of producer nations are, of course, symbolic to make the point rather than representing actual numbers. Of the approximately 200 nations in the world, virtually all produce textile and apparel products—and most of them produce at least some products for world markets.

As a result, global competition in textiles and apparel has made this a difficult and sensitive sector. Because of the significant role the sector plays as a major employer in both the developed and developing countries, many issues related to international production and trade of textile and apparel products have become political in nature, often taking on seemingly disproportionate importance in broader relationships among nations. Because of these sensitive aspects of textile and

apparel trade, the institutional arrangements (agencies, trade policies, and other special treatment) that exist to handle problems in the sector are unique and elaborate compared to most other sectors. Later sections of the book will cover the special international and U.S. provisions that exist to resolve the complexities of global textile and apparel trade.

SUMMARY

As a leader in the Industrial Revolution, first in England and later in the United States and other parts of Europe, the textile industry played a key role in major industrial movements. In both Europe and the United States, the economic and social changes effected by the textile industry shaped the nations in a broad sense. Examples of ways in which the industry was a leader included the launching

FIGURE 2–4
In recent years, the number of nations exporting to world markets has expanded greatly—while the international market demand has increased minimally.

TEXTILE-PRODUCING COUNTRIES

TODAY
little growth in world market

of the Industrial Revolution through use of machine rather than hand labor, the development of the first factories, the impetus for the establishment of the earliest mill towns, widespread employment of women outside the home, and industrial reform resulting from worker abuse. Other industries followed many of these early developments of the textile sector. Similarly, many additional countries imitated England, other parts of Europe, and the United States in using the textile sector as the first industry through which to pursue economic development.

Shifts in the economy and the trade climate from one period to another influenced significantly the development of a global textile complex. Capitalism and more liberal political and economic thinking replaced the mercantilism of the seventeenth and eighteenth centuries, leading to expanded trade. The period between the Napoleonic Wars and World War I

(1814–1914) were particularly significant to the development of an international economy. Specialization among nations developed; market forces rather than governments regulated trade; and a sense of international economic interdependence developed during this era. By the late 1800s and early 1900s, economic nationalism emerged, however, bringing with it measures to protect markets from imports. The United States became a major force in world trade, but was one of the first nations to increase tariffs. International trade became more volatile than had been true earlier, and shortly after World War II, measures were taken to provide greater cooperation and stability. These included the establishment of the International Monetary Fund (IMF) and the General Agreement on Tariffs and Trade (GATT). By 1971, however, the Bretton Woods gold exchange standard was replaced by the floating exchange rate system.

Expansion of international trade in much of the twentieth century bridged the oceans between continents and countries, creating the global textile and apparel market that exists today. As growing numbers of developing countries started textile and apparel production and looked to exports for their growth, the industry in the United States and most other developed countries felt the impact of the growing competition. As a result of intense international competition, the textile and apparel industries became forerunners to similar trade problems in other sectors.

GLOSSARY

Capital is a factor of production defined to include all aids produced by people to further production; in addition to monetary resources, capital includes physical inputs, such as buildings and machinery, used in the production process.

Capitalism is an economic system in which investment in and ownership of the means of production, distribution, and exchange of wealth are made and maintained chiefly by private individuals or corporations rather than by government.

Capitalists are individuals who have capital, often extensive capital, to invest in businesses.

Devaluation of currency refers to the deliberate reduction of the value of a country's currency in relation to that of other countries. The lower value of the currency means that products from other countries are more expensive in home markets, thus encouraging use of domestic products over imports. Moreover, this practice makes the home country's exports more attractive in other countries.

Economic nationalism refers to the tendency of countries to focus only on their own economic interests.

Embargo is a prohibition on exports or imports.

Exports are goods and services sold to other countries.

Floating exchange rates are prices of one currency in terms of another in a system that permits the value of currencies to fluctuate with supply and demand.

Free trade is international trade that is not restricted by government measures aimed at protecting domestic industries.

Gold-exchange standard established a system of fixed exchange rates; under this system, the dollar could be converted (for official purposes) to gold at a fixed price. This system was used from 1944 to 1971.

Gold standard was the international monetary system used from about 1880 to 1914; gold was the international reserve.

Imports are goods and services purchased from other countries.

Import substitution refers to the substitution of domestic products for previously imported goods.

Industrial Revolution is the name for the complex social and economic changes resulting from the mechanization of production processes, which began in England in the mid-1700s.

Industrialized countries are those countries whose economies are heavily dependent on mechanized industry. This term is often used synonomously with the term "developed countries." In general, the industrialized countries are the more prosperous countries of the world.

International monetary system consists of the rules, customs, instruments, facilities, and organizations for effecting international payments (Salvatore, 1987).

Labor is the term for the services provided by all types and skills of workers.

Labor-intensive industry is one in which a high labor-to-capital ratio exists; that is, a great deal of labor (relative to capital) is required for production. In addition, a high ratio of production workers to all workers is typical. Grunwald and Flamm (1985) note that a labor-intensive industry is defined as a sector in which the proportion of unskilled labor is 160 percent or more of the fraction of unskilled employed in all industries. *Labor-intensive goods* are those made under the conditions of a high ratio of labor to capital.

Mercantilism is a belief that a country's wealth depends upon its holdings of treasure, usually gold. Under this economic philosophy, exports should exceed imports as a means of increasing wealth.

Protection (or *protectionism*) is a term for measures taken to "protect" domestic markets from imports. Protection may include tariffs, quotas, trade policies, and numerous other types of measures.

Protective tariffs are those tariffs imposed on imported goods primarily to discourage shipment of the products to a country trying to protect its domestic market.

Tariff (also known as a *duty*) is a tax on imported goods.

Trade refers to the voluntary exchange of goods and services between two or more countries.

SUGGESTED READINGS

Addy, J. (1976). *The textile revolution*. London: Longman.
This study of the English textile industry traces the evolution of the industry and its impact on economic development and trade.

Crawford, M. (1959). The textile industry. In J. G. Glover & R. L. Lagai (Eds.), *The development of American industries*. New York: Simmons Boardman.
A review of early development of the U.S. textile sector.

Ellsworth, P. T., & Leith, J. C. (1984). *The international economy*. New York: Macmillan.
A historical review of international economic developments and theories.

Foner, P. (Ed.) (1977). *The factory girls*. Urbana, IL: University of Illinois Press.
A collection of writings on life and struggle in the New England textile mills.

Jeremy, D. (1981). *Transatlantic industrial revolution: The diffusion of textile technologies between Britain and America, 1790–1830s*. Cambridge, MA: MIT Press.
A study of the westward diffusion of early industrial textile technology and its role in economic development.

Kidwell, C., & Christman, M. (1974). *Suiting everyone: The democratization of clothing in America*. Washington, DC: Smithsonian Institution Press.
A review of the development of mass-produced apparel in the United States and the role of that clothing in the "democratization of America".

Mantoux, P. (1927). *The Industrial Revolution in the eighteenth century*. New York: Harcourt Brace Jovanovich.
This book provides a useful account of the role inventions played in the Industrial Revolution. Important early textile developments are discussed.

Poulson, B. W. (1981). *Economic history of the United States*. New York: Macmillan.
This book traces changes in economic, social, and political institutions and how these changes influenced American economic development.

Stein, L. (Ed.). (1977). *Out of the sweatshop*. New York: Quadrangle.
This book of readings on early days of the U.S. garment industry focuses particularly on labor concerns.

Tucker, B. (1984). *Samuel Slater and the origins of the American textile industry, 1790–1860*. Ithaca, NY: Cornell University Press.
A study of Slater's introduction of the British textile manufacturing system in America and the impact of this system on industrial development.

3

The Setting— An Overview

INTRODUCTION

Although the global economy has increased interdependence among countries, we still exist in a world of vast differences in the way we live our lives and conduct business affairs. Participating in a global economy requires an appreciation for the differences we find in the international setting. Moreover, our global citizenship requires that we keep in mind that we are part of a much larger picture and that there are many "right" ways of functioning. In short, we must be sensitive to the differences in our worldwide environment, in the broadest sense of the word, to function effectively in it. The main goal of this chapter is to focus on various aspects of the international setting that influence textile and apparel production, trade, and consumption.

A crucial aspect of studying textiles and apparel in the international economy will be to review the geographic shifts of production around the world and the resulting trade shifts fostered by this trend. As we study these shifts, we will be making repeated references to various country groupings. Thus, an overview of the major categories of countries provides a common language for further discussions.

A review of country groupings will be followed by a brief overview of economic systems, political systems, and cultural environments that affect the climate for global textile and apparel production and trade. Special attention will be given to the division between the developed countries and the developing countries.

Staying informed about the international setting has become increasingly difficult in recent years. Geographic and political boundaries have been dramatically altered as old alliances dissolve and new ones emerge. For

FIGURE 3–1

"A victory for blue jeans over concrete" Globally, many barriers have been removed in recent years, changing the world profoundly and bringing the people of the world closer together. No event in modern history, however, has equaled the crumbling of the Berlin Wall—both literally and figuratively—to free millions who were isolated from the rest of the world. Amid the euphoria, as the world watched the liberation of Eastern Europe and the former Soviet Union, there before our eyes was *"a victory for blue jeans over concrete."* The visual span of blue denim worn by those who had surmounted the wall seemed to depict the common threads shared with humanity elsewhere.

Source: Photo © 1994 David Burnett/Contact Press Images.

example, the former Soviet Union became 15 different countries; East and West Germany became one; and Yugoslavia splintered into many war-torn states. Names of states and major cities changed, and sometimes factions have been unable to agree on the names or the spelling of the names for the areas. World map publishers have not struggled this hard to stay current since 1960, when 17 African nations asserted independence and adopted new names. Nevertheless, all of us who wish to exert influence on our fate in today's interdependent world must strive to comprehend the social, economic, and political dimensions of our global community.

COUNTRY GROUPINGS

Country groupings used in industry or trade discussions are often based on levels of **development** or **economic development**. Most of the distinctions made among countries in the various groupings relate to differences in average incomes. A term often used to express relative wealth (or for many countries, the lack of wealth) is **gross national product (GNP)**[1] or

---

[1]Some sources use gross national product (GNP) as a measure of national productivity or output; others use **gross domestic product (GDP)**. See the glossary for distinctions between these two terms.

per capita gross national product. Additionally, however, the groupings have different economic and political frameworks, varying levels of economic development, and many other divergent socioeconomic conditions.

International agencies, scholars, and others concerned with international activities use a variety of groupings and terms to classify and describe countries. Since these various categorization systems and terms appear in the literature and often are used interchangeably, two sets of terminology are identified here.

The first set of country groupings are those used most often in this book and which correspond closely to those of the United Nations. These groupings are as follows:

- *Developed countries*[2] (also known as the industrialized countries) are those that have achieved a high level of physical and material well-being. This category includes Western Europe, some countries in Eastern Europe, the United States, Canada, Japan, Australia, New Zealand, and South Africa. The largest flow of trade occurs among these countries, although these nations account for less than one-fifth of the world's population.
- *Centrally planned economy countries* are those that are governed by single-party communist regimes. As a result of the move away from communism to market economies in the former Soviet Union and Eastern Europe (now known by some international organizations as "economies in transition"), the number of these countries has decreased dramatically in recent years. Remaining countries include China, North Korea, Vietnam, and Cuba.

- *Developing countries*[3] are those in which the population as a whole has a lower level of physical and material well-being than exists in the developed countries. This category includes other countries not in the above groupings—particularly in Latin America, Asia, and Africa (with the exception of oil-rich exporting nations). Most of the Eastern European countries are in a transitional or developing stage rather than at the level of developed countries. Although rapidly progressing in development, Hong Kong[4], Taiwan, South Korea, and Singapore[4] are often included in this grouping. Overall, the developing countries account for a large portion of the world's population but a small amount of its wealth.
- *Newly industrialized countries (NICs)* (also known as the "newly industrialized economies") are frequently included with developing countries rather than identified as a separate category; however, the rapid development and rising levels of material well-being in these countries distinguish this group from other developing countries. In fact, when this small group of NICs is included in the developing country grouping, this upper tier represents a concentration of the greatest industrial and social progress in the group. These nations may still resemble developing countries in some ways (for example, the advancements may not be dispersed broadly among the population), but most have a significant

---

[2] Some sources are now using terms such as "more developed" and "less developed," particularly as some previous distinctions are now blurred. Other sources (e.g., World Bank) also refer to "high-income," "middle-income," and "low-income" countries.

[3] At times, the World Bank and other international organizations group together the low-income economies and the middle-income economies into this one group.

[4] Hong Kong and Singapore are city-states rather than countries; however, rather than having to draw this distinction each time, these two will be included in references to countries. Hong Kong is technically a British colony but will revert to control by China in 1997. In this book we shall use the term *country* as the United Nations does to refer also, as appropriate, to territories or areas (United Nations, 1990).

degree of industrialization as well as fast-growing economies. Many of the NICs export a substantial volume of manufactured goods. Major NICs include Hong Kong, South Korea, Taiwan, Singapore, and Brazil; the first three are among the most important NICs in the global textile and apparel sector. (Some classifications place South Africa in the NIC category rather than in the developed country grouping.)

The other common system for classifying countries to distinguish between levels of development is as follows:

- *First-world countries* are the free, well-off industrial market economies, which may also be known as the developed or industrialized countries.
- *Second-world countries* are those moderately well-off nations making the transition from centrally controlled economies to market economies. The United Nations refers to these as "economies in transition." These are the Baltic States and the Commonwealth of Independent States (CIS) from the former Soviet Union, plus the Eastern European countries.
- *Third-world countries* are the poorer countries of the world. These are also commonly known as the less developed countries (LDCs) or the developing countries in the categories previously listed (Thompson, 1978). These are generally disadvantaged, "have-not" nations.
- *Fourth-world countries* is a label sometimes applied to the poorest countries in the world. These are the most underdeveloped of all nations. This designation is not very common; usually, all the developing countries are considered in the Third-World classification.

World Bank Categories

The World Bank (the International Bank for Reconstruction and Development), an organi-zation originally established to make loans for postwar reconstruction, exists primarily to make long-term loans to the less-developed countries. The World Bank collects extensive data on the economic status and other demographic characteristics of nations. Table 3–1 displays the broad range of GNP per capita among countries with a population of over one million. In many cases, the middle-income economies differ from the low-income economies because they are oil exporters or because they export a substantial volume of manufactured products. Life expectancy is shown as a measure of the general **level of living** and well-being within countries. Figure 3–2 gives a global view of GNP per capita among countries. (This map will also serve as a useful reference as the reader uses the book.)

This table and map show that much of the world is made up of what we might call developing or less-developed countries. More than half the population of the world lives in countries where the annual per capita GNP is less than $500.

Despite the well-being many individuals in more developed nations have experienced as a result of technological revolutions of the twentieth century, "more than one billion people (one-fifth of the world's population) live on less than one dollar a day—a standard of living that Western Europe and the United States attained two hundred years ago" (World Bank, 1991, p. 1.) The number of people living below the poverty line increased 40 percent over a 20-year time span. Although urban poverty is growing in the developing countries, the rural poor still account for over 80 percent of the poor people, according to a recent United Nations study (United Nations, *NGLS*, 1992). Furthermore, the per capita GNP for the more-developed and the less-developed countries of the world reflects a growing gap between the two groups. Sadly, gains by the developed nations and the upper tier of developing countries are not shared by their poorer brethren.

FIGURE 3–2
The world: GNP per capita, 1992.

Source: Data from *World Bank Atlas* 1994, p. 20; reprinted courtesy of World Bank.

Almost all the low-income countries are located in Asia and Africa. The middle-income countries are more dispersed. The Latin American countries are for the most part in the middle-income grouping.

Whatever grouping or term is used, the developing countries as a rule face many serious problems related to health and other basic human needs (as shown in Table 3–1 by the lower life expectancy in those countries), such

as lack of education, internal political strife, growing debt, difficulty in participating competitively in global trade, and a population growth that exceeds available resources.

As developing countries attempt to strengthen their economies, many shift from the export of primary products (such as food, agricultural products, and minerals) to the export of manufactures. A large portion of these countries tie their hopes for economic development and improved quality of life to textile and apparel production as one of their first industries.

TABLE 3–1
GNP per capita and life expectancy among countries with a population over one million

	GNP per capita ($) 1992	Life expectancy at birth (years) 1992			GNP per capita ($) 1992	Life expectancy at birth (years) 1992
Low-income economies	**390 w[a]**	**62 w**	36	Lesotho	590	60
Excluding China and India	**370 w**	**56 w**	37	Egypt, Arab Rep.	640	62
			38	Indonesia	670	60
1 Mozambique	60	44	39 * Myanmar	..	60
2 Ethiopia	110	49	40 * Somalia	..	49
3 Tanzania[b]	110	51				
4 Sierra Leone	160	43	41 * Sudan	..	52
5 Nepal	170	54	42 * Yemen, Rep.	..	53
6 Uganda	170	43	**Middle-income economies**	**2,490 w**	**68 w**
7 Bhutan	180	48	**Lower-middle-income**	**.. w**	**67 w**
8 Burundi	210	48	43 Cote d'Ivoire	670[d]	56
9 Malawi	210	44	44 Bolivia	680	60
10 Bangladesh	220	55	45 Azerbaijan[c]	740	71
11 Chad	220	47	46 Philippines	770	65
12 Guinea-Bissau	220	39	47 Armenia[c]	780	70
13 Madagascar	230	51				
14 Lao PDR	250	51	48 Senegal	780	49
15 Rwanda	250	46	49 Cameroon	820	56
			50 Kyrgyz Republic[c]	820	66
16 Niger	280	46	51 Georgia[c]	850	72
17 Burkina Faso	300	48	52 Uzbekistan[c]	850	69
18 India	310	61				
19 Kenya	310	59	53 Papua New Guinea	950	56
20 Mali	310	48	54 Peru	950	65
			55 Guatemala	980	65
21 Zambia	310	48	56 Congo	1,030	51
22 Nigeria	320	52	57 Morocco	1,030	63
23 Nicaragua	340	67				
24 Togo	390	55	58 Dominican Republic	1,050	68
25 Benin	410	51	59 Ecuador	1,070	67
			60 Romania	1,130	70
26 Central African Republic	410	47	61 Jordan[e]	1,120	70
27 Pakistan	420	59	62 El Salvador	1,170	66
28 Ghana	450	56	63 Turkmenistan[c]	1,230	66
29 China	470	69	64 Moldova[c]	1,300	68
30 Tajikistan[c]	490	69	65 Lithuania[c]	1,310	71
			66 Bulgaria	1,330	71
31 Guinea	510	44	67 Colombia	1,330	69
32 Mauritania	530	48				
33 Sri Lanka	650	72	68 Jamaica	1,340	74
34 Zimbabwe	570	60	69 Paraguay	1,380	67
35 Honduras	580	66	70 Namibia	1,610	59
			71 Kazakhstan[c]	1,680	68
			72 Tunisia	1,720	68

+ Economies classified by the United Nations or otherwise regarded by their authorities as developing.

[a] w = weighted averages. [b] In all tables GDP and GNP data cover mainland Tanzania only. [c] Estimates for economies of the former Soviet Union are subject to more than usual range of uncertainty and should be regarded as very preliminary. [d] Data refer to GDP.

* For years or periods other than those specified.

	GNP per capita ($) 1992	Life expectancy at birth (years) 1992		GNP per capita ($) 1992	Life expectancy at birth (years) 1992
73 Ukraine^c	1,820	70	Low-and-middle-income	1,040 w	64 w
74 Algeria	1,840	67	Sub-Saharan Africa	530 w	52 w
75 Thailand	1,840	69	East Asia & Pacific	760 w	68 w
76 Poland	1,910	70	South Asia	310 w	60 w
77 Latvia^c	1,930	69	Europe and Central Asia	2,080 w	70 w
78 Slovak Republic	1,930	71	Middle East & N. Africa	1,950 w	64 w
79 Costa Rica	1,960	76	Latin America & Caribbean	2,690 w	68 w
80 Turkey	1,980	67			
81 Iran, Islamic Rep.	2,200	65	Severely indebted	2,470 w	67 w
82 Panama	2,420	73			
83 Czech Republic	2,450	72	High-income economies	22,160 w	77 w
84 Russian Federation^c	2,510	69			
85 Chile	2,730	72	110 Ireland	12,210	75
86 * Albania^c	..	73	111 New Zealand	12,300	76
87 * Mongolia	..	64	112 +Israel	13,220	76
88 * Syrian Arab Republic	..	67	113 Spain	13,970	77
			114 +Hong Kong	15,360	78
Upper-middle-income	**4,020 w**	**69 w**	115 +Singapore	15,730	75
89 South Africa	2,670	63	116 Australia	17,260	77
90 Mauritius	2,700	70	117 United Kingdom	17,790	76
91 Estonia^c	2,760	70	118 Italy	20,460	77
92 Brazil	2,770	66	119 Netherlands	20,480	77
93 Botswana	2,790	68			
			120 Canada	20,710	78
94 Malaysia	2,790	71	121 Belgium	20,880	76
95 Venezuela	2,910	70	122 Finland	21,970	75
96 Belarus^c	2,930	71	123 +United Arab Emirates	22,020	72
97 Hungary	2,970	69	124 France	22,260	77
98 Uruguay	3,340	72			
			125 Austria	22,380	77
99 Mexico	3,470	70	126 Germany	23,030	76
100 Trinidad and Tobago	3,940	71	127 United States	23,240	77
101 Gabon	4,450	54	128 Norway	25,820	77
102 Argentina	6,050	71	129 Denmark	26,000	75
103 Oman	6,480	70			
			130 Sweden	27,010	78
104 Slovenia	6,540	73	131 Japan	28,190	79
105 Puerto Rico	6,590	74	132 Switzerland	36,080	78
106 Korea, Rep.	6,790	71	**World**	**4,280 w**	**66 w**
107 Greece	7,290	77			
108 Portugal	7,450	74			
109 Saudi Arabia	7,510	69			

Source: From *World Development Report* 1994 by World Bank, 1994, Washington, DC: Author. Reprinted by permission.

Relevance to Textiles and Apparel

An understanding of the type of countries that constitute each of these categories is important to a global study of textile and apparel production and trade. Characteristics of different countries account for shifts in production and trade for these sectors. In recent years, the difficulties in textile trade have often reflected the dichotomy between the developed countries and the developing nations. Moreover, the political dimensions of textile trade problems have *intensified* the division between the richer and the poorer nations. The textile and apparel sectors represent a particularly critical area of trade because these industries account for about one-third of the manufactured exports of the developing countries. In some cases, textile products constitute more than one-half of the exports; for many, the industry is the primary export sector.

As we will discuss more in detail later, because of the unique role that the textile and apparel sectors play in the economies of both developed and developing countries, many of the issues surrounding textile trade have significant social and political repercussions.

REGIONS OF SPECIAL SIGNIFICANCE IN TEXTILE AND APPAREL PRODUCTION AND TRADE

Although a good case could be made for giving special attention to many specific countries or regions, space does not permit. Selected regions are shown in the following maps to aid in following frequent references to these areas. These are areas of particular significance at the present in textile and apparel production and trade.

Economic integration, the removal of economic barriers between or among nations, characterizes a number of these regions. The major forms of economic integration are: **free trade area (FTA)**, **customs union**, **common market**, **economic union**, and complete **economic integration**. In general, economic integration facilitates trade and resource flows: resources flow to efficient producers, and economies of scale often occur as markets grow.

Western Europe

According to De Vorsey (1992), Western Europe is home to some of the world's most productive and prosperous people, who inhabit only 3 percent of the earth's total land surface. Western Europe is composed of diverse countries with distinctive histories, languages, and traditions—and pride in these national heritages. Compared to some regions of the world, the Western European nations share many common characteristics: healthy, well-fed populations, birth and death rates far below world averages, incomes far above the world average, predominantly urban populations, industrially oriented economies, and market-oriented agriculture sectors. Although three countries (Spain, Portugal, and Greece) are not as advanced in economic development as some other parts of Western Europe, they are members of the European Union. The Western European culture, although not as old as some others, has profoundly shaped the world as we now know it. Today, many other parts of the world accept and aspire to the European way of life.

The following country groupings, with relevance for trade, exist in Western Europe.

The European Union (EU) (also European Community)

The European Economic Community (EEC), also known as the "Common Market" when it was originally established in 1952 (with six Member States), was established first to foster economic cooperation and integration. Later, member countries gradually began to cooperate on a broad range of issues. As Member States have expanded their common agenda beyond economic matters, they have become known as the **European Community**, or **EC**, and more recently as the **European Union (EU)**.[5]

Readers should be familiar with the composition of the EU. Many parallels in the history and status of the textile and apparel sectors bind the EU and the United States into common positions on many textile and apparel trade matters.

The European Union is a group of 12 West European nations that have joined together for cooperation on a variety of economic, social, and other issues. The EU includes the following Member States as shown in Figure 3–3: Belgium, Denmark, France, Great Britain, Greece, Ireland, Italy, Luxembourg, the Netherlands, Portugal, Spain, and Germany. A number of other European countries aspire to join the EU. Among the first group likely to be included are Austria, Finland, Norway, and Sweden. The next candidates are the Czech and Slovak Republics, Hungary, and Poland.

The European Economic Community was originally a customs union formed to eliminate barriers and discrimination in trade among members and to harmonize trade policies for its Member States with the rest of the world. In most matters, member countries still govern themselves independently of each other and retain national identities. However, certain matters are decided at the Community (now Union) level in Brussels and the Community (Union) makes policies and laws that apply in all its member countries.

The European Union has moved toward increasingly integrated plans for cooperation. The EU began as a **customs union**, later

became a **common market**, and now embodies essentially **complete economic integration**. Plans to include other European countries are underway.

European integration has occurred in phases. On December 31, 1992, the EC entered a new stage in integrating member countries into a unified European market. The European Community embarked on a plan for further refinement of a goal it started in 1957: a single internal market with freedom of movement for goods, services, people, and capital. The unified market permits the 12 nations to function more as one coordinated unit in world trade and gives the EU a more favorable competitive position in its dealings with the United States and Japan in particular. Although countries are not expected to abandon their national identities, the unification permits the EU to focus more efficiently on a wide range of common matters, including social problems and environmental concerns (*European Union*, 1992).

The unified European Union is one of the world's largest markets, with 345 million consumers (This includes the number resulting from the reunification of Germany [Price Waterhouse, 1991]). In addition, the elimination of trade barriers among member countries is having a significant impact on traditional methods of producing, marketing, and distributing. Changes permit manufacturing in different European countries, centralized shipping, elimination of delays crossing borders, and smoother accounting and billing procedures. Moreover, the changes affect other nations that conduct business with Europe, as well as altering commercial relationships within the EU. The strength of the unified market permits the EU to wield increased power in global trade relationships. Activities in the global textile and apparel sectors are affected by this change.

EU integration into a unified Europe has not been easy. Centuries of tradition for each

---

[5]The name *European Union* is being widely used; however, many among the Member States' residents continue to use the term *European Community*. Even new publications from the official government body, the Commission, are inconsistent in their references.

FIGURE 3–3

Western Europe: the European Union and members of the European Free Trade Association (EFTA).

member country have led to reluctance in adopting new European Union ways of viewing life and going about business. A great deal of bickering has characterized the progress to date, and the average citizen has shown little sign of enthusiasm for a new pan-European identity. Historic resentments have remained the greatest obstacle to closer integration, but cross-border contact appears to be easing old tensions (Horwitz, 1993).

EU members agreed on another step toward deepening integration by signing the

Treaty of Maastricht in February 1992. The Maastricht Treaty represents efforts to move toward a full-fledged European Union through establishment of closer economic and political integration. Although the Maastrich Treaty was greeted with hostility by many citizens, particularly in Denmark and England, its final goal focuses on an Economic and Monetary Union (EMU) with the establishment of a single currency by 1999. Not only has the EU strengthened its own 12-country integration, but the Union has also widened its associations to include two other groups of countries, as noted in sections that follow.

European Free Trade Association (EFTA)

Another example of economic integration, the European Free Trade Association (EFTA), was formed in 1960. EFTA includes Austria, Iceland, Liechtenstein, Norway, Sweden, Switzerland, and Finland (see Figure 3–3). In this *free trade area*, member countries eliminated tariffs on manufactured goods and agricultural products that originate in and are traded *among member countries*. This group of European nations sought the benefits of free trade among members but preferred that each country retain its own external tariff structure for trade with other countries.

As following sections indicate, EFTA nations have joined the EU to form the European Economic Area (EEA), which means that nearly all barriers between the two groups related to the flow of people, products, capital, and services were eliminated except for the sensitive agricultural sector for which special arrangements exist. The future of EFTA may be somewhat in question because Austria, Finland, Norway and Sweden have applied for full membership in the EU.

European Economic Area (EEA)

In January 1993, the EU and five nations of the European Free Trade Association (EFTA) (Austria, Sweden, Norway, Finland, and Iceland) implemented a historic agreement, forming the European Economic Area. Switzerland and Liechtenstein have not ratified the EEA agreement. This accord creates a free trade area with 380 million people and 40 percent of the world's GDP ("European Economic", 1994; Rapoport, 1992), including some of the world's most affluent consumers in the EFTA nations. This agreement results in a GDP of about $7 trillion and accounts for about 40 percent of world trade (Tully, 1991). Formation of the EEA was the first step for some EFTA members to seek full membership in the EU.

"Greater Europe"

Another agreement may expand trade ties so far that the region will be known as "Greater Europe"—a huge trading area of 450 million people in at least 25 countries (Hammes, 1991). For this expansion, the EU has signed agreements with some of the countries of Eastern Europe that have sought preferential access to the EU market. A 1991 agreement provides improved access for Hungary, Poland, plus the Czech and Slovak Republics, paving the way for complete free trade with the EU within 10 years. This agreement may have been even more significant than that with EFTA countries because the EU and EFTA already had close trade ties and conducted a great deal of business in each other's markets. That is, the ties with Eastern Europe represented new markets for EU firms. This agreement was of limited value to the Eastern European nations, however, because the EU retained stiff barriers on agricultural and other "sensitive sector" products such as textiles, apparel, steel, and iron—the most important products to the economies of those former communist countries.

Eastern Europe, Commonwealth of Independent States (CIS), and Baltic States

Prior to the fall of communism in Eastern Europe and the former Soviet Union, most of these countries were characterized as having centrally planned economies and nondemocratic political systems. This region includes a number of countries whose identities have changed significantly—some are new, in most cases a portion of a larger nation that existed earlier. The former Soviet Union emerged as 15 newly independent states; Czechoslovakia became the Czech and Slovak Republics; Yugoslavia splintered into many new states; and East Germany reunited with West Germany. (Figure 3–4 provides an overview of the region.)

Revolutionary changes are underway in Eastern Europe, the CIS[6], and the Baltic States,[7] with economies in transition from the old order of central planning to new market economies. In many respects, the transition has been painful and costly in economic terms. Citizens, excited over the new freedom from communism, were not prepared for the difficulties in store or for the time required to make the transition. No formula existed to guide a country through this process; no precedent existed.

Previously, many of these countries participated in the Council for Mutual Economic Assistance (CMEA or COMECON) and were major trading partners with one another. In the transition to market economies, a new trading system based on convertible currency transactions and world market prices was implemented. A lack of convertible currencies and workable payment mechanisms caused all the countries in Eastern Europe and the former Soviet Union to reduce their trade with one another. Many of the intermediate materials for production had been obtained

from other trading partners in the region; therefore, when trade among countries slowed dramatically or stopped, manufacturing suffered. Different states were at varying stages in developing political and institutional changes in their economies; this, too, affected intra-group trade and payment relations. A domino effect from all these factors led to severe economic disruption. In the former Soviet Union, a year after the transition began, national income was at least 15 percent under what it had been the prior year. As United Nations (1992) writers noted, "By all economic indicators, the region is in the grip of a savage economic contraction. The fall in economic activity is without precedent in industrialized countries. Levels of output were no higher than ten years ago" (p. 24).

Unemployment rose to high levels in some of these economies—in a few cases, four to six times the normal rate. Real wages and salaries declined; therefore, household incomes plummeted. Public expenditures for health and education services declined. Poverty grew. Impatience and disenchantment led to worries that if more authoritarian forms of government appeared to represent stability, democratic reforms might be at risk. United Nations (1992) authors summarized the situation as follows: "Although individual freedom has been strengthened by the weakening of various forms of authority and previously accepted values of collectivism, in a sense society has become more fragile" (p. 26).

A ray of hope exists in the fact that some of the countries that began the process first have stabilized somewhat; serious shortages of products have improved. Some of these countries are making a concerted effort to reorient their foreign economic ties "outward." A few have trade arrangements with Western Europe. For others, however, this goal has not been easy because they have lacked manufactured products that are competitive in world markets.

---

[6]As the book goes to press, the Commonwealth of Independent States (CIS) includes the Russian Federation, Kazakhstan, Kyrgyzstan, Tajikistan, Turkmenistan, Uzbekistan, Azerbaijan, Armenia, Ukraine, Moldova, Belarus, and Georgia.

[7]Baltic States include Estonia, Latvia, and Lithuania.

FIGURE 3–4
Eastern Europe, Commonwealth of Independent States (CIS), and Baltic States.

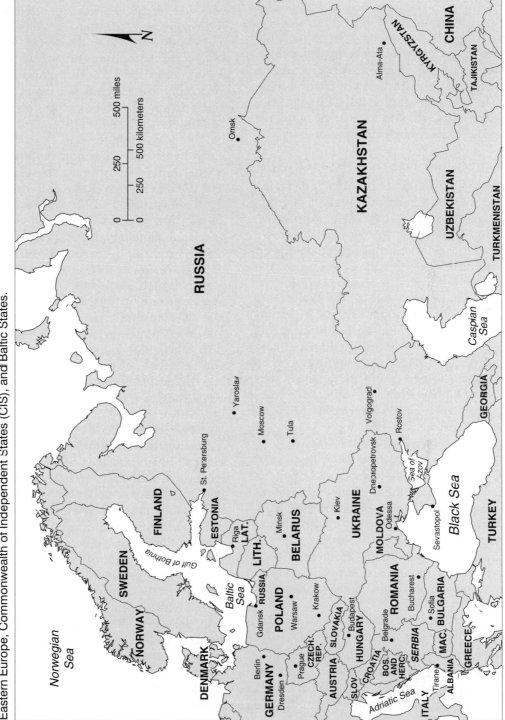

The Americas

Following Europe's trend toward broader economic integration, Canada, Mexico, and the United States began to develop integrated markets as well. So far, agreements to strengthen these trade associations have occurred in two stages. Like Europe, the countries of North America have plans for more extensive economic integration.

The Canada-U.S. Free Trade Area (CFTA)

In 1989, Canada and the United States entered into an agreement to establish a free trade area between the two countries. Although nearly 80 percent of the trade between the two countries already occurred with no tariffs or restrictive regulations, the agreement removed barriers to trade for the remaining 20 percent—which included textile and apparel products. The agreement included a gradual phasing out of all tariffs and quotas within a 10-year period. U.S. textile and apparel industry leaders were opposed to the agreement; they feared that Canada would become a conduit for low-wage imported products directed to U.S. markets (Wall & Dickerson, 1989).

In the first years under the Canada-U.S. agreement, the United States appeared to benefit more than Canada. Many Canadians blamed the pact for the economic slump that increased Canada's unemployment rate from 7.5 percent to 11.6 percent in the three years following the agreement ("No gain," 1992). However, as we shall discuss further in Chapter 6, the textile and apparel industries in both countries gained as a result of the agreement.

North American Free Trade Area (NAFTA)

In August 1992, Canada, Mexico, and the United States signed an agreement to take effect on January 1, 1994, to eliminate all tariffs on trade between the three countries over a 15-year period. Final passage required ratification by legislative bodies in the three countries. The combined market, stretching from the Yukon to the Yucatan, is one of the largest and richest markets in the world, with a $6.5 trillion annual output and encompassing 370 million consumers. Formation of this trade area will have a significant impact on textile and apparel producers and consumers, not only in North America but also for producers in other parts of the world.

The three NAFTA nations already had strong trade relationships. The United States and Canada were already each other's leading trade partner, and Mexico was the United States' third largest partner, following Canada and Japan. Similarly, Mexico's most important trade partner and greatest source of **foreign direct investment (FDI)** has been the United States, which accounted for 70 percent of Mexico's trade in 1991 and 61 percent of the FDI by value as of June 1992 (USITC, 1993b).

NAFTA plans met with considerable concern, particularly among certain industries and segments of the population in Canada and the United States. Moreover, until the late 1980s, Mexico's closed economy had not made the nation an attractive free trade partner. However, more recent progressive leadership radically trimmed protectionist policies that made it difficult for other countries to conduct business with Mexico. Although Mexico made tremendous advancement in its economic and political structures, many Canadians and Americans feared that free trade with a lower-wage nation might take jobs from their countries. Although many U.S. and Canadian industry groups saw the advantage of selling into one of the fastest growing markets in the world, with a population of more than 90 million persons, other industries and labor groups were less enthusiastic. The fact remained, however, that these countries *were already important trade partners with one another*—NAFTA merely facilitated trade by removing some of the existing impediments.

Enterprise for the Americas Initiative (EAI)

NAFTA is seen as an important step towards free trade in the Western Hemisphere. In 1990, President George Bush announced his vision for a free trade area that would extend from Alaska to Argentina to be known as the Enterprise for the Americas Initiative (EAI). The EAI would incorporate trade, investment, and debt reduction to bolster the economies in the Americas.

The Caribbean Basin Area

The Caribbean basin area (Figure 3–5) has grown rapidly as a major apparel production area for U.S. markets, particularly as a result of trade policies intended to aid the region. Textile and apparel products have been very important to these economies, and the impact of this production has been significant, particularly for the U.S. industry and for some Asian producers.

The Caribbean region is "an ethnic blend of almost all the peoples and cultures of the world" (Knight, 1990, p. 308), resulting from early colonization by Great Britain, France, Spain, the Netherlands, and North American colonies—a colonization that left its stamp on the language, religion, music, dress, and even the work orientation of the separate peoples. Colonization also left an economic legacy. Colonial powers sought raw materials and sold finished products there; agriculture products and extracted natural resources became important exports from the region. The Caribbean economies depended heavily on exports and foreign capital; industrialization was limited (Axline, 1979; Balkwell & Dickerson, 1994; Knight, 1990).

After World War II, most of the Caribbean colonies gained independence, sought national identities, and tried to expand industrialization. Manufacturing generally consisted of assembly operations that used components made in the developed countries. The apparel industry was a leading industry in this development. Although the Caribbean economies made significant strides, the difficult world economy of the mid-1970s led to large government debts, diminished optimism, and, in some cases, widespread discontent.

Beginning in the early 1980s, the United States enacted trade policies to bolster the Caribbean region. Particularly since the 1986 enactment of these policies, which provided special access to the U.S. market for apparel assembled in Caribbean basin countries, many U.S. apparel firms have shifted production to the region. In fact, virtually all Caribbean-produced apparel is destined for U.S. markets; (U.S. Department of Commerce, 1993; Steele, 1988). Manufacturers who have production in the Caribbean are taking advantage of labor that is far less costly than that in the United States, yet the location is much closer to the domestic market than Asia. In response to the potentially large loss of business, a number of Asian producers have established production sites in the Caribbean region themselves, specifically to ship to U.S. markets. Moreover, Asian producers who face tightened **quota** restraints on products made in their home countries established Caribbean production as a way to have access to U.S. markets.

The North American Free Trade Agreement, which gives Mexico greater trade privileges with the United States than exists for the Caribbean Initiative countries, has been a concern for those manufacturers involved in Caribbean production. Therefore, Caribbean producers and U.S. firms with production in the Caribbean have sought equal treatment (*parity*, in trade terms) with Mexico (author's visits with industry sources, 1994; Barrett, 1993).

The Caribbean Economic Community (CARICOM). This grouping of Caribbean economies was formed to reduce trade barri-

FIGURE 3–5
The Caribbean basin area.

ers among member nations and is moving toward a customs union with a common external tariff for goods entering the community. CARICOM's long-term goals are to enhance economic development and reduce the region's external dependence.

Asia

The area, often called Monsoon Asia by geographers, is the southeastern quadrant of the Eurasian land mass. This includes regions sometimes designated as East Asia, South Asia, and Southeast Asia. This area accounts for about 7.2 percent of the earth's total land surface (excluding Antarctica and Greenland), but has about 56 percent of the world's population (just under 3 billion in 1990) (Pannell, 1992). Figure 3–6 shows the countries of Monsoon Asia.

Asian countries have relied heavily on textile and apparel production in their economic development process. Therefore, many of these countries have had enormous influence on the global picture for textile and apparel production and have accounted for the greatest shifts in production and trade in recent decades.

East Asia

This region, often referred to in the past as the Orient or the Far East, has been transformed remarkably in little more than a decade. Economic growth and development are among the fastest growing in the world. East Asia boasts countries that are some of the major suppliers in today's international textile and apparel market. Many of these countries (for example, Japan, Hong Kong, South Korea, and Taiwan) have well-developed production and marketing structures and exert a powerful influence on global markets for the sector. Japan was clearly the early leader in developing its industry and exporting products to other parts of the world. Not long ago, China was at the early stages of developing its textile and apparel industry, but it rapidly became a major force in global markets. By the early 1990s, China had become the world's leading apparel exporter.

Hong Hong, Taiwan, and South Korea have been called the "Big Three" because of the major role they have played in global production and trade for these industries. China is often added to the Big Three, constituting a group known as the "Big Four" in textile and apparel trade. Although other countries in Asia are at varied stages of economic development, and textiles and apparel may be among those nations' primary exports, the industries in those nations have not yet exerted the impact on global markets equal to that of the Big Four.

Southeast Asia

Mainland Southeast Asia (sometimes called Indochina because of its interface between India and China) includes Thailand, Laos, Myanmar (formerly Burma), Vietnam, Kampuchea (formerly Cambodia), and western Malaysia. Island countries include the eastern portion of Malaysia, Indonesia, Singapore, the Philippines, and Brunei.

Levels of economic development vary greatly among the region, ranging from Singapore, which ranks next to Japan in prosperity (based on per capita GNP) in Monsoon Asia (Pannell, 1992), to other countries with large populations living in poverty. The region is a mosaic of people with disparate national histories, cultural heritages, political allegiances, and religious followings. Agriculture remains important in most of the countries; however, economic development has been dramatic in some, such as Malaysia, Indonesia, and Thailand. In many of the Southeast Asian countries, the textile and apparel sector has led the way in economic growth.

FIGURE 3–6
Asia

Some of the Southeast Asian countries have entered into economic integration efforts.

Association of Southeast Asian Nations (ASEAN) ASEAN represents the first major Asian effort toward integration; cooperation has occurred on development and trade mat-ters, despite the cultural disparity among the countries. Organized in 1977, the ASEAN net-work includes Malaysia, Singapore, the Philippines, Thailand, Indonesia, and Brunei.

Rapid growth in textile and apparel pro-duction in the ASEAN nations was spurred first by investments from Japan and the Big Three. This shift of production to ASEAN nations occurred in many cases as Japan and the Big Three experienced tightened quotas for shipping to U.S. and EC markets. That is, Japanese and Big Three suppliers established production in ASEAN countries where more abundant quotas permitted shipping the products to major developed markets. Additionally, Japan, the Big Three, and other countries looked to the ASEAN nations for low-wage labor as workers for the textile and apparel industry became scarce and more costly in their home countries.

In late 1992, the ASEAN group agreed upon the main elements for a free trade area among members (the ASEAN Free Trade Area, or AFTA), with tariffs for trade with one another reduced to 0 to 5 percent in the year 2008. The Asian free trade area is intended to foster trade among the region that encompasses 330 million consumers, to attract foreign investment, and to counteract the economic integration occurring in Europe and North America (*IAF Newsletter*, 1992; United Nations, 1993). (Discussion on the emergence of powerful trading blocs will follow in this chapter.)

South Asia

South Asia, known also as the Indian subcontinent, consists of three countries with very large populations (India, Pakistan, and Bangladesh), plus Sri Lanka, Nepal, and Bhutan. Also included is Afghanistan, which is an interface state with historic ties to both South Asia and the Middle East. Exceeded only by China, India is the second most populous country in the world. Although the countries of South Asia have different levels of economic development, all are considered poor by Western standards. Political disputes and military conflict have kept these nations from reaching their potential (Pannell, 1992).

For most of the South Asian countries, textile and apparel production has been extremely important to the developing economies. For example, in 1991 textile and apparel exports accounted for 65 percent of Pakistan's merchandise exports. Similar exports represented 31 percent of India's merchandise exports (GATT, 1993) and perhaps would have been even greater had not India's closed economy made it very difficult for more developed nations to invest and produce there, as had occurred in the ASEAN nations. In the early 1990s, India made progress in opening its economy and encouraged foreign investment more than in the past. South Asia is expected to continue to be an important textile and apparel region.

Asia Pacific Economic Cooperation Conference (APEC)

In 1989, 15 nations, including the ASEAN countries, Japan, South Korea, China, Hong Kong, Taiwan, Australia, and New Zealand, plus the United States and Canada, formed the Asia Pacific Economic Cooperation Conference. The group's purpose is to encourage freer trade and to encourage major economies in particular to settle their differences without retaliating against countries perceived to be engaged in unfair trade (*IAF Newsletter*, 10/92). This group is not technically a trade bloc since it includes trading partners outside Asia. The group's goals are to make the region a major exporting force in the world economy, to attract investment, and to be an Asian counterpoint to the European and North American trade blocs (United Nations, 1992, 1993).

FORMATION OF REGIONAL TRADING BLOCS

In recent years, increased economic integration has led to the formation of regional **trading blocs**. Following the EC unification efforts, other countries grew concerned that they might have more limited access to the large EC market—i.e., that the EC might become "fortress Europe." As a result, EC unification spurred a continuing trend toward

FIGURE 3–7
The formation of regional trading blocs has the potential for being divisive rather than forming a broader global trading community.

Source: Illustration by Dennis Murphy.

formation of regional trade blocs. In fact, the proliferation of these agreements, as shown below, reflects the growing interest in trading with neighbor nations—as well as the fear of being excluded from existing blocs. Some of these trading blocs have been mentioned earlier in sections on country groupings; as a review, those are included briefly along with others. The three major blocs are

- *The European bloc.* As the European Union moves through successive stages of integration (unification of its 12 members, adding EFTA countries, and developing cooperative agreements with Eastern Europe), this large and powerful bloc will

be known as the European Economic Area (EEA) and later as Greater Europe.
- *The Americas bloc.* With conclusion of the NAFTA agreement, this region represents another important trading bloc. Further, if the Enterprise for the Americas Initiative becomes a reality, this will unite the Western Hemisphere into a formidable trading bloc.
- *The Asian bloc.* Seeing the formation of the European bloc and the NAFTA bloc, Asian countries became increasingly motivated to unite into a bloc to offset the effects of the other two. Although Japan represents the major industrial trading power in the region, that nation has not taken leader-

ship in the formation of the Asia Pacific Economic Cooperation Conference (APEC). Rather, Singapore has been the leader. As the ASEAN nations unite in APEC with other economies in the region, this bloc will also be a powerful force in the global economy, representing a majority of the world's consumers and many fast-growing economies.

Other regional or sub-regional trading arrangements (some of which are or may be included in the larger blocs above) are

- *The Association of Southeast Asian (ASEAN) group.* This group, which was discussed earlier, has moved from an association that was less integrated on economic issues toward becoming a regional common market known as the ASEAN Free Trade Area (AFTA).
- *The Caribbean Economic Community (CARICOM).* Although this group was established in the 1970s, finally in the early 1990s it became a common market with a common external tariff among members.
- *The Andean Pact.* In January 1992, a free trade pact among Bolivia, Colombia, and Venezuela became effective, with plans for Ecuador and Peru to follow. The original agreement did not specify a common external tariff, but since most of these countries have reduced tariffs in recent years, the common external tariff is expected to be 5 to 20 percent when pact members reach this stage (United Nations, 1992).
- *Southern Cone Common Market ("Mercosur").* In March 1991, Argentina, Brazil, Paraguay, and Uruguay completed a common market agreement that not only removed barriers to trade but also included plans for coordination of policies on broader industrial and financial matters. Trade has expanded among members, and firms in the region have changed investment strategies as a result of the agreement (United Nations, 1992).

- *Central American Common Market.* Although a regional economic group existed in the 1960s, it dissolved after a few years. In the early 1990s, Costa Rica, El Salvador, Guatemala, Honduras, Nicaragua, and Panama agreed to re-establish a common market among members.
- *Black Sea Economic Cooperation Region.* This grouping consists of Turkey, Bulgaria, Romania, and the Republics of Armenia, Azerbaijan, Georgia, Moldova, Russia, and Ukraine. The group was formed to help members integrate with the world economy and resolve regional problems (United Nations, 1992).
- *African Economic Community.* In June 1991, members of the Organization for African Unity signed an agreement to begin dealing with trade barriers, with the long-term goal of becoming a free trade area and later a continent-wide customs union.

Pros and Cons Concerning Trade Blocs

Trading blocs are a fact of life in today's global economy. As the number of trade blocs continues to grow and as the three major blocs expand, concern exists that these regional groupings will be a divisive influence in the world economy—that is, that blocs may fragment efforts to form a global trading community. As the General Agreement on Tariffs and Trade (GATT, which is explained in greater detail in later chapters) attempts to foster world trade by removing various kinds of barriers, some sources feel that the proliferation of regional trading blocs may undermine the broader effort (Magnusson, 1992).

On the positive side, trading blocs encourage member nations to participate in trade, at least to an extent. That is, a country that has been an isolated, closed economy may participate in a regional arrangement more readily than in a broader one, thus learning the benefits and skills involved in trade. In this case, the regional bloc may be a stepping-stone to broader participation. Second, since consumers generally benefit from free trade, it follows that consumers in a region should find advantages in having more choices and better prices from a greater number of producers in the region compared to only the home country.

On the negative side, trade blocs may simply divert trade rather than create it. There is a tendency to substitute products in the region for those from the rest of the world, causing a reduced demand for products from outside the bloc. Additionally, powerful trade blocs may be inclined to push for trade policies that benefit them, whereas individual countries not in blocs will be at a disadvantage (United Nations, 1992).

In reflecting on trade blocs, United Nations (1992) writers concluded: "The costs of consolidation of the world into a few large trading blocs would probably be borne not by the countries in the blocs, but by those left out. Those would most likely be small, open, export-oriented countries—especially developing ones—that thus far have gained the most from a strong and liberal multilateral trading system" (p. 61).

THE DIVISION BETWEEN NORTH AND SOUTH

Of all the country groupings relevant to the study of global textile and apparel production and trade, the division between developed countries and developing nations merits special attention. Terms for the division between the "North" and the "South" come from an imprecise reference to the fact that the industrial market economies are in the Northern Hemisphere (Australia and New Zealand are important exceptions), and the greatest proportion of the developing countries are in the Southern Hemisphere.

Economic concerns, including trade in particular, have led to these divisions. This North-South split has become especially sensitive on nearly all global economic and trade matters in recent decades and is a key point in the difficulties associated with global textile and apparel production and trade.

In this section, we will review the division between North and South. In the next chapter, this division will be considered within a framework of *development* theory. In various portions of the book, the reader will see the division between developed and developing countries as a repeated theme in discussions of textile and apparel production and trade.

First, a brief historical review will be helpful in understanding the origins of the relatively recent division between the developed countries and the LDCs. In the nineteenth and early twentieth centuries, international trade provided opportunities for growth and prosperity for the dominant nations of the times. During this era, the economies in newer countries such as the United States blossomed. Since World War I, however, global trade has grown more slowly than it had earlier. The volume of international trade grew 270 percent between 1850 and 1880, 170 percent between 1880 and 1913, and only 57 percent between 1928 and 1958 (Nurkse, 1961).

After World War II, a wave of decolonization swept the world, liberating the peoples of Africa and Asia. The newly independent states were said to be "sovereign and equal to other nations, old and new, large and small" (Agarwala, 1983, p. viii). The developing countries' admittance to the United Nations reinforced their status of sovereignty. In the years that followed, however, a large proportion of the developing countries began to feel they had ended an era of *political* colonization only to enter one of *economic* colonization. Many of these Third-World countries embarked on plans for national economic development. They attempted to pattern themselves after the earlier industrialization strategies of the developed countries; this approach had been relatively successful in some of the Latin American countries. Goals for economic growth in developing countries were formally included in the official development strategies of the First and Second United Nations Development Decades (the 1960s and 1970s).

The developing countries expected trade to play a major role in their economic advancement, as it had for the developed countries. However, Third-World countries' success in trade fell short of expectations.

Until 1953, world trade in general expanded more rapidly than global production output, but, after that, trade grew more slowly than output. Trade no longer fueled growth and prosperity as it had earlier. Developing countries that aspired to the same kind of economic development they had observed in the industrialized countries felt their opportunities had been stymied by the wealthier nations. The developed countries increasingly restricted the developing countries' exports of agricultural commodities and manufactured goods such as textile products and leather goods. A growing sense of frustration mounted as the developing countries expressed resentment that the international economy was not functioning in their interests.

Other factors affected relationships between the developed and the developing countries in the early 1970s. First, the Middle East oil embargo of 1973–1974 led to quadrupled oil prices that affected both groups of countries. During this time, some Third-World nations became aware of their important roles as sources of major natural resources on which the developed countries depended. Thus, some developing nations discovered their ability to wield a certain amount of economic and political power. This power was minimized, however, because the economic conditions of both the developed and the developing countries deteriorated seriously in the mid-1970s. Problems in the developed countries that included inflation, unemploy-

ment, and unused industrial capacity focused concerns on *domestic* economies—with less interest in assisting the Third World (Agarwala, 1983).

All these factors caused leaders in many countries to realize that problems associated with the North-South split must be addressed as part of a changing international economy. Consequently, this concern stimulated a host of declarations and studies by the United Nations and the international community at large. Several efforts relevant to discussions on the division between North and South are described below.

- *United Nations Conference on Trade and Development (UNCTAD)* has played an active role in attempting to coordinate the relationships between the developing countries and the industrialized nations. UNCTAD focuses on such areas as commodities, manufacturing, shipping, and other trade concerns. It was at the first UNCTAD session in Geneva in 1964 that developing countries began to express a strong, collective voice regarding their frustrations with the world economy. The developing countries began to pressure the industrialized countries to give preference to manufactured exports from the developing countries. This was the beginning of what is now known as the North-South dialogue.
- The *North-South dialogue* is a term for the discussions that resulted from protests of the developing countries regarding their status in the world economy. This dialogue has continued since 1974, with the primary concern of the developing countries focused on how to transfer wealth from the developed countries to the poorer, developing nations. Key issues addressed in these dialogues have been reduction of trade barriers in the developed countries, increased aid and investment, stabilization of export earnings and commodity prices, and repayment of debts. In general, the

developing countries made greater demands than the industrialized countries were willing to meet.

- The *Group of 77* is a coalition of developing countries (originally 77 countries—now well over 100) within UNCTAD that coordinated the efforts of the LDCs in requesting fuller participation in the world economy. In recent years, the Group of 77 has focused a great deal on concerns related to the effect of trade barriers on their exports to industrialized countries.
- *A New International Economic Order (NIEO)* emerged as an agenda issue at the 1974 meeting of the UN General Assembly. The developing countries, aware of economic leverage because of their control of the supply of a number of important fuels and raw materials—as well as being purchasers of about 25 percent of the developed world's exports—felt that the existing global economic system was inadequate for their future growth.

  Increasingly dissatisfied with the way in which the world economic system affected the developing countries, the LDCs pressed for a "new international economic order" to address their needs. They proposed that this include (1) greater control by the LDCs over their own economic fate, (2) a reduction in the gap of per capita income between developing countries and the industrialized nations, and (3) an increased share of the world's industrial production occurring in the LDCs. To achieve these goals, the LDCs requested tariff preferences for their exported products (that is, that their products would have reduced tariffs when shipped to the developed countries), increased transfer of funds to the LDCs from the industrialized countries, and maintenance of prices on LDC commodities (Ellsworth & Leith, 1984; Mansfield, 1983).
- *Organized in 1961, the Organization for Economic Cooperation and Development (OECD)* is composed of 24 primarily industrial, market economy countries—i.e., the North. Many persons outside the organization call it the "rich man's club" because member nations are the most prosperous in the world. OECD was formed to assist member governments in formulating policies to promote economic and social welfare and to stimulate and coordinate members' assistance to developing countries. Although the goals of OECD include far more than trade and economic issues, these concerns have taken on special significance in recent years. One should also note that OECD was organized before the North-South division erupted.

- Issues related to the North-South dialogue are particularly relevant to the position of textiles and apparel in the international economy. Later discussion will relate the intense divisions between the North and the South on textile trade matters. In fact, the sensitive and difficult aspects of global textile trade are tied to the divisions between these two groups of countries and the role of the textile and apparel industries in each grouping.

ECONOMIC SYSTEMS

According to Schiller (1983), the **economy** is an abstraction that refers to the sum of all our individual production and consumption activities. Schiller also compares "the economy" to a family. What we collectively produce is what the economy produces, and what we collectively consume is what the economy consumes.

An **economic system** is the way of organizing the production of goods and services that people want and then distributing those products to the end use consumer. The economic system determines the allocation of resources within a nation—that is, the control of economic activity and the ownership of factors of production (for example, land and capital). In **capitalist economic systems**, the **factors of production** are owned by individuals, and allocation decisions are made by market forces (see the following discussion on market-directed systems). In contrast, in **socialist economic systems**, all nonlabor means of production have been owned by the state, which controls resource allocation (see the following discussion on centrally planned economic systems). We must keep in mind, however, that these systems have changed in a number of countries. The type of economic system present in a country significantly affects both the environment for domestic textile and apparel production and distribution, as well as the conditions for international trade for these products.

The Market-Directed Systems

Mansfield (1983) defines a **market** as a group of firms and individuals that are in touch with each other in order to buy or sell some good (this definition may also be expanded to include services). Consumers and producers come together in a market, although this may be through systems that do not require that all the players interact in person. In *market-directed economic systems*, consumers have the opportunity to make the choices they wish from the array of goods and services available at any given time, and firms are given the freedom to respond to consumer demand in ways perceived to be most beneficial to each company. In addition, firms are given the freedom to stimulate consumer demand. Individuals who exchange their goods and services in the marketplace for those produced by others are submitting to the market mechanism. Consumer response may occur in a *domestic* market or, as has been more typical in recent years, consumers are participating increasingly in the *global* market system.

Price becomes the regulator of supply and demand and determines shifts in resources from one area of production to another. Prices regulate local, domestic, and worldwide markets, and the free market inhibits those who provide unwanted goods or attempt to price goods above the market price. This system rewards the workers and companies who respond most sensitively and competitively to consumers' desires. When this idea is applied on a global scale, economists contend that protecting an industry from foreign competition reduces that industry's need to function at its best to remain competitive. Debate over this point as it relates to the textile and apparel sector will be covered in a later section. Cateora (1987) summarizes well the market system in its ideal state as follows: "Theoretically, the market is an automatic, competitive, self-regulating mechanism providing maximum consumer welfare and regulating the use of factors of production" (p. 47).

In reality, however, perfect market economies do not exist. Market-directed economies and centrally planned economies are ends of a continuum, and perfect examples do not occur. Economies more strongly resembling the market-directed type have been successful in many of the major developed countries. Most of the rest of the world considers the U.S. market as a good example of a prosperous market economy; however, several limiting factors in the United States prohibit the operation of a perfect market economy. Limiting factors include government policy and labor unions, which provide mechanisms that restrict the influence of market forces.

Centrally Planned Systems

Governments play a primary role in determining the allocation of a nation's resources in a **centrally planned system**. Rather than permitting consumers and producers to compete and be rewarded on the basis of price as the market-directed system does, countries with central planning allocate resources according to government goals. The government may establish what will be produced, by whom, and for whom. Often the goal in central planning focuses on political objectives rather than the efficiencies that bring greater reward in the form of profits. Because of the emphasis on goals other than meeting consumers' needs, the centrally planned systems experience a variety of problems. Often supply and demand are mismatched, and frequently the production of component parts is not synchronized in timing or volume to the production of end products.

China and Vietnam are examples of centrally planned economies. Both of these nations, however, have incorporated into their economic systems an increasing number of features that permit free market operations to function.

Under the former Soviet Union's centrally planned system, widespread shortages of many basic goods[8] were a fact of life. However, the political changes and resulting freedom in the former USSR and Eastern Europe have permitted citizens of those countries in many cases to witness the greater availability of consumer goods in market-directed systems. In short, the dramatic alterations of the political climate in the former Soviet bloc countries have fostered equally significant changes in the economic systems.

Mixed Economies

Most markets are a combination of market systems and centrally planned systems. For exam-

ple, the U.S. market is characterized by a certain amount of intervention in the form of government regulations. Trade restraints are one example. Similarly, China and Vietnam have embraced an increasing number of market economy concepts. Other countries are much more clearly mixed economies; as an example, France has private ownership of businesses but maintains strong central control.

Contrast of the Systems

Try for a moment to envision the contrast in the two systems in relation to apparel production, particularly for fashion products for which there is a concern regarding the timing. (Admittedly, in the past, the matter of timing of fashion goods has been less an issue in many of the centrally planned countries. In recent years, however, an increasing desire to export has increased this sensitivity. In addition, the new freedom in countries that had centrally planned systems has permitted greater interest in fashion products.)

Consider the difficulties of coordinating component parts involved in apparel production when influences other than market forces determine availability. Think of the phases of production involved in manufacturing a garment, going back to production or harvesting of fibers, through to the assembly of the garment (for example, a shirt). Fiber producers may have little incentive to match the type and amount of fiber to the shirt producer's end product. Perhaps the shirt producer was geared to manufacture 1,000 dozen Pima cotton men's shirts. However, because of the limited incentives to satisfy customers (in this case, "customers" also included producers at various stages of the chain), the intermediate producer at each stage modified the amount and type of fabric according to that mill's convenience. By the time the fabric reached the shirt producer, the factory received homespun (i.e., rough, nubby weave) cotton yardgoods

---

[8]A 1989 study by the USSR State Committee for Statistics (Bogert, 1989) reported that 1,000 out of 1,200 basic consumer goods were hard to find in at least some regions of the Soviet Union. Half of all communities surveyed indicated shortages of cotton underwear. Also in short supply were towels, men's cotton socks, children's shoes, men's and women's boots, and children's tights.

of the incorrect colors, the incorrect width, and in yardage to produce only 600 dozen men's shirts. Consider the added dilemma if the original shirt orders had been from a market-oriented country in which the particular shirt ordered had current, immediate fashion appeal. Contrast this to production in a market economy where the producer at each stage prospers or suffers according to the profit-oriented company's ability to respond efficiently.

Few centrally planned economies remain. However, many countries in Eastern Europe and the former Soviet Union have struggled from the long-term effects of central planning as they make the transition to market economies. Workers have had to accept the idea that a job and an income are no longer guaranteed, as they were previously by the state, regardless of one's productivity. They have learned that incentives come with meeting customers' needs and doing it well. Factories and other business enterprises have had painful adjustments while learning how to function with profit as an end goal. For example, one German consultant who advised textile companies in Eastern Europe reflected on the difficulty of assisting industry personnel who had no concept of what interest rates on capital meant (IAF Conference, 1991).

Market-directed economies also have their share of problems. Examples are extremely unequal distributions of wealth and income, large and unpredictable shifts in economic activity and indicators, the tendency toward monopolies with attendant dysfunctions, and high social costs such as wasteful abuse of the environment.

POLITICAL SYSTEMS

Just as different economic systems determine how textile and apparel industries will function both domestically and internationally, the type of political system in existence in a country also has a great influence on how textile and apparel production and trade occur. A **political system** is built around ideologies (a body of constructs, theories, or what we might commonly call the *philosophy* of a society) and provides a means of integrating a society into a functioning unit. Political systems are closely tied to economic systems in the operation of a country. Moreover, a good portion of today's societies are *pluralistic*, which means many ideologies are held by groupings of the population rather than having only one ideology supported by everyone. Although there are many different divisions for political systems, a more simplified approach is considered here.

Democratic Political Systems

Under this type of system, individuals have the right and responsibility to be involved in decision making that involves their well-being. At least theoretically, all persons have equal rights under democratic systems. Because of the difficulty of having the masses participate in decision making, various forms of *representative* participation occur. As an example, individual consumers may not have a first-hand opportunity to vote on congressional trade legislation; however, all citizens do have an opportunity to vote to choose the elected representative who will speak for them.

Nondemocratic Political Systems

In nondemocratic systems (totalitarianism or authoritarianism), individuals have little right of participation in decision making. A select few individuals, who generally do not permit opposition, hold the power and make the decisions. Totalitarianism exists in numerous forms, but one of the most common is communism. Truly totalitarian communism exists today in only a few countries—North Korea,

Cuba, and China, to name three. It also exists in military dictatorships such as Libya or religious states such as Iran.

Relationships of Economic and Political Systems

Although some types of economic systems are more commonly found within certain political systems, there are too many exceptions to generalize. A look at the common patterns may be helpful, however, in trying to remember or to apply the categories presented previously. Often, countries with centrally planned economies have nondemocratic political systems in which the factors of production are state owned. Similarly, market economies are more commonly found in countries with democratic political systems that permit public ownership of the factors of production. Keep in mind that exceptions to these obser-

vations are plentiful. For example, France's democratic socialism assumes that the democratically controlled economy requires regulation by an elected government. Several communist countries are experimenting with combined systems that do not fit the typical patterns. Some totalitarian governments may have economic systems that are in effect state capitalism. China represents a notable example of state capitalism.

WHY DO THE ECONOMIC AND POLITICAL SYSTEMS MATTER FOR TEXTILES AND APPAREL?

The following example illustrates the impact of the broader economic-political system on the textile and apparel sector. This example using blue jeans illustrates how the mecha-

---

 CHINA: BOOMING STATE CAPITALISM

Southeastern China, from Hong Kong to Shanghai, is leading the country to become an economic powerhouse. Gone are the days of Mao's baggy blue suits and isolation from the rest of the world. Foreign investment is pouring into China, exports are exploding, and the gross domestic product is expected to double by early next century. Although per capita income is low compared to that of some of its Asian neighbors, China's budding middle class is emerging and spending on luxuries such as makeup, clothing, and color televisions.

Although capitalism appears to be flourishing, the Chinese economy is a form the world has not seen before. China is not expected to embrace Western-style capitalism; rather, it is a mixed economy in which the leadership intends to keep the means of production in the public

sector. Beijing is giving provinces and towns the opportunity to operate quasi-public companies. A new class of managers, who may drive Mercedes but are card-carrying members of the Communist Party, is emerging. Along with decentralization of economic control, there is also an effort to extend reform and growth to the pennies-per-hour workers in interior provinces so these regions may share some of the boom experienced by the coastal areas.

Whatever form China's emerging economy continues to take, there is little question that this nation will become one of the world's top economic powers in the next century. Home to one-fourth of the world's inhabitants, China's influence will be felt around the world (Barnathan, Curry, Einhorn, & Engardio, 1993).

nism of the capitalistic market economy responds to serve the needs of consumers. We shall use China's transition from its totally centrally controlled status to a quasi–market economy as an example. For our product examples, let's think about the shift from Mao's traditional baggy blue suits to jeans.

When consumers want to wear blue jeans rather than baggy blue pants, mechanisms of the capitalist system encourage producers to recognize consumer wishes. Profits accompany the production of what the consumer wants (the jeans), and production is increased to meet the demand. Baggy blue pant production decreases because declining demand reduces the possibility for making a profit. A limited market for baggy blue pants may continue, but production shrinks to match the shrinking demand.

In countries with centrally planned economies where profits may not exist, mechanisms in the economic system do not encourage production to respond to what the consumer wants. Instead, the government must anticipate consumer needs. To make matters more complicated, the government's decisions may be based on some objective considered more important than satisfying consumers' needs—for example, providing employment. This has been true in China in the past. In centrally controlled economies, shortages occur in goods that are in demand, and a strong black market demand for jeans results. On the other hand, overproduction of goods that consumers no longer want is common. The mismatch of supply and demand occurs when market mechanisms are not present to reward prompt response to changes in consumer demand. Without the market mechanism, the manufacturer of baggy blue pants does not receive the message to switch to jeans. Or, even if the baggy blue pant producer did receive the signals to switch to jeans, no reward system in the form of profit makes it worthwhile for the manufacturer to go through the inconveniences of shifting

production lines. Only when a government official notices that one product is selling and another is not can production shifts be made.

Try to imagine the monumental task of balancing production and demand from a centralized agency, as was true earlier in Beijing, China's capital. As a way of attempting to visualize the difficulty of this coordination (or control) function, envision being the individual in your town who has been appointed to oversee this task. (Although this hypothetical exercise is oversimplified, it may be helpful in considering how the broader economic-political system influences production for the sector.) The coordinator must attempt to balance all the clothing produced for your area with the needs of all the individuals who live there. Consider changing desires for various fashion goods (although this was not an issue previously in China). Think of the mobility of residents and how your supply would be affected as people come and go. (Mobility was restricted by Beijing, in China's case.) Are the sizes what the residents need? Now, try to envision being asked to expand your role to being the clothing supply and demand coordinator for your country. The prospects of the task seem overwhelming. This assignment would involve added headaches if you also knew that the government's main goal for the textile and apparel industry was to provide jobs for a large number of unemployed persons rather than to satisfy consumer needs.

Although we have said China is a mixed economic and political system, perhaps this mental exercise will be helpful in contrasting the merits of the capitalistic market system to those of a socialist centrally controlled system—particularly for a sector such as textiles and apparel. The market system appears to offer many advantages for a sector in which the products often play an important role in personal identity (that is, being able to find the products the consumer believes to be "right" for him or her) and for which timing for products is important. We must keep in mind, however, that individuals in other parts of the world may not view clothing as playing this role in personal identity in the way many persons do in the developed countries. The market system provides an environment in which fashion-related industries often respond to new trends with remarkable speed (at least this is the ideal and it does occur with amazing regularity). Moreover, those businesses that do not respond to what the consumer wants have a limited life.

Trade between countries with centrally planned economies and those with market economies can pose difficulties, however. In the late 1980s, when the People's Republic of China applied for membership in the General Agreement on Tariffs and Trade (GATT), the primary international forum for trade matters, many market economy countries were concerned about China's participation. Concerns stemmed from the unequal conditions for trade in the centrally controlled Chinese economy. For example, since the Chinese government chose textiles as a primary industry to develop and expand within their economy, the government funneled vast resources toward building the industry. Market economy countries felt that it would be difficult to accept as equal trading partners (within GATT) countries whose government made production decisions and subsidized the industry. In other words, if one nation is dependent upon market forces to compete and the other is not, they are not on equal footing. If profits are required to survive, competing against producers who need not concern themselves with profits can be a serious disadvantage. We must also clarify here, however, that government subsidies and production decisions that result from government policy occur in market-directed economies as well as centrally planned economies.

An understanding of the different economic and political environments in various countries is helpful as we examine textiles and

apparel in the global economy. The varied environments have implications both for the production of textile and apparel goods within countries and for exploring the potential for marketing products to nations with diverse systems.

CULTURAL ENVIRONMENTS

As the textile and apparel industries have become global in nature, individuals associated with the sectors must be increasingly sensitive to cultural differences in various parts of the world.[9] To function effectively and responsibly in the global arena—whether in production, marketing, or other activities—industry representatives must be aware of the important role the cultural environment plays.

Because all the activities of a business are performed by people, human differences give rise to different business practices in various parts of the world. Although there may be variations within a country, generally certain physical, demographic, and behavioral norms are present, which may influence the way in which business is conducted from one nation to another. Business activities are unlikely to succeed if differences in cultural environments are ignored. In fact, U.S. business representatives often have been criticized for

---

[9]**Culture** is defined as the *learned* behaviors, beliefs, attitudes, values, and ideals generally shared by members of a group. Stokes (1984) suggests that one way to understand the concept of culture and how it affects social behavior is to think of culture as the script of a play. Although the actors may vary their performances somewhat, the script provides the basic plot, defines the roles, and provides the dialogue. The script gives the play its basic shape, as culture shapes human behavior. Culture shapes our views on appropriate behavior for various occasions, beliefs about what is right and wrong, concepts of beauty or ugliness, the appropriate clothing to be worn for various occasions, the meaning of symbols such as a flag or a cross, the meaning of gestures, and other details of life.

their lack of sensitivity to cultural differences in other countries and their tendency to assume that "the American way is better"—an attitude known as **ethnocentrism**.

One of the difficult aspects of ethnocentrism is that we become blind to the fact that we live within a culture and our views of what is appropriate have been shaped by that

MORE THAN THE MANNERS YOUR MOTHER TAUGHT YOU

Remembering the good manners your mother taught you is not enough to succeed in conducting business in other countries in which cultural differences dictate a different set of social behaviors. Although your mother was probably right for the setting in which you lived, she didn't anticipate the fast approach of a global economy in which many of us would interact with individuals whose mothers (and others, of course) had taught them a *different* set of social customs and expectations. Therefore, today's global business climate requires that we *learn about* and *be sensitive to* these cultural differences if we are going to succeed in international commercial endeavors. The following are a few examples of how international behaviors vary:

- *Talking business.* In some parts of Europe, talking business after the work day ends may turn off hosts. On the other hand, the Japanese spend many of their evenings with business associates in restaurants or bars, and whether talking business or not, the purpose is business. Declining an invitation for after-work socializing may jeopardize a business deal. However, talking business after just meeting a Japanese person is not considered appropriate.
- *Space relationships.* In conversations, Latin Americans and Middle Easterners stand very close to others—sometimes toe to toe or side by side brushing elbows, whereas North Americans feel comfortable standing two to three feet apart. When Middle Easterners and Americans talk, the Middle Easterner will move closer as the Americans back away.
- *Greetings when meeting.* Although the Japanese prefer to greet one another by bowing, they cater to Westerners by shaking hands. How-

ever, when Middle Easterners and Far Easterners shake hands, they prefer a gentle grip. Although North Americans are taught that a firm grip shows genuine warmth, Far Easterners may feel this suggests aggressiveness.

- *Eye contact.* North Americans are taught to look individuals directly in the eyes in conversations and when greeting others. Japanese and Koreans are taught to do the opposite, to avoid direct eye contact; to them, eye contact may suggest disrespect, intimidation, or even sexual overtones.
- *Exchanging business cards.* When a North American receives another person's business card, he or she quickly stores the card in a pocket or other safe place. In contrast, Japanese and other Far Eastern individuals attach special meaning to one's association with a company and therefore accept a card with great respect. Consequently, when receiving a business card from a Japanese or Far Eastern person, one should treat it with a great deal of respect and study it carefully before putting it away.
- *Conversation.* Europeans follow international affairs and read publications that provide worldwide coverage; therefore, it is important to follow world events to engage in conversations with Europeans. In most parts of the world, politics, religion, and personal matters represent sensitive conversation areas. In some Asian countries, however, individuals are quite curious about visitors, so one should not be too startled if asked one's weight, height, or even income.

Source: From *Do's and Taboos Around the World* by R. Axell (Ed.), 1990, New York: John Wiley & Sons; "Foreign Exchange" by R. McGarvey, June 1992, U.S. Air Magazine, pp. 58–65; and author's experiences.

culture. We make the mistake of assuming that our way is the "natural" or only way.

Culture includes all parts of life. In the study of humanity's way of life, anthropologists focus on several dimensions of social heritage that constitute culture. If we look at culture from the anthropologist's perspective, this gives us a framework for considering the elements of a cultural environment in which international commerce occurs. Each of these elements influences the ways in which business is transacted from one country to another. Various authors define and categorize the elements of culture differently. Herskovits (1952) defined them as follows.

Material Culture

Material culture consists of (1) technology and (2) economics. Technology refers to the techniques and know-how of a society that are used in the creation of material goods. Economics (from the anthropologist's perspective) refers to the way in which people employ their capabilities and the resulting benefits. Both the type of economic organization and the technology employed in a country have a profound impact on the production, distribution, and use of textile and apparel product within a country.

Material culture determines the quality, type, and quantity of products required for maintaining the cultural system and the means of producing and distributing them. As an example, clothing demands and the means employed for producing that clothing vary considerably from a developing country like Nepal to a developed nation like the United States. As a contrast in level of demand, a family in Nepal would have difficulty finding storage space in its modest home for the volume of clothing owned by the average U.S. consumer.

Social Institutions

Social institutions include (1) social organization, (2) education, and (3) political structures. These include ways in which people relate to one another, live in relation to one another, govern themselves, and pass on to other generations the expectations for appropriate behavior. Differing social institutions

FIGURE 3–8
In this alley sewing operation in Mali, men are the operators. In many African countries, men commonly perform sewing operations, whereas in some regions of the world, many men would consider these sewing jobs inappropriate for male participation.

Source: Photo courtesy of International Labour Office, Geneva.

affect such areas as work relationships, political environments for business, and appropriate appeals for marketing products. For example, in some countries, women's roles are defined in such a way that women would not be permitted to work in textile and apparel production jobs outside the home. In other regions, women constitute nearly all the production work force for sewing operations, but men would never consider those jobs as being consistent with the definition of the male role. On the other hand, in some regions, men have become quite willing to perform sewing operations.

Humanity[10] and the Universe

This includes religion, belief systems, superstitions, and their related power structures. Religion and other belief systems can have an all-powerful impact on how people live their lives, the products they use or do not use, when and how they will work, and many other activities related to international business. In many countries, religion and other belief systems play an important role in deter-

---

[10]This is an adaptation of Herskovits's category, which referred to *mankind*.

A CASE OF CONFLICTING WORK ETHICS

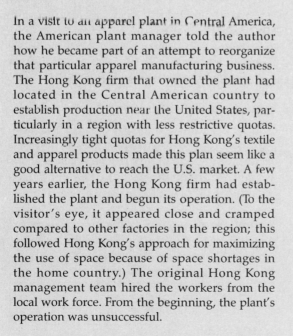

In a visit to an apparel plant in Central America, the American plant manager told the author how he became part of an attempt to reorganize that particular apparel manufacturing business. The Hong Kong firm that owned the plant had located in the Central American country to establish production near the United States, particularly in a region with less restrictive quotas. Increasingly tight quotas for Hong Kong's textile and apparel products made this plan seem like a good alternative to reach the U.S. market. A few years earlier, the Hong Kong firm had established the plant and begun its operation. (To the visitor's eye, it appeared close and cramped compared to other factories in the region; this followed Hong Kong's approach for maximizing the use of space because of space shortages in the home country.) The original Hong Kong management team hired the workers from the local work force. From the beginning, the plant's operation was unsuccessful.

The Hong Kong management team was unable to understand and accept the work ethic of its local work force. In contrast to the Asian work ethic, which required few rules or punishments to stimulate productive employment, the local Central American work force defined the balance between work and leisure quite differently. After a difficult and unsuccessful attempt to make the factory succeed, the Hong Kong firm was prepared to close the plant. The American, an experienced apparel plant manager who was looking for a new career challenge, proposed to the Hong Kong owners that he manage the plant for a year and attempt to mediate the expectations of the Hong Kong owners and the local work force. At the time of the visit, the manager had made strides in balancing the two diverse work ethics.

mining appropriate dress. In certain countries, religion plays an important role in the work ethic. For example, Max Weber, a German sociologist, at the turn of the century observed that the predominantly Protestant countries were the most economically developed. The Protestant ethic attached great importance to work. That Protestant ethic appears to have shifted away from the developed countries to other regions of the world ("What Is Culture's," 1986).

Superstition may also play an important role in some parts of the world. For example, Malaysian factory workers have been known to experience attacks of hysteria from seeing a particular variety of ghost. Workers may fall to the floor in convulsions, screaming, and soon the hysteria spreads up and down the assembly line. Sometimes the plant must be closed for a week or more to exorcise the "spirits" (Ehrenreich & Fuentes, 1981).

The importance of religion and belief systems may be seen in textile and apparel factories in various parts of the world. For example, in Taiwan small shrines may be found in garment factories; these are to ward off bad luck. In Mexico, a predominantly Catholic country, many garment workers have small shrine-like arrangements near their work areas reflecting their faith (Figure 3–9). In Islamic countries, small mosques may be found in some garment factories so that workers may worship during the day. Although certain textile production requires continuous operation for either technical or economic reasons, religious restrictions in some countries (e.g., Israel) may prohibit continuous production.

Aesthetics

Aesthetics include arts, folklore, music, drama, and dance. Aesthetics play an important role in the definition of what is attractive and desirable within a culture. A person or a product considered attractive in one culture may not be in another. Therefore, for a textile or apparel firm to successfully market its products in other parts of the world, its marketers must be sensitive to the aesthetic values for that country or region. This may mean that products require modification for another market, and promotion of the product will vary greatly. For example, France's uninhibited television commercials for undergarments would be considered quite offensive in many parts of the world.

Aesthetic values may also affect perceptions of quality from one part of the world to another. Workers in countries like Japan, where perceptions of quality are largely similar to those of the industrialized West, may be better prepared to produce items suited for export to the West than are workers in some developing countries who have limited technological capacity for producing and limited experiences in understanding Western concepts of quality or aesthetics. Conversely, traditional aesthetic standards in some new exporting countries may require enormous labor-intensive and costly attention to detail in the manufacture of certain products. Such products may be unable to garner enough market share to make their introduction to the international marketplace profitable.

Although firms in many countries have been sensitive to these cultural differences and have adapted products and marketing approaches to local export markets, many firms have not. Unfortunately, in the past, some American firms have viewed foreign markets as a place to dispose of products that were not selling well in the domestic market rather than viewing foreign markets as new opportunities to build long-term sales. This difference in attitude affects the extent to which the firm will adapt to the local culture's aesthetics.

Language

Understanding the language of a country or region is critical to conducting business in

FIGURE 3–9

Workers bring their religious beliefs with them to the workplace. In the shipping department of a garment plant in Taiwan, workers have a small shrine to keep away evil spirits (a). In Mexico, with its devout Catholic population, it is common in apparel factories to see small shrines near an employee's work area—such as the one over the computer table (b).

Source: Photos by Kitty Dickerson.

other parts of the world. If textile and apparel firms have production facilities in other countries, plant managers from the firm's home country must be able to communicate with local workers. If companies intend to market their products in other nations, they must have staff who know the language. Often, firms find it advisable to work with the assistance of a national (a local person) in the country to relate effectively in another production or marketing environment.

In addition to the dictionary translation of the language, companies must have representatives who are sensitive to the idiomatic interpretation as well. Humorous stories of advertisers' blunders in language usage remind us of the importance of language in relating to local markets to sell American products.

Educational systems in many countries have fostered the study of foreign languages to a far greater extent than has the U.S. system. Because of the geographic size of the United States, and to some extent because of the global power wielded in the past, Americans have not been motivated to learn foreign languages to the same degree as people in many other countries. As a result, Americans typically expect representatives from other countries to communicate with them in English.

More recently, however, the world economy has fostered an increase in the number of Americans learning second languages. Many U.S. companies recognize that to compete overseas they must have multilingual employees, as many of their global competitors do. As a result, enrollment in foreign language courses has grown dramatically. Moreover, a noticeable shift from European languages to Asian languages is apparent.

SUMMARY

This chapter provided an overview of several areas important to the understanding of how the textile and apparel industries fit into a larger global context. An understanding of

MULTICULTURAL CORRECTNESS IN LANGUAGE—SOME SURPRISES

Many companies have made embarrassing errors in translating products' brand names or features into other languages. The General Motors phrase "body by Fisher" was translated in Flemish as "corpse by Fisher." Mitsubishi planned to introduce a new car called "Pajero," which turned out to be Latin American slang for compulsive sexual behavior. Colgate-Palmolive's Cue toothpaste was introduced in France without changing its name; unfortunately, this name had a pornographic connotation to the French. "Come alive with Pepsi" almost appeared in a popular Chinese magazine as "Pepsi brings your ancestors back from the grave." Similarly, in a German edition of the same magazine, the ad said, "Come alive out of the grave." Schweppes Tonic was advertised in Italy as "bathroom water." The Chevrolet's "Nova" meant in Spanish "It doesn't go." When Parker launched a sales campaign in South America, a less than accurate Spanish translation promised buyers that the new ink would prevent unwanted pregnancies.

Sources: From *Consumer Behavior* by J. Engel & R. Blackwell, 1982, New York: Dryden Press; "Multicultural Correctness," January 1993, *World Trade*, p. 28; *International Business Blunders* by D. Ricks, M. Fu, & J. Arpan, 1974, Columbus, OH: Grid.

differing economic, political, and cultural environments in the international setting is critical to functioning effectively in the global textile and apparel markets.

A review of country groupings included the common categories used in discussions on trade, with per capita GNP as a common measure used in making these distinctions. These country groupings reflect dramatic differences in relative wealth and prosperity—differences often resulting from varying levels of trade activity.

A number of regions of special significance to textile and apparel production and trade were presented. Because of references throughout the book to these regions, this chapter helps the reader become familiar with the regions and have an understanding of the major economic and political changes that have and are taking place there. In today's global economy, these changes have an impact not only on the textile and apparel production and trade for the respective country or region, but also for the industry in many other countries. The formation of regional trading blocs was also considered along with brief discussion on the implications of these blocs for the broader global trading community.

The differences in relative wealth of nations have led to a division between the developed countries and the developing nations. That is, many developing countries planned their economic development around industrialization and trade, attempting to imitate the successful strategies of the developed countries. Unfortunately for many developing countries, these aspirations have never materialized. Through what is known as the *North-South dialogue*, the developing nations have become increasingly vocal in asking that their needs be considered more fully. The North-South division is particularly relevant to textile and apparel production and trade.

Different types of economic and political systems make a dramatic difference in the environment in which a country's textile and apparel industrial and trade activities occur.

These environments affect the ways in which all segments of a textile complex might respond to meeting consumer needs, with quite varied end results.

The cultural environment from one country to another influences the way in which textile and apparel firms conduct business. Whether a company is establishing production operations in another country or attempting to sell its products in another market, sensitivity to differing cultural environments is critical to success and to understanding the impact of business practices on the participants.

GLOSSARY

Capitalist economic systems are those in which the factors of production are owned by individuals, and allocation decisions are made by market forces.

Centrally planned system is an economic system in which governments play a primary role in the allocation of the nation's resources.

Common market has the characteristics of a custom union but also eliminates restrictions on factor mobility (that is, resources used to produce goods and services—e.g., labor and capital—may be transferred at least to a certain degree across national boundaries).

Culture is defined as the learned behaviors, beliefs, attitudes, and values generally shared by members of a group. Culture refers to the social heritage of the human race—"the totality of the knowledge and practices, both intellectual and material of society. . . . [It] embraces everything from food to dress, from household techniques to industrial techniques, from forms of politeness to mass media, from work rhythms to the learning of familiar rules" (Guillaumin, 1979, p. 1).

Customs union is a form of economic integration that eliminates internal tariffs and establishes a common external tariff.

Development, as defined by Fisher (1992), is "the process by which the political, social, and especially economic structures of a country are improved for the purpose of assuring the well-being of its populace" (p. 15).

Economic development is "a process of improvement in the material conditions of people through diffusion of knowledge and technology" (Rubenstein, 1992, p. 302).

Economic integration is the removal of economic barriers between or among national economies.

Economic system is the way of organizing the production of goods and services that people want and then distributing those products to the end use consumer.

Economic union is similar to a common market but has a degree of harmonization of national economic policies.

Economy is an abstraction that refers to the sum of all our individual production and consumption activities.

Ethnocentrism is the belief that one's own group or culture is superior, the tendency to view other cultures in terms of one's own. An ethnocentric attitude in international business usually means that a firm believes that what worked at home should work abroad and ignores differences in the culture and the environment.

Factors of production are the resources used to produce goods and services to satisfy wants. Land, labor, and capital are three basic factors of production.

Foreign direct investment (FDI) is foreign investment in plant(s) and equipment. This generally refers to ownership or part ownership of foreign production facilities.

Free trade area (FTA) is a form of economic integration in which tariffs are removed among members but each member maintains its own tariff against non-FTA countries.

Gross domestic product (GDP) is a yardstick of economic activity in a country. It is the market value of the final output of goods and services *produced domestically* in a country in a year. Unlike GNP, it excludes profits made by overseas operations of a country's firms. By the same token, if temporary migrant workers are employed in a country, the output of these workers is included in gross domestic product. In short, GDP is a measure of all the goods and services produced by workers and capital *located in a country* regardless of its ownership or the origin of the workers.

Gross national product (GNP) is a measure similar to GDP, except that it is the value of output *produced by domestic residents.* Although data from many sources are available only in GNP terms (e.g., some international agencies), in today's international economy, the GDP measure may be more appropriate as workers go to other countries to work and as corporations move their capital to other countries to produce.

Level of living refers to the material well-being of individuals or families. This includes the basics of food, clothing, and shelter, and for more affluent societies, distinctions in level of living may include many other things beyond these basics.

Market refers to a group of firms and individuals that are in touch with each other in order to buy or sell some good or service (Mansfield, 1983).

Per capita GNP is the country's GNP divided by mid-year population.

Political system is built around ideologies (a body of constructs, theories, or what we might commonly call the *philosophy* of a society) and provides a means of integrating a society into a functioning unit.

Quota is a limit on the quantity of a good that may be imported in a given time period.

Socialist economic systems are those in which all nonlabor means of production have been owned by the state, which controls resource allocation.

Subsidies (government subsidies) are a form of government payment or support to exporters so they may compete more effectively in world markets. **Indirect subsidies** are applied to components (e.g., the fabric for shirts) that become part of exported products. Indirect subsidies may also include low-cost loans, state health insurance, etc.

Trading blocs are groups of countries participating in a special trade relationship that encourages and facilitates trade within the region, often in preference to that with outside nations.

SUGGESTED READINGS

Axtell, R. (Ed.). (1990). *Do's and taboos around the world.* New York: John Wiley & Sons.
   A guide to international behavior and protocol.

Axtell, R. (Ed.). (1991). *Gestures: The do's and taboos of body language around the world.* New York: John Wiley & Sons.
   A guide to multicultural interpretation of gestures.

Barnathan, J., Curry, L., Einhorn, B., & Engardio, P. (1993, May 17). China: The emerging economic powerhouse of the 21st century. *Business Week*, 54–68.
   An overview of China's burgeoning economic power.

Cooper, H. (1988). Foreign language and today's interdependent world. *National Forum*, 68(4), 14–16.
   This article addresses the importance of foreign language education.

Ehrenreich, B., & Fuentes, A. (1981, January). Life on the global assembly line. *Ms.*, 54–71.

This article reviews important economic, political, and cultural issues associated with work "on the global assembly line."

Ellsworth, P. T., & Leith, J. C. (1984). *The international economy.* New York: Macmillan.

This book provides a helpful overview of the international economy; its approach blends theory, history, institutions, and policy.

Hamilton, J. A. (1991). Worlds apart: The high price of ethnocentricity for clothing and textiles and the cultivation of a global perspective. In S. B. Kaiser & M. L. Damhorst (Eds.), *Critical linkages in textiles and clothing subject matter: Theory, method, and practice* (pp. 257–263). Special Publications Monograph of the International Textile and Apparel Association, Vol. 4.

This paper encourages the development of a global perspective for clothing and textiles studies.

Harris, M. (1985). *Culture, people, nature* (4th ed.). New York: Harper & Row.

An introduction to general anthropology.

Mansfield, E. (1983). *Economics.* New York: W. W. Norton.

A general economics textbook with a useful section on international trade.

Price Waterhouse. (various dates, usually current). *Doing business in _____.* Various countries: Author.

A series of publications on business conditions in the countries in which Price Waterhouse has offices or does work.

Rubenstein, J. (1992). *The cultural landscape: An introduction to human geography* (3 ed.). New York: Macmillan.

An overview of the cultural characteristics (such as language, social customs, and industry) of the world presented with a topical approach.

Thompson, W. (Ed.) (1978). *The Third World: Premises of U.S. policy.* New Brunswick: Institute for Contemporary Studies.

Papers on U.S. policy for a changing Third World.

Trade and culture (monthly).

This magazine helps in understanding the cultures and the countries involved in conducting international business.

United States Chamber of Commerce (International Division). (1989). *Europe 1992: A practical guide for American business.* Washington, DC: Author.

This book provides a good overview of EU integration and the implications for firms in other countries that wish to conduct business in the unified EU.

United States International Trade Commission (1985, July). *Emerging textile-exporting countries, 1984.* (USITC Publication 1716). Washington, DC: Author

A study of emerging textile-exporting countries expected to become increasingly important in global trade.

World Bank (annual). *World Bank atlas.* Washington, DC: Author.

An annual source of economic and social indicators that describes trends and characterizes differences among countries.

World Bank (annual). *World development report.* Washington, DC: Author.

An annual review of social and economic conditions of the world, with a special emphasis on the developing countries. Each annual volume focuses on a timely area of concern.

4

Theoretical Perspectives

INTRODUCTION

The subject of textiles and apparel in the international economy is so extensive that focusing in a meaningful way on what is happening may be difficult. Because so many things happen simultaneously, it is difficult to sort the meaningful occurrences from those that are not, without using some kind of "organizing concepts." These organizing concepts are needed to focus attention on the important aspects of a situation and may be thought of as the building blocks for theories (McNeill, 1986).

Theories from a number of fields provide a helpful framework in which to consider the economic, political, and social concerns associated with textiles and apparel in the international economy. Although many aspects of production, and even trade, of these goods occurred before the theories developed, these theories help to provide systematic approaches for considering this important area of study. Theories help to explain existing situations or to speculate on the ideal that perhaps *should* prevail. The goal of this chapter is to present several relevant theories and models that apply to the focus of this book and is not intended to include all existing theories that might be considered.

REASONS FOR TRADE

Trade between nations occurs for the same reasons that trade takes place within a nation—people seek to enjoy higher levels of living and therefore greater satisfaction. As individuals or families, most of us choose to participate in the exchange of goods and services rather than to be self-sufficient. Others can produce various products and services more efficiently than we can, so we choose to exchange the money we receive from producing our goods or services (that is, what we do "for a living") for those produced by others. As an example, most of us would not choose to produce our own shoes. We lack the skills to produce shoes that would be comfortable and durable. Instead, we exchange some of the money we earn in selling our own goods and services (our income) for shoes produced by firms employing machines and people who have the skill to make shoes of the quality we want to wear.

Trade among nations can provide the same advantages we identified in choosing to have others make our shoes. According to traditional theories, trade fosters specialization, and specialization increases output. When countries trade, one nation can specialize in goods and services it produces particularly well and can trade these for goods and services other countries are good at producing. A particular country as well as its trading partners benefit because of the exchange.[1] As consumers come to depend on products that originate in many other countries, we discover that trade has contributed importantly to the global interdependence that characterizes the latter part of the twentieth century.

In this chapter we consider some of the classical economic theories on trade. We also consider some of the newer theories—coming from a variety of disciplines—that give differing perspectives on why trade occurs and who benefits from this trade.

---

[1]This perspective reflects the neoclassical international trade theory of Adam Smith and David Ricardo, whose theories are discussed briefly early in this chapter. We must keep in mind that this is orthodoxy and not everyone believes it (McGowan, 1989).

BASIC ECONOMIC CONCEPTS AND TRADE

Ankrim (1988) distilled basic economic concepts into what he considered five "concept clusters" that underlie all economic theory. In other words, human behavior related to economic activities might be explained to a great extent by these five clusters. These concepts are basic to economic activity whether on the local, national, or international level.

Scarcity and Choice

No society can provide everything its people want. Resources of time, labor, machinery, and land are scarce. Therefore, our wants generally exceed our resources—especially since humans tend to have insatiable wants. Consequently, scarcity requires that we choose between competing demands on resources. Economics, as a discipline, is based on the concept of choices that are necessitated by scarcity.

Opportunity Costs

The **opportunity cost** of using resources a certain way is the value of what these resources could have produced if they had been used in the best alternative way. That is, the sacrifice a person or country incurs to produce a product might be considered in view of what the next best application might have been. For example, growing cotton in New York City would make no sense because of the sacrifice of valuable land resources to produce something of limited value compared to other more profitable uses for the land. This far-fetched example suggests that the opportunity costs of growing cotton in New York City are too great. A key point is that the sacrifices affect the values of products. If cotton were grown in New York City, the price of the cotton would be prohibitively high because of the potential for other, more profitable use of the land. In other words, cotton simply will not be planted in New York City because the opportunity costs are too high.

Rationing and Incentives

Because our collective wants exceed the available supply of goods and services, we must devise ways of rationing (distributing) the scarce supply. Rationing systems are devised to distribute the scarce goods and services, and people respond to rationing schemes to get some of the supply. For example, in the United States, goods and services are usually given to persons willing to sacrifice the most money. In short, in market economies, prices determine who will receive scarce commodities. In centrally planned or mixed economies, people respond to the rationing systems that operate there. People respond to incentives in predictable ways. This provides an opportunity to predict behavior and forecast consequences of that behavior.

Laws of Supply and Demand

These relationships are described by two separate theories that have proven true so consistently that they have been labeled *laws*. Both show how people respond to incentives, particularly in market-directed economies.

Law of Supply

The **law of supply** is a general statement about how producers adjust the quantity of goods or services available in relation to incentives (prices, in market-directed economies). *When the reward offered for a specific product rises, this reward provides an incentive to produce more of the product.* For example, the popularity of cotton textile products among consumers has attracted a number of U.S. farmers to produce cotton as an income crop. The following newspaper account illustrates this law:

Cotton is king again in southeast Missouri. . . . Record yields and near-record prices on world commodity markets have pushed the value of Missouri's 1987 cotton crop to $92 million. . . .

Perfect weather, newfangled technologies and a growing demand for cotton products—especially among members of the baby boom generation—have contributed to an avalanche of cotton that has left veterans of the trade shaking their heads in disbelief.

During the past two years [1986–87], cotton acreage in the state has increased more than 25 percent. That trend was expected to accelerate as more farmers forsake soybeans and grains to cash in on the cotton bonanza. . . . [The author also noted that domestic prices stabilized at about 64 cents per pound, after having been as low as 23 cents a pound earlier.][2] (Keller, 1987, pp. 33–34)

To illustrate further the law of supply, we might consider the hypothetical case in Figure 4–1.

Other textile examples help to illustrate this concept. Vicuna fiber from the endangered vicuna found in the Andes—a prized and precious wool once reserved for clothing for Incan nobility—has sold in recent years for between $3,000 and $4,000 *per yard* in Europe. The vicuna population, reported at 250,000 in the late 1950s, was devastated by uncontrolled hunting, causing a drop to 7,500 vicunas in the late 1960s. Unlike most other specialty hair animals, vicunas must be killed to harvest their wool. Until recently, marketing of vicuna wool was banned; however, the ban meant big profits for poachers and the underground vicuna trade. By the late 1980s, Peru's vicuna population had reached nearly 120,000. By 1989, Peru was permitted once again to harvest vicuna wool and transform it into cloth. If we apply the law of supply, we might speculate that most Peruvians made an effort to protect vicunas not only to preserve

---

[2]For our illustrative purposes here, we are not considering the added complexity of federal price support programs for cotton farmers.

EXAMPLE OF SUPPLY CURVE

The supply curve shown in Figure 4–1 relates the quantity of cotton supplied to prices; the upward slope indicates that the quantity supplied increased as prices increased. Just as Missouri farmers increased the supply of cotton as it became more profitable, we see a similar occurrence in this hypothetical example. At $200 per bale, 10,000 bales were supplied, but at $300 per bale, 39,000 were supplied. The shift of the supply curve from S to S₁ represents an increase in supply that may occur for various reasons. In addition to increased cotton prices, the relative prices for other crops influence farmers to choose one crop over another. Improved technology (for example, advanced mechanical pickers and chemicals that defoliate the plants, control plant height, fatten the bolls, and speed ripening) has been an important factor. A decrease in supply would be represented by a shift of the curve to the left.

FIGURE 4–1
Example of supply curve.

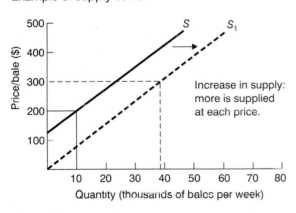

Increase in supply: more is supplied at each price.

the species but also to reach a point once again to be able to harvest this treasured wool fiber bringing exhorbitant prices (Scott, 1989).

In another instance, Australian wool growers began witholding wool from the market in an attempt to raise prices. Because of sluggish international demand resulting from depressed economic conditions in the major consuming countries, Australian wool growers attempted to reduce the supply and raise prices. This strategy was not very successful, however, because consumer demand was never adequate for the large supply on hand during this period ("Australian Growers," 1993).

Law of Demand

The **law of demand** is a general statement about how individuals respond to changes in price. This may apply to individual consumer or **aggregate** (combined) **demand**; aggregate behavior is considered market demand. *Rising prices for a product usually cause a drop in demand*—that is, there is a tendency to "economize." For example, when cotton prices have been unduly high at times, consumers have been willing to accept products of other fibers when they might have preferred cotton. Both producers and consumers respond to changes in product prices in predictable ways. Rising prices are a market signal to producers to supply more and an incentive to consumers to demand less of a good. As Figure 4–2 illustrates, when prices fall, this is an incentive to producers to supply less—but an incentive to consumers to demand more of a product.

Other textile examples illustrate how the law of demand works. For example, if we refer back to the earlier vicuna example, we can guess with reasonable accuracy that demand for vicuna wool fabric selling at $3,000 to $4,000 per yard was quite limited. Only elite customers of European fashion houses might seek fabrics in that price range. That is, demand diminished as prices increased.

EXAMPLE OF DEMAND CURVE

In the hypothetical example illustrated in Figure 4–2, the demand curve shows how individuals respond to changes in price for cotton products. At $200 per bale, the demand is 57,000 bales per week; at $300 per bale, the demand is 19,000 bales per week. Demand may increase because of a rise in income, a rise in the price of a substitute, change in taste favoring the commodity, or an increase in the population. In our cotton example, demand may increase also because of fashion preference of natural fibers or perhaps because rayon prices increase (that is, creating less price advantage for rayon over cotton).

FIGURE 4–2
Example of demand curve.

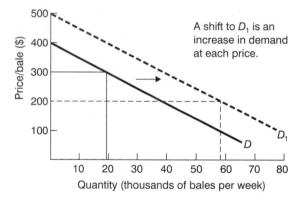

A shift to D_1 is an increase in demand at each price.

In another instance, cashmere prices began rising in China, where about 60 percent of the world's cashmere—and generally the best quality cashmere—is produced. Already an expensive luxury fiber, shortages of cashmere caused prices to increase by as much as 50 percent. These shortages boosted the prices of apparel using cashmere fiber; that is, the garment factories were forced to charge more to cover the rising cost of the cashmere yarn. As a result, the increased price of cashmere garments reduced the demand by consumers unwilling to pay the higher prices (Ehrlich, 1989a).

Equilibrium Price

And finally, Figure 4–3 illustrates another important related concept, **equilibrium price**, which is the price at which the quantity demanded equals the quantity supplied. Our cotton example also illustrates this concept.

Gains from Voluntary Exchange

In a voluntary exchange—that is, buying and selling of goods and services—both parties must feel they are benefiting. Both parties are pursuing their own best interests and believe they will be better off as a result of the trade.

Ankrim (1988) concluded that the economic perspectives in the five concept clusters are applicable to studying both world trade and the U.S. economy. These clusters are helpful in understanding how resources are allocated—at the global, national, or other level—for the use of humans.

Although underlying human motives for improving one's level of living may be basic to all people, the circumstances under which these are applied vary greatly from one part

EQUILIBRIUM PRICE

In the example illustrated in Figure 4–3, the equilibrium price is $260 per bale. At a price of $260, the quantity demanded equals the quantity supplied. At prices above the equilibrium, there will be excess supply and downward pressure on price. At prices below equilibrium, there is excess demand and upward pressure on price. Equilibrium prices are not permanent; rather, they may change quickly as market conditions change.

FIGURE 4–3

Equilibrium price.

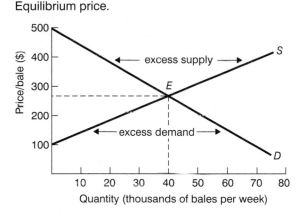

of the world to another. Diverse cultural and political backgrounds as well as different economic systems in various countries mean that these concepts tend to be applied quite differently from one place to another.

BASES FOR TRADE

International trade occurs when both the buyer and seller expect to gain from the exchange. Otherwise, there would be no reason for the trade. Therefore, participants in world trade are responding to the positive incentive to gain. Both importers and exporters believe they are trading something that is relatively less valuable for something that is relatively more valuable in their country. As participants in trade, most countries *specialize* in production of various goods and services—at least to some extent. It is important to consider what constitutes the basis for this specialization and trade.

The type and the quantity of resources a country has—human and nonhuman resources— provide important bases of specialization for trade among nations. Specialization occurs to some extent because of unequal distribution of resources. If countries have natural resources such as farmland and minerals or human resources for a workforce, specialization for trade usually takes advantage of those plentiful resources within each country. Although almost all theories acknowledge the importance of resources, some newer approaches emphasize the importance of *how a nation uses its resources* as more important.

Additionally, we must remember that the bases for specialization change over time as the resources and priorities in countries change. As a result, shifts in international specialization—and, therefore, trade—will occur. For example, changes in international specialization dramatically affected trade in textiles and apparel, accounting for many of the difficulties in this sector. That is, as many developing countries shifted labor and other resources from agricultural production to textile/apparel manufacturing, this change altered earlier global patterns of specialization dominated by the developed countries.

TRADE THEORY

Most traditional trade theories are based on the economic concept clusters discussed previously. These classic theories have been a useful means of examining what products or services might be produced most competitively in certain nations as well as where one might produce and sell products most advantageously. An understanding of both the classic as well as the newer trade theories also helps one to consider potential impact of trade policies. The following sections provide a brief review of some of the more relevant trade theories for the purposes of this book, beginning with theories that were important historically and including later theories as well.

Mercantilism

During the era between 1500 and 1750 when **nation-states** began to emerge, the dominant powers of the time such as England, France, and Spain competed and often fought to acquire colonies and gold. **Mercantilism** was actually an economic philosophy built around the idea that a country's wealth depended upon its holdings of treasure—in particular, gold. Mercantilism today might be called *economic nationalism* because of the emphasis on building domestic industries and domestic economies. A nation's prosperity was usually achieved at a loss to other economies.

Leaders believed that their nations gained from participation in trade—only if they had a favorable **balance of trade** (a balance in which the value of exports exceeded that of imports). Therefore, governments established policies that emphasized exporting more than importing and sought the *continuous inflow of gold from their trade surpluses*. Under this philosophy, the main goal was to make one's nation rich and powerful through regulation of trade and the domination of its colonies.

Strict trade rules promoted exports and limited imports. **Merchandise trade balances** were carefully monitored. Since textile products were among the earliest manufactured goods traded, a mercantilist climate meant that England tried to force its colonies to buy the British textile goods and refused to accept the colonies' textiles. The British went so far as to ban the sale of textile equipment to the colonies to keep the colonists dependent on imported fabrics.

Although mercantilism declined in popularity by 1800, this philosophy left an imprint on the terminology used to discuss trade. We still refer to a "favorable" balance of trade when exports exceed imports or an "unfavorable" balance when the reverse is true. Because of the typical interpretation of these words, we tend to think of *favorable* as beneficial, whereas economists now often disagree that a favorable balance is beneficial. In the mercantilist era, the difference in trade (the "imbalance") was made up by transfer of gold, but today credit is granted to the deficit country. (As a result of today's U.S. trade imbalance, other nations are using the accumulated U.S. currencies to buy U.S. assets—land, companies, and buildings.)

Absolute Advantage

Adam Smith (1930/1776) developed the theory of **absolute advantage**, which suggests that different countries can produce certain goods more efficiently than others. In contrast to mercantilism, which had promoted national self-sufficiency and local production, Smith questioned why consumers in a country should be required to buy domestic goods when they might purchase foreign-made items more cheaply. His views fostered the idea of international **division of labor**. In his book *The Wealth of Nations* (1930/1776), Smith challenged the mercantilist view that a nation's wealth depends on its stockpile of treasure. Instead, Smith believed that the real wealth of a country consisted of the goods and services available to the citizens. In contrast to the mercantilist views that emphasized the well-being of the nation-state, Smith's emphasis was on the welfare of the individual. He believed that individuals and businesses, given the freedom of choice, would look after their own self-interests, providing the most effective regulation of commerce and trade. This became known as his laissez faire or let-alone philosophy.

As part of Smith's theory, he advocated that nations be free to trade with one another without restrictions. The opportunity to trade freely would encourage nations to specialize in the product areas in which each had an absolute advantage. Thus, this theory encouraged a nation to concentrate on industries in which its costs are lowest. It suggested that a country trade part of its output for goods that other nations can produce more cheaply. That is, a nation exports a product if it is the world's low-cost producer. Trade on this basis, according to Smith, provided all nations with a greater quantity of goods at more efficient costs.

According to Smith's theory, nations would shift resources to those industries in which the country could be most competitive and labor (the workforce) would shift accordingly. The "advantage" in this theory included either

1. a natural advantage available to produce a product because of climate or natural resources, or
2. an acquired advantage achieved through technology or skill that enables the country to produce a differentiated product.

In the textile sector, a country may have a natural advantage in producing certain vegetable fibers such as cotton or ramie because of the availability of agricultural land and a suitable climate, but the country may have limited technical capabilities to produce man-

ufactured fibers. Certain regions of China and India would fit this description. Another country may have the technical sophistication to produce synthetic fibers but lack the land to produce cotton or ramie. Japan would be an example here. Under Smith's theory, each of these countries would shift resources to the production in which it had an advantage and would specialize in these areas in world trade.

Let's consider a hypothetical example[3] to illustrate how absolute advantage might work. In the following example, Panama produces shirts efficiently but does not produce computers efficiently. Using the labor and equipment available in each country, it takes a worker in Panama one hour to produce a shirt and ten hours to produce one computer.

	Time to make 1 shirt	Time to make 1 computer
Panama	1 hour	10 hours
Canada	1.5 hours	4 hours

On the other hand, Canada has the resources (the skilled labor and equipment) to produce computers more efficiently than Panama, but, in our hypothetical case, Canada does not produce shirts as efficiently. In this example, if Panama and Canada decide to specialize in what they produce best, Panama will produce shirts and Canada will make computers, as depicted in Figure 4-4. If we considered the difference in output for a work week, the results would make an even stronger case for specialization. Admittedly, this is an oversimplified example because international trade involves many different products and countries. The general principle holds, however, that if each country specializes in producing

---

[3]The time given to make the products in each country is strictly hypothetical and is not intended to reflect on the country or its workforce. Additionally, the discussion is intended to be illustrative and not prescriptive.

those items in which it has competitive advantages and trades with other countries, more goods and services are available for everyone.

Comparative Advantage

Adam Smith's theory of absolute advantage came under criticism because it assumed that an exporting nation must have an *absolute* advantage—that is, it must be able to outproduce its competitor nations. Critics believed this theory overlooked the nations who had no superior production areas. Many poor countries were not superior producers in any area, while a few countries were able to produce nearly all products at an absolute advan-

FIGURE 4–4
Each nation gains by producing and trading those products and services in which it has some natural or acquired advantage.

Source: Illustration by Dennis Murphy.

tage; thus, Smith's theory did not encompass these extremes. In the early days of textile trade, a few countries had the absolute advantage in the elementary production available at that stage, whereas most of the smaller or poorer countries had an advantage in few or no textile production areas. Smith's theory might have suggested that the poorer countries had no justification for entering textile trade.

David Ricardo, one of the most significant writers of the nineteenth century in influencing trade theory, extended Smith's work by showing that even countries without absolute advantages could benefit from specializing in goods that had comparatively low production costs, particularly in comparison to nations with which trade is intended. Ricardo's theory relied heavily on the *labor theory of value*, which asserted that the value of any commodity was determined by its labor cost: "The value of any commodity . . . depends on the relative quantity of labour which is necessary for its production" (Ricardo, 1960/1817).

This principle of relative labor cost determines the value of exchange for goods. For example, if it takes ten worker-hours to produce a computer and two worker-hours to produce a shirt, then the value of the computer will be five times as high as that of a shirt.

Ricardo used this labor theory of value to develop his theory of **comparative advantage** (or relative advantage), which advocates that a country will produce and export products that use the lowest amount of labor time relative to foreign countries and import those products that have the highest amount of labor time in production relative to domestic products. Further, only *relative* amounts of labor matter.

In the last example, Panama had an absolute advantage in producing shirts, and Canada had an absolute advantage in making computers. We will consider now an example in which one country has an absolute advantage in the production of both computers and shirts and will consider whether countries should still trade.

	Time to make 1 shirt	Time to make 5 shirts	Time to make 1 computer
Panama	2 hours	10 hours	15 hours
Canada	1 hour	5 hours	5 hours

In this example, Canada has an absolute advantage in producing both shirts and computers. This does not mean that Panama should refrain from producing both items because it has a disadvantage in both. In this case, according to Ricardo, if the countries decide to specialize and trade, Canada should specialize in manufacturing the product in which its *advantage is comparatively greatest* (computers) because Canada is ten hours more efficient in making each computer, whereas it is only one hour more efficient in making each shirt (or for five shirts—the same time required for making a computer—Canada is only five hours more efficient). According to this theory, Panama should specialize in shirts—in which its *disadvantage is comparatively less* (a difference of five hours for making five shirts, compared to ten hours for a computer). This is what is known as comparative advantage. As a result, both nations gain if they specialize in production of those things they can produce at the lowest relative cost.

Ricardo's theory, which focused on comparative cost, was an advance over Smith's philosophy. A country can be at an absolute disadvantage in all lines of production, yet be an active participant in global trade. Perhaps a country needs to have only a comparatively *smaller disadvantage* and not necessarily an absolute advantage. Countries with comparative advantage in most production areas may gain more from trade by focusing on the areas in which they have the greatest comparative advantage. In short, Ricardo's theory was based on differences in labor productivity from one country to another.

COMPARATIVE ADVANTAGE IS NOT FOREVER

Countries may have a comparative advantage in some type of production at one point and later discover that new developments have left them with almost no market at all. As an example, Tanzania was once one of the major world producers of sisal, and production of this fiber was a mainstay of the country's economy. However, the introduction of manufactured fibers virtually eliminated demand for sisal because the new fibers were cheaper and functioned as well or better than sisal. As a result, sisal can be sold on world markets at prices dramatically under those it formerly brought.

Both Ricardo's and Smith's theories were based on assumptions that should be clarified. (1) Both assume that resources were fully employed—that is, that no shirt makers or computer makers were experiencing unemployment. (2) The theories also assume that countries are primarily interested in profit maximization or maximum efficiency when, in fact, the nation may be more concerned about other objectives than output efficiency. An example of this would be the textile and apparel industry in China where providing employment has been more important than output efficiency. (3) Ricardo's example, like the one above, uses two countries and two commodities, which may not be very realistic. (4) Neither theory considers the cost of transporting products. (5) Both theories assume that resources can move from one good to another domestically but are not free to move internationally. Although Ricardo's theory and the modifications of it that followed had shortcomings, this philosophy was important in articulating the gains from trade. Ricardo's theory of comparative advantage shaped trade philosophy until well into the twentieth century and is still a fundamental concept of trade and in shaping many nations' trade policies.

International trade in today's world is far more complex than the simple examples used to illustrate absolute and comparative advan-

tage. Nations generally specialize, however, in producing those things for which they have an absolute or comparative advantage. Increases in international trade have encouraged specialization; in turn, this specialization has helped to increase the total amount of goods and services produced in the world.

Factor Proportions Theory

Ricardo's comparative advantage theory is based on the relative differences in the productivity of labor among nations; however, the theory fails to explain *why* this comparative advantage (relative efficiency of labor) exists. Secondly, although Smith's and Ricardo's theories show how specialization increases the output of different countries, these theories give no clues in identifying the product areas in which countries might have their greatest advantage. Instead their theories depend upon the influence of the free market to determine in what areas countries might compete most effectively.

Two Swedish economists, Eli Heckscher and Bertil Ohlin, expanded on Ricardo's comparative advantage theory when they developed the *factor proportions theory*. This theory is based on two requisite **factors of production**—capital and labor. According to the Heckscher-Ohlin theory, differences in countries' endowments of labor relative to their endowments of land or capital explain differences in factor costs. For example, if labor were *abundant* in relation to land and capital, labor costs would be low and land and capital costs high. On the other hand, if labor were *scarce*, then the cost of labor would be high in relation to that for land and capital. In other words, that which is scarce is dear.

According to the Heckscher-Ohlin theory, a country should specialize in and export those commodities that use resources in good supply (and which are, therefore, cheaper). Capital-abundant countries will export products that use a great deal of capital in their production (**capital-intensive products**). For example, Switzerland might be expected to export hi-tech textile production machinery because of the capital required for its production.

Countries with a good supply of labor, compared to capital, should have a comparative cost advantage in the production of commodities that use more labor than capital. Therefore, this theory suggests that the countries with abundant labor should export labor-intensive products (for example, labor-intensive apparel products) and import capital-intensive ones (hi-tech industrial textile equipment) from countries with relatively abundant supplies of capital.

When examining relationships of land and labor, we note that observations of global production and trade support the notion that where there are many people (labor) in relation to the amount of land, land prices are quite high. Manufacturing follows this pattern as well. As an example, land in Beijing, China, is scarce in relation to the number of persons and is quite expensive. Apparel production is an ideal industry because it requires little space per worker and factories can be several stories high. On the other hand, the open, abundant land in rural mainland China (where there are fewer people in relation to the amount of land) is ideal for growing cotton.

In contrast to what might be expected under this theory, studies of land-to-capital relationships have produced surprising findings. These studies have found that U.S. exports were less capital-intensive and more labor-intensive than U.S. imports. This may be explained because the Heckscher-Ohlin theory did not take into account the differences in labor (skills, training, and education) in various countries. Thus, this theory is valid only when human capital in the form of training and education (requiring capital expenditures that do not show up as traditional capital outlay) are included in the calculation of a nation's capital stock.

Although the Heckscher-Ohlin theory has been helpful in explaining trade on the basis of relative use of factors of production, this theory has shortcomings today. For example, much of the current trade in manufactured products takes place between countries with *similar factor endowments.*

The Product Cycle Theory

Theories discussed up to now apply for the most part to standardized or homogeneous products. In addition, there is also a need for theories that have some predictive ability; this is particularly true for new products. Vernon (1966) and others developed a body of theory in the 1960s that built upon the stages of a product's life and postulates that certain kinds of products go through a cycle consisting of four stages: introduction, growth, maturity, and decline. Although Vernon's original product life cycle theory was not related to location, later he argued that each phase had important implications for location in terms of both production and demand. Adding the location dimension, Vernon speculated that production moves from one country to another as the product's life cycle changes; the stages are on a continuum rather than being distinct. This theory attempts to explain why a country may have a technological advantage in producing a particular product at a particular time. As a way of making the stages more relevant, let us consider development and production of popular running shoes as an example.

1. *Introduction*. According to the product cycle theory, producers in a country (most often, a developed country) observe a need and a potential market for a product to fill the need. New products are more likely to be developed in response to *domestic* rather than foreign needs because the producer is able to observe the potential market close at hand compared to that in another country. At the early stage, technology to assist in production is undefined, and product development expenditures may be relatively high. Advocates of the product cycle theory believe that new products are more apt to be produced in the industrial countries. Most production at this stage is focused on the domestic market, with a limited amount of the product exported to other countries. Usually these exports go to other industrialized countries where consumers have heard about the new product and have the financial means to purchase it.

Running shoes were developed as an adaptation from what were once known as "tennis shoes" to fit the needs of the American population as large numbers of persons became increasingly physically active. Early production was based on research of users' needs, and product development was quite costly in the early stages as the leading producers "reinvented" a shoe for active wear.

2. *Growth*. In this stage, according to the theory, sales may increase in both domestic markets and in foreign markets where consumers have the financial means of purchasing the product. The originating country's exports may increase noticeably. Competition increases as other producers enter the market by adapting the product slightly to avoid patent infringements. At this stage, machinery and other technology are likely to be developed for large-scale production.

Some foreign production begins at this stage, most likely in other industrial countries; many developing countries may lack the resources for startup operations. At this point, foreign countries may erect tariffs on the product to encourage their own production. Or the costs of transportation and tariffs may encourage the original producer to establish a manufacturing base abroad.

Running shoes quickly became popular, despite relatively high prices for high-quality lines. Additional manufacturers adapted the leading firm's product. Mass production soon developed. Production soon occurred in other countries.

3. *Maturity*. In the mature stage, products become quite standardized and price becomes a more competitive factor. The original producing country probably no longer has a production advantage as more countries enter production. Changes in comparative advantage encourage movement of production to the developing countries where unskilled, low-wage labor can be employed to produce the standardized product more cost efficiently. The extent to which industries relocate in developing countries will depend for the most part on the extent to which unskilled labor can contribute to reducing the costs of production.

Production of running shoes shifted to developing countries, first to the NICs and later to less developed countries, where unskilled labor was an advantage in production costs. Additionally, shoes could be marketed in those countries.

4. *Decline*. Finally, as products reach this stage, most production occurs in the developing nations and the innovating country becomes a net importer. By this stage, production of running shoes for U.S. firms shifted almost entirely to developing countries.

Although many products fit into the product life cycle theory, several do not. Among the exceptions are products with short life cycles (for example, fashion items) that may not permit the global shifting, luxury goods for which price is not an issue, and products for which transportation costs are too high to encourage export sales (Giddy, 1978). Other arrangements that affect the validity of this theory are (1) multinational firms' introduction of products in several countries at the same time and (2) international subcontracting (sending products to low-wage countries for assembly operations).

In short, Vernon's product cycle theory introduced important concepts of location into trade theory. For example, Porter (1990) noted that the product cycle notion was the beginning of a truly dynamic theory in suggesting the importance of home markets on influencing innovation. In general, however, even Vernon himself (1971) believes this approach has too many shortcomings to explain current trade patterns because of reasons noted in the previous paragraph

PORTER'S COMPETITIVE ADVANTAGE OF NATIONS

Michael Porter, a faculty member in Harvard University's Business School, has been a leading innovator in developing new approaches to studying the competitiveness of industries and why firms based in particular nations succeed internationally in certain industries and certain segments (Porter, 1980, 1985, 1986, 1990). In *The Competitive Advantage of Nations* (1990), Porter looked specifically at the "decisive characteristics of a nation that allow its firms to create and sustain **competitive advantage** in particular fields" (p. 18). Rather than considering the usual economic question of why some nations succeed and others fail in international competition, he focused on:

"Why does a nation become the home base for successful international competitors in an industry? Or to put it somewhat differently, why are firms based in a particular nation able to create and sustain competitive advantage against the world's best competitors in a particular field? And why is one nation often the home for so many of an industry's world leaders?" (p. 1).

Porter believes that classical trade theory has been inadequate to explain trade patterns in today's global market in terms of how certain industries in certain nations succeed while others do not. His approach draws extensively on the theory of competitive strategy plus insights gained from a broad range of disciplines. In his efforts to develop a comprehensive theory of the competitive advantage of nations, he studied a wide range of nations and many industries within those countries. He noted that although the basic unit of analysis for understanding national advantage is the industry, nations succeed not in isolated industries but, rather, in *clusters* of industries and their relationships. Although it is difficult to provide a summary from Porter's extensive work, a few highlights will give the reader a sense of his ground-breaking theories.

In Porter's efforts to examine why a nation achieves international success in a particular industry, he concluded that four broad attributes of a nation shape the environment in which local firms compete. These promote or impede the creation of competitive advantage. He termed these the *determinants of national advantage* and portrayed them as a system in the diamond model shown in Figure 4–5.

Porter found that "four broad attributes of a nation shape the environment in which local firms compete that promote or impede the creation of competitive advantage" (p. 71). The determinants that form the diamond in Porter's model are

FIGURE 4–5
Porter's determinants of national advantage.

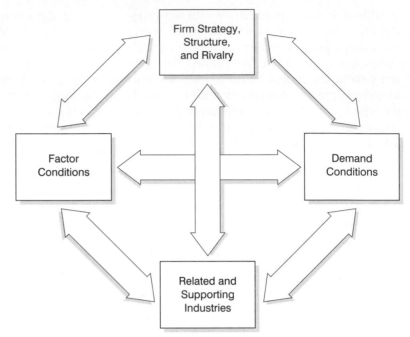

Source: From *The Competitive Advantage of Nations* (p. 72) by M. Porter, 1990, New York: Free Press. Reprinted by permission of The Free Press.

1. *Factor conditions*. Although factors of production such as labor supply and infrastructure are important, Porter believes it is where and how effectively factors of production are deployed that proves more decisive than the factors themselves in determining international success. Contrary to earlier theories, Porter asserts that the factors most important to competitive advantage in most industries, particularly the industries critical for productivity growth in advanced economies, "are not inherited but are created within a nation" (p. 74).

2. *Demand conditions*. Porter found that the nature of demand in home markets played a significant role in shaping the rate and character of improvement and innovation by a nation's firms. Nations develop a competitive advantage in industries and industry segments when the home buyers (either industrial buyers or consumers) pressure local firms to continually improve and innovate quickly. Sophisticated, demanding buyers force local firms to meet high standards in product quality, features, and service. This forces firms to be sensitive to trends in buyers' needs and to be able to respond quickly to those needs. Demanding home buyers help to position a company, and even an industry, into an advantageous role in competing internationally. The pressure to continually upgrade makes the firm or industry more competitive with international rivals and, in addition, embodies potential mechanisms through which the nation's products or services are "pulled" abroad (e.g., multinational buyers, foreign demand for products, etc.).

3. *Related and supporting industries*. Here, Porter refers to the presence or absence in the nation of supplier industries and related industries that are internationally competitive. His premise is that "competitive advantage in some supplier industries confers potential advantages on a nation's firms in many other industries, because they produce inputs that are widely used and important to innovation or to internationalization" (p. 100). Among the potential advantages are rapid access to the most cost-effective inputs, partnerships with world-class suppliers that are in the process of innovating and upgrading, related industries that share technology development (e.g., Japan's water jet weaving machines that weave long-filament synthetic fibers), and that success in one industry boosts international sales for complementary products or services.

4. *Firm strategy, structure, and rivalry*. This refers to "the conditions in the nation governing how companies are created, organized, and the nature of domestic rivalry" (p. 71). Characteristics of a nation are often reflected in how firms are managed and run, such as the training and "orientation of the leaders, group versus hierarchical style, the strength of individual initiative, the tools for decision making, the nature of relationships with customers, . . . the attitude toward international activities, and the relationship between labor and management" (p. 109). These features create advantages or disadvantages in competing in certain kinds of industries. Porter asserts that nations will succeed in industries where the goals and motivations of employees and managers are aligned with the sources of competitive advantage. In some cases, national pride or a long tradition in an industry represents a competitive advantage; generally, where employees and shareholders have a sustained commitment to the firm and the industry, firms have a competitive advantage if other determinants are favorable. Moreover, domestic rivalry that forces firms to compete vigorously in the home market often leads to competitive advantage internationally because those firms have been forced to improve and innovate.

Porter's determinants provide the setting in which a nation's firms compete. As he notes:

> Firms gain competitive advantage where their home base allows and supports the most rapid accumulation of specialized assets and skills, sometimes due solely to greater commitment. Firms gain competitive advantage in industries when their home base affords better ongoing information and insight into product and process needs. Firms gain competitive advantage when the goals of owners, managers, and employees support intense commitment and sustained investment. Ultimately, nations succeed in particular industries because their home environment is the most dynamic and the most challenging, and stimulates and prods firms to upgrade and widen their advantages over time. (p. 71)

Porter concludes that nations are most likely to succeed in industries or industry segments where the national "diamond" is most favorable. This does not mean that all firms will survive in this environment, but those that do emerge will succeed in international competition.

Moreover, Porter views the diamond as a mutually reinforcing system in which the effect of one determinant is dependent on the state of the other. Additionally, advantages in one determinant can create or upgrade advantages in others.

WHY FIRMS TRADE OR INTERNATIONALIZE

Most classic trade theories focus on *countries* and their participation in trade. Countries are the focus because of common economic characteristics typically found within a nation's borders. Except in centrally controlled economies, decisions to participate in trade are not made at the country level, however. Instead, *decisions are made at the firm level.* Firms may choose to trade or internationalize their business activities by importing and exporting or through a variety of other structural arrangements. In all cases, the reason is the capitalistic *drive for profit*. That is, companies trade or participate in other international activities when they believe they will gain from importing, exporting, or other arrangements (i.e., that these activities will increase or sustain profitability). Like individuals, companies have limited resources and invest them where rewards are greatest. Decisions on whether to participate in domestic or international business activities will be influenced by this basic economic concept. Now, we shall consider two major categories of firms' participation in trade or internationalization activities.

Arm's Length Trade

In the first of these categories, firms may participate in conventional **arm's length trade**. In this form of trade, producers in one country trade goods with buyers in other countries. Business relationships may be defined simply as buyers and sellers. Examples might include the sale of Swiss watches to customers in other countries, the sale of Italian shoes in other nations' markets, or the exporting of U.S.-made jeans into Turkey's markets.

Companies may choose to *export* for the following reasons:

- *Increased profitability*. Cultivating markets abroad may vastly increase the potential to sell products, compared to focusing on just the domestic market. Levi jeans can be sold in nearly all parts of the world; this dwarfs the market for selling in the United States alone.
- *Survival*. Some countries do not represent an adequate market for a company to survive; the firm needs far broader markets to survive. For example, Swiss textile machinery producers could not survive if they were limited to the relatively small textile industry in Switzerland.
- *Cost reduction*. Serving international markets permits the firm to take advantage of

economies of scale; the increased output may reduce unit costs of production.
- *Balancing variable demand*. If a recession or other cyclical factors affect sales in certain countries, demand in other parts of the world may offset these slumps. For example, if the textile market is sluggish in the United States, major textile firms such as Milliken and Company may benefit from having established markets in other countries not experiencing the downturn.

Companies may choose to *import* for the following reasons:

- *Cheaper inputs or products*. The importing firm may import components or completed products to save costs. Apparel manufacturers may import fabrics that are less expensive than those obtained in the domestic market; fabric producers may import their yarns for the same reason; or textile producers may even purchase imported **greige goods**, which are then printed and finished before selling to *their* customers. In a study of U.S. textile CEOs, nearly 52 percent of the executives indicated their firms use some imported materials in their production (Hooper, Dickerson, & Boyle, 1994).
- *Unique products*. Companies may supplement domestic production with imported products that provide distinction. For example, a company selling coordinated sweater and skirt sets may produce the skirts domestically but import the sweaters to add design interest to the line.
- *Expanding the supplier network*. Developing alternative suppliers, including those in other countries, makes a firm less dependent on a single supplier.

Intra-Firm Trade or Activity

Our second category of firms' participation in trade or internationalization is that of **intra-firm trade** or activity. In recent years, these forms of international participation in business have become increasingly important.

In intra-firm trade, a company has operations in other countries in addition to the home country. Firms of this type are known as **multinational corporations (MNCs)** or **transnational corporations (TNCs)**. Many international organizations and some writers prefer the term *transnational corporation* because it can be applied more broadly. Dicken (1992) believes the term *multinational corporation* suggests operations in a substantial number of countries; *transnational corporation* suggests operations in at least two countries. According to Dicken, all multinational corporations are transnational corporations—but not all transnational corporations are multinational.

Transnational corporations have had a profound influence on the global economic system. TNC activities have had far-reaching influence according to where and how they have invested in operations in other countries, how they have secured component parts, how they have marketed the products, and the extent to which they have transferred technology and other expertise. Although the typical image painted of the transnational corporation is that of firms from the developed nations setting up operations in developing nations, this is only one scenario. Actually, much TNC activity is among the developed nations; more recently, some of the NICs have established TNCs. Because most TNCs are based in the industrialized nations, their influence, particularly on developing economies, has often been dramatic. Although the TNCs have often provided much-needed jobs, some sources consider their influence in Third-World countries questionable in the long run. This notion will be explored further later in this chapter.

We should note here that TNCs render traditional trade theories of comparative advantage inadequate in terms of explaining why and where a nation exports. Whereas classic trade theory assumes that trade is subject to

external market prices, the intra-firm trade of the TNCs is subject to the *internal decisions of the firm*. Rather than simply importing and exporting, the TNC also may compete in other countries with its own subsidiaries located in those countries or regions.

Intra-firm trade as executed by transnational corporations—that is, trade between parts of the same firm across national boundaries—accounts for a substantial amount of world trade. Dicken (1992) suggests that increasing proportions of world trade in manufactured products is *intra-firm*, rather than *international trade*. Because most countries do not collect trade data in a manner that can separate out intra-firm trade, the exact extent is difficult to determine. This information does exist for the United States and Japan, and Dicken (1992) notes that more than 50 percent of total trade (imports and exports) for both these countries is TNC trade. Dicken, who is British, believes that possibly 80 percent of the United Kingdom's manufactured exports result from UK firms with foreign operations or from foreign-owned operations in the UK. The type and extent of intra-firm activity varies from one industry to another.

In summary, theories are helpful in examining textile and apparel trade. The theories provide various scholars' views on how we might consider the larger picture and examine trade in a systematic manner. Various theories help us to look more objectively at what is happening in trade and to explain shifts that have "reorganized" textiles and apparel in the global economy. At the same time, however, trade theories have their limitations and cannot account for all the complexities involved in trade, particularly textile and apparel trade.

DEVELOPMENT THEORY

Development, or international development, concerns focus on the imbalances in the distri-

THE ROLE OF TRANSNATIONAL CORPORATIONS (TNCS)

A United Nations report noted that the textile and apparel industries have "played a significant role in the industrialization process of a number of developing countries and in the growth of their manufactured exports" (United Nations, Centre on Transnational Corporations, 1987, p. x). Authors note that the two sectors are major examples of *international industrial relocation* and of the *international restructuring of the world economy*. They consider that transnational corporations (TNCs), also known as multinational corporations (MNCs), have been determining factors in that process.

Because of the intensive use of low-skilled labor in most segments of the textile and apparel industries, TNCs have limited potential for deriving firm-specific advantages from **direct foreign investment** in the textile/apparel sector. That is, firms desire the advantages of the low-cost labor but may prefer minimal capital commitments. For that reason, other forms of transnational activity have figured significantly in the internationalization of the textile and apparel industries. These include international subcontracting of assembly operations, brand name and trademark **licensing**, and importing finished garments.

On the other hand, the complex technology of the *manufactured fiber industry* offers greater opportunities for TNCs to exploit their firm-specific advantages through direct foreign investment. The Japanese textile sector has participated extensively in TNC activity as a means of ensuring markets abroad for Japanese manufactured fibers. That is, the Japanese have established textile production in other countries to be sure they can sell their products in those markets. Although U.S. textile firms have participated in TNC efforts, U.S. firms have engaged in transnational production less in the past than Japanese firms because of the extensive domestic American market.

Transnational activity in *apparel production* most often includes foreign assembly of apparel or licensing programs. Further, some countries—for example, Germany and the United States—have national legislation that provides tariff concessions for the foreign processing of apparel; this has provided an added impetus to the internationalization of the industry. Most often, however, the sewing plants in the LDCs are dependent on TNCs to provide market outlets for their products (United Nations, Centre on Transnational Corporations, 1987).

bution of resources between the rich and the poor of the world. For the most part, this imbalance is between the North and the South, and development efforts are aimed at reducing the gap.

Reasons for the gap between the rich and the poor countries is easily observed. Rich countries have economic systems that are very productive because they are able to produce a surplus over and above what is required for the population to survive. The surplus permits the rich countries to continually improve the population's standard of living as well as to make investments that further enhance productivity. In contrast, the economic systems in poor countries are relatively unproductive because production is barely adequate for a subsistence level of existence for the population. These countries have little surplus to use for investments that would increase productivity and reduce poverty. That is, the rich countries get richer because their investments continue to improve productivity, whereas the poor countries cannot take food from the mouths of the population to make similar investments.

Munck (1984) considers development as "the historical process of capital accumulation and the extension to the far reaches of the globe" (p. 1). Although economic conditions are basic to the disparity between the rich and the poor nations of the world, development issues are seen generally as extending more broadly to social and political concerns as well.

In a landmark perspective on development, Pope Paul VI's 1967 Encyclical entitled "Populorum Progressio" ("the development of peoples") introduced the phrase "development is the new name for peace" to emphasize the importance of integral human development (Carr, 1987). Even today, in the New York United Nations headquarters, this phrase is displayed frequently in connection with UN development projects. In the Encyclical, development was defined as a process aimed at creating conditions to provide the material necessities of life and bring about changes in oppressive social structures. Development, according to this view, includes economic growth, self-reliance, and social justice (Carr, 1987).

As scholars have studied international development, various schools of thought have evolved. As we have seen, the same was true for the emergence of theories related to international trade. We will review some of these briefly after considering why development issues are relevant to our study.

Trade and Development

In the past, trade has been an "engine of growth" that often stimulated a country's development (Robertson, 1938, p. 48). Trade in general exerts an important influence on economic development. Textile and apparel production and trade, in particular, play a vital role in economic development. This was true in the early industrialized nations more than 200 years ago. It remains true today for much of the developing world.

As we study the impact of international trade on global interdependence, we become aware of evolving patterns of development among nations of the world. Levels of development typically change to a degree over time in a particular country. We would hope these development changes represent improvements. It is important to keep in mind, however, that as each country changes, the relationships of nations to one another are shifting as well.

Development patterns are particularly significant as we study textiles and apparel in the international economy. As we look at textile and apparel production and trade for a particular country, we must be aware of where these sectors fit into the overall development scheme for that country. That is not enough, however. We must look also at what is happening more broadly in the world. Acquiring an understanding of *global development patterns* is equally important in comprehending how the domestic industry will be affected by worldwide shifts in production capabilities and other aspects of development.

Particularly in view of the fast spread of textile and apparel production to the developing countries, development theory provides another systematic means of studying production and trade shifts for these sectors. Development theory is quite complex because of its interdisciplinary nature; therefore, we can consider here only a brief overview to provide another perspective for analyzing shifts in this global sector.

Emergence of Development Theory

Development theory represents a body of scholarly approaches for attempting to understand and explain the imbalances between the rich and the poor nations of the world. Development scholars have tried to explain the nature of the imbalances and how these differences evolved; many have attempted to identify strategies for improving conditions

FIGURE 4–6

Bangladesh women who have lacked education and other opportunities learn skills so they may earn a modest income. Training is frequently in the textile and apparel areas. In the mid-1980s, upon completion of their training at centers like this one, women received a modest loan of $20 to start their own businesses.

Source: Photo by S. Paul, reprinted courtesy of United Nations.

for the disadvantaged nations. Development theories vary drastically in orientation; disagreement among various schools of thought has been common. A unified theoretical framework for development has not emerged in the past. Nor is a single unifying theory likely in the future because of the complexity of the problems along with the ideological and political differences (Bernstein, 1973; Schiavo-Campo & Singer, 1970).

Modern development theory emerged just after World War II. Interest in development increased after the war as European colonies in Asia and Africa began their struggle toward political independence and were thought of as potential Western allies in a world that was divided by the Cold War.

When scholars made their first attempts to construct development theories, the concepts of development and economic growth were often considered the same thing. Therefore, most early development theories came from the economics field. For example, the work of two well-known leaders from the classical period of economic thought—Smith and Ricardo—provided important links in early development theory. Smith's and Ricardo's economic theories promoted division of labor and distribution of production among various classes of society—along with international trade. Sociology also contributed importantly to early development theory.

The Mainstream/Modernization Theories of Development

In the late 1940s and early 1950s—the early days of development theory—**underdevelopment** was seen as the difference between rich and poor countries. The problem of underdevelopment was considered one of a *shortage of capital*. Development was seen as the process for bridging the gaps by having the poor countries imitate the industrialized nations.

In the late 1950s, the theory of development began to expand beyond its roots in economics and sociology. Scholars in several fields began to study the ways in which developing countries attempted to imitate the industrialized countries in the development process. Economists continued to examine the economic structure; other scholars analyzed social institutions; and some studied human behavior involved in development. Soon, the theory of development became interdisciplinary in nature as anthropologists, political scientists, and psychologists joined the economists and sociologists in focusing on these changes.

According to one group of scholars, development was considered an evolutionary process through which the less-developed countries would eventually assume the qualities of the industrialized nations. McGowan (1987) combines the development theory of this school in his mainstream/modernization model (see Table 4–1). In essence, McGowan's model provides an umbrella under which several theories with similar characteristics are grouped. Theories represented by this model may be called *mainstream* theory, *modernization* theory, and *conventional* or *traditional* develop-

ment theory. To a great extent, theories of this school were based on the notion that development and growth were synonymous; that is, development was closely tied to the idea of capital formation. *Modernization*, a key aspect of this approach, followed George's (1984) growth/trickle down model in which results of economic growth and modernization of the industrialized countries would trickle down gradually to the poor nations.

Rostow's (1960) "theory" or model[4] of economic development—considered important during the late 1950s and 1960s—reflected the perspective common to mainstream theories. His approach, used to classify countries by stages of economic development and to show growth from one stage to the next, identified five stages (countries in the first three were considered *underdeveloped*):

1. *The traditional society*. Countries are limited in their production capabilities by their levels of knowledge and technology.
2. *The pre-take-off stage*. Characteristics of the traditional society begin to disappear as the beginnings of modern technology are applied to agriculture and production. Transportation, communications, education, and other components of the infrastructure are initiated.
3. *The take-off*. A growth pattern emerges. Human resources are cultivated to sustain development. Industrial modernization becomes significant with certain sectors taking the lead.
4. *The drive to maturity*. Progress is maintained; technology is extended to all fronts of economic activity. The country becomes involved in international economic activities. Specialization develops.
5. *The age of high mass consumption*. Citizens can satisfy most of their basic needs and

---

[4]Some sources (e.g., Cateora, 1987) refer to Rostow's effort as a model, but others (e.g., Blomström & Hettne, 1984) refer to it as a theory.

TABLE 4–1
The mainstream/modernization model of development.

	Per Capita GNP 1992[a]	Life Expectancy at Birth[a]	Year Drive to Modernize Began[b]
DEVELOPED COUNTRIES			
Switzerland	$36,080	78	1798
Japan	28,190	79	1868
Sweden	27,010	78	1809
USA	23,240	77	1776
NEWLY INDUSTRIALIZED COUNTRIES			
South Korea	$6,790	71	1910
Mexico	3,470	70	1867
Brazil	2,770	66	1850
LESS DEVELOPED COUNTRIES			
Ghana	$450	56	1957
Bangladesh	220	55	1973
Ethiopia	110	49	1924

Tradition > Preconditions > Take-off > Maturation > Mass Consumption
FIVE STAGES OF DEVELOPMENT[b]

[a]Source: World Bank, 1994
[b]Walt Rostow, *The Stages of Economic Growth: A Non-Communist Manifesto,* 1962.

Source: From "Key Concepts for Developmental Studies" by R. McGowan, in *The International Development Crisis & American Education* (p. 45) edited by C. Joy and W. Kniep, 1987, New York: Global Perspectives in Education. Modified and used courtesy of The American Forum for Global Education.

consumption shifts to durable consumer goods and services. Income rises, with greater amounts of discretionary income available.

McGowan's (1987) mainstream/modernization model of development incorporates Rostow's stages of development. This model attempts to show the perspectives of modernization theorists who believe that all countries must go through the stages of development experienced by the already developed countries. These theorists believe that the LDCs can and will develop as others have "if they are patient and politically stable, open their economies to foreign investment and technology, reform their cultural and social institutions . . , and adopt correct economic develop-

ment policies emphasizing comparative advantage in their exports and less state intervention in their domestic economies" (McGowan, 1987, p. 46).

Although Rostow's approach helped to explain the economic evolution within a country, his efforts were characterized by the shortcomings later associated with the mainstream/modernization theories. A common limitation of development theories from this school was the notion that poor, developing countries must follow in the tracks of the United States and Western Europe to be on the proper road to development.

The mainstream/modernization approaches of Rostow's era told the poor of the world that if they wished to develop, they must pursue individual self-interests—like

Americans and Europeans. For many of the world's peoples, following this pattern is not possible, and many would not wish to imitate this strategy even if it were possible because they value community, religion, or family more than individual achievement. The modernization perspective dominated several social sciences in the 1950s and 1960s. Blomström and Hettne (1984) contend that the modernization approach had widespread appeal in the North because of the paternalistic attitude toward non-European cultures. Further, they believe the modernization theory established the rationale for foreign aid and the form it took. These authors concluded that the general outlook of modernization theory constitutes what still prevails as the popular image of developing nations in the developed countries.

A later group of scholars decried the mainstream/modernization development models—asserting that to apply the Western experience of development over the past 200 years to the rest of the world is ethnocentric and biased.

Despite the criticism of the mainstream/modernization theories, this school of thought tends to reflect the massive changes taking place in the developing countries as they move toward adoption of Western culture. Adoption of lifestyles, consumer products, and bureaucratic administration are seen in the proliferation of three-piece suits, fast-food restaurants, supermarkets, and rock music in urban areas around the world.

We are reminded that modernization is not the same as development. Although the two may be related, there is also some evidence that diffusion of Western practices and beliefs may hinder development. The author is reminded of hearing a teacher from a poor developing country relate the story of residents in the countryside who had purchased a refrigerator because they desired the status this piece of equipment represented. However, the family had no electricity to run the refrigerator; it simply sat there with no cooling capabilities. In this case, the desire to imitate the West (i.e., modernization) did little for development.

According to the later group of scholars, it makes no sense to expect that the development experience of Ecuador or Nepal should follow the earlier patterns of the United States or France. Consequently, the modernization approach was contested by another group of scholars by the early 1970s.

Structural Theories of Development

A later group of scholars formulated theories that were quite different from the mainstream/modernization approaches for explaining the imbalances between the rich and the poor of the world. McGowan (1987) combines several of these later approaches into what he calls *structural theories*. A few scholars had proposed a structural approach in the 1950s, but these views were not generally accepted until the 1970s. In fact, it is important to keep in mind that the structural theories still represent a minority view.

Van Benthem van den Bergh (1972) used a sports analogy to explain development from the structuralist perspective. He suggested that rather than viewing the process of development as a race, we might think of it as a league of commercially run football teams. We might assume that some of the teams are more successful than others. The more successful teams have the ability to attract and purchase the poorer teams' best players. As a result, the poorer teams tend to deteriorate even further, and prospects for improving their league standing virtually disappear.

Keeping this example in mind, then, development according to the structuralists' views is no longer thought of as a race in which some of the participants have fallen behind. Underdevelopment is considered a problem of *structural relations* rather than a problem of scarcity. Development for one of the parties generally suggests underdevelopment for the other.

A major limitation of the modernization approach to explaining development is that it treats underdeveloped nations as isolated units. That is, a nation is considered to succeed or fail in its development efforts because of internal factors—societal beliefs and values, government systems, organization of the economic system, and so on. This isolated perspective fails to recognize the profound influence the more developed nations have had on the poorer nations. For example, many of the underdeveloped nations emerged as independent states after a long history as colonies of the Western powers. Critics of the modernization approach often assert that the poorer countries are still "economic colonies" because of their relationships with the developed world.

Theorists in this school believe that certain *structural* factors required alternative models for development in the underdeveloped countries. These structural factors included those that existed between the North and South as well as those within the underdeveloped countries, such as the permanently high level of unemployment. For example, the North has the ability to produce high value-added manufacturers whereas the South relies heavily on agriculture, natural resources, and simple manufacturers—resulting in decreasing terms of trade. Thus, we see a vicious cycle in which the disparity between the North and South increases rather than decreases. Consequently, the structural theories were based on the notion that the relationships between North and South restricted development for the less developed nations.

Theorists of this school are hostile to the idea that diffusion of modern attitudes and behavior from the developed to the underdeveloped countries is the answer to economic development. From the structuralists' point of view, the long and continuing history of contact between the rich and poor countries is the *cause* of underdevelopment. These scholars believe that all nations of the world are locked together in a single system, which includes a network of economic, social, and political exchanges, all of which work to the disadvantage of the poorer nations. The structuralists generally view the relationships as exploitative of the developing countries.

Advocates of structural development theories consider that transnational corporations have played a key role in the exploitation of the periphery. Structuralists are troubled because although the TNCs provide low-paying jobs for workers in a host country, the corporate headquarters in core nations benefit most.

According to the structuralists, the notion that underdeveloped countries could imitate the industrialized countries seemed unlikely. The optimism regarding underdeveloped countries' development prospects was toned down, and economic models of the day were no longer seen as useful in analyzing the problems of development. Underdevelopment could no longer be explained by a lack of capital. In short, despite economic growth in a number of the underdeveloped countries, significant progress appeared unlikely. A number of studies began to refer to "growth without development" (Blomström & Hettne, 1984).

Structural theories provided another way of viewing the problems of underdevelopment. We have noted that these theorists believe underdevelopment is the result of structural problems, but how did those problems occur? McGowan (1987) suggests that structural theories are based on global processes of development as they unfolded in history. Two striking facts about world history over the last 500 years count heavily in the structural approaches:

1. The world became "an integrated and interactive system characterized by sharp

inequalities between a minority of well-off people and a majority of poor people" (p. 49). Except for Japan, the rich part of the world is European or of European origin, while the poor part represents the non-Western peoples of the world.

2. "Structural models recognize that this world-division did not always exist: the development gap is a product of modern history" (p. 49).

If these world divisions did not always exist, how did Western Europe and its overseas extensions, such as the United States, come to dominate the world—economically, politically, and culturally? How did China and the Islamic civilizations end up as part of the world's poorer regions?

McGowan's (1987) structural model of development is also an umbrella approach for grouping together a number of theories with similar characteristics. His structural model integrates views of a number of development scholars (including Raúl Prebisch and Immanuel Wallerstein, two influential writers) and attempts to describe how these major divisions in levels of development occurred. According to McGowan, **dependency theory** and **world-systems theory**, other important development theories instrumental in the break from mainstream theory, are repre-

sented in this model. For example, Wallerstein's world-systems approach considers "zones" of development similar to those shown in McGowan's model in Figure 4–7.

As McGowan traces the divisions that emerged, he notes that major changes began to occur about 1000 A.D. as "the trade network of Eurasia became ecumenical, embracing all substantial blocs of population in its tentacles for the first time" (McNeill, 1986, p. 223). From that time on, major Old World civilizations were linked through trade of items such as silk and spices. Until about 1450, trade had not influenced development differences among trading regions; however, it produced two changes in Europe that were of monumental importance in altering global development relationships in the future. The two significant changes in Europe were

1. The Italian trading states developed *merchant capitalism* and *banking*. The capitalist-oriented market behavior that spread around the world during the next 500 years changed the world dramatically.
2. By 1450, wealthy European aristocrats had developed a *taste for the luxury goods* that resulted from trade. European leaders also felt the need to increase their incomes to support their armies and to pay for their luxury goods. Thus, the European civiliza-

---

 EMERGENCE OF THE DEVELOPMENT GAP

McNeill's (1965) *The Rise of the West* helps us to understand that the development gap is a fairly recent occurrence when viewed in the history of the world. During the fifteenth century there were slight developmental differences among the major civilizations, and the differences that did exist favored the Islamic civilizations of the Middle East and India over Western Europe and China. Contrary to what might have been expected in the fifteenth century, China and the Islamic civilizations became the world's poorer regions. In general, European countries and nations of European origin became the wealthy regions of the world while non-Western regions became the poor regions.

FIGURE 4–7
A structural model of development

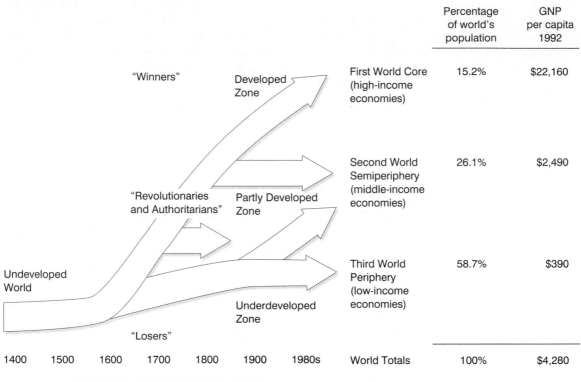

	Percentage of world's population	GNP per capita 1992
First World Core (high-income economies)	15.2%	$22,160
Second World Semiperiphery (middle-income economies)	26.1%	$2,490
Third World Periphery (low-income economies)	58.7%	$390
World Totals	100%	$4,280

HISTORICAL "DEVELOPMENT" PATHS

Source: Updated data from *World Development Report 1994* by World Bank, 1994, Washington, DC: Author. Chart originally from "Key Concepts for Development Studies" by P. McGowan, in *The International Development Crisis & American Education* (p. 50) edited by C. Joy and W. Kniep, 1987, New York: Global Perspectives in Education, Modified and used courtesy of The American Forum for Global Education.

tions were expanded to other parts of the world, and by 1900, "Europe and its overseas extensions such as the United States ruled the world" (McGowan, 1987, p. 51).

According to McGowan's (1987) structural model, the time between 1450 and 1600 A.D. marked a turning point—*the beginning of the divergent paths in worldwide development*. Up to that time, most of the world was *undevel*oped—that is, civilizations were roughly similar in their wealth, power, and other achievements. After 1500, however, the spread of capitalism and the "rise of the West" caused

the development paths of the world's peoples to diverge markedly. Thus, these historical differences in development paths are basic to development theories that advocate that the underdeveloped countries must pursue strategies other than trying to imitate the industrialized countries. These divergent paths set the stage for the problems in structural relations mentioned earlier.

As capitalism and the Western influence spread around the globe in the next 500 years, various regions of the world developed differently. The controlling influence of the more powerful nations caused regions to develop in widely divergent paths. Consequently, according to a number of development theories and models, three different zones emerged (at least one theory suggests four zones). Note that these zones roughly parallel the country groupings discussed in the prior chapter. Descriptions of the zones follow.

First-World Core

This group consists of 24 democratic, industrialized countries of North America, Europe, and Japan. Chirot (1977) noted that as this group emerged, its member nations acted like the "international upper class" (p. 8). Members are rich, economically diversified, and industrialized powers who have dominated the world scene. Wallerstein (1974) uses the term *core societies* for the rich societies whose success changed the rest of the world. This group has the smallest proportion of the world's population—somewhat over 800 million persons.

Second-World Semiperiphery

This is an intermediate zone of partial development consisting of societies that acted as an "international middle class." Many in this group have tried to catch up to the rich and have taken advantage of poorer societies to use them in their catch-up efforts (Wallerstein, 1974). This zone consists of three distinct types of societies and regions:

1. *Formerly communist ruled*. This is the oldest grouping, consisting of countries in East Europe and the former Soviet Union. The economies of many of these countries have been in a fragile state during the transition to market economies.

2. *The NICs*. These are former underdeveloped, peripheral societies such as South Korea, Taiwan, and Brazil that have moved up to the next level of development. Some development models are based on the belief that all countries can move to the NIC status and

beyond. The structural approach, however, accepts the likelihood that only a limited number of countries can move to this stage. This outlook is based on the fact that there is not enough world income and it is too unequally distributed to buy the products of 50 South Koreas (McGowan, 1989).

3. *The OPEC countries*. Most of these countries were in the periphery prior to 1973 when their oil wealth provided greater opportunity for development and began to influence world financial markets.

Third-World Periphery

As a result of colonialism, imperialism, and unequal trading relationships imposed by the core countries, McGowan (1987) asserts that this zone—which represents almost 60 percent of the world's population—did not experience development within the world system. Chirot (1977) described this group of societies as filling the role of an "international lower class" who provides cheap labor, certain raw materials, and certain agricultural products; they have remained poor, weak, and overspecialized in a limited number of export products. Limited manufactures have been produced through low-wage, low-technology processes. This zone includes more than 3 billion people in countries and territories in the Caribbean, Latin America, Africa, the Middle East, and Asia.

Underdeveloped countries constitute the periphery. Within structural approaches, *underdevelopment* is the term for the condition in which a country becomes (i.e., this is not a God-given condition [McGowan, 1989]) specialized in production of low-wage, low-technology products. Long-term prospects are quite different for countries characterized as underdeveloped in contrast to being on a path of "development." The latter brings with it prospects for higher wages and advanced technology. Nearly all countries in the periphery countries are poor and agrarian. The limited industry present in these countries is generally controlled by the core countries (McGowan, 1987). Often an additional factor is the presence in the periphery countries of a comprador (local agent) who stands to benefit from this structure (personal correspondence with S. Douglas, 1989). World Bank data in Table 4–2 provide a summary of the world's population and wealth. The World Bank categories correspond roughly to the structural model's zones.

A quick analysis of the Table 4–2 data provides a jolting awareness of the contrasts from one zone to another. The core's 24 countries account for only about 15 percent of the world's population but nearly 80 percent of the wealth. In contrast, the more than 100 countries in the periphery represent 58.4 percent of the world's population but account for only about 5 percent of its income. Although a large number of countries constitute the periphery, China and India dominate this group in both size and population. The semi-periphery represents slightly over one-fourth of the world's population and about 16 percent of its income.

United Nations population experts project that the population growth in the regions representing the periphery will continue to increase at a far greater rate than will be true in the developed or core countries. Figure 4–8 illustrates this dramatic growth expected in the periphery. The reader is also reminded of earlier discussions regarding the relative decline of incomes in the developing nations compared to those of the developed countries.

Structural Theories: Relationships Among the Zones

Various structural theories of development (including dependency theory and the world-systems approach) focus on examining the relationships among the zones. Consequently, the structural approaches do not present a very flattering picture of the core countries. In fact, some of the structuralist views are considered radical in the core countries and, as a result, have not been accepted widely. Resulting structural models suggest that the world's development inequalities are not just the result of different resource endowments and economic performances—rather, the differences are politically created and maintained. Chirot (1977) asserted that the periphery countries are not poor merely because of internal conditions but because of their relationship with the rich societies—that is, as a result of structural relations, a concept we have noted earlier as basic to structural theories and/or models.

TABLE 4–2
The world's GNP and population, by major country groupings.

Country Grouping	1991 GNP (billions of dollars)	% of World GNP	1991 Population (millions)	% of World Population
Low income	1,097	5.1	3,127	58.4
Middle income	3,474	16.2	1,401	26.2
High income	16,920	78.8	822	15.4
World	21,464	100.0	5,351	100.0

Note: Totals may not equal 100 percent due to rounding

Source: Adapted from *World Development Report 1993* (p. 199) by World Bank, 1993, Washington, DC: Author.

FIGURE 4–8
Population projections by region

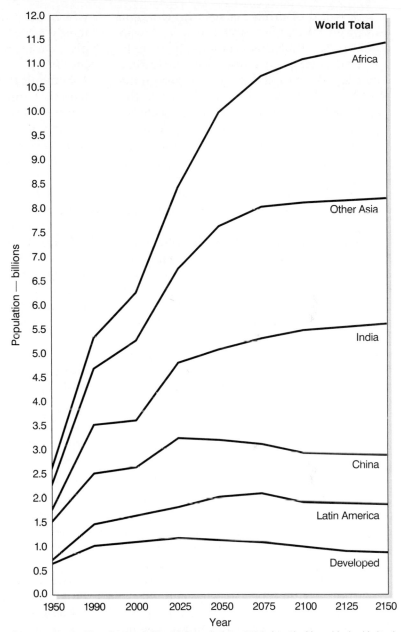

Source: From *The State of World Population 1993* (p. 6), New York: United Nations Population Fund. Reprinted by permission.

In a world of profit makers (the workers) and profit takers (the capitalists), McGowan (1987) noted that this relationship usually takes advantage of workers in periphery countries. Of all capitalists and workers in the world, workers in the periphery have the least power of all. Most have no advocates to represent their interests. Moreover, policies in underdeveloped countries have been developed and supported many times by individuals or groups that prosper under current conditions: import-export firms or others serving as local agents for participating in various forms of trade.

Therefore, we find a remarkable phenomenon within our world: "The exact same job earns very different wages depending upon where it is located" (McGowan, 1987, p. 55). As a result, we find apparel workers earning a fraction of the wages in poor, developing periphery countries that their counterparts earn in North Carolina. Scholars who support the structural views on development reject the economists' views of comparative advantage. Structuralists believe the notion of comparative advantage gives license to exploit the developing countries.

Chirot (1977) asserted that the capitalist leaders in core societies have not been interested in making poorer regions independent and prosperous. Instead, it is to the advantage of the core countries to keep the poorer areas dependent and overspecialized in the production of certain cheap goods. This is not intended as a "plot" by the rich against the poor, but rather the result of "interconnected forces within rich societies and within the entire world system" (Chirot, 1977, p. 9). As a consequence, according to McGowan, profits are transferred from the periphery to the core, and high-wage core societies grow richer faster while low-wage peripheral societies lag behind—with the development gap growing rather than diminishing. Thus, we are reminded of the football league analogy and the premise of the structural approach,

which asserts that underdevelopment is primarily a *problem of relations* rather than simply a problem of scarcity (Blomström & Hettne, 1984).

Some of the newer development perspectives that emerged—such as dependency theory—encouraged representatives of Third-World countries to demand changes in the world economy. Otherwise, many believed that the LDCs may be "stuck" permanently in their underdeveloped conditions; they believed the industrialized nations would continue to take advantage of the low-wage labor and other resources needed to make profits. Hence, LDC concerns of this type stimulated several efforts discussed in an earlier chapter: the North-South dialogue, the emergence of the Group of 77, and the pressure from the LDCs for a "new international economic order."

Development and Textiles and Apparel

Development theories and models are relevant and useful in studying global textile and apparel production and trade in the following ways:

- Development approaches provide another means for viewing the larger picture of global textile and apparel production and trade and for explaining the global dispersion of these industries.
- Development perspectives help us to consider certain social and political dimensions of textile/apparel production and trade that traditional economic theories, for example, may not offer.
- We have a better understanding of why in recent years so many countries participate in simple textile and apparel production. Further, we may comprehend more clearly that many developing countries have few other prospects for participating in world trade.

• By viewing the world in this perspective, we can see that developing countries are likely to continue to be important textile and apparel producers.

A Promising Future or Stuck at the Bottom?

If we reflect on the two major types of development theories considered, we can see that the future role of the developing countries will be quite different in the two.

If one subscribes to the *mainstream/modernization approach*, developing countries involved in the simplest textile/apparel production—that is, agricultural production and simple manufacturing—might consider simple production a transition stage in their development. Operating under this model, nations might look forward to advancing eventually to the levels of the NICs or the developed countries. This strategy remains

the one which almost all Northern conventional economists, core governments, and several key international organizations (World Bank, International Monetary Fund, United Nations organizations, and GATT) say the LDCs should follow (McGowan, 1989).

If one subscribes to the *structural approaches*, developing countries involved in these simple production stages may be stuck at that level of development. Companies in the industrialized countries find the low-priced labor and other resources in the periphery countries attractive in furthering profits for the core countries.

Structuralists would consider many textile and apparel jobs in the periphery to represent exploitation. Other persons might consider, however, that these jobs represent an opportunity because the sector provides valuable employment to workers. For many individuals in developing countries, agrarian fiber pro-

FIGURE 4–9
According to the mainstream/modernization theories, underdeveloped countries may progress toward more advanced levels of development. This Laotian pilot spinning plant reflects the efforts to bring about industrial development.

Source: Photo by J. Maillard, photo courtesy of International Labour Office, Geneva.

FIGURE 4–10
According to the structural theories, underdeveloped countries may be unable to achieve development that expands beyond agricultural production and simple manufacturing. These views suggest that the work of this Bedouin family in Tunisia typifies the long-term prospects for the periphery. The family shears sheep inside their tent home.

Source: Photo by K. Bader, reprinted courtesy of United Nations/United Nations Development Program.

duction or apparel assembly may provide the only available means of earning an income.

Various development theories suggest implications for future relationships between the North and the South in textile and apparel production and trade. Development perspectives may provide clues as to which countries or regions of the world are apt to be involved in various production and trade activities for the sector. For example, analyzing the global picture through a development approach may suggest which regions will be competitors in the textile and apparel sector. That is, if a substantial number of countries move to more advanced stages of development, global competition will become more intense in those segments. For example, if significant numbers of Third-World periphery nations advanced to the NIC level of development, competition among those countries for certain segments of the global market would be even more intense than at present. On the other hand, to companies in the core, models may provide clues on long-term prospects for a low-wage work force to perform apparel assembly operations.

As we consider the development process (or lack thereof) of nations, it is also useful to consider typical stages through which the textile and apparel industries evolve. Because of the important role of the textile/apparel sector in the development process of many nations, changes in the sector often parallel national development. We shall discuss these concepts in greater detail in Chapter 5.

THE NEW INTERNATIONAL DIVISION OF LABOR

The concept of an international division of labor is not new; however, as a global economy becomes an increasing reality, this production strategy has gained special attention. Moreover, in recent decades, this concept has taken on a new dimension. The notion of the **new international division of labor** borrows from economics, in some ways resembling Adam Smith's division of labor and Ricardo's comparative advantage; it also relates to development models, embracing some of the perspectives of the structural theories.

As advances in communication and transportation systems have transformed the world from comparatively independent national economies to an integrated system of worldwide production, a changing international division of labor between the industrialized nations and the developing countries has emerged. As production is segmented into tasks that can be dispersed to various regions of the world, an "internationalization" results from the complementarity between factors of production in developed and developing nations.

In essence, the *new international division of labor* refers to the restructuring of the global economy in which we see a shift of industrial production from the core economies to the periphery. The publication of *The New International Division of Labour* by Fröbel, Heinrichs, and Kreye (1980) provided groundbreaking perspectives on this phenomenon, and, interestingly, Fröbel et al. focused on the textile and apparel industries. In this type of international activity, we must keep in mind that we are not referring to trade but, rather, to *having different aspects of individual firms' production take place in different parts of the world.* (This corresponds to *intra-firm activity* discussed earlier in this chapter.) Dicken (1992) asserts that the transnational corporation is the most important factor to have influenced the global shifts in production to which we are referring.

The *new international division of labor* breaks down complex manufacturing into small, simple production processes that are contracted out to various parts of the world. Production is reduced to simple tasks that can be performed by unskilled labor who can be quickly trained. By contracting production to low-wage countries, manufacturers in the industrialized core countries are able to replace skilled labor receiving high wages with unskilled or semiskilled labor receiving much lower wages. At the same time, the more technical aspects of production, requiring more highly skilled workers, generally occur in countries with greater technological and financial resources.

A worldwide reservoir of labor has become available for industrial employment as Third-World workers have begun to shift away from primitive agricultural production to seek industrial jobs. In some ways, this shift of the populations from agriculture to industrial employment is similar to that which occurred in Europe and the United States more than 200 years ago.

Another concept, the **internationalization of capital**, is related to the international division of labor and suggests that as industrialization begins to occur in developing countries, it is often a result of investments from the core societies. Many developing countries have pursued economic development through strategies that Sklair (1989) has given the acronym ELIFFIT: export-led industrialization fuelled by foreign investment and technology. In fact, many Third-World nations receive the foreign capital to start industrialization because of policies that promote "investment by invitation"—that is, many developing countries actively seek foreign investments through a variety of incentives and concessions, often competing against other Third-World countries to attract investment and production.

Typically, the industries employing the new international division of labor use widely understood technology to make relatively simple products, apparel being an especially important example; such production has led the growth of manufactured exports from the developing nations. Firms in the industrialized countries have found the low wages in Third-World countries particularly attractive as labor costs have risen in their home countries. Therefore, the developing countries' desire to increase industrialization and exports complements the needs of corporations in the industrialized nations to find sources of less costly labor. Hence, since the 1950s, transnational corporations have frequently split their production processes to have the more labor-intensive assembly operations occur in the Third World.

Various writers have applied a number of terms to the resulting co-production relationships dispersed around the globe. Drucker (1977) coined the term *production sharing* for this arrangement. Grunwald and Flamm (1985) refer to the *global factory* as they concluded that the 1960s and 1970s ushered in a new stage in the evolution of the world capitalist system as U.S. (and the same could be said for European) transnational firms switched, on a fairly large scale for the first time, to overseas production of manufactured exports for the domestic market.

As firms in the industrialized countries view developing countries for possible location of simple production processes, they consider a country with a good supply of nonunionized labor, political stability, developed **infrastructures**, and other incentives as "an appropriate investment climate."

The relocation of industrial investment and the new international division of labor require a number of technological developments, most of which are readily available. Today's transportation and communication systems permit certain industries, such as textiles and apparel, to be located almost anywhere in the world. Fröbel et al. (1980) noted that air freight cost for a garment from Southeast Asia to Western Europe was only between $0.50 and $1.00 at the time of their study. Garments and most other textile items are low-bulk, low-weight commodities ideally suited to the new international division of labor.

Although the shared production arrangements have advantages to both the investor firms and to the host nations, conflicts are inherent. Moreover, many scholars are critical

of these arrangements, with arguments that closely resemble those of theorists who believe the structuralist development theories. That is, conflicts reflect a struggle between the North and the South, the have and the have-not nations. Although the shared production arrangements provide export earnings and jobs for large unemployed labor pools in the developing countries, critics see many limitations. For example, Fröbel et al. (1980) charged that "this process also perpetuates those structures which generate dependency and uneven development and the marginalisation of a large part of the population without creating even the most rudimentary preconditions for alternative development" (p. 404). Similarly, Sklair (1989) concluded that the goal of these relationships is to ensure the continued accumulation of capital at home and abroad—as has always been true for global capitalism. Additionally, Pantojas-Garcia (1990) asserted that the arrangements benefit class interests rather than all of society. He believes these arrangements often falsely portray economic development for the masses; however, in many cases special interest groups have designed strategies to benefit themselves.

Thus, critics believe that assembly operations condemn host countries and workers to continued underdevelopment. Because transnational corporations generally make decisions in their headquarters located in the developed nations, the host country's potential supplies of intermediate inputs may be ignored, development of local management and other skills are often overlooked, and the use of technology along with research and development from the investor nation neglects the nurturing of these activities in the host country. As a result, the international division of labor may do little to help the developing economy to advance to stages in which *local* management, investment, technology, and research and development would play a dominant role in the production process. Moreover, wage increases may be difficult to pursue for local workers, because host countries often worry that increasing labor costs may cause the investor firm to move to more favorable settings in other countries.

Critics use other arguments to illustrate that shared production arrangements are detrimental to host economies and that underdevelopment will be perpetuated under these schemes. For example, critics assert that TNC investor firms may have a negative impact on local industry structure in the developing country, often building too many plants or plants of inappropriate size in their efforts to capitalize on market position at a given time. Furthermore, the powerful TNC may have the potential to exploit economies of scale, product differentiation, technological advantages, marketing advantages, and vertical integration, which may be significant entry barriers to local firms in the host country.

The new international division of labor also has critics in the developed countries, with most attention focused on the job losses caused by the transfer of production elsewhere. Although many Third-World nations have welcomed foreign companies and investors, and those economies are booming, the older industrialized economies have flourished far less in recent years. As Dicken (1992) noted, unemployment in the Western industrialized countries reached levels in the 1970s and early 1980s unknown since the Great Depression of the 1930s. Employment in the world's seven richest nations, the Group of Seven, has fallen in recent years, with more then 25 million people out of work, and the numbers are growing (Farrell, Mandel, Javetski, & Baker, 1993). Factory closings, job losses, and shifts from manufacturing to service jobs have fostered the term *deindustrialization* to describe the developed economies—often with older industrialized regions in each nation facing the greatest unemployment. Ironically, it is often the dilemma of competing with lower-cost imported goods from developing countries that leads to a firm's decision to relocate its own production abroad. As might be expected, labor unions in the developed nations believe jobs have been lost as a result of foreign assembly and are opposed to this "export" of jobs. These issues will be debated further in later chapters of this book.

In conclusion, many textile and apparel production processes are scattered around the globe. This globalization of the industry is the single most significant change affecting the textile and apparel sectors in recent decades. Familiarity with the new international division of labor concept provides another useful way of considering in a broad perspective what is happening in global textile and apparel production and trade.

SUMMARY

Theories are helpful in focusing on global shifts in textile and apparel production and trade. Theories and concepts help us to see the broad picture and examine these global trends in an organized manner. Further, theories may help to explain what is and what could be produced competitively in a given area.

Several trade theories provide various perspectives on why production and trade occur as they do. Mercantilism provided groundwork for the idea that a favorable balance of trade is desirable. Adam Smith's theory of absolute advantage suggested that a nation concentrate on industries in which its costs are lowest and that the country trade part of its output for goods other nations can produce more cheaply. Ricardo's theory of comparative advantage shows that a country can specialize and develop a "comparative" advantage although it has no absolute advantage. Smith's and Ricardo's theories focused on the question: Is trade beneficial? Both these writers emphasized benefits for all countries through trade.

Later theories focused on the question: What should be produced where? The factor proportions theory suggests that relative factor endowments of land, labor, and capital will affect the relative cost of these factors, therefore determining the goods a country can produce most efficiently. The product cycle theory suggests that products will shift locations for production according to stages in the product's life cycle.

More recently, Michael Porter's *The Competitive Advantage of Nations* (1990) provided new perspectives on why some nations succeed in certain industries and certain segments. His determinants of national advantage shape the environments in which a country's firms compete to promote or impede international competitiveness.

Although trade theories examine global exchange on a country-to-country basis, decisions to trade or not to trade are generally made by firms within those countries. Firms may trade to use excess production capacity, to lower production costs, or to spread risks.

Development theories and models are relevant and useful in studying international textile and apparel production and trade. Although development theory has its roots in economics, development approaches extend to historical, social, and political issues as well. As we observe the emergence of textile and apparel production in nearly all Third-World countries, development theory helps us to understand these global trends. Moreover, various development approaches provide insight into the long-term outlook for the role of the textile and apparel sectors in various regions.

Early *mainstream/modernization theories* of development relied on the premise that poorer countries would imitate the development patterns of the industrialized nations. Newer theories, grouped into what McGowan

(1987) calls *structural theories*, reject the notion that the poorer countries are likely to develop in patterns similar to the richer nations. The structural theories, which McGowan considers to include dependency theory and world-systems theory, are based on the idea that problems in structural relations existed because of vastly different historical paths of development for three major groups of countries or societies: the core, the semiperiphery, and the periphery.

The concept of the new international division of labor, which borrows from both economic and development theories, refers to the breaking down of complex manufacturing into small, simple production processes that are contracted out to low-wage countries. *Internationalization of capital* refers to the investment by core nations in the periphery regions to use the LDCs for low-wage production processes. These global shifts in production and investment offer advantages to both transnational corporations and to host economies in the Third World. At the same time, these strategies have been subject to criticism from various quarters.

GLOSSARY

Absolute advantage exists when one nation can produce more of a commodity with a given amount of resources than another country can.

Aggregate demand is the sum of a group of individuals' demand; this represents market demand.

Arm's length trade occurs when producers in one country trade goods with buyers in other countries. Business relationships may be defined simply as buyers and sellers.

Capital-intensive products are those that result from production with a high capital-to-labor ratio; that is, a great deal of capital is required for production.

Balance of trade measures the difference between the value of a nation's exports and the value of its imports. The balance of trade includes services in addition to merchandise.

Comparative advantage is a concept in trade theory that suggests that a country "should specialize in producing and exporting those products in which it has a comparative, or relative, cost advantage compared with other countries and should import those goods in which it has a comparative disadvantage. Out of such specialization, it is argued, will accrue greater benefit for all" (Dicken, 1992, p. 92).

Competitive advantage refers to whatever it is that enables a firm to beat its competition in the marketplace.

Dependency theory (in Spanish, *dependencia*) originated in Latin America as the LDCs concluded they were too dependent on the sale of a few primary commodities and/or too dependent on a limited number of developed countries as customers and suppliers. According to dependency theory, industrialized countries have dominated and exploited the Third World.

Development, in addition to the definition given in Chapter 3, focuses on the imbalances in the distribution of resources between the rich and the poor of the world. Development efforts are aimed at reducing the gap.

Direct foreign investment refers to ownership or part ownership of foreign production facilities.

Division of labor refers to the division of production jobs or tasks because certain groups of workers are presumed to provide efficiencies in the use of resources (for example, labor costs, skills, technology, and so on).

Equilibrium price is the price at which the quantity demanded equals the quantity supplied.

Greige goods are unbleached, unfinished fabrics that will receive further processing, which may include dyeing, printing, or other finishing.

Factors of production are the basic inputs required for production; these include natural resources (land and raw materials), capital, labor supply, knowledge resources, technology, and infrastructure.

Infrastructures are the underlying systems or frameworks within a country that support the activities of industry or other operations; these include communication networks, energy, roads, railroads, and seaports (and some sources include education). Infrastructures reflect a nation's level of development and affect the country's ability to participate in global commerce. For example, if an LDC produces a large volume of cotton but does not have the infrastructure to transport it to ports, the country has little opportunity to export the cotton.

Intra-firm trade occurs when trade takes place between two or more units of the same company across national boundaries.

Law of demand suggests there is an inverse relationship between market price and the quantity demanded when other factors remain constant. That is, as price increases, demand decreases; as demand increases, price decreases.

Law of supply suggests there is a relationship between quantity supplied and prices; as the price for a product rises, this encourages producers to increase output.

Licensing (or licensing arrangements) involves an agreement between a firm in one country and a foreign manufacturer to use the former's trademark and expertise to produce and market the product (for example, garments) in the foreign manufacturer's country.

Mercantilism was an economic philosophy built around the idea that a country's wealth depended upon its holdings of treasure—particularly gold.

Merchandise trade balance. The merchandise trade balance is the difference between the amount of money a country receives from selling its goods (merchandise) abroad and that which it pays to buy goods from other countries.

Multinational corporations (MNCs) are those that own, control, or manage production and distribution facilities *in more than two* countries.

Nation-state is what we now call a country.

New international division of labor refers to reducing complex manufacturing into small, simple production processes that are contracted out to other parts of the world to be performed by low-cost labor.

Internationalization of capital refers to investments by core countries in the early industrialization efforts (also mines and plantations) of periphery nations. Often, this is associated with contracting simple production processes to the LDCs.

Opportunity cost is the cost of using resources for a given purpose, measured by the benefit or revenues given up by not using them in their best alternative use.

Society, as it is often considered in international business, is the nation-state because of the basic similarity of people within national boundaries.

Transnational corporations (TNCs) are those that own, control, or manage production and distribution facilities *in at least two* countries.

Underdevelopment has varied definitions in different development theories. In the *mainstream/modernization view*, underdevelopment is the difference between the rich and poor countries. According to this view, underdeveloped countries are characterized by capital shortages. In the *structural approaches*, underdevelopment refers to a country's or a region's specialization in the production and export of low-wage, low-technology products.

World-systems theory, which followed dependency theory, emphasizes "the capitalist world economy as one integral system covering the whole globe and being moved by a single dynamic system overpowering the individual states that make up the system; . . . this central power, which is in the process of expansion, has forced peripheral areas under its control" (Blomström & Hettne, 1984, pp. 186–88). Immanuel Wallerstein is the scholar best known for extending this approach beyond dependency theories.

SUGGESTED READINGS

Bernstein, A., Konrad, W., & Therrien, L. (1992, August 10). The global economy: Who gets hurt? *Business Week*, pp. 48–53.
This article examines the impact of global shifts of production on workers in the developed countries.

Blomström M., & Hettne, B. (1984). *Development theory in transition*. London: Zed Books, Ltd.
This book emphasizes the importance of dependency theory in the formulation of broader development theories.

Caporaso, J. (Ed.). (1987). *A changing international division of labor*. Boulder, CO: Lynne Rienner.
A volume of papers that focuses on the international division of labor, with special emphasis on the role of the working class.

Dicken, P. (1992). *Global shift: The internationalization of economic activity* (2nd ed.). New York: Guilford Press.
This book provides an excellent multidisciplinary examination of global shifts in production, with particular emphasis on the role of TNCs.

Edwards, C. (1985). *The fragmented world.* London: Methuen.
Chapter 1 provides a useful summary of the world division of labor and economic theories.

Ellsworth, P. I., & Leith, J. C. (1984). *The international economy.* New York: Macmillan.
A study of international economics; the authors blend theory, history, and policy.

Farrell, C., Mandel, M., Javetski, B., & Baker, S. (1993, August 2). What's wrong? Why the industrialized nations are stalled. *Business Week,* pp. 54–59.

Fishlow, A., Diaz-Alejandro, C., Fagen, R., & Hansen, R. (1978). *Rich and poor nations in the world economy.* New York: McGraw-Hill.
This book addresses the political economy of North-South relations and includes a useful section on development strategies.

Fröbel, F., Heinrichs, J., & Kreye, O. (1980). *The new international division of labour.* Cambridge: Cambridge University Press.
A study of the new international division of labor; the study focuses on West Germany's textile and apparel industries.

Grunwald, J., & Flamm, K. (1985). *The global factory.* Washington, DC: The Brookings Institution.
An important study on foreign assembly and international trade.

Joy, C., & Kniep, W. (Eds.). (1987). *The international development crisis & American education.* New York: Global Perspectives in Education.
A review of challenges, opportunities, and instructional strategies related to development education.

O'Reilly, B. (1992, December). Your new global work force. *Fortune,* pp. 52–66.
An article on how firms are tapping the world's skilled labor pool.

Pollard, S. (Ed.). (1990). *Wealth & poverty.* Oxford, England: Oxford University Press.
A well-organized and illustrated economic history of the twentieth century.

Porter, M. (1990). *The competitive advantage of nations.* New York: Free Press.
The author builds on his earlier works to develop a new paradigm for analyzing international competitiveness that may replace the classic concept of comparative advantage.

United Nations, Centre on Transnational Corporations. (1987). *Transnational corporations in the man-made fibre, textile and clothing industries.* New York: Author.
A study of transnational corporation activities in textiles and apparel.

Ward, K. (Ed.). (1990). *Women workers and global restructuring.* Ithaca, NY: ILR Press.
An examination of how women workers are affected by global restructuring.

World Bank (annual). *World development report (year).* Washington, DC: Author.
Each annual volume focuses on a special development theme or issue and also provides an update on world development data.

III

An Overview of the Global Textile and Apparel Industries

Part III provides a general survey of the textile and apparel industries in the global economy and global shifts for these sectors. These chapters are designed to help us understand and appreciate the magnitude of the global textile complex and the role the industries play in virtually every country of the world.

Chapter 5 provides an overview of the global textile complex, including a brief historical perspective. The chapter also considers the stages of industry development in relation to a country's or region's overall development.

Chapter 6 reviews the textile complex in select regions of the world, particularly in relation to the restructuring of the industry that is occurring on a global scale. We will consider significant changes that are shaping the nature of the global industry. In this chapter, wherever possible, an effort is made to relate the discussion to various stages of development considered in earlier chapters.

In Chapter 7, we examine global patterns of textile and apparel production, employment, consumption, and trade. We will consider the noteworthy patterns that have emerged and some of the implications for producers, workers, and consumers in various regions of the world.

5

An Overview of the Global Textile Complex

INTRODUCTION

Textile and apparel production plays a vitally important role in supporting and sustaining human life around the world. Beyond providing clothing as a basic human necessity, the production of textile and apparel goods provides a means for earning a livelihood for an impressive portion of the world's population. Whether we are considering textile workers in a major industrialized country or those involved in elementary production in the poorest countries in the world, this industry provides employment for a vast number of the world's occupants. Employment in the complex is vital to most of these workers, regardless of the region of the world, because individuals may have few or no other options to obtain earnings to sustain themselves and their family or household members.

World trade in textiles and apparel has been given special attention for many years. Global trade in the sector has become quite sensitive because of the unique role the industry plays as a major employer. Moreover, because of the industry's important role in providing employment for workers in virtually every country, trade problems have become quite politicized and difficult to resolve. As might be expected, nearly all countries with a textile industry want an opportunity to compete in world markets. In short, increased global participation in textile/apparel production has led to an overcapacity to produce for existing markets, and intense competition has resulted. Hence, the attention given to textile trade may seem disproportionate to the economic contribution of the sector to the global economy. The fact remains, however, that textile and apparel production is one of the top manufacturing employers in the world (International Labour Office, 1992; United States International Trade

Commission, 1982). If accurate reports of **cottage industry** employment could be documented, the industry is perhaps *the* largest global manufacturing employer.

This chapter presents (1) an overview of the global textile complex, including a brief historical perspective, (2) a review of global patterns of development for the textile complex, (3) consideration of changes in the textile complex in relation to a nation's development, and (4) a brief reflection on global supply in relation to demand.

BRIEF HISTORICAL PERSPECTIVE

The textile industry led the early industrialization process in regions of Europe and the United States. Similarly, as other countries moved toward economic development, the textile sector played a vital role in industrialization efforts. Later, as apparel production became an "industrial" activity, both sectors became significant components of a changing global economy. Although we have noted the increased global participation in these sectors, words fail to reflect the chaos and political drama that have accompanied global shifts in production, employment, and trade.

Production and trade shifts for textiles began to occur in the early part of the twentieth century. As these changes began to affect the textile industries of the developed countries, global textile activity began to take on turbulent characteristics that would intensify in later decades. A brief historical review of global shifts will provide a helpful perspective as we examine these trends in greater detail in this chapter and the one that follows.

Early Twentieth Century

At the turn of this century, Britain accounted for 70 percent of the world's textile trade (Aggarwal, 1985). According to Maizels (1963),

world textile production increased by about 90 percent between 1900 and 1937, and significant changes in *where* production would occur began during this era. Although absolute global production increased, the contribution of textiles as a portion of all manufacturing production in the developed countries began to decrease by 1900. The increased proficiency of a major new producer nation, Japan (a developing country at that time), partly accounted for the drop in the industrialized countries' production as a portion of total manufacturing activity.

After the Depression began in 1929, challenges to the dominant positions of the textile and apparel industries in the industrialized countries set the stage for what would follow for much of the century. Japan's economic development from the 1920s through the 1950s paralleled earlier patterns in the United States and certain European countries by relying heavily on textile production to lead the industrialization process. By 1933, Japan had become the primary exporter of cotton textile products in the world (Aggarwal, 1985; General Agreement on Tarrifs and Trade, 1984). Japan's textile competitiveness was affected seriously, however, by World War II; more than three-fourths of her textile production capacity was destroyed.

Mid-Twentieth Century

After the war, the U.S. and British industries expanded vigorously while the textile and apparel sectors in most other countries rebuilt production facilities. By 1947, the U.S. textile and apparel industries enjoyed an impressive trade surplus and began to consider the surplus as normal. Consequently, U.S. manufacturers willingly supported efforts to help Japan rebuild her industry (Aggarwal, 1985; Destler, Fukui, & Sato, 1979). The struggling nation depended heavily on textile production for rebuilding her economy, and, by the

1950s, Japan again became a major contender for global textile markets. American manufacturers began to worry about the impact of Japanese imports in U.S. markets. These events set the stage for similar shifts that would occur in the decades that followed.

In the 1950s and 1960s other developing countries and a few nations in Eastern Europe began to pattern economic development strategies after the industrialized countries. The **newly emerging countries** hoped that similar industrialization would permit them to become important forces in world markets and would bring to their economies some of the prosperity they observed, particularly in the United States and Western Europe. Japan was a role model many developing countries attempted to emulate. (The reader is reminded that the development theories in vogue during this era suggested that the LDCs would be able to imitate the industrialized countries in their development process. Japan was an impressive example of the progress believed to be possible by advocates of the mainstream/modernization approaches.) Japan's rapid rebuilding and economic evolution represented progress other countries hoped to repeat. Of particular significance is the fact that most of the emerging nations chose textile production as a major sector (more often, *the* major sector) in which to concentrate their investments, their efforts, and their dreams for advancing economically.

Textile production was a natural first industry for developing countries to choose. Then and now, the textile complex provided an easy entry for **new producer nations.** Simple textile/apparel production required limited capital and technology—resources in short supply in the developing countries. Portions of the industry are quite labor intensive, and emerging nations usually have an abundance of low-cost labor. Such countries usually have large populations in need of jobs to help the nation earn foreign exchange and improve the local level of living. In addition, unskilled workers are able to assume simple production jobs in the textile complex with little training.

Following Japan's example, a number of less-developed nations began to produce and export cotton products. (Keep in mind that this was prior to widespread production of manufactured fiber products.) Soon, Hong Kong, South Korea, India, and Pakistan joined Japan in exporting growing amounts to the markets of the developed countries. Although imports accounted for only about 2 percent of the U.S. textile market by 1955, domestic manufacturers became increasingly concerned over the threat from exporting countries (Aggarwal, 1985). Similarly, by 1958, British textile and apparel producers became alarmed that their country, which had launched the Industrial Revolution with textiles, was importing more cotton cloth than she was exporting.

As competition for world markets increased in the mid- to late-1950s, early efforts began in both the United States and Europe to stem the flow of textile products from low-wage countries into the developed countries' markets. Although problems associated with global textile trade began to seem difficult in that era, the 1950s were a mere prelude to the growing clash between exporting and importing nations.

Late Twentieth Century

The number of nations producing for the international textile and apparel market has multiplied many times over since the 1950s. As the number of textile-producing nations grew, the competition for market access became increasingly intense. Further, at a time when the number of producer nations increased, textile product consumption slowed in the major markets—those of the developed countries. As a result of the increased competition and the perceived

threat of imports, textile and apparel manufacturers in the industrialized nations began
to demand trade policies to protect domestic
markets. Trade policies related to the textile
sector will be presented in more detail later in
the book.

GLOBAL PATTERNS OF DEVELOPMENT FOR THE TEXTILE COMPLEX

Although the relative importance of textile
and apparel production varies (both in relative terms in global markets and in relative
terms within a country), virtually every country in the world produces at least some textile
products. This production ranges from making simple textile components (fibers, yarns,
fabrics) to sophisticated end-use products. For
some nations, production of textile and
apparel products represents a vital means of
economic survival; for others, this industry
has taken on a less important role.

Stages of Development in the Textile Complex

Toyne et al. (1984) have provided a helpful
conceptual approach for considering the
extent to which the textile complex has developed in various countries or areas of the
world. Toyne and his research colleagues
described different levels of development on
a continuum "ranging from embryonic to
declining" (p. 20). All the stages of development can be found in various parts of the
world today, and the industries in many
countries are evolving from one stage to
another.

The notion of "stages of development"
(Toyne et al., 1984) in textile and apparel production parallels, in many ways, the discussion in Chapter 4 regarding overall develop-

ment within cou
lels will be discu

Toyne's stages
consider the maj
textile complex
scale. Although
countries as exa
important to reme
we would find ma, countries and regions of
the world.

Although these stages of development do
embody some characteristics of the main-
stream/modernization development theories
and models, these stages are primarily
descriptive of the textile complex as we might
find it throughout the world today. That is,
the stages are descriptive rather than prescriptive. Although the textile and apparel
industries in some countries have moved or
will move through most or all of the stages,
this evolution will not be possible in many
nations.

The stages developed by Toyne et al. have
been modified and updated from the original
scheme. As we consider the stages, we must
keep in mind that a country or region's textile
complex may be represented by more than
one level.

1. The *embryonic stage* is typically found in
the poorest and least developed countries.
The industry is often little more than a collection of cottage industries, and most production is for domestic consumption, such as that
in Figure 5–1. Production consists primarily of
making simple fabrics (usually by hand-pro-
duced methods) and garments from natural
fibers. These countries typically import component parts if they can afford to do so. Production of natural fibers for export, particularly cotton, may be one of the few ways in
which some countries at this stage can earn
foreign exchange. The textile/apparel sectors
in many countries in Africa are presently at
this stage of development.

...mitive type of loom, this village woman ...or is weaving sisal to make sacks. (Photo ...esy United Nations.)

2. *Early export of apparel* occurs because low-wage labor is used for labor-intensive operations to produce garments for which there is a market in other countries. This may be assembly of component parts of garments from other countries, the production of ethnic clothing, or products with extensive hand work. Often products from countries at this stage of development are for the low end of the market in developed nations, and, in many cases, price is the primary appeal for consumers who consider the products. Often when a nation is at this stage, some of the technical aspects of garment production are not yet perfected and quality may be unpredictable. Examples of countries in this stage are Nepal, Bangladesh, Sri Lanka, and several Latin American and Caribbean countries. Some of the ASEAN countries (Association of Southeast Asian Nations) have been in this stage, but certain members are advancing to the next levels.

3. *More advanced production of fabric and apparel* occurs at this stage of development. Domestic production of fabric improves a great deal in volume, quality, and sophistication, and fabrics may be exported to other countries. As countries become more advanced at this level, they may develop their own fiber production, including manufactured fibers. During this stage, apparel production is expanded and upgraded. Garments may be made from fabrics and component parts (**intermediate inputs**) produced within a country rather than simply assembling components from other countries, more typical in the second stage. In general, the textile complexes at this level "become larger, more diversified, more concentrated, and more internationally active" (Toyne et al., 1984, p. 20). Some of the more advanced ASEAN countries are in this stage of development. Mainland China is in this stage and is making rapid advances toward self-sufficiency in manufactured fiber production (Ehrlich, 1988b; McMurray & McGregor, 1993).

As Toyne et al. noted, large manufacturers and retailers in more developed countries provide assistance at this stage, which fosters advancement from one level to the next. Large manufacturers and retailers assist by investing in the emerging countries' industries, by contracting, and by providing information on technical aspects of production, marketing, and management. Further, movement to this level of production is often encouraged by local government policies that encourage **import substitution**, and by initiatives that foster exporting. (We should note that government support also occurs in the first two stages. Often it is government support, however, that permits movement to this third stage.)

4. *The "Golden Age" stage* of development is characterized by increasingly enlarged and sophisticated textile and apparel production as well as large trade surpluses for the sector.

BANGLADESH: POOR AND LOSING A MAJOR INCOME PRODUCER

Bangladesh, India, and China have been major producers of jute, a natural fiber used for bagging, carpet backing, and a variety of low-grade textile applications. Jute production is an agricultural activity particularly important to these poor developing countries, especially in rural regions that do not have the means for industrialization. China and India have large internal economies that use the bulk of jute produced within each country. Bangladesh, on the other hand, uses only about 10 percent of its jute output and relies on exporting. Jute is one of the few areas in which Bangladesh seems to have a comparative advantage. Jute production is an agriculture mainstay in this country with a population of about half that of the United States and an average per capita income of $220 per year—one of the poorest countries in the world (World Bank, 1994).

Competition from the olefins, particularly polypropylene, has taken a significant portion of the jute market. When polypropylene is slit into narrow strips and stretched before winding, it behaves more like a textile than plastic, making it suitable for weaving. In this form, polypropylene has been used for many of the applications for which jute once had an almost exclusive market. Additionally, newer processes lowered costs of producing polypropylene for these applications. Thus, as costs dropped, this created even more difficult market conditions for jute. As a result, jute has been forced to meet the challenge by keeping prices very low: 1993 prices were about the same as those in 1960.

Jute is biodegradable and may have some advantages over its competitors. This quality may be used in future jute promotions. However, it is expected that the jute market will continue to shrink and that Bangladesh will bear the heaviest burden in the battle between jute and the substitutes. This will be unfortunate for this poor country for which jute is one of the few cash crops to support the rural economy. Further decline in the jute industry will result in further economic and social difficulties than exist today. Although competition among fibers is nothing new, this example illustrates the plight of poor developing countries with high levels of dependence on natural fiber production and few means for improving the lives of their people (Mackie, 1993).

Manufactured fiber production becomes more advanced and increases in volume. The domestic textile industry is capable of supplying a good portion of the fiber and fabric needed to make garments or other finished products. The textile complex diversifies its product mix and in general becomes a more powerful force in international markets.

Rather than being on the receiving end of contractual arrangements with firms in other nations, industry leaders in a country at this stage initiate joint arrangements for their own firms. That is, textile/apparel firms in coun-tries at this stage now invest in the industry in other countries—much like the more advanced countries once invested in them. Korea and Taiwan are presently examples of countries at this stage ("Taiwanese Firm", 1988 Westbrook, 1992). Hong Kong's apparel and fabric sectors are also at this advanced level, but geographical (space) limitations have restricted development of the manufactured fiber sector. Firms from these three major Asian sources have invested in segments of the industry in other countries that are at earlier stages of development.

MAKING A SACRIFICE TO EXPORT TEXTILES

In their desperate attempts to secure foreign exchange to help their national economies, African governments have at times promoted use of the most fertile land to grow cotton (and a few other crops) for export—rather than growing food for their populations. In the late 1980s, some of the countries most affected by the African famine were building surpluses in crops for which a world market glut existed. For example, in the mid 1980s, Sudan's cotton crop expanded to 550,000 bales (worth over $500 million at the time), but an excess supply in world markets made it difficult to sell. Unfortunately, Sudan relied on cotton for about 50 percent of its export earnings at the time (Clark, 1986).

By this stage, a country's level of industrialization and development may affect the importance attached to the textile complex. Nations with increased sophistication in sectors requiring more technology and capital

FIGURE 5–2
Child labor is common in many parts of the developing world, and sometimes in the more developed countries as well.

Source: Photo courtesy of United Nations.

may start to favor certain other industries and depend less on the textile complex.

5. *Full maturity* represents the fifth stage of development. As Toyne et al. (1984) noted, although total output may continue to increase at this stage, employment in the textile complex starts to decline; the drop in employment is particularly noticeable in the apparel sector. The industry may become more concentrated; products and processes tend to be at a fairly advanced level such as that shown in Figure 5–3. The production of manufactured fibers and relatively complex textile mill products are characteristic of this stage. As the industry in countries at this stage attempts to compete in world markets, a good deal of the production is fairly capital intensive. Large capital investments are used to offset the labor advantages in competing nations and also may be required for more complex products.

Toyne et al. placed the United States, Japan, and Italy in this stage but noted the major differences among the three. Of the three, the U.S. complex is the largest; Japan's complex is most vertically integrated and perhaps makes most extensive use of **offshore production** and contracting; and the Italian textile complex receives fairly extensive assistance from the government.

CHILD LABOR COMMON IN EARLY STAGES

In the early stages of a nation's development when many income-earning activities are quite labor intensive, child labor is a common practice. When a great deal of labor is necessary in production, every pair of hands is an asset—including those of children. Although most nations have child labor laws, many violations occur. Many of these are in the textile and apparel complex.

In the late 1980s, the International Labour Organization in Geneva estimated that 88 million children between the ages of 11 and 15 were in the work force. The numbers are probably much higher because many children *under* that age are also employed, and because it is impossible to have an accurate count of children who work in factories that many authorities would prefer not be seen. India, for example, has termed child labor a necessary evil but has vowed to end the practice eventually. Although Indian law bars jobs for children under 14, the government estimates that 17 million of them work, mostly in match and glass making, diamond polishing, and carpet weaving. Private estimates put the number at 55 million ("India Defends," 1993).

Reporters from Cox Newspapers traveled all over the world investigating child labor practices, from which they developed a poignant series entitled *Stolen Childhood* (Albright & Kunstel, 1987). The Cox team found shameful demands and conditions for children. In Morocco, the Cox reporters found a factory they described as "one piece of a global shame" (p. 4) in which more than 250 girls and young women work 55 hours per week, sitting elbow to elbow in a "one-room carpet factory where the sweet, sickly odor of wool dust hangs in air" and lighting is so poor one could not see without strain. One-third of the workers looked no older than 10. The manager talked to reporters and said, "We prefer to get them when they are about 7. Children's hands are nimbler. . . . And their eyes are better, too. They are faster when they are

small" (p. 4). The reporters visited 14 Moroccan carpet factories, were welcomed (unannounced) at 11, and saw large numbers of children in all of them. The operations appeared profitable. Even mid-level managers at some of the factories drove Mercedes Benz sedans.

The Cox reporters found similar shameful conditions in garment factories in the Philippines, Thailand, and other countries. They saw thousands of children working at sewing machines for as many as 90 to 110 hours per week, often so exhausted that they slept next to their sewing machines. Some of the children were ill and suffered from lack of sleep.

One Filipino factory manager commented to the Cox team, "The very sad reality is that we're part of the Third World. . . . We're part of the dumping ground where cheap labor is the main attraction. For investors, cheap labor is the main attraction of the Philippines at this point in time." Cox reporters noted that the factory manager's remarks "reflect the mind-set shared by many intellectuals in the Third World: that child labor and child exploitation may be inevitable as the country struggles to keep up with competing Third World nations in the race for development" (p. 11).

Cox reporters commented, "The defect of this argument is that greed and grimness observe no national borders. In the global competition to offer cheap labor, some other country will always hold wages even lower. And the net result is that children are paid so little that their labor often verges on servitude" (p. 11).

Children yield cheap labor and produce merchandise that represents bargains to buyers for fashionable stores in the developed countries. New York department stores carrying the brand of Moroccan rugs found in the factories visited refused to speak to Cox reporters.

A sad dilemma is that attractive alternatives for Third-World children may not be readily available. For many, the work fends off starva-

CHILD LABOR COMMON IN EARLY STAGES *(continued)*

tion for themselves and their families. For others, work in the grim factories may be preferable to alternatives such as prostitution (child prostitution is common in Thailand, for example). And in many countries there are not enough schools to accommodate the children even if they were not working.

A number of transnational firms have developed policies that take a stance against doing business with factories in countries where child labor is common. For example, Levi Strauss & Co. has in its *Business Partner Terms of Engagement and Guidelines for Country Selection* a provision against use of child labor. Levi Strauss & Co.'s

policy clearly states: "Use of child labor is not permissible.... We will not utilize partners who use child labor in any of their facilities" (Levi Strauss & Co., no date). Moreover, the company has withdrawn contract arrangements with firms found to violate this policy.

Bills were introduced in both houses of Congress in 1993 to deal with issues of child labor, using a two-pronged approach: (1) setting criminal sanctions for U.S. employers who violate child labor laws and (2) banning imports from industries abroad that employ children under 15 ("Child-labor," 1993).

6. *Significant decline* is characteristic of the final stage of development. Both the number of firms and the number of workers in the textile complex decrease significantly at this stage, and trade deficits occur in many segments, particularly apparel and fabric. Survival patterns are quite mixed because while some segments remain healthy, others are in serious trouble and perhaps cannot be revitalized. Figure 5–4 illustrates a possible outcome

FIGURE 5–3
High-tech textile production, such as that required to produce manufactured fibers, characterizes more advanced stages of development in a textile complex.

Source: Photo courtesy of DuPont Fibers.

at this stage. Offshore production increases significantly. Toyne et al. considered several European countries to be at this stage: the United Kingdom, West Germany,[1] France, Bel-

gium, and the Netherlands. Although the textile complexes in all these nations are basically in the declining stage, the decline occurred in differing degrees and sometimes because of quite different approaches by respective governments. For example, West Germany intentionally shifted away from segments of the industry that are labor intensive and require less technical production. As a technologically advanced nation, West Germany assumed a position of retaining the more sophisticated

---

[1]Toyne et al. (1984) made these observations prior to the reunification of Germany. The reference would apply only to the mature industry in the former West Germany. Much of the industry in the former East Germany is at much less advanced stages and struggles to remain viable.

ASIAN CHEMICAL PRODUCTION

Asia's fast-growing economies are the site of rapid emergence of chemical plants that reflect the advancements in the region's development. High economic growth rates and escalating regional demand account for the rapid construction of petrochemical complexes. A number of new petrochemical plants will convert crude-oil byproducts into ethylene for use in making many products "from plastic packaging to pipes to polyester" (McMurray & McGregor, 1993, p. A1).

Rapid growth of this sector in Asia means that the global balance of power in petrochemicals will tilt toward the Pacific Rim region within the decade. The region's annual chemical output is expected to more than double by 2002, accounting for 35 percent of the world market, edging out the United States as the world leader by a few percentage points. Pacific Rim chemical exports are beginning to take some of the market that European and U.S. producers have had in Asia. For example, South Korea has about 25 percent of the Asian ethylene capacity and exports about half its production (McMurray & McGregor, 1993).

The strong Asian emergence in chemical production has several relevant points for our study. First, this trend reflects the overall advancement of the region into sectors that require higher technology, skill, and increased capital expendi-

tures. Second, the trend means that the Asian countries are striving to become independent by producing their own intermediate inputs. That is, when a nation can produce all its own textile inputs, then it no longer must purchase those from other countries. If, for example, China can produce all its own manufactured fiber and fabrics for the garments exported, then the profits and the jobs accrue to China rather than to a country from which textile inputs may have been purchased previously. Therefore, these shifts have important implications not only for the new chemical-producing country but also for those that may have previously supplied the textile inputs. In our example, if China produces all the manufactured fiber needed, then the manufactured fiber producers in other countries that previously sold to China will lose that market.

European and U.S. chemical producers are keenly aware of the implications, and many are investing heavily in the Asian expansion. For example, DuPont will spend $2 billion on Asian projects, with half that going toward a synthetic fiber plant in Singapore. Western chemical firms also worry that by aiding the expansion of the chemical industry in Asia, they may also be hurting themselves by increasing the supply on the world market, which could lead to forcing down world prices (McMurray & McGregor, 1993).

FIGURE 5–4
More than 600 British workers lost their jobs when this textile mill closed down.

Source: Photo by Jacques Maillard, courtesy International-al Labour Office.

portions of the textile complex, such as chemical fiber production. A substantial portion of the labor-intensive apparel production is sent to low-wage countries for the sewing operations. This is another case in which the role of government affected dramatically the nature of a country's textile complex. Therefore, the decline in West Germany occurred because of government priorities despite the fact that individual firms within the complex may have desired greater government assistance.

TEXTILE AND APPAREL STAGES OF DEVELOPMENT IN RELATION TO BROADER DEVELOPMENT

As we have noted earlier, the "stages of development" for textile and apparel production

generally parallel the developmental stages of a nation or region. The reader may wish to reflect on the discussions on development in the last chapter. Figure 5–5 provides a graphic way to help us think of these parallels.

Keeping these parallels in mind, we find that examining the stages of development of the textile complex within various regions of the world gives a reasonable indication of the overall economic and other development in these areas. Perhaps this could also be said of some other industries; however, this is particularly true because of the significant role this sector plays in the early development of most countries. Additionally, the parallels are particularly evident in less-developed areas where the textile complex is often at the forefront of broader economic and industrial development, and in many ways, the same may be true for other regions as well.

Developing Stages

Figure 5–6 provides a way of considering the textile and apparel industries in the early development process of a country or region. Although this model may convey the optimism of the mainstream/modernization

FIGURE 5–5
Stages of development for the textile complex generally parallel the development stages of a nation or region.

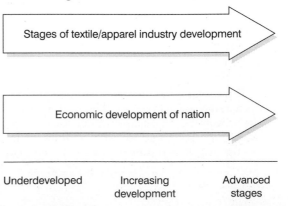

| Underdeveloped | Increasing development | Advanced stages |

approach, textile/apparel production in most countries does evolve through at least some of these stages. For this model, let us consider that the underdeveloped countries are participating in the most elementary forms of textile and apparel production. This might be the production of natural fibers (that is, agricultural activities such as growing vegetable fibers such as cotton or producing animal fibers such as wool) or participating in simple apparel assembly processes. All of these are labor-intensive, low-capital, low-technology areas of textile and apparel production.

Simple textile or apparel production is often the first attempt toward industrialization in underdeveloped or newly developing countries (the Third-World periphery). Countries with little capital and technology can provide the labor required to grow fiber crops, raise sheep, or assemble garments. Typically, assembly operations are being performed for firms headquartered in the First-World core—which is where the profits go, too. Production occurs in the periphery regions because wages are a fraction of what they are in core states and the activities are

labor intensive. At this stage, periphery countries gain little more than jobs paying extremely low wages for performing the assembly operations. (However, we must not minimize the significance of those jobs and the resulting modest wages in terms of what they contribute to workers in poor nations.)

In recent decades, nearly all developing countries that were not already producing textiles and apparel for world markets have become players in this highly competitive sector. As Figure 5–7 attempts to illustrate, an extensive number of nations at varying developing stages now compete. The newest entrants include some of the most underdeveloped countries with the fewest resources to start and operate their own industry. The large number of participants that we see here adds to the overcapacity of global production, creating a difficult trade scenario for these countries as well as for those at more advanced stages.

If we refer back to Figure 5–6, our model suggests that as countries develop, if they are able to do so, they eventually move into somewhat more advanced levels of textile and

FIGURE 5–6

Textile and apparel production in a nation's early development.

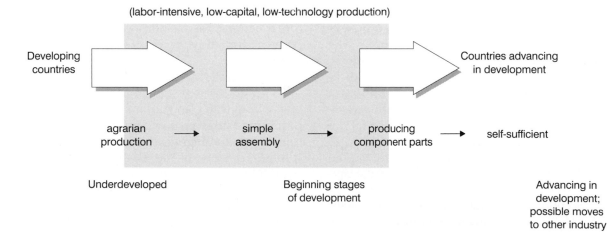

FIGURE 5–7
Developing Stages: Nearly all developing nations of the world have entered textile and apparel production and are at varying stages of development for the sector, as this figure attempts to illustrate. The large number of producer-nations account for the intense global competition. The countries and regions named here are intended only to be illustrative of countries at various stages rather than a complete list.

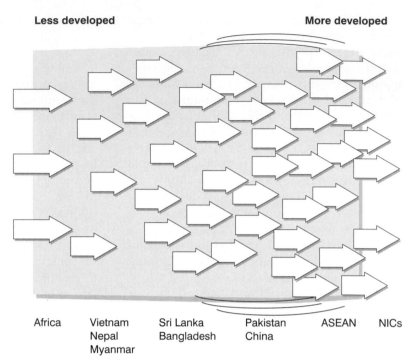

Less developed   More developed

Africa	Vietnam	Sri Lanka	Pakistan	ASEAN	NICs
	Nepal	Bangladesh	China		
	Myanmar				

apparel production. Fairly predictable changes may occur as a country advances beyond the elementary stages.

First, if the country continues in textile and apparel production, its textile/apparel sector may become capable of producing its own component parts. Up to this point, the workforce may have simply assembled garments from fabrics and other components supplied by more advanced countries. As the industry in a developing nation begins to produce its own components for production (that is, the yarns, fabrics, and other intermediate inputs), the sector not only becomes more self-sufficient, but the production that occurs is at a more advanced level. For example, the technical aspects of manufacturing yarns or fabrics on a mass production scale (as opposed to simple hand methods) require more capital and technological expertise than does the simple assembly of garments.

Second, as a nation's textile/apparel sector develops its technical capabilities, it may

become increasingly competitive in a wider range of textile and apparel production. For example, many of the Asian NICs have become competitive in manufactured fiber production—this represents one of the more technologically advanced aspects of the global textile complex. In some of the more developed NICs—for example, South Korea and Taiwan—the fiber production facilities may be owned by local sources. In less developed nations, the facilities, the expertise, and the capital may be provided by foreign sources.

And, finally, if the nation continues to advance in the development process, a move away from textile and apparel production into other industries may occur. Other industries may command higher wages and yield higher profits. For some of the Asian NIC nations to whom textile/apparel production was once so important, other industries such as computers or electronics may provide greater financial benefits.

Whether a country moves to more advanced textile/apparel production or into other industries, generally the country gains more than it did in performing only simple assembly tasks for apparel production. In simple assembly operations, the host nation gains little more than low-paying jobs for its workforce. Few profits remain in the country and the workforce is given little opportunity to advance its technological capabilities.

The model in Figure 5–6 is based on the assumption that some development will occur over time within a country. Our prior discussion suggests, however, that development may be limited in some nations. That is, textile and apparel production may not advance beyond agrarian production and simple assembly operations. For many underdeveloped countries in the Third-World periphery, the structural model of development suggests that low-wage, low-technology production may become their "specialization" for a long, long time.

On the other hand, some of the NICs such as Singapore, Taiwan, and South Korea have developed to a stage in which other industries are seen as more promising in their contributions to national economies. In the latter case, the countries have moved into other industrial production and have less emphasis on textiles and apparel. When the NICs move to other manufacturing sectors, textile and apparel production often shifts to lower-wage locations that may include Mauritius, Vietnam, the Philippines, or Indonesia.

Developed Stages

As the textile and apparel industries mature, and as countries are more developed, we see several scenarios that occur as the industry starts having difficulty in competing in the domestic market. Several factors contribute to this difficulty in competing, with less expensive imports often being a major one. Consequently, critical changes are made to make the industry more competitive. As Figure 5–8 indicates, these changes may include (1) having assembly take place in low-wage nations to save on labor costs, (2) investing in

FIGURE 5–8
More Developed Stages: When the textile complex reaches more developed stages, a variety of strategies may be used to retain competitiveness.

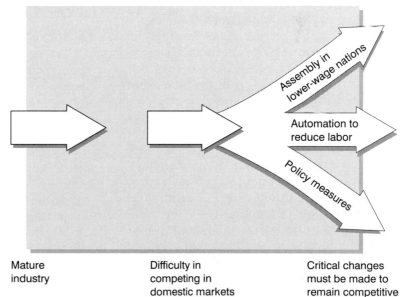

Mature industry

Difficulty in competing in domestic markets

Critical changes must be made to remain competitive

Assembly in lower-wage nations

Automation to reduce labor

Policy measures

improved automation and other technology to reduce labor costs and improve production speed and quality, and (3) securing government policies that generally are designed to aid the domestic industry in a number of ways, particularly in shielding domestic producers from the competition of Third-World imports.

Many manufacturers in the developed nations (and more recently, the NICs) have chosen to move their garment assembly operations to low-wage countries. Besides looking for lower wages, companies often turn to production in developing countries that have quota availability (a topic we shall consider in greater detail later in the book). As examples, U.S. apparel manufacturers turn to the Caribbean and Mexico; the Germans produce in Turkey; the Japanese have assembly done in China; the Taiwanese turn to Indonesia; and the South Koreans use assembly operations in Vietnam. Often, however, this strategy has ironic side effects.

As Figure 5–9 suggests, the strategy of moving production to low-wage countries has been responsible for establishing and expanding production in many underdeveloped countries that would otherwise be less able to participate in textile and apparel manufacturing for the world market. Firms in the more developed countries provide the investment, production expertise, technology, and marketing know-how to develop the industry and promote the products. Consequently, this strategy has led to a significant increase in the number of producer nations that have been able to become suppliers for the world's consumers. Although this strategy has benefited workers in the developing nations as well as corporations in the developed economies seeking to lower production costs, the point to be made here is that this strategy has expanded quite significantly the number and proficiency of competitor countries. Producers in both the developed nations and the devel-

oping countries are affected by this added competition.

As an example of this point, Dicken (1992) noted the important role of the Japanese textile firms and the general trading companies (the *sogo shosha*) in starting the first major wave of shifting production to less-developed nations in the 1960s. According to Dicken, the Japanese textile firms had a strongly vertically integrated system in Japan, and the *sogo shosha* handled a large proportion of Japanese imports and exports through a well-organized international network. In the early 1960s, when the United States started to impose restrictions on Japan's textile products, the Japanese textile producers and *sogo shosha* established a network for their operations in East and Southeast Asia. Working with local producers to have manufacturing occur in those countries for shipment to the United States, Japanese firms were able to avoid the trade restrictions on products *from Japan.*

THE TEXTILE COMPLEX— A GLOBAL BAROMETER OF DEVELOPMENT

As we have indicated, as the textile complex of a nation or region matures and goes through growth stages and perhaps even eventual decline, the status of this sector is often a fairly reliable barometer of broader development and industrial progress (although keep in mind that this can be altered rather significantly by various factors such as government policy, as in the case of the former West Germany).

If one is willing to consider the concept that patterns of development in the textile complex reflect the broader economic and industrial status within regions or nations, this provides an opportunity for interesting observations from a global perspective. There-

FIGURE 5–9

As manufacturers move their assembly operations to less-developed nations, they are also hastening the development of additional proficient competitors.

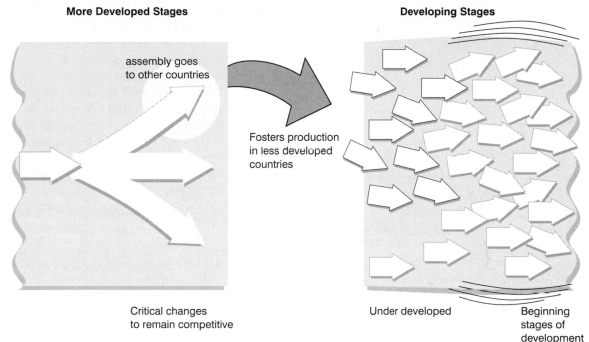

fore, if we could view the stages of development in the textile complex within countries and regions around the world, this would provide a "snapshot" view of total global economic and industrial development. Admittedly, generalizations are difficult because exceptions are always apparent; however, it may be helpful to consider this approach a bit further as a way of looking at the larger international picture.

In our global overview, for example, we might see that for decades some countries have had the capabilities for certain kinds of textile and apparel production, whereas they may have had limited production capabilities in more advanced processes. In Figure 5–10, we might consider that all of the countries identified here—developed nations, NICs, and a large developing nation—have had the

capabilities for apparel assembly operations for several decades.

On the other hand, if we were to look for more advanced types of textile and/or apparel production, the status of those segments of the industry reflects varying degrees of overall development for the country or countries. In contrast to Figure 5–10, in which we see that all the nations have been capable of assembly operations, we see in Figure 5–11 that these nations have differing years of experience in manufactured fiber production, particularly when the country was able to produce fiber in volume.

Only when each country had reached a certain level of development—with technological expertise, capital inputs, infrastructure, and other necessary factors associated with development—was that country able to pro-

FIGURE 5–10
Apparel assembly and broader development: Nations at varying levels of overall development may be able to perform certain types of activities in the textile complex—such as apparel assembly.

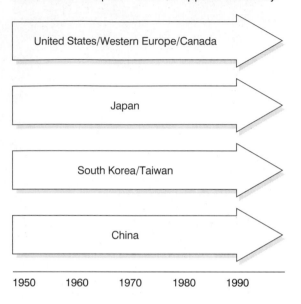

duce manufactured fiber. Hence, our global snapshot tells us something about the countries or regions according to which have the capabilities for certain types of production.

The textile complex in the major developed countries (the United States, Canada, nations in Western Europe, Japan, and Australia) typically led the industrialization process within each nation. In each country the sector became quite advanced and competitive as a producer for textile and apparel markets and eventually evolved to "full maturity" stages; textile complexes in some of these countries have begun to decline while others have not. The point of special significance is that the textile complex has been typically one of the earliest sectors to "mature" in a country. Although other mature industries such as steel and ship building experience similar shifts, the textile complex has often been the first or one of the first to do so.

Characteristics of the textile complex—such as serving basic human needs, labor intensity, and easy entry because of low capital and technology requirements—account for many of the global shifts that affect both the industrialized and developing countries. If we continue with our snapshot approach, we will see the most elementary textile production taking place in the poorest and most underdeveloped countries. This might be portions of Latin America, Africa, or parts of Asia. In these regions, textile production began because it was perhaps the only possibility for elementary industrialization and economic development for countries with few resources other than a large workforce. Therefore, a profile of

FIGURE 5–11
Manufactured fiber production as a reflection of broader development (volume production): In contrast to Figure 5–10, certain types of activities in the textile complex usually can be performed only when the overall level of development for the nation can provide the elements needed. Manufactured fiber production is one of the most advanced activities of the textile complex and has begun in each of countries or regions shown as overall development reached certain levels.

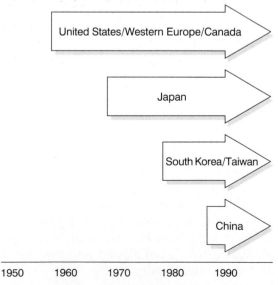

the textile sector in a less-developed country gives a fairly accurate reading of where that country stands in its overall economic development. Often this profile for a number of adjoining countries provides an overview of the development of a region or, in some cases, large portions of continents.

Even the nations and regions that seem most remote are no longer isolated. Now that national economies have become increasingly interlinked and interdependent in recent years, the textile complex in any advanced economy is influenced in various ways by its less-developed counterparts in poor, remote villages that may be halfway around the world. For example, the low-wage labor used in the fledgling industries in the LDCs is often viewed as a threat to the textile complex in an industrialized country. On the other hand, as we noted earlier, some portions of the complex in developed countries, such as the apparel segment, utilize the less costly labor in the LDCs for labor-intensive assembly operations. In this case in the global snapshot, one would see movement of industry segments to take advantage of certain resources, with the most obvious being the shifts that continually seek the lowest labor costs available. Again, reviewing the status of the textile complex in these global shifts provides insight into the broader stages of development of both the country that is the host site of textile production as well as the "investor" country seeking low-wage production in the LDCs.

In short, our global snapshot permits us to observe patterns that reflect the economic and development theories considered earlier. We can see patterns of production (that is, who is producing what) that reflect comparative advantage, factor proportions utilization, and Porter's determinants of competitive advantage. Similarly, we can see various stages of development and relationships among countries that reflect the development theories considered previously.

A BROAD PERSPECTIVE ON GLOBAL SUPPLY AND DEMAND

As we reflect on our discussion in this chapter, we note that two major changes have occurred as countries have advanced in their overall development and as the textile complex in various regions has gone through several stages of development: (1) The *number* of textile/apparel producer nations has increased dramatically as Third-World countries used this sector to begin industrialization, and (2) many of the earlier developing countries that established textile/apparel production became *much more proficient* producers, capable of manufacturing products in a broader spectrum in terms of technical expertise. In short, these two factors have led to an enormous global capacity to supply the consumers of the world. In fact, this large number of producers has led to what could accurately be called a *global overcapacity* that has resulted in extremely competitive global market conditions.

Moreover, the new textile- and apparel-producing nations—like other developing countries that had begun textile and apparel production earlier—viewed the markets in the industrialized countries as the ideal recipients for their products. Whereas manufacturers in the developed countries had depended primarily on their home markets for growth, *producers in the developing countries looked to exports for growth*. To producers in many developing countries, the markets in the developed countries have been perceived as composed of affluent consumers with insatiable appetites for textile and apparel goods. And as we noted in Chapter 4, most of the world's wealth does reside in the developed countries. Consequently, the competition for the same markets has grown intense.

In short, we can conclude that the global supply perhaps exceeds the global demand for the textile/apparel sector. In addition to the fact that consumer spending has been sluggish in the developed countries, it is important to remember that many consumers in the developing world do not have the purchasing power to obtain products they may need or desire. If all consumers—in both the developed and developing world—had unlimited funds to buy textile and apparel products, perhaps the global production capacity could be fully used without the harsh competitive conditions. However, such is not the case, and those conditions do exist, as we shall explore further in the book.

SUMMARY

Global shifts in textile and apparel activity (production, employment, and trade) began to occur in the early part of the twentieth century. As Japan and other new textile- and apparel-exporting countries relied significantly on the sector in their nation's economic development, international relocation of these industries began.

Because of the fragmented nature of the global textile complex, production can be located in almost any part of the world. This means that various regions of the world are engaged in a wide range of textile and apparel activities. A global perspective reveals that textile and apparel sectors may be found at various stages of development on a continuum "ranging from embryonic to declining" (Toyne et al., 1984, p. 20). The stages of development for the textile complex permit us to consider the major stages through which the textile complex is passing on a worldwide basis. This does not mean, however, that the sectors in all countries will go through all stages. The stages are: (1) the embryonic stage, (2) the early export of apparel, (3) the more advanced production of fabric and apparel, (4) the "Golden Age" stage, (5) full maturity, and (6) significant decline.

Focusing on the stages of development of the textile complex within various regions of the world gives an indication of the overall development in these areas. In many respects, a global "snapshot" of stages of the textile complex in various regions or nations would likely reveal a great deal about the country or region itself—for example, its relative resources or its technological and industrial advancements.

Considering the stages of development of the global textile complex also permits us to look at these relative to the economic theories and the development theories considered earlier. These theories help us to see why the resources of certain nations permit some types of production but not others, or we may see why the relationships among nations seem to dictate particular types of production. Theories help to explain, for example, why Bangladesh produces jute and the United States produces polybenzimidazole.

The growing number of producer nations, along with the increasing proficiency of already established textile/apparel producer nations, has led to a massive supply capacity for the world market. Moreover, the developing countries have directed most of their textile/apparel products for the export market, creating intense competition for the same developed country markets where consumers have greater spending potential.

GLOSSARY

Cottage industries are decentralized industries in which production occurs in homes or other small facilities; because the workplace is removed from the more formal manufacturing system, this production is difficult to document in many countries and may operate in ways inconsistent with governmental regulations.

Foreign exchange is currency that one country uses to pay for goods and services it buys from another country; that is, an instrument for making payments abroad.

Import substitution refers to producing goods domestically that were previously imported. Often, import substitution involves subsidizing the home industry and restricting imports to allow the domestic industry to grow.

Intermediate inputs, for our purposes, are the textile components used in producing finished or more nearly finished goods. These include the fibers, yarns, and fabrics sold to producers at the next stage of the production chain.

New producer nations are developing countries that have just begun to produce textiles and/or apparel for the international market.

Newly emerging countries are nations that have made some degree of progress in economic and other aspects of development. In reference to textiles and apparel, the term is often used to refer to underdeveloped countries that have become increasingly important producer nations.

Offshore production is the term used when an apparel firm's manufacturing occurs in another country. It also includes the practice of exporting finished (component parts) or semifinished manufactures to lower-cost countries for completion. The finished products are then reexported for distribution.

SUGGESTED READINGS

Anson, R. (forthcoming). *World textile trade and production trends*. London: Textiles Intelligence Limited.
   A summary of global textile production and trade; major regions are considered also.

Carpenter, B. (1993, February 8). Defusing the bomb. *U.S. News and World Report*, pp. 52–55.
   An update on world population trends.

Ehrlich, P. (1988, June 7). Chinese fiber plants diminish need for imports. *Daily News Record*, p. 12.
   This article reports on an example of a country's move toward self-sufficiency in the textile complex.

General Agreement on Tariffs and Trade (1984). *Textiles and clothing in the world economy*. Geneva, Switzerland: Author.
   A study of the global textile complex and the sector's contributions to the international economy as well as the economies of main regions.

General Agreement on Tariffs and Trade (1987, November 30). *Updating the 1984 GATT Secretariat study: Textiles and clothing in the world economy*. Geneva, Switzerland: Author.
   An update of the 1984 textile/apparel study.

Keesing, D., & Wolf, M. (1980). *Textile quotas against developing countries*. London: Trade Policy Research Center.
   A study of barriers developed to prevent the developing countries from exporting textile products to the industrialized markets.

Maizels, A. (1963). *Industrial growth and world trade*. Cambridge, England: Cambridge University Press.
   A study of industrial production patterns and the relationship to trade.

McMurray, S., & McGregor, J. (1993, August 4). New battleground: Asia targets chemicals for the next assault on Western industry. *Wall Street Journal*, pp. A1, A4.
   This article reports on Asia's move toward competitiveness and self-sufficiency in the chemical industry.

Textile Institute. (1993). *Asia and world textiles* Textile Institute Conference Proceedings (Hong Kong). Manchester, England: Author.
   A collection of papers presented at the Textile Institute's annual meeting; provides excellent information on the industry in Asia.

Toyne, B., Arpun, J., Ricks, D., & Shimp, T. (1984). *The global textile industry*. London: George Allen & Unwin.
A study of major trends affecting international competition in the textile mill products industry.

United Nations Population Division, New York, NY.
A source of publications and databases on world population trends.

United States International Trade Commission. (1985, July). *Emerging textile-exporting countries*. Washington, DC: Author.

A study of textile-exporting nations expected to become increasingly important producers for the global market.

United States International Trade Commission (1987, December). *U.S. global competitiveness: The U.S. textile mill industry*. (USITC publication 2048). Washington, DC: Author.
A study of factors influencing the global competitiveness of the U.S. textile mill industry.

The Textile Complex in Select Regions of the World

INTRODUCTION

In this chapter, we shall look briefly at the textile complex in select regions of the world and consider the **restructuring** of the industry that continues to occur on a global basis. Although it would be useful to cover regions and countries in far more detail, unfortunately space does not permit. Full books are, in fact, written about the textile complex in individual regions and countries. Therefore, it is our intent to provide a brief overview that gives the reader a basic understanding of the industry in these regions, particularly in relation to previous discussions on stages of development for the textile complex and overall development of nations and regions.

ASIA

We shall begin with Asia in these discussions for two reasons. First, this has been the fastest growing part of the world economy for more than a decade, with significant shifts in world textile and apparel production moving toward this region. Second, parts of this region illustrate vividly some of the concepts discussed in Chapter 4 and later in this chapter.

East Asia

East Asia has been a powerhouse of growth. During the 1980s, the region led the world economy with annual average growth rates of around 5 percent for Northeast Asia and over 7 percent in Southeast Asia, compared to only 2 to 3 percent average annual economic growth for the rest of the world (Fayle, 1993). Figure 6–1 illustrates the relative growth of this region compared to other parts of the world. (Note: This is *total* GDP for regions, not the *per capita* GDP we have considered in previous chapters.)

FIGURE 6–1
Estimates of the growth of GDP
for various country groupings.

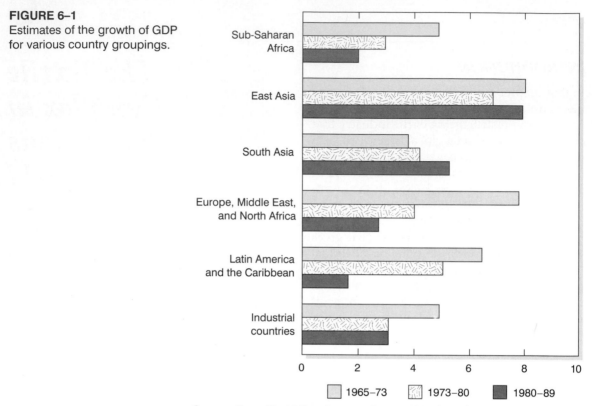

Source: From *World Development Report 1991* (p. 19) by World Bank, 1991, Washington, DC: Author. Reprinted by permission.

A common element in the economic success of the region has been an emphasis on export-oriented industries. For all of these countries, the textile complex has been a major contributor to growth and development, but for the more developed economies in the region, the industry's role has diminished in recent years.

As Fayle (1993) noted, the time lag between the introduction of new technologies in the developed countries and their diffusion to economies at lower levels of development has been shortened. Moreover, the newly maturing economies, the NICs, are maturing more rapidly than did Japan because the pace of structural change has been compressed as the pace of technological change has accelerated.

Some of these nations that are more advanced in textile and apparel production have found it increasingly difficult to ship their products to the long-time primary markets in North America and Western Europe. Quantitative limits (quotas) on imports from major Asian suppliers have increased in number. Moreover, the quick response demanded by retailers in both regions has caused the distance between those markets and the Far East to be a growing disadvantage.

In the more advanced economies of East Asia, income levels have been rising, creating greater demand in domestic markets. In a *Business Week* article, Engardio, Barnathan, and Glasgall (1993) note that "East Asia is generating its own wealth on a speed and scale that probably is without historical precedent" (p. 100). This trend, along with high population growth in the region, will make East Asia a major market area in the future.

Japan

Japan was clearly the leader in industrialization and development in this region and continues to be the most technologically and economically advanced. The early establishment of the textile complex as an important component of Japan's export-oriented economy is undisputed. In fact, Japan's strategies for economic development and her early reliance on the textile complex for that development served as a model followed by the NIC economies of Hong Kong, South Korea, Taiwan, and Singapore. More recently, other developing nations in Asia have followed similarly.

Yeung and Li (1993) have provided a helpful summary of the stages of development for Japan's textile industry, using stages outlined by Toyne et al. (1984). Table 6–1 shows Yeung and Li's summary of Japan's progression through the various stages of development.

Japan's arrival at the "full maturity" stage (that is, a **mature industry**) reflects advanced levels of production capabilities, particularly in terms of capital and technology inputs; the **value added** has been increased. Labor shortages are a problem for the apparel industry, particularly in urban areas. As we have noted earlier in this chapter, Japan began foreign investment in other Asian nations quite early in relation to some other advanced economies. That practice continues to be a major part of Japan's textile and apparel production strategy. Although Japan's textile industry is one of the most technologically advanced in the world, a growing trade deficit plagues the sector. Even manufactured fiber output has declined slightly from that in the mid-1980s (Fiber Economics Bureau, various years; Watanabe, 1992).

Fayle (1993) noted that Japan's appreciation of the yen caused the nation's labor costs to rise, making production in many of Japan's

TABLE 6–1
Stages of Development of Japan's Textile Complex

Embryonic	*Initial Export*	*Advanced Production*		*Golden Age*	*Full Maturity*
Manual production for local consumption Silk export Net importer of textile products	Infant cotton spinning sector Initial export of cotton yarn	Textile production extended into cotton, rayon fabric, and garments Textile production rose and trade surplus increased Above 50% of total exports	War time	Rapid growth of manmade fibre sector Expanding trade surplus Intensified foreign investment Leading world textile exporter	Enhanced top-end textile production technology Sophisticated product development Employment decline Expanding trade deficit Intensified foreign investment
1890	1910	1940		1970	1990

Source: From *Education for a Changing World* by K. Yeung and S. Li, May, 1993. Paper presented at the meeting of the Textile Institute, Hong Kong. Used by permission.

industries uncompetitive. Japan's foreign investment and offshore production increased, first to the Asian NICs, then to the Association of Southeast Asian Nations (ASEAN) region and China to take advantage of even less-costly labor. Fayle described the resultant trend as the "flying geese pattern"—one which became self-reinforcing. That is, as Japan shifted to less labor-intensive industries, it benefited from the demand of the NICs and ASEAN for intermediate inputs, technology, and capital equipment. Similarly, the NICs later restructured to move toward more capital-intensive industries when they experienced wage pressures from lesser developed Asian nations and labor shortages in their own countries. The NICs similarly relocated labor-intensive production to the ASEANs and China. Fayle cautioned, however, that one must not assume that the other Asian economies followed the exact path of Japan; each was unique because of differing national characteristics.

Taiwan

Taiwan's textile complex has developed in a similar pattern to that of Japan. Having a much later start, both as a nation and an industry, Taiwan has made remarkable progress in developing the textile complex. Yeung and Li (1993) plotted Taiwan's progress in Table 6–2, using stages from Toyne et al. (1984).

Taiwan has gone from being one of the world's largest apparel exporters (for a time in the 1980s, it was the leading apparel exporter to U.S. markets) to one that is quickly losing ground in the more labor-intensive segments of the industry. Rising wages, labor shortages, appreciation of the New Taiwan Dollar, and other problems have created increasing difficulties for Taiwan's apparel industry. To ease the worsening labor shortfall, a long-standing ban on employing foreign workers was lifted in 1991. However, the number of workers was subject to a strict quota limit, and workers were permitted mostly in dyeing and finishing sectors (Taiwan Textile Federation, 1992). Consequently, increasing amounts of apparel for Taiwanese firms is being sewn in lower-wage Asian nations.

The commentary in Taiwan Textile Federation's (1992) industry summary might have been written by industry counterparts in any of the more-developed countries. The report noted that for those apparel manufacturers not moving offshore, a marketing orientation must be emphasized to provide quick response and efficiencies in the marketing channels.

In recent years, Taiwan's textile industry has grown to a fully integrated fiber-textile-finishing industry (Bai, 1992). Because Taiwan does not produce natural fibers, the fiber production sector has focused on the production of manufactured fibers. Taiwan has developed a sophisticated textile industry, and in 1991 it ranked after the United States as the second largest producer of manufactured fiber in the world (Taiwan Textile Federation, 1992).

Hong Kong

Hong Kong's textile complex has developed somewhat differently from those of Japan and Taiwan. Originally developed by refugees fleeing the communist rebellion in China in the late 1940s, the Hong Kong industry benefited from leaders who had been industrialists and entrepreneurs in Shanghai with experience in textile manufacturing. Hong Kong became the world's leading exporter of apparel products in the 1970s and 1980s, holding this lead until outpaced recently by China. Still, textile and apparel products accounted for nearly 40 percent of Hong Kong's domestic exports in 1990, 23 percent of her merchandise **re-exports**, and 43 percent of her employment (Hong Kong Government Industry Department, 1992). Yeung and Li (1993) have shown Hong Kong's stages of development in Table 6–3.

TABLE 6–2

Stages of Development of Taiwan's Textile Complex

Embryonic	Initial Export	Advanced Production	Golden Age
Handicraft and machine production of textiles for domestic consumption Net importer of textile products mainly from Japan Little export of silk cocoons and linen fibre to Japan	Substantial development of textile industry under government support Early export of textile products mainly to S. E. Asia	Development of clothing sector Expansion of textile and clothing exports Start of man-made fibre production	One of the leading textile and clothing exporters Expanding textile trade surplus Rapid growth of man-made fibre sector Intensified foreign investment in S. E. Asia
1950	1960	1970	1990

Source: From *Education for a Changing World* by K. Yeung and S. Li, May, 1993. Paper presented at the meeting of the Textile Institute, Hong Kong. Used by permission.

Hong Kong apparel has been valued as high-quality products desired by major consumer markets in the United States and Western Europe. In recent years, however, Hong Kong's cost advantages have become increasingly difficult to sustain as real estate and labor costs have increased dramatically. Additionally, Hong Kong has experienced a labor shortage, even though the government has permitted limited importation of workers. Therefore, companies have found it increasingly difficult to maintain production. Many

FIGURE 6–2

Because of increasingly competitive conditions in Taiwan that make it difficult for clothing producers to compete, this apparel firm owner points to a section of his factory in the background which was not working and said, "It is asleep."

Source: (Photo by Kitty Dickerson).

TABLE 6–3
Stages of Development of Hong Kong's Textile Complex

Embryonic	*Initial Export*	*Advanced Production*	*Golden Age*
Small scale cottage type textile production for domestic consumption Net importer of textile products	Establishment of cotton textile industry Expansion of textile export mainly to developed countries	Rapid growth of the clothing sector Textile production was diversified into cotton/manmade fibre blend products 50% total production was for export One of the leading exporters of clothing products	World's leading clothing exporter Revitalisation of re-export trade mainly in textile and clothing that led to expanding textile trade surplus Intensified foreign investment in S. E. Asia Contraction of the industry
1950	1960	1970	1990

Source: From *Education for a Changing World* by K. Yeung and S. Li, May, 1993. Paper presented at the meeting of the Textile Institute, Hong Kong. Used by permission.

other Asian countries have lower wages, as well as greater labor availability; therefore, Hong Kong has had difficulty in competing (Au, 1992). As a result of these problems plus quota limitations on their exports, Hong Kong firms have various arrangements with partners in less developed countries. For example, many Hong Kong firms engage in **outward processing arrangements** (OPA). In addition, many firms have invested in other locations throughout the developing world, from most regions of Asia to the Caribbean and South America. Steele (1990) noted that "Hong Kong producers sometimes liken themselves to textile gypsies—forever 'moved on' from country to country, forever denied a permanent home capable of accommodating their energies and way of life" (p. 94). Hong Kong apparel manufacturers who retain production there will have to continue reinvesting and modernizing to compete (Au, 1992).

Textile production has always been a challenge for Hong Kong because it has no domestic source of fiber, making it dependent on imports for these materials (Steele, 1990). Much textile manufacturing has become increasingly ill-suited to Hong Kong's urban setting with high land costs, labor costs and shortages, and the costs of complying with environmental regulations. As a result of these factors, Hong Kong's position as a textile producer seems in question. As Yeung and Li (1993) note, "there is no sophisticated manufacturing/finishing production in Hong Kong, and the change from labour-intensive to capital-intensive production, as in the case of Japan, seems highly unlikely" (p. 4).

Although Hong Kong manufacturers have needed **quota** to ship their apparel products to the United States and Western Europe, the total amount of quota available to Hong Kong was among the most generous provided to any major textile/apparel exporting economy. Hong Kong, as an early producer, was granted generous quota allowances before the number of producer nations mushroomed. The export system is managed by the Hong Kong Trade Department, which must grant export authorization—an export license—to manufacturers before they can export their products. When the author visited the Trade Department, the long lines of individuals representing companies waiting to secure export licenses were hard to believe but served as an affirmation of the volume of textile trade from this city-state.

A substantial portion of Hong Kong's textile and apparel trade consists of re-exports. Nearly all of Hong Kong's current apparel re-exports are from China. Moreover, Steele (1990) noted that Hong Kong's growing apparel re-export trade reminds one of earlier visions of Hong Kong in the nineteenth century as an **entrepôt** for China's trade with the outside world. A report from the Hong Kong Government Industry Department (1992) indicates that when re-exports are included, Hong Kong is the world's third largest exporter of textiles. The issue of re-exports is quite controversial because some are legal, but others are not. Companies with operations in China that do not have quota to export *from* China smuggle clothing into Hong Kong and export products as locally produced—sometimes known as the *submarine trade* (presumably because it is out of sight). Other countries with quota shortages use Hong Kong to participate in similar **transshipping** activities.

Hong Kong has successfully established a growing reputation for high fashion. Many large U.S. and European manufacturing and retail firms have offices there. Fashions are marketed in part by the Hong Kong Trade Development Council (HKTDC), which has a sophisticated system for promoting Hong Kong's products to markets around the world. The HKTDC is funded by a small levy on all Hong Kong exports. In fact, Hong Kong will continue as a major marketing center, in many cases, for products manufactured elsewhere, even if the apparel manufacturing base continues to shrink within Hong Kong itself.

For a time, uncertainties associated with Hong Kong's return to China in 1997 cast a shadow over this booming city's future. Large numbers of the educated elite sought citizenship in the developed countries. Many feared that China might not provide the freedom required to run the free-market system that led to Hong Kong's prosperity. More recently, however, foreign investors have been ignoring these concerns and pouring billions of dollars into Hong Kong's blue chip stocks (Engardio et al., 1993).

South Korea (Republic of Korea)

South Korea, like her neighbors discussed above, represents an economic and development success story. According to Sakong (1993), "Korea in the early 1960s was a typical developing nation caught in a vicious circle of underdevelopment. With an annual per capita GNP of less than $100, domestic savings were negligible, and accordingly, foreign aid financed over 50 percent of the nation's investment. Over 40 percent of the population was suffering from absolute poverty" (p. xv). In 1991, after three decades of hard work and careful planning, Korea was the eleventh largest trading nation in the world. Korea's 1991 *national* GDP was exceeded in Asia only by that of Japan and China.

Korea's textile complex played a major role in the country's development and economic success—i.e., its "liberation from poverty" (Kim, 1992, p. 115). For example, in 1970, textiles and apparel accounted for 41 percent of Korea's exports (Sakong, 1993). As Japan saw the need for industrial restructuring and moving out of labor-intensive industries, the Japanese provided significant foreign direct investment (FDI) for Korea's textile complex. As an important first industry, Korean textile

FIGURE 6–3

The Hong Kong Trade Development Council sponsors an annual Fashion Week, during which Hong Kong and international garment manufacturers and exporters establish business contacts. Here, interested trade buyers gather in a Hong Kong firm's booth during Fashion Week.

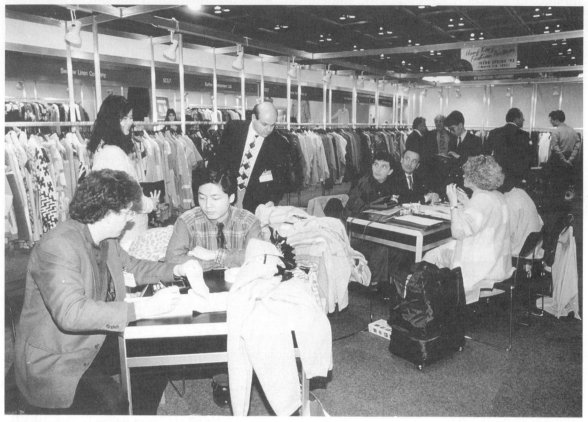

Source: Photo courtesy of Hong Kong Trade Development Council.

and apparel manufacturing evolved through many of the stages similar to those of Asian neighbors discussed previously, losing some of its competitiveness in the mid-1980s (J. Lee, 1993). Rhee (1992) noted that the chemical fiber industries in Korea have been growing remarkably, in both quantity and quality. Proficiency in more complex types of production reflects Korea's overall advanced development.

Presently, the Korean textile and apparel industry faces two major structural problems—labor shortages and rising labor costs. Recently, Korean firms have been investing in other countries to take advantage of less-

developed countries' different factor endowments—i.e., labor. Korean textile, apparel, and footwear FDI has been substantial in Asia (45 percent) and in the Central and South American nations (32 percent) (Sakong, 1993).

Korean textile and apparel exports are not expected to grow as much in the future as they have in the past; however, the textile complex will remain an important export industry for some time. As recently as 1987, textiles and apparel represented a significant portion (31.7 percent) of Korea's manufactured exports (Noland, 1990). The industry is attempting to improve its competitiveness through restructuring, modernization, and offshore production. A population with increasing incomes will add to domestic demand, with an upward shift in fashion and quality to respond to more fashion-conscious consumers (COMITEXTIL, 1992a; Shin, 1993).

China (People's Republic of China)

Although most Asian nations have had a profound impact on the global textile and apparel picture, as we someday read the history of the world textile complex, perhaps none will equal the impact of Mainland China—particularly because of the nation's large labor force and production potential, along with rapid entry into world markets. Until China's economic reform in 1979, textile and apparel production was for the domestic market. The government determined what would be produced, and there was no attempt to tie what would be produced to demand; however, that has now changed as China has embraced a unique form of market economy. Since the reform, China has placed great emphasis on labor-intensive manufactures to increase exports, a pattern we have discussed previously as common in a country's development. Now China is the world's leading supplier of apparel (and footwear) products. With a population of more than 1.3 billion persons (about 24 percent of the world total), impressive growth in labor-intensive production is not surprising.

Since the reform in 1979, China's annual GNP growth has averaged 9–10 percent, one of the highest growth rates in the world. Additionally, China expects its GDP to grow by 10 percent annually through the 1990s. China's booming economy has made the nation something it never was before—a major economic force, if not the dominant market in Asia in the next century (Borris & Engardio, 1993; Hu, 1993; Tanzer, 1992). Two regions have led the country in this economic boom: (1) Shenzhen economic zone in southern China near Hong Kong, and (2) Shanghai, the largest city, which has a long history as the country's most cosmopolitan region.

The Chinese population has benefited as the textile complex has advanced. Guobiao (1993), president of China Textile Engineering Society, noted that China's supply system, which had required coupons for textile products for about 30 years, was eliminated in 1983. He reported that the annual per capita consumption of fibers in 1991 had increased 1.7 times that of 1978, from about 5 to 9 pounds. He concluded, "Thus, the problem to keep people warm has been solved" (p. 1).

According to Guobiao (1993), textile and apparel output has increased significantly in recent years. The figures in Table 6–4 will give the reader an idea of the massive **shipments** (i.e., output) of China's textile complex, as well as the increases in a short time.

Chinese leaders identified the textile complex as a major sector to expand in the nation's economic development strategy. Statistics show that the industry expansion has been dramatic. For example, since 1977 China has had one German company *alone*, Zimmer AG, build 45 major synthetic fiber plants in the country, including the world's largest polyester plant ("More Poly," 1994). Guobiao (1993) reported that output from the textile complex accounted for 16 percent of the total national industrial output in 1992. About 13 million workers are employed in the industry (16 percent of the industrial workforce); however, this number does not include the large numbers employed in informal cottage industries or in natural fiber production (which are classified as agricultural employment). Massive numbers of workers are required to produce the annual output of natural fibers, as shown in Table 6–5

China also has a large textile machinery industry, consisting of 800 factories. Of these, only 39 are said to make updated machines. According to Chinese authorities, the technology is ideal for developing countries. The price is more affordable for countries that cannot afford to buy the expensive, leading-edge machines from Europe or Japan. According to Bow (1993b), Chinese producers complain

TABLE 6–4
China's Textile Complex

Product	1992 output	% increase over 1987
Manufactured fibers	2.08 million tons	77
Yarn	4.90 million tons	12
Fabric	18.5 billion tons	7
Woolen fabric	300 million meters	11
Garments	2.9 billion pieces	28

Source: Guobiao, 1993.

that no matter how careful the worker, the end product can be only medium quality at best. (The reader should take note that this discussion applies to some *textiles* rather than apparel.) Chinese textile producers use Chinese machines because most have no alternative and lack the capital to do otherwise; however, it is reported that most would prefer to have a foreign partner to provide capital to obtain the high-tech machines produced in Europe or Japan. Faced with declining markets for its machines in China, the textile machinery industry plans to export.

Textile and apparel exports from China have increased dramatically within a five-year period. The total export volume was US$24.6 billion in 1992, 2.6 times that in 1987. Just as planned in the government leaders' strategy, textile and apparel exports became China's leading export industry for earning foreign exchange—accounting for 29 percent of China's total exports in 1992, compared to 24 percent in 1987. Of the total 1992 textile/apparel exports, apparel exports represented 63 percent (Guobiao, 1993).

China's textile and apparel exports face serious trade restraints in the major markets in North America and Western Europe; these restraints will continue to be a problem for China. Severe restraints on China's products have resulted from the concerns of manufacturers in the developed countries who fear being overwhelmed by Chinese imports. Moreover, many Chinese exporters' efforts to illegally bypass quota limits on shipments have created ill will in the United States and Western European countries.

Labor costs in China have been very low, ranging from US$40 to $80 per month for six-day work weeks (Braithwaite, 1991). Many new workers just out of school, about 15 years of age, have sometimes earned only $10 per

TABLE 6–5
Annual Output of Natural Fibers

Cotton	5 million tons
Silk	60,000 tons (nearly 60% of world output)
Linen and ramie	200,000 tons (nearly 2/3 of world output)
Cashmere	5,000 tons (nearly half of world output)
Rabbit hair	10,000 tons (nearly 2/3 of world output)

Source: From Guobiao, 1993.

month in recent years[1] (author's visit to Chinese garment plants, 1991).

The Communist Party's presence is evident in the Chinese textile and apparel industry. For example, when the author visited garment factories in China in 1991, some had armed guards at the entrance (perhaps not uncommon for security purposes in some other parts of Southeast Asia). Another factory displayed awards given by the Party for the establishment's fine work (Figure 6–4). In **joint venture** operations, if a board of directors is formed for a company, local government officials (who represent the Party) may sit on the board.

Foreign investment has been important in establishing China's textile complex since the reform. Between 1979 and 1991, the government's China National Textile Council (formerly the Ministry of Textile Industry) approved over US$3 billion of foreign investment for China's textile complex; the industry also obtained more than $400 million in foreign loans. Of the foreign investors, 85 percent were from Hong Kong, Macao, and Taiwan, 5 percent were from Japan, and 3 percent from the United States. Foreign investors have been encouraged to establish factories in the countryside where the population has fewer job opportunities. Therefore, textile enterprises have invigorated the econ-

---

[1]Although this sounds very low, readers are reminded that in China at that time, these wages were much more significant than the amount would suggest if considered in the United States or Western Europe.

FIGURE 6–4
A Chinese apparel firm proudly displays the awards presented to it by the Chinese government officials.

Source: (Photo by Kitty Dickerson).

omy in rural regions and created jobs for the younger generation and the "surplus labor force" (Leung, 1992).

China will continue to be a major influence in world textile and apparel production. Quality will continue to improve, and manufacturing facilities will be upgraded. However, Sung (1993) noted that China lacks the financial base to import large amounts of modern machinery. Therefore, as he spoke of China in particular, he projected, "Modernization is a long-term business, and the average Asian mill (textiles) will have changed very little of its current appearance by the year 2001" (p. 5). Although he clarified that many facilities will be up to date, other mills will not replace their present machines simply because newer ones are available.

Association of Southeast Asian Nations (ASEAN)

As the more established economies of East Asia moved to more advanced stages, the ASEAN (Singapore[2], Indonesia, Malaysia, Philippines, Thailand, and Brunei[3]) economies benefited. In fact, these are among the fastest growing economies in the world. The reader is reminded of Fayle's (1993) flying geese analogy. Figure 6–5 illustrates this concept as it applies to the Asian region. As the more advanced economies, particularly Japan, Taiwan and South Korea, restructured their own industrial bases, many began to reduce manufacturing in labor-intensive industries. As a result, many economies began to provide foreign investment in the ASEAN region where large pools of less-expensive labor were available. Although Singapore had

started to industrialize and emphasize exporting in the 1960s, other ASEAN members had arrived at this stage of development in the 1970s and 1980s—about the time the more advanced East Asian neighbors were looking for other locations in which to invest and have production occur.

The ASEAN nations were also attractive locations for textile and apparel production because many had quota available for shipping their products to the North American and Western European markets. Consequently, during the 1980s the textile and apparel industries in most of the ASEAN group developed rapidly. Government policies in these countries encouraged the growth of textile and apparel production. These countries have actively encouraged direct involvement of foreign textile and apparel corporations and offered incentives to attract foreign investment. Foreign licensing arrangements and other forms of **technology transfer** have been encouraged (Finnerty, 1991; Shin, 1993).

As a result of the various changes, the ASEAN region became an increasingly important contributor to the world textile and apparel market. This led to a greater international division of labor—a concept discussed in Chapter 4. That is, we began to see more specialization in production among Asian countries. Some countries became more specialized in manufactured fiber production, some in garment assembly, some in natural fiber production, and so on.

The ASEAN region is expected to continue to be an attractive destination for foreign investment and for textile and apparel production. However, Fayle (1993) noted that the most rapid growth in investment may have passed. She also projected that during the 1990s some of the ASEAN economies will encounter shortages of skilled labor. Moreover, she noted that the shortages reflect the fast economic growth and, in some cases, too little expenditure on educating and training the population (referred to as human resource development)—far lower in ASEAN than the

---

[2]Singapore is much more advanced in economic development than other ASEAN members. Singapore is generally considered a NIC and has a per capita GNP that is exceeded in Asia only by that of Japan.

[3]Brunei differs from ASEAN neighbors because of its relative prosperity from oil. Limited textile and apparel production occurs there.

FIGURE 6–5

In the flying geese pattern of development, less-developed nations often perform more of the assembly operations while more advanced countries are likely to provide the intermediate inputs for production.

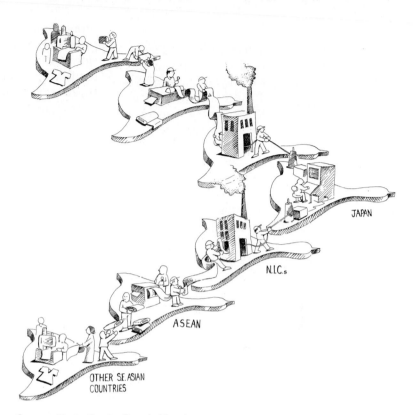

Source: Illustration by Dennis Murphy.

more advanced Asian economies discussed above. Fayle believes this forthcoming shortage of skilled labor has been intensified by accelerated technological change and *leapfrogging* ("adopting an advanced technology without going through the technological stages that preceded it" [p. 6]). She believes ASEAN economies will feel this in the earlier stages of industrialization and perhaps even more as they attempt to move out of labor-intensive activities and into higher **value-added production**.

ASEAN textile and apparel exports will continue to expand for some time yet to come and will continue to represent serious competition to manufacturers in North America and Western Europe. ASEAN producers, some of whom are owned by firms in more developed Asian countries, work regularly with retail buyers in the developed countries who

seek out the products made there. Moreover, many manufacturers in most regions of the developed world have at least explored the **sourcing** possibilities in the ASEAN region or, in other cases, have relocated production there.

Eventually, most of the ASEAN nations—like their more-advanced Asian neighbors—will move out of more labor-intensive industries and into others. As we have seen in other instances, this means that certain segments of the textile complex will shift toward other nations with suitable conditions. As incomes increase in the region, along with population growth (although some are trying to reduce their high population growth), the ASEAN region will be an increasingly important market.

At this point, we shall look briefly at each of the major ASEAN nations in relation to textile and apparel production.

Indonesia

According to Finnerty (1991), Indonesia's textile and apparel industry has developed "initially along the classic Indonesian pattern of a heavily protected producer of import substitutes . . . to become the country's second largest industrial employer" (p. 47). The government started putting an emphasis on exports in the mid-1980s, but exports did not take off until 1986. Textile and apparel products are now Indonesia's leading manufactured exports and leading source for earning foreign exchange other than petroleum products. More than 7 million workers are employed in over 2,000 large and medium firms, in addition to thousands of small-scale and home producers (Zwirn, 1992).

A great deal of foreign investment has gone into Indonesia's textile complex, particularly from the more advanced Asian economies, with Japan, Taiwan, and Korea as the leading investors. In 1990 Taiwan and Indonesia entered into an agreement through which Taiwan is relocating plants (including apparel) to Indonesia. In the first stage, 40 plants, providing 10,000 jobs, were relocated from Taiwan to Indonesia (Finnerty, 1991).

Japan established a few large manufactured fiber spinning operations in Indonesia in the 1970s. Most manufactured fiber plants built since then have been Indonesian-owned. Although some cotton is grown in Indonesia, most cotton has to be imported because of the unpredictable climate in many areas. The apparel industry has grown dramatically in recent years and is likely to continue to do so for some time because of the very low wages in Indonesia (Braithwaite, 1991). Although the large population of Indonesia represents a major market, an annual per capita GNP of $670 (World Bank, 1994) represents limited purchasing potential.

Malaysia

Malaysia's textile complex started to grow in the late 1970s, leading to the establishment of more than 3,000 firms by the early 1980s. A global recession in the early 1980s led to a slowdown in the industry. A 1985 government study of the industry described the sector as fragmented and not very viable. Industry restructuring resulted as weak companies were taken over by stronger ones, leading to fewer companies. By the end of 1985, the industry began to boom, and exports expanded significantly (Douglas, 1989; Finnerty, 1991).

Malaysia's textile complex is smaller than that of some ASEAN neighbors, but the industry has developed a reputation for good quality. The government has actively promoted exports, and textile and apparel exports have represented about one-fourth of all manufactured exports. Products are manufactured for leading branded-apparel firms in the United States and Europe. The industry has attracted investment from the region, particularly Singapore (Braithwaite, 1991; Douglas, 1989; Finnerty, 1991).

Malaysia and Singapore are the most progressive ASEAN members. Both have vigorous private sectors and the highest per capita GNP in the region; however, Singapore is considerably ahead of Malaysia. Malaysia is generally considered to be approaching NIC status (Douglas, 1992).

Philippines

The Philippines textile complex developed as an import substitution strategy, initiated by former traders and importers and fully supported and protected by the government. As a protected industry, the sector was not efficient or competitive (Finnerty, 1991). However, despite serious recessions in the Philippines, typhoons, earthquakes, floods, political turmoil, and a relatively poor infrastructure, exports eventually expanded in the mid-1980s (Braithwaite, 1993). Apparel exports account for about four-fifths of exports from the textile complex. The United States is by far the main market for these products.

The Philippine population growth rate is high, and the country remains poor. Wages have risen somewhat, with rates higher than some other ASEAN countries. Political instability has created an undesirable investment climate in the Philippines. Sustained stability would be the greatest asset for this nation and for the textile complex there. In terms of economic development and political stability, the Philippines lags behind most other ASEAN members.

Singapore

Like Hong Kong, this city-state has limited land and natural resources but has been enterprising in developing its manufacturing base and becoming a major world trade center. Speculation exists that Singapore may acquire some of Hong Kong's commercial activities because of Hong Kong's uncertainty under China's rule. Singapore is prosperous and successful. Textile and apparel production were important earlier in Singapore's industrialization, but labor shortages and increasing wages have created conditions in which many of these manufacturers, particularly in apparel, cannot remain competitive. Therefore, many of Singapore's apparel manufacturers have capitalized on lower labor costs in Indonesia and Malaysia to remain viable and competitive (Douglas, Douglas, & Finn 1994).

In keeping with the city-state's role as a major trading center, in 1993 Singapore opened TradeMart Singapore, Asia's first wholesale fashion mart. Modeled after the CaliforniaMart, Singapore's mart is a business center where companies from every segment of the fashion industry—from designers to zipper suppliers, from manufacturers to retailers—are based in one location. Because of the international nature of the business, the offices are accessible 24 hours a day throughout the year. Seminars and trade events are held in the center, and various services such as fashion trend reports are available to serve the industry.

Thailand

Emerging in the 1950s, Thailand's textile complex had become the largest among the ASEAN nations by the 1970s (Finnerty, 1991). Thailand became an increasingly important producer for world markets, having a well-developed textile and apparel sector. The labor force is skilled and has acquired a growing reputation for producing good quality products—entering the league with Korea, Taiwan, and Hong Kong on quality.

The textile complex accounts for about one-third of the manufacturing workforce and represents one of the major export sectors for Thailand. Apparel accounts for about 70 percent of the exports from the textile complex. However, Thai garment firms must rely on imported textiles for a large portion of the fabrics needed to produce clothing to export.

Thailand's low labor costs and skilled workers caused more U.S. apparel manufacturers, as well as retailers, to look to that nation for merchandise for the U.S. market. Several U.S. firms have opened offices in Thailand. For example, May Department Stores opened a buying office in Bangkok in the late 1980s. Buyers noted, "It's second to Taiwan in terms of good supplies of raw materials. The factories are very professional and the workmanship is very good." The Thai government offered numerous incentives to attract business to the country (Ehrlich, 1988e).

Although Thailand has the potential of becoming one of the next NICs, the growth of the Thai textile complex has slowed. As the country advances in its development, labor costs have risen, causing this nation to lose some of its competitive advantage in the sector. Wages in Thailand are now five times higher than in neighboring Vietnam and about three times higher than in Indonesia. Consequently, foreign investment in the industry from Japan, Taiwan, and Korea will likely move to Indonesia, China, and Vietnam (Witchuroj, 1993). Another prospect is that

Thailand will turn to more developing neighbors such as Laos or Kampuchea (formerly Cambodia) to find lower-cost labor. Again, this will reflect the flying geese pattern of development.

Other Southeast Asian Countries

Other countries in Mainland Southeast Asia (Indochina) include Laos, Myanmar (formerly Burma), Vietnam, and Kampuchea. All of these are very poor and have populations in need of jobs. Wages are very low. Although all of these have been or are torn with political strife and war, they are likely to be growth areas for textile and apparel production at the earlier stages of development. In fact, garment assembly already occurs there. These are likely production sites for more advanced Asian countries as well as for joint ventures with more adventuresome Western manufacturers. For now, at least, these countries are on the trailing end of the flying geese pattern.

South Asia

The Indian subcontinent has many countries (India, Pakistan, Bangladesh, Sri Lanka, Nepal, and Bhutan) that are already major textile and apparel producers for the world market. For most of these countries, this sector has been vital to overall development, and textile and apparel products account for a significant portion of the nation's total exports. The large populations in India, Pakistan, and Bangladesh represent large labor pools of workers. In fact, the combined population of these countries exceeds that of China. This group of countries merits much more discussion than space permits.

India

India's population is second only to China, representing masses in need of a livelihood. The country has a long history in textile pro-

duction, but early industry advancement was stifled when the country was under British rule. Textile and apparel exports together constitute about one-fifth of India's total exports; apparel alone represents one-eighth of the country's total exports. India accounts for a large volume of products on the world market—the fifth largest exporter of clothing to the European Union, the sixth largest exporter of textiles to the EU, and a large exporter of cotton garments to the United States (Janardhan, 1993; Khanna, 1991; U.S. Department of Commerce, 1993).

Although the Indian textile complex is large, internal problems and production shortcomings threaten the Indian industry's future as an exporter, however. Koshy (1993), an Indian professor at the National Institute of Fashion Technology in New Delhi, surveyed importers in Western countries and found that many were shifting away from Indian products. Importers noted the following problems: too far behind the fashion wave, fabrics of limited range and quality, slow shipments, problems with documents, and lack of familiarity with the workings of other countries. Khanna (1993), a University of Delhi marketing professor who studied the Indian industry, also noted that export firms should be motivated to overcome narrow product specialization. Perhaps it is significant that for many years India had a very **closed economy**, making it difficult for foreign investors to have businesses there. As a result, Indian firms failed to gain the benefits of upgraded production processes and marketing expertise that usually accompanies foreign investment in Third-World enterprises. Most experts (e.g., World Bank, 1991) believe that countries have developed more quickly as an *active* part of the world economy rather than in *isolation*. Various sources indicate that India's recent policies toward a more **open economy**, plus the importance of the textile complex to the country's economy, has

VIETNAM: ADVANCING WITH APPAREL, NOT THE ARMY

After decades of political and economic turmoil under the influence of the Japanese, then the French, later the Americans, and finally the rigid communist system, the industrious Vietnamese are shaking the effects of their tumultuous past and are turning their country into one of the promising economic "frontiers" of the decade. Although the country remains under communist rule, the Vietnamese people are moving whole-heartedly toward a capitalist market economy in an effort to increase their average annual per capita incomes beyond the $200 to $300 typical in the early 1990s.

As Vietnam strives to move beyond its desperately poor stage, the nation's reliance on the apparel industry represents for our study a text-book example of the important role the textile complex plays in the overall development of a country. Since the Vietnamese government's 1986 reforms to permit foreign investment and to abandon central planning, the textile complex has been one of the few sectors to cope successfully with a free market system in a socialist political framework.

Starved for capital, Vietnam cannot enter industries requiring major investments unless foreign partners provide the funding. Yet the population is in critical need of employment and income. Consequently, the nation's economic future depends greatly on the textile complex, particularly the apparel industry. Priority has been given to export-oriented industries, with textiles and apparel as the leading export-earner. In the early 1990s, about 700,000 workers were employed in the textile complex, and more than 70 percent of the country's manufactured goods were textile/apparel products (Shelton, 1993). More than 90 million apparel items were produced in Vietnam in 1992. A small percentage of the plants, particularly the larger ones, remain state owned (Bow, 1993a; Fearon, 1993; "Vietnam Hopes," 1992).

Vietnam's apparel industry is more competitive than the textile sector. A skilled workforce with a strong work ethic produces garments acceptable in many of the European markets. Foreign investors have helped to purchase newer equipment in many Vietnam production facilities. The Vietnam National Union for Textile Production and Export-Import Enterprises (TEXTIMEX) reported that the textile mills have primarily outdated equipment, producing low quality products that are unable to meet domestic or export requirements ("Vietnam Hopes," 1992). (This reflects the stages of development we have discussed earlier, in which developing countries often are proficient in assembly operations but do not have the capital and technology to produce high-quality fabrics and other inputs.) Infrastructure problems, typical in developing countries, are prevalent in Vietnam. Poor transportation systems make it difficult to get raw materials in and finished goods out. The power supply is undependable, with frequent power cuts.

After the former Soviet Union withdrew from Vietnam, several Asian countries moved rapidly into the poor Asian nation—particularly to take advantage of the labor force; most did so because of acute labor shortages at home. Average apparel wages of less than 20 cents per hour are an important factor (Shelton, 1993). More advanced Asian neighbors have provided investments and market connections that Vietnam did not have. Moreover, the Vietnam apparel industry needed the more-advanced textiles (fibers, yarns, fabrics, etc.) that Vietnamese mills were unable to produce to standards required in export markets. In turn, this represented new markets for the more-advanced Asian textile producers.

For nearly 20 years, U.S. investment in Vietnam or trade with Vietnam were not permitted because of an embargo from the mid-1970s,

VIETNAM: ADVANCING WITH APPAREL, NOT THE ARMY
(continued)

enforced under the Trading with the Enemy Act. Americans began to move beyond the bitterness of defeat in Vietnam, and many U.S. companies wanted to establish operations there. The United States was the only developed country with an embargo on Vietnam goods. The Vietnamese considered the U.S. embargo a major obstacle to their export development, particularly in the textile and apparel sector. Outgoing President George Bush, and later President Clinton, began to ease the embargo, particularly as the Vietnamese government began to cooperate on investigations of missing U.S. servicemen. In early 1994, the U.S. trade embargo was lifted (Barnathan, McKinnon, & Harbrecht, 1994; Bow, 1993a; Fearon, 1993; Greenberger, 1993; Marshall, 1992).

encouraged a new outlook for India's textile and apparel sectors ("Textile professionalism," 1993).

Pakistan

Pakistan's overall development is tied closely to the textile complex. Cotton production has long been a major source of income, and textile mills to produce fabrics from cotton are important industrial contributors to the economy. In fact, Pakistan is the third largest producer of cotton in the world. Much of the fabric has been exported as greige goods for further processing in countries that have highly developed converting industries. In more recent years, Pakistan has given emphasis to production of apparel for the world market and has promoted these through highly advertised trade fairs. Manufacturers in some of the developed nations have established joint ventures in Pakistan. For example, Sara Lee has manufacturing in Pakistan. The United States is the largest importer of Pakistan's textiles and apparel.

Bangladesh

Bangladesh is the world's largest exporter of jute. Rural areas of this poor nation depend on a jute sector that will meet increasingly difficult competition from manufactured fiber substitutes. Bangladesh has also developed a substantial apparel industry that is a major export sector for the nation; apparel accounts for 44 percent of the country's total export earnings (Hossain, 1991). Bangladesh is the seventh largest apparel exporter to the United States and the tenth largest to the EU (U.S. Department of Commerce, 1993). As for many newly developing nations, quality has been unpredictable in many instances. However, because of the extremely low wages, it has become a growing site for apparel operations.

Sri Lanka

Sri Lanka has become a significant apparel producer for world markets. Apparel represents almost 80 percent of Sri Lanka's trade. The industry is more highly developed than that of Bangladesh, and therefore quality is usually more consistent. Like the other countries above, exports from this sector are extremely important for this Third-World nation. The United States is Sri Lanka's leading market for apparel products (U.S. Department of Commerce, 1993). Sri Lanka's textile industry produces for the domestic market, and exports are minimal. Sri Lanka welcomes foreign investment, particularly for the textile segment, because about 90 percent of the fabrics needed for the garment industry must be imported (Gunawardena, 1993). The reader will recall that this follows the development patterns discussed in Chapter 5, in which developing countries at the early stages of production must obtain components from more advanced nations.

Nepal and Bhutan

These countries have begun producing for the export market. Both have potential for growth, particularly with foreign investment.

NORTH AMERICA

Canada and the United States are major trading partners with one another, as are Mexico and the United States. Trade among the three nations will grow even more under the North American Free Trade Agreement (NAFTA). The reader may wish to refer back to Chapter 3 for an overview of trade relationships. In this section, we shall focus more specifically on the textile complex in Canada and Mexico, with further discussion on the United States in later chapters.

Canada

Geographically, Canada is the world's second largest country, comprising nearly 4 million square miles. About 27 million Canadians inhabit this vast country; however, the population is concentrated in a few areas, with an east-west dispersion that causes high transportation and distribution costs. Canada has official bilingualism, with about 20 percent of Canadians speaking French as their first language (Barry, 1992; Wall & Dickerson, 1989).

Canada is a trading nation, with over 30 percent of the GDP coming from exports (all sectors). Between 1980 and 1990, Canada moved from being the tenth to the seventh largest trading nation in the world. Canada and the United States are the world's two largest trading partners. For overall trade in 1992, about 77 percent of Canada's exports went to the United States, and about 65 percent of Canada's imports came from the United States (*Statistics Canada*, 1993).

As an affluent, high-tech industrial society, Canada closely resembles the United States in its market-oriented economic system and patterns of production. The two countries have fairly comparable levels of living and consumer lifestyles (Wall & Dickerson, 1989). In the 1980s, Canada registered one of the highest rates of real growth among the OECD countries. However, in the early 1990s, Canada suffered from a serious recession that affected all sectors, including the textile complex.

Canada's textile complex remains an important industrial sector despite a number of factors that have created difficult competitive conditions. Textile/apparel shipments in 1992 were valued at nearly C$13 billion (Canadian Textile Institute, 1993). Difficulties faced by the industry included a recession, high labor costs, a 7 percent goods and services tax (GST) imposed by the government in 1991, and cross-border shopping. When the GST is combined with provincial taxes, an average 15 percent sales tax burden has encouraged Canadian consumers to drive to the United States to purchase lower-priced products. Many Canadian consumers are attracted to U.S. apparel brands because they are exposed to the same advertisements as their neighbors to the south.

Canada's textile and apparel industry is concentrated geographically. Production is concentrated in Quebec (mostly Montreal and the Eastern Townships) and Ontario (mostly in Toronto and South Western Ontario). Eighty-eight percent of Canada's apparel firms employ fewer than 100 workers; however, the larger firms (only 12 percent of the total) account for more than 50 percent of the employment and value of shipments (USNTDB, 1993). Table 6–6 gives an overview of the Canadian textile complex.

Quebec's large concentration of industry is significant in view of the province's continued discussions about separating from the rest of the country (it is important to remember this has been a possibility for a long time). This separatist sentiment was evident at the 1992 Winter Olympics when some Canadian athletes flew the provincial rather than the national flag. Quebec depends heavily on exports to other Canadian provinces; therefore, secession may not be helpful to the industry (Abend, 1992; USNTDB, 1993).

A number of Canadian apparel manufacturers have developed a successful high-fashion niche of well-made, European-styled clothing that appeals to fashion-conscious U.S. consumers. Canadian firms producing for this market have created a unique niche for themselves not filled by U.S. apparel makers. These high-end producers have created distinction and respect for the "Made in Canada" label. Consequently, some U.S. retailers have bought these lines because of the forward fashion, high quality, value, and fast delivery due to proximity.

Canadian manufacturers have invested heavily in new technology in the last 15 years. Investments have been largely in textile manufacturing rather than in the apparel sector, however.

Although most Canadian and U.S. textile/apparel manufacturers generally opposed the Canada-U.S. Free Trade Agreement (FTA) (Canadian textile manufacturers supported it), trade trends indicate that both countries benefited substantially from increased trade resulting from the tariff reductions. Many manufacturers on both sides of the border protested the agreement because they believed it would lead to the demise of their respective industries. Producers in each country believed themselves to be the losers; however, the data on Canada's trade with the United States, shown in Table 6–7 indicate quite the contrary.

The United States is the major destination of Canada's textile and apparel exports, accounting for nearly 75 percent of all exports from this sector (Canadian Textile Institute, 1993). Moreover, since the FTA has been in effect (as of January 1, 1989), Canada's textile/apparel exports to the United States have grown more than exports to all other countries. As the data above indicate, Canada's exports to the United States generally have shown a greater increase than imports from the United States. In 1992, 37 percent of

TABLE 6–6

An Overview of Canada's Textile and Apparel Industries

		Textiles	Apparel
Shipments (1992)	(Can$ million)	6,752	5,993
Employment (1990)	(number)	62,732	103,431
Total wages & salaries paid (1990)	(Can$ million)	1,657	1,976
Investments, 1983–1992	(Can$ million)	4,469	601

Source: Personal communication with Canadian Textiles Institute staff, 1993.

TABLE 6–7
Canada's Textile and Apparel Trade with the United States

	Textiles (% increase over previous year)		Apparel (% increase over previous year)	
	Exports to U.S.	*Imports from U.S.*	*Exports to U.S.*	*Imports from U.S.*
1990	28.5	2.6	25.7	31.2
1991	15.5	9.8	33.6	14.5
1992	26.5	12.1	60.1	37.0

Source: Personal communication with Canadian Textile Institute, 1993

Canada's textile/apparel imports came from the United States. For textiles alone, 58 percent came from the United States. According to U.S. Department of Commerce sources (Watters, 1992), U.S. apparel exports to Canada tripled in the first three years of the FTA. Similarly, some Canadian apparel producers credit the FTA for sensitizing them to greater export potential (Abend, 1992). Moreover, benefits from the FTA helped offset the impact of the recession for Canada's textile complex (Barry, 1993).

In 1993, the Canada-U.S. Free Trade Agreement reached its half-way point toward full phase-out of tariffs on textile and apparel products. This meant that in 1993, U.S. products were subject to only half the tariff applicable to other countries. Under the FTA, textile/apparel tariffs are being reduced by one-tenth each year. As of January 1, 1998, textile and apparel trade between Canada and the United States will be free of all tariffs.

Although Canada and Mexico have had relatively limited textile/apparel trade with one another, the North American Free Trade Agreement will foster additional trade. A likely prospect is that Canadian apparel producers may turn to Mexico for lower-wage assembly operations, and Canadian textile manufacturers may seek markets for their products in Mexico.

Canada's government provided $5.2 million in 1993 to create the Canadian Apparel Federation. The goal of the Federation is to contribute to apparel industry competitiveness through various means; among them, distributing consumer trade and market information, developing industry partnerships, and enhancing communication between industry and government ("Canadian Group," 1993).

In short, the Canadian textile complex remains a vibrant sector (Barry, 1993). This industry has weathered a recession, a period of significant restructuring, and a transition toward free trade with the United States. Although some Canadian manufacturers have not survived these challenges, most have shown their resilience and are more viable than before to face global competition.

United States

Because later chapters in this book focus in considerable detail on the United States textile complex, information will not be included here. The reader may wish to refer to Chapters 8 and 9.

Mexico

The growth of Mexico's textile complex has paralleled the country's economic growth and overall development. Until the mid-1980s, Mexico remained a closed market, isolated from competitive forces that make industries and firms more efficient. (The reader may wish to refer back to Porter's determinants of competitive advantage in Chapter 4.) The closed markets meant that many Mexican industry segments were inefficient, prices were high because competition was reduced, and many products were of poor quality. Since 1986, when Mexico joined the GATT, Mexico's more open economy has been reflected in the softgoods industry. The textile and apparel industry has had to adjust to the added competition that came with opening Mexico's markets to products from other countries; these adjustments generally meant that companies had to become more efficient and produce higher quality products at competitive prices. Although perhaps challenging, the changes were helpful to the industry in the long run. Previously, Mexican manufacturers had a captive market; however, they are now faced with a consumer market that is *importing* more and consuming fewer Mexican textile and apparel products, with imports representing about 50 percent of the domestic market (Mexican Investment Board, 1993a).

Mexico's textile complex makes a valuable contribution to the country's economy, representing more than 2.2 percent of Mexico's GDP, exceeding the 2.0 percent share held by the country's booming automobile industry. Within the manufacturing sector, the textile complex accounts for 9.8 percent of Mexico's GDP. The industry is expected to play an important role in the next stages of Mexico's overall development. Moreover, since the demand for textiles is closely linked to the GDP, the rise in GDP expected in the years ahead will result in growth opportunities in this sector (Mexican Investment Board, 1993b).

Mexico produces both natural and manufactured fibers. In the agricultural sector, cotton, wool, and sisal are produced. The manufactured fiber sector segment of the industry is perhaps the strongest in the textile complex, with world-class technology and ties to major world producers through joint ventures. Mexico's petroleum resources are an asset to this segment of the industry. Manufactured fibers account for about 65 percent of Mexico's fiber consumption.

Certain segments of the **textile mill products industry**, however, lack state-of-the-art technologies; plants are operating at only about 70 percent of their capacity. According to some U.S. industry reports, Mexico has modern spinning technology but lacks, for example, state-of-the-art finishing capabilities—a segment of the industry where much of the value is added to yarns and fabrics. The industry is facing pressure to modernize and form strategic alliances or mergers with U.S. producers (Cates, 1992; Farley, 1993; Mexican Investment Board, 1st & 3rd qtr. 1993; Reed & Montero, 1993; Silva, 1993). Because this segment of Mexico's industry is not competitive, many U.S. textile firms are capitalizing on the market potential there.

The Mexican apparel sector is quite fragmented, with over 5,000 firms; when the footwear and accessory industries are added, this amounts to nearly 10,000 firms. A majority are family-run and over 70 percent have 15 employees or fewer (USNTDB, 1993; Silva, 1993). Most of these small shops lack sophisticated technology, strong capital bases, and a well-developed supply chain. Since Mexico's entry into GATT, more than 500 weak textile and apparel companies, once protected by restricted trade, have closed (Reed, 1993).

Maquiladora operations, manufacturing plants that assemble components and re-export garments to the United States, are an important component of Mexico's apparel industry. Approximately 60,000 workers are involved in these plants, located mostly along the U.S. border. U.S. apparel manufacturers have used these border plants to retain proximity to the U.S. market, yet to gain the advantage of Mexico's lower wages (Silva, 1993; USNTDB, 1993). With the implementation of NAFTA, the Mexican Investment Board (1993) projected that employment in the *maquiladora* apparel sector will increase threefold by the year 2000. Ironically, foreign investment data show that assembly operations may be growing *at the expense of* investment in facilities in Mexico. The Mexican Investment Board noted the trend shown in Table 6–8. This decline may suggest that Mexico has become, in a sense, increasingly the "sewing room" for the United States. That is, although apparel production in Mexico has increased and exports to the United States have grown dramatically, greater portions of the production appear to have occurred in *maquiladora* arrangements rather than through building Mexican factories that would be owned or partially owned by the investor firm.

Of all segments of Mexico's textile complex, the apparel industry industry is the most likely to be affected by trade with the United States, particularly under NAFTA. Mexican consumers are attracted to U.S. brands. The appeal of U.S. apparel brands, plus the size and relative efficiency of some U.S. apparel firms, caused some Mexican producers to fear competition from the "gorillas to the North" (Mexican apparel manufacturer's comment to author, 1992).

A study of Mexican consumers commissioned by the U.S. Department of Commerce affirmed Mexican consumers' appetite for U.S. fashions. The report noted, "Justifiably or not, there is a widespread idea that the quality of Mexican apparel is inferior to American goods. This is capitalized on by Far East manufacturers who label their products in English, which leads many people to believe that the garments are American" (Ramey, 1992a, p. 16). Although U.S. apparel exports to Mexico have grown, these represent *a declining share* of the Mexican market because of increased Asian apparel imports. Hong Kong is the second largest supplier, representing 23.3 percent of the import market in 1990, up from 4.6 percent in 1988 when Mexico began to lower tariffs and open her markets to imports (Ramey, 1992a).

A government-sponsored Program to Promote Competitiveness and Internationalization of the Textile and Apparel Industries offers a wide range of investment possibilities to assist the Mexican textile/apparel industry in acquiring new technology to modernize. This program will promote exports through trade fairs and other strategies and will coordinate joint efforts between different segments of the industry. A Mexican Fashion Institute is being established as part of this program (Mexican Investment Board, 1993b).

Mexico's retail sector is fragmented, and distribution channels are different from those in the United States. However, some U.S. retailing firms have expanded into Mexico. Many see Mexico as having great potential compared to the United States, where retail growth has been sluggish. Well-known U.S. retail chains such as J.C. Penney, Kmart, and Wal-Mart have stores there. One of Wal-Mart's first stores there, a Sam's Club store, part of a joint venture with the Mexican retailer Cifra SA, recorded higher sales per square foot than any other Sam's Club store at the time. Similarly, when a new Wal-Mart Supercenter opened in Monterrey, the biggest city in Northern Mexico, more than 12,000 people came on the first day, causing store

TABLE 6–8
Trends in Foreign Investment in Mexico

Year	Foreign investment (US$ millions)
1989	46.4
1990	22.4
1991	19.4

Source: International Apparel Federation, 1992)

managers to halt access for a time until some shoppers left—the first time company executives remember ever having to do so ("New Wal-Mart," 1993). It is noteworthy that Sears Roebuck has a chic image in Mexico. At a time when the company's U.S. image plummeted, Sears de Mexico waged a successful campaign to woo Mexico's most affluent 10 percent of the market and carved an enviable niche in the market (Moffett, 1993).

THE CARIBBEAN BASIN AREA

Early colonization of the Caribbean islands created an economic legacy of dependence that has been difficult for the region to shed. The reader may wish to review the overview of this region in Chapter 3. After gaining their independence after World War II, many of the new Caribbean nations began industrialization efforts in which the apparel industry (primarily assembly operations) played a major role. For two decades, the new Caribbean nations achieved economic progress; however, by the mid-1970s, large national debts, diminished hopes, and widespread discontent were serious problems (Axline, 1979; Balkwell & Dickerson, 1994; Knight, 1990; Sklair, 1989).

Two overriding factors led to the development of the Caribbean basin region as a major apparel producing area. First, the United States had substantial interest in assuring the economic and political stability of a region of strategic importance to the nation. During the Cold War era, concerns about communism making inroads into the region was a factor. Second, the Caribbean had great potential for providing the low-cost production many U.S. apparel manufacturers needed to compete with imports. As low-cost imports increased in domestic markets, U.S. manufacturers found that they, too, must become active participants in the global economy. At this same time, pressures on the U.S. government to

restrict imports had led to increasingly restricted trade policies on products from East Asia—particularly from the Big Three (Hong Kong, Taiwan, and South Korea). As wages in those countries increased and shipping rates grew, the increasing costs of sourcing (also known as **outsourcing**) from Asia fostered an interest in finding less costly sources of production. As retailers demanded faster deliveries, a closer manufacturing location became desirable. Apparel production in the Caribbean basin area became the answer to many of these concerns.

The U.S. government's concerns for stability in the Caribbean led to several special trade policies to aid these economies. Although apparel assembly operations had occurred in the Caribbean for decades, measures were included in some of the later Caribbean trade policies to assure that the entire integrated textile-apparel production process would not move offshore from the United States to that region. That is, most Asian imports had been fully assembled garments generally made from non-U.S. fabrics. To ensure that the total garment production process and the use of U.S. textiles in those garments would not be lost in Caribbean production, the trade policies included provisions to encourage use of U.S. fabrics and to retain part of the production process in the United States. These provisions reinforce the notion that the Caribbean apparel industry, and the policies that governed this trade with the United States, reflected the requirements of the U.S. market.

The U.S. trade policies relevant to Caribbean production follow.

- *9802 (formerly 807) production.* Since 1963, a special provision (paragraph 807, now 9802) in the U.S. tariff regulations permits cut garments to be exported for assembly and reimported into the United States, with the exported garment components excluded from duty charges when finished garments were returned to the domestic market. That is, tariffs are charged only on the value added in the production process, and garments were subject to regular quota rules. Although the 9802/807 provisions are not limited to the Caribbean, this region has become the major user.

- *The Caribbean Basin Initiative (CBI)* (officially known as the Caribbean Basin Economic Recovery Act). The CBI was enacted in 1983 to boost the economies of 22 Caribbean countries by providing special trade privileges for those nations. In 1987, it was permanently expanded to include 27 nations. Although the CBI provided tariff-free access for most Caribbean products shipped to the United States, tariffs *continued* on textile and apparel products.
- *The Caribbean Basin Textile Access Program* (also known as 807A or "Super 807"). Under this 1986 agreement, Caribbean textile and apparel products are given a more liberal quota system for access to the U.S. market if fabrics are *both made and cut* in the United States. A similar provision for Mexico, known as the Special Regime, has been replaced by the free trade rules of NAFTA.
- *Caribbean Parity*. This program refers to efforts on the part of U.S. firms with production in the Caribbean to secure trade privileges for this region similar to those for Mexico under NAFTA. A 1993 U.S. Congressional bill proposed this "parity" for the Caribbean. Without parity, the Caribbean is likely to lose production to Mexico, which has virtually *free* trade with the United States.

Generally speaking, each subsequent trade policy afforded increased privileges for Caribbean apparel production and access to U.S. markets. Consequently, shipments from the region have grown dramatically, particularly since passage of the Textile Access Program. In fact, textile and apparel products have become an increasingly important portion of total U.S. imports from the Caribbean. Similarly, Caribbean apparel imports have grown faster than other textile/apparel imports in U.S. markets.

Of the CBI countries involved in apparel production (very little textile production occurs in the region, particularly for export), the Dominican Republic is by far the largest in terms of annual shipments (by value). Other top contributors in order are Costa Rica, Guatemala, Honduras, Jamaica, and El Salvador. Haiti has been an important site for apparel assembly in the past; however, civil unrest drastically reduced industry activities there.

Wages in the Caribbean are comparable to those in many less-developed regions of Asia; however, labor costs are considerably lower than those found in Hong Kong, Taiwan, and South Korea. As might be expected, wages are much lower than in the United States. In 1993, wages, including benefits, in many of the Caribbean countries was under $1.00 per hour (Cedrone, 1993). Only the U.S. territories, Puerto Rico and the Virgin Islands, had wages even close to U.S. rates.

A number of East Asian manufacturers, particularly from South Korea and Hong Kong, have also been attracted to the Caribbean region. The Asian firms have sought Caribbean production for many of the same reasons U.S. firms have—the proximity to U.S. markets and the availability of low-cost labor. However, the Asian producers have moved to the Caribbean for another important reason. As U.S. quota restraints became increasingly tight on major Asian suppliers, these manufacturers established operations in the Caribbean so that their products could be shipped to the United States under Caribbean trade policies, rather than under the more limiting policies that applied to goods produced and shipped from their home countries. However, to get the unlimited access to the U.S. market under the 9802A (807A) provisions, garments had to be *made of U.S. fabrics and cut* in the United States, therefore making the situation less attractive to Asian producers in the Caribbean. As one might guess, this provision was by design. That is, U.S. manufacturers influenced trade policy so that Asian producers would not have equal access to the U.S. market. Another handicap some Asian manufacturers have experienced is a cultural barrier in persuading Caribbean workers to adopt their work ethics.

Apparel assembly in the Caribbean for U.S. firms typifies the new international division of labor considered in Chapter 4. (For further information on this topic, the reader may wish to see Balkwell & Dickerson, 1994.) Because of the nature of apparel production, manufacturing can be broken into separate processes that can be contracted out to lower-wage countries. The production of fabrics, the apparel product development, and cutting operations are performed in the United States. The cut garments are sent to the Caribbean region for labor-intensive assembly and returned to the United States, where marketing and distribution take place.

Some Central American and South American countries have developed their apparel sectors as a result of being part of the special

U.S. policies for the Caribbean basin, and it is likely that others will be the site of textile and apparel industry development in the future. Particularly as trade becomes more integrated in the Western Hemisphere, additional nations can be expected to place greater emphasis on developing their textile/apparel sectors.

WESTERN EUROPE

The textile complex in Western Europe has an illustrious past that includes England's launching of the Industrial Revolution with textile production to France's leadership as the fashion mecca of the world for more than a century. Parts of Western Europe's industry have been pacesetters for fashion trends, the benchmark for quality, the elite in the use of certain industrial technology, and a dominant force in world trade.

Industrialized countries, in general, have faced problems in their economies since the 1970s, and Western Europe's textile complex reflects the problems in adjusting to new global competitive forces. As a mature indus-

---

   MIAMI: "THE HONG KONG OF THE 21ST CENTURY"

Caribbean apparel assembly has turned South Florida, particularly Miami, into a hub for 9802 (807) and 9802A (807A) operations. Textile exports (primarily cut fabrics) increased 78 percent from 1989 to 1993, and imports of finished apparel have grown 218 percent over the same time period. Activity in Miami's airports and harbors reflect the increased Caribbean production. Miami's airport is now second in the U.S. only to New York's Kennedy Airport in international

cargo handled (G. Lee, 1993b). Caribbean production has spawned an entire industry of consultants, insurance firms specializing in cargo, freight forwarders, lawyers specializing in offshore production and shipping contracts, and customs brokers to handle extensive paperwork associated with shipments. G. Lee (1993a) noted that some individuals have speculated that Caribbean production may make Miami "the Hong Kong of the 21st century" (p. 12).

try, the textile complex in Western Europe has much in common with its counterpart in the United States. In this section, most of our discussion will focus on the European Union (EU), with some brief coverage of the European Free Trade Association (EFTA) countries (most of which are expected to join the EU to become the European Economic Area, or EEA). (See Chapter 3 for a review of these country groupings.)

Despite some decline in the European Union textile complex, the industry still ranks among the largest EU industries in output, employment, and exports. In a 1993 EU Commission (the governing body of the EU) study, 1992 combined output for textiles and apparel put the sector in *sixth* place. The combined textile-apparel-fiber complex accounted for 2.7 million workers in 1992, generally estimated to be about 9 percent of the workforce (EU Commission, 1993). Additionally, EFTA countries were reported to have 170,000 workers in the textile/apparel sectors (COMITEXTIL], 1993b). Various sources have reported that the EU textile complex lost some 450,000 jobs from 1988 to 1992. Nearly 70 percent of the EU **redundant workers** (a term to describe workers who are no longer needed) in manufacturing during this period were in the textile complex; industry leaders fear the trend will continue unless the EU industrial policy becomes more favorable to the industry (COMITEXTIL, 1993b; Gälli, 1993).

A Kurt Salmon Associates (KSA) study (1993) on the EU industry reported that as a result of poor domestic market conditions, both the EU textile and apparel industries had cut back on their domestic production. For example, Germany's textile companies were reduced by 207 to 1,097 between 1986 and 1990; the Netherlands suffered the greatest closures—37 percent (Gälli, 1993). Germany's losses are particularly significant in view of the fact that for decades the nation has been the leading textile exporter in the world— with a long history in advanced manufactur-

ing and technology, a strong technical textiles industry, an emphasis on high-technology production rather than labor-intensive processes, and a strong textile machinery industry.

Social charges (or **social costs**)—the European term for employee benefits, particularly those required by the government (for example, comparable to U.S. Social Security levies)—are seen as having a profound negative impact on the EU textile and apparel industries. In 1991, EU employers were required to pay 33 percent in various social charges compared to less than 14 percent in the United States. When these social charges are added to already-high wages, EU textile and apparel manufacturers are dealt a tremendous competitive disadvantage. As unemployment in Europe grows, a paradox occurs: the fiscal base decreases, and the tendency to increase social charges increases. Moreover, growing unemployment means fewer and fewer workers are contributing to the social charges fund from which benefits are paid (author's discussion with government and industry sources, Brussels, 1994; COMITEXTIL, 1993c).

The 12 countries of the European Union have vast differences in their levels of overall development, and, consequently, the nature of the textile complex in each. The EU contains some of the most highly industrialized countries of the world (predominantly in the north—Germany, for example) and also includes some of its newest members (primarily in the south—Greece, Portugal, and Spain) that resemble developing countries in some regards (e.g., wages). These contrasts may be seen in the differences among the textile complexes. Other factors have influenced the nature of the textile and apparel industries in each; among these are the extent to which the government emphasizes and supports the industry (for example, Germany does not attempt to support its declining apparel sector), the traditions of specialization for the industry (e.g., France's *haute couture* or Italy's emphasis on high quality), workforce availability, labor costs in the country, and so on. Four countries dominate the European textile and apparel industries: Germany, Italy, Great Britain, and France (Subhan, 1993).

COMITEXTIL (1993b) reported that the EC textile complex accounted for over 220,000 enterprises. In both textiles and apparel, a great many small operations exist. For the EU as a whole, textile firms have an average of 21 employees; the figure drops to 11 for apparel firms. For apparel, small operations account for over half the workforce. The proportion of small establishments appears to vary by country, with many firms employing fewer than 20 persons in Italy, for example, compared to much larger companies in Great Britain and Germany.

Although the EU textile and apparel industries vary greatly from one country to another, the EU industry as a whole has experienced a growing trade deficit. Figure 6–6 illustrates the EU's growing trade deficit in external trade (i.e., trade with countries outside the EU, in contrast to intra-trade among members).

The EU apparel sector has been affected much more by imports than the textile industry. As might be expected, these are generally imports from low-wage, developing countries. In fact, it is the apparel sector that accounts for a large part of the deficit for the EU textile complex as a whole. However, when apparel products are imported, it is important to keep in mind that EU textile producers lose, too. Textile firms have, in effect, lost the market they would have had if the apparel had been produced domestically with EU-made fabrics. EU textile firms have offset this to an extent, however, by exporting fabrics to those countries that ship apparel to the EU market. In fact, in 1991, for the first time in a decade, more EU textiles were shipped to *developing nations* than to the traditional industrialized countries (the OECD group) (COMITEXTIL, 1992b).

Textile and apparel trade among West European countries or with others in the region (that is, intra-Western European trade) accounts for a significant volume of trade from the region. For example, in the late 1980s, slightly more than half the EU trade in apparel was intra-trade (Fitzpatrick Associates, 1991). Or, to consider this in a global perspective, in 1992 all world trade in textiles was valued at $117 billion; *intra*-Western European trade accounted for $43 billion of the world total. For apparel, *intra*-Western European trade represented $43.5 of the world total of $131 billion (GATT, 1993).

For the most part in the past, *exports* from the EU to countries outside the Community have been shipped primarily to high-income countries. This is still true for apparel; however, for textiles, the developing countries have replaced the OECD group as the major customers (COMITEXTIL, 1992b). EU clothing *imports* generally come from low-cost countries that enter EU markets under one of three different trade policies (these may include garments that are made fully in other countries, as well as those assembled elsewhere):

1. The EU gives preferential treatment to a group of Mediterranean basin countries such as Cyprus, Egypt, Morocco, and Turkey. If these countries' textile and apparel products are limited, restrictions are generally more favorable than for most other supplier countries.
2. The EU has also given preferential treatment to developing countries identified in the Lomé Convention. The Lomé Convention describes the European Union's financial and technical assistance programs to more than 60 "Associated Countries of Africa, the Caribbean, and the Pacific"— known as the "ACP countries" (many former European colonies). The agreement gave preferential treatment to the ACP countries' products in EU markets by permitting goods to enter free of customs duties.

FIGURE 6–6
European Union Textile and
Apparel Trade, 1974–1992 (with
trade partners outside the EU).

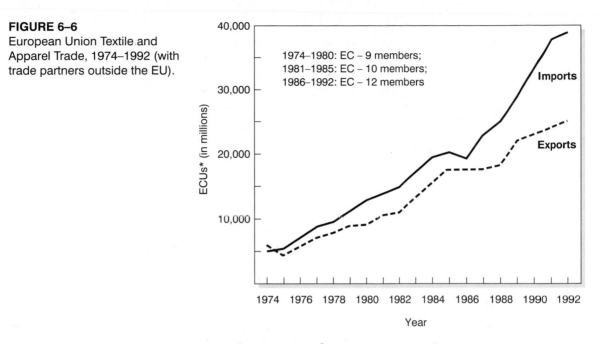

1974–1980: EC – 9 members;
1981–1985: EC – 10 members;
1986–1992: EC – 12 members

*The European currency unit (ECU) is a composite of several national currencies weighted according to the relative GNP of each country and each country's share of intra-European trade.

Source: From "The E.E.C.'s External Trade in 1992" by COMITEXTIL, 1993, *COMITEXTIL Bulletin*, 93/3, p. 18. Reprinted by permission.

3. Products from Asian suppliers are controlled under an international trade policy called the Multifiber Arrangement (MFA) that will be discussed in detail later in the book. In fact, the Asian suppliers were the biggest gainers in EU markets in the 1980s in both textiles and apparel (COMITEXTIL, 1992b, 1993a).

Labor rates are very high in the more advanced West European economies. Because of high wages, many apparel producers have their production operations performed in lower-wage countries. The Europeans refer to this as **outward processing** or **outward processing trade (OPT)**. (At this point, the reader may wish to reflect back to discussion in Chapter 4 on the new international division of labor.) This is an arrangement similar to U.S. manufacturers' 9802/807 production in the Caribbean basin region.

Enormous growth of OPT represents one of the most significant factors influencing the Western European textile complex. Growth in OPT production is in fact causing a major restructuring of the European industry. As more EU firms engage in OPT activities, the domestic industry will continue to be affected. The growth of OPT trade accounts in part for the dramatic job losses in the EU apparel industry. Western Europe's outward processing arrangements are with partners in Eastern Europe, many of the Mediterranean countries, and select African countries (mostly North Africa, near southern Europe). These regions have two factors in common: They are relatively close to the EU market, particularly in comparison to East Asia, and the labor rates are generally a fraction of those in the EU.

Data from L'Observatoire Européen du Textile et de L'Habillement (OETH) (1993) indicate that OPT imports from the major partner countries in Eastern Europe, the Mediterranean region, and North Africa have increased dramatically in recent years. OPT clothing imports increased 22 percent in 1991 and 13 percent in 1992. Germany has been the leading EU country to use OPT because of the nation's emphasis on high-technology manufacturing rather than on labor-intensive industries. Germany is still the largest OPT importer, accounting for 61 percent of the EU imported apparel in 1990. The report suggests that OPT activities will continue to grow at a fast rate as more West European firms engage in this form of production. For example, Italy and Great Britain used little of this production in the past but are expected to turn increasingly to OPT trade ("Some Lesser Known," 1993).

A disadvantage of the OPT strategy is that it reduces the incentive to upgrade technology. Moreover, arrangements of this type have risks involved. For example, the former Yugoslavia was the largest OPT clothing producer for the EU, accounting for 31 percent of the EU OPT imports for 1990. However, when political and military turmoil devastated this region, EU manufacturers scrambled to save the garment shipments that were at risk of being destroyed or lost. Moreover, EU manufacturers who had established working relationships with contractors in the former Yugoslavia found themselves temporarily without partners to sew their apparel. More recently, however, most of the OPT arrangements with the former Yugoslavia have moved to other parts of Eastern Europe.

EU production, imports, and exports all went up since 1985; however, imports more than doubled during that period ("Some Lesser Known," 1993). The KSA study (1993) projects that textile and apparel imports from outside the EU (this includes OPT imports) will take increasing market share over the next few years. By the end of the decade, KSA predicted that *70 percent* of the EU's annual

consumption of a projected 8.8 million pieces of clothing will be imported, compared to 54 percent of the 6.4 million garments sold in 1991. Already the share is over 90 percent in some apparel categories (Gälli, 1993; International Apparel Federation, 1993).

Although the EU textile/apparel industries have felt the impact of global competition in these sectors and will continue to do so, it is important to remember that the EU is still a very important international producer and trader, particularly in the high-value market sectors. Subhan (1993) asserts that even in today's **postindustrial** Western Europe, these are still major industries—much larger, for example, than the high-tech office and data processing machinery industry.

Even Western Europe's legacy as the fashion capital of the world is being transformed as a result of globalization, however. In earlier decades, European designers provided the inspiration for new directions, and the latest trends took as long as two years to filter down to the mass market. Today's international media coverage and instant communications have spawned consumers who see television clips from the European shows and expect to find the newest fashions in the stores within the same season. Consequently, in his article, "European Fashion in Recession," Stogdon (1993) asserts that couture has been replaced to an extent by ready-to-wear that is rapidly available for the mass market. In view of the growing dependence on imports made in countries some distance away, this creates a special challenge in being able to respond quickly to consumer demand for the latest "look." In a 1992 study, the Institut Francais de la Mode (IFM) (1993) found that the average lead time for orders from EU manufacturers was two to four weeks compared to four to five months from East Asian suppliers. Speed of delivery will help to offset lower prices available from distant locations.

European producers are affected by yet another trend. As the EU moved toward unification, firms in other parts of the world saw unified Europe as potentially becoming "Fortress Europe." That is, that the EU would become a trade bloc difficult for foreign companies to penetrate. Therefore, companies that wished to sell in EU markets established European production bases to be able to produce and sell in those markets. Perhaps the most notable example is the Japanese Toray Textiles Europe Ltd. in England, which represents the largest single investment in a spinning and weaving mill in British textile history. Toray will sell not only to British apparel manufacturers but also to apparel producers in other European countries as well (Gälli, 1993).

In addition to the products from low-wage countries brought into the EU through out-ward processing arrangements, retail buyers also add to imports through their sourcing efforts. In fact, Gälli (1993) notes that 64 percent of all imports from outside the EU enter Europe's markets through large volume traders such as department stores, mail-order houses, chain stores, and supermarkets. In a study of European retail buyers, IFM researchers identified patterns of retail sourcing from three geographical groupings, with certain product and market characteristics associated with each:

1. *European Union*:
   quick response (fashion);
   high technical requirements (e.g., tailored
      clothing);
   upmarket brands and styles;

 ISO 9000

ISO 9000 refers to a set of international standards that companies will have to meet if they hope to sell in Europe. Rather than being product standards, ISO 9000 is a series of standards for *quality management* and *quality assurance* for both manufacturing and service operations. Standards are generic, not specific to any industry. Although legally required only for safety-sensitive products, ISO 9000 certification is seen increasingly as a competitive necessity for international firms. A growing number of European companies will not buy or take bids for products from foreign suppliers that do not meet the ISO 9000 standards.

The International Organization for Standardization (ISO) is the specialized international agency for standardization, comprised at present of the national standards bodies of 91 countries. ISO 9000 represents a set of standards developed by the group to cover *quality control systems* for product development, design, production, management, and inspection. Companies can benefit by building quality into their product or service instead of costly after-the-fact inspections, warranty costs, and re-work.

Companies may have their quality systems registered by having an accredited independent outside party conduct an on-site audit of the firm's operations against the requirements of one of the standards (there are several under the ISO 9000 umbrella). Upon successful completion of the audit, a firm receives a registration certificate and is considered "certified." ISO 9000 audits can be costly for companies; however, many are considering it as another cost of doing business. Although some sources believe that the underlying principles of ISO 9000 are credible, others think the standards are another way of restricting other countries' products from EU markets (that is, a non-tariff barrier, a term covered in Chapter 10) (author's discussion with industry source, 1994; International Apparel Federation, 1993; Pechter, 1992).

TURKEY: A FOOT ON EACH CONTINENT—AND MOVING FAST

Located partly in Asia and partly in Europe, Turkey is positioned between the East and the West. In recent years, this country, which aspires to join the European Union, has become one of the fastest-growing textile and apparel exporting nations.

The Turkish textile industry began industrial manufacturing in 1836 in the days of the Ottoman Empire and has been a leading industrial sector through the decades. Between 1913 and 1915, 28 percent of the businesses employing more than 10 workers and 48 percent of employees in those workplaces were in the weaving industry (Yilmaz, 1991). With the end of the Empire and founding of the Turkish Republic, the textile industry was given priority as an industrial sector by the 1930s. The apparel industry developed much later as part of the nation's emphasis on exports in the 1970s. The new export-oriented economic model adopted by Turkey in the 1980s, along with export credits and other incentives, fueled apparel exports from $130 million in 1980 to $2.8 billion in 1990—a 22-fold growth in 10 years (Ilyasoglu & Duruiz, 1991). In 1992, textiles accounted for 11 percent of Turkey's merchandise exports; apparel, 28.5 percent—*together almost 40 percent of Turkey's total merchandise exports.* Turkey was the world's eighth largest apparel exporter in 1992 (GATT, 1993).

In the early 1990s, the Turkish apparel industry received a significant boost when both the United States and the EU granted much more generous quota allowances to Turkey. Because Turkey had been an ally during the Gulf War—including the use of Turkish air bases—the additional quota allowances were granted. The additional quota meant that Turkish manufacturers could export much more apparel to both U.S. and EU markets. More recently, however, Turkey's labor costs have risen significantly (from $1.80 in 1990 to $3.10 per hour in 1991). As a result, Turkish manufacturers are establishing ties in Eastern Europe, including joint ventures in Uzbekistan to take advantage of less-costly labor.

In a visit to Istanbul, the author visited IPAS (pronounced "E-pash"), a Turkish clothing firm owned and managed by the Ayan family (see Figure 6.7). IPAS, a manufacturer of moderate-price women's and junior sportswear, is listed in the top Turkish 500 industrial firms (all industries) and is the largest apparel firm to produce and export. From the moment of arrival in the foyer resplendent with brass and marble (and President Erkan Ayan's impressive collection of antique sewing machines) to the CAD operation to the spacious showroom, the author gained an appreciation for the level of development of some of Turkey's apparel industry. Employing the company's own stylist, IPAS sells primarily in the European market, particularly in Germany, the Netherlands, and Austria. IPAS offers 120 to 150 new items each month and participates in four European trade fairs a year, presenting 1,400 new designs at each. Pre-ticketing is available to retail customers if they desire it. Most employees are women between the ages of 16 and 20 and unmarried. Once married, husbands want them to stay home. All sample makers are men, however, who were tailors previously. The factory provides its employees with a clinic, free lunches, a small mosque (Turkey is 99 percent Moslem), German courses, dance classes, and recreational activities such as basketball, volleyball, and ping pong. Most work decisions are made democratically; workers have input on nearly everything. Most Turkish factories have a workers' syndicate (similar to a union). Workers decide whether or not they want the syndicate in their factory. IPAS is one of only eight or nine apparel factories that do not have a syndicate, which is a compliment to the quality of the management. Erkan is regarded fondly by employees; he and his family are invited to all the workers' weddings. At least 10 had named sons after him at the time of the author's visit.

In short, IPAS could be a model for apparel manufacturers in many other parts of the world.

fabric as the key to product appeal;
short production runs or the possibility for automation.

2. *Neighboring countries* (Mediterranean and Eastern Europe):
semi-quick response (fashion);
high technical requirements and labor content;
medium-high range of brands and styles;
fabric is key to product appeal;
medium production runs or the possibility of automation.

3. *Distant countries*:
high labor content;
long production runs;
standardized items;
raw materials is not key to product appeal or local raw material is very competitive in price (IFM, 1993, p. 126).

The IFM study (1993) concluded that distant sources may not always yield the greatest overall profit for EU importers when all relevant costs, including risk, are taken into account. Also, researchers found no conclusive evidence that consumers benefited from the lower prices of imports. The OETH study (1993) found that estimated apparent consumption of clothing in the EU fell slightly in 1992 compared to 1991 (using constant prices). Between 1990 and 1992, prices rose about 2 percent, using constant prices.

EASTERN EUROPE, COMMONWEALTH OF INDEPENDENT STATES (CIS), AND BALTIC STATES

The economies of this region became integrated after World War II through economic and social strategies patterned after those of the former Soviet Union. Under the Soviet type of command economic systems, state planning agencies—following Communist Party directives—managed the economy with the production and utilization of goods determined by political objectives that were centrally prescribed. Channels and prices of procurement and sales were determined by the authorities. The textile industries had been well developed and internationally recognized in some countries, such as the former Czechoslovakia and East Germany; however, the Soviet type of economic system sup-

FIGURE 6–7
E. Ayan visits with a member of his design staff for IPAS.

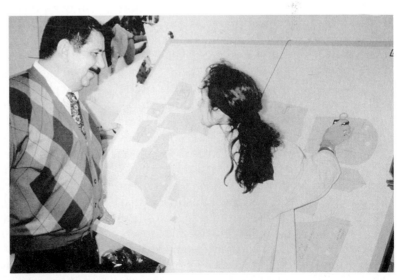

Source: Photo by Kitty Dickerson.

pressed the industry. Priority was given to **heavy industry** and manufacturing producer goods (used in the production of other commodities) rather than to the production of consumer goods (ECHO, 1991; Thiede, 1992).

Prior to the fall of communism, countries in this region were members of the Council for Mutual Economic Assistance (CMEA, or Comecon), an organization established by the Soviets to control and integrate trade within Soviet bloc countries. Patterns of specialization developed among many of the countries, and, in many cases, the council filled the needs of member nations. However, trade for these countries was most often with one another—not with the rest of the world.

The effects of centrally controlled economies and isolation from the world market had a crippling effect on the region. The economies became shortage economies in which the ability to generate income was limited; technology and management had not kept up with the rest of the world; and although workers had jobs, earnings and consumption were very low. Infrastructures such as roads, telephones, and energy were poorly developed and remain woefully inadequate by Western standards. Particularly in today's information-driven society, communication links are poor; even in capitals and major cities, only about half the time one gets a dial tone when attempting to place a call (Enderlyn & Dziggel, 1992; Thiede, 1992).

As a result of the Soviet system, the textile and apparel industries lacked modern technology and relied heavily on unskilled or semi-skilled labor. Although the industries grew, quality and competitiveness lagged. Because the textile and apparel industries had been isolated from world markets, these sectors had not experienced the adjustments that the Western European textile complexes had made in the 1960s. In short, Eastern Europe's industry lagged 20 to 25 years behind that of Western Europe (ECHO, 1991). Enderlyn and Dziggel (1992) noted that factories and technology in the region for most sectors are comparable with that in Western nations in the 1940s.

The textile and apparel industries in this region are experiencing painful adjustments and transformation. Through **privatization**, giant state enterprises with thousands of employees have been divided into smaller units, often with direct ties to other countries, not to the state authorities. According to Gälli (1992b), 4 to 5 million people were employed in the textile complex, all in state enterprises. The system also included such things as company housing, hospitals, ambulances, kindergartens, leisure and holiday centers, sports clubs, and canteens—and, of course, political education. That is, the state provided not only jobs, but also a way of life.

Although the end of the communist era was celebrated throughout the region, most citizens were not prepared for the difficulty of adjusting to the realities of a market economy. The old way of life had provided a significant degree of comfort and security that no longer exists. Gälli (1992b) noted that Western experts project that the textile and apparel output of the region can be achieved with *a mere one-third of the former workforce*. Therefore, many employees will become redundant workers. Gälli noted that women, in particular women such as those shown in Figure 6–8, will be affected disproportionately because of their high degree of representation in the textile complex. For large proportions of these workers, no alternative employment exists.

Moreover, leaders in the textile complex in countries in this region must make enormous leaps to overcome the stifling effects of a socialist command economy to participate in a global market economy. Many qualities at the heart of market competition must be recultivated—such as initiative, flexibility, business acumen, and specialization. The old system had provided no incentive for workers to be efficient and more productive; workers were not rewarded for extra effort. The author

FIGURE 6–8

As the textile complex in the former Soviet bloc shifts from state-owned enterprises toward privatization, many workers such as these will lose their jobs, becoming what is known as "redundant workers."

Source: Photo by J. Maillard, courtesy of International Labour Office.

heard a German textile advisor speak of the difficulty of assisting firms in this region whose executives had no concept of what interest on capital meant. Even modern bookkeeping is unknown to many. Other challenges include logistics, marketing, and sensitivity to fashion in international markets. In the past, firms needed only to turn out products that were "inexpensive, warm and lasting," but now they must be "competitively priced, of a quality appropriate to market demand, and 'fashionable'" (Gälli, 1992b, p. 116).

Some of the East European countries—particularly Poland, Hungary, Romania, and Bulgaria, plus the Czech and Slovak Republics (as was true for the former Yugoslavia before the political turmoil)—are becoming increasingly important suppliers for the EU market. In the future, these countries are likely to take an increasing share of the EU market now supplied by East Asian producers. Gälli (1992b) noted that many of these Eastern European countries are becoming "Europe's sewing rooms." Apparel assembly operations (OPT) account for large portions of exports from the region. In Poland, for example, assembly operations account for 93 percent of the country's textile/apparel exports; 90 percent for Hungary; 88 percent in Romania; and 63 percent for the Czech and Slovak Republics.

Some countries in the region are putting great effort into reviving their traditional **light industry**, which includes shoes, leather, and apparel. Many see these industries as being the engines of growth for their economies, as was true of the "Four Dragons" of East Asia. Western inputs of capital, technology, and marketing expertise will be necessary for companies in Eastern Europe, the CIS, and the Baltics to fulfill these aspirations. Economic reforms must find a way to rekindle workers' incentive and motivation. One may speculate that the textile complex will play a crucial role in the future economic, social, and political prospects for the region. Already, we know of the important role the industry plays in early development in most countries. Coupled with the specter of increasing disenchantment in the region because of difficult adjustments and hardships from the transition from communism to democracy, the industry may play a critical role in maintaining overall stability in the region.

The populations of these countries face grim economic realities of high inflation, declining industrial sectors, and rising unemployment. Consequently, many persons find it difficult to make a living. Those fortunate enough to have jobs typically earn between $25 and $75 per month for an average working individual. Leaders face an ongoing challenge to keep citizens from feeling they were better off under communist rule. Many older people are inclined to believe they were better off under communism; however, the younger generation believes a market economy will work and that it takes time (Frazier, 1993).

Eastern Europe, the CIS, and the Baltics will become increasingly important as players in textile/apparel world markets. In fact, Gälli

(1992b) notes that a textile development "axis" is forming across Central Europe over the Baltic to the CIS. Additionally, the growing trade connections between the East and the West make this a significant region to watch in the future.

At this point, we shall look briefly at these countries by groups.

Eastern Europe

Hungary, Poland, Romania, and Bulgaria, plus the Czech and Slovak Republics, share the characteristics described above for the overall region, as does the former East Germany during the transition stages to becoming part of unified Germany. However, some variations exist among the group. The Czech and Slovak Republics and former East Germany were the most advanced textile producers, with Poland and Hungary following them. Bulgaria and Romania have the least advanced textile and apparel industries of the group (along with the former Soviet Union—now the CIS and the Baltic states).

Although the Czech and Slovak Republics' textile industries were more advanced, their difficulty in remaining viable and competitive characterizes the difficulty experienced in all these countries. The former Czechoslovakia had a long history of textile production, and in the CMEA division of labor was the textile machinery producer. However, estimates indicate that in the industrial restructuring that followed economic reforms, some 30 percent to 50 percent of the textile and apparel producers are on the verge of collapse. Modernization has been limited, however, by financial restraints. Although the Republics have the potential to export, the relatively low-quality products offer limited prospects for penetrating foreign markets. Although the industry had developed traditional skills over decades, the sector's weaknesses become more apparent when subjected to a market economy. Domestic demand is unlikely to increase in the face of stagnating incomes and unemployment ("Czechoslovak Constraints," 1992).

This group of countries has much closer ties to the EU than does the CIS or the Baltic states. Gälli (1992b) projected that these countries will replace the Mediterranean countries in the role as lead supplier to the EU market; however, much of the trade consists of assembly operations. Some members of this group already enjoy special trade provisions with the EU; some aspire to become EU members after their economies have stabilized.

The Commonwealth of Independent States (CIS)

The CIS is a loose-knit community of independent states (see Chapter 3 for a review of the members) without the legal formalities of a nation or commonwealth of nations. Because of its transitory nature, statistics on the industry are difficult to obtain. Glasse (1993) notes, however, that the CIS is one of the world's three largest producers of fiber, yarn, and fabric. Although the CIS is 95 percent self-sufficient in the manufactured fibers needed, it faces serious shortages in many other raw materials. As relationships between former republics have deteriorated, light industries such as textiles and apparel have faced shortages of intermediate inputs but lack the foreign exchange to purchase these elsewhere. Workers are sent home on unpaid leave because the yarns, fabrics, etc., are not available for production. Glasse (1993) cited a Moscow radio report that indicated one million workers in the textile/apparel industry would lose their jobs in an unspecified period of time.

CIS wages are low by world standards. The average wage for a Moscow apparel worker ranges from $.50 to $1.00 per day ("Apparel Russia," 1993). The average Russian textile worker's monthly income is about $50, which Pennar (1992) reports to be about three times

as high as that of workers in other industrial sectors.

Although a few factories have state-of-the-art technology, most of the CIS industry uses outdated machinery and processes, which are often slow and inefficient. Product quality is low, and sometimes reliable deliveries of products are a problem. Some textile mills employed 5,000 to 6,000 workers, which made them inefficient. The emphasis was on quantity rather than quality. Since the fall of communism, the CIS population has become more aware of what is going on in other parts of the world. Therefore, many consumers want better quality and more fashion-sensitive apparel than the CIS industry has provided them in the past, and many have money to spend but little to spend it on because of shortages in consumer goods ("Apparel Russia," 1993; Glasse, 1993). This trend has implications for CIS producers who must upgrade products to retain the domestic market or for firms in other countries that desire to sell in the CIS markets.

Glasse (1993) noted that anecdotal stories on doing business in the CIS abound. One businessman reported visiting a CIS plant that produced yarn and sewing thread. "Although the yarn should have been twisted in a different direction from the thread, the factory was twisting both yarns and threads in the same direction. As a result, the thread produced was unravelling. When asked why the company was doing this, the spinning mill spokesman said the plant was paid on the basis of the number of kilos of product produced and that it was easier to twist yarns and threads in the same way" (p. 60). This story reflects many CIS manufacturers' lack of understanding of market forces.

Most of the CIS exports go to Eastern Europe. However, Western Europe is a growing market for CIS products.

CIS textile and apparel firms desperately need capital to upgrade production technology. Consequently, foreign partners are needed to provide the necessary investment and expertise. A few apparel plants have computerized machinery and CAD/CAM technology that has been purchased through a barter system of paying for the equipment with apparel from the factories (Knobel & Carey, 1993). Glasse (1993) reports that firms from various EU countries, China, South Korea, and Australia have launched operations there, but those to date are only a modest beginning for the enormous task of rescuing the CIS industry.

DuPont has an office in Moscow and has sold Lycra into the CIS since the late 1980s. A DuPont representative noted that it has been harder to do business since the collapse of communism because they have no direct partner now. Former textile ministries were abolished or turned into trade associations. Identifying decision makers is often difficult. Now, DuPont must deal directly with textile mills that do not have the capital to purchase the products. Although many CIS firms want DuPont's technology and products, they do not have the ability to purchase them (Glasse, 1993).

Now that former Soviet states have more autonomy, they are asserting their independence even in textile trade. For example, Uzbekistan currently produces two-thirds of the overall cotton crop of the former Soviet Union, or about 5 million metric tons (one metric ton equals 2204.6 pounds). Under the old system, the Soviet Union exported a great deal of cotton, but very little of the proceeds accrued to Uzbekistan. Now, Uzbekistan considers the vast cotton crop an asset and is using it in trade, frequently in barter arrangements, to purchase essential imports ("Cotton," 1992).

Several ventures are under way to bring Western-style retailing to Moscow. The German department store Karstadt opened a store in Moscow because its owners are convinced that Russians are ready to buy fashion. Moscow's premier department store, GUM, has been privatized and is seeking to establish itself among Europe's best retailers by attracting international brands and investors. GUM is one of the world's largest department stores, covering an entire block opposite the Kremlin. Raper (1992) noted that GUM has a long way to go, however; after being "smothered in bureaucracy, buried under decades of grime, and screaming for a major overhaul, GUM remains one of the few stores that still double-checks computer inventories with an abacus" (p. 24). GUM needs cash registers and contemporary technology to manage the inventory, but as long as salaries are low, it is less costly to pay people than to buy machines. Sales clerks earn about $20 per month; the GUM president earns about $65 per month.

Glasse (1993) predicts that the successful transition to a market economy will take 10 to 15 years even under the best of circumstances. Although foreign capital is necessary for the CIS development, investors are cautious because so many uncertainties exist.

The Baltic States

The three Baltic states of Lithuania, Latvia, and Estonia were the first to break away from the former Soviet Union. The textile complexes in these countries were important, well-established industries in each case before being absorbed into the Soviet empire. Under communism, the industries deteriorated in ways similar to those described for the CIS. Fifty years of socialist planning and production only for CMEA markets resulted in outdated, out-of-touch industries ill prepared to compete in a market economy (Gälli, 1992a).

Technology is inadequate; supplies of raw materials are a serious problem; quantity was emphasized over quality and design; privatization is occurring too slowly to have gained the desperately needed capital from outside partners; and foreign investors are restrained in their business activities (for example, in

Lithuania and Estonia, foreigners may not buy property but can only take 99-year leases). Weighty bureaucracies, poor infrastructures, and little appreciation for the importance of quality and responsibility are also matters of concern for potential partners (Gälli, 1992a).

Despite the shortcomings, the textile complex remains critical to the economies of these three break-away states. In 1990, Lithuania's textile sector contributed 40 percent of the country's industrial output; Latvia's complex accounted for 82 percent of the country's light industry; and Estonia's industry represented 24 percent of total industrial output. Wages are similar to those in the CIS (Gälli, 1992a).

AFRICA

A brief overview of Africa's textile and apparel industry is merited because so little has been written on the African textile complex and because of the likelihood that at some future time Africa will be the site of substantial industry development. That is, the movement of parts of the industry from developed to developing nations means that Africa will gain in the future. As wages continue to rise in Asia and Latin America, it seems likely that Africa will be seen as the last reservoir of plentiful, low-cost labor for certain labor-intensive aspects of textile/apparel production. Africa's future potential is enormous.

Africa is a huge continent of 53 states, with a population of 682 million people in 1992 and more than 2,000 languages and dialects. The United Nations predicts the population will exceed 856 million in the year 2000 and will be more than 1.5 billion by 2025. In rural villages, Africans may go about a traditional tribal way of life, although in urban centers, a western lifestyle is common. Some cities boast skyscrapers and a cosmopolitan outlook. Economic systems range from market economies

to those that are centrally controlled. Political systems range from multiple party representation in parliamentary settings to military dictatorships and Marxist governments. On the positive side, Africa has abundant natural minerals, some emerging market economies, and close ties to major industrial powers; however, the continent also suffers from drought, famine, poverty, disease, political unrest, foreign debt, and poor infrastructure in many regions (United Nations, 1993; Werbeloff, 1987; World Bank, 1993).

Werbeloff (1987) noted that despite the global attention focused on the African continent in recent years, relatively little has been known about the full extent and structure of its fiber, fabric, and garment sectors for the continent as a whole. A major reason for the lack of continent-wide data is that collecting comparable, reliable, up-to-date, and comprehensive data is difficult because of political bias in official data, nonreporting by industries and governments, and disruption of statistical surveys by civil wars, shortages of government funds, or droughts.

Africa has produced cotton since the early Egyptian civilization, and South African wool and Tanzanian sisal have been sold internationally for most of the century. Apparel manufacturing began in South Africa in the early 1900s, and the Egyptian textile industry began in the 1920s. Following the independence of African countries in the 1950s and 1960s, textile and apparel factories began to develop in many regions. Because the African countries had been colonies of various European countries, ties through investments and trade have continued in varying degrees. Today a wide range of yarns, fabrics, and finished products are produced in Africa; however, exporting is still relatively limited (Werbeloff, 1987). Unless the African textile and apparel industry exports, however, opportunities for growth are limited because of the almost non-existent purchasing power in many of these countries. Africa's average annual fiber consumption per person is less than three pounds, compared to 57 pounds for U.S. residents (Food and Agriculture Organization of the UN [FAO], 1993).

In a large number of African states, the textile complex has played a major role in industrial development, generally out-paced only by food in terms of the total manufacturing value added. Although some large plants exist, most of the apparel industry is composed of small enterprises, often organized on an informal basis, with fewer than 50 workers (often fewer than 10). Although these play a critical role in providing clothing and employment, these operations struggle to survive. A number of modern textile plants have been built, and as a result, much of the small-scale, informal textile production—often making high quality hand-woven traditional African fabrics—is being replaced. Although modern textile factories exist, Werbeloff (1987) noted that some have been erected with political motives, rather than based on economic feasibility studies, and these have had chronic underutilization. A World Bank story (1992b) from a related industry, shoe production, illustrates this practice. The Morogoro Shoe Company in Tanzania started business in 1980 with World Bank financing, with plans to be one of the largest shoe factories in the world and intending to export 80 percent of its production. Inadequate planning led to capacity use of *less than 4 percent* and a pair of shoes was never exported, despite a cost to the economy of $500,000 a year to keep the firm in business, not counting the interest and principal on $40 million of capital investment costs.

A few African nations represent examples of the export potential possible for the continent's textile complex. Morocco, Tunisia, and Mauritius have developed fast-growing textile and apparel export businesses, particularly with the European Union and to a lesser degree with the United States. Morocco's and Tunisia's proximity to the EU countries puts them in advantageous positions similar to those of Caribbean nations in relation to the United States. All three countries have attracted offshore textile and apparel plants and foreign investments that have substantially increased employment and foreign exchange. For example, employment in the Mauritius apparel sector quadrupled from

FIGURE 6–9
This informal operation is typical of much of Africa's textile complex. Women are sewing fabric manufactured at the Gonfreville textile mill in Côte d'Ivoire.

Source: Photo courtesy of World Bank.

1982 to 1991 (International Labour Office, 1993). Apparel exports represented *nearly half* Mauritius's total merchandise exports in 1991 (Personal communication with GATT economist, 1992). The dynamic growth of the industry has raised the level of living dramatically on this tiny Indian Ocean island off the coast of Africa. More recently, however, the Mauritius apparel industry growth has slowed because of labor shortages, rising wages, and other factors. Now, Mauritius manufacturers have begun to outsource in Madagascar, where wages are lower (COMITEXTIL, 1992b).

As our models for economic development and stages of industry development (in Chapter 5) would have us expect, some of the more industrialized Asian nations are moving their production to African nations to take advantage of the labor availability and low costs. Equally important is the freedom from quota limits on shipping apparel to the United States and the EU. For example, Hong Kong, Taiwanese, and Chinese firms have operations in Mauritius (as do France, England, and Germany). Another report indicates that Hong Kong–based apparel manufacturers have invested in the tiny West African nation of Gambia, formerly Britain's oldest colony in West Africa, which is sandwiched between Senagal and Gineau-Bissau. Skilled workers in Gambia earn little more than $2 per day. Investments in less industrialized nations like Gambia help Hong Kong apparel manufacturers solve problems related to a labor shortage and avoid the high prices on quota for U.S.-bound products (Ehrlich, 1988c).

In sharp contrast to most of Africa, the Republic of South Africa is the continent's most-developed nation. The South African textile and apparel industries are well established and face many of the challenges confronting the industry in other industrialized nations. The channels of production and distribution are at a roughly comparable level to those in the EU or the United States (Buirski, 1992; Vigdor, 1992a, 1992b).

SUMMARY

In this chapter, we have considered the textile complex in select regions of the world (1) to gain an understanding of restructuring of the global industry as a whole and (2) to examine the industry in various geographical areas in relation to stages of development for the textile complex and the overall development of nations and regions.

Asia represents the region of most dramatic overall development and growth in the latest decade or more. All Asian economies have been fueled by export-oriented industries, and the textile complex has led the way in virtually all these nations. Typically, the textile complex accounts for a high proportion of industry output, employment, and exports in the early days of the country's development. Then, as wages rise and labor shortages occur, labor-intensive portions of the production process have been sent to less-developed neighbors. The more advanced partners provide the more technically advanced components to the less-developed neighbors, who assemble the components into final products. As each nation or group of nations advances, the relationships continue to be much the same; however, the partners change—leading to the "flying geese" pattern of development discussed in the chapter.

First, Japan's reliance on the textile complex for her economic development led the way. The NICs followed, first performing the least technical aspects of textile/apparel production and then advancing rapidly. As the NICs moved through various stages of development, manufacturers in most of these nations sent a significant portion of their labor-intensive production to the neighboring ASEAN members. More recently, several members of the ASEAN group have approached NIC status and are losing their competitive advantage in the labor-intensive aspects of production. In the flying geese scenario, some of the ASEAN producers (along with their advanced neighbors) have established assembly operations in the least-developed countries in Asia; among these are Vietnam, Bangladesh, Sri Lanka, and China. Throughout Asia, the international division of labor is evident, and production sites often change quickly as some of Asian nations escalate rapidly through the earliest stages of development to more advanced stages in which wages increase, labor shortages occur, and other sectors are emphasized more. Additionally, many of the Asian nations have moved into one of the most complex segments of the textile complex, manufactured fiber production.

In North America, free trade on the continent will be the way of the future. Despite protests to the Canada-U.S. Free Trade Agreement from textile and apparel manufacturers on both sides of the border, trade figures show that producers in both countries have benefited from the pact. Although the Canadian textile complex has faced a number of challenges, the industry has remained viable and competitive. Apparel manufacturers, for example, have established a successful niche in high-quality, European-styled clothing. New challenges and new opportunities exist as the three North American countries move toward free trade under the North American Free Trade Agreement (NAFTA). Unlike the Canada-U.S. agreement, NAFTA incorporates a partner at a different level of development—a fact that will surely lead to some restructuring of the textile complex on the continent. Mexico has a well-developed manufactured fiber industry but needs textile mill products. Mexico's wages are low, and *maquiladora* operations are common in the apparel sector. U.S. apparel brands are popular among Mexican consumers; however, Asian producers have taken a growing share of the market.

The Caribbean basin area has developed as a significant apparel assembly area for U.S. manufacturers, under a variety of policy provisions designed to aid the region and U.S. manufacturers at the same time. Caribbean assembly operations represent a classic example of the new international division of labor. Caribbean apparel operations have turned Miami into a hub of activity related to this form of offshore production.

Although the textile and apparel industries in Western Europe have faced problems in adjusting to new global competitive forces, these sectors still rank among the largest industries in output, employment, and exports, particularly in the Economic Union. The textile complex in the 12 EU member countries vary greatly from one to another, as might be expected because the countries are very different. Because of high labor rates, and accompanying high social costs, in most of Western Europe, many apparel producers have their manufacturing activities located in lower-wage countries under a strategy the Europeans call outward processing trade (OPT). Escalating growth of OPT activities represents one of the major restructuring activities of the Western European textile complex. Low-wage locations for Western European manufacturers include several Mediterranean countries, Eastern Europe, parts of North Africa, and Asia. Predictions are that through a combination of OPT garments and imported apparel secured by large volume retailers, imports will account for 70 percent of EU apparel consumption by the year 2000.

The economies of Eastern Europe, the Commonwealth of Independent States (CIS), and Baltic states are making a painful transition from the crippling effects of being isolated and centrally controlled under the old Soviet system. Although the textile and apparel industries varied considerably among the countries of the region, all lacked modern technology and an understanding of how to respond to market forces. Managers are having to learn basics of business acumen and how to develop a system that provides incentives for workers. Responding to fashion is a new concept for manufacturers. As enterprises are privatized, high unemployment is a problem. However, some countries in the region are placing increased emphasis on light industries such as apparel, aspiring to have these sectors become the engines of growth for the economies. For several of these countries, the textile complex already accounts for a significant portion of industrial output. Some parts of Eastern Europe are becoming increasingly important suppliers to the Western European market—a large portion of the exports represent outward processing trade (OPT), however.

Africa already has textile and apparel production in many areas; however, for the most part, this continent is largely underdeveloped both in a general sense and in terms of the textile complex. Particularly as firms in more developed nations seek low-cost labor, Africa will likely be an area of growth in the future. Having received outside investment, Morocco, Tunisia, and Mauritius represent examples of countries that have developed significant export industries; these are largely apparel production operations (OPT). In contrast, the Republic of South Africa has a well-developed textile complex that faces many of the same challenges as mature industries in other more industrialized nations.

In summary, textile and apparel production is changing rapidly around the world. This chapter's overview helps us to see not only the emergence of many new, important producer nations, but also to see the degree of global interdependence that exists among textile/apparel producer nations. Nations and firms no longer look exclusively within their domestic boundaries for either production or distribution. Individuals involved in the soft-goods industry will find it necessary to be aware of global shifts and accompanying competitive conditions to function effectively in the future.

GLOSSARY

Closed economy (or market) describes a country that has a variety of measures to restrict the products and services from other countries. Nations that have closed economies generally take these measures to protect domestic industries and to force buyers within the country to buy domestic products (import substitution).

Entrepôt is a center or warehouse for the distribution or transshipment of goods.

Heavy industry refers to "manufacturing that uses large amounts of raw materials—such as coal, iron ore, and sand—and that has relatively low value per unit of weight" (Fisher, 1992).

Joint venture refers to the partnership between a foreign-owned firm with a partner in another country. More than two partners may be involved.

Light industry refers to manufacturing that uses small amounts of raw materials and employs small or light machines (Fisher, 1992). Apparel production is considered light industry, whereas automotive manufacturing would not be.

Maquiladora operations are assembly plants, mostly along the U.S.-Mexico border, in which garments are assembled from U.S.-cut parts and shipped back to the United States.

Mature industry refers to an advanced stage of development for an industry. Often these are the industries that were first established in a country and have "matured" to a stage in which competitiveness is a problem in some respects. Although products and processes may be at a high level, a decline in employment is typical.

Open economy describes a nation that has few barriers to trade for other countries that attempt to sell products and services there.

Outsourcing broadly refers to components and finished products supplied to the transnational firm by independent suppliers around the world. This term is also narrowly defined, and more frequently used, to indicate the extent of components and finished products supplied to the firm by independent suppliers located in developing countries (Kotabe, 1992). The term is often used interchangeably with *sourcing*.

Outward processing or *outward processing trade (OPT)* is the European term for sending cut garments to lower wage countries for final assembly. In Hong Kong, the term used is *outward processing arrangement (OPA)*.

Postindustrial society refers to an evolving society in the major industrialized countries in which traditional manufacturing activity is replaced gradually by high-technology industry, and employment emphasizes services, government, and management-information activities (Fisher, 1992).

Privatization is the process of transferring state-owned industries (and farms) to partial or full private control.

Quotas are limits on the volume of garments or other products that can be shipped into an importing country such as the United States. Quota limits are established generally through negotiations under global trade policies for textiles and apparel. (Under previous trade policies, the United States may also set quotas unilaterally—that is, without negotiation—and has done so in the past in a limited number of cases).

Redundant workers are employees who become "redundant," or unnecessary, through industrial restructuring or market changes. Although the term may appear to be an unkind label, this is a common term in industrial and economic literature.

Re-exports consist of the outward movement of nationalized goods, plus goods which, after importation, move outward from bonded warehouses or free zones *without having been transformed*. Nationalized goods consist of imported goods in free circula-

tion in the home territory that are subsequently exported *without transformation* (Jackson, 1989).

Restructuring refers to a shift in emphasis in economic sectors or activities. For example, restructuring the textile complex in the developed countries may include transferring some labor-intensive operations to low-wage countries. Or, in another example, restructuring in the developing economies may include a shift from agriculture to industrial production.

Shipments refer to the goods produced by manufacturers; the term is often used to refer to a country's domestic manufacturers' output.

Social charges (or *social costs*) include everything being paid by the employer (but not directly to the worker). These may include vacation pay, medical benefits, unemployment benefits, etc. These vary greatly from one country to another. In some developing countries, this might even include free meals (personal communication with R. Verret, 1989).

Sourcing refers to the process of determining how and where manufactured goods, or components, will be procured (obtained). The term *sourcing* seems to have rather imprecise meaning—sometimes referring to procurement of finished goods, sometimes to components, and at times to outward processing arrangements for having assembly operations performed in low wage countries. The reader should also note the definition for *outsourcing*; these terms are often used interchangeably. Sourcing is a part of business for both manufacturers and retailers.

Technology transfer, as we will be using it in this book, refers to having technological developments diffused beyond the country in which the innovations occurred. The transfer may occur through exported products, industrial processes, and skills required for technical improvements or innovations in production and other operations. Technology transfer can occur domestically, too—from one industry to another, from academe to industry, or in other ways.

Textile mill products industry refers to the conversion of fibers into finished fabrics; this includes spinning and texturing yarns; knitting, weaving, and tufting; and dyeing, printing, and other finishing.

Transshipment occurs when manufacturers in one country ship products to a second country with unused quota to take advantage of that available quota. This strategy is a means of circumventing the producing country's quota limitation in the importing market.

Value added is the value, in dollars or other monetary terms, added to a product during the last stage of production. *Value added* refers to the difference between the value of component parts used to produce a good and the value of the end product— basially, the "value added" by the manufacturing process. **Value added products** or **value added production** generally refer to those products or processes with a high value-added content.

SUGGESTED READINGS

Caribbean/Latin American Action. (1993). *Caribbean basin databook*. Washington, DC: Author.
A handbook of current information on economic and social factors in more than 40 countries in the Caribbean basin.

ECHO. (1991). *Textiles and clothing in Eastern Europe*. London: The Economist Intelligence Unit.
An overview of the industry in Eastern Europe, including the former Soviet Union (written after some of the changes occurred in the region).

Enderlyn, A., & Dziggel, O. (1992). *Cracking Eastern Europe*. Chicago: Probus.
Detailed information for marketers interested in Eastern Europe.

Finnerty, A. (1991). *Textiles and clothing in Southeast Asia*. London: The Economist Intelligence Unit.
An industry overview for several countries in the region.

Fitzpatrick Associates. (1991). *The clothing industry and the single European market*. London: The Economist Intelligence Unit.
An overview of the EC apparel industry and future prospects in a unified Europe.

Price Waterhouse. (various dates). *Doing business in ____*. Various countries: Author.
Guides to conducting business in various countries, giving a good overview of business conditions in each country presented.

Sakong, I. (1993). *Korea in the world economy*. Washington, DC: Institute for International Economics.
An overview of Korea's rise from a developing to a newly industrializing nation.

Steele, P. (1988). *The Caribbean clothing industry: The U.S. and far east connections*. London: The Economist Intelligence Unit.
A profile of Caribbean apparel manufacturing.

Steele, P. (1990). *Hong Kong clothing: Waiting for China*. London: The Economist Intelligence Unit.
An overview of Hong Kong's industry, with prospects for the industry as China assumes rule of Hong Kong.

Textile Institute (1993). *Asia and world textiles*. Textile Institute Conference Proceedings (Hong Kong). Manchester: Author.
A collection of papers presented at the Textile Institute's annual meeting; this source provides excellent information on the industry in Asia at the time of the conference.

United States Chamber of Commerce. (1992). *North American Free Trade Agreement*. Washington, DC: Author.
An overview of the agreement and implications for business.

United States Department of Commerce. (Monthly on CD rom). *United States national trade data bank (USNTDB).* Washington, DC: Author.

Ward, K. (Ed.). (1990). *Women workers and global restructuring.* Ithaca, NY: ILR Press.
An examination of how women workers are affected in global restructuring; includes various industries.

Werbeloff, A. (1987). *Textiles in Africa: A trade and investment guide.* London: Alain Charles Publishing Ltd.
An overview of the African textile and apparel industry. Because of difficulty in securing data on African nations, this may be one of the few sources of its type.

7

Global Patterns of Textile and Apparel Activities

INTRODUCTION

This chapter presents an overview of global trends in textile and apparel production, employment, consumption, and trade, with particular attention given to major global shifts for these activities. Most of the information in this section focuses on recent decades for three reasons: (1) the textile and apparel sectors became particularly significant in international commerce in the years following World War II; (2) many significant changes affecting the worldwide textile complex occurred since the 1950s; and (3) data on the global industry were either unavailable or of poor quality until after World War II, and, although shortcomings are still present, statistics have improved since that time.

Even in years to come, when the situation for the international textile and apparel sectors may change, this period is likely to remain an important one in the history of the global textile complex. The textile and apparel sectors were affected profoundly by the linking of national economies into a global economy that occurred during this period. Related to the globalization of the economy were the rapid worldwide expansion and development of the textile and apparel industry to an extent that the capacity to produce exceeded demand; this created intense competition never experienced prior to this era.

GLOBAL PATTERNS OF PRODUCTION

As noted earlier, the global picture for textile and apparel activity began to change markedly in the 1950s. Both the emergence of a growing number of producer nations and the globalization of the economy created a new environment in which the global textile complex would function.

Changes in worldwide textile and apparel production patterns—that is, who produces for the consumers of the world—have had a dramatic effect on other economic activities for the global sector. Logically, employment and trade patterns are tied closely to production. Consequently, the shifts in production sites—from certain countries and regions to other countries and regions—have had a tremendous impact on the global textile complex.

Although new countries entered global textile production in the 1950s and 1960s and manufacturers in the developed countries began to worry about imports, production in the industrialized countries continued at a healthy pace during this period. Textile and apparel production in the developed countries increased on average between 3 and 4 percent a year between 1953 and 1973.

Textile Production

Although textile production in the developed countries sustained a healthy growth rate (based on average annual rate change in volume[1]) between 1953 and 1973, production in the developing areas was growing more rapidly. Between 1963 and 1973, the Eastern trading area (the former Soviet bloc) also sustained a healthy growth rate.

Textile production increased dramatically in Japan between 1953 and 1973, with growth exceeding all other countries. It should be noted that even after having to rebuild after the war, Japan was soon again considered an important industrialized nation, rather than a developing one. Pro-

duction in the developing economies of Asia increased significantly from 1953–1963 but slowed somewhat afterward.

Although the United States' textile production grew at a healthy pace from 1963–1973, the annual rate of change in volume declined markedly after 1973. The European Economic Community (which eventually became the EU) growth rate was lower, however, than that of the United States after 1963.

In 1973, the global economy was affected severely by an increase in oil prices. *Worldwide* textile production slowed, as well as that in all regions of the world. In many ways, this was also a critical turning point in global shifts in textile and apparel production.

From 1973 on, the strongest textile production growth rates were in the developing areas and the Eastern trading area. By this time, more and more of the risks associated with international marketing were minimized for these areas as contracting importers, retailers, and producers in the developed countries (many of these would be considered transnational corporations) provided manufacturing and marketing assistance. By the 1980s, growth in the former Soviet bloc had fallen behind that for the developing areas. By this time, the developing areas exhibited clearly the strongest growth.

Among the major textile-producing nations at the time, Japan's production slowed more than that of any other country—going from being the country with the strongest growth rate in the 1950s and 1960s to the weakest from the 1970s on. The reader must keep in mind that we are referring to average annual *growth rates*, rather than to absolute levels of production. Japan's slowdown may be attributed to restrictions on Japanese textile products being shipped to the EC (now EU) and U.S. markets (the Multifiber Arrangement, which will be discussed in Chapter 10, became effective in 1974) and to Japan's shift to more technologically advanced manufac-

---

[1]In this usage, *volume* is an economic term referring to deflated values—that is, data in current values adjusted for inflation. This adjustment is made by dividing the current values by the appropriate price indices.

TABLE 7–1
Textile Production in Select Areas

	EC (12)	USA	*(Index 1973 = 100)* Japan	Hong Kong*	S. Korea
1974	96.4	90.9	85.0	na	102.9
1978	94.1	102.8	84.7	na	212.6
1982	91.5	92.7	82.3	94.5	299.7
1988	97.7	111.5	77.2	166.5	448.8
1992	92.7	118.5	68.2	187.5	412.7

Source: Personal correspondence with GATT staff (1993, 1994), based on national statistics.

turing areas, other than textiles and apparel. The developing Asian countries experienced the strongest growth rate in textile production from 1973 on.

Table 7–1 gives an indication of the trends in several major textile producing countries or regions for nearly three decades. The **indexes**[2] illustrate Japan's declining production, the stagnant (and sometimes declining) growth of the EU and U.S. textile industries, and the growth of an important new Asian producer, South Korea.

Over the nearly four decades reviewed, the growth rate for textile production in the developed countries diminished while production in the developing countries grew rather steadily. The developing countries as a group doubled their *share* of global (market economies only) textile production between 1953 and 1980 (from 18 to 35 percent). Keep in mind that the **share** of global textile production (or employment or trade) is not the same as the *absolute level* of production (or employment or trade). That is, a declining

share does not necessarily mean a decline in absolute level of production, employment, or trade.

Apparel Production

Although average annual growth rate for *worldwide* apparel production grew at a healthy rate in the 1960s, this trend slowed markedly between 1973 and the late 1980s. The developed countries dropped to near-zero growth during the 1973–1987 period (with a slight negative change when considered for 1980–1987 only).

The most noticeable pattern of change in apparel production was that while all other geographic areas experienced *reduced* average annual growth rates over time, the *developing areas sustained healthy increases*. While growth rates declined for the United States, Japan, and the EC (now EU), the developing economies experienced an 11.5 percent annual growth rate during the 1980s. Although a similar pattern occurred for textile production, the shift is far more pronounced for apparel production. The labor-intensive nature of apparel production and the ready adaptability of unskilled, low-wage labor to garment assembly accounted for this marked shift. As we have noted earlier, many develop-

[2]An index is often used as a means of overcoming problems associated with incompatible data that come from a variety of sources. Each region is compared with itself over time. Indexes are established by assigning a value of 100 to a given year, and other years are adjusted in relation to the base year.

ing countries began participating in the global textile complex by performing apparel assembly operations, usually for firms headquartered in the industrialized core countries.

An examination of apparel production indices (as shown above for textiles) reveals a similar pattern to that for textiles, except more exaggerated in some cases. For example, EU apparel production declined even more than EU textile production. Korean apparel production grew even more than textiles, going from an index of 131.2 in 1974 (1973 = 100) to 559.7 in 1992.

The developing countries' share of global (market economies only) apparel production more than tripled between 1953 and 1980, going from 8 to 25 percent.

In summary, the economic theories and development theories covered earlier help us to understand many of the major shifts occurring in the global textile and apparel industries in recent years. The cost advantage in many developing nations explains the shift of production—particularly the labor-intensive apparel production—to those areas. Similarly, the competition from low-cost producers has encouraged industrialized countries like the United States to focus more on production for which it has special advantages over many of the LDCs. Examples include more technologically advanced manufactured fiber production; use of more capital-intensive equipment and processes to automate and speed production and distribution; and development of higher-volume production.

Textile and apparel production in both the developed and developing countries is affected seriously by macroeconomic conditions of global markets. For example, the textile complexes in all the developed countries experienced the following recessionary periods: 1974–1975, 1977–1978, 1980–1982, and the early 1990s. Similarly, the industry in developing countries also felt the impact of the recessions in the more-developed nations. Slowed

consumption in the developed areas naturally affects the market potential for products from the exporting nations.

Textile and Apparel Production as a Share of All Manufacturing

Although absolute textile production increased after the war until the early 1970s, the share of the textile industry as a part of all manufacturing began to decline in the postwar years for most regions. By this, we mean that although textile production was increasing, it was doing so more slowly than the rest of manufacturing. For the developing countries as a whole, the share of textile output as a part of all manufacturing is about two and one-half times larger than in the developed countries (in 1980, 11.5 percent compared to 4.4 percent) (GATT, 1984). These statistics reflect the relative importance of the textile sector in the economies of the developing countries.

In North America, the European Community (when it had nine members), and other countries in Western Europe, apparel production experienced a steady decline as a share of all manufacturing production. Although apparel production increased as a share of manufacturing in some developing country regions, it declined in others. Even so, apparel production as a portion of all manufacturing was nearly twice as high for the developing countries as it was for the developed countries (in 1980, 4.5 percent compared to 2.8 percent) (GATT, 1984). Apparel production as a percentage of all manufacturing is much lower than textiles for the developing countries; this may be attributed in part to the more limited domestic demand for ready-made apparel in developing countries. Another explanation is that a large part of small-scale manufacturing, of which apparel production is an important part, goes unrecorded (Jackson, 1989).

QUALIFYING STATEMENTS ON DATA

Although the data for production, employment, and consumption used in this chapter come from the most respected international and national sources, even the "best" data have inherent limitations. "Perfect" data for these global textile/apparel activities do not exist. Therefore, the reader should be aware of a number of limitations associated with even the most conscientiously compiled international textile and apparel data. Limitations include the following:

- The data are subject to frequent revisions.
- Regional definitions can vary among international organizations and over time.
- Prior to the expansion of the EC to 12 Member States, some GATT papers classified Greece, Portugal, and Spain as developing countries. EC data that do not include these last three members are identified in this chapter.
- Data from which some regional aggregates are calculated are limited in terms of country coverage and quality of the data.
- Country groupings have changed markedly in recent years (for example, the breakup of the former Soviet bloc), making it difficult or

impossible to have continuous data for some areas over time. For example, GATT began a new country grouping system in 1990 to reflect changes in the former Soviet bloc. Therefore, GATT data for certain country groupings before and after 1990 are not directly comparable.

For example, the world and centrally planned economies' aggregates used in this chapter *do not include* China. Furthermore, since China is not classified as a developing country by the United Nations or GATT, China is not included in the developing areas in data from those organizations.

Similarly, data from the developing countries are scarce. The only global indicator available is the UN index; therefore, any index from this group of countries is going to be rough because of limited data from certain countries or some years. Missing data are statistically estimated time series (usually by regression analysis), as is the case with the UN index. Consequently, although these are the most accurate data available in the world today, shortcomings are inherent (Jackson, 1989).

GLOBAL PATTERNS OF EMPLOYMENT

Although the textile and apparel industries contribute to the international economy in many ways, their important role as a major employer of people around the globe accounts for their prominence and special attention as a sector in global commerce. The textile complex is among the largest sources of manufacturing jobs in both the developed and the developing countries.

If comprehensive data were available to review total employment in these sectors, sta-

tistics would likely confirm that the textile and apparel industries comprise the largest source of manufacturing jobs. However, employment in cottage industries or other informal arrangements, particularly in the developing countries, is difficult to determine; therefore, employment statistics do not accurately reflect the large numbers of workers employed in these decentralized arrangements such as the one shown in Figure 7–1. The lack of documentation on workers in the textile and apparel industries is not limited to the developing countries, however. Unregistered labor may be found in the developed

FIGURE 7–1
Workers in informal establishments, such as this one in India, frequently are not counted in employment figures. These home textile industries provide a living for many people, including children.

Source: Photo courtesy International Labour Office.

countries as well. Italy is the most obvious example, but many undocumented workers may be found also, for example, in the New York garment district and in areas of Los Angeles. Keep in mind, as global employment patterns are discussed, that large numbers of workers who have never been officially reported are not included. Therefore, most statements about numbers of workers tend to understate total *actual* workers' contributions.

Employment in Textiles

Figure 7–2 displays annual growth rates of employment in textiles by main areas. Aggregate employment data are not available after 1987. Although the International Labor Orga-

nization has textile and apparel data for many countries, more recent aggregate data appear not to exist. The author believes the trends shown in the figures have continued and intensified since 1987.

Over the nearly four decades shown, a declining average annual percentage rate of change in textile employment is evident. Even in the 1950s, the long-term decline in employment in the textile sector in the developed areas began. Between 1973 and 1985, textile employment in absolute terms in the developed countries as a group declined by 30 percent (GATT, 1987). Although employment in all areas declined during the 1980s, the developing areas experienced an increase overall for the three continuous periods shown (that is, from 1953–87).

FIGURE 7–2
Employment in textiles by main areas. Notes: No world data or former Soviet bloc data are available for 1953–1963. Country groupings for 1953–1973 are not strictly comparable to country groupings for 1973–1987.

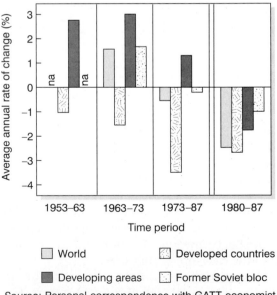

Source: Personal correspondence with GATT economist, 1988.

Employment in Apparel

Slightly more than half the workers employed in the global textile complex are employed in the apparel sector. Employment in apparel production has grown more rapidly in recent years than has textile production or manufacturing as a whole. Figure 7–3 displays employment in apparel production by main areas.

Employment in apparel production has declined for the developed countries from 1963 on; however, average annual growth rates for the developing countries has been substantial. Although the developing areas' employment growth rates slowed during the

FIGURE 7–3

Employment in apparel by main areas. Notes: No world data or former Soviet bloc data are available for 1953–1963. Data for the former Soviet bloc include leather and footwear. Country groupings for 1953–1973 are not strictly comparable to country groupings for 1973–1987.

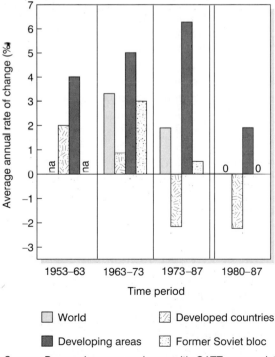

Source: Personal correspondence with GATT economist, 1988.

1980s, employment increased an average of 6.3 percent annually from 1973 to 1987.

Apparel employment, perhaps more than any other area of activity for the global textile complex, reflects the shifts that may be explained by economic theories and development theories considered earlier. As a large number of developing countries attempted to advance their development, many employed masses of workers in labor-intensive apparel assembly operations. The sector was easy to enter, and large numbers of workers could be employed; wages were substantially lower than in many other countries, thereby resulting in low-cost garments for world markets.

Nearly all the increases in employment in the global (market economies only) textile complex since 1970 resulted from growth in the developing countries. Absolute employment in the developing countries more than doubled in the apparel industry and increased more than 40 percent in the textile industry between 1970 and 1981.

In reviewing the shifts in shares of the global (market economies only) employment from 1953 to 1980, the developing countries increased by half their share of jobs in the textile sector, from 52 to 73 percent. For apparel, the developing countries nearly doubled their share of jobs during the same period, with most of the increase occurring in the Asian countries (GATT, 1984).

Both textile and apparel employment declined in the developed countries during the period when the number of workers grew in the developing countries. Between 1973 and 1985, apparel employment in the developed countries declined by 18 percent (GATT, 1987). The same pattern of decline was evident in the *shares* of global employment for both the textile and apparel sectors in the developed countries.

A number of factors account for the decline in textile and apparel employment in the developed countries in recent decades. Among the causes are stagnant consumption, use of labor-saving equipment that also increased **productivity**, and increased imports from the developing countries (USITC, 1985a). Although low-cost imports are viewed by manufacturers in the developed countries as the primary cause of the decline in employment, a number of sources (for example, Cline, 1987; Keesing & Wolf, 1980) suggest that productivity gains account for much of the drop in the number of jobs (it is virtually impossible to determine job losses by cause).

Wage Differences as a Factor in Employment Shifts

The high labor content of many textile products, and apparel in particular, accounted for much of the dramatic shift in production to the developing countries. The labor-intensive aspects of apparel production make garment assembly quite costly in countries where wages are high.

Compared to most other product manufacturing, apparel production typically requires a great deal of processing by human hands to assemble garments from two-dimensional fabric to fit the three-dimensional human body. Automation has not been readily available to handle limp fabrics, the basic component of apparel production. Therefore, a great deal of labor goes into assembling garments. In the United States, for example, labor costs typically account for about one-third of the wholesale value of garments (USITC, 1985a). Thus, the availability of low-cost labor in the developing countries provides an advantageous match for the high labor requirements of apparel production.

Wage differences are a key factor in the global shifts in textile and apparel production, and thus are at the heart of the complexities associated with international trade in this sector. Table 7–2 provides a comparison of hourly labor costs in selected countries for the *textile* industry (comparable data are not available for the apparel industry).

In Table 7–2, the hourly labor cost comparisons developed by Werner International

include all worker benefits paid by the employer (but not directly to the worker). These may include vacation pay, holiday pay, medical benefits, unemployment benefits, and so on. These vary greatly from one country to another. In some developing countries, these benefits might even include free meals (author's visits, various years; Verret, personal communication, 1989; Verret, 1993).

Although many of the developing countries have relatively poor productivity levels in textile and apparel production, typically the hourly costs of labor are so much lower than wages in the developed countries that the LDCs continue to have a significant competitive advantage in world markets. Whereas textile productivity rates have increased in the United States, developing countries showed marginal productivity growth. One must keep in mind, however, that developing countries continue to improve productivity rates. Productivity in the apparel industry increased somewhat in the United States but declined in the developing areas (Cline, 1987; Wolf, Glismann, Pelzman, & Spinanger, 1984). The entry of new producer nations, most of whom rely more heavily on apparel production than textile production, accounts for much of the drop in productivity rates for apparel manufacturing in the developing nations. Productivity levels are generally quite low in countries that have just begun production. Moreover, for many LDCs in early stages of development, providing employment for a large and otherwise unemployed workforce may be more important than trying to improve productivity rates. Further, new technology to improve productivity usually is not an option for manufacturers in the poorer countries.

Textile and Apparel Employment as a Share of All Manufacturing Employment

Employment in both the textile and apparel industries in the developed countries

TABLE 7-2
Labor Cost Comparison-Summer 1993 (in U.S.Dollars)

Rank 1993	Country	Hourly Cost US$ 1993	Ratio 1993* USA = 100
1	Japan	23.65	204
2	Switzerland	22.32	192
3	Belgium	21.32	184
4	Denmark	21.32	184
5	Holland	20.82	179
6	West Germany	20.50	177
7	Austria	18.81	162
8	Norway	18.46	159
9	Sweden	17.22	148
10	France	16.49	142
11	Italy	16.20	140
12	East Germany	14.17	122
13	Canada	13.44	116
14	Finland	11.86	102
15	U.S.A.	11.61	100
16	Australia	10.84	93
17	United Kingdom	10.27	88
18	Ireland	9.18	79
19	Spain	7.91	68
20	Israel	7.20	62
21	Greece	7.13	61
22	Taiwan	5.76	50
23	Turkey	4.44	38
24	Hong Kong	3.85	33
25	Portugal	3.70	32
26	South Korea	3.66	32
27	Singapore	3.56	31
28	Uruguay	3.09	27
29	Tunisia	2.97	26
30	Mexico	2.93	25

* Based on USA = 100. Ranking: 1 = Highest; 58 = Lowest.

declined since the 1950s as a share of all manufacturing employment, with the decline less dramatic in North America than in other developed regions. In most developing countries, employment in textile production declined as a share of total manufacturing employment. However, apparel production employment in the developing countries as a group became increasingly important as a portion of all manufacturing employment. In 1980, apparel production employment in the developing countries accounted for 10.9 per-

TABLE 7-2 *(continued)*

Rank 1993	Country	Hourly Cost US$ 1993	Ratio 1993* USA = 100
31	Argentina	2.47	21
32	Venezuela	1.90	16
33	Colombia	1.85	16
34	Hungary	1.80	16
35	South Africa	1.64	14
36	Morocco	1.47	13
37	Brazil	1.46	13
38	Czech Republic	1.43	12
39	Peru	1.43	12
40	Mauritius	1.42	12
41	Slovakia	1.29	11
42	Malaysia	1.18	10
43	Syria	1.12	10
44	Thailand	1.04	9
45	Philippines	0.78	7
46	Egypt	0.57	5
47	India	0.56	5
48	Zimbabwe	0.47	4
49	Pakistan	0.44	4
50	Indonesia	0.43	4
51	Nigeria	0.41	4
52	Sri Lanka	0.39	3
53	Vietnam	0.37	3
54	China PR	0.36	3
55	Zambia	0.32	3
56	Kenya	0.31	3
57	Bangladesh	0.23	2
58	Tanzania	0.22	2

* Based on USA = 100. Ranking: 1 = Highest; 58 = Lowest.

Source: From *Spinning and Weaving Labour Cost Comparisons* Summer 1993, by Werner International, 1993, New York: Author. Reprinted by permission.

cent of all manufacturing jobs, compared to 5.7 percent for the developed countries (GATT, 1984). These figures highlight the importance of the apparel industry in providing jobs in the developing countries.

GLOBAL PATTERNS OF CONSUMPTION

Consumer demand (also referred to as consumption) for textile and apparel products is

LABOR COSTS ARE ONLY ONE FACTOR IN COMPETITIVENESS

Although the low wages in the developing areas provide important cost advantages to the developing countries, other factors affect the competitiveness of the textile/apparel industry. Other significant factors include productivity rates, costs of other factors such as raw materials and energy, plus noncost factors such as quality, styling, and services to customers. We see that labor costs are only one factor to consider when we compare the hourly labor costs of the largest exporter nations of textiles and apparel.

Ormerod (1993) gives examples in which wage rates have declining significance in terms of where profitable textile operations are located (this may apply less to apparel). Similarly, in viewing GATT data for 1992, we see that of the ten largest exporter nations of textiles (see Table 7–7), six can be considered high-wage countries, two are NICs with escalating wages, and two are low-wage countries. In apparel (Table 7–9), four of the top ten exporters are high-wage countries and two are NICs with higher wages. The countries are identified and discussed more in detail later in this chapter; the reader may wish to consider those countries in relation to the wages given in Table 7–2.

---

the leading force in determining the levels of production and employment discussed in prior sections. Demand for final end-use products such as clothing, home furnishings textile products (for examples, draperies, linens, carpets), and other products containing textiles such as tires, luggage, and sporting goods also affects the demand for intermediate inputs of fibers, yarns, and fabrics. Consequently, a healthy and sustained rate of consumption of textile and apparel products is critical to the prosperity of the global textile complex.

Changes in consumption levels can have a widespread impact on the global textile complex. First, a drop in consumption leads to a ripple effect backward through several stages in the production chain. For example, a decline in clothing demand reduces fabric demand; this is followed by similar reductions in yarn and fiber demand. Second, in the global fragmentation of the textile and apparel industries, a number of countries may be involved in making "global products" and, consequently, are affected by the changes in demand.

According to Anson and Simpson (1988), worldwide fiber consumption has grown more between 1950 and 1986 (259 percent) than during the first half of the century (141 percent). Anson and Simpson based their conclusions on fiber production data, assuming that at the aggregate (world) level, production and consumption are roughly similar. These researchers noted that fiber consumption growth rate was especially strong from 1950 to 1973, but since the oil price increases in 1973, growth has been at a far slower pace (26 percent from 1973 to 1986).

In the following sections, we will consider two types of measures for examining consumption patterns. These include (1) **fiber consumption** data and (2) **consumer expenditure** data. The two types of data may be used in a complementary manner. One measures fiber demand at one end of the textile chain and *demand for final textile products* at the other.

Fiber Consumption Measure

Fiber consumption data may be considered in a variety of ways. We might think of the collective fiber consumption of a country or a region and make comparisons on that basis. Similarly, we might make comparisons among groups of countries such as the developed countries and the developing countries. On the other hand, we might consider the average fiber consumption of individuals, that is, comparing individual consumption from one country to another.

One definition of **textile consumption** has been offered by Toyne et al. (1984) as follows: "The sum of a region's production and its net trade (imports minus exports) is the amount of a commodity that a region *consumes*, ignoring stocks held in inventory. Consumption on a per capita basis is both a measure of welfare of the consumers of a region and a measure of the potential market from the firm's point of view" (p. 62, italics added). Toyne et al., like many others who analyze global textile and apparel activities, used the term **per capita fiber consumption** to refer to the average number of pounds (or other measures of weight) of fiber consumed per individual on an annual basis. This is usually calculated for a defined area—a country, a region, or the world.

Using the per capita measure, total world fiber consumption has shown little or no growth since the late 1970s. Particularly in the early 1980s, per capita consumption declined, reflecting the slowed demand for apparel and also the reduced demand for such products as carpets, autos, and furniture that contain textile materials (USITC, 1987b). World fiber consumption was depressed in the early 1990s as a result of sluggish economic conditions, particularly in Western Europe, the United States, and Japan. For example, world fiber consumption grew by only 1.3 percent in 1992; however, this was an improvement over growth in 1991 (*Fiber Organon*, 1993).

The per capita consumption measure is useful in making intercountry and regional comparisons. Figure 7–4 shows the relative per capita consumption for select countries

and country groupings.[3] The developed countries account for the largest per capita fiber consumption of textile products, with the United States and Japan accounting for the greatest per capita consumption.

We must keep in mind that the *per capita* data in these comparisons represent only one way of considering fiber consumption patterns. For example, if we look at *collective consumption* for the developed countries and the developing nations, we may arrive at different conclusions. Although the developing countries are relatively marginal consumers on a per capita basis, as shown in Figure 7–4 in absolute terms (that is, based on total fiber availability in 1990 [1989 for developing countries]), their *total consumption* was not much below that for the developed countries. The developing countries consumed 14.6 million tons of fibers compared to 22.4 million tons for the developed countries (FAO, 1993). The England-based Textiles Intelligence Limited developed the estimates shown in Figure 7–5 for three points in time. As the figure indicates, estimates project the *total consumption* of fibers for the developing countries to be roughly equal to that of the total for the developed countries by the year 2002 (Coker, 1993).

As we noted, the per capita measure is useful in allowing us to observe certain consumption patterns. For example, the United States and Western Europe experienced serious declines in per capita fiber consumption from 1979 through the early 1980s. During this period the U.S. per capita fiber consumption dropped to the lowest level since the mid-1960s but experienced a healthy recovery by 1986 (Fiber Economics Bureau, 1989). Western

---

[3]The FAO definition of developed countries includes centrally planned countries in Eastern Europe, including the former USSR. Their definition of developing countries includes China (and this probably also means that Taiwan data are included with those for China).

FIGURE 7–4
Per capita fiber consumption in selected areas. (Latest data are 1990 for developed countries and 1989 for developing countries.)

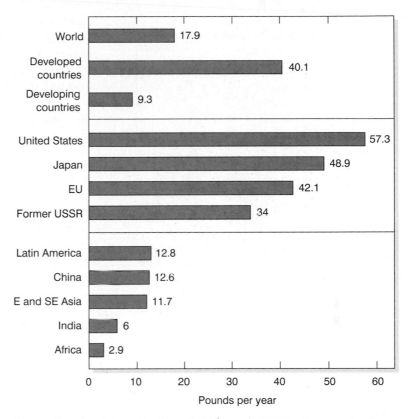

Source: Based on information from *World Apparel and Fiber Consumption Survey,* 1992, by Food and Agriculture Organization of the United Nations, 1993. Rome: Author.

European consumption has lagged because of a prolonged recession there.

In the decade between 1982 and 1992, the U.S. population grew 9.9 percent. During this time, the per capita GDP increased 19.1 percent (in constant 1987 dollars), and consumption of all fibers rose 54.7 percent. In 1992, U.S. per capita consumption of all fibers rose 8.2 percent over that for 1991 (Fiber Economics Bureau, May 1993).

A few observations might be made in reviewing what occurred during the early 1980s global recessionary period. First, the widespread recessionary patterns illustrate the interlinking of nations in recent years into a global economy. Second, textile and apparel consumption is affected significantly by the broader economic trends. And third, economic changes in the industrialized countries have a serious impact on the global textile complex.

As an example of the importance of the economies of the developed countries, in 1989 the United States, which has only 5 percent of the global population, consumed over 17 percent of the fiber produced worldwide for the year (FAO, 1993). Together, all Europe and the United States accounted for 15 percent of the world's population in 1989 but jointly consumed more than 39 percent of the world fiber output for the year (FAO, 1993).

In addition to being affected by broad economic changes, two other key factors influence global consumption of textile and apparel products. These are *changes in world population* and *income levels*. Changes in the

FIGURE 7–5

Final consumption of textile fibers 1992–2002

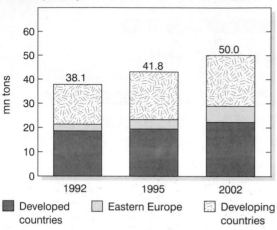

Developed countries   Eastern Europe   Developing countries

Source: Textiles Intelligence estimates and forecasts

Source: From "World Textile and Clothing Consumption: Forecasts to 2002" by John Coker, November 1993, *Textile Outlook International*, p. 37. Reprinted by permission of Textiles Intelligence Limited.

total population can have a significant impact on consumption; the location of the changes may be equally significant. As we learned in Chapter 4, the world's population is shifting from the industrial nations of the North to the developing nations of the South. The Population Reference Bureau (1993) predicts that by the year 2010, over four-fifths of the world's population will be concentrated in developing countries.

Although dramatic population growth may occur in some parts of the world, the economic means for acquiring additional textile and apparel products may be limited. Thus, total *personal income* is another variable to consider in consumption levels of textile and apparel goods. The following chart (see Figure 7–6), developed by Textiles Intelligence Limited (Coker, 1993) from the FAO database, illustrates fiber consumption relative to income. A statistical technique called regression analysis was used to show how fiber demand varies with income in a number of

countries. Keep in mind that *per head* is another term for *per capita*, and because fiber consumption is given in kilograms per head, one should remember that one kilogram is equal to 2.2046 pounds.

Consumer Expenditure Measure

Although fiber consumption data may be used as an indicator of consumption trends for textile and apparel products, GATT economists caution against basing the economic analysis of consumption of *finished* textile and apparel products on fiber consumption data alone (GATT, 1984). They have noted that the fiber consumption data omit other inputs (including labor and capital) for all the processing stages up to and including the one that produced the consumer end product. That is, the "other inputs" are much more important in value terms than the fiber content of the final products (GATT, 1984).

Moreover, GATT experts noted that using weight to express per capita consumption fails to consider the differences in prices and values of different products, treating a pound of one product as equal in value to a pound of any other. For example, the "weight approach" might include comparisons of pounds of silk to pounds of jute—hardly a realistic comparison in terms of the weight/value relationship. Further, the measure does not account for the trading up toward higher-quality, higher-priced items that tends to occur. Trading up occurs particularly as a result of quota restrictions, which encourage producers to maximize the value of products that can be shipped in restricted quantities. Similarly, GATT sources have noted that technological innovations have caused a decrease in fiber usage by weight. For example, many manufactured fiber products tend to be lighter in weight and more lasting than similar products of certain natural fibers; thus the increased production and use of manufactured fiber products would be

FIGURE 7–6
Fiber consumption and income per head for selected countries, 1990

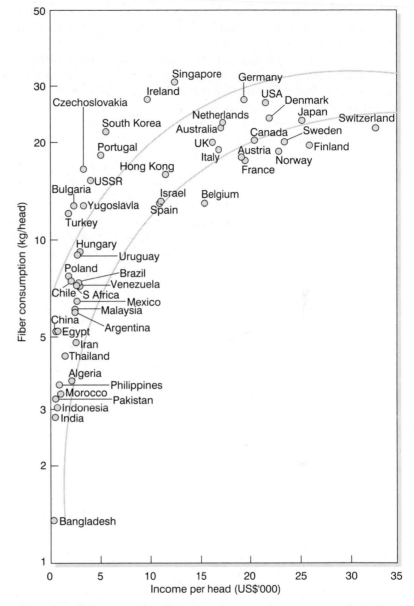

Source: From "World Textile and Clothing Consumption: Forecasts to 2002" by John Coker, November 1993, *Textile Outlook International*, p. 20. Reprinted by permission of Textiles Intelligence Limited.

underestimated in the per capita consumption data based on weight measures.

Although the fiber consumption measures are quite useful, GATT economists like to consider also a second approach—the use of consumer expenditure data—as a complementary way of studying the demand for textile and apparel products. The GATT staff believes that fiber consumption data and consumer expenditure data are not measuring the same thing.

That is, fibers are at one end and consumer expenditure at the other end of the textile chain. In other words, GATT economists believe that although the fiber consumption data are useful, this information is not the same as *final demand* for textiles and clothing.

Table 7–3 shows changes in consumer expenditure on clothing (including footwear) in relation to total consumer expenditure for the United States, Japan, and the EU. Complete and reliable data are not available for the developing countries. This table shows the average annual percentage rate of change in volume (real consumer expenditure; that is, data in current values deflated by price indices).

Changes varied within the three main developed areas shown. The European Union and Japan experienced the greatest slowdown in apparel expenditures, whereas similar expenditures in the United States grew faster than total consumer expenditures. Despite more positive growth in the United States, the slow growth in total clothing expenditures for the developed countries from 1973 through 1992 affected seriously the global textile complex.

Figure 7–7 compares the percentage share of consumer clothing expenditure as a part of total consumer expenditure in 1973 and 1992 for three developed areas.

We note that clothing's share of total expenditure dropped in Japan and the EU but increased in the United States during this period. Comparable data are not available for the developing areas. As we have noted earlier, however, the developed countries consume the largest proportion of fibers per person.

Although the expenditure data avoid the shortcomings of the per capita fiber consumption measures based on weight, many of the consumption/demand patterns shown here are quite similar to those noted in the earlier analysis. Both approaches reflect a marked drop in consumer demand or purchase of textile and apparel products from the early 1970s to the early 1990s. A key point to remember is that the *declines in production and employment* discussed earlier were tied closely to this *reduction in consumer spending in the developed countries.*

The Impact of Reduced Consumption

The period of stagnant consumption occurred at a particularly critical time in the broader development of the global textile and apparel

TABLE 7–3
Total Consumer Expenditure and Expenditure on Clothing in Selected Developed Countries (Selected years 1963–1992)

		Average Annual Percentage Rate of Change in Volume		
		1963–1973	1973–1992[a]	1980–1992[a]
United States	Total	4.5	2.5	2.6
	Clothing	4.0	3.6	3.4
Japan	Total	8.5	3.4	3.4
	Clothing	7.0	1.4	1.5
EC(12)[b]	Total	4.5	2.5	2.3
	Clothing	4.0	1.7	1.5

[a]For developed countries as a group, last year was 1992; Japan (clothing) was 1991.
[b]Data 1963–1973 refers to the EC (9).

Source: Personal correspondence with GATT economist, based on OECD National Accounts and national statistics.

FIGURE 7–7

Share of clothing (including footwear) in total consumer expenditure, select developed countries, 1973 and 1992 (1980 prices).

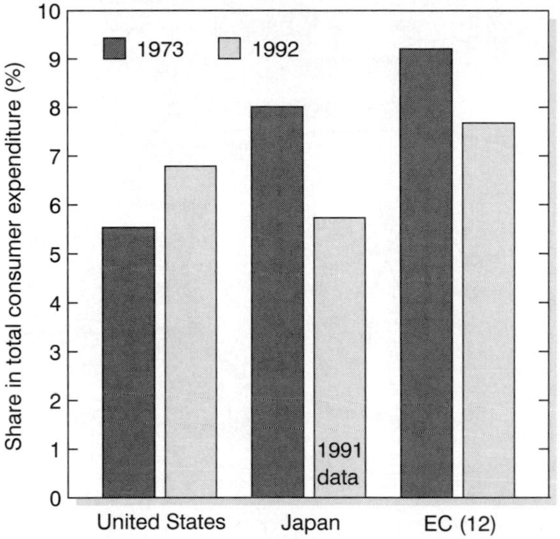

Source: Personal correspondence with GATT economist, based on OECD National Accounts and National Statistics

share of the market, as depicted in Figure 7–8, while the market has not grown appreciably.

GLOBAL PATTERNS OF TRADE

Whereas textile and apparel producers in the industrialized countries depended upon home markets to use the products they manufactured, the developing countries concentrated on exports as the source of their growth. They, too, looked to the markets of the developed countries to buy and use their products. Thus, as the developing countries increased their production capacity and could offer many products at lower prices because of labor costs, significant global shifts in trade occurred. Consumers in the developed countries saw an increase in the number of products in their markets made in other countries.

Shifts in textile and apparel trade are particularly important to examine in a study of the textile and apparel sectors in the international economy. Trade shifts are at the heart of the controversy associated with international commerce for the textile complex. After all, production and employment shifts are seen as problems only as they affect trade. That is, as textile and apparel manufacturers in the developed counties have experienced declines in production and employment, the trade shifts are typically viewed as the cause. Furthermore, logic would suggest that the domestic textile and apparel industries in the industrialized countries would be negatively affected when other producers compete for and successfully acquire a sizeable portion of the home markets. After all, consumption did not grow adequately to absorb the increased worldwide production that occurred.

Another reason that global trade for textile and apparel products merits special attention is that trade is one of the most accurately measured economic activities for the sector. Regardless of how conscientious international

industry. It was during these same years that the number of textile and apparel producer nations proliferated as an increased number of newly developing countries looked to this sector as an important cornerstone in their economic development plans. Consequently, *slowed consumption of textile and apparel products in the developed countries caused competition for world markets to intensify.* At the same time that textile and apparel manufacturers in the developed countries attempted to adjust to the reduced demand in their domestic markets, they also found they had many new global competitors.

Slowed demand coupled with the proliferation of producers led to fierce international competition for market share. Simply put, an overcapacity for production has the potential to create easily a glut of products in relation to global levels of consumption. In short, more and more countries have competed for a

FIGURE 7–8

In this illustration, representatives of many countries of the world vie for a "piece of the U.S. pie." As the nation with the highest per capita fiber consumption, producers in most exporting nations view the U.S. market as a desirable place to sell their textile and apparel products.

Source: From American Fabrics and Fashions (cover), issue number 131, 1984. *Reprinted courtesy of Bobbin Blenheim Media Corporation.*

agencies attempt to be in their analyses of production and employment data, statistics on those activities often are subject to question. For example, some countries have fairly limited reporting and record-keeping systems. Moreover, many production and employment statistics are dependent upon producers to report on their own operations, leaving room for omissions and inaccuracies to occur. In contrast, records on trade are more accurate. As products are traded, **exports** and **imports** must pass through customs agencies operated by national governments. Records of these

transactions are more precise and provide more comparable documentation of what occurred than is true for some of the production and employment records. Further, a number of international organizations (the United Nations, the Organization for Economic Cooperation and Development [OECD]) collect and publish these trade data in consistent, comparable form, which permit meaningful analyses of trade patterns on a global basis.

A good portion of world data on textile and apparel trade is classified according to the

WHO PAYS MORE DEARLY FOR CLOTHING?

Although persons in the developing countries consume a much smaller volume (in pounds, kilograms, and so on) of fiber than do persons in the industrialized countries, another striking comparison should be considered. In the developing countries, a far higher percentage of the household consumption expenditure is required for clothing (and footwear) compared to the developed countries.

As one of the basic necessities of life, clothing—like food—must be obtained before other things may be purchased. Once basic needs are satisfied, relatively higher proportions of income are spent on other goods. For some of the poorer nations of the world, however, the inhabitants never move beyond the necessities. More accurately, many never have adequate amounts of the necessities. World Bank data provide this startling contrast:

	GNP per capita	Percentage of household consumption on clothing and footwear
Tanzania	$ 110	10
Nepal	170	12
Rwanda	310	11
Ecuador	980	10
Turkey	1,630	15
United States	21,790	6
Switzerland	32,680	4

Source:: From *World Development Report, 1992* (Tables 1 and 10) by World Bank, 1992, Washington, DC: Author. Reprinted by permission.

Standard International Trade Classification (SITC) system. Textiles are classified under SITC 65 (textile yarn, fabrics, made-up articles, not elsewhere specified, and related products), and apparel is classified under SITC 84 (articles of apparel and clothing accessories) (USITC, 1985b).

Although it is important to continue studying the most current textile and apparel trade data, a review of a span of years in which there was dramatic change for the complex provides a useful perspective on how the textile and apparel industries are affected by broader economic changes and by the inter-

meshing of national economies. Charting historical data permits us to discover patterns that are useful for current analysis and prediction. In this sense, studying historical trends is as important as studying current data. Historical trends often provide an important basis for government and business decisions.

This section provides an overview of global patterns of textile and apparel trade and considers shifts in trade that have occurred in the postwar years. After an overview, trade for the two industries will be considered separately. Although trade patterns for textiles and apparel have much in common, for the most

FIGURE 7–9
As the developing countries became more proficient producers for the global textile and apparel market, consumers began to see growing evidence of the globalization of the textile complex.

part, the unique aspects of each sector account for differing trade shifts.[4]

An Overview of Textile and Apparel Trade

World trade in textiles and apparel, *as measured by the value of world exports*, grew considerably—almost 18 percent—between 1970 and 1980 to $97.4 billion. However, the worldwide economic recession that began in the early 1980s had a serious impact on consumer demand for all products and severely affected global trade in this sector. Textile and apparel trade grew slowly during the first half of the 1980s but accelerated considerably by 1986. By 1990, textile and apparel trade increased more than 56 percent over 1980, accounting for $224 billion in 1990. That year apparel was the tenth largest trade category as a share of all world **merchandise trade** (exports); textiles was the eleventh largest category (GATT, *International Trade*, various years). Table 7–4 summarizes global textile and apparel trade as a share of merchandise trade and as a share of total manufactures in trade for 1992.

When we consider textile and apparel trade combined, we see the following distribution by major areas[5] in Figure 7–10. It is significant to note that for combined textile and apparel trade, the developing countries

_____

[4]In considering textile and apparel trade data, we must keep in mind that the recording of offshore assembly trade (known in Europe as outward processing trade) and exports from **free trade zones** is not consistent among countries. This trade may be excluded entirely from recorded export statistics (e.g., Mexico). It may be lumped together with other products in the "not elsewhere specified" section (e.g., China, Philippines, Sri Lanka), thus escaping inclusion in textiles, apparel, and manufactures on the exports side. It would appear in import figures, however. Thus, for example, U.S. clothing imports from Mexico in 1985 were over double the value reported in the Mexican export statistics. A discrepancy of this magnitude cannot all be a result of valuation and reporting time lag differences (Jackson, 1989).

_____

[5]The reader must keep in mind that because of major changes in the world, particularly in Eastern Europe and the former USSR, country groupings used in trade data

TABLE 7–4
Global Textile and Apparel Trade, 1992

| | Share of Textiles and Apparel in Total (%) | | Value of Exports ($US billions) |
	Merchandise Exports (%)	Exports of Manufactures (%)	
Textiles	3.2	4.4	$117
Apparel	3.6	4.9	$131

Source: Personal communication with GATT economist, 1994.

account for slightly more of the total than the developed countries. Table 7–5 provides an overview of world textile and apparel trade by main areas for 1990 and 1992.

As we study trade shifts in this section, we must keep in mind the effects of changes in currency **exchange rates** (see boxed insert). For example, trade for a country may appear high, due in part to the valuation effects of exchange rates. For example, in the mid-1980s, the devaluation of the dollar resulted in textile and apparel growth rates that appeared very high for some of the West European nations whose currencies appreciated against the dollar. In terms of their national currencies, however, those countries' growth rates for textile exports declined. For example, France went from an average annual growth rate in textiles of 0.7 percent from 1980 to 1986 to a growth of

17.4 percent in 1987 when measured in dollars. When measured in francs, however, France's textile exports went from an average annual 9.4 percent growth rate to 1.5 percent.

The Importance of Textile/Apparel Trade to Developing Countries

Since the 1970s, the most important influences on global textile trade were the growing number of producer nations and the increased

FIGURE 7–10
Textile and apparel trade, 1992 (billion dollars).

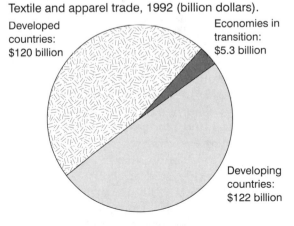

Developed countries: $120 billion

Economies in transition: $5.3 billion

Developing countries: $122 billion

Total trade: $247.6 billion

Note: Sum of categories might not equal due to rounding.
Source: Personal correspondence with GATT staff, 1993, 1994.

have changed. In 1990, the GATT began a new system of country groupings which means that data from similar groupings before that time *are not comparable* with the new system. This prevents making comparisons of trade over a period of recent decades up to the present.

Current GATT country groupings are:

Developed countries: Canada, United States, Japan, European Union (excluding former East Germany), and EFTA.

Developing countries: Latin America, Western Europe not elsewhere specified, Romania, Africa not elsewhere specified, Middle East, and Non-OECD Asia.

Economies in transition: Former USSR and Central/Eastern Europe (without Romania).

Hong Kong re-exports are not included.

TABLE 7–5
World Textile and Apparel Trade by Main Areas, 1990 and 1992 (billion dollars)

	Destination							
	World[a]		Developed countries		Developing countries		Economies in transition	
Origin	1990	1992	1990	1992	1990	1992	1990	1992
World								
Textiles	104.75	116.80	65.74	67.72	34.08	44.80	4.27	3.98
Apparel	106.45	130.80	93.09	113.90	9.63	13.96	3.59	2.88
Developed countries								
Textiles	65.55	68.80	49.79	49.60	13.50	16.49	2.19	2.63
Apparel	45.24	51.53	39.48	44.15	4.47	6.23	1.27	1.13
Developing countries								
Textiles	37.85	46.70	15.19	17.14	20.23	28.15	1.83	1.22
Apparel	58.80	75.30	51.73	65.97	5.12	7.71	1.85	1.58
Economies in transition								
not available								

Imports—read down.
Exports—read across.
Example: Developing countries exported $17.14 billion in textiles to developed countries in 1992.
Developing countries imported $16.49 billion in textiles from developed countries in 1992.
[a]Includes unspecified destinations
Source: Personal communication with GATT economist, 1994.

proficiency of the developing country producers. As noted earlier, the textile and apparel industries have been particularly important in the economic development of many developing countries. Table 7–6 illustrates the importance of textile exports to a number of these countries.

We see, for example, that in 1992, Pakistan's combined textiles and apparel accounted for nearly 70 percent of all merchandise exports. In some countries (for example, South Korea), we see that textiles and apparel have declined as a portion of all exports, while others such as China, Sri Lanka and Turkey have experienced substantial increases in textiles and apparel as a portion of all exports.

The reader should also keep in mind that these percentages are even higher when considered as a share of exports of manufactures.

Trade in Textiles

Patterns of Trade

The increased textile production capacity of the developing countries has accounted for significant shifts in trade. Textile exports both in the *value* and the **share** of trade from the developing countries grew at a faster rate than exports from the developed countries. Although the developed countries continue to lose in their combined share of world trade,

THE IMPACT OF EXCHANGE RATES

Many trade shifts for the textile complex may be attributed to the price effects caused by changes in exchange rates among currencies. Ghadar, Davidson, and Feigenoff (1987) noted that the consequences of strengthening the dollar on industries with low profit margins, such as textiles and apparel, are long term. When the U.S. dollar weakens against other currencies, this means that the dollar buys less abroad; therefore, U.S. consumers are more likely to buy domestic products. At the same time, foreign currencies are stronger against the dollar, resulting in greater purchasing power for buying U.S. products. Conversely, when the U.S. dollar strengthens against other currencies, the effects are reversed.

Figure 7–11 summarizes the influence of movements in the exchange rate for the U.S. dollar. Although this graphic summary may be an oversimplification, it is provided as an aid in remembering typical effects of exchange rate shifts related to discussions on textile trade.

Movements in exchange rates create price effects on foreign demand for U.S. textile and apparel exports. Thus, as the dollar weakens against another currency, an increase in U.S.

exports toward that currency generally occurs. Or, when the dollar strengthens against another currency, imports grow.

As an example, between 1979 and 1982, the U.S. dollar strengthened against other major currencies. As expected, exports declined and imports increased. U.S. textile imports increased 22 percent in 1981 over 1980, and exports fell by 0.4 percent (Toyne et al., 1984). Although the U.S. International Trade Commission (1983) found in a study on a limited number of products that many other factors were as important as changes in exchange rates in affecting trade, experts (e.g., Ghadar et al., 1987; Toyne et al., 1984) generally agree that where exchange rates shift in relation to one another, trade flows are affected significantly.

In terms of impact on a domestic industry, Ghadar et al. (1987) noted that because of the low profit margins in textiles and apparel, even small increases in the value of the dollar can foster the failure of firms that might have remained healthy otherwise. U.S. trade with some of the major East Asian textile- and apparel-producing countries may not be affected, however, because those currencies are tied to the value of the U.S. dollar.

FIGURE 7–11
Typical effects of exchange rate shifts.

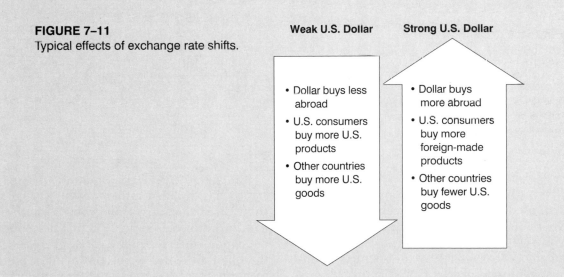

Weak U.S. Dollar

- Dollar buys less abroad
- U.S. consumers buy more U.S. products
- Other countries buy more U.S. goods

Strong U.S. Dollar

- Dollar buys more abroad
- U.S. consumers buy more foreign-made products
- Other countries buy fewer U.S. goods

TABLE 7–6

Share of Textiles and Apparel in Total Merchandise
Exports Selected Economies, 1973 and 1992[a]

| | Percentage Share in Total Merchandise Exports | |
	1973	1992
Bangladesh	50	66.9
Brazil	5.1	3.8
China[b]	4.5	29.8
Colombia	6.2	8.9
Hong Kong	41.4	27.0
domestic exports	na	40.4
re-exports	na	21.1
India	26.7	30.2
Indonesia	0.2	20.5
Japan	na	2.3
Korea (South)	36.8	19.5
Macau	77.1	77.2
Malaysia	1.5	6.0
Mauritius	3.1	51.1[c]
Mexico[b]	7.5	3.3
Morocco	6.8	24.5
Pakistan	48.9	69.4
Portugal	28.3	29.9
Singapore	7.6	4.6
Spain	5.8	3.6
Sri Lanka	0.9	55.0
Taiwan	28.9	14.4
Thailand	8.0	15.5
Tunisia	4.0	36.6[c]
Turkey	11.5	39.5
United States	2.2	2.2
Uruguay	11.3	15.1

[a]Or nearest year.

[b]Includes exports from processing zones.

[c]Apparel only; country exports virtually no textiles, if any.

na = not available

Source: Personal Communication with GATT staff, 1988, 1993, 1994.

they remained the major exporters of textiles. Although the developed countries still accounted for nearly 60 percent of all textile exports in 1992, this is a decline from 80 percent in 1955 and 70 percent in 1980. (Please remember that after 1990 the country groupings were modified by GATT, so this is not a precise comparison of the same countries.)

Although the developed countries' share of *exports* has declined rather steadily for more than three decades, this group's share of *imports* has increased. In 1955, the developed countries were recipients of slightly more than half all world exports in textiles; more recently, the developed countries imported about two-thirds of the worldwide output.

Origin and Destination for World Trade in Textiles

Figure 7–12 shows a summary of origin[6] and destination for world trade in textiles in 1992. Figure 7–12 shows the origin and destination by major country groupings as well as for the major trade regions. This figure permits us to focus on relative trade flows, with trade among major areas shown with arrows (which also show the direction and value of trade). The amount of trade occurring within each area is shown within the circle, with relative amounts represented roughly by the size of the circles.

The left portion of Figure 7–12 reveals that more than 40 percent of world trade in textiles

---

[6]*Origin* as used here may be where the goods are produced, or it may refer to the country from which the goods are shipped (Jackson, 1989).

was mutual trade among developed countries. That is, in 1992, total world exports were $116.8 billion; of that, $49.6 billion was developed country intra-trade (i.e., trade *among* developed countries). Similarly, intra-trade among developing countries is substantial. It is significant to note that the developing countries' textile exports were greater *to other developing countries* than to the developed countries ($28.2 billion compared to $17.1 billion).

Although the developing countries have increased in their importance as textile exporters, often trade reports give the impression that nearly all textile trade is flowing *from* the developing countries *to* the developed countries. These figures tell us that the developed countries are recipients of only a portion of the LDC exports. As we learned in Chapter 6, many of the more-advanced Asian nations have become proficient textile suppliers to other Asian countries in the region that do not

FIGURE 7–12
Textile trade flows, 1992 (billion dollars)

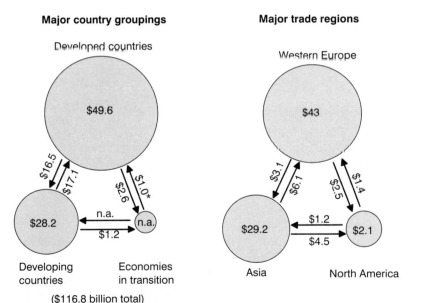

Major country groupings

Developed countries

$49.6

$16.5 $17.1 $2.6 $1.0*

$28.2   n.a.   n.a.

$1.2

Developing countries   Economies in transition

($116.8 billion total)

Major trade regions

Western Europe

$43

$3.1 $6.1 $2.5 $1.4

$29.2 $1.2 $2.1

$4.5

Asia   North America

*Data from the economies in transition are either unavailable or unreliable at this time. Estimates of exports to developed countries are based on developed country data.
Source: Based on data from personal communication with GATT economist, 1993, 1994.

have the technical or financial capabilities for complex textile production. In many cases, however, when intermediate textile inputs are shipped from one developing country to another, the second country may be producing finished products for export to markets in developed countries.

The right portion of Figure 7–12[7] reveals that the intra-trade in textiles for Western Europe is substantial ($43.1 billion of $116.8 for the year, or 37 percent of all world textile trade). In fact, West European countries account for the largest proportion of world

trade in textiles. Intratrade among Asia[8] is quite significant for reasons noted previously. North America is by far the weakest trading region in textiles, both in terms of intra-trade and exporting to other trade regions.

Leading Textile Exporters

Table 7–7 provides a more detailed listing of the top 15 textile exporting nations (using value data) over a period of time. Of particular significance in this table are the following:

---

[7]Ohmae (1985) refers to these regions as the *power trade triad*.

[8]The primary reason that Asia's textile trade is greater in the power trade triad than the figure for the developing countries in the left part of Figure 7–12 is that Japan is not a developing country. Therefore, Japan's textile trade adds to the total for Asia.

TABLE 7–7

Leading Exporters of Textiles, 1963, 1973, and 1992 (billion dollars)

	1963		*1973*		*1992*
Japan	0.92	Germany, Fed. Rep.	3.04	Germany	13.9
United Kingdom	0.71	Japan	2.45	Hong Kong[a]	11.0
France	0.63	France	1.69	domestic exports	2.2
India	0.54	Belgium-Luxembourg	1.69	re-exports	8.8
Germany, Fed. Rep.	0.53	Italy	1.53	Italy	10.2
				China[b]	8.6
Italy	0.53	United Kingdom	1.45	Korea, Rep.	8.2
Belgium-Luxembourg	0.51	Netherlands	1.29		
United States	0.49	United States	1.22	Taiwan	7.6
Netherlands	0.36	India	0.69	Japan	7.1
Switzerland	0.21	Hong Kong[a]	0.67	Belgium-Luxembourg	6.5
				France	6.3
Hong Kong[a]	0.14	Switzerland	0.64	United States	5.9
Austria	0.11	China	0.60		
China[b]	0.10	Taiwan	0.56	United Kingdom	4.3
Portugal	0.09	Austria	0.45	Pakistan	3.6
Pakistan	0.09	Pakistan	0.44	Netherlands	3.0
				Indonesia	2.8
				Switzerland	2.3
Above countries as a percentage of world exports	84.0		79.0		79.0

[a]Includes re-exports. Domestic exports were $0.11 billion in 1963, $0.46 billion in 1973, and $2.05 billion in 1987.
[b]Includes trade through processing zones.
Source: Personal communication with GATT economist, 1988, 1994.

(1) the shifts in relative importance of various countries over time, and (2) the large portion of all world textile exports that are provided by only 15 nations.

In 1963 and 1973, except for India and Hong Kong, the top ten textile exporters were developed countries. By 1992, only six of the top ten were the traditional developed countries (including Japan). For a period in the late 1980s, the United States was no longer among the top ten textile exporters, but by the early 1990s it was in tenth place, barely making the list. The growing importance of the major East Asian countries became quite apparent as Hong Kong (includes re-exports), China, and South Korea entered the top five, and Taiwan entered the top ten. All four of these newer East Asian suppliers had passed the United States, Japan, and the United Kingdom—the earlier textile powers.

Although the composition of the list of major textile exporting countries changed, the top 15 exporters command a fairly constant share of world textile exports, accounting for 79 percent in 1992, the same as in 1973 (personal communication with GATT economist, 1988, 1994).

Leading Textile Importers

In the past, as might be expected, the top importing nations were the major developed countries. As Table 7–8 reveals (using value

TABLE 7–8
Leading Importers of Textiles, 1963, 1973, and 1992 (in billions of dollars)

1963		*1973*		*1992*	
Germany, Fed. Rep	0.77	Germany, Fed. Rep.	2.74	Hong Kong	13.1
United States	0.68	United States	1.58	retained imports[c]	4.3
United Kingdom	0.41	France	1.40	Germany	12.4
Netherlands	0.07	United Kingdom	1.26	United States	8.2
USSR[a]	0.30	Japan	1.13	China[d]	7.0
				France	7.5
Canada[a]	0.27	Netherlands	1.10		
Australia	0.24	Belgium-Luxembourg	1.01	United Kingdom	6.9
Belgium-Luxembourg	0.23	Hong Kong[b]	0.94	Italy	5.6
Sweden	0.22	Italy	0.91	Japan	4.2
Hong Kong[b]	0.20	Canada[a]	0.78	Netherlands	3.6
				Belgium-Luxembourg	3.6
South Africa	0.20	USSR[a]	0.63		
France	0.19	Australia	0.62	Korea, Rep.	2.6
Italy	0.15	Sweden	0.51	Spain	2.5
Denmark	0.15	Switzerland	0.50	Canada[a]	2.5
Switzerland	0.15	Austria	0.48	Singapore	2.0
				retained imports[c]	1.1
				Portugal	2.0
Above countries as a percentage of world imports.	64.0		67.0		60.8

[a]Imports f.o.b.

[b]Includes imports for re-export. Re-exports amounted to $0.025 billion in 1963, $0.210 billion in 1973, and $3.6 billion in 1987.

[c]Retained imports are defined as imports less re-exports. The 1992 data reflect a newer approach for separating out re-exports.

[d]Includes trade through processing zones.

Source: Personal communication with GATT economist, 1988, 1994.

data), Germany (the former West Germany) and the United States were consistently the major importers; this continued through the late 1980s. However, by 1992, Hong Kong had become the leading textile importer, primarily because of textiles being imported for re-exporting purposes.

Several observations are helpful in understanding the broad patterns. First, 9 of the top 15 leading textile importing nations in 1992 were also among the group in 1963; however, relative rankings changed. Although Australia, Sweden, South Africa, and Denmark were among the top textile importing nations in 1963, they are no longer in the group. By 1973, Japan and Austria were newcomers among the top 15 textile importing nations, and, by 1992, Hong Kong (mostly from re-exports), China (includes imports through processing zones), South Korea, Spain, and Portugal were among the group. The top 15 importing countries accounted for a smaller portion of total world textile imports, going from 67 percent in 1973 to 60.8 percent in 1992 (personal communication with GATT economist, 1988, 1994).

Japan's presence on the 1973 list of leading textile *importers* is a point of interest. We recall from earlier discussion that Japan had been considered by the developed countries as the major threat as a textile *exporting* nation in the 1950s and 1960s.

China's recent presence among the top importing nations reflects the more active status of the textile complex in that country and its reliance on other countries for certain fibers and other basic textile inputs. A good portion of China's textile imports were manufactured fibers because of its limited high-technology production facilities until recently. This is a temporary stage for China, however, as its textile industry moves toward a more advanced and self-sufficient level in its development. The country is attempting to move toward self-sufficiency in manufactured fiber production. The other major source of China's

imports is through processing zones such as Shenzhen, outside Hong Kong, where cut garments are sent for assembly and other production operations (Cut garments are counted as *textile imports* for China in that stage).

Hong Kong was the largest textile importer in 1992; however, about two-thirds of these textile imports were for re-export. Additionally, because of limited space and environmental concerns, Hong Kong has very limited textile production to support the extensive apparel industry; therefore, textiles from elsewhere are a necessity.

A review of the major textile importer list, particularly in relation to the major exporter list, provides an interesting opportunity to reflect on both the application of economic (trade) theory and the stages of development for the textile complex within various countries. Questions to consider are: (1) why are some countries both major exporters and major importers? and (2) why do some countries appear on one list but not the other? (For example, why is Canada a major importer but not a major exporter?)

Trade in Apparel

Patterns of Trade

Although certain global apparel trade patterns were similar to those for textiles, significant differences also occurred. The labor-intensive characteristics of apparel, along with the minimal technology and capital requirements for its production, fostered expanded apparel trade in ways that differed from textile trade. In reviewing Table 7–4, we see that apparel was a greater share of total worldwide exports (both merchandise and manufactures) than textiles. The value of total apparel trade (exports) was greater than that for textiles ($131 billion compared to $117 billion).

When we reviewed the relative importance of the major country groupings for textile exports for the postwar period, we saw a steady decline in the developed countries' share of world exports and a marked increase in the developing countries' share. A similar pattern occurred for apparel trade, except that *the shift toward the developing nations was even more dramatic.*

The export shifts favoring the developing countries reflected those nations' dependency on the apparel sector for export earnings and the ability of those countries to produce apparel at attractive prices for the global market, principally because of lower wages. Figure 7–13 illustrates the export orientation of the developing countries.

The developing countries' share of world exports increased from about 10 percent in 1955 to 58 percent in 1992. In contrast, the developed countries accounted for 71 percent

FIGURE 7–13
A number of developing countries have actively promoted their textile and apparel products in the global market. Bangladesh, for example, has sponsored a textile and apparel exposition to attract buyers to see the country's products. This advertisement appeared in various trade publications.

Source: Reprinted courtesy of Bangladesh Garment Manufacturers and Exporters Association.

of world apparel trade in 1955 and 39 percent in 1992 (GATT, *International Trade*, various years; personal communication with GATT staff, 1988, 1993, 1994). The reader is reminded again that these major groupings are not exactly comparable because of GATT's new data system in 1990.

Another global shift for apparel occurred in the postwar period. The developed countries accounted for a growing percentage share of apparel imports, and the developing nations represented a declining share. As the exports from developing countries grew rather dramatically during this period, the developed countries became increasingly important as the recipients of those goods.

Origin and Destination for World Trade in Apparel

Figure 7–14 shows a summary of origin and destination for world trade in apparel in 1992. The origin and destination are shown by major country groupings as well as for the major trade triad.

The left side of Figure 7–14 reveals that mutual trade among developed countries was also important in apparel, accounting for nearly 34 percent of the total world trade. The figure also supports the assertion that developed countries were by far the major recipients of apparel in global trade. In 1992, the developed countries purchased more than 87 percent of all world exports in apparel—of which, nearly 39 percent came from within the developed countries, and nearly 58 percent came from the developing areas.

Whereas trade among developing countries is important for textiles (24 percent of total developing country textile exports), trade among these countries is rather limited for apparel (about 10 percent of their total apparel exports). As Figure 7–14 shows, the developing countries concentrate on exporting to the developed countries, where demand is greatest.

The right portion of Figure 7–14 reveals that two regions account for more than three-fourths of world apparel exports: (1) Western Europe and (2) the Asian suppliers. A sizeable

FIGURE 7–14
Apparel trade flows, 1992 (billion dollars)

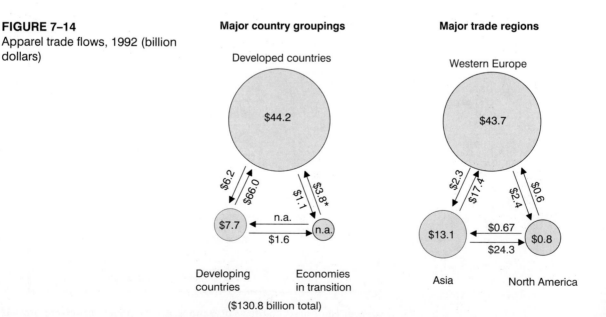

Major country groupings

Developed countries

$44.2

$6.2 $66.0 $1.1 $3.8*

$7.7   n.a.   n.a.

$1.6

Developing countries   Economies in transition

($130.8 billion total)

Major trade regions

Western Europe

$43.7

$2.3 $17.4 $2.4 $0.6

$13.1 $0.67 $0.8

$24.3

Asia   North America

Source: Personal communication with GATT staff, 1988, 1994.

portion of the apparel trade for Western Europe came from within the region. (U.S. readers may wish to think of this as somewhat similar to trade among the U.S. states, particularly as Western Europe becomes more of an integrated trade area). In particular, exports from Greece, Turkey, and Portugal expanded rapidly. In some respects, these latter countries had many of the characteristics of the developing countries, compared to their West European neighbors. As countries with many of the qualities of less-developed areas, these nations relied heavily on apparel production for further economic development. Therefore, apparel production with an export orientation toward nearby markets represented a logical strategy for those countries. In some respects, the shifts of apparel production to lower-wage European countries resembles the earlier shift of the industry from the northern United States to the South to find a more receptive workforce and lower wages (due in part to the general absence of labor unions).

By far, the major growth for apparel exports has been from the Asian region. Marked increases in the share of apparel exports have come from the four main East Asian suppliers: China, Hong Kong, South Korea, and Taiwan. Japan is not a major exporter of apparel. Figure 7 14 shows that major markets for Asian apparel are Western Europe and North America, with the latter as the single most important market.

Similar to the situation for textiles, North America is by far the weakest player for apparel exports among the major trade regions. North America has not accounted for a significant share of the supply of apparel for the global market, even for trade within North America. Among the factors accounting for the limited apparel exporting from North America are: (1) the relative disadvantages in labor costs compared to other regions (although the same could be said for Western Europe; however, shipping costs for Western

Europe's intra-trade would be to that region's advantage); (2) the strength of the dollar for several years, which made U.S. exporting more difficult to some areas such as Western Europe; and (3) the serious lack of an export orientation on the part of most of the U.S. apparel industry.

Apparel import increases to North America have been most dramatic from Asian suppliers. At times in the 1980s, however, apparel imports from Western Europe increased in North America more rapidly than imports from other regions. This may be attributed to (1) the lack of restrictions on products from Western Europe compared to rather restrictive limits on products from the East Asian and many other supplier countries (through an informal **gentlemen's agreement**, the United States and the EU do not place import restrictions on each other's textile/apparel goods), and (2) the exchange rate advantage at times on the part of the West European countries.

Leading Apparel Exporters

Table 7–9 provides a more detailed listing of the top 15 apparel exporting nations (using value data) over a period of time. As we review the shifts among producer nations, the reader may wish to reflect on the stages of development discussed in previous chapters to help understand the changing positions of countries involved in apparel trade.

Between 1963 and 1992, the number of developed countries in the top 15 exporters went from 11 to 7. (When Portugal and Greece joined the EC (now the EU), they were reclassified as developed countries.)

Although the number of developed countries dropped, Italy and Germany (now unified Germany, but earlier only West Germany) were in the top 5 throughout the period. The ranking of the United States among the top apparel exporters continued to drop. At times in the late 1980s, the United States was not among the leading 15 apparel exporting countries, but, as the 1992 listing indicates, the

TABLE 7–9
Leading Exporters of Apparel, 1963, 1973, and 1992 (in billions of dollars)

	1963		*1973*		*1992*
Italy	0.34	Hong Kong[a]	1.42	Hong Kong[a]	20.1
Hong Kong[a]	0.24	Italy	1.30	domestic exports	10.0
Japan	0.21	France	1.04	re-exports	10.1
France	0.20	Germany, Fed. Rep.	0.91	China[b]	16.7
Germany, Fed. Rep.	0.15	Korea, Rep. of	0.75	Italy	12.2
				Germany	8.4
United Kingdom	0.11	Taiwan	0.71	Korea, Rep.	6.8
Belgium-Luxembourg	0.10	Belgium-Luxembourg	0.57		
United States	0.09	United Kingdom	0.44	France	5.3
Netherlands	0.07	Netherlands	0.41	United States	4.2
Switzerland	0.04	Japan	0.37	Turkey	4.2
				Taiwan	4.1
Austria	0.04	United States	0.29	Portugal	4.0
Yugoslavia	0.02	Poland	0.28		
Portugal	0.01	Romania	0.25	Thailand	3.8
Canada	0.01	Finland	0.21	United Kingdom	3.7
Taiwan	0.01	China	0.20	Indonesia	3.2
				India	3.1
				Netherlands	2.7
Above countries as a percentage of world exports	75.0		73.0		70.5

[a]Includes re-exports. Domestic exports were $0.24 billion in 1963; $1.39 billion in 1973; and $8.36 billion in 1987.
[b]Includes trade through processing zones.

Source: Personal communication with GATT economist, 1988, 1994.

nation regained a position among the group. Japan was the third highest exporter in 1963 but dropped to ninth place in 1973; by the late 1980s, Japan was no longer among the top 15 exporters of apparel. To a great extent, Japan's decline as a major apparel exporter was intentional. Japanese policy makers encouraged manufacturers to de-emphasize this segment of the textile complex and focus on areas that took greater advantage of the nation's technological capabilities.

On the other hand, the major East Asian countries continued to increase their relative rankings (excluding Japan). Of these, China moved up most rapidly. In 1963, China was not among the top 15 suppliers but, by 1992, was the second largest apparel exporter. If Hong Kong's re-exports were excluded, China would replace Hong Kong as the top apparel exporter. Since a large portion of Hong Kong's apparel exports are from China, the latter may be easily counted as the leading apparel exporting nation in the world. Major apparel export growth in Turkey, Portugal, Thailand, Indonesia, and India boosted these countries to the list of top exporting nations. For all these nations, apparel accounted for a growing and significant share in each respective nation's total merchandise exports.

In addition to the changing composition of the group of top 15 apparel exporters, the share of worldwide apparel exports accounted for by this group has decreased. The top 15 apparel exporters accounted for 75 percent of world exports in 1963, but the top 15 represented 70.5 percent in 1992. This decline reflects the growing number of countries involved in apparel production, particularly the entry of many newly developing countries in recent years (personal communication with GATT economist, 1988, 1993, 1994).

Leading Apparel Importers

Table 7–10 provides a summary of the top 15 apparel importing nations (using value data) from 1963 to 1992.

Several observations from the table are useful in understanding broad apparel trade patterns. First, all the major importers are developed countries, except for Hong Kong, whose imports are primarily for re-export. Second, 13 of the top 15 importers for 1992 were also among the top 15 in 1973, although the relative rankings shifted. Denmark was no longer among the top group, and the former USSR no longer exists. Hong Kong was a newcomer, due to imports for re-export.

The top 15 countries absorbed a large portion of all world apparel exports, although the concentration among the top 15 is less than in previous years shown. The most dramatic change was in the increased portion of world apparel exports absorbed by the United States and Germany, particularly the United States. In 1992, the United States imported 28 percent of all world apparel exports, compared to only 17 percent in 1973. The United States and Germany together accounted for more than 49 percent of total world imports of clothing (personal communication with GATT economist, 1988, 1993, 1994).

TABLE 7–10

Leading Importers of Apparel, 1963, 1973, and 1992 (billion dollars)

	1963		*1973*		*1992*
USSR[a]	0.52	Germany, Fed. Rep.	2.54	United States	33.0
United States	0.39	United States	2.17	Germany	24.8
Germany, Fed. Rep.	0.26	USSR[a]	1.06	Japan	11.2
United Kingdom	0.18	Netherlands	0.86	Hong Kong	10.3
Netherlands	0.15	United Kingdom	0.82	retained imports[b]	0.3
				France	9.8
Switzerland	0.09	France	0.59		
Sweden	0.09	Japan	0.57	United Kingdom	7.9
France	0.07	Belgium-Luxembourg	0.56	Netherlands	5.8
Belgium-Luxembourg	0.07	Switzerland	0.50	Italy	4.3
Canada[a]	0.06	Sweden	0.40	Belgium-Luxembourg	4.2
				Switzerland	3.6
Norway	0.05	Canada[a]	0.33		
Denmark	0.03	Norway	0.20	Spain	3.2
Singapore	0.03	Austria	0.20	Austria	2.6
Italy	0.03	Italy	0.19	Sweden	2.6
South Africa	0.02	Denmark	0.18	Canada[a]	2.4
				Norway	1.4
Above countries as a percentage of world imports	92.0		89.0		85.1

[a]Imports f.o.b.

[b]Retained imports are defined as imports less re-exports.

Source: Personal Communication with GATT economist, 1988, 1993, 1994.

For all of the top 15 apparel importers (except for Hong Kong, which represents a different situation), the shares of apparel in each country's total merchandise imports increased in *every* case.

A review of the major apparel importer list, particularly in relation to the major apparel exporter list plus the similar rankings for textiles, provides additional opportunities to reflect on the application of economic theory and stages of development for the textile complex within various countries. For example, what characteristics distinguish the textile exporters from the apparel exporters? In general, how do apparel exporters differ from apparel importers? Why are most of the major apparel importers developed countries?

Influences on Trade

A number of factors influence trade in general and, therefore, also affect textile and apparel trade. These factors affect what countries produce, what they trade, and what they seek in exchange when they trade. Although some of the influences on trade have been mentioned in this chapter, a summary may be helpful at this point.

General Economic Conditions

Although positive economic growth since World War II fostered trade, the postwar decades were also marked by periods of decline and expansion of trade. When economic conditions are booming, trade often grows more rapidly than production. In a sluggish economy, however, trade increases at a rate lower than production. Moreover, changes in global prosperity affect dramatically the type of products traded and their relative importance in trade. Increased production in a country increases employment; thus the purchasing power of the population increases. As noted in examples in this chapter, when the economies of the major textile/apparel markets slowed, consumption decrease caused a ripple effect that led to reduced production, employment, and trade for textiles and apparel globally.

Stages of Economic Development

The stages of development for the various economies of the world range from the poorest, who are at beginning stages, to the most affluent, whose populations enjoy sophisticated products from around the world. Nations at early stages are limited in what they can sell to the rest of the world to gain foreign exchange. These developing countries need the means of gaining foreign exchange so they can buy advanced equipment and other technology not available in their own countries but which are necessary to move forward with their aspirations to become more industrialized. On the other hand, in the mature economies, consumers have substantial purchasing power and satisfy their needs with products from many countries. These products are from both the industrialized nations and the developing countries; therefore, worldwide trade occurs.

Trade patterns shift over time as certain economies mature and newer ones emerge. Some countries, such as Japan and Germany, made conscious decisions to de-emphasize certain labor-intensive portions of the textile complex and to give greater priority to more technologically advanced production. As a result of the development and maturing of the economies of many countries, trade shifts have been quite apparent for the global textile and apparel industries. A number of the developed countries that led the Industrial Revolution—with the textile industry in the forefront—experienced severe declines in their domestic textile/apparel industries. At the time, producers in a number of developing countries became significant competitors.

Types of Economy

Market-directed economies permit individual firms to participate in world trade in a variety of arrangements that satisfy consumer demand and render a profit to the firms involved in importing or exporting. Although government policies often influence trade, a market-directed economy permits participation in world trade according to market mechanisms in ways similar to the participation in domestic markets. *Centrally planned economies*, on the other hand, monitor trade according to government goals. Both exporting and importing are controlled by central sources rather than by consumer demand or the motivation for profit. Many of the centrally planned economies of Eastern Europe have shifted toward market-directed economies, and look to the textile complex in their countries for economic growth. China is an example of a textile- and apparel-producing country with a centrally planned economy that embraces many aspects of a market-driven economy. North Korea, in contrast, is clearly centrally controlled.

Differences in Natural Resources

The earth's resources are not evenly distributed, and, as a result, trade is the means by which those who do not have all they want or need can secure resources from those willing to sell. In much of the under-developed world, human energy (labor) is one of the most abundant resources; and usually, because of its abundance, it is inexpensive. When textile and apparel goods are produced with this abundant resource, products therefore are much less expensive than those supplied by countries where human input is more costly. Other natural resources affecting textile and apparel trade include land for natural fiber production, climates for growing fibers such as cotton, and petroleum and chemicals for manufactured fiber production. As we recall from Adam Smith's theory of absolute advantage, these resources represent a *natural*, as opposed to an *acquired*, advantage in trade.

Worldwide distribution of natural resources may become involved in textile and apparel trade in another way. Since many of the developed countries are short on certain raw materials vital to their economies or needed for the manufacture of goods, the industrialized countries are dependent upon many developing countries to supply these needs. As developed countries apply restrictions on textile and apparel products from the developing areas, the industrialized countries cannot forget their own dependency upon their LDC trading partners to supply certain needs.

Technology

Technological changes both in the products available and the processes by which they are produced affect the relative positions of countries in global trade. Demand for new products and for the technology to produce those products provides a ready incentive for trade. In some cases, the new technology provides production efficiencies that give a competitive advantage over prior processes in both price and response time. A major textile development of recent decades was the refinement and mass production of manufactured fibers— a development that revolutionized global textile trade. Table 7–11 illustrates the impact of manufactured fiber production on the global textile market. Moreover, as the table shows, the growth of manufactured fibers occurred over a relatively short period of time.

Manufactured fiber production was a technological advancement that clearly favored the developed countries with the expertise and capital to nurture this segment. In contrast, up to that time countries had been dependent upon natural resources for fiber production. As in the case of most technological developments, manufactured fiber production originated in the industrialized (richer) nations, and few developing countries

TABLE 7–11
World Fiber Production, 1900–1992 (millions of metric tons)

| | Natural Fibers | | Manufactured Fibers | |
| | | | Artificial (Cellulosic) Fibers | Synthetic (Noncellulosic) Fibers |
Year	Cotton	Wool		
1900	3,162	730		
1950	6,647	1,057	1,608	69
1960	10,113	1,463	2,656	702
1970	11,784	1,659	3,579	4,818
1973	13,738	1,497	3,856	7,767
1980	14,040	1,599	3,557	10,625
1986	15,196	1,701	3,276	13,765
1992	18,115	1,676	2,620	17,213

Source: Personal communication with Comité International de la Rayonne et des Fibres Synthétiques, 1987, 1994.

had the means to expand into this production. Entry into manufactured fiber production is a significant accomplishment for a nation as its textile complex moves through the various stages of development. Overall, however, availability of manufactured fiber production technology had a profound impact on global textile trade.

Traditions of Specialization

Some countries established traditions of specialization and continue to foster skills and talents that enable them to produce distinctive goods in demand by persons in other parts of the world. Although perhaps originally tied to resource endowments, many of these products require expertise that is difficult to duplicate to produce the distinctive items (an *acquired* advantage rather than a *natural* advantage). Therefore, countries or regions with these traditions of specialization engage in trade of the products valued by individuals in other parts of the world. Examples of these include stylish, high-quality Italian shoes; British woolen goods; high-fashion women's clothing from Paris; and distinctive batik fabrics from Indonesia.

The trade advantages acquired through traditions of specialization are rarely permanent. Shifts in trade patterns occur for products of this type as readily as other trade shifts occur. Producers of these products must retain the distinctive product qualities and yet respond to global market changes, knowing that other suppliers can replace them. For example, Japan's emphasis on quality and high fashion have led some sources to predict that Japan (or some other Asian center) may replace Paris eventually as the center of high fashion.

Political Objectives

Both internal and external political concerns can influence dramatically the trade for a country. Often governmental influence on trade cannot be justified by economic reasoning. Because of the importance of textile and apparel production in providing employment, political objectives influence trade.

Internally, pressure from domestic industries often influences governments to raise barriers to imported goods. An argument often used to seek protection from imports is that essential domestic industries must be protected during peacetime so that the country will not be dependent upon foreign sources in case of war. (See "Minimum Viable Production" in Chapter 12.) In the United States, for example, industry sources have argued the need for a healthy textile and apparel industry to produce uniforms, parachutes, and other textile-related defense items.

Externally (that is, beyond the boundaries of one's country), political concerns may influence trade in a variety of ways. Political allies may receive more favorable trade agreements than countries with fewer advantages (bargaining chips) to offer. As an example, the United States and Western Europe do not impose quotas on textile and apparel products

---

                 ## POLITICS AND TEXTILE/APPAREL TRADE

Political objectives have frequently influenced U.S. textile and apparel trade policies. Examples are:

- *South Africa.* In 1986, the United States imposed trade sanctions on South Africa's products because of that country's apartheid policies (a government policy that mandates racial discrimination). Although the U.S. House of Representatives had *already* voted to impose trade sanctions that would bar imports from South Africa, U.S. textile negotiators finalized a textile agreement with South Africa to permit an annual 4 percent increase in textile and apparel products in U.S. markets. Members of Congress were outraged. After an affirmative Senate vote for the sanctions, all imports—including textiles and apparel—were barred from U.S. markets. Eventually, after South Africa dismantled its apartheid policies, trade was resumed.
- *Vietnam.* In the early 1990s, as firms from other countries descended on Vietnam to take advantage of the booming growth, the low wages, and the excellent labor force, U.S. firms were not among them because of trade sanctions. After the Vietnam war and the communist takeover, the United States ended trade relations with the nation. By the early 1990s, many U.S. investors pressed the government to lift the sanctions so they might also do business in Vietnam. Trade sanctions were lifted in early 1994.
- *Myanmar (formerly Burma).* In 1991, the United States did not renew its textile bilateral agreement with Myanmar, in retaliation for Myanmar's failure to reduce opium production and ease political repression ("U.S. Textile," 1991).
- *Egypt.* In 1994, as U.S. government sources monitored import shipments, the volume of men's and boys' woven shirts coming from Egypt appeared to pose a risk of disrupting the U.S. market (i.e., a threat to U.S. producers). Through a "consultation call," a trade policy mechanism used to handle cases of this type, the U.S. government asked for a negotiation with the Egyptian government. However, the matter occurred just as Secretary of Commerce Ron Brown had been in Egypt—a visit perceived by the Egyptians as a goodwill visit to foster trade between the two countries. Because of the timing, the issue of men's and boys' woven shirts escalated to a problem to be handled at top government levels. Because of the pending Middle East peace process and Egypt's strategic role as a U.S. ally in the region, the matter required high-level and delicate diplomacy. In the end, Egypt was given a quota that permitted shipment of 870,000 dozen men's and boys' woven shirts per year—less than the Egyptians wanted and more than the United States would have permitted under other circumstances. The new quota level was generous, given the sensitivity of the shirt category and in fairness to other trading partners (confidential conversation with U.S. government source, May 1994).

traded with one another (that is, the gentlemen's agreement) although both have extensive restrictions on products from many developing countries. As might be expected, this is a sensitive point to the LDCs, whose products are subject to restrictions in both markets. The comparable economies and similar wage structures are given as reasons to justify this; however, favorable treatment of political allies appears to be an important issue as well.

Shifts in Exchange Rates

Although we considered earlier the effects of changes in exchange rates, we are reminded here that trade is influenced significantly by these changes.

SUMMARY OF GLOBAL TEXTILE/APPAREL ACTIVITY

As we reflect on the patterns for global textile and apparel production, employment, and trade covered in this chapter, we find that one common pattern prevails. These textile/apparel activities have shifted increasingly to favor the developing countries. Although the nature of the shifts and the magnitude of the shifts vary, in general the developing countries have accounted for a growing share of textile and apparel production, employment, and trade, while the developed countries account for a declining share. As many of the more advanced Asian countries have

increasing incomes—and, in some cases, wealth—consumption has increased markedly. Figure 7–15 depicts the shift in activity from the developed countries to the developing areas.

SUMMARY

In this chapter, we have examined global trends in textile and apparel production, employment, consumption, and trade. For each of these areas, we have seen rather distinct trends, and, in most cases, global shifts in these activities.

New countries entered the global textile/apparel markets in the 1950s and 1960s, and production maintained a healthy growth rate between 1953 and 1973. Production slowed in all the main areas after 1973 because of recessionary effects from the oil price hike; however, textile production growth rates in the developing areas far outpaced those in the developed countries. The developing countries increased substantially their *share* of global production.

Similarly, total worldwide apparel production increased at a slow rate after 1973. Global sites for apparel production changed far more dramatically than was true for textile production. Apparel production in the developed countries experienced almost no growth and, in fact, had a negative growth rate in the 1980s. By contrast, apparel production in the developing areas continued to increase at a

FIGURE 7–15
Global textile/apparel activity. Note that textile trade and apparel trade indicate greater participation in trade, as well as growing receipt of products by developing countries.

Developed countries

Textile production
Apparel production
Textile employment
Apparel employment
Textile trade
Apparel trade

Developing countries

healthy pace, with the developing Asian countries representing a large portion of the growth.

Although employment data do not reflect large numbers of undocumented workers, the global textile complex provides one of the largest sources of manufacturing jobs. Textile employment began declining even in the 1950s in the developed countries and continued to have a negative growth rate through the present. The developing areas increased employment between 1953 and 1987.

Annual growth rate of employment in apparel declined also in the developed countries during this period. Apparel employment, perhaps more than any other area of activity for the global textile complex, reflects the shifts toward the developing countries. Wage differences are seen as the key factor in the global shifts of both textile and apparel production and employment.

Global textile/apparel consumption patterns have a widespread impact on both production and employment trends. Most segments of the textile complex are affected by consumption patterns, as are many countries involved in this globalized sector. Consumption trends may be examined by two types of measures: (1) fiber consumption data and (2) consumer expenditure data. These use two different types of data, which are complementary in considering textile and apparel consumption. One measures fiber demand at one end of the textile chain and demand for final textile products at the other.

Fiber consumption data show that the total (based on fiber availability) consumed by the developing countries is about two-thirds the amount consumed in the developed countries. Although the developing countries have modest per capita consumption levels, the total consumption is relatively high because the population in this group of nations accounts for a large share of the world's inhabitants.

Worldwide recessionary conditions affected consumption both in the developed and the developing countries. Because of the large per capita fiber consumption patterns in the major developed country markets compared to the rest of the world, a decline in consumption in those countries has a significant impact on many exporting nations. In addition, changes in world population and income levels play an important role in global consumption patterns.

Consumer expenditure data provide another means of studying consumption patterns. These data reflect demand for final textile products and clothing. Although all consumer expenditures in major developed countries slowed from 1973–1992 compared to 1963–1973, clothing expenditures (with the exception of the United States) slowed even more. This decline seriously affected the global textile complex.

Stagnant consumption patterns occurred at a difficult time in the broader development of the global textile complex. At the same time that consumption slowed, a growing number of producer nations entered the global market, adding to an existing problem of overcapacity.

And, finally, we examined trade patterns in this chapter. As the developing nations expanded textile and apparel production, most looked to exports as a means of growth. In contrast to the industrialized countries where manufacturers focused primarily upon home markets, the LDCs concentrated on exports. Consequently, the volume of global textile and apparel trade has expanded greatly, and producers in both the developed nations and the developing areas compete for the same key markets—those in the more affluent industrialized nations. Labor cost advantages in the LDCs favor production and, therefore, trade for the developing countries.

Textiles and apparel ranked eleventh and tenth among major product groups as a share of world merchandise trade in 1992. Textile exports from the developing countries grew at a faster rate than exports from the developed countries. Although the developed countries still account for nearly 60 percent of all textile exports, this group's share has continued to decline while the share from the developing areas increased. Major East Asian suppliers accounted for substantial growth for the latter group.

Western Europe and the United States have been major recipients of textile imports; however, some of the East Asian nations grew increasingly important as textile importers. A good portion of the Asian increase appears to have been products destined for re-export.

Overall, about 40 percent of world trade in textiles was mutual trade among developed countries; 37 percent was intra-EU trade. The developing countries were the destination for growing imports of the textile exports from other developing nations.

Patterns for apparel trade were similar to those for textile trade except that apparel's shift toward the developing nations was even more dramatic. This shift reflects the LDCs' dependency on apparel production for export earnings (and the trend for core firms to take advantage of low-wage periphery labor costs). As the apparel exports from the developing countries grew from the 1970s to the present, the developed countries became increasingly important as the recipients of those goods.

Western Europe and the four main East Asian suppliers accounted for a large portion of all apparel exports; however, a sizeable portion of Europe's exports were directed to countries within the region. The main East Asian suppliers grew in importance as suppliers. In 1992, the United States and Germany were the leading apparel importers, providing a market for 49 percent of all world apparel exports.

Mutual trade among the developed countries accounted for 34 percent of the total world trade for apparel. The developed countries received more than 85 percent of all world apparel exports in 1992; of their total apparel imports, 44 percent came from within the developed countries.

A number of factors influence textile and apparel trade. These include general economic conditions, stages of economic development for countries or regions, types of economy, differences in natural resources, technology, traditions of specialization, political objectives, and shifts in exchange rates.

GLOSSARY

Consumer expenditure data refers to final demand for apparel and other textile products at the end of the textile chain.

Exchange rates refers to the number of units (i.e., the "price") of one currency required to secure one unit of a currency for another country.

Exports, imports. For customs purposes, exports and imports are defined as movement of goods across customs frontiers. Customs data are generally used by governments in recording merchandise trade. Data in this chapter are customs data.

Fiber consumption or *per capita fiber consumption* refers to the average number of pounds (or other measures of weight) of fiber consumed per individual on an annual basis. Per capita fiber consumption is usually calculated for a defined area—a country, a region, or the world.

F.O.B. refers to *free on board.* This means that the exporter or seller has included in the price of the goods the transportation to port as well as the handling and loading aboard the vessel.

Free trade zone (also called free zone, free port, or foreign trade zone) is an area within a country where goods can be imported, stored, and/or processed without being subject to customs duties and taxes.

Gentlemen's agreement was an informal agreement between U.S. and EU textile trade officials that they would not impose restraints on each other's textile/apparel products.

Index for production, employment, or other economic activity is often used to avoid problems of incompatible data gathered from numerous sources. In effect, each region is compared with itself over time.

Manufactures are manufactured goods that are referred to by this term to distinguish them in the economic analysis of trade flows as *one* of the categories of merchandise trade.

Merchandise trade refers to trade in all goods that add to or subtract from the material resources of a country as a result of their movement into or out of the country. In the economic analysis of trade flows, merchandise trade is often divided into broad product groups. The main ones are agriculture, mining, and **manufactures**. Textiles and apparel are included in the manufactures group.

Per capita fiber consumption is the average volume (pounds, kilograms, and so on) of fiber consumed per individual for a given time period, usually per year.

Productivity refers to the output produced per unit of input. This frequently refers to labor productivity, measured by output per hour worked.

Share of global production, employment, or consumption refers to a nation's or area's portion of the total activity (as we use it here, of *global* activity). This is not the *absolute level* of that activity. For example, an area's absolute level may increase while the share decreases.

Textile consumption has been defined as "The sum of a region's production and its net trade (imports minus exports) is the amount of a commodity that a region consumes, ignoring stocks held in inventory. Consumption on a per capita basis is both a measure of welfare of the consumers of a region and a measure of the potential markets from the firm's point of view" (Toyne et al., 1984 p. 62).

SUGGESTED READINGS

Anson, R., & Simpson, P. (1988). *World textile trade and production trends.* Special Report No. 1108. London: The Economist Intelligence Unit.
A summary of global production and trade; major regions are considered.

Anson, R., & Simpson, P. (1994, January). World textile trade and production trends. *Textile Outlook International*, pp. 9–51.
An overview of textile production and trade through 1992.

COMITEXTIL bulletin (bimonthly). Brussels: Author.
This publication addresses trade issues relevant to the textile industry in the European Union. Features in the Bulletin often address global textile and apparel production, consumption, and trade issues.

Ford, J. (1986). World trade in textiles. *Textiles, 15*(3), 72–77.
An overview of global textile trade.

GATT (annual). *GATT International Trade (annual)*. Geneva, Switzerland: Author.
This annual publication provides useful information on all global trade and includes sections on textile and apparel trade.

Ghadar, F., Davidson, W., & Feigenoff, C. (1987). U.S. *industrial competitiveness: The case of the textile and apparel industries.* Lexington, MA: Lexington Books.
Although this book focuses primarily on the U.S. textile and apparel industries, it presents the domestic industries in a global context.

International Textile Manufacturers Federation. (1993). *Overcapacity—the global challenge.* Vol. 16. Zurich: Author.

Proceedings from the annual ITMF meeting in which overcapacity for global textile production was addressed.

Toyne, B., Arpan, J., Barnett, A., Ricks, D, & Shimp, T. (1984). *The global textile industry.* London: George Allen & Unwin.
A study of major trends affecting international competition in the textile mill products industry.

United States International Trade Commission (1983, September). *The effect of changes in the value of the U.S. dollar on trade in selected commodities.* Washington, DC: Author.
A study of the impact of changes in exchange rates on trade.

United States International Trade Commission (1985). *Emerging textile-exporting countries.* (USITC Publication 1716). Washington, DC: Author.
A study of the textile-exporting nations expected to become increasingly important in global textile/apparel trade.

IV

The U.S. Textile Complex in the Global Economy

 Part IV gives an overview of the U.S. textile and apparel sectors and presents the domestic industry within the broader international context. More specifically, the objectives of Chapters 8 and 9 are (1) to provide a profile of the U.S. textile and apparel industries, (2) to show the role of the textile and apparel sectors as significant contributors to the U.S. economy, and (3) to convey an understanding of the position of the U.S. textile and apparel sectors within the broader global setting.

Chapter 8 provides an overview of the total U.S. textile complex and presents information common to various segments of the complex. Chapter 9 presents an overview of the U.S. textile and apparel sectors. Chapter 9 includes sections on production, employment, markets, and trade for both sectors. An examination of these various areas is intended to help the reader understand these unique industries, their role in the domestic economy, and factors that affect their international competitiveness. Emphasis is on an economic and performance profile rather than on providing technical details of production.

Although this section focuses primarily on the U.S. textile complex, efforts are made whenever possible to relate the position of the U.S. industries to the broader global perspective. Because of today's interlinking global economy and particularly because of the position of the textile complex in that global economy, no country's textile and apparel industries can be considered in isolation. Since the U.S. textile complex has been shaped profoundly by international market forces, this section is intended to convey a profile of the U.S. domestic sectors—sectors that are part of a larger global picture.

8

An Overview of the U.S. Textile Complex

INTRODUCTION

The textile complex can claim the longest history of any industrial sector in the United States. Moreover, the textile complex's role as a vital segment of the American economy has continued since the early days of cottage industries and mill villages. As a long-established basic industry, the textile complex has contributed immeasurably to the economic development of the United States. The industry has been the means by which untold numbers of families and individuals have sustained themselves with the basic necessities of life. Moreover, employment in the textile complex permitted many to enter the mainstream of American life that went beyond a subsistence level. As a source of employment for many generations of workers engaged in their first industrial jobs, workers have been able to improve their living conditions, send children to college, and enjoy at least a degree of the prosperity that characterizes this country compared to a great portion of the world. In many respects, the U.S. textile complex still fulfills this basic role in providing employment for an enormous workforce composed of individuals who in many cases have few other job alternatives.

Still today the fiber-textile-apparel complex represents the largest manufacturing employer in the U.S. economy, providing jobs for nearly 2 million workers, or almost 10 percent of the domestic industrial work force. When cotton and wool production are included, the number employed exceeds 2 million. Production facilities are located in every state, and the industry is the largest manufacturing employer in nearly a dozen states. Moreover, textile and apparel firms are often the primary employer in rural regions, yet the apparel sector is also a major source of jobs in metropolitan areas, particularly in the Middle Atlantic states and California. Figure 8–1 depicts the importance of the textile and apparel industries in providing employment in the United States.

As an industry that led the way for widespread employment of women outside the home, the textile complex is still the leading manufacturing employer of women. Similarly, the textile and apparel sectors are a leading industrial employer of minorities. Moreover, many new immigrants entering the United States still find these industries, particularly apparel production, to be one of the most readily available and accepting sources of employment.

Not only does the U.S. textile complex contribute directly to the U.S. economy in important ways, but it also contributes indirectly through close ties with other industrial and agricultural sectors. A number of other industries are closely linked to the textile complex; therefore, the activities and general status of the textile and apparel industries have a more significant impact on the economy beyond that for the complex itself. In addition to the number of workers directly employed in the textile complex, it has been estimated that the textile and apparel industries provide jobs for several hundred thousand persons in service and other related support industries (U.S. Congress, Office of Technology Assessment [OTA], 1987). Examples are cotton growing, the production of dyestuffs and fabric finishes, and providing merchandise for an area vital to the retailing industry. That is, apparel sales are the most important merchandise category for department stores, mass merchandisers, and specialty stores (Ghadar et al., 1987).

The textile complex is large and highly fragmented. It represents a production and marketing chain in which fiber is made into various fabric products for sale to consumers and industrial users. Major segments include fiber producers, yarn and fabric manufacturers, and finished goods manufacturers, including apparel producers. These segments have unique business structures and unique histories and employ quite different technologies. Yet, many industry segments are integrated with one another in important ways, thus making producers dependent upon upstream and/or downstream activities for ultimate success.

The comprehensive, yet fragmented, nature of the textile complex is both an asset and a liability. The flexibility of the system has matched products to markets through a range of changes in styles and production technologies. On the other hand, the fragmentation has made the industry more vulnerable in facing global competition. Segments of the textile complex are affected by trade in different ways, yet most producers share a common concern for retaining the U.S. market and for remaining competitive in an increasingly challenging international market, of which they are a part.

Various sectors of the industry complex compete in a variety of markets, ranging from the trade of cotton on exchange markets to the retail distribution of apparel goods. All of these markets have become global in nature. Manufacturers have come to realize that even the domestic market, which they had considered their "own" market, is now an important part of a global market.

The purposes of this chapter are to provide an overview of the U.S. textile complex on the following: (1) contributions to the U.S. economy; (2) impact of consumer demand; (3) challenges to the textile complex; (4) changes in the complex; and (5) participation in international trade. For the most part, this chapter examines the textile complex as a whole—that is, common areas affecting most segments of the industry. The following chapter focuses on the textile and apparel industries as separate sectors.

FIGURE 8-1

The geographic distribution of textile and apparel employment by state, 1992 (includes fiber production)

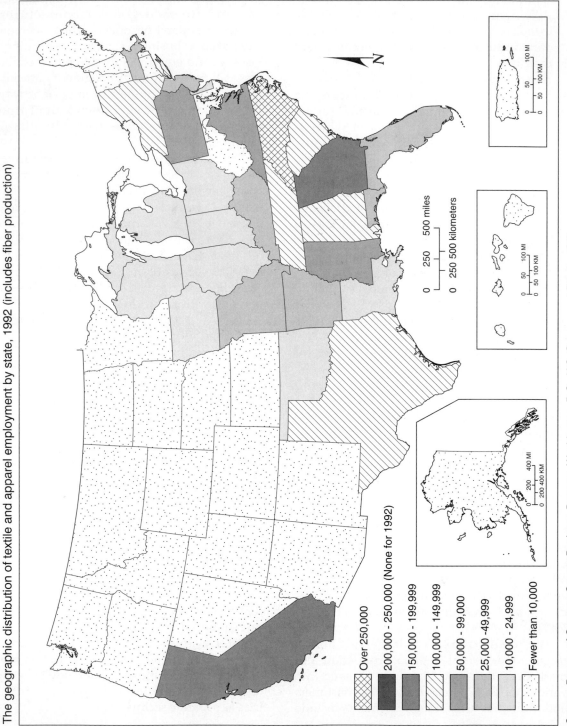

Over 250,000

200,000 - 250,000 (None for 1992)

150,000 - 199,999

100,000 - 149,999

50,000 - 99,000

25,000 - 49,999

10,000 - 24,999

Fewer than 10,000

Source: Bureau of Census, *County Business Patterns,* Washington, D.C.: U.S. Government Printing Office.

MAJOR SEGMENTS OF THE TEXTILE COMPLEX

Activities of the textile complex include:

1. the processing of natural fibers and the production of manufactured fibers
2. the conversion of those fibers into intermediate textile mill products such as yarns and fabrics
3. the manufacture of **end-use products** from the intermediate components. End-use products include apparel; interior furnishings textile products such as carpet, draperies, and bed linens; and industrial applications such as tires and erosion-control webbing

Traditionally, the industry has been structured so that each production segment is fairly separate from the other. Producers in each segment provided the intermediate products used by manufacturers in the next phases of the production chain. In the traditional industry structure, for example, a cotton producer sold to a fabric manufacturer, who in turn sold to an apparel producer; then the apparel was sold to a retailer who sold to the consumer. This production-marketing chain, also known as the **softgoods chain**, has become more integrated in recent years, however.

As U.S. manufacturers strived for advantages over their foreign competitors, new relationships and new alliances developed within the U.S. industry. Domestic manufacturers, individually and collectively, have worked toward greater speed, efficiency, and production of quality products through more integrated relationships within the chain. With more emphasis on fast and continuous flow, **vertical integration** means that traditional links in the chain are more susceptible to either **backward** or **forward integration** efforts than in the past.

Vertical integration led to increased **concentration** within the industry as one segment acquired capacity in other segments. Integration occurred forward or backward to merge production stages in the chain. As examples, fabric producers integrated backward to acquire fiber or yarn production capabilities and apparel producers acquired fabric manufacturing facilities. As an example of forward integration, apparel producers moved into the retail segment of the chain. A number of major apparel manufacturers have developed successful forward integration into retailing through outlet stores. Moreover, as the linkages within segments altered the industry structure, the era of a textile complex composed mostly of the small, decentralized family-owned and -operated **firms** has passed (except in apparel production). Although the concentration varies from one segment to another (and remains low compared to other industries [USITC, 1987]), further integration, particularly for fibers and fabrics, will continue. The growth of multinational firms with diversified production capabilities and market-oriented organizations will continue to alter the **industry structure** as it existed in the past (OTA, 1987b).

Despite changes in the structure of the textile complex through integration and concentration, the various segments of the complex can be identified according to rather distinct activities. That is, the basic activities of the different segments remained the same: Fibers are made into intermediate products, those products are developed into end-use goods, and the finished products are made available to end-use consumers, including industrial consumers. Rather, many changes took place in the fiber-fabric-apparel-retail *organizational structures and relationships* through which these activities occurred.

Although industry segments will be covered more in detail in the following chapter, an overview is presented here to provide a broad perspective of activities of the textile complex.

Production of Fiber

Fibers are the raw materials—that is, the basic components—for all the activities and resulting products that occur in later stages in the textile complex. In other words, without fibers the textile complex as we know it today could not exist.

Fibers are categorized into two basic groupings: (1) natural and (2) manufactured fibers (known previously as "man-made" fibers). Production processes vary greatly according to whether the fibers are natural or manufactured. Natural fibers include cotton, wool, silk, linen, ramie, hemp, jute, and several less prominent fibers. Most of these are products of agriculture and play important roles in international trade, particularly for the agricultural sector. Only cotton and wool are produced in the United States at present; however, products made of other natural fibers (particularly silk, flax, and ramie) became common in U.S. markets in recent years as a result of foreign trade.

Manufacture of Textile Mill Products

The manufacture of textile mill products represents the intermediate segment of the textile complex and consists of three primary operations: (1) yarn spinning, (2) fabric forming, and (3) fabric finishing. This segment also includes the production of a number of finished nonapparel consumer products such as sheets and towels. Although many small firms perform specialized aspects of these operations, a large number of textile mills have integrated operations from yarn spinning through fabric finishing.

Yarn

Yarn is used generally in the production of other goods. Most frequently, the textile yarn is used to weave or knit fabric or to tuft carpet, but other products may include cordage and a variety of strand products.

Fabric

In fabric manufacturing, yarn is transformed into fabric through weaving or knitting; for nonwoven fabrics, fibers are bonded or interlocked by mechanical, chemical, or thermal means to form the fabrics. The resulting fabrics are a fundamental intermediate textile mill product, used in a large portion of the end-use products that come from the textile complex.

Dyeing and Finishing

Newly produced fabric from the loom or knitting machine usually requires additional dye-

FIGURE 8–2
Many textile workers, like this woman, perform operations that produce fibers as well as intermediate and end-use products from fibers.

Source: Photo courtesy of DuPont Fibers.

ing and/or finishing from the unfinished (greige) stage to make it desirable for consumer end use. Dyes and finishes add important aesthetic properties, comfort, ease of care, and durability—all of which are critical to customer appeal and satisfaction.

A number of the processes for manufacturing textile mill products are quite knowledge- and capital-intensive; thus these characteristics differentiate global production sites to some extent. The production of manufactured fiber yarns, and particularly the blending of multiple fibers into a single yarn, require sophisticated manufacturing capabilities. In addition, a number of the finishing processes are also quite knowledge- and capital-intensive, giving the United States and other more developed countries an advantage in production.

Manufacture of End-Use Products

Manufactured end-use products made from textiles include apparel, home furnishings textiles, and textiles for industrial applications. The apparel industry accounts for nearly half of all textile and apparel sales. Although apparel has dominated this category of U.S. production in the past, in recent years finished products for interior furnishings and industrial use have experienced stronger growth than domestic apparel (U.S. Department of Commerce, 1993).

The apparel segment of the textile complex is the most labor-intensive, fragmented, and price competitive (Toyne et al., 1984). Whereas other aspects of the industry are shifting from small firms to larger and more vertically integrated operations, apparel production continues to be dominated by small manufacturers, jobbers, and contractors. Because apparel production tends to be labor-intensive and U.S. wages are high compared to those of many other countries, this segment of the U.S. complex is most affected by production in other regions of the world.

A Related Sector: Textile Machinery Manufacturing

The U.S. textile complex is dependent upon the textile machinery industry to provide new equipment, which will not only increase productivity and quality, but will also develop new products and processes. The U.S. textile machinery industry was the primary supplier of domestic machines until the early 1960s. Since that time, other major suppliers have entered the global machinery industry; the most prominent ones include Germany, Switzerland, Italy, and Japan. Although the U.S. textile machinery industry exports for 1992 were about $583 million (40 percent of the machinery produced), imports were $1.3 billion. Since 1984, 50–60 percent of the U.S. textile machinery market has been supplied by other countries (U.S. Department of Commerce, 1993).

Similarly, foreign companies supply industrial apparel production equipment to the domestic market. Union Special Corporation and Reece were the last major U.S. suppliers of industrial sewing machines. However, both have been bought by firms in other countries in recent years.

CONTRIBUTIONS OF THE TEXTILE COMPLEX TO THE U.S. ECONOMY

Contribution to Gross National Product

The textile complex contributes to the U.S. economy in a number of important ways. The gross national product (GNP) generated by the textile and apparel industries compared to selected other U.S. sectors is shown in Figure 8–3.

Contributions to Employment

Although growth in employment for the textile complex lagged behind that for the indus-

FIGURE 8–3
Contributions of some major U.S. industries to the GNP (in billions of dollars, 1990, GNP).

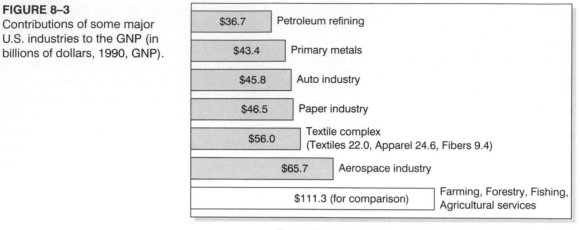

Total U.S. GNP in 1990 = $5,522.2

Source: U.S. Department of Commerce (Bureau of Economic Analysis) and American Textile Manufacturers Institute, 1993.

trial sector as a whole, in recent years nearly 10 percent of the U.S. manufacturing work force has been employed in the textile and apparel industries.

Table 8–1 displays employment statistics for the textile and apparel industries for more than a decade. Textile and apparel employment is shown in relation to (1) total nonagricultural employment and (2) all manufacturing employment. Note that a net decline in employment occurred for both textiles and apparel.

One should keep in mind that the decline in employment cannot be attributed only to negative influences. For example, improved technology and other operating efficiencies brought about increased productivity levels; thus fewer workers were needed to perform the same production tasks than were required earlier. Domestic production has increased, in fact. In this sense, these were shifts because of operating efficiencies that made the U.S. industry more competitive globally by reducing labor costs.

The textile complex has played a particularly significant role in providing jobs for women, minorities, and new immigrants. A number of segments of the textile complex employ about twice as many women, blacks, and persons of Hispanic origin as all manufacturing; the contrast is not quite as great when compared to all manufacturing of **nondurable goods** (some sources consider these manufacturing areas to require lower skill levels than other areas of manufacturing—i.e., **durable goods** manufacturing).

Contributions to Other Sectors

Value Added

A number of other important U.S. industries are linked closely to textiles and apparel. According to the Office of Technology Assessment (1987), only about one-fourth of the valued added by production and sale of textile goods and fabricated textile products goes to textile and apparel firms, although about 40 percent of the value added from production and sales of fabrics and apparel remains within the industry. According to OTA, the rest of the value from textile/apparel sales is distributed broadly throughout the economy. That is, many other sectors benefit from the

TABLE 8–1

Employment Statistics for the U.S. Textile and Apparel Industries, 1974–1993 (in thousands)

	Total Nonagricultural Employees	All Manufacturing Industries	Textile Mill Products Industry	Apparel & Related Products
1974	78,265	20,077	965	1,363
1975	76,945	18,323	868	1,243
1976	79,382	18,997	919	1,318
1977	82,471	19,682	910	1,316
1978	86,697	20,505	899	1,332
1979	89,823	21,044	885	1,304
1980	90,406	20,285	848	1,264
1981	91,160	20,171	823	1,245
1982	89,570	18,783	750	1,161
1983	90,200	18,434	741	1,163
1984	94,496	19,378	746	1,185
1985	97,519	19,260	702	1,121
1986	99,610	18,994	705	1,106
1987	102,101	19,104	730	1,113
1988	106,025	19,538	726	1,096
1989	107,894	19,391	720	1,076
1990	109,423	19,078	691	1,036
1991	108,259	18,406	670	1,006
1992	108,518	18,041	672	1,005
1993	110,173	17,804	666	978

Source: U.S. Department of Labor, Bureau of Labor Statistics.

value that is added at different levels of textile and apparel production.

Jobs Created

The U.S. Office of Technology Assessment (1987) found that $1 million output from the U.S. textile/apparel industry created between 26 and 30 full-time equivalent jobs (depending on the segment of the industry) in other areas of manufacturing, natural resource industries, construction, and so on. The OTA staff noted the important linkages with the service industries, particularly transportation and trade, as well as the highly paid "transactional" services like finance, insurance, and business services.

In a study funded by a U.S. textile/apparel industry group, the Economic Policy Institute (1993) found that for every 100 manufacturing jobs in textiles, another 267 jobs were generated in a "multiplier" effect. Similarly, the group found that 100 apparel jobs generated 207 secondary jobs.

Other Contributions

The U.S. Congress, Office of Technology Assessment (1987) estimates of full-time job equivalents generated by textile/apparel jobs did not include retailing. A large number of additional persons in the retail sector depend upon the domestic complex to produce the goods they sell. Similarly, the OTA estimates do not include persons employed through new equipment purchases or plant modernization. (As we shall see later, however, a substantial portion of the production equipment is secured from other countries.)

Overall, the textile complex is vital to the U.S. economy in a number of ways: through contributions to the gross national product, by providing more manufacturing jobs than any other industrial sector, and by contributing importantly to other sectors through a variety of linkages. In addition to overall contributions to the U.S. economy, the importance of the industry and its linkages is intensified in regions such as the southeastern United States where textile and apparel manufacturing represents one of the primary sources of employment. The industry represents the lifeblood of many of those regions, and its success or decline has a severe impact on those communities and regions.

THE IMPACT OF CONSUMER DEMAND

Consumer demand has a profound impact on the economic health of the textile complex and similarly on the total softgoods chain. Consumer spending for clothing and **semidurable** home furnishings products generates the basic demand that extends back through the production and marketing chain, back as far as the initial fiber production. Consumer demand in other areas affects the textile complex. For example, since automobiles contain textile components, consumer demand for autos influences the textile complex rather significantly.

As we noted in an earlier chapter, which focused on the global perspective, consumer demand is also referred to as *consumption* by certain sources that collect industry data. Both U.S. consumption data and production data for recent years are given in Table 8–2.

TABLE 8–2
U.S. Textile and Apparel Production and Consumption

| | [1]Production (1987 = 100) | | | Consumption [2]Consumer sp. (bil. $) | |
Year	Textile Mill Products	Total Apparel Products	Industrial	Clothing	Semi-durable House Furns.
1992	104.7	92.3	106.5	195.7	23.6
1991	96.9	91.9	104.1	181.6	21.9
1990	97.0	92.2	106.0	175.7	21.2
1989	100.3	95.0	106.1	170.1	20.4
1988	98.6	98.1	104.5	158.7	19.4
1987	100.0	100.0	100.0	148.6	17.9
1986	93.9	96.3	95.3	138.8	17.2
1985	89.7	92.6	94.4	129.3	15.7
1984	93.7	95.7	92.8	120.9	14.9
1983	93.2	93.8	84.9	110.3	13.5

[1] Federal Reserve Board
[2] Dept. of Commerce

Source: Standard and Poor's *Industry Surveys* and *Textiles, Apparel and Home Furnishings—Current Analysis* (1994), p. T81, based on data from the above sources.

An index is used for production comparisons (based on assigning a value of 100 to production in 1987), whereas consumption is shown in billions of dollars. Of particular note, in 1992 U.S. consumers spent $196 billion for clothing and $23.6 billion for semidurable home furnishings products.

The impact of consumer demand on the total chain might be compared to a train in which the consumer and consumer spending provide the momentum for the overall operation. In other words, consumer spending is the engine of activity for the softgoods chain. Although the industry is becoming more integrated, making it more difficult to identify the distinct segments as clearly as Figures 8–4 and 8–5 suggest, the train analogy may be a helpful way to conceptualize the impact of consumer demand.

In this case, positive consumer spending created demand at the retail level. In turn, the sales activity for the retail segment of the chain required increased production from apparel manufacturers. As apparel producers responded to orders, these manufacturers required additional textile mill products (going back to the fiber stage) to meet demand. When business conditions are optimum, different segments of the softgoods chain usually respond and work together with reasonable effectiveness (often with

remarkable effectiveness), especially considering the volatile nature of fashion products (hence, the speed and timing involved) and the fragmented nature of the chain.

Sometimes, however, a variety of factors can influence consumer spending and create conditions in which the softgoods chain loses its momentum. When consumer demand slows, especially if it occurs rather abruptly, the train analogy might appear as Figure 8–5.

Just as consumer demand extended backward in the softgoods chain when spending was at a healthy pace, a *decline* had a braking effect backward in this case. As consumer purchases slowed, retailers experienced excessive inventory buildups. Not wishing to add to existing inventory excesses, retailers reduced orders to apparel manufacturers. Since apparel manufacturers no longer had the anticipated retail orders to fill, they had no need for the textile mill products they had projected using. Like the retailers, the apparel manufacturers did not wish to have an excess of potentially unsaleable inventory, so they, too, reduced orders to textile producers. Keeping in mind that several operations occur within the textile production portion of the chain, multiple effects may have occurred within the segment. In short, the change in consumer demand had an adverse effect on the total softgoods chain.

FIGURE 8–4
Using apparel purchases as an example, the train—led by consumer spending (the engine)—moves at a healthy rate and the segments are moving together.

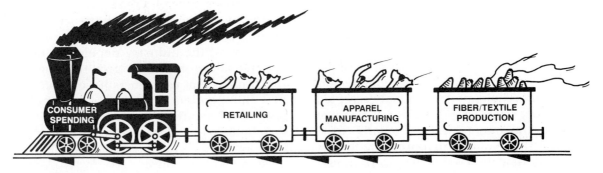

FIGURE 8–5
This train shows the impact of a sharp slowdown in consumer spending.

A number of examples, often with different causes, can be given to illustrate the slow-down effect on the total chain caused by a decline in consumer spending. Apparel demand in particular is unpredictable, causing manufacturers to face cyclical patterns of production. Factors influencing demand include shifts in the economy, styles, consumer interests (other than style), demographic changes in the market, and changes in lifestyle. Two examples follow, which illustrate the effect of slowed demand as it extended through the production and marketing chain. The examples are followed by some of the lessons learned.

Slowed Demand Due to Style Changes

Slowed demand occurred because of style changes in 1988, resulting from the fashion industry's unsuccessful attempt to introduce the mini-length skirt as the primary fashion length in women's apparel. Although short skirts did become more commonly accepted by the early 1990s, in 1988, many independent women consumers, and particularly those who felt the mini was inappropriate for the new professional roles they had worked hard

to attain, rejected the industry's attempts to shift preferences to a new length. Consequently, apparel retailers found the mini-length skirts remained on their racks to a great extent, as did coordinating pieces including matching jackets and other items that were often of minimum use without the accompanying skirts. Consequently, the industry effort to introduce the mini-length skirt left many consumers disappointed in fashions for the season, and, as a result, purchases declined. Not only were women's apparel sales affected, but men's purchases were influenced as well. Because women are the primary purchasers of men's apparel, when female consumers were unenthusiastic about shopping for themselves, they were not in stores at the usual frequency to notice and to buy men's apparel. Consequently, ill-fated efforts to change fashion lengths created a decline that extended through the various segments of the industry dependent upon apparel sales for healthy growth. Stogdon (1993) notes that consumers have asserted a new independent spirit toward changing fashions. Consumers are now more likely than in the past to choose a "look" that seems right for the individual rather than following the dictates of fashion.

Slowed Demand Due to Economic Changes

The period of the early 1990s illustrated dramatically the impact of economic changes on demand—which in turn affected the entire textile complex. During this time, recessionary conditions prevailed in the United States, affecting **consumer confidence**. Consumer confidence, as measured by established survey procedures, provides an indication of consumers' perceptions of general economic well-being at a given time. The resulting consumer confidence index provides a rough indicator of consumers' willingness to spend. Trends in consumer confidence, which affected demand, are shown in Figure 8–6.

Consumer demand was sluggish in the early 1990s, causing the period to be a particularly difficult one for most segments of the softgoods chain. As retailers attempted to respond to erratic sales and carrying costs, they tightened their inventories and placed smaller-than-usual orders. In effect, this meant that retailers shifted the financial burden of holding existing warehouse inventories onto manufacturers rather than securing the inventories themselves as was originally intended. In addition, some retailers were slow to pay manufacturers. Manufacturers' profit margins suffered.

The October 1987 stock market crash was another example of how changing economic conditions affected the textile complex. Consumer confidence dropped, and retailers became cautious about future buying plans. Although consumer expenditures remained high as a result of heavy discounting and promotions on the part of retailers, new orders for textile mill products began to reflect concern over economic uncertainties (Standard & Poor's, 1988).

FIGURE 8–6

Consumer confidence, based on an index of 100, in 1985.

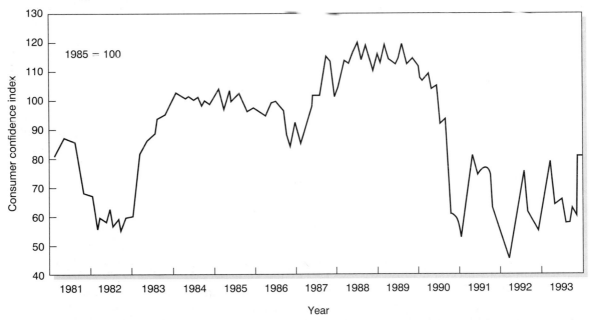

Consumer confidence index

1985 = 100

Year

Source: Reprinted permission of Standard and Poor's 1990, 1994, *Industry Surveys* and *Textiles, Apparel and Home Furnishings—Current Analysis*.

More Careful Inventory Management

During economic slumps like that of the early 1990s, all segments of the industry become more proficient at careful **inventory management**. Many learned this hard lesson in the early 1980s. Since manufacturers and retailers often borrow to finance production or inventory for forthcoming seasons, periods of high interest rates such as those in the early 1980s (interest rates were in the 14–17 percent range) caused carrying charges to be exorbitant. As retailers and manufacturers alike experienced losses associated with the excessive inventories and high interest rates, companies at all levels became sensitive to more careful inventory management. In the textile sector, overproduction and forced liquidation of apparel fabrics taught mill management to be more sensitive and skilled in scheduling production. Textile manufacturers learned to work more closely with apparel manufacturers and retailers to gauge consumer demand.

Greater Emphasis on a Marketing Orientation

Difficulties experienced by the textile complex in the early 1980s encouraged both textile and apparel manufacturers to focus on a stronger marketing orientation. Although the unsuccessful attempt to revive the mini-length skirt in 1988 indicated that the industry can still miscue at times, manufacturers have become much more sensitive to the importance of responding to consumers' needs and desires through improved marketing efforts.

Although consumer demand influences the production chain for any sector, the extent of consumer impact on both upstream and downstream segments of the industry is exaggerated in the textile complex and in the total softgoods chain. The "perishable" nature of fashion goods and the seasonal characteristics of many of the products mean that excessive inventory from one season can seldom be held for a following season.

Major Trends That Affect Consumer Demand

At best, prediction of the consumer's textile and apparel (particularly apparel) purchases is difficult. To be in touch with consumer demand, the industry must be sensitive to major demographic shifts occurring in the population. Manufacturers must be alert to changes in the age of the population, shifts in households, household composition, geographic shifts, income shifts, and other demographic patterns that affect total consumer spending on textile and apparel goods.

The following sections give examples of major shifts that generally affect demand for textile and apparel products in U.S. markets.

A Major Shift to an Older Population

As the U.S. population increases, the changing composition by age groups will have a significant impact on consumer purchases. In general, the population in older age groupings continues to increase while younger groups are decreasing as a portion of the total population. In particular, the "baby-boomer" generation has matured, and many of these individuals are in the 40–50 age group, which is expected to continue to increase significantly through the year 2000. The U.S. Census Bureau has indicated that the largest population growth is in the 40–58 age group, which has the most money to spend on apparel and home furnishings. On the other hand, the group that spends the greatest portion of disposable income for apparel (not textiles)—young adults under age 25—will decline over the same period.

Textile and apparel manufacturers must be alert to the implications of these shifts for their markets. Staff at the Marketing Research Corporation of America (MRCA) (Tugman, 1989)

THE FICKLE CONSUMER

A textile or apparel company's market position is often exclusively a function of product. Fashion trends thus have a pronounced effect on profitability, regardless of aggregate industry conditions. A manufacturer's performance frequently is subject to the demand of a fickle consumer. For example, corduroy and polyester double-knits, once best sellers, are now almost nonexistent.

Crystal Brands Inc., formerly known as the General Mills Fashion Group, is a case in point. The company's central product line was its Izod Lacoste sportswear (known by its crocodile emblem). Originally sold through specialty outlets like pro shops, Izod Lacoste products were worn mostly by a core group of men and women for sporting activities, such as golf and tennis. In the early 1980s, the company began to experience rapid growth, principally due to a surge in demand related to the "preppie" fad, and distribution expanded to general retail outlets. Sales of Izod Lacoste sportswear increased four-fold. In the wake of such explosive growth, management invested heavily in expanding personnel, manufacturing facilities, advertising, and inventory.

The company's sales projections ultimately proved too optimistic when the preppie fad waned. Added capacity made matters worse as margins narrowed significantly when sales slid. Following this reversal, the company adopted a strategy of reducing overhead and other costs to a level consistent with the reduced sales level. Crystal Brands reported a return to profitability for a time; however, the company has been in serious financial trouble in recent years.

While Crystal Brands miscalculated that the preppie style would have more permanence, others mistook just the opposite in the fleecewear boom. Though many thought the fitness fad wouldn't last, a more affluent, leisure-oriented society adopted sweatpants and sweatshirts as a uniform. After their stock of sweatshirts and sweatpants sold out in 1986, companies such as Tultex Corp. and Russell Corp. rapidly expanded production to meet the increased demand. Earnings of these companies rose dramatically. This is a perfect example of how the consumer drives the market unrelated to industry conditions in the aggregate and how management can be caught by surprise, either overly optimistic or underestimating consumer response to their product.

---

observed that apparel manufacturers had not changed to match the needs of the new consumer mix. In both the men's and women's apparel market, 1989 sales deteriorated most for the 16–24-year-old segment compared to the prior year. Increases were greatest among the groups 45 years and older. MRCA staff noted that the age distribution of the population has changed dramatically, but the more mature age segments have not increased apparel purchases enough to offset the decreased purchasing of the younger segments that have driven the industry in recent years.

On the other hand, as the population grows older, consumers may spend more money on their homes. In this case home furnishing will get a bigger share of discretionary income.

Southward Geographic Shifts

The U.S. population continues to shift to the sunbelt—from Virginia to California. The shift southward is expected to continue at least through the turn of the century, with most of the regions to the north of the sunbelt declining in population. Population age groups vary by geographic areas as well. For example, the

South will continue to have a high population growth of persons over age 65.

Lifestyle and seasonal apparel needs vary greatly according to regional characteristics. Therefore, producers in the textile complex must be sensitive to geographic shifts because these have a significant influence on both the national and regional markets.

Increases in the Education and Income of the Population

As education and income levels of the population continue to increase, the number of white-collar workers who have a greater need for dress apparel will also increase. This shift has been especially significant among women. Since the early 1970s, the increase in the education and income levels of career-oriented women (income was up 30 percent during the 1980s) has had a significant impact on the professional women's apparel market.

In general, market analysts portray today's apparel consumer as one with a sophisticated taste level, a high income level, and a high education level—particularly in comparison to recent decades. In recent years, both men and women have become more sensitive to the communicative aspects of their clothing in career advancement. As a result of these changes, apparel consumers have become more interested in better quality, longer-life garments. The consumer of the 1990s is one who is value-oriented; this consumer wants a quality product at a reasonable price and may be less influenced by labels compared to the 1980s consumer. Higher education and income levels have influenced both apparel and home furnishings markets and will continue to do so in the future.

Changes in Household Formations

Changes in household formations have a significant impact on both the apparel and home furnishings markets. Although the number of households has increased in the 1990s, husband-wife households are expected to increase at a slower rate. During the same period, divorce rates and postponement of marriage are projected to have increased single adult (both female and male) households substantially. Composition of households affects income levels, sometimes positively and sometimes negatively. For example, the two-career household may have generous spending potential. Or, a single-career household resulting from divorce may decrease spending potential. In addition, shifts in the presence of children in various household formation arrangements affect the children's wear market.

Shifts in household formations are also particularly important for the home furnishings market. Increases or decreases in household formations have a significant impact on purchases of carpet, rugs, draperies, upholstered furniture, and other textile goods.

Forbes writers Feldman and Levin (1993) assert the 1990s is the decade for consumers to focus on the home. They believe the 1980s was the decade to "drape the body" and the 1990s is the decade to "drape the home" (p. 64).

CHALLENGES TO THE U.S. TEXTILE COMPLEX

Recent decades have been difficult, particularly at times, for all segments of the U.S. textile complex. One must also keep in mind that the textile complexes in most other industrialized market economy countries experienced similar periods of growth and decline.

Following World War II through a good portion of the 1960s, U.S. producers enjoyed a fairly captive market. The large and relatively affluent U.S. market absorbed most of the shipments from domestic textile, home furnishings, and apparel manufacturers. Although foreign competition became a concern to certain segments of the textile complex by the 1960s, U.S. producers enjoyed for the most part a prosperous growth period. By the early 1970s, textile and apparel employment reached a peak of 2.3 million workers.

In the 1970s, the competition from producers in other countries began to have a serious impact on the U.S. textile complex (as it did on the industry in virtually all other developed countries). Previously secure domestic markets became threatened by an influx of products from an increasing number of producer nations, many of whom offered products at considerably lower prices than U.S.-made products because of wage differences. As evidence of the increased shipments, the U.S. textile and apparel trade deficit for 1972 was $2.4 billion compared to $191 million in 1961, representing more than a 12-fold increase in slightly more than a decade. During this time the newly industrialized countries (NICs) emerged as major competitors to the U.S. textile and apparel industries. By 1974, imports from Hong Kong, Korea, Taiwan, and China accounted for 56 percent of the apparel imports entering U.S. markets. By the 1970s, Japan had moved toward more advanced industrial manufacturing and accounted for only 8 percent of the U.S. textile/apparel imports in 1974 (Ghadar et al., 1987).

Moreover, imports escalated during the period when U.S. consumption had slowed markedly. For nearly two decades, U.S. expenditures for apparel, for example, rose only slightly. Consequently, the combination of increased import shipments and sluggish demand heightened competition for the existing U.S. market.

As a result of the intense competition during the 1970s, the U.S. textile complex faced the reality that its ultimate survival was in serious jeopardy. Manufacturers who wanted to survive realized that previous approaches to business were no longer adequate. Business failure rates for the textile complex were substantial, particularly for apparel. In 1975, for example, the business failures in the textile

complex accounted for almost one-third of all U.S. manufacturing business failures. For most years between 1960 and 1990, the textile complex business failures represented about 10 percent of those for all manufacturing.

Although imports were taking a greater portion of the U.S. market, one must not conclude that all the business failures in the textile complex could be attributed to imports. According to Standard & Poor's (1984), the textile complex included more than 15,000[1] firms in the early 1980s, many of whom produced a rather narrow range of products. As a result of the large number of domestic firms, competition *among* U.S. producers was excessive as well. Therefore, many manufacturers in the U.S. textile complex were unable to survive in the increasingly competitive domestic business environment.

Some segments of the industry—the apparel segment in particular—are easy to enter (that is, they have few **barriers to entry**) because of limited capital and technology requirements (the same reasons for easy entry for developing countries). Because a number of minimally qualified entrepreneurs start operations, the fallout rate has tended to be high. In short, even without the growth in imports, many of the U.S. firms would have failed. However, imports perhaps hastened the failure of marginal firms as foreign competition accelerated changes that were already occurring. In particular, imports placed downward pressure on prices; thus profit margins of U.S. manufacturers tended to be lean, and firms found it increasingly difficult to generate capital for modernization and expansion (Arpan et al., 1982).

Although manufacturers and workers affected by company failures surely would not agree, some business experts concluded that the industry as a whole became stronger

---

[1]Some sources, such as the American Apparel Manufacturers Association, give a larger number.

and more competitive after market forces "weeded out" some of the weak companies. In fact, economists might view the loss of the weaker firms as the early stages of **industrial adjustment**. In efforts to restore competitiveness for an industry, adjustment may occur through the **rationalization** of existing firms and facilities in order to establish fewer, more efficient producers and a number of specialized companies. Market forces required that firms either adapt or close. For textile and apparel firms, adapting to the demands of market forces required a variety of strategies. Examples were updating facilities and production methods, changing product lines, perhaps horizontal or vertical integration, and "otherwise finding means of improving competitiveness or redeploying resources to other industries" (Ghadar et al., 1987, p. 2).

The 1970s and 1980s were critical transition years for the U.S. textile complex. Many changes occurred within the complex as a whole and within individual firms, creating a production and marketing chain quite different from that of the 1950s and 1960s. Although many companies were no longer in business and a majority of the firms that survived experienced difficult times, the adjustment process prepared many of the survivors to function more effectively in increasingly competitive markets. The textile complex made changes "affecting the nature of the products produced; how they are produced; how they are marketed; the structure, scale, and scope of the enterprises producing them; and the nature of jobs created directly and indirectly by the industry" (U.S. Congress, OTA, 1987, p. 3).

CHANGES IN THE TEXTILE COMPLEX

According to a study by the U.S. Office of Technology Assessment (1987), a combination of international competition and new technology forced the domestic textile complex through its "most profound transformation since the industrial revolution" (p. 3). During the 1970s, certain segments of the textile complex made significant progress in achieving the adjustment necessary to counter increasing international competition. Adjustment varied, however, in different segments of the textile complex. Because of the textile industry's technology and capital orientation, modernizations and efficiencies for that segment were more readily implemented than was the case for the labor-intensive and more fragmented apparel industry. Within the textile industry, productivity also grew at a much faster rate than the economy as a whole.

Manufacturers achieved this through investing in new plants and equipment that increased operating efficiencies and produced more sophisticated products with shorter start-up times. These changes typically increased specialization and were intended to enhance the U.S. industry's position in market segments where U.S. products already enjoyed strong acceptance.

In contrast, the nature of the apparel industry made change more difficult for that sector. The apparel industry has been characterized by a high degree of family ownership, a large number of small companies employing an average of fewer than 50 workers, with many producing quite limited product lines; therefore, changes have been more difficult to implement. The process of constructing garments from limp fabrics was more difficult to automate than was true for most of the textile mill operations. Moreover, the sophisticated production that was being developed for the apparel industry by that time was often so costly that only the largest companies could justify (or afford) the expenditures. Plants (**establishments**) employing fewer than 50 workers did not have the financial means of investing in advanced technology to improve productivity.

Although change occurred more slowly, the apparel segment did make strides to improve productivity; in fact, apparel productivity grew slightly faster during the 1970s than manufacturing as a whole. The share of total output produced by larger firms increased; capital and knowledge intensity of the segment grew; and many firms broadened and upgraded product lines (Ghadar et al., 1987; Standard and Poor's, various years).

Overall, the textile complex performed strongly during the 1970s, with growth in some segments equal to, or in some cases better than, the U.S. industrial complex as a whole. **Shipments** (that is, the goods U.S. manufacturers produced) increased steadily in dollar value after the 1975 recession, growing by 24 percent for the decade (adjusted for inflation); also, exports doubled. Although total employment in the complex declined by 44 percent between the early 1960s and mid-1980s, the decline has been fairly gradual in recent years.

As foreign competition intensified during the early 1980s, many segments in the U.S. textile complex found it increasingly difficult to maintain the momentum established in the 1970s. Domestic firms continued their capital investment efforts; for example, the textile segment nearly doubled its investment outlay between 1975 and 1984, going from $1 billion to $1.9 billion annually. Despite the increased investments, productivity growth, and, in many cases, improved quality, imports continued to account for an increasing share of the U.S. textile and apparel market (USITC, 1987b).

Between 1980 and 1992, textile and apparel imports increased 256 percent in volume terms; the increase was 332 percent in value terms (D. Link, personal communication, 1993). Apparel imports grew substantially, which meant that not only were U.S. apparel manufacturers losing a substantial portion of their market, but also that textile producers who previously had supplied the fabrics for domestic apparel production lost a major portion of their market as well. Figure 8–7 shows the increase in textile and apparel imports that occurred during this period and the trade deficit that resulted.

According to Ghadar et al. (1987), the rise in the value of the dollar correlated closely with the dramatic growth in textile and apparel imports. Although some sources (GATT, 1984; USITC, 1983) note that shifts in exchange rates have not been proven to affect trade in specific sectors, patterns of textile and apparel trade were altered dramatically as the value of the dollar began to increase in 1981. Within 18 months, the surge of imports began to occur, and, even more quickly, exports began to decline. The inordinately strong U.S. dollar added to trade shifts already affecting the U.S. textile complex. The strong dollar meant that U.S. importers and retail buyers found foreign buying particularly attractive because the dollar purchased more than ever in many regions of the world (but keep in mind that the currencies in several of the Asian NICs are closely tied to the U.S. dollar). Conversely, U.S. textile and apparel products became less attractive to foreign buyers because the change in exchange rates made U.S. goods more costly to purchase.

Although the U.S. textile complex had attempted to improve its competitiveness through increased investments and operating efficiencies, the impact of growing foreign competition and the shift in exchange rates continued to create challenges for the domestic industries. This led to the growing realization that much of the domestic market could not be held on the basis of reducing manufacturing costs alone, but that attention must be given to other competitive factors as well. The textile complex's attempts to retain or regain a competitive position included the following efforts (some industry efforts that have been discussed up to this point are included in the summary to provide an overall review).

FIGURE 8–7
U.S. textile and apparel trade.
(U.S. Department of Commerce.) (c.i.f. import values;
f.a.s. export values)*

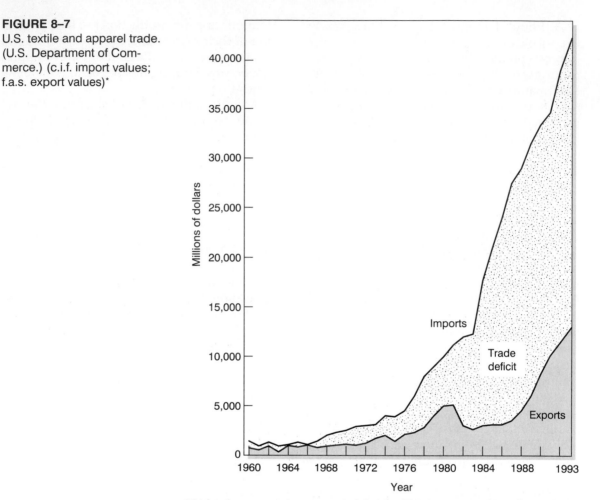

*C.i.f. refers to cost, insurance, and freight. This is a pricing term that includes insurance and freight charges. F.a.s. refers to free along side. This is a pricing term under which the seller must deliver the goods to a pier and place them within reach of the ship's loading equipment.

Closing or Revitalizing Outmoded and Inefficient Plants

Manufacturers closed or remodeled obsolete production facilities. Or, in some cases, market forces eliminated producers who could not compete under the conditions that existed. In the textile sector alone, for example, more than 350 plants were closed between 1981 and 1986 (Standard & Poor's, 1987).

Restructuring Through Acquisitions, Consolidations, and Mergers

Several manufacturers made acquisitions to add vertical stages of the business to their operations (vertical integration); some integrated horizontally (**horizontal integration**). A number of consolidations occurred to de-emphasize import-battered segments of the market. In general, the consolidations and mergers strengthened many companies and therefore improved the overall competitiveness of the industry.

A number of major apparel firms made acquisitions either to move into new product areas or to penetrate different levels of the retail market. VF Corporation did both. VF Corporation acquired H D Lee, Vanity Fair, Vassarette, Barbizon, Blue Bell, Girbaud, Bassett-Walker, Jantzen, Health-Tex, and several other companies. In addition to the obvious range of products produced by the VF companies, many of these provided access to different distribution channels for the same product lines. The latter point is important because brand-name apparel manufacturers have learned they cannot sell nearly identical merchandise to both department stores and discount stores; once products are in discount stores, they have lost their appeal to department stores. Therefore, VF Corporation's spectrum of jeans companies permits VF to be in three channels of distribution: Rustler and Wrangler jeans for the discounters; Lee jeans for department and specialty stores; and the Girbaud line for upscale department stores. Similarly, VF's underfashion companies penetrate different channels.

Not all the restructuring in the industry was voluntary or beneficial, however. Despite conscientious efforts of Burlington and J. P. Stevens to restructure, both of these industry giants later faced another threat of the 1980s—hostile takeover attempts by other companies. The restructuring that followed meant that these two former industry giants no longer remained the sector's leaders they were in earlier years. As Burlington successfully fought the takeover, management was forced to sell major segments of the company to pay debts. In its efforts to fend off the takeover, Burlington became a **privately held firm** and was highly leveraged. The company fought valiantly to recover from bankruptcy and, in 1991, became a **publicly held firm** once again as Burlington Industries Equity,

later emerging once again as Burlington Industries, Inc. J. P. Stevens, which had been the second largest publicly held U.S. textile company, after Burlington, did not fare as well. The industry was stunned by the break-up of J. P. Stevens, splitting into portions known as JPS Textile Group, West Point-Pepperell, and Forstman. Later Farley Industries (now Fruit of the Loom) tried unsuccessfully to buy West Point-Pepperell; the company eventually emerged as WestPoint Stevens. Changes in these companies reflect the refigurations occurring in the industry during recent years.

Not all consolidations and acquisitions resulted from textile or apparel firms buying other companies in the complex. For example, Sara Lee—better known for cakes and pies—became the largest publicly held apparel conglomerate in the United States. Through acquisitions and strategic planning, Sara Lee quietly grew, almost unnoticed by many industry peers, to become an apparel giant with sales in its Personal Products Division of over $6 billion in 1993, compared to over $2 billion in 1988. Sara Lee has such well known brands as Hanes, Bali, Playtex, L'eggs, Champion fleece and activewear, and a number of international brands.

Investments in Equipment and Technology

As noted earlier, manufacturers invested substantially in new, more productive equipment. Although plant closings occurred, the textile sector's Federal Reserve production index grew 14 percent from 1980–1992 (D. Link, personal communication, 1993). The installation of more technologically sophisticated, less labor-intensive equipment accounted for this increase. In the last decade, the textile industry has averaged about $2 billion per year in investments to upgrade production (Standard & Poor's, 1992). The apparel sector's investment in equipment and technology was considerably under that of the textile industry.

The apparel industry has invested more in recent years than was true in the past, however.

Efforts to Improve Productivity Levels

Operating levels and output have increased for the complex, particularly in certain segments. Improved productivity is closely tied to the first three strategies above but may be affected also by a variety of management and operating efficiencies. The American Textile Manufacturers Institute noted that the textile sector's productivity gains of 3.3 percent annually from 1973 to 1988 were much higher than the 2.3 percent gain for the total U.S. industrial sector (D. Link, 1993). Productivity for the apparel sector improved but not nearly as much as the increase for the textile industry.

Developing a Greater Sensitivity to Market Needs

Having been privileged to have a somewhat captive and secure market for decades, many segments of the textile complex had become insensitive to customer needs, including the needs of industrial customers. In many cases, the industrial customers were manufacturers at other stages of the softgoods chain. Some manufacturers who had prospered for many years by producing what they wanted to produce often had not been responsive to customers' desires. As an example of the lack of responsiveness, President Irving Spitalnick (1985) of Spitalnick and Company cited difficulties in convincing U.S. textile mills to provide distinctive fabrics for his apparel lines. As he and other apparel manufacturers approached fabric producers with special product requests, they frequently encountered a "take it or leave it" attitude on the part of textile mills.

However, foreign manufacturers' production efficiencies and their desire to produce according to customers' needs helped U.S. manufacturers realize the necessity and benefits of responding more effectively to the needs of the market. In fact, virtually all segments of the textile complex have placed added emphasis on marketing programs, which help them (1) to serve more effectively their customers at various positions in the chain, and (2) to be more efficient in inventory management by anticipating more accurately what will be purchased by those customers.

Closer Working Relationships within the Softgoods Chain

The textile complex is a fiber-to-end-use system composed of many independent enterprises, which, by the nature of the industry and the products produced, need to work together closely. In the past, however, the system has not functioned at its best because of poor communication among fiber, textile, apparel, and retail operations. In recent years, various segments within the production and marketing chain came to realize that a more cooperative and helpful working relationship with one another served the interests of all members of the larger complex.

In an industry in which intense domestic competition has been a fact of life and the relationships between suppliers and buyers often tended to be adversarial, the threat of foreign competition provided an incentive to various segments of the industry to work together more closely. For example, textile producers learned that they must be concerned not only about making their own products competitive with imports but must also strive to assist their customer, the apparel manufacturer, in being more competitive with apparel imports and to meet more effectively the needs of the U.S. retailer.

Although developing a marketing orientation was part of the effort to work more effectively with other segments of the softgoods chain, the improved climate that began to develop represented a new era of more cooperative working relationships. U.S. manufacturers began to realize that to produce and market textile and apparel goods (and particularly fashion goods) quickly, efficiently, and with improved quality levels—and to be able to compete more effectively with foreign products—new working relationships were required. Examples of the cooperative linkages are the following networks:

- *The Textile, Apparel and Sundries Linkage Council (TALC/SAFLINC)*: This is a network of U.S. apparel, sundries, and textile industries dedicated to eliminating redundant business operations and decreasing overall response time. This group emphasizes quick response strategies and partnerships as overall critical business issues (S. Black, 1993). This is a merger of the former Textile and Apparel Linkage Council (TALC) and the Sundries and Apparel Findings Linkage Council (SAFLINC).
- *The Voluntary Interindustry Communications Standards Committee (VICS)*: VICS was developed to provide a network among textile and apparel manufacturers and retailers. VICS' early objectives included establishing standard item identification and a standard data transmission format for computerized data interchange systems within the chain. In addition, VICS has provided education for companies in the softgoods industry (Tahmincioglu, 1989).

Concentrating on Market Segments in which the United States Has Greatest Advantages

In a market that continues to grow increasingly global, many U.S. textile and apparel manufacturers have attempted to specialize and identify competitive market niches. In some cases domestic manufacturers have focused on capital- and knowledge-intensive production areas for which many of the developing countries are not prepared to compete. Or, some U.S. producers have found they may remain competitive where technology can be used to provide efficiencies to offset production costs. In other cases, domestic manufacturers have determined they cannot be competitive in certain highly labor-intensive areas. As examples, two apparel manufacturing areas illustrate these divergent strategies: (1) men's underwear (particularly knit briefs) has been a highly standardized product area for which automated production has been quite successful; therefore, several U.S. producers have remained competitive in domestic production; (2) on the other hand, the labor-intensive characteristics of women's bras has forced most U.S. bra firms to move the intricate sewing operations to countries with lower labor costs.

Although focusing on specialized market niches has been advantageous for many U.S. manufacturers, producers have no assurance of retaining those markets. In earlier years, apparel imports were mostly in lower-priced lines. Some domestic manufacturers tried shifting to higher value-added lines to avoid the intense foreign competition. Over the years, however, as overseas manufacturers attempted to maximize the value of products they could ship to the United States under quotas allotted to them, the producers in other countries have also tended to move toward higher value-added market areas.

Shortening Response Time

Efforts to streamline production and delivery of products within the textile complex are by far the most evident outcome of closer working relationships among segments in the softgoods chain. A variety of strategies known as **Quick Response (QR)** has evolved to shorten delivery times and provide other efficiencies in the production and marketing chain.

Global competition and the resulting uncertainty over future markets encouraged domestic producers to develop a number of Quick Response approaches, which enhanced one of their major competitive advantages— *proximity to domestic markets.*

Quick Response systems combine effective management techniques with new communication and information processing technology, along with new production technology, to reduce delivery times throughout the chain. Through computer linkages, each segment responds with the merchandise or product components needed for a quick response to orders for the end-use customer. The computer linkage system is based upon availability and use of **point of sale (POS) information** that is fed back to successive stages in the production chain (Figure 8–8). That is, through use of computerized registers, retailers capture at the point of sale detailed information on products sold (vendor, style, size, color, etc.). The point of sale data is captured by stockkeeping units (SKUs)[2]. Subsequently, the information is communicated through computer linkages to apparel manufacturers who respond by providing items needed to replenish stock. Linkages may extend backward to fabric and fiber producers as well. In short, the computer linkages set in motion automatic reordering known by industry terms such as *automatic replenishment* or **just-in-time (JIT)** responses. Cooperative efforts such as that of the VICS group have been helpful in implementing Quick Response programs.

The close communication required under QR systems necessitates that each segment of the industry be closely in tune with the needs of its customers. The primary goal of the whole Quick Response initiative, which incidentally was developed by the *manufacturing segments* of the softgoods chain, was originally focused on efforts to attract U.S. retailers to buy domestic textile and apparel products rather than imports. The incentive to retailers to participate in QR efforts is that they might hold inventories low and avoid overstocking, while still ensuring that merchandisers would be able to stock what customers wanted to buy. Today, fast response has become increasingly a basic expectation on the part of retailers as a condition of doing business with manufacturers.

If we refer again to the train analogy used earlier to illustrate the impact of consumer demand on the flow for the entire softgoods chain, we might think of QR as providing rapid communication back through the individual sections of the train so that each unit can anticipate the speed of the train. In keeping with the high-technology character of Quick Response, we might think of QR as providing a monitor in each car on which relevant data related to the engine's speed are made available. Consequently, because each segment has been able to anticipate the engine's speed, costly "mishaps" are less likely to occur.

In addition to helping retailers serve customers more effectively with minimal inventory backlog, firms at all stages of the production chain have the potential of reducing costly inventory investments by participating in Quick Response efforts. Ideally, companies at each stage may reduce inventories of whatever they contribute to the production-marketing chain because they could expect fast service from their suppliers.

Quick Response works when products flow quickly through the pipeline to the consumer. By reducing the production pipeline,

---

[2]**Universal Product Coding (UPC)**, often called *bar coding*, plays an important role in Quick Response. Apparel manufacturers affix on their garments a 12-digit UPC identification that provides details on vendor, style, color, and size. Stores may add price—if they choose not to use the manufacturer's suggested price—and other information, if needed. Retail scanning equipment reads the UPC labeling, capturing point of sale information on the products sold. This information is fed back to manufacturers to give an indication of actual consumer demand.

FIGURE 8–8
Quick Response (QR) is based on closer linkages and an integrated system that shortens delivery times throughout the softgoods chain to improve service to the retailer and the end-use consumer.

Source: Illustration by Dennis Murphy.

stock can be replenished quickly at the retail level and retailers avoid costly **stockouts** and **markdowns**.

Furthermore, a faster-responding pipeline reduces the investment retailers must make in inventory at a given time. These improvements in the pipeline can greatly improve the financial performance, the "bottom line," for retailers. Moreover, QR reduces risks for the retailer because buying decisions are made closer to the selling season. For example, QR advocates believe that with two-season product lines, retail buying decisions might be made as late as eight weeks prior to the selling season compared to the traditional five to six months for domestic suppliers. The contrast is even greater in considering foreign suppliers who may require seven to eight months in lead time.

Promoting Domestic Products

As a result of a number of consumer studies that showed strong consumer preference for U.S.-made apparel, manufacturers in the textile complex joined forces to make consumers more aware of domestic-made products. Known as the "Crafted with Pride in U.S.A." campaign, a national labeling and promotion effort developed under the leadership of the Crafted with Pride in U.S.A. Council, which represents several hundred members. The council's statement of purpose is:

> The Crafted with Pride in U.S.A. Council is a committed force of United States cotton growers, labor organizations, fabric distributors, and manufacturers of manmade fibers, fabric, apparel, and home fashions, whose mission is to convince consumers, retailers, and apparel manufacturers of the value of purchasing and promoting U.S.-made products.

Figure 8–9 is the logo for the Crafted with Pride campaign. Campaign backers designed the logo to be an easily recognized symbol of U.S.-made products.[3]

---

[3]Industry leaders who initially developed the Crafted with Pride logo intentionally designed it to be somewhat "generic" with the expectation that other U.S. industries might wish to join the campaign to promote domestic products. Manufacturers of a number of other product lines have used the logo on their products.

QUICK TRANSFER OF QUICK RESPONSE

The Quick Response effort was begun by U.S. textile and apparel manufacturers in an effort to regain domestic markets from foreign suppliers. QR is based on the idea that U.S. manufacturers can serve retailers more quickly and more efficiently because they are located in U.S. markets. In general, the U.S. industry perceived QR as *its* brainchild and *its* strategy for competing against imports. Not long after U.S. manufacturers launched the Quick Response strategy, the author was in meetings with apparel producers (mostly contractors) in Costa Rica and learned that manufacturers in that country viewed Quick Response—by the same name—as a strategy for Costa Rican producers as well. Moreover, Costa Rican manufacturers employed basic technology associated with QR. Both the strategy and the technology to support it diffused quickly to Costa Rica and surely to many other countries. No doubt the transfer was hastened by the volume of Costa Rican production under contract for U.S. manufacturers.

FIGURE 8–9
Crafted with Pride in U.S.A. logo.

Source: Reprinted courtesy of the Crafted with Pride in U.S.A. Council, Inc.

with widespread geographical dispersion. As a result, W. Cline (1987) noted that special interest groups representing the textile complex have strong political power at the national level. According to Aggarwal (1985), Keesing and Wolf (1980), Toyne et al. (1984), and numerous others, the U.S. textile complex has been particularly effective in influencing both national and international trade policies in efforts to restrict foreign imports. Although the textile complex has felt battered by foreign competition and would like increasingly strengthened trade policies to protect their interests, Aggarwal (1985), W. Cline (1987), Keesing and Wolf (1980), and Toyne et al. (1984) noted that, compared to almost all other industrial sectors, the textile and apparel industries have in fact been successful in acquiring considerable protection in a variety of forms.

Major retailers such as Wal-Mart and J.C. Penney have been supportive of the industry's efforts by emphasizing U.S. products. In fact, Wal-Mart Stores, Inc. has made a conscious effort to secure as many of its lines as possible from domestic suppliers to preserve domestic jobs. This program is discussed in greater detail in a later chapter, which focuses on retailers.

In addition to the industry-sponsored Crafted with Pride effort, a federal law has required since 1984 that labels on domestically produced garments show that items were produced in the United States. Prior to that time, only foreign country of origin labeling was required.

Influencing Public Policy

Various segments of the textile complex are located in every state, and in total these industries and those dependent upon the complex represent a large number of voters

THE U.S. TEXTILE COMPLEX IN THE GLOBAL MARKET

By any measure, the U.S. textile complex is a major force in global markets. Moreover, most other countries look to the United States in one way or another as a major player whose textile and apparel trade activities will affect significantly their own sectors as well as their respective nation's economies. For example, the United States is a major market for many countries' products; or other nations may buy intermediate textile products to use in production of their own finished goods. In total, many aspects of the U.S. textile complex's production, consumption, and trade (including trade policies) often have a broad ripple effect through the global textile complex.

In addition to the historical strength of the United States in general trade matters, the magnitude of the U.S. market coupled with the size and diversity of the textile complex make these U.S. sectors important globally.

Toyne et al. (1984) provided a helpful view for putting the U.S. textile complex in perspective from a world view. Toyne and his colleagues noted:

> Although most countries manufacture textile products, most lack the supply and demand conditions necessary to support entire textile complexes. For example, not all countries are endowed with the land or climatic conditions necessary for the production of agricultural products such as cotton or wool. Some countries do not have the indigenous technological or financial capabilities to develop and support chemical complexes capable of producing manmade fibers, or textile machinery. Others lack the necessary internal markets required to achieve economies of scale in the production of man-made fibers, chemicals and "mature" textile fabrics. As a result, there is considerable variation between [sic] countries in their manufacturing industries, their dependence upon foreign inputs and/or markets, and their abilities to compete internationally. (p. 8)

The U.S. textile complex encompasses all the elements to which Toyne refers and has had size, production, and marketing sophistication at most levels, which have made it one of the largest and most comprehensive globally.

Many other countries are dependent upon the U.S. market for sale of their textile and apparel products. According to data cited in a prior chapter, the U.S. market was the third-highest recipient of worldwide textile exports in 1992 ($8.2 billion) and was by far the major recipient of worldwide apparel exports for the same year ($33.0 billion) (personal communication with GATT economist, 1993, 1994). Figure 8–10 shows the primary sources of textile and apparel imports in U.S. markets in 1993.

Although the U.S. market is a major recipient of textile and apparel goods from other regions of the world, the domestic industry has not attained a comparable position as an exporter to the markets of other countries. Various segments of the U.S. textile complex

FIGURE 8–10

Major sources of U.S. imports of textiles and apparel, 1993.

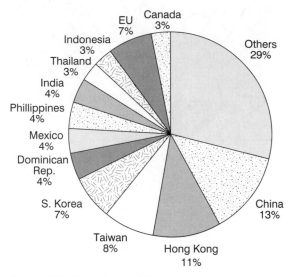

Source: U.S. Department of Commerce.

differ greatly in their export performance. For example, the manufactured fiber industry has been relatively successful in exporting, whereas the apparel industry has not in the past.

Many U.S. textile and apparel firms have operations in other countries. For decades, some of the major manufactured fibers firms such as DuPont have had multinational operations. In recent years, a growing number of apparel manufacturers have had sewing plants in other countries, particularly in the Caribbean basin region and along the Mexican border. More recently, however, several U.S. firms have acquired companies in other countries as part of their strategy to penetrate markets in those regions. DuPont acquired the nylon operations of ICI Fibers, a British firm, and in exchange ICI acquired DuPont's acrylic operations.

At least two major apparel firms have made acquisitions to have access to markets in other countries. Sara Lee has acquired Montreal-based Giltex (a Canadian hosiery manufacturer), Mexico's Mallorca, S.A. de C.V. (the second largest sheer hosiery producer in that country), Italy's Filodoro Group (a hosiery manufacturer), Maglificio Bellia (the leading Italian men's and women's underwear manufacturer), Dim (a French hosiery line and the largest in Europe), Pretty Polly and Elbeo brands in the United Kingdom, and Nur Die and Bellinda brands in Germany. Sara Lee is now the leading hosiery producer and marketer in Europe (Sara Lee Corporation, 1993). This acquisition strategy provides Sara Lee access to channels of distribution for the company's U.S. brands such as Hanes, in addition to those produced by the acquired companies. VF Corporation has pursued a similar strategy of acquiring companies in other countries.

FOREIGN INVESTMENT IN THE U.S. TEXTILE COMPLEX

The term *globalization of the textile industry* has taken on new meaning in the United States in recent years as a growing number of foreign firms have invested in the domestic textile industry. Investing in the United States has become increasingly attractive because of current high operating rates and the perception that the United States is a safe economic and political haven. During 1987, for example, a total of 51 foreign companies moved to or expanded operations in South Carolina alone; the majority were in the textile and apparel industries (Standard & Poor's, 1988). Foreign investment in the U.S. industry accounts for about 2 percent of the establishments and about 5 percent of the employment and shipments of the overall textile industry. Foreign-owned U.S. facilities are somewhat more heavily concentrated in the thread, nonwoven fabric, and cordage industries (U.S. Dept. of Commerce, 1993).

Increased foreign investment is yet another dimension in the restructuring of the U.S. industry. This trend also helps us to understand that we must view textile (and generally apparel) production and trade in a broad global perspective rather than as simply domestic matters.

SUMMARY

The U.S. textile complex has a long history of contributing to the American economy. The fiber-textile-apparel complex represents the largest manufacturing employer in the U.S. economy, providing jobs for approximately one of every ten industrial workers. Production facilities are located in every state.

The textile complex is a major contributor to the U.S. gross national product, ranking as one of the top manufacturing sectors in its contribution. Although the number of jobs has declined, the complex remains the leading U.S. manufacturing employer. Textile and apparel manufacturing has played a particularly significant role in providing jobs for women, minorities, and new immigrants. In addition, the complex contributes importantly to other U.S. sectors through a variety of linkages.

Major activities of the textile complex include the production of fibers, the conversion of those fibers into intermediate textile mill products, and the manufacture of end-use products from the intermediate components. In the past, each segment operated more or less separately, producing intermediate products for the next stage of the production chain. More recently, however, more integrated relationships developed as the domestic industry sought advantages over their foreign competitors. As a result, the U.S. textile complex has experienced a significant level of restructuring. For example, many manufacturers have engaged in vertical integration—both forward and backward integration—and mergers and acquisitions have led to greater concentration in the industry. The basic production activities remained similar to those in the past (although updated by technology), but major changes occurred in the *organizational structures and relationships* through which these activities took place.

Consumer demand (consumption) provides the momentum for activity in the total softgoods chain. Favorable consumer spending fosters activity among all segments in the chain; a decline in spending creates a slowdown in activity in all segments. Factors influencing demand may include shifts in the economy, style changes, consumer interests, demographic changes, and changes in lifestyle.

Affected by demand as well as other factors, the U.S. textile complex, like those in most other industrialized countries, has experienced periods of growth and decline. Increased foreign competition occurred at a time when domestic consumption slowed markedly. As a result, the combination of increased import shipments and sluggish demand heightened competition for the existing U.S. market.

The 1970s and 1980s were critical transition years for the U.S. textile complex. International competition and new technology forced the domestic textile complex through "its most profound transformation since the industrial revolution" (OTA, 1987, p. 3). Changes included the nature of the products produced; how they are produced; how they are marketed; the structure, scale, and scope of the enterprises producing them; and the nature of jobs created directly and indirectly by the industry.

Efforts of the U.S. textile complex to retain or regain a competitive position included the following: closing or revitalizing outmoded and inefficient plants; restructuring through consolidations and mergers; investments in equipment and technology; efforts to improve productivity levels; developing a greater sensitivity to market needs; establishing closer working relationships within the softgoods chain; concentrating on market segments in which the United States has greatest advantage; shortening response time; promoting domestic products; and influencing public policy.

In considering the U.S. textile complex in the international economy, we see that the magnitude of the U.S. market—coupled with the size and diversity of the textile complex—make these U.S. sectors important globally. Moreover, the economies of many other nations are affected by activities of the U.S. complex. And finally, another form of globalization of the industry has occurred as a significant number of foreign firms are buying U.S. textile firms.

GLOSSARY

Backward integration means that a firm extends its operation into a previous stage of the production process. For example, a fabric producer adds yarn production capabilities.

Barriers to entry are those factors that make it difficult to enter an industry. Examples include capital, high-technology demands, or monopolistic market conditions.

Concentration or *concentration ratio* refers to the portion of total business in a given industry that is handled by a specified number of the largest firms—generally expressed as the percentage of business assets, production, sales, employment, or profits accounted for by the largest firms (usually the largest three to eight firms) (OTA, 1987).

Consumer confidence refers to consumers' outlook on the economy, particularly in terms of how they will be affected by the general state of the economy. Consumer confidence is measured by periodic consumer surveys.

Domestic production refers to production that occurs within one's country.

Durable good is a good that yields its services gradually over an extended period of time; examples are automobiles and household appliances.

End-use products are those textile products ready for use or application whether apparel, interior furnishings, or industrial/specialty goods.

Establishment (or plant) is a single productive unit; a firm may have one or more establishments.

Firm (or *company*) includes all manufacturing establishments owned by the firm, plus all manufacturing establishments of subsidiaries or affiliates over which the company has acknowledged control.

Forward integration means that a firm extends its operations into later stages of the production process. For example, a yarn producer acquires fabric manufacturing capabilities, or an apparel producer adds retailing operations.

Horizontal integration occurs when a firm expands into the production of new products that are competitive with older ones—that is, integration of production at roughly the same stages in the manufacturing process. For example, a weaving firm that has produced denim expands to include an operation that produces broadcloth.

Industrial adjustment (also known as *adjustment* or *structural adjustment*) means restoring productivity of an industry so that it remains competitive in the overall industrial scheme of the economy (Ghadar et al. 1987).

Industry structure refers to the number and sizes of firms in a given industry and the type of competition that exists among them (OTA, 1987).

Inventory management refers to matching inventory as closely as possible to demand to reduce investment costs and losses from excessive stock. (As a result of increasingly difficult conditions of the 1980s, all segments of the softgoods industry became more attentive to careful inventory management.)

Just-in-time (JIT) inventory management refers to inventory control systems that control the inflow and outflow of parts, components, and finished goods so that minimal inventory is kept on hand.

Markdown is a retail price reduction on merchandise. These reductions may be planned for promotional purposes or unplanned for merchandise that does not sell at the original price.

Nondurable good yields its services within a more immediate and shorter term, especially in comparison to durable goods; examples are apparel and food.

Point of sale (POS) information refers to the data captured at the point of sale through sophisticated computerized registers. In Quick Response systems, this information is fed back to successive stages in the production chain.

Privately held companies are those owned privately by individuals or groups rather than shareholders.

Publicly held companies are those owned by shareholders who have purchased stock in the company.

Quick Response (QR) is an industry initiative that at first focused on shortening production cycle time based on extensive use of electronic data transmission from the retailer to various segments of manufacturing. The concept evolved into a transformation of the way in which apparel is made and distributed and is based largely on closer working relationships between suppliers and retailers.

Rationalization refers to the elimination of "excess" steps in the labor (production) process. (Also see glossary for Chapter 12.)

Semidurable good yields its services within a term between that of a durable good and that of a nondurable good; home furnishings textile products such as carpet and draperies may be considered in this category. (Some sources consider apparel to be a semidurable good.)

Softgoods chain refers to the total textile and apparel production-distribution chain. This includes the manufacturing of products through retailing and other distribution phases associated with making products available to the consumer.

Stockout is a term used when customers want merchandise that is not available in the store.

Universal product coding (UPC) is the bar coding used on products so relevant data may be captured by retail scanning equipment. The 12-digit UPC identification shows the retail price to be charged to the customer. However, capturing other point of sale information on products sold permits the retailer to quickly replenish products of certain styles, sizes, or colors, for example, as items are sold.

Vertical integration occurs when a single firm operates at more than one stage of production. This might include any combination of stages of production, but the most comprehensive type of vertical integration includes operations from processing the raw material for fiber to the completion and distribution of the finished product.

SUGGESTED READINGS

American Apparel Manufacturers Association (AAMA) (Annual). *Focus: An economic profile of the apparel industry.* Arlington, VA: Author.
Annual industry profile.

American Textile Manufacturers Institute (ATMI). (Quarterly). *Textile hi-lights.* Washington, D.C: Author.
Quarterly reviews of textile industry performance; some data on broader textile complex.

Arpan, J., de la Torre, J., Toyne, B., Bacchetta, M., Jedel, M., Stephan, P., & Halliburton, J. (1982). *The U.S. apparel industry: International challenge, domestic response.* Atlanta: Georgia State University Press.
A study of the U.S. apparel industry's international competitiveness and how domestic companies responded to the global competition.

Fibers, Textiles, and Apparel Industry Panel, Committee on Technology and International Economic and Trade Issues (1983). *The competitive status of the U.S. fibers, textiles, and apparel complex: A study of the influences of technology in determining international industrial competitive advantage.* Washington, DC: National Academy Press.

Finnie, T. (1992). *Textiles and apparel in the U.S.A.: Restructuring for the 1990s.* London: The Economist Intelligence Unit.
An overview of major factors leading to a restructuring of the U.S. industry.

Ghadar, F., Davidson, W., & Feigenoff, C. (1987). *U.S. industrial competitiveness: The case of the textile and apparel industries.* Lexington, MA: Lexington Books.
This book examines global and domestic forces that affected the performance of the U.S. textile complex.

Spitalnick, I. (1985, May). Coming home. *Apparel Industry Magazine,* pp. 48–54.
Spitalnick's report on returning to U.S. production when he was president of Evan-Picone and his frustrations in working with domestic suppliers when he started Spitalnick and Company.

Standard & Poor's. *Industry Surveys.* (Annual). *Textiles, apparel and home furnishings—Basic analysis. Annual overviews of industry performance.*

U.S. Congress, Office of Technology Assessment. (1987). *The U.S. textile and apparel industry: A revolution in progress.* Washington, DC: U.S. Government Printing Office.
An overview of structural adjustment in the U.S. textile complex.

U.S. Department of Commerce. *U.S. industrial outlook* (annual). Washington, DC: Author. *A concise overview of the status of various industry sectors for the current year.*

U.S. International Trade Commission (1987, December). *U.S. global competitiveness: The U.S. textile mill industry.* (USITC Publication 2048). Washington, DC: *An in-depth study of the U.S. textile mill sector.*

9

The U.S. Textile and Apparel Industries and Trade

INTRODUCTION

Within the comprehensive textile complex, the textile and apparel industries are closely related yet distinct sectors. Despite the fact that the textile and apparel sectors have a great deal in common as part of an integrated production and marketing chain, each has distinct characteristics and unique problems—features that position the two quite differently in terms of competitiveness and trade. In this chapter, we shall give an overview of each industry, with special emphasis on issues that influence each sector's ability to compete in the global economy.

PRODUCT CLASSIFICATION SYSTEMS

Both international and U.S. industrial classification systems define products included in the categories considered *textiles* and *apparel*. Unfortunately, the system used for international trade data is not directly comparable to the domestic system; that is, the categories and definitions for international data are not the same as those used for U.S. production categories. The two classification systems are as follows:

Standard International Trade Classification (SITC) (International)

This system was introduced by the United Nations in 1950 to promote international comparability of world trade data. Textile products are classified under **SITC** 65, which includes textile yarns, fabrics, made-up articles not specified elsewhere, and related products. These may be natural fibers, manufactured fibers, or blends of these fibers. This UN sys-

FIGURE 9–1
The U.S. textile and apparel industries represent a large and comprehensive collection of enterprises that includes operations at all stages of manufacturing and distribution.

Source: Illustration by Dennis Murphy.

tem groups apparel products under SITC 84, articles of apparel and accessories.

Standard Industrial Classification (SIC) (United States)

The **SIC**, established and maintained by the U.S. Office of Management and Budget, is designed to classify U.S. establishments into industry groupings on the basis of their primary economic activity. Table 9–1 provides a listing of classification categories for both textiles and apparel. The following are relevant categories to our study:

- *Textile mill products* comprise major *group 22 (SIC 22)*.
- *Apparel* constitutes major *group 23 (SIC 23)*.
- *Manufactured fibers* (because of their chemical origin) are in the *chemical and allied prod-*

ucts grouping (SIC 28), rather than with textile mill products.
- *Textile machinery* is classified in *group 35 (SIC 35)*, specifically as 3552.

The first two digits define the major SIC classification (i.e., "major group"). Typically, the third digit defines a grouping (i.e., "group") of products. Examples are: the 232 group consists of men's and boys' furnishings, work clothing, and allied garments; the 233 group consists of women's, misses', and juniors' outerwear; and the 234 group consists of women's, misses', children's, and infants' undergarments.

Within the SIC category system, some types of knitted apparel may fall in the textile group while other kinds may be considered part of the apparel group. Under this classification system, apparel constitutes major

TABLE 9–1
SIC codes for extiles and apparel

SIC 22 Textile Mill Products		*SIC 22 Textile Mill Products (continued)*	
2211	Broad woven fabric mills, cotton	2297	Nonwoven fabrics
2221	Broad woven fabric mills, man-made fiber and silk	2298	Cordage and twine
		2299	Textile goods, not elsewhere classified
2231	Broad woven fabric mills (including dyeing and finishing)		
2241	Narrow fabrics and other smallwares mills: cotton, wool, silk, and man-made fiber	*SIC 23 Apparel and Other Finished Products Made from Fabrics and Similar Materials*	
2251	Women's full-length and knee-length hosiery	2311	Men's and boys' suits, coats, and overcoats
2252	Hosiery, except women's full-length and knee-length hosiery	2321	Men's and boys' shirts
2253[a]	Knit outerwear mills	2322	Men's and boys' underwear and nightwear
2254[a]	Knit underwear and nightwear mills	2323	Men's and boys' neckwear
2257	Circular knit fabric mills	2325	Men's and boys' trousers and slacks
2258	Lace and warpknit fabric mills	2326	Men's and boys' work clothing
2259	Knitting mills, not elsewhere classified	2329	Men's and boys' clothing, not elsewhere classified
2261	Finishers of broad woven fabrics of cotton	2331[b]	Women's, misses', and juniors' blouses and shirts
2262	Finishers of broad woven fabrics of man-made fiber and silk	2335[b]	Women's, misses', and juniors' dresses
2269	Finishers of textiles, not elsewhere classified	2337[b]	Women's, misses', and juniors' suits, skirts, and coats
2273	Carpets and rugs	2339[b]	Women's, misses', and juniors' outerwear, not elsewhere classified
2281	Yarn spinning mills		
2282	Throwing and winding mills		
2284	Thread mills	2341[b]	Women's, misses', children's, and infants' underwear and nightwear
2295	Coated fabrics, not rubberized		
2296	Tire cord and fabric	2342[b]	Brassieres, girdles, and allied garments

group 23 (SIC 23) officially entitled Apparel and Other Finished Products Made from Fabrics and Similar Materials (U.S. Executive Office, 1987). Garments such as sweaters and sweatshirts knitted directly from yarn or made from fabric knitted in the same establishment are classified in SIC 22, Textile Mill Products. The major difference between SIC 22 and 23 is that the latter involves firms cutting and sewing *purchased* fabrics, whereas the former involves mills knitting apparel in a vertical operation either from yarn or from fabric knit in the same mill. In addition, as the last portion of Table 9–1 shows, several other types of apparel and accessories are included in other SIC classification categories.

THE U.S. TEXTILE INDUSTRY

Although the term *textile* was derived from the Latin verb *texere*, which means "to weave," modern usage includes a far more comprehensive interpretation. Our discussion on the textile industry will focus on fibers and textile mill products:

- *Fibers* represent the basic component and the initial production phase for the entire textile complex, regardless of the form the final product takes.
- *Textile mill products* include the following groupings: yarn, thread, cordage, twine, woven fabrics, knitted fabrics, carpets and

TABLE 9–1 *(continued)*

SIC 23 Apparel and Other Finished Products Made from Fabrics and Similar Materials (continued)	2396 Automotive trimmings, apparel findings, and related products
	2397[a] Schiffli machine embroideries
	2399 Fabricated textile products, not elsewhere classified

2353	Hats, caps, and millinery
2361[b]	Girls', children's, and infants' dresses, blouses, and shirts
2369[b]	Girls', children's, and infants' outerwear, not elsewhere classified
2371	Fur goods
2381[a]	Dress and work gloves, except knit and all-leather
2384[a]	Robes and dressing gowns
2385[a]	Raincoats and other water-proof outerwear
2386[a]	Leather and sheep-lined clothing
2387[a]	Apparel belts
2389[a]	Apparel and accessories, not elsewhere classified
2391	Curtains and draperies
2392	Housefurnishings, except curtains and draperies
2393	Textile bags
2394	Canvas and related products
2395[b]	Pleating, decorative and novelty stitching, and tucking for the trade

Others

2823	Artificial (cellulosic) fibers
2824	Synthetic (noncellulosic), organic fibers
3552	Textile machinery
3069[a]	Fabricated rubber products, not elsewhere classified (insofar as it includes vulcanized rubber clothing)
3079[a]	Miscellaneous plastic products (insofar as it includes plastic clothing)
3151[a]	Leather gloves and mittens
3842[a]	Orthopedic, prosthetic, and surgical appliances and supplies (insofar as it includes surgical corsets, belts, trusses, and similar articles)
3962[b]	Feathers, plumes, and artificial flowers (insofar as it includes artificial flowers)

[a]Branch of industry specializing in producing articles of apparel for both sexes.
[b]Branch of Industry specializing in producing women's and children's apparel.

Source: U.S. Executive Office of the President, Office of Management and Budget, *Standard Industrial Classification Manual* (1987).

rugs, interior furnishings such as bedding and towels, and other products such as nonwoven fabrics (USITC, 1987b).

The U.S. textile industry represents more than 5,000 firms (and far more establishments); (various sources give differing statistics) ranging from large sophisticated companies to small plants performing rudimentary production processes. Products range from technologically advanced fibers to simple products manufactured in plants that have changed little over time. Most firms manufacture intermediate or finished products for mass markets; this market orientation has resulted in long production runs and standardized products. The mass production emphasis has been both good and bad for the textile sector. Although this strategy resulted in products representing high quality for the cost, emphasis on volume runs also has resulted in a degree of insensitivity to customer needs.

The textile industry is a large and important industrial sector in the U.S. economy. Despite a number of difficult foreign and domestic challenges in recent decades, most segments of the textile industry have remained competitive. Although the industry has experienced hard times, some of the resulting adjustments have made the sector more efficient and more viable for competing in today's international market.

Brief Historic Review

Archaeological evidence suggests that textile products have been basic to humankind for centuries. Because textile production has existed for so long in most regions of the world, the textile industry's history may account for some of the sector's current problems. The industry's long history means that the global market suffers from an overabundance of producers. Moreover, as a leader of the Industrial Revolution, the industry has been developing technically for hundreds of years; therefore, the industry suffers from certain problems typical of "mature" industries.

As a producer of goods vital to human life and a provider of jobs for the masses, the textile industry established a powerful place for itself in both the global economy and in the U.S. economy. Despite a dramatic technological and social transformation of the industry since its early days, textile production has remained a primary industrial sector in the United States.

For much of its existence, the textile industry has faced a constant need for renewal and modernization. In recent decades in particular, the industry has faced difficult challenges because of intense competition from foreign producers and among domestic producers. Global market conditions and other economic changes have placed intense pressures on the U.S. textile industry to restructure in order to survive. Consequently, the last three decades have been among the most eventful—and trying—in the history of the U.S. textile sector.

Historically the U.S. textile sector has had little product differentiation and a relatively low concentration of manufacturing. The lack of concentration within the textile sector, particularly when compared with other major industrial sectors, accounts for some of the competitive climate in the industry. In contrast to some industries where barriers to entry exist—such as large **economies of scale**, a high degree of product differentiation, high absolute costs, large capital requirements, control of input supplies, ownership of key patents and institutional or legal factors (Toyne et al., 1984)—many aspects of textile production are relatively easy to enter.

In short, the combination of (1) producing relatively homogeneous products, (2) developing limited specialization and concentration, and (3) posing few barriers to entry into the industry led to intensely competitive conditions for most of the textile sector.

The Fiber Industry

Sectors that produce the two major types of fibers—natural fibers and manufactured fibers—represent a sharp contrast to one another. Natural fiber production is part of the agricultural sector; manufactured fiber production is part of the technologically advanced chemical and allied products sector. Despite the contrasting modes of production, most fibers can be substituted for each other. Manufactured fibers not only compete with one another but also with natural fibers. Moreover, fashion changes, other consumer preference trends, and various economic conditions have caused fairly dramatic shifts from one group to the other.

Worldwide demand by fiber categories varies from that for the U.S. market. In particular, cotton accounts for a much higher market share globally than is true in the United States. U.S. consumption of manufactured fibers exceeds that of natural fibers, but we must remember that these figures reflect interior furnishings and industrial use, along with apparel use. The worldwide demand for cotton relative to manufactured fibers also reflects the availability of cotton compared to manufactured fibers in the developing countries.

In today's global economy, worldwide fiber demand can affect the U.S. softgoods industry and the U.S. consumer. As an example, the global demand for cotton may exceed the supply in years when crop production is poor. As a result, availability and prices for cotton and cotton products for U.S. markets are affected.

Natural Fibers

Cotton is the primary natural fiber produced and consumed in the United States, accounting for over 90 percent of natural fiber used. Wool is produced in limited amounts; other natural fibers are relatively important in the U.S. market but are imported. For the most part, natural fiber production has increased slowly in the United States because of the strong competition from manufactured fibers; however, the resurgence of popularity of natural fibers for apparel in the late 1980s increased demand noticeably.

Manufactured Fibers

Manufactured fibers represent a milestone development for the global textile complex in the twentieth century. The technology and capital requirements for this chemical-based industry determined for at least a time the locations in which world fiber production occurred. In addition to the capital- and knowledge-intensive aspects of manufactured fiber production, this is one segment of the textile complex for which significant economies of scale existed. Another barrier to entering manufactured fiber production has been limited access to distribution channels. As a result of these characteristics, manufactured fiber producers were in the past located in the developed countries and were typically part of large, diversified, multinational chemical companies. In the past, a large portion of the manufactured fiber industry used similar manufacturing processes; products were substituted for one another easily, markets were similar, and most companies had comparable **research and development (R&D)** expenditures.

Manufactured fibers consist of two types: (1) **artificial fibers** (also known as cellulosic fibers)—such as rayon, acetate, and triacetate—which come from naturally occurring cellulose sources (generally trees), and (2) **synthetic fibers** (also known as noncellulosic fibers)—such as nylon, polyester, and acrylic—which are petrochemical derivatives. Manufactured fiber production is so much a part of the chemical industry that within the U.S. Standard Industrial Classification (SIC) system, this segment is grouped with the chemical and allied products series rather than with textile mill products (Table 9–1).

Presently, the United States is the leading world producer of manufactured fibers, with this segment being one of the most competitive of any in the U.S. textile complex involved in global trade. Yet, the U.S. manufactured fiber industry consists of a small number (approximately 15) of large multinational corporations, which are horizontally integrated. DuPont, Monsanto, and Allied are American-owned companies and are among the world's largest firms. The top 10 producers in the United States account for more than 90 percent of U.S. production (OTA, 1987). Manufactured fiber producers compete for the markets of seven distinct fibers: polyester, nylon, acrylic, polyethylene, polypropylene, rayon, and acetate. In 1993, an estimated 56,400 persons were employed in the U.S. manufactured fiber industry (U.S. Department of Commerce, 1994).

Trade

The discussion in the earlier section on fiber markets included several relevant points on trade. Manufactured fibers have been a major export category for the U.S. textile complex, with exports growing from less than $200 million in 1972 to an estimated $1.7 billion in 1992 (U.S. Department of Commerce, 1993). Manufactured exports decreased 1 percent in 1993 because of the slowdown in the global economy (U.S. Department of Commerce, 1994). Moreover, as developing nations increase their manufactured fiber production capacity, U.S. manufacturers' share of the world market has decreased. As an example, U.S. synthetic fiber producers' share of the world market dropped from 33 percent in 1979 to 18 percent in 1991 (Fiber Economics Bureau, March, 1986; U.S. Department of Commerce, 1993).

Overall, the U.S. fiber sector suffers from problems of production overcapacity and saturated markets—a condition evident in many instances in which various segments compete against one another for a share of the market. The saturated and overcapacity market conditions also apply in considering competition between natural and manufactured fibers in a range of product areas. Finally, the glutted market conditions are most evident in considering the mix of domestic and imported products—a situation in which producers from many other countries compete with domestic manufacturers for the U.S. market. DuPont, a leader in manufactured fiber production, has **restructured** its fiber business in response to this competition. As part of this restructuring, hundreds of jobs have been eliminated.

The global cotton market is intensely competitive because of the large number of countries producing this fiber. U.S. cotton producers supply fiber for both the domestic market and the international market. In fact, the United States is the second largest world producer of cotton—with Japan, South Korea, and other Pacific Rim nations accounting for the major purchases of U.S. cotton (OTA, 1987).

Developing countries will continue to be major cotton producers because many economies in those nations depend on cotton as a primary source of earnings, employment, and trade. Many of those countries lack the resources for other production. Because of lower production costs, those countries sell cotton at attractive prices in world markets and are likely to continue doing so.

As additional developing countries gain the capabilities for producing manufactured fibers, many are doing so not only for domestic import substitution but also as part of global trade strategies. That is, as the developing countries mature, they strive to produce all the component parts for the end products they export, whereas in earlier stages they tended to assemble products from components made elsewhere. As a result of this maturing of industrial sectors in many developing countries, particularly many Asian nations, competition for U.S. manufactured fiber producers will continue to intensify.

In the last decade, the greatest growth in manufactured fiber production has been in the developing countries. Western Europe, the United States, and Japan account for declining shares of manufactured fiber production, and the greatest increases have been in China and other Asian countries (Fiber Economics Bureau, various years).

The U.S. fiber industry, in its present form, is vulnerable in a number of respects. High investments in equipment intended to enhance competitiveness have been focused on mass production of basic fibers. That is, U.S. producers who have the history and technical expertise to continue being the vanguard fiber industry of the world have for the most part produced basic commodity fibers, that is, relatively common fibers produced in large quantities. Following this strategy means that U.S. fiber producers have attempted to compete on a price basis for the *same high-volume markets* as the new entrants in the developing countries. Although the United States has been a leader in developing specialty fibers (both new generic groupings as well as highly specialized variations within established generic groupings), most of the industry output has been in the commodity fiber area. In contrast, the industry in Western Europe (the industry most comparable to that in the United States) has placed added emphasis on specialization and service rather than production of homogeneous, standardized products.

Although the U.S. fiber industry has been a leader in manufactured fiber development, the industry is dependent to a large degree upon foreign producers of textile machinery for the equipment required for the production. For both natural and manufactured fiber producers, much of the technology required to maintain a competitive lead in the industry globally comes from producers in Germany, Switzerland, Japan, and Italy. Equipment changes frequently, making technology an important factor in competition and making fiber producers quite dependent on the manufacture of machinery. Moreover, the same modern equipment sold to U.S. producers is also available to the industry in any country with the capital and skills to obtain and use it. In this regard, newly established plants in developing countries may start production with state-of-the-art machinery whereas established fiber producers in the developed countries can seldom start over with all new production equipment.

Problems facing the domestic fiber industry, particularly the manufactured fiber industry, are a part of the broader phenomenon occurring in the United States. In sector after sector, domestic industries are losing their competitive edge in world markets, including many of the knowledge- and capital-intensive areas ("Can America compete?", 1987, "Fixing America's," 1992). The fiber segment of the U.S. textile complex, in many ways thought to be the most "secure" of the sectors within the complex because of its barriers to easy entry (high knowledge and capital requirements, along with other reasons given earlier), appears to be no exception to this difficulty in maintaining global competitiveness.

The Textile Mill Products Industry

The conversion of fibers into finished fabrics requires a variety of complex steps—including spinning and texturing yarns; knitting, weaving, and tufting; and dyeing, printing, and other finishing—resulting in an extensive textile mill products industry to perform these operations. This intermediate segment of the textile complex accounts for a majority of the establishments and workers within the "textile" sector. Although the mill products segment is quite fragmented, many areas are also highly specialized (Figure 9–2).

The total number of textile mill industry establishments has decreased somewhat since the early 1980s. The overall decrease can be attributed to a number of factors: plant closings as firms leave the industry, plant closings from consolidation of operations by some firms, and also the effects of mergers and acquisitions that have restructured the industry.

Although the textile mill products industry is dispersed throughout the United States, concentration is greatest in the Southeast. Location varies somewhat by sectors.

The textile industry **capacity utilization rate** has been healthy in recent years—generally around 90 percent—exceeding that for all manufacturing. As a result, textile industry performance from 1986 through 1988 began to provide an improved outlook for the sector. Although profit levels dipped periodically, overall performance was more positive than for some earlier periods in the 1980s. In fact, certain aspects of the textile sector's performance improved so dramatically that industry critics began to question why the textile industry needed increased protection from imports.

The recession in the early 1990s caused a significant slump in capacity utilization and corporate profit patterns. Nevertheless, the textile mill products industry fared better on both measures than U.S. manufacturing as a whole.

The textile sector has a commendable record of investing in advanced technology to

FIGURE 9–2
This father-son team, Farrell Hussey (left) and J. C. Hussey, illustrates the important role the textile industry has played for generations of workers. The Husseys are performing a slashing operation in Burlington's Asheboro, North Carolina, plant.

Source: Photo courtesy of Burlington Industries, Inc.

improve labor productivity. The textile industry's record of investing its profits has been comparable to that for all U.S. manufacturing. Textile production technology advanced dramatically in the 1970s, and forward-thinking companies invested heavily in the new generation of technology.

Although many textile firms have invested heavily in the technological advances, not all production facilities use state-of-the-art equipment. In general, however, where newer technology was incorporated into production operations, fewer workers were required.

The textile industry's investment in modernization has improved **productivity** and, as a result, has generally sustained profits. Increased productivity has aided profit performance primarily by reducing labor requirements, thus, labor costs. When productivity is improved, employment usually drops. In other words, fewer plants with fewer employees are producing greater output. Although productivity improvements make the industry more competitive, a negative effect is job loss. Now, it is not uncommon to find only one or two workers in charge of large spinning rooms that once would have required dozens of employees to run. Consequently, some **structural unemployment** has occurred.

The U.S. textile sector's increased productivity helped to position the industry at a greater advantage in international markets than would have been true without the improvements. Belaud (1985) reported in a European study that the U.S. achievements in productivity have made the country's textile industry quite competitive globally:

Some Western industries—especially the United States'—have achieved considerable gains in productivity thanks to the modernization and automation of the production. In 1980, the U.S. textile industry recorded the highest productivity per employee amongst the major industrialized manufacturing countries, thereby enabling it to achieve the lowest unit production costs amongst the same industrialized countries. . . . The labor cost per unit produced in the United States is therefore closer to that of Portugal than that of the major European manufacturers, and closer to the unit cost in Pakistan than to the unit cost in Belgium or Germany. As a result, U.S. producers have been able to achieve price levels approaching those of some "low cost" Asiatic or Mediterranean countries. (p. 37)

In the past, U.S. companies in the textile mill products industry have focused most efforts on the domestic market. In the early

1980s when the dollar was strong, exports accounted for only 3 percent of the total industry shipments. Consequently, the domestic market accounted for approximately 97 percent of the business for the textile mill products industry (USITC, 1987b). More recently, this industry segment (at least *some firms* in the segment) have begun to place more emphasis on exporting. According to *U.S. Industrial Outlook, 1994* (U.S. Department of Commerce, 1994), exports accounted for nearly 7 percent of total industry shipments in 1993. In a survey of textile CEOs, Hooper, Dickerson, Boyle (1994) found that 60 percent of the chief executives said their company planned to expand exports in the coming year. Another 22 percent said exports would remain the same.

As might be expected, the U.S. textile market is for the most part mature and saturated—especially in the segments that produce standardized, nonspecialty items.

Moreover, the overcapacity of the industry and the easy substitutability of products add to market problems for the mill products sector. Modest growth in the domestic markets, at a time when imports have increased dra-

matically, intensified competition for markets among domestic producers. Many older plants have closed, with attrition particularly high in the apparel fabrics sector. Many manufacturers have shifted to markets in which they expected less foreign competition and improved profit performance. Examples are the shifts from apparel fabric production to the home furnishings area in which sales have been healthy, import competition less intense, and automation more readily adaptable to the production processes. The interior textiles market began to slow down in 1992, however. As baby boomers moved beyond the prime marrying years, the segment of the market furnishing new homes has declined.

Changes in demand for textile products have a severe impact on mill **operating rates**. In Figure 9–3, mill operating rates reflect fluctuations in demand; and it follows that mill operating rates are reflected in the pretax profit margins for the industry. As Figure 9–3 illustrates, when increases and decreases in demand affected mill operating rates, pretax profit margins generally reflected the overall trend of the fluctuations.

FIGURE 9–3

Operating rates versus pretax margins (in percent, quarterly).

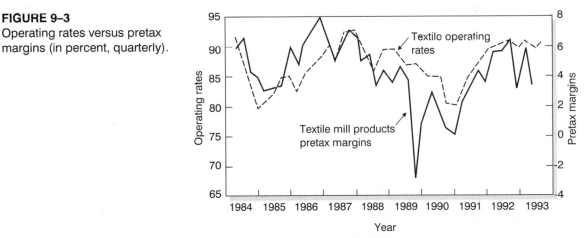

Source: Reprinted courtesy of Standard and Poor's; based on operating rates from Department of Commerce and pretax margins from Federal Trade Commission.

Employment in the textile mill sector peaked at almost one million in 1973 and declined to 593,000 in 1993. (U.S. Department of Commerce, 1994). The largest drops in employment occurred in the recession years of 1974 and 1982. Employment in the textile mill products area declined steadily until 1991, when employment began to remain relatively stable compared to the downward trend that occurred for several years. The improved employment trend also included increased hours worked and a decline in unemployment. Within the textile mill industry, changes in employment varied within selected industry segments.

Employment declines for the textile mill industry can be attributed to three major causes: (1) the increasing share of the U.S. textile market being supplied directly by imports; (2) the declining demand for apparel fabrics by U.S. apparel producers as imports have taken an increasing share of the U.S. market; and (3) the reduced need for production workers as modern, labor-saving equipment has been installed to improve productivity and competitiveness.

Trade

Although most areas of the U.S. textile mill products industry have experienced the effects of import competition, the domestic industry supplies the bulk of the U.S. market. As USITC staff (1987b) noted, the U.S. industry has advantages related to distribution costs, expenses associated with travel, communication, and paperwork costs and can provide savings through lower inventories because of the possibility for reordering during a season. U.S. mills also are able to produce large runs of many standard fabrics, which provide economies because of the continuous operations. Many foreign producers find it difficult to compete with the U.S. industry in certain areas, such as heavier-weight fabrics sold in large volume. Foreign suppliers have been more successful in the lighter-weight fabric market where transportation is a smaller part of total cost. These may be low-priced commodity fabrics or high-quality fabrics with distinctive design qualities, often made available in smaller quantities than U.S. mills have been willing to produce in the past.

Imports. Global competition has had an impact on the textile mill sector. U.S. textile mill product manufacturers had a relatively large and secure market for years. Consequently, the loss of portions of the market to imports has been difficult to accept and has required a number of dramatic changes in nearly every aspect of industry operations in order to remain competitive.

Determining the extent to which imported textiles account for a portion of the U.S. market is one of great controversy. The **import penetration ratio** is the measure of imports as a percentage of **apparent U.S. consumption**. Trade data may be examined in different ways, resulting in quite different conclusions about the level of import penetration in U.S. textile markets. The perceived severity of the import problem can vary greatly according to how the issue is examined. Therefore, reports on import penetration levels must be interpreted with care. An understanding of the different ways in which import penetration is reported is important as one begins to consider textile and apparel trade policy issues.

The two primary ways of examining import penetration ratios are:

1. *By using physical quantities*—usually **square-meter equivalents (SMEs)**—previously square-yard equivalents (SYEs), or, in some cases, weight. Industry sources believe this measure is appropriate because imports displace U.S. products in physical amounts. That is, the SMEs in an imported item represent a

comparable amount that a domestic manufacturer might have produced.

2. *By using the value of shipments*—W. Cline (1987) believes this measure is more appropriate because imports tend to be cheaper products. That is, since imports are usually cheaper products, SMEs overstate the real economic value of imported goods compared to domestic output. This approach generally gives a more conservative estimate of the domestic market taken by imports than measures based on physical quantities.

Textile import data will be shared in various forms—(1) to show the levels of import shipments in various product areas and (2) to illustrate how import penetration ratios vary by the approach used.

Import Penetration Based on Physical Measures

Table 9–2 displays import penetration in the total U.S. market for all textile products (this includes apparel). These figures are based on a physical measure, millions of pounds—an appropriate measure for fiber usage; similar summaries are available using the square-meter equivalent measure. (Here we must remember that trade data based on pounds are reported by major fiber groupings. That is, "fibers consumed" include textile mill products as components in end-use products. Table 9–2 includes mill consumption.) Imports in all textile product areas accounted for 10.6 percent of the quantity of U.S. fiber consumption in 1979, growing to 16.4 percent in 1982 and to 34.5 percent in 1993. The final column gives the portion of imports consumed (as a percentage of total textile/apparel consumption) in U.S. markets, based on this measure.

Figure 9–4 gives a graphic summary of U.S. imports of textile manufactures; this graph is based on square-meter equivalents,

another *physical* measure. It provides a quick review of imports by major categories for more than a decade.

Import Penetration Based on Value

Import penetration based on value—rather than volume—appears in Table 9–3. The "nominal" values are the *current* dollar values at the time. The "real 1982 prices" are the adjusted dollar amounts for each year, using the price index for U.S. domestic product shipments (from the U.S. Department of Commerce). That is, the nominal dollar amounts were adjusted to obtain figures that could be compared meaningfully over the time period shown. When this method is used to consider import penetration ratios for textiles, ratios are significantly *lower than the ratios based on physical measures.*

During the period shown, imports increased rapidly at times from one year to the next; at other times, the increase was slight. W. Cline (1987) noted that from 1961–1962 to 1972–1973, imports averaged an annual increase of 7 percent, but then declined slightly and slowed until 1980. Imports began to increase in the early 1980s and in 1984 jumped 34.4 percent in real terms. Foreign shipments were somewhat less in 1985 but increased by nearly 18 percent in 1986 (W. Cline, 1987; personal communication with U.S. Department of Commerce staff, 1990). Cline speculated the large increases resulted from a combination of some remaining impact from the strong dollar plus the anticipation of tighter import restrictions when the major textile trade agreement, the Multifiber Arrangement, was renegotiated in 1986. Import penetration levels were highest from 1985 through 1991 for three decades, from the 1960s to the present. However, estimates for 1992 and 1993 are the highest in history (U.S. Department of Commerce, 1994)

TABLE 9-2
Cotton, wool, and manufactured fibers consumed in textiles: U.S. mill consumption, exports, imports, and apparent consumption, 1979–1992 (millions of pounds)

Year	Mill Consumption				Exports				Imports				Apparent Consumption				Ratio of Imports to Consumption (total) (%)
	Cotton	Wool	Manufactured Fiber[a]	Total	Cotton	Wool	Manufactured Fiber	Total	Cotton	Wool	Manufactured Fiber	Total[b]	Cotton	Wool	Manufactured Fiber	Total[b]	
1979	3,077	111	9,585	12,773	478	15	597	1,090	746	110	525	1,381	3,345	206	9,513	13,064	10.6
1980	3,033	123	8,734	11,890	523	24	772	1,319	811	103	541	1,455	3,321	202	8,503	12,026	12.1
1981	2,716	138	8,694	11,548	367	12	638	1,017	962	114	639	1,715	3,311	240	8,695	12,246	14.0
1982	2,488	116	6,775	9,379	253	12	439	704	897	112	698	1,707	3,132	216	7,034	10,382	16.4
1983	2,808	138	8,173	11,119	220	21	460	701	1,121	150	889	2,160	3,709	267	8,602	12,578	17.1
1984	2,716	142	7,966	10,824	206	19	488	706	1,447	210	1,115	2,772	3,957	340	8,593	12,890	22.8
1985	2,813	117	8,226	11,156	213	18	449	680	1,604	210	1,334	3,203	4,204	364	9,111	13,679	23.4
1986	3,256	137	8,652	12,045	270	16	506	793	1,885	265	1,684	3,841	4,871	393	9,830	15,093	25.4
1987	3,784	143	9,047	12,974	298	23	592	913	2,336	272	1,805	4,417	5,822	396	10,260	16,478	27.0
1988	3,482	144	9,215	12,841	330	31	685	1,046	2,119	276	1,736	4,097	5,271	355	10,266	15,892	26.0
1989	4,046	135	9,219	13,559	507	66	1,061	1,709	2,354	242	1,716	4,958	5,893	291	9,873	16,808	29.5
1990	4,115	133	9,047	13,445	665	60	1,339	2,155	2,416	222	1,750	5,040	5,867	279	9,458	16,330	30.1
1991	4,348	152	9,102	13,724	723	63	1,400	2,280	2,593	206	1,769	5,221	6,218	299	9,471	16,665	31.0
1992	4,762	151	9,743	14,762	845	72	1,418	2,427	3,193	211	2,127	6,211	7,110	316	10,450	18,546	33.5
1993	4,939	160	10,179	15,383	958	78	1,388	2,522	3,575	237	2,221	6,767	7,555	343	11,012	19,628	34.5

[a]Beginning in 1982, consumption of nontextile glass fiber (such as that used in insulation and other building materials) is not included. The quantity of such fiber has been sharply increasing in recent years, amounting to about 1.0 billion pounds per year.

[b]Also includes flax and silk after 1988.

Note: Because of rounding, figures may not add to the totals shown.

Source: Cotton and Wool-Situation and Outlook Yearbook, U.S. Department of Agriculture, Economic Research Service, CWS-69, August 1992; *Cotton and Wool-Situation and Outlook Report,* U.S. Department of Agriculture, Economic Research Service, CWS-75, February 1994.

FIGURE 9–4
U.S. imports of textile manufactures (in millions of square meters).

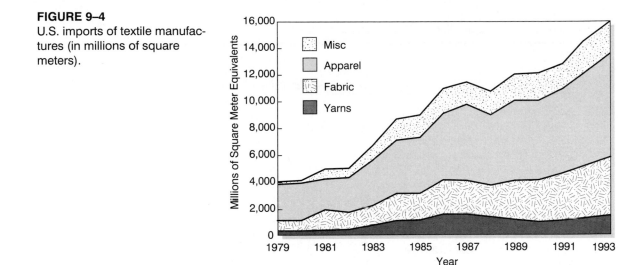

Source: Reprinted courtesy of American Textile Manufacturers Institute.

Although import penetration ratios are substantially lower when based on value data than on physical quantities, Table 9–3 shows that imports have taken an increasing share of the U.S. textile market even when calculated in *real value* terms.

The import data based on *value*, which is presented in Table 9–3, gives imports at the prices valued in processing through U.S. Customs. Figures for import shipments in these terms represent the **customs value**. Cline (1987) noted that other costs of obtaining imports must be added to these values in order to make accurate comparisons with the wholesale values of domestic output. Insurance and freight costs must be added to the customs values to permit meaningful comparisons; similarly, **tariffs** must be added to give the price for domestic consumption. According to the Department of Commerce (1985), in 1984 the **c.i.f. values** for textiles and apparel were 7.5 percent higher than the customs values. In addition, tariffs averaged 27 percent for apparel and 15 percent for textiles in recent years. Cline's analysis revealed that import values were 37 percent above customs valuation for apparel and 24 percent above customs valuation for textiles after adding tariffs, insurance, and freight. Table 9–4 shows the adjusted import penetration ratios based on c.i.f. values plus tariffs.

Cline's analysis, including added costs for importing, showed that apparel imports accounted for about 31 percent of the value of U.S. consumption for apparel in 1986, somewhat less than 10 percent for textiles, and a combined total of 22 percent. These import penetration levels were considerably greater than those based on value for the same years in Table 9–4.

"Indirect" Imports

The portions of the U.S. market taken by imports, as shown in these tables and Figure

TABLE 9–3
Trade and domestic consumption: textiles (millions of dollars)

Year	Nominal M	X	TB	C^b	Real 1982 Prices[a] M	X	TB	C^b	Import Penetration (M/C) (%)
1961	590	320	−270	13,151	1,016	551	−465	22,657	4.5
1962	699	300	−399	14,435	1,190	511	−679	24,584	4.8
1963	745	307	−438	15,136	1,562	644	−918	31,742	4.9
1964	759	340	−419	16,292	1,532	686	−846	32,885	4.7
1965	858	391	−467	17,547	1,690	770	−920	34,554	4.9
1966	941	405	−536	18,837	1,857	799	−1,058	37,177	5.0
1967	803	377	−426	18,928	1,542	724	−818	36,347	4.2
1968	934	351	−583	21,097	1,679	631	−1,048	37,928	4.4
1969	970	418	−552	22,007	1,686	726	−960	38,248	4.4
1970	1,058	461	−597	21,709	1,910	832	−1,078	39,188	4.9
1971	1,248	465	−783	23,221	2,285	851	−1,434	42,521	5.4
1972	1,345	603	−742	26,644	2,389	1,071	−1,318	47,326	5.0
1973	1,423	926	−497	29,550	2,260	1,470	−790	46,923	4.8
1974	1,407	1,284	−123	31,000	1,944	1,774	−170	42,840	4.5
1975	1,107	1,157	50	29,158	1,585	1,657	72	41,760	3.8
1976	1,392	1,399	7	34,253	1,874	1,883	9	46,106	4.1
1977	1,489	1,345	−144	38,198	1,958	1,769	−189	50,239	3.9
1978	1,855	1,466	−389	40,590	2,351	1,858	−493	51,438	4.6
1979	1,834	2,130	296	42,349	2,205	2,561	356	50,909	4.3
1980	2,034	2,488	454	44,320	2,245	2,746	501	48,922	4.6
1981	2,482	2,326	−156	47,897	2,503	2,346	−157	48,303	5.2
1982	2,225	1,766	−459	45,375	2,225	1,766	−459	45,375	4.9
1983	2,557	1,560	−997	51,482	2,523	1,539	−984	50,796	5.0
1984	3,539	1,541	−1,998	54,256	3,390	1,476	−1,914	51,979	6.5
1985	3,697	1,462	−2,235	52,382	3,575	1,414	−2,161	50,660	7.1
1986	4,225	1,653	−2,572	54,920	4,212	1,567	−2,645	52,701	8.0
1987	4,699	1,891	−2,808	64,167	4,699[c]	1,891[c]	−2,808[c]	64,167[c]	7.3
1988	4,458	2,339	−2,119	65,994	4,400[c]	2,309[c]	−2,091[c]	65,146[c]	6.8
1989	4,711	2,842	−1,869	68,810	4,571[c]	2,765[c]	−1,818[c]	66,936[c]	6.8
1989	4,786	2,803	−1,983	72,516	4,501[c]	2,636[c]	−1,865[c]	63,691[c]	7.1
1990	4,888	3,636	−1,252	71,126	4,508[c]	3,353[c]	−1,155[c]	61,090[c]	7.4
1991	5,375	4,101	−1,274	71,915	4,913[c]	3,749[c]	−1,165[c]	60,824[c]	8.1
1992[d]	5,843	4,467	−1,376	74,630	5,306[c]	4,056[c]	−1,249[c]	62,461[c]	8.5
1993[e]	6,179	4,690	−1,489	75,312	5,600[c]	4,250[c]	−1,349[c]	62,649[c]	8.9

M = imports; X = exports; TB = trade balance; C = apparent consumption.

[a]Deflating by textile product shipments price index, US Department of Commerce.

[b]Equals production *plus* imports *minus* exports.

[c]Real 1987 prices.

[d]Estimate, except exports and imports.

[e]Estimate.

Source: From *The Future of World Trade in Textiles and Apparel* (p. 35) by W. Cline, 1987, Washington, DC: Institute for International Economics. 1986–1993 updates from U.S. Department of Commerce.

TABLE 9–4

Adjusted import penetration ratios, value basis[a] (in percent)

Period	Textiles	Apparel	Textiles and Apparel
1961–1965[b]	6.0	3.7	4.9
1966–1970[b]	5.7	6.0	5.9
1971–1975[b]	5.8	10.7	8.2
1976–1979[b]	5.2	16.3	10.8
1980	5.6	18.4	12.1
1981	6.3	19.5	13.2
1982	5.9	19.9	13.7
1983	6.0	21.6	14.4
1984	7.9	27.3	18.6
1985	8.5	29.6	20.5
1986	9.5	31.1	22.0

[a]U.S. Department of Commerce Import Data (customs value) adjusted upward for insurance and freight and for import duties. Import penetration ratios are equal to adjusted imports divided by apparent consumption (domestic output plus adjusted imports less exports).

[b]For multiple years: averages.

Note: Methodology not available to provide comparable update after 1986.

Source: From *The Future of World Trade in Textiles and Apparel* (p. 49) by W. Cline, 1987, Washington, DC: Institute for International Economics. Reprinted by permission.

$$\frac{\begin{bmatrix}\text{Combined total of} \\ \text{imports of fabric of} \\ \text{a type used in apparel}\end{bmatrix} + \begin{bmatrix}\text{estimated fabric} \\ \text{equivalent of imports} \\ \text{of finished apparel}\end{bmatrix}}{\begin{bmatrix}\text{estimated fabric equivalent} \\ \text{of domestic} \\ \text{consumption of apparel}\end{bmatrix}}$$

Using this calculation, the ratio for imports was an estimated 52.4 percent for apparel in 1986 and 16.6 percent for the industrial and home furnishings market; the resulting combined total is 35.6 percent (USITC, 1987b, taken from ATMI sources).

This calculation of "indirect" imports provides yet another means of reporting the extent of import penetration in the domestic market. Although one can understand why the domestic textile mill products industry would want to have import penetration calculated in this manner, certain U.S. Department of Commerce officials object to this approach, which they consider "double counting." Although the calculation of "indirect" imports represents another example of using statistics to support a political position, it is also understandable that domestic textile producers would perceive their market losses in this manner.

Textile mill producers have felt most competition from imports in the lower-priced, lower-quality product lines or in the high-priced, high-fashion products. Heavy import penetration into those markets means that domestic manufacturers supply most of the broad middle segment of the market; however, import restraint policies tend to encourage foreign producers to move upward from the lower quality/price ranges into the mid-range as well. Foreign producers also supply products typically not produced in the United States such as handmade carpets, products of certain vegetable fibers, and hand-loomed or cottage industry products. Further, foreign producers have been willing to supply products in small runs, often providing unique design qualities not readily obtained from U.S. manufacturers.

9–4, are only those in *direct* competition with each of the textile mill product sectors. Textile mill producers believe the effect of the *indirect* competition, although much harder to measure, is perhaps an equal threat to the domestic mill products industry. Since the U.S. textile mill industry considers that the growing quantity of end-use imports (particularly apparel) has taken a sizeable portion of the market for which it would otherwise have provided the fabrics (and other components) for production, the industry has attempted to measure this combined impact of imports. For apparel, for example, the estimate was calculated as follows:

CHOOSING AN APPROACH FOR STATING IMPORT PENETRATION LEVELS

As we have seen in the prior discussion, two differing approaches may be used to state import penetration levels. We might ask why it matters which is used or what difference it makes which we choose. For the most part, the answer lies in the message we wish to give. Although certain sources use both approaches, others representing special interest groups tend to report the status of imports in the way that makes the strongest case for that group's position. This means that as textile industry sources attempt to make a case regarding the threat of imports and the need to restrict foreign products, industry leaders generally use import data based on *physical quantities*. This approach is logical for that group because the *physical quantity data indicate that imports have taken a much larger share of the domestic market* than is shown in using value data (however, W. Cline's [1987] adjusted ratios in Table 9–4 showed that value data may also reflect high import penetration, especially for apparel).

On the other hand, the special interest groups that want to continue importing substantial quantities of textile and apparel products—without added restrictions—tend to choose the *value approach*. These groups include importers and retailers who wish to minimize concern over the threat of imports in the U.S. market. Thus, those who want to be free of trade restrictions (the "free traders") like to use import data based on *value*. And, this approach is logical for the free traders because the *value data indicate that imports have taken a much smaller share of the domestic market* than is indicated by using physical quantity data. We must keep in mind that Cline (1987) generally represents a free trade perspective.

We may ask: Which approach is correct? The answer is both.

The significance of this point for us is that in politicized areas such as textile trade, we must remember to consider the source of our information and the position represented by that source. We can benefit by considering a wide range of perspectives, but then we must weigh each carefully to determine the approach that appropriately represents our views on an issue.

In 1992, the imports of textile mill products to U.S. markets came from the following countries and regions:

Country/Region	Value[a]	Share(%)
Canada and Mexico	520	8.9
European Union	1,514	25.9
Japan	620	10.6
East Asia NICs	1,788	30.6
South America	272	4.7
Other	1,129	19.3
World Total	5,843	100.0

[a]Value in millions of dollars.

Source: From *U.S. Industrial Outlook 1994* by U.S. Department of Commerce, 1994, Washington, DC: Author.

Product Shipments as a Reflection of a Nation's Development

The types of products shipped to U.S. markets by various countries often reflect both the level of overall development of the supplier countries and the stage of development of the textile complex in those countries. A look at the changes in Asian suppliers of textile mill products to the U.S. market illustrates this point. For example, the East Asian NIC suppliers initially gained shares of the U.S. market by supplying low-cost textile products, usually for lower-priced apparel and household textile markets. Early Asian producer nations supplied low- to medium-quality standard construction fabrics, often in greige goods state. As technical capabilities in a particular country grew and as wages increased with the development of competing industries, the country typically moved toward production of more advanced textile products, which provided increased value added as exports. This development within supplier nations has been evident in the types of products shipped to U.S. markets by the Asian countries. Japan and Hong Kong were once the leading suppliers of ordinary greige goods but both have moved toward higher quality, higher priced fabrics and other products often with more distinctive design qualities. (However, Hong Kong's fabrics are most often re-exports.) Similarly, Taiwan, Korea, and even China are moving toward product lines that are more sophisticated and have increased value added.

Many supplier nations would prefer to export more finished products such as apparel rather than textile mill products to increase the value added for their exports. For countries with high wages, however, this may be unlikely to occur because of the high labor content of apparel. Some countries—which not long ago were the low-wage countries themselves—are achieving the value-added product strategy by having the labor-intensive assembly operations performed in current low-wage countries. For example, Japanese and NIC firms contract to have apparel assembly operations performed in less-developed Asian nations.

Although U.S. textile mill product manufacturers may be inclined to speak against imports, a significant proportion of the domestic producers are actually importers themselves. In one study, nearly 52 percent of the participating firms said they use some imported textile mill products themselves (Hooper, Dickerson & Boyle, 1994). This means that some textile mill producers import intermediate inputs to produce their firms' mill products. For example, weaving mills may import yarns for their production of fabrics.

Exports. As noted earlier, nearly all U.S. textile mill product shipments have been directed toward domestic markets in the past. Perhaps this domestic focus resulted from a tradition in which U.S. producers were privileged to a nearly captive U.S. market—that is, before competition from imports for U.S. markets became intense. In earlier decades, U.S. producers had no need to focus on foreign markets for their products because of vast opportunities provided by the large, affluent domestic market.

Consequently, few manufacturers acquired an export orientation and few developed international marketing staffs with the skills and sensitivities to function effectively in foreign markets where language differences, cultural differences, and varied marketing structures were a challenge. In short, few U.S. manufacturers thought of a global market or developed global proficiencies to perform in those markets.

Many challenges accompany exporting, including fluctuating currency exchanges and red tape. In fact, of the U.S. manufacturers who earlier had developed promising markets in other countries—particularly in Western Europe—many experienced significant losses in the early 1980s because of changes in the value of the dollar against other currencies.

For many U.S. producers, supplying foreign markets requires increased domestic investment in production facilities to provide adequate quantities of textile products. Because many of the export-oriented firms have experienced poor performance in foreign markets, many have been reluctant to invest in additional production capacity. Moreover, many other countries have restricted their markets as a way of protecting domestic textile and apparel industries; thus one must not assume that U.S. manufacturers have had free access to foreign markets.

U.S. textile exports have increased in the last few years, generally with annual double-digit increases, almost doubling exports between 1989 and 1992, going from $2.8 billion in 1989 to $4.7 billion in 1993. Leading export markets have been Canada, Mexico,[1] and the European Community (U.S. Department of Commerce, 1994). In fact, during these years, export expansion softened the blow of the domestic recession for the textile industry.

Textile producers have been assisted by the comprehensive export development program sponsored by the U.S. Department of Commerce that has given added visibility to U.S. textile firms. Companies have been assisted through seminars, overseas trade shows, trade missions, and by being matched with potential partners in other countries. This assistance has given U.S. firms added confidence in their ability to sell in other countries.

Outlook for the U.S. Textile Mill Products Industry

Although the U.S. textile mill products industry has experienced several traumatic decades as a result of import competition, in many ways the industry is stronger and more focused as a result of that competition. Industry restructuring has included the closing of outmoded plants, investing in technology and automation to increase productivity, and focusing on market niches that are less labor intensive and more service oriented to avoid import competition. The industry that has emerged is one that is leaner, more efficient, and more competitive.

The textile mill products industry has invested heavily in sophisticated microprocessor-controlled technology. Technological advances are directed toward three goals: (1) reducing the labor required, (2) increasing product quality, and (3) developing flexibility in production. Productivity improvements have been dramatic, rising at a rate greater than that for all U.S. manufacturing or for the textile industries in most other industrialized nations (Edwards, 1988).

Although competitive conditions are expected to continue, the present revamped mill products industry is much better prepared to hold its own in global markets than was true for the sector a decade ago. The viability of the U.S. textile sector is evident in the fact that the industry was the *fourth highest* U.S. industry in terms of financial performance in 1993 (over 1994) according to *Business Week* ("Finding Gems," 1994).

The Textile Machinery Industry

In 1992, the U.S. textile machinery industry included nearly 500 plants and employed 15,000 workers—about two-thirds of whom are in production (U.S. Department of Commerce, 1992). Although the textile machinery industry is not part of the SIC 22 classification, the sector is part of the broader U.S. textile complex and is particularly important to the textile industry. This sector is classified as SIC 3552, Textile Machinery, rather than as part of SIC 22, Textile Mill Products.

The availability of advanced machinery—whether to improve products, to reduce labor, or to speed production—is critical to the competitiveness of the U.S. textile industry. In fact, for the most part, the textile industry can advance only to the extent that it can obtain increasingly sophisticated equipment. Many of the manufacturing advances in the textile complex have resulted from utilizing new equipment produced by equipment firms.

---

[1]U.S. export figures include the value of exports to off-shore assembly operations under a special tariff provision (9802, formerly 807) (discussed later in this chapter) for eventual re-importation into the United States. Government sources are unable to separate those exports from exports that are wholly consumed abroad; therefore export data—particularly for Mexico (prior to NAFTA) and the Caribbean countries—should be considered with the understanding that a substantial volume of trade under provision 9802 (807) is included (U.S. Department of Commerce, 1993).

From the early days when textile-producing technology was smuggled into the United States from England and through the development and refinement of the domestically produced equipment, the textile machinery industry was one of the first capital goods industries to develop in the United States. The ability of U.S. textile machinery producers to develop and modify production equipment was critical to the major strides the domestic industry made in most of the history of the U.S. textile industry. Moreover, the domestic textile machinery industry supplied most of the needs of U.S. mills until recent decades.

As recently as 1970, U.S. textile machinery manufacturers supplied nearly 70 percent of the domestic market. The market share dropped to 47 percent by 1984 and to about 40 percent in 1987; and whereas earlier sales had been for new, complete machines, later sales tended to be predominantly parts. The shift toward supplying parts kept existing equipment functioning; however, servicing a parts market is not equal to sales of new equipment in terms of the outlook for the domestic textile machinery industry. Spare parts represented by far a higher proportion of shipments for the U.S. industry than was true for the industry in other countries; 92 percent of all U.S. sales were for parts compared to 27 percent for Italy, 49 percent for West Germany, and 51 percent for Great Britain (USITC, 1987b, 1990). The heavy sales of U.S. spare parts reflects favorably on a U.S. machinery industry in the past but offers limited prospects for future markets for complete machines.

Although the market for machinery to support the U.S. textile industry is presently the second largest in the world (after China), domestic machinery manufacturers continue to lose the market to foreign suppliers. Increasingly, U.S. machinery producers are supplying less sophisticated equipment for the industry, while foreign competitors take not only more of the domestic market but also the global market of which U.S. manufactur-

ers once had a larger share. In short, the U.S. textile machinery industry is no longer a strong force in producing for the textile machinery market. Instead, the U.S. has become increasingly dependent upon producers in other countries to provide the highly specialized equipment necessary to sustain its competitiveness.

As the USITC staff (1987b) noted, the decline of the textile machinery industry coincided with—and perhaps resulted from—the structural changes that occurred in the textile industry. The major textile machinery producers were acquired by large, publicly owned conglomerates who later sold the operations as profits of the parent companies declined. While the domestic industry was **adjusting** to major changes in the 1960s, many foreign firms with technologically advanced products and accompanying customer service orientations took sales from U.S. suppliers.

Recapturing earlier positions in the textile machinery market requires significant research and development (R&D) investment on the part of U.S. manufacturers—a difficult hurdle for most firms who lack either the necessary means or the momentum. The primary cause of the decline of the domestic industry was the technologic superiority of foreign machinery, stemming from the R&D investment of the industries in the EU and Japan. In contrast, during the 1960s and 1970s, U.S. manufacturers were devoting fewer resources to developing new equipment. Further, foreign suppliers have representatives who work closely with their customers and reportedly gave better delivery and service than U.S. textile machinery manufacturers (U.S. Congress, 1987; USITC, 1987b).

Debate surrounds the question of whether the competitive status of the U.S. textile machinery industry affects the competitiveness of the domestic textile industry. A dependency upon foreign suppliers means that new technology is made available to worldwide producers rather quickly because equipment suppliers want to sell as much of their equipment as possible; however, some suppliers have established research centers in the United States to respond to needs of some of their major customers. USITC sources (1987b) noted that although the United States has become increasingly dependent on foreign manufacturers, the domestic textile industry's competitiveness does not appear to be affected. At times, however, exchange rate fluctuations have caused the prices of imported machinery to increase significantly.

Although the U.S. textile industry is the second largest of any country in the world, the sector's increasing dependency on textile machinery produced in other nations illustrates vividly the growing globalization of the textile complex. Although representatives of the U.S. textile industry often protest against imported products, which they believe infringe on their markets, many are at the same time growing increasingly dependent on foreign machinery for their own production. Further, as the domestic textile industry promotes restraints on imports of foreign textile and apparel products, those same U.S. manufacturers would be severely handicapped if similar limitations were placed on foreign-made equipment.

THE U.S. APPAREL INDUSTRY

Although the apparel industry is part of the textile complex and is closely tied to the textile industry, the apparel sector is a large and distinct segment of the U.S. industrial base. A profile of the U.S. apparel industry and an overview of the apparel sector's competitiveness in the international economy differ markedly from a similar review for the textile industry.

In brief, the U.S. apparel industry is composed of a great many more firms and has a much larger work force than the textile sector.

As a sector that is quite fragmented with a larger number of small firms, the U.S. apparel industry experiences greater difficulty in competing with foreign producers in markets both at home and abroad than the textile sector. Since the apparel sector is the largest user of textile products such as fabric, a healthy apparel industry is vital to the textile complex. The apparel sector produced shipments of $68 billion in 1993 compared to $13 billion for the manufactured fiber and nearly $69 billion for the textile mill products industries (U.S. Department of Commerce) (1994). Apparel firms range from large, highly sophisticated businesses producing a variety of products to other companies operating with limited equipment and expertise.

In 1993, U.S. consumers spent $209 billion on apparel.[2] To most consumers, clothing produced by the apparel industry represents the most tangible and most easily recognized aspect of what we consider more broadly as the textile complex. Consumers can identify clothing and understand that an industry produces clothing, whereas most consumers are less likely to understand the term *textiles* or to identify the many ways in which other textile products are part of their lives.

Apparel production includes the manufacture of men's, boys', women's, girls', children's, and infants' apparel and apparel accessories. Items are produced primarily by cutting and sewing woven and knit textile fabrics (SIC 23). Garments knitted directly from yarn or knitted in the same establishment are considered apparel, but are classified in SIC 22, Textile Mill Products. Other items considered as apparel or apparel accessories (SIC 23) may be made by cutting,

---

[2]U.S. expenditure/consumption figures vary according to the source of data; in some cases, the difference reflects inclusion of other categories such as shoes or accessories. The figure given here is from the U.S. Department of Commerce, Bureau of Economic Analysis (BEA) 1994. The figure given above does not include shoes.

FIGURE 9–5
Production workers like this woman constitute a significant portion of the large apparel industry work force.

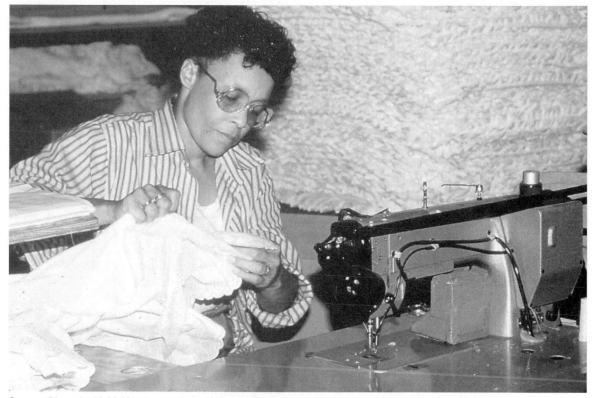

Source: Photo by K. McKenna, courtesy of Kellwood Company.

sewing, cementing, or fusing such materials as rubberized fabrics, plastics, furs, and leather. Footwear is not considered part of the apparel sector; however, the footwear industry has many characteristics similar to the apparel industry: the products are a necessity, products are influenced by fashion, and both apparel and footwear production are labor intensive.

The apparel industry is by the far the most labor-intensive and most fragmented sector in the U.S. textile complex, operating 23,515 establishments in 1991. The apparel sector is characterized by many small firms, employing an average of 43 workers per establishment. In 1991, approximately 63 percent of the plants (perhaps more appropriately called *shops* in the case of operations this small) employed fewer than 20 workers; this represented only 9 percent of all apparel workers, however. On the other end of the spectrum, 20 percent of the firms (that is, the large ones) account for 78 percent of the employment. (U.S. Department of Commerce, 1991, *County Business Patterns*). A relatively small percentage of U.S. apparel firms have sales over $200 million per year. In fact, sales of the larger apparel firms increasingly account for a growing share of all apparel sales.

Of the segments of the textile complex, the apparel industry has the lowest entry barriers in terms of capital and technical knowledge requirements, ready access to production equipment, and broad availability of raw materials. The ease of entry also accounts in part for the small size and the rather high failure rate of firms and establishments. Traditionally, the apparel sector has been a creative, price-competitive business, with a large number of family-owned firms.

As an Office of Technology Assessment report (1987) noted, the apparel industry comes close to representing textbook conditions for "perfect competition," but production operations are kept small, in part because of the specialization that each has in a particular narrow product line. Competition is intense—both among domestic companies and with foreign producers. Intense competition has been reflected in apparel prices that generally have risen less than most other consumer expenditures.

Typically, apparel firms produce narrow product lines. Only the larger firms produce garments in more than one category (for example, women's outerwear, men's furnishings, and children's sleepwear). Further, most firms produce garments in a fairly specific price and fashion range. As examples, firms that produce high-fashion women's suits usually do not produce inexpensive nightwear. Or, firms that produce inexpensive children's sleepwear typically do not produce trendy men's sportswear.

The U.S. apparel industry is more scattered across the United States than the textile industry. Although most states have a certain amount of apparel production, this sector also has areas of heavy concentration, particularly in the Northeast, the Southeast, and California. Many apparel plants are located in small towns across the country and play crucial roles in local economies. As we shall discuss in more detail later in this chapter, many U.S. apparel firms are participating increasingly in **offshore production** of their garments.

Characteristics of the Apparel Industry's Products That Account for Unique Challenges for the Industry

Some of the following aspects of garment production offer unique challenges to the industry and perhaps account for some of the fragmented structure of this sector.

Difficulties in Manufacturing Products Made of Limp Fabrics

The manufacture of garments from limp fabrics makes the apparel industry quite labor intensive. The process of making a garment for a three-dimensional human body from two-dimensional fabric has required up to this time a large amount of human handling in the production processes. Whereas mechanical equipment has long been available to handle and position rigid metal, plastic, or even paper, similar mechanization has not been developed significantly to pick up single layers of fabric for processing through various production stages. Although automation for apparel production has been developed more rapidly in recent years, equipment manufacturers have found it challenging to invent machines that could pick up a single ply of fabric or that could automatically perform more than a limited number of assembly steps. For example, jean pocket-setting machines have been available for a number of years. For the most part, however, workers are still required to move the garment pieces from one operation to the next and usually must position the piece in place for the automatic operation to occur.

Limitations on Large Production Runs

Many aspects of apparel production, particularly of fashion items, discourage efficiencies of production possible with other products. This occurs in at least two ways:

- *The desire for "exclusive" products.* Consumers want, and often demand, a degree of exclusivity in clothing; the more costly the garment, the more this holds true. Even at moderate price levels, however, consumers want a certain degree of distinctiveness in the clothing they buy and wear. Because clothing is used as a form of expressing their individuality, most U.S. consumers are looking for more than a uniform look. For the apparel industry, particularly for fashion items, this means that the efficiencies of large-volume runs are not possible as they are in many other industries. For example, the manufacturers of snow shovels or tooth brushes need not be concerned about limiting volume production because consumers would not want to see their neighbors using the same products.

- *The changing nature of fashion.* The transient nature of fashion poses special challenges to apparel manufacturers. The fashion at a given time may have unique features for which specialized production equipment and specially trained workers are needed. As an example, when monogrammed shirts were a popular fashion item, production would have been enhanced greatly by the availability of special-purpose machines to perform the monogramming operation. Large firms might easily invest in the equipment to produce the item; however, smaller firms might have difficulty justifying the investment in special equipment for a passing fashion. Adapting to fashion is a constant challenge that includes producing garments from a wide range of fabrics, using diverse construction techniques that are both functional and decorative and that incorporate style variations that range from use of lace trims to rivets.

The Transient, Unpredictable Nature of Fashion

The fashion areas of the apparel industry are unpredictable, particularly since consumer interests can change quite rapidly. Although the industry as a whole is placing greater emphasis on marketing efforts, and even before that, well-managed apparel firms were in tune with consumer demands, responding to fashion whims can be difficult. Even if an apparel firm is sensitive to a new fashion trend as it develops, the company may have difficulty in securing the component parts from the multiple stages in the production chain in time to respond to a rapid fashion change. Or, even more difficult are the times when a firm is in the middle of production on a line only to learn that the fashion item has gone into a rapid downward trend.

The Challenge of Timing

Other aspects of timing related to apparel production represent difficulties for apparel manufacturers. As an example, seasonal production is particularly critical in some areas of the country. Consumer demand for swimsuits and coats are hardly interchangeable. If coat-weight fabric suppliers do not respond on time, coat producers may have difficulty in providing coats for the appropriate season. Retailers, who are in turn responding to consumer demands, have limited patience if coats are not available from manufacturers when needed. In their attempts to respond to consumers, retailers will seek other coat suppliers to fill their needs. This is another application of the train analogy discussed in Chapter 8; consumer demand sets the pace for the production and marketing chain.

Seasonal concerns are only one aspect of timing for the industry. In general, the industry is a dynamic one in which timing and speed typically are quite remarkable considering the multiple stages involved in producing and selling garments. Responding to the demands of appropriate timing is a constant challenge, however.

We might also reflect here that the industry itself has fostered some of these characteristics that pose a challenge. For example, the industry promotes fashion change as an inherent aspect of the business. An emphasis on the latest "new look" generates excitement and sales for the industry. Therefore, coping with the fast turnover of fashion—that is, implementing this emphasis in the production and distribution aspects of the industry—is a natural consequence of the sector's focus on change.

Types of Operations

Apparel production may occur in different types of operations. The principal domestic ones are as follows:

- *Manufacturers* are responsible for the entire range of operations for apparel production, from the initial designs to shipping. Although manufacturers are responsible for all aspects of garment-making and may perform most or all the production in their own factories, many also contract at least a certain amount of their work to outside shops, particularly during peak production periods.
- *Jobbers* are responsible for their own designs, acquire the fabric and other necessary components for production, and arrange for sale of finished garments. Jobbers may perform cutting operations but typically contract out most other production operations.
- *Contractors* are independent producers who perform sewing operations, and sometimes the cutting, for apparel manufacturers and/or jobbers (and increasingly for retailers). Typically, contractors receive cut garments in bundled form and process them into completed garments. Many contractors and manufacturers have long-standing working relationships and function virtually as partners in producing garment lines. Contractors may be located in the United States or in other countries where labor

and appropriate skills are available. Additional options for combining domestic and offshore production are considered later in this chapter.

Advantages and disadvantages are present under the different manufacturing arrangements. When manufacturers perform all their own operations, they maintain greater control over quality and avoid the added demands of moving the goods. On the other hand, this arrangement requires investment in production equipment and a commitment to retain employees during both peak and slow periods. In contrast, using contractors may give the manufacturer greater flexibility to expand and contract output without the added investment in equipment or the responsibility of maintaining a large production work force. Contracting requires the physical movement of goods, however, and the manufacturer loses some control over quality and delivery dates. In recent decades, the use of contractors and jobbers has grown in relation to manufacturing.

Factors Affecting Competitiveness

Since its early development, the apparel industry has been characterized by relatively simple technology and a high degree of labor intensity. According to Ghadar et al. (1987), the apparel industry was estimated to be only 5 percent automated in the early 1960s, and, by the early 1970s, the rate had increased to 15 percent. Boosted by the rapid development of technology generally, the apparel industry's extent of automation reached 25 percent by the later 1970s and increased to about 40 percent by the mid-1980s.

Because of the amount of labor involved in apparel production and because of the labor-cost advantages in many developing countries, if industrialized countries are to remain competitive in global markets, increased automation appears to be essential. Automation can reduce labor costs, add production flexibility, and standardize quality. New technological developments and adaptations offer a great deal of potential for improving productivity in the apparel industry.

As part of his study, W. Cline (1987) noted that the apparel sector as a whole had invested in capital equipment to improve its operations to a very limited extent. In recent years, however, an increasing number of apparel manufacturers have undertaken major capital investment programs. One should keep in mind, however, that major reinvesting may not have been a realistic option for a good many U.S. apparel manufacturers (including jobbers and contractors). The fragmented nature of the apparel industry and the high proportion of small firms may account for some of the low reinvestment pattern for the industry. A significant number of small operators are independent manufacturers, jobbers, and contractors for whom it is unrealistic to think of reinvesting in costly state-of-the-art production equipment. A shop employing 20 workers could hardly afford high-technology equipment; neither could it make adequate use of costly new equipment to justify the expenditure. Many small establishments survive on slim margins, and, further, the size of the business in many cases would hardly justify or utilize effectively expensive equipment. So, although Cline's observations may have been valid for many larger firms and for the total sector, many small operators might have had limited opportunity to reinvest.

Although Arpan et al. (1982) found that limited **production economies of scale** existed for the apparel industry, the very small size of some establishments is a serious disadvantage. Limited opportunities for investment or employing staff with expertise in major functional areas jeopardizes the success of the small operations.

Foreign competition has placed increased pressure on domestic apparel manufacturers to find ways to reduce costs and enhance productivity. In response, many of the forward-thinking apparel firms, which are often the larger companies, have taken bold steps toward improving productivity through technological advances. In fact, larger companies with significant production volume are the ones who might most effectively utilize automation and other technology to improve productivity.

Particularly from a global perspective, however, reinvesting to improve international competitiveness is a matter of serious concern facing the U.S. apparel industry. As a "mature" industry, some of the U.S. apparel sector's plants and equipment resemble garment plants as they were established decades ago. Companies are able to function satisfactorily in many cases with basic sewing, cutting, and pressing equipment far short of state-of-the-art quality. In contrast, however, as garment plants have been established in recent years in major competitor countries, some of those operations begin with modern equipment. This would be true particularly in the NICs but would not be the case for most poorer, developing nations who use outdated, second-hand equipment.

"Pattern of Work"

In focusing on the need to have modern production equipment for a competitive advantage, we must remember, however, that technical improvements represent only one side—albeit an important side—of worker productivity. Another significant component of worker productivity is what Arpan et al. (1982) referred to as the "pattern of work." The pattern of work is tied closely to the employee's commitment to work. Measurable components of the pattern of work are attitudes toward work; willingness to work efficiently on a scheduled, dependable basis; the speed at which work is done; the number of hours worked; absenteeism; turnover; and the quality of work. As Arpan noted, the major Asian exporting countries appear to have work patterns equal to or better than that in the United States. Expressing similar views in a *Wall Street Journal* article, Stabler (1986) shared Peter Berger's observation on shifts in work ethic in today's global economy:

> "The old Protestant ethic, which isn't very significant today in its countries of origin, is alive and well in Seoul, in Soweto and in Santiago de Chile." It is operating there, he added, much as it did in Europe and North America in an earlier period, "by inculcating moral values and attitudes that are conducive to success in a nascent capitalist economy." (p. 1)

Technology Transfer

Changes in technology have benefited companies that have used the advancement effectively. For most firms, new technology has improved international competitiveness for at least a time. Despite the increasing cost and sophistication of new technology, the competitive advantages of this technology usually last for a short time, however. New technology—whether it takes the form of new equipment or other products, industrial processes, or the skills needed to apply technical knowledge—spreads worldwide with amazing speed.

In today's global economy, rapid technology transfer around the world is a fact of life. The pace of technological diffusion is increasing—as a result of technology itself. International data networks provide global access to information in some areas, and new telecommunications systems permit even closer ties on matters of production and marketing. Technology transfer also occurs when U.S. retailers and manufacturers contract with foreign producers. Under various offshore arrangements, foreign firms that lack the technical and managerial/marketing skills

often gain those skills from the U.S. firms with whom they have contracts. Technology transfer does not always occur, however, because in some cases developed country firms try to prevent it from happening, not wanting their competitive position weakened by allowing host countries to strengthen their own capabilities. At any rate, technological development must be a continuous process in order to maintain a competitive edge.

Sourcing

Sourcing is an industry term to describe the process of determining how and where manufactured goods, or components, will be procured. The industry uses the term also for having production or assembly done elsewhere. Although both manufacturers and retailers participate in sourcing activities as a normal part of business operations, our focus in this chapter will be primarily from the perspective of the U.S. apparel firm. For many years, U.S. apparel companies had two options: they could manufacture garments in their own plants or they could contract the work to another producer. Now, however, apparel companies have a wide range of sourcing options both domestically and internationally. For many apparel executives, worldwide sourcing strategies are basic to their operations.

Eight major sourcing alternatives available to U.S. apparel firms, as identified by the American Apparel Manufacturers Association (AAMA) (1984), follow.

Domestic Production, Domestic Fabric. Under this arrangement, manufacturers produce garments in their own plants, and, in doing so, manufacturers have greatest control over timing and quality of their lines. However, firms need to invest in technology to be competitive; equipment can become easily outdated. Wages are higher than in many other countries.

Domestic Contractor Production, Domestic Fabric. As noted earlier in this chapter, use of contract operations reduces investments and the need to maintain employees to meet production schedules. Contractors may produce overflow for manufacturers with limited capacity, may produce specialized products for manufacturers who lack a particular expertise, or may be the primary production site for marketing-oriented firms who have little or no production capacity. The potential for losing control over quality and delivery encourages many apparel executives to limit contractor sourcing to a set percentage of total production.

Domestic Production Plus 9802 (Formerly 807) Production, Domestic (and Foreign) Fabric. A combination of domestic production with a special type of offshore production now designated as **9802 production** (formerly **807 production**) gives greater control over a portion of the firm's manufacturing operations but adds the economy of lower labor rates.

Some 9802/807 plants are owned by U.S. firms; others are contract or joint-venture plants. The use of 9802/807 production may allow a firm to operate domestic plants at a level production rate while adjusting 9802/807 sourcing to meet market fluctuations. Since the main reason for using 9802/807 sourcing is labor cost, high labor content (relative to weight) is a critical criterion for this strategy because of shipping costs, possibly lower productivity in developing countries, and tariffs. Under 9802/807 operations, recourse on poor merchandise or service may be difficult.

In addition, many retailers are now using this sourcing strategy to obtain apparel. In doing so, this means that retailers bypass U.S. apparel manufacturers in having merchandise made by foreign producers.

Foreign Contractor, U.S. Fabric. This sourcing option differs little from the last one and differs from 9802/807 production because cut parts are not shipped from the United States under this plan. This strategy gives the U.S. manufacturer increased control over the quality of fabrics used and also may be an advantage for coordinated lines, which are sourced from both foreign and domestic sources. The use of U.S. fabric typically adds to product costs because of shipping expenses.

Owned Production Overseas. As one of the least common sourcing alternatives, foreign apparel production in a firm's own plants includes both manufacturer-owned plants as well as joint venture arrangements. (See Chapter 12 for further discussion on these arrangements.) Having company-owned foreign plants offers greater opportunity to control quality than may be possible in foreign contracting, especially if local managers run the plant according to the parent company's expectations. Furthermore, product cost is lower from owned plants than from a foreign contractor, since no contractor profits are included. On the other hand, owning plant facilities adds to the company's investment and risk. In some countries that have a volatile political climate, firms have less flexibility in moving operations to another region or country if they own manufacturing plants. Moreover, given certain other (host) countries' investment policies, owning production facilities often is not possible.

Combination Options. Many firms use a mixture of sourcing options, with the sourcing mix quite varied from one company to another. Given the uncertainties in the apparel industry itself and in global competition, a combination of strategies provides managers with flexibility to shift sourcing as conditions dictate. Mixed sourcing plans permit a firm to have greater stability and control in production in its own plants and, at the same time, to assume somewhat more risk in offshore sourcing for other parts of the business. Although a firm may want to have some basic production capacity and own some of its

9802 (FORMERLY 807) PRODUCTION

Item 807 of the former, and now nonexistent, Tariff Schedule of the United States (TSUS) permitted the export of garment pieces to low-wage countries for assembly, with the re-entry duty paid essentially only on the value of the assembling (the "value added"). This provision for production still exists but under a new tariff classification system called the Harmonized Tariff Schedule, often called the "Harmonized System." (This program was developed to have a common system for tariff nomenclature and categories usable by a large number of the world's trading nations rather than each having its own unique system.)

Although the industry has known this as "807 production" for a long time, *the new classification under the Harmonized Tariff Schedule is 9802.* As before, production under this special provision allows an article that has been assembled in a foreign country "in whole or in part of fabricated components, the product of the United States" (USITC, 1994) to enter the United States with the special tariff concessions. (Under this provision, garment parts must be cut in the United States; fabrics may be from elsewhere.) That is, tariff is paid on the "value added" rather than on the total value of merchandise produced under other arrangements.

Under this provision, however, merchandise is subject to the *same quota rules* as other apparel from foreign shippers. *Quotas* are limits on the volume of a product that can be shipped into the United States (other importing countries also impose quota limits). This means that when apparel producers in a foreign country ship assembled garments to the United States under the 9802 provision (formerly 807 provision), they are using a portion of the country's quota allowance to do so when quota allowances exist.

Earlier, U.S. producers used the Far East for 807 production, but, more recently, production has shifted to Mexico and the Caribbean basin countries because of proximity to the domestic market.* An added provision in the Tariff Schedule, under a Special Access Program, has been **Item 807A**—also known as "Super 807" (perhaps to be known as 9802A). The Special Access Program gives Caribbean countries added quota allowances (known as **guaranteed access levels** or **GALS**) when fabric are *both made and cut* in the United States. If foreign-made trim is used, it may not exceed 25 percent of the total value of the garment (Gelber, 1989).

---

*Now that NAFTA is a reality, provisions of that agreement are more favorable for Mexico; therefore, Mexico uses NAFTA provisions rather than 9802 (807) for the country's apparel trade with the United States.

own equipment, the company may also want to limit its investment and take advantage of contractor services, perhaps in another country where wages are lower.

The nature of the apparel products, the market, the cost of various sourcing options, the availability of attractive sourcing options for the type of product, and many other factors determine the sourcing mix. Overall, however, a combination of sourcing arrange-ments gives the apparel firm a hedge against uncertainties inherent in apparel production. Companies can monitor investments, control risks to varying degrees, and also take advantage of certain low-cost sourcing options. Since retailers are now becoming "manufacturers" themselves by bypassing apparel firms and going directly to foreign producers to have their apparel lines made, U.S. apparel companies can counteract this trend to some

9802 (FORMERLY 807) PRODUCTION *(continued)*

FIGURE 9–6
Apparel producers' use offshore assembly.

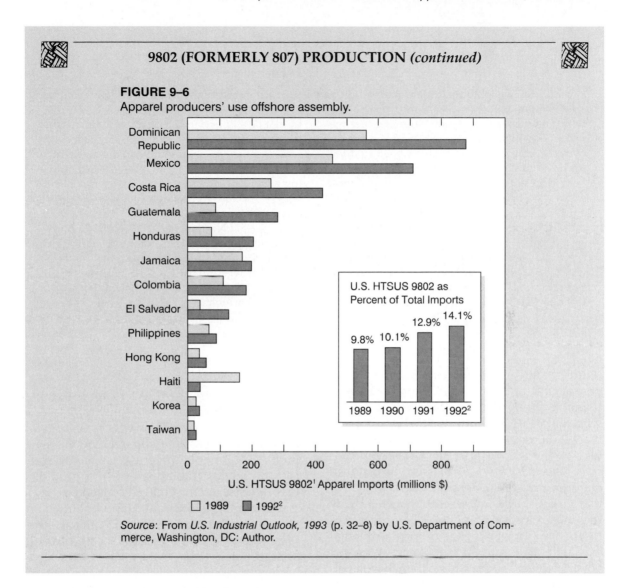

Source: From *U.S. Industrial Outlook, 1993* (p. 32–8) by U.S. Department of Commerce, Washington, DC: Author.

degree by developing their own competitive sourcing strategies. AAMA (1984) has provided useful models to assist manufacturers in determining the most advantageous sourcing options for their particular businesses.

Markets

Of all markets in the U.S. textile complex, the apparel market is in many respects the most competitive and most difficult. In no other segment of the complex is the potential for overcapacity and oversaturation quite so great as in apparel. The potential to produce more than the market can absorb causes intense competition and fosters a "survival of the fittest" climate for producers in this sector. In the United States alone, more than 23,500 establishments compete for the market, although their specialized production areas

THE IMPORTANCE OF ACCESS TO QUOTA

At least until well into the twenty-first century, a quota system will affect textile and apparel trade with many countries. Under sourcing arrangements in which garments are made in another country, shipments often are subject to quota limitations. Foreign apparel producers must have access to some of their country's quota allowance to ship garments to the importing country. For example, a Hong Kong producer must have access to Hong Kong's quotas granted by the United States to ship to the United States.

Quotas are distributed to apparel manufacturers in various ways from country to country. Therefore, U.S. manufacturers using sourcing options that involve foreign assembly or total production must take care to work with contractors who have quota rights. Otherwise, garments cannot be shipped to U.S. markets. Quotas must be purchased in certain countries, and earlier, as trade restrictions became tighter, quotas became more scarce and more valuable. As a result, rising and unpredictable quota prices have been both a risk and a growing expense when using certain of these strategies.

Under the North American Free Trade Agreement, quotas are much less of an issue for Mexican production than in the past. Similarly, the special provisions for the CBI countries mean that quotas are not an issue if U.S. fabrics are used and garments are cut in the United States.

---

reduce the degree to which all of them compete against one another. Add to the scores of domestic producers large numbers of nations who are also competing for the U.S. apparel market. *In contrast to certain segments of the textile sector for which only a limited number of countries participate in global markets, virtually all countries are active in apparel manufacturing.* For many LDCs, apparel assembly may provide the only industrial employment and may represent the primary means of earning foreign exchange. The intense global activity in the apparel sector accounts for extremely competitive conditions both in the international market and in the U.S. market. The U.S. market would be oversaturated, perhaps, even without the added pressure from imports.

Apparel manufacturers serve the following two markets:

1. *The retail market*, composed of retailers who are the buying agents for their apparel customers and
2. *The consumer market*, composed of those who use the apparel.

The Retail Market

Since retailers are the direct customers of the apparel producer, the relationship between these two industry segments is of special importance. Unless the apparel manufacturer produces garments and offers service that satisfy the retailer, the apparel firm's products may never reach the end-use consumer.

Department stores and department chain stores (including J.C. Penney, Sears, and Wards) have been the largest source of retail apparel sales. However, as consumers have become more cost conscious in recent years, they are seeking less-expensive clothes at less-expensive places. Department stores are losing market share to discount stores and other lower-cost forms of retailing. Apparel specialty stores have felt the impact of this shift. For example, two specialty chains that had outstanding success in the 1980s, The Limited and The Gap, have struggled in the early 1990s.

Moreover, apparel distribution channels have become increasingly complex as retailers have consolidated or otherwise grown into

MANUFACTURING COST COMPARISON

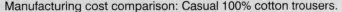

Kurt Salmon Associates, Inc. (KSA) has developed models for calculating sourcing options given a specific set of sourcing and inventory parameters for a specific product. Silva, a KSA vice-president, noted that one of the keys to success involves calculating **lead times** and **velocity costs** as well as labor, transportation, and startup costs in a sourcing strategy. Velocity costs include interest on holding inventories, markdowns, extra handling costs, etc. Generally, the higher the labor content and the lower the weight of the product, the more reasonable it is to consider sourcing outside the United States. (The reader is reminded of the theoretical discussions in Chapter 4 that considered why apparel is frequently involved in the international division of labor.) The following KSA graph shows the combined costs of manufacturing casual cotton trousers in seven countries. In this comparison, even though Indonesia has far lower wages, Mexico would offer the most economical production when all things are considered (Silva, 1993).

FIGURE 9–7

Manufacturing cost comparison: Casual 100% cotton trousers.

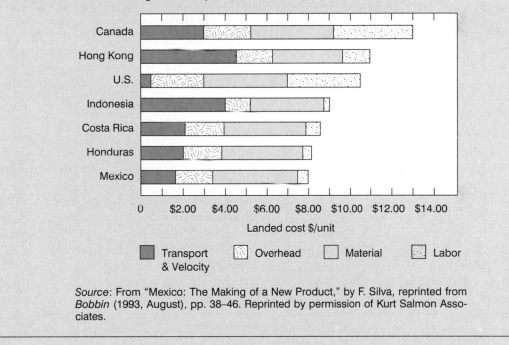

Source: From "Mexico: The Making of a New Product," by F. Silva, reprinted from *Bobbin* (1993, August), pp. 38–46. Reprinted by permission of Kurt Salmon Associates.

mega mass-merchandisers. This means that buying decisions are concentrated in the hands of fewer and fewer buyers. Additionally, retailers are demanding increased financial and service privileges. As the largest apparel manufacturers continue to grow larger, similar to what is happening in retailing, we see a pattern one industry consultant described as "the big tend to dance with the big" (Standard & Poor's, 1992, p. T81).

THE NORTH AMERICAN FREE TRADE AGREEMENT

When the NAFTA went into effect on January 1, 1994, textile and apparel trade between the U.S. and Mexico took on a new character. For the first time in more than two decades, the U.S. moved toward textile and apparel trade without restraints on products from Mexico. Prior to NAFTA, a great deal of apparel production for U.S. firms occurred in Mexican plants, frequently under the *maquiladora* arrangements. Shipments from the Mexican assembly operations were limited, however, under an agreement called the Special Regime, similar to the Special Access Program for Caribbean nations. To avoid quotas under the Special Regime, garments had to be both made and cut from U.S. fabrics. Tariffs were levied on the value added for finished garments when returned to the United States. The Special Regime under NAFTA swept away all quota restrictions if products made in Mexico are from U.S.-formed and U.S.-cut fabric. The remaining limitation on trade was that garments must be made from components "from the yarn forward" that originated in North America. This was a provision of NAFTA to satisfy U.S. textile producers who wanted to be sure Mexican garment firms used North American fabrics rather than those from Asian suppliers. And, if textile and apparel products meet these rules, products may qualify for duty-free entry into the U.S.

Once NAFTA became a reality, Caribbean nations were at a disadvantage in apparel production compared to Mexico, because Caribbean production still had to meet the stipulations of the Special Access Program to avoid quotas and had to pay duties on the value-added portion of the garment when returned to U.S. markets. Caribbean nations sought parity with Mexico as a site for U.S. apparel production.

The overcapacity and oversaturation in the apparel sector mean that competition is intense for manufacturers to obtain and to keep retail accounts. If a manufacturer is unwilling to respond to a retailer's needs (and, in some cases, demands), an exceptionally large number of other producers—both global and domestic—are ready to respond with attractive offers. Retailers also have faced difficult competitive conditions in recent years; therefore, they have found it necessary to seek the most attractive prices for the garments they buy for their stores. For many retailers, the choice has been to buy imports for a growing share of the store's apparel selections.

As a result of retailers' increasing purchase of foreign-made apparel in recent years, working relationships between apparel manufacturers and retailers have been strained. Representatives of the U.S. textile and apparel industry have viewed retailers as playing a primary role in the continued increase of imports in U.S. markets. Retailers have sought apparel made in other countries for several reasons, such as attractive prices, distinctive designs, and variety. Unquestionably, attractive prices have been a primary reason, however, as retailers have pursued the low-cost labor advantages of products made in developing countries. In some cases, retailers have found foreign suppliers more willing than U.S. firms to respond to their needs. Many domestic textile and apparel firms take the skeptical view, however, that retailers' offshore sourcing is a way of adding excessive markups to extend profits—at the expense of domestic manufacturers. (However, as a growing number of U.S. apparel manufacturers engage in offshore production, fewer are in a position to criticize retailers.)

As manufacturers recognized the powerful position of retailers in bypassing the U.S.

apparel sector for their purchases, the domestic industry initiated special efforts to improve service to retailers and to mend relationships between the two sectors. The Quick Response program initiated by the U.S. textile and apparel industries has been a significant effort directed toward these goals. The Quick Response concept offers many advantages to retailers; it has the potential for reducing investments, providing better service to the end-use customer, and enhancing profit margins.

Manufacturers and retailers have cultivated closer working relationships, as both sectors realize that they can serve the end-use customer more effectively by working together. Moreover, apparel manufacturers have placed added emphasis on marketing strategies to aid in responding to customers' needs—an approach that is useful also to retailers. In general, the U.S. apparel industry has made strides toward establishing a partnership climate with its retail customers.

Consumer Markets

Apparel manufacturers have the challenging task of producing garments with style and quality to appeal to end-use customers. Moreover, these garments must be offered at prices that are competitive in both the retail and consumer markets. Apparel must be sold at prices at which retailers can earn a profit, and, at the same time, items must be offered at prices competitive with those for comparable garments produced by other domestic suppliers and with those made in low-wage countries.

Various demographic shifts can have a significant impact on consumption. For example, apparel expenditures in the 1960s and early 1970s were boosted by the maturing of the postwar baby-boom generation to the teen and young adult years when apparel expenditures are high. Similarly, changes in the economy have a dramatic impact on consumer apparel expenditures. For example, in the

1980s, consumers placed emphasis on apparel expenditures and were even somewhat extravagant in their purchases. Consumer apparel expenditures nearly doubled in the 1980s, increasing from $90 billion in 1980 to $170.3 billion in 1989, for an average annual growth rate of 7.3 percent. By 1990, the impact of the recession, little growth in disposable personal income and high unemployment caused consumers to be more cautious in their apparel spending, resulting in a 3.1 percent increase in 1990, 1.3 percent in 1991, and about 2.9 percent in 1992 (Standard & Poor's, 1992, 1993). This slowdown in consumer apparel expenditures illustrates why many apparel firms experienced poor financial performance in the early 1990s.

Marketing Strategies

A major change in the U.S. apparel industry has been the increased emphasis on a **marketing orientation**. Earlier, apparel firms tended to have primarily a **production orientation** and "thought of their business and markets in terms of *what their plants could produce*" (AAMA, 1984, p. 55). Although the apparel industry's increased marketing emphasis is part of a broader focus in the textile complex, a marketing orientation is especially critical for apparel manufacturers. First, it is the apparel manufacturer who transforms intermediate textile inputs into products that go to retailers and consumers. If the apparel firm miscues, it is the most immediate segment of the production chain to suffer a loss (and, as a result, suppliers share in that loss). Second, a marketing focus took on added importance to apparel manufacturers as it became apparent that retailers were bypassing the domestic apparel industry to buy many of their apparel lines in other countries. Apparel firms realized the increased importance of being sensitive to both retail market and consumer market needs. Consequently, **apparel marketing** and

apparel merchandising have become increasingly important activities in successful apparel firms.

Some of the special difficulties resulting from foreign competition encouraged U.S. apparel manufacturers to develop more thoughtful marketing plans. Increasingly competitive conditions no longer permitted the losses that accompanied a less-focused hit-or-miss approach used by some. A number of manufacturers who had failed to tie their apparel production to sound marketing strategies (which, for example, acknowledged imports in their specific markets) found their businesses quite vulnerable to import competition. Many firms that had specialized in a specific product or a narrow product line found they were unable to respond to an influx of imports by shifting product lines. Similarly, firms that had concentrated production in price-sensitive, high-labor, and low-fashion garment lines, such as men's and boys' shirts, found their domestic markets disappearing because a large share of foreign producers aimed for this market as well.

The Workforce and Wages

The apparel industry employs just under one million workers, of whom a large majority are production employees.[3] The large work force is a reflection of the labor-intensive nature of the apparel industry. Also reflecting the high labor requirements, apparel production workers account for about 85 percent of the total workforce, compared to 68 percent in U.S. manufacturing overall (U.S. Department of Commerce, 1993). Women and minorities constitute a large portion of the apparel workforce, particularly when compared to other

industries or to U.S. manufacturing as a whole.

In short, the apparel industry provides jobs to a large component of the U.S. industrial workforce. Perhaps many of those workers would have no other source of gainful employment in their regions without the apparel jobs, and many workers lack the financial resources to relocate for other employment. Moving from rural communities to urban environments to take similar jobs hardly seems an attractive alternative. In a sense, the apparel industry makes a social contribution in providing employment for many workers with few job alternatives. One might even speculate that for a significant number of U.S. workers, apparel employment provides the same beginning for those workers who are in their first (and perhaps only) industrial jobs and who have few other alternatives, just as the industry does in many developing countries.

Since its beginning, the apparel industry has been known for its low wages (the reference is to production wages). Work in the needle trades has long been undervalued, as Plant (1981) noted:

> The fact that practically every woman and most men could ply a needle, and indeed that even little girls in most families learnt to sew at an early age, meant that for many workers sewing was the only skill they had to offer. The introduction of the hand or treadle sewing-machine did little to change their situation, since it was a simple device to master. One thinks of the penniless immigrants arriving in New York, there to make garments for the new nation, or of oppressed minorities in other countries, not allowed to own land and debarred, as a rule, from practising the more prestigious crafts, starting with little more than a needle and thread. (p. 57)

Data on earnings in the apparel industry show that workers in the sector are paid significantly less than employees in other manufacturing industries and other selected sectors.

---

[3]According to the Bureau of Labor Statistics, the apparel industry employed 977,000 persons in 1993. This figure is slightly higher than Department of Commerce figures for the year.

Average hourly earnings in most segments of the garment industry were only about 60 percent of the wages paid to workers for all manufacturing.

Speculation on the reasons for the large disparity in industrial wages leads to a number of questions. Although economic justification can be given, no doubt, for the large wage differences, one might ask if the skill levels required in the apparel industry are that different from those in the automobile industry. Is the skill required to make a collar that much less than is required to perform routine assembly line tasks to attach a fender in an automobile plant? Yet, most automobile workers earn more than twice the amount paid to garment workers. One might ask to what extent low apparel wages are associated with the predominance of female (and minority) workers. Is it more than coincidental that the manufacturing sector with the highest proportion of women and minority workers is the one with the lowest wages? Given the history of a gender gap in wages in the United States and the probability that a predominantly female workforce has been in the past more passive in terms of employment demands, it does not seem unreasonable to speculate on the association between gender (and perhaps other characteristics associated with limited power) and wages for the industry. (If the reader wishes to pursue this topic, a useful source is Leiter's [1986] study of Southern textile workers.)

In W. Cline's study (1987) of the U.S. textile and apparel industries, he found that wages in the apparel industry have declined in relative terms over time. Cline questioned the continued decline of relative wages for apparel workers, particularly in light of what he perceived as "healthy" profits for the apparel sector. (Readers who wish to pursue Cline's concern over what he calls the "profits paradox" may wish to read his 1987 book. Although some sources find his conclusions useful, others question his access to reliable profit data for making the assertions found in his book.)

Employment in the apparel sector declined gradually from 1972–1973. Employment dropped from a peak of 1.4 million workers in 1973 to slightly under one million in recent years.

Industry sources typically view textile and apparel imports as the cause for declining employment in the domestic sectors. Basic logic suggests that the large influx of imported goods in U.S. markets in recent years has displaced some of the domestic market share and, hence, affected employment. A number of researchers (Frank, 1977; Grossman, 1982; Isard, 1973; Krueger, 1980; Martin & Evans, 1981) have attempted to determine to what extent imports and productivity influence industry employment. In general, these researchers have concluded that labor productivity growth (and, for textiles, slowed consumption) had a much more serious impact on employment than did imports. Another factor to consider is that productivity rates may have increased as a *result* of the threats posed by imports; therefore, it may be difficult to separate the effects of the two forces. We may also conclude, however, that imports played a more significant role in declining employment for the apparel sector than for the textile sector.

Labor Shortage

The declining employment status of the apparel industry has another dimension. A number of U.S. apparel manufacturers have begun to experience difficulty in securing production workers. In regions where the labor force has various employment options, workers may choose jobs in sectors where wages are higher. A number of far-sighted apparel executives have begun to establish day-care facilities and provide other incentives as a possible way to attract and retain the workers needed, a high proportion of whom are women.

Trade

Since the early 1960s, the U.S. apparel industry has faced increasing competition from foreign apparel suppliers who offered attractive prices on garments because of lower labor costs in their countries. Although the influx of imports has been detrimental to the domestic industry in several respects, the import threat also provided the stimulus for industry efforts to maintain and enhance the U.S. industry's position—both in domestic and international markets. In short, although the competition has been painful, the U.S. apparel industry that has emerged is a more viable one.

The Trade Status for Apparel Compared to Textiles

The trade picture for the apparel sector differs markedly from that for the textile sector. Although the two industries share many common trade concerns, the impact of low-cost imports has been much greater for apparel than for textiles. Two primary explanations account for the more dramatic increases in apparel import shipments compared to textile imports:

1.   Apparel production has been difficult to automate to reduce the amount of labor required to make garments. Other characteristics of the market also reduce the efficiencies that go with high-volume production possible in other industries. As a result of these peculiarities of apparel production, industrialized countries like the United States are generally at a disadvantage in competing in the international market or even in their own domestic markets.

2.   The labor-intensive nature of apparel production makes it one of the most suited early industries for developing countries to enter in their quest for economic development. High labor requirements for apparel assembly are well suited to the "factor endowment" of the developing countries. (The Heckscher-Olin theory suggests that a nation will rely heavily on producing and exporting products that use more of the country's abundant—and cheaper—factor.) Many developing countries have abundant unskilled labor and limited capital and technical expertise. Not only is the apparel industry an attractive first industry for many newly developing countries, it may be the *only* industry for which it has the necessary factors to enter production, particularly for export.

In contrast, production in the textile sector is not as prone to relocate to the developing countries. The capital and technology requirements for textile production, particularly of any advanced nature, make the textile sector less attractive to the poorer, developing countries. Furthermore, textile manufacturers in the developed countries have been able to use technology to reduce labor costs in textile production.

Global Shifts in Apparel Production

Apparel production has become dispersed around the globe, shifting as comparative advantage changes in various regions of the world. Most shifts occur to take advantage of cheaper labor and to avoid trade restrictions that prevent a country's products from entering the U.S. or other importing markets.

Both apparel firms and retailers in the United States and other developed countries have *fostered* the international shifts in apparel production as they seek the benefits of the developing countries' comparative advantage. Moreover, these representatives from the importing countries have provided technical assistance to the producers in low-wage countries so apparel suppliers might improve styling and quality features of the garments they make for customers in the developed countries.

Global apparel production and trade patterns cannot be explained entirely by labor costs. (See Chapter 5 for review of this point.)

Although apparel assembly operations continue to spread to newly emerging (in economic development) countries such as Bangladesh, Nepal, and Sri Lanka where labor is among the cheapest, the major apparel suppliers are China and the NICs in East Asia (Hong Kong, Korea, and Taiwan).[4] These NICs have the advantage of having been established in production for a longer period of time. Most ASEAN nations are close behind at present, however. Perhaps, more importantly, apparel producers in these countries have developed successful working relationships with importing apparel firms and retailers in the developed countries, and many have a record of providing responsive, reliable service in delivering good-quality products. In these relationships, firms from the United States and other developed countries have fostered development of the industry in the NICs and other countries.

An irony of the global shifts occurring in apparel manufacturing is that now even the NICs participate in their own version of "offshore production." Particularly as NIC wages have risen and as quota restrictions limit shipments from the NICs into U.S. markets, apparel firms from those countries have established production operations in other countries that have few or no quota restraints. For example, as the United States tightened quotas on apparel shipments from the "Big Three" Asian exporters, manufacturers from those nations opened sewing plants in Caribbean countries to avoid tight quota limits and also to be closer to U.S. markets. (And, for that matter, Hong Kong firms in particular appear to have established plants in a number

of strategic markets, including *in* the United States and England.)

In another type of arrangement, called transshipment, the Asian NICs and China, in particular, shipped products to other countries—usually other nearby Asian countries—which had unused quota. Products were then shipped to the United States or other markets from the second country, taking advantage of the second country's unused quota. Transshipment was curtailed somewhat for a time by revised U.S. country-of-origin trade regulations enacted to eliminate the circumvention of quota limits. By the early 1990s, however, transshipment had become one of the major U.S. textile and apparel trade problems.

U.S. Apparel Trade Trends

Apparel import shipments in U.S. markets have increased rather significantly, and, with the exception of the garments that apparel firms imported themselves, these imports represented competition for the domestic industry. Apparel trade in relation to domestic consumption is presented in Table 9–5 .

According to Cline's (1987) analysis, real apparel imports (value adjusted by a domestic product shipments price index) grew 15.5 percent annually (compared to increases in annual consumption of 3.6 percent) from 1961–1962 to 1972–1973. Increases in imports slowed to 9.7 percent annually (real consumption was only 1.7 percent annually) from 1972–1973 to 1981–1982. Although the annual import growth of 9.7 percent was still quite high, Cline attributed the drop in the growth of imports from the earlier decade to the new trade policies that went into effect in the 1970s and 1980s to limit imported textile and apparel products. By 1983–1985, the overvalued dollar contributed to import growths of 16.5 percent in 1983, 37.4 percent in 1984, and 10.4 percent in 1985. Consumption increased 16.1 percent during the period (W. Cline,

---

[4]Italy, Germany, and France are also top global suppliers of apparel. Much of this apparel is produced, however, by use of low-cost labor in the member EU countries of Portugal, Spain, or Greece or through outward processing arrangements with other low-wage nations. Furthermore, a substantial portion of these apparel exports are for intra-EU trade.

TABLE 9–5

Trade and domestic consumption: apparel (millions of dollars)

Year	Nominal				Real 1982 Prices[a]				Import Penetration (M/C)
	M	X	TB	C[b]	M	X	TB	C[b]	(%)
1961	283	159	−124	13,212	648	364	−284	30,273	2.1
1962	374	152	−222	14,170	838	341	−497	31,767	2.6
1963	400	158	−242	15,060	901	356	−545	33,934	2.7
1964	481	196	−285	15,799	1,062	433	−629	34,887	3.0
1965	568	177	−391	16,817	1,254	391	−863	37,135	3.4
1966	637	188	−449	17,757	1,389	410	−979	38,726	3.6
1967	692	207	−485	18,968	1,416	424	−992	38,823	3.6
1968	900	220	−680	20,308	1,764	431	−1,333	39,811	4.4
1969	1,149	242	−907	21,952	2,123	447	−1,676	40,555	5.2
1970	1,286	250	−1,036	21,430	2,192	426	−1,766	36,531	6.0
1971	1,574	258	−1,316	23,003	2,650	434	−2,216	38,726	6.8
1972	1,967	300	−1,667	25,581	3,470	529	−2,941	45,133	7.7
1973	2,261	381	−1,880	27,850	3,773	636	−3,137	46,472	8.1
1974	2,465	593	−1,872	28,727	3,726	896	−2,830	43,425	8.6
1975	2,775	603	−2,172	29,270	4,124	896	−3,228	43,498	9.5
1976	3,912	740	−3,172	33,191	5,516	1,043	−4,473	46,801	11.8
1977	4,393	859	−3,534	38,767	5,796	1,133	−4,663	51,148	11.3
1978	5,722	1,035	−4,687	42,352	7,315	1,323	−5,992	54,372	13.5
1979	5,902	1,387	−4,515	41,865	7,163	1,683	−5,480	50,810	14.1
1980	6,543	1,604	−4,939	45,232	7,428	1,821	−5,607	51,349	14.5
1981	7,752	1,628	−6,124	50,198	8,122	1,706	−6,416	52,592	15.4
1982	8,516	1,236	−7,280	53,961	8,516	1,236	−7,280	53,961	15.8
1983	10,018	1,049	−8,969	58,392	9,918	1,039	−8,879	57,812	17.2
1984	14,001	1,026	−12,975	63,647	13,632	999	−12,633	61,968	22.0
1985	15,711	991	−14,720	65,424	15,044	949	−14,095	62,646	24.0
1986	18,171	1,178	−16,993	68,480	17,445	1,116	−16,329	65,258	26.7
1987	21,503	1,491	−20,012	83,068	21,503[c]	1,491[c]	−20,012[c]	83,068[c]	25.9
1988	22,170	1,955	−20,215	85,478	21,570[c]	1,902[c]	−19,668[c]	83,165[c]	25.9
1989	23,722	2,602	−21,120	90,625	22,322[c]	2,448[c]	−19,874[c]	85,276[c]	26.2
1989	25,372	2,362	−23,010	109,829	24,093[c]	2,243[c]	−21,850[c]	80,199[c]	30.0
1990	26,602	2,864	−23,738	112,302	24,573[c]	2,646[c]	−21,927[c]	79,163[c]	31.0
1991	27,230	3,708	−23,522	113,401	24,616[c]	3,352[c]	−21,264[c]	77,898[c]	31.6
1992[d]	32,462	4,625	−27,837	124,414	28,633[c]	4,079[c]	−24,553[c]	81,105[c]	32.8
1993[e]	35,449	5,556	−29,893	130,803	30,938[c]	4,849[c]	−26,089[c]	83,219[c]	37.2

M = imports; X = exports; TB = trade balance; C = apparent consumption.

[a]Deflating by apparel product shipments price index, US Department of Commerce.

[b]Equals production *plus* imports *minus* exports.

[c]Real 1987 prices.

[d]Estimates, except exports and imports.

[e]Estimate.

Source: From *The Future of World Trade in Textiles and Apparel* (p. 40) by W. Cline, 1987, Washington, DC: Institute for International Economics. 1986–1993 updates from U.S. Department of Commerce.

1987). In nominal terms, imports increased at an annual rate of nearly 20 percent during the 1982–1987 period.

In the 1990s the extent of apparel import growth varied considerably, whether in nominal or real values. In nominal values, 1991 imports increased only 2.4 percent over 1990; 1992 imports grew by about 19 percent; and estimated data show a 9.2 percent growth for 1993. In real terms, apparel imports did not increase substantially between 1989 and 1991; however, imports grew by 16.3 percent in 1992 and by 8 percent in 1993, based on estimates. The real prices for 1987 through 1993 are not directly comparable to earlier real prices.

A review of apparel exports is important also as we consider trade for the sector. Apparel exports were never great in volume; however, they increased at a healthy pace from 1973 to 1980, growing 16.2 percent annually in real terms. The increase in exports was of somewhat limited significance because the base (the export shipments on which the percentage increases were based) was small. Between 1980 and 1985, exports declined by half, primarily because of the strong dollar (Cline, 1987). From 1986 on, apparel exports began to increase again. Growth has been encouraging in the 1990s, albeit from what is still a relatively small base. In real terms, 1990 exports increased 18 percent over the previous year; 1991 exports represented a 26.7 percent increase; 1992 exports grew by 21.6 percent; and according to estimated data, 1993 exports were an increase of about 18 percent. Exports have not been successful, however, in offsetting the shipments of imports to reduce the trade imbalance for the sector.

The last column in Table 9–5 shows the growing increase of apparel imports as a percentage of U.S. consumption, that is, the import penetration ratio. This ratio grew from slightly over 2 percent in 1962 to more than 37 percent in 1993.

Cline (1987) noted two aspects of the import penetration trends that he considered paradoxes. First, he observed that the apparel sector was successful in getting protection against imports in the early 1960s when the ratio of imports was actually quite low. Cline attributed this early protection to a strong U.S. textile and apparel lobby. Second, he noted that imports rose quite rapidly despite increased protection through trade restrictions during the period. Cline believed that **product upgrading** accounted for the strong continued growth. Although trade restrictions continued to tighten, the *value* of import shipments continued to grow significantly because of product upgrading. That is, tightened quotas encouraged foreign suppliers to produce more costly garments, therefore increasing the value of shipments.

Variation in Import Penetration. Import penetration has varied greatly among apparel categories. In some categories, imports represent a small portion of the U.S. market; in a few other cases, imports account for more sales than U.S.-made products. The differences in import penetration rates by type of apparel may be explained to a degree as follows:

- Products with high labor requirements are difficult for U.S. firms to produce competitively. Two prime examples are gloves and bras. As a result, high import penetration exists in these product areas.
- Price-sensitive lines of apparel typically have had high import penetration levels. Examples are men's and boy's dress shirts and knit shirts. Arpan et al. (1982) suggested that high levels occurred in these areas because retailers could buy lower-priced imports and either offer products to consumers at attractive prices or benefit from a higher profit margin by selling the cheaper import at a price close to that for the U.S. product.

- U.S. production processes may not have been competitive in certain areas. Sweaters are an example. Imports accounted for a large portion of the U.S. sweater market before domestic producers adapted production methods to produce quality sweaters at competitive prices.
- Success in automating production helped retain large shares of the U.S. market in certain categories; automation reduced costs and kept domestic production competitive. Men's knit briefs are an example for which automation has been applied quite successfully. Staple product lines such as underwear also provide economies of volume production and do not face the risks associated with fashion lines.

Table 9–6 lists the major sources of U.S. apparel imports, ranked by *physical quantity* shipped to the U.S. market. Perhaps it is significant to note that no traditional developed country is among the top group, based on quantity shipped to U.S. markets. The table also gives the value of shipments, but the reader will note that rankings are somewhat different according to value of imports. For example, Bangladesh is the seventh largest provider of U.S. apparel imports in terms of quantity, but, in value terms, it ranks twelfth. If countries were ranked according to the value of apparel imports, Italy would be thirteenth; however, the nation does not provide a quantity of imports comparable to those on the list shown.

As Table 9–6 indicates, 1993 U.S. apparel imports in value terms were more than $28.2 billion. Of that, the East Asian NICs provided $7.8 billion, or 27.8 percent of the total, based on value. When China is added to the East Asian NICs, the "Big Four" accounted for $11.3 billion, or 40 percent of all U.S. apparel imports, based on value. More than $3.9 billion came from Caribbean Basin Initiative (CBI) countries; most of these would have been from 9802 (807) production (U.S. Department of Commerce report, 1994).

TABLE 9–6

1993 U.S. imports of apparel (all MFA fibers) by major suppliers

	Millions of square meter equivalents[a]	Millions of dollars
World	7,546.0	28,217.2
China	935.4	3,448.8
Hong King	772.1	3,776.5
Taiwan	652.4	2,196.6
Dominican Republic	488.2	1,409.9
South Korea	427.6	1,883.7
Philippines	393.0	1,261.7
Bangladesh	355.4	741.1
Mexico	321.4	1,127.2
Indonesia	260.4	978.4
Costa Rica	240.6	652.6
Sri Lanka	237.0	805.0
India	232.1	889.9
Thailand	227.7	823.5
Jamaica	158.0	388.9
Guatemala	156.6	545.7
Honduras	152.8	506.2
Malaysia	139.7	609.3
Pakistan	124.2	357.0
Singapore	115.7	516.6
Turkey	105.5	368.4

[a]The square meter equivalent is a common unit of quantity, across all categories. Conversion factors are used to convert garments into square meter equivalents for trade purposes.

Source: From *Major Shippers Report by Category, 12/93 data* by U.S. Department of Commerce, 1994, report available from U.S. Department of Commerce.

Two points should be made regarding the share of imports in U.S. markets. (1) We noted earlier that the actual degree of import penetration (that is, to what extent imports account for a share of the U.S. market) is controversial. (2) Of the volume of imports shown for the U.S. market, apparel manufacturers themselves accounted for a significant portion of those products through various sourcing arrangements. The U.S. Department of Commerce indicated that about 15 percent of all apparel imports result from 9802 (807) production. U.S. manufacturers are the primary users of these strategies (U.S. Department of Commerce, 1994). When apparel firms import products, this is done to further their own business efforts. Under these circumstances, it seems inappropriate for apparel manufacturers to say that imports have "taken" domestic market share. (Because apparel manufacturers have participated increasingly in foreign assembly and other sourcing operations, AAMA no longer takes a hard-line position against imports.)

Export Potential. The apparel industry has been criticized for its lack of an export orientation. For example, Vigdor, a consultant who assists firms in exporting, noted, "The U.S. textile and apparel industries in particular are being extremely slow in awakening and reacting to the facts of global economic life. With or without the government, businesses in practically every industry must plan an increasingly larger role in the global economy as sellers and marketers. This could well mean a company's survival—let alone its prosperity" (1989, p. 58).

Critics believe more active export programs would help to offset the growth of imports. Apparel exports in 1993 were about $4.6 billion (U.S. Department of Commerce, *U.S. Export Markets by Group,* p. 31, 1994); these resulted from the export efforts of only a handful of companies.

FIGURE 9–8
Untapped apparel markets appear to await U.S. producers willing to explore the potential and to assume the risks of entering the export market.

Source: Illustration by Dennis Murphy.

The lack of export orientation is unfortunate because certain U.S. apparel products appear to have appeal in various other parts of the world.

Jeans and T-shirts are examples of U.S. apparel that have widespread global appeal, having become "the ultimate transatlantic uniform. The streets of Paris, London and Tokyo are filled with young men and women wearing jeans and T-shirts in a variety of ways—including dressing them up with jackets—looking very much like their counterparts in New York, Chicago and Los Angeles" (Kissel and Spevack, 1989, p. 1). American fashion looks have a great deal of appeal in many overseas markets. Jeans and T-shirts are one of the easiest ways for young Europeans and Japanese to dress with American flair. One manufacturer noted, "When I walk the streets of Paris or London, I see more American and California influences than their own. Jeans and T-shirts—that's all they're wearing. I was surprised by how much denim they actually wear. They really know how to make a fashion statement with a basic t-shirt and jeans" (Kissel & Spevack, 1989, p. 46).

Although few products can compare with the classic Levi jeans example, a number of other U.S. apparel products are attractive to consumers other countries. European women have begun to imitate the more casual dress of U.S. women and like U.S. casual wear. Moreover, consumers in certain countries attach status to having U.S.-made garments.

Licensing is an alternative to exporting—often used by apparel firms unable (or sometimes unwilling) to ship products to countries where demand exists for their garments. Licensing may provide another source of profit to apparel firms. Generally, under the licensing agreement, the U.S. apparel firm agrees to permit foreign manufacturers to use the company's trademark, its production technology, and its marketing skills to produce and sell garments in other countries. Although U.S. firms face risks of losing control over their trademarks and expertise, carefully controlled licensing agreements may be profitable enough to apparel firms to justify the potential risk. AAMA sources (1984) cautioned that licensing arrangements require long-term commitments from U.S. firms because of the time needed to develop markets in another country.

SUMMARY

Change in the international economy has been influential in reshaping the U.S. textile and apparel industries. Both sectors have changed markedly in the last three decades.

Prior to the 1960s, the textile industry focused on serving a domestic market and had relatively little competition in that market. Even in the 1960s, the textile sector enjoyed buoyant growth, but in the 1970s, stagnated markets and increased raw material prices had negative effects on the industry. Further, as other countries began to produce textile products—particularly mill products—U.S. manufacturers began to feel the impact of foreign competition. Many of the newly developing countries produced with exporting in mind, and U.S. markets were a natural target for those shipments.

The U.S. textile industry's response to foreign competition has resulted in a significantly transformed industry. Textile production has moved from a craft-oriented industry to one of high technology. The industry's willingness to invest in new technology has greatly enhanced its position in world markets. Investments in technology have increased productivity and reduced labor requirements—and, therefore, labor costs. In addition to the capital- and knowledge-intensive nature of the textile industry, productivity improvements and reduced labor costs gave the U.S. industry an improved competitive position in maintaining domestic markets—and in exporting to an extent. Various restructuring efforts, which often included vertical or horizontal integration of businesses, improved the efficiency and profit positions for a number of firms.

The outlook is less optimistic, however, for another sector important to the competitiveness of the U.S. textile industry—the textile machinery industry. As the U.S. textile machinery industry has declined, domestic textile producers find they have become increasingly dependent on foreign machinery producers. Once a strong force in the global market for textile machinery, the U.S. industry has now become a supplier of less sophisticated equipment and a source for spare parts. U.S. textile producers must now rely to a great extent on equipment developed by major firms in other countries.

The U.S. apparel industry, like its counterparts in other developed countries, faces a long-term international shift in comparative advantage toward developing countries. The primary component in the shift of comparative advantage toward developing nations is the lower labor cost. Virtually all aspects of the U.S. apparel industry have been affected profoundly by the influence of low-wage imports. In addition to the labor cost differences, other characteristics of apparel products—such as fashion and timing—add to manufacturers' challenges to produce efficiently and competitively for both domestic and global markets.

The U.S. apparel industry has made significant advances in rethinking the manufacturing-distribution system to serve its customers more effectively. Increasingly, marketing strategies are driving the activities of U.S. apparel firms. Many companies now think of manufacturing in terms of global sourcing plans. Forward-thinking companies have invested significantly in technology that improves both production and distribution functions, but many U.S. apparel firms have been slow to invest in their future through capital expenditures. In many cases, firms are too small to have adequate resources to make these investments.

Many apparel firms participate in various types of sourcing strategies. These strategies include numerous combinations of both domestic and foreign production, using varying combinations of domestic and foreign-made fabrics. Worldwide sourcing is basic to many U.S. firms, and offshore assembly known as 9802 production (formerly 807) is one of the most common strategies.

Although foreign competition has posed serious challenges for the U.S. apparel industry, at the same time that competition has fostered advances in production, marketing, and distribution that have made the domestic industry a more viable one. The fragmented nature of the industry will continue to pose a challenge, however, for the maintenance and growth of a healthy U.S. apparel sector in an increasingly competitive international market.

GLOSSARY

Adjustment means restoring productivity of an industry so that it remains competitive in the overall industrial scheme in the economy. In essence, adjustment is an industry's response to changing comparative advantage. Adjustment may include, as examples, industry contraction ("downsizing") in both employment and output and productivity growth through modernization.

Apparel licensing involves an agreement (i.e., a "licensing agreement") between a U.S. apparel firm and foreign manufacturers to use the U.S. company's trademark plus the technology and expertise needed to produce and market the garment in those countries. (We should add also that an apparel firm may grant other *domestic* firms licensing privileges; e.g., Levi Strauss & Co.

licenses the use of its name on hosiery that is made domestically.)

Note: The reader should also be aware that the term "licensing" is used in another manner in trade as well. **Import licenses** refer to government procedures in certain countries that have been established to regulate the flow of goods. In these cases, potential importers or exporters must secure permission—i.e., the "license"—before conducting trade transactions.

Apparel marketing, as defined by Frank (1985), focuses on broadly defining a company's market and characteristics. The marketing function of a firm identifies new opportunities for growth through self-analysis and market research and promotes a company's image and products.

Apparel merchandising in a manufacturing firm is more specific than marketing, concerning itself with the development, execution, and delivery of the product line. With its close ties to the market segment it serves, the merchandising function is not only able to adjust to market variations rapidly, but is capable of actually anticipating and helping to create market changes (Frank, 1985).

Apparent consumption of textiles (and/or apparel) refers to U.S. production plus imports minus exports.

Artificial fibers (cellulosic fibers) come from naturally occurring cellulose sources; examples are rayon, acetate and triacetate.

Capacity utilization rate refers to the extent to which production facilities are operating, based on the premise that 100 percent capacity utilization rate represents operating at full capacity. The capacity utilization rate provides an important measure of industry activity at a given time. For the textile mill industry, for example, the number of spindles and looms in place, the number of these that are active, and the hours these are operating provide an indication of the capacity and the utilization rates for the spinning and weaving segments of the industry (USITC, 1987b). This measure is generally about 5 percent lower than "operating rates" (below) because, for utilization rates, the Federal Reserve Board employs a broader definition of available capacity (Ringlestein, 1989).

C.i.f. values include the cost, insurance, and freight. When foreign products are bought under this term, the seller quotes a price including the cost of the goods, the insurance, and all transportation charges to the named point of destination. When two values are given for import shipments, the c.i.f. value is higher than the customs value because the c.i.f. figure includes insurance and freight costs.

Customs value is essentially the price of goods received by the foreign exporter. When two values are given for imports, this is the lower one.

Economies of scale occur when advantages of larger, more concentrated production operations account for savings that can be reflected in lower production costs. For example, output or some other measure of productivity may increase as the size of the firm or establishment increases.

807 production. Under the former Tariff Schedule of the United States (TSUS), Item 807.00 enabled apparel manufacturers to send *U.S.-cut* garment parts to low-wage countries to have labor-intensive sewing operations performed. Although this term is still used in the industry; this is actually 9802 production now.

807A or (*"Super 807"*) (9802A arrangement). Although textiles and apparel were treated as an exception to the Caribbean Basin Initiative (CBI), subsequent agreements increased U.S. *quota* allotments—known as **guaranteed access levels** or **GALS**—to CBI countries and Mexico. Under the guaranteed access levels, extended quota levels are available to eligible countries assembling apparel *from fabric both made and cut* in the United States. Eligibility for GALs requires that items be classified under a category that has been negotiated for inclusion in this program by that country (Gelber, 1989).

Greige goods are unbleached or undyed cloth and yarn.

Import penetration ratio is the measure of imports as a percentage of apparent consumption for a country. Import penetration ratios may be calculated for all textile and/or apparel imports for the country, or more specifically, for product categories.

Lead time for manufacturers refers to the time required between the execution of production and the delivery of finished merchandise.

Marketing orientation for a firm means that the company focuses on the consumer's needs and wants, and this emphasis is backed by an integrated effort within the firm to satisfy the customer. The company's focus on satisfying the customer is seen as the means for achieving the firm's financial return objectives. More recently, the textile complex, and particularly the apparel industry, has placed increasing emphasis on serving both retail and end-use consumers.

9802 production. Under the new tariff classification system, the Harmonized Tariff Schedule, Item 9802.00 permits the same offshore production arrangement as under 807.

Offshore production refers to having some or all of a firm's apparel lines produced in another country.

Operating rate, like capacity utilization rate, refers to the extent to which plants are operating as a percentage of full operating capacity. As noted above, this measure tends to be higher than capacity utilization rate because of the definition of available capacity.

Product upgrading occurs when textile trade policies limit the *volume* (SMEs) of import

shipments. Since the limits are on *volume* and not the *value* of import shipments, this provides an incentive to foreign producers to upgrade apparel lines. As a result of the volume limits, enterprising foreign suppliers upgrade product lines to obtain the greatest value within their shipment limits.

Production economies of scale are those efficiencies of production that occur as a result of forming larger manufacturing operations.

Production orientation for a firm means that the company places greatest emphasis on what its plants produce and how it fulfills the production role. Until the mid-1980s, the apparel industry (and, for that matter, the textile complex broadly) focused most of its efforts on refining production processes, believing this approach would be the key to future successes.

Productivity refers to the ratio of output to employment; labor productivity refers to the output per worker.

Research and development (R&D) refers to those operations in a firm devoted to developing and improving products, production processes, or other aspects of the business that will make the firm more competitive.

Restructuring refers to the changes a sector or a company goes through in its efforts to remain competitive in response to changing market conditions. Restructuring of a sector may occur as part of the adjustment process.

Square-meter equivalent (SME) is the unit of measure—in physical terms—for imports of textile and apparel products. With the exception of fabric, all apparel and textile products are assigned a conversion factor that converts units into equivalent square meters. For example, a dozen men's or boys' woven shirts represents X equivalent square meters. The SME measure is used in trade agreements that set limits on imports from various countries.

Standard Industrial Classification (SIC) system is a U.S. system established and maintained by the U.S. Office of Management and Budget (originally developed in 1972; revised in 1987) to classify U.S. establishments into industry groupings on the basis of their primary economic activity. Although the categories are not totally distinct, most segments of the textile industry are under SIC 22, and most apparel is under SIC 23. The SITC and SIC systems use different categories and definitions; data are not comparable.

Standard International Trade Classification (SITC) system is an international system introduced by the United Nations in 1950 to promote international comparability of world trade data. This system is used by the UN and a number of other international organizations for collecting and analyzing trade data. Textile products are under SITC 65; apparel is included under SITC 84.

Structural unemployment occurs as a result of restructuring or when the decline of an industry or a change in the demand for its products results in reduced demand for workers' traditional skills.

Synthetic fibers (noncellulosic fibers) are in most cases petrochemical derivatives; examples are nylon, polyester, and acrylic.

Tariff (also referred to as duty) is a governmental tax applied to goods from another country.

Velocity costs refer to costs that may not be readily apparent when considering sourcing options, according to Kurt Salmon Associates, Inc. (Silva, 1993). Among these costs are interest on holding inventories, markdowns, and extra handling costs.

SUGGESTED READINGS

American Apparel Manufacturers Association. (annual). *Focus: An economic profile of the apparel industry*. Arlington, VA: Author.

Annual economic profile on the U.S. apparel sector.

American Apparel Manufacturers Association. (1984). *Apparel manufacturing strategies*. Arlington, VA: Author.

A review of various sourcing strategies for apparel manufacturers.

American Apparel Manufacturers Association, Apparel Research Committee. (1987). *Managing an industry in transition*. Arlington, VA: Author.

A review of challenges in managing an evolving apparel industry.

American Apparel Manufacturers Association, Technical Advisory Committee. (1987). *Getting started in Quick Response*. Arlington, VA: Author.

A reference notebook on Quick Response.

American Fiber Manufacturers Association, Inc. (periodic). *Manufactured fiber fact book*. Washington, DC: Author.

Manufactured fiber profile.

American Textile Manufacturers Institute. (quarterly). *Textile Hi-Lights*.

Quarterly update on textile industry performance.

Arpan, J., de la Torre, J., Toyne, B., Bacchetta, M., Jedel, M. Stephan, P., & Halliburton, J. (1982). *The U.S. apparel industry: International challenge, domestic response*. Atlanta: Georgia State University Press.

A three-year study of the U.S. apparel industry's international competitiveness and the industry's response to the competitive environment.

Can America compete? (1987, April 20). *Business Week*, pp. 44–69.

This special report reviews the U.S. decline in productivity and competitiveness; included are various perspectives on ways to restore the U.S. position.

Cline, W. (1987). *The future of world trade in textiles and apparel*. Washington, DC: Institute for International Economics.

An economic review of the U.S. textile and apparel industries, with a critical analysis of trade policy for the sectors.

de la Torre, J. (1984). *Clothing-industry adjustment in developed countries*. London: Trade Policy Research Center.

A critical review of adjustment and its costs in the OECD countries.

de la Torre, J., Jedel, M., Arpan, J., Ogram, E., & Toyne, B. (1978). *Corporate responses to import competition in the U.S. apparel industry*. Atlanta: Georgia State University.

An in-depth study of ten apparel firms' responses to import competition.

Fiber Economics Bureau. (monthly). *Fiber Organon.*

Statistical update on textile industry performance.

Finnie, T. (1992). *Textiles and apparel in the USA: Restructuring for the 1990s*. London: The Economist Intelligence Unit.

An overview of the U.S. industry and restructuring for the 1990s.

Fixing America's economy. (1992, October 19). *Fortune*. Special feature issue.

Examination of U.S. problems in the economy and global competitiveness, with a focus on how these might be improved.

Ghadar, F., Davidson, W., & Feigenoff, C. (1987). *U.S. industrial competitiveness: The case of the textile and apparel industries*. Lexington, MA: Lexington Books.

An examination of global and domestic forces that affected the textile and apparel industries.

Glock, R., & Kunz, G. (1990). *Apparel manufacturing: Sewn product analysis*. New York: Macmillan.

A comprehensive analysis of apparel manufacturing, with special emphasis on factors that determine cost, price, quality, performance, and value of garments.

Kotabe, M. (1992). *Global sourcing strategy*. New York: Quorum Books.

This book explores the market performance of various global sourcing strategies employed by multinational firms.

Kurt Salmon Associates (Annual). *Textile profile—The KSA perspective.*

Annual U.S. textile industry performance profile of publicly held firms.

National Cotton Council of America. (annual). *Cotton counts its customers: The quantity of cotton consumed in final uses in the United States*. Memphis: National Cotton Council of America.

Statistical report on quantities of cotton and competing materials consumed in textile products manufactured in the United States.

Olsen, R. (1978). *The textile industry: An industry analysis approach to operations management*. Lexington, MA: Lexington Books.

Overview of process technology and market structure of the industry; includes four case studies.

Tugman, J. (quarterly). *MRCA Soft Goods Information Service Reports*. Stamford, CT: Author.

Quarterly summaries of softgoods market activity.

U.S. Department of Commerce (annual). "Apparel" and "Textile" chapters, *U.S. Industrial Outlook*, Washington, DC: U.S. Government Printing Office.

Annual review of textile and apparel industry performance.

U.S. Department of Commerce, Office of Textiles and Apparel. (annual). *Foreign regulations affecting U.S. textile/apparel exports*. Washington, DC: Author.

A summary of trade requirements and restrictions of 135 countries, which may affect textile and apparel export sales.

U.S. International Trade Commission (1987, December). *U.S. global competitiveness: The U.S. textile mill industry*, USITC Publication 2048. Washington, DC: Author.

An in-depth study of the U.S. textile mill sector and its relative competitiveness in global trade.

U.S. Office of Management and Budget (1972; 1989). *Standard Industrial Classification Manual*. Washington, DC: U.S. Government Printing Office.

SIC codes for the U.S. industrial classification system.

V

"Managing" Textile and Apparel Trade in the Global Economy

As global textile and apparel production and trade increased, the problems associated with growing international competition led to a complex system of trade policies and structures to "manage" that trade. As one of the most sensitive and difficult sectors in world trade, textile trade came to be managed by a unique international "regime." Both at the international level and at the national level in many countries, textile and apparel production and trade concerns have attracted special attention and provisions to attend to those concerns.

Chapter 10 provides an overview of the evolution of policies affecting trade in textiles and apparel. As the international perspective is presented in this chapter, special attention is given to the U.S. position within the broader context of global policy development and implementation. Major textile and apparel trade policies are presented; in some instances, these policies are contrasted to those for trade in general.

Chapter 11 presents an overview of the major global and U.S. structures for facilitating or managing the textile and apparel trade. The goal of this chapter is to help the reader understand how the trade policies operate at both the global and national levels as well as the ways in which the policies and their implementation may be influenced by various groups. Key organizations and their roles in textile and apparel trade are discussed.

10

Textile and Apparel Trade Policies

INTRODUCTION

Textile and apparel production is vital to the economies of both the developed and the developing countries. Although the textile complex has declined in the industrialized nations, it remains a top manufacturing employer in most of these countries. At the same time, textile and apparel production may be the only industry through which a relatively large number of developing nations can participate in international trade. For many other LDCs and NICs, textile and apparel products are a main source of export earnings and employment.

By the 1960s and 1970s, growth in the number of textile and apparel producers for the world market led to a growing overcapacity for production. Expanded capacity for producing textile and apparel goods greatly exceeded growth in demand. As a result, global competition grew intense and difficult. As producers in the developed countries attempted to protect their markets from imports from low-wage countries, country-by-country trade policies emerged. Later, global textile trade policies[1] developed in an attempt to mediate the problems associated with the worldwide surplus. The policies that developed represented a compromise with which almost no players have been satisfied.

Although textile trade policies are in the process of changing markedly, a review of the development of these policies is important to an understanding of the complex nature of global trade in this sector. A review of these trade policies and how they developed pro-

---

[1]In trade policy discussions, *textile* or *textiles* is often used as a shortened label when referring to both the textile and apparel industries. If one were speaking of textile trade policies, these would apply to both textiles and apparel.

vides an understanding of the political tensions and drama that have unfolded as nations often have fought bitterly to protect their respective textile and apparel interests—because these industries are vital to most nations' economies. Moreover, textile trade represents one of the most phenomenal studies of trade politics in all history. Although textile trade policies are changing, this history may suggest to us that the politics of textile trade will not disappear.

In this chapter, we will review the evolution of policies affecting trade in textiles and apparel. We will consider different types of regulations on textile trade—both at the international and national levels—and how these are implemented. Discussion will also point to the unique trade policies for textile and apparel trade in contrast to those for trade in general.

HISTORICAL PERSPECTIVE

Historically, textile and apparel trade has been a ready target for regulations to restrict or "manage" that trade. In part, this may be due to the important role textile and apparel products play in satisfying humans' needs to clothe themselves and furnish their dwellings. Consequently, most countries have wanted to have their respective domestic industries supply the needs of the population. Second, the industries have played vital roles in the economic development and economic health of country after country. Countries have wanted to reap the economic benefits from production. In short, the desire by most countries to control production has made textile trade regulations almost as common as the production itself. Broader international relations often have suffered as a result of various countries' efforts to control certain portions of the production and trade of textile and apparel products.

Early Development and Regulation of Textile Trade

One of the earliest recorded efforts to regulate textile trade occurred in England in the late 1600s when the British Parliament prohibited Indian cloth so that the fledgling English industry might develop. The industrialization that soon followed in England made it possible to produce growing amounts of fabric.

England's early textile industry developed when mercantilism was the common economic philosophy of the day. Governmental manipulation of trade regulations assured that exports were greater than imports as a means of increasing wealth. By the 1800s, however, merchants and industrialists wanted to broaden their markets through freer trade. Adam Smith's *laissez faire* philosophy supported the English capitalists' desires to have fewer regulations and to be able to expand more freely to other countries. The English cotton textile manufacturers took advantage of the changing mood and soon developed a successful export business. The open trade fostered development of the textile industry, making textile goods one of England's major export products by the end of the 1800s.

The American textile industry began to develop in the 1700s, despite England's efforts to guard its early spinning and weaving technology from being transferred out of the country. The British authorities believed the colonies should absorb products from the mother country. In contrast, the colonists became eager to produce their own textile goods and reduce their dependence on England. Eventually, the colonists secured the necessary technology to do so.

Both England and the United States became protective of their respective textile industries. Because textiles was the first real "industry" for both nations, a great deal was at stake. England tried to impose laws on the colonists to force them to buy British textiles. In turn, as the American industry became established, Congress imposed a duty in 1808 on foreign textiles to protect the growing U.S. industry. Later, during the War of 1812, foreign textile goods were embargoed.

The textile industries in both England and the United States were boosted in their early development by government policies that provided substantial protection from imports. The trading partner with more power at a given time usually exerted control in trade. England dictated trade policies to the colonies. Later, however, as the United States became independent and more powerful, the new country was in a position to issue its own rules.

The nineteenth century was an important expansion period for both the English and American textile industries. Boosted by the open trading system that evolved in England, the British textile industry developed an impressive textile trade. By 1900, Britain accounted for 70 percent of the world's textile trade (Juvet, 1967). While Britain's textile industry was expanding in global markets, the U.S. industry was developing and expanding rapidly in its own home market. The U.S. cotton industry was relatively minor at the beginning of the 1800s, but by 1860 it was the country's leading manufacturing industry (Poulson, 1981). In contrast to England's export growth, the U.S. industry grew to a great extent because of **import substitution**. **Tariffs** and embargoes imposed on foreign textiles protected the U.S. industry from competition and encouraged the substitution of domestic textiles for previously imported goods. Although the U.S. textile industry had grown to be one of the world's major textile industries, its focus was primarily on the domestic market.

By 1900, the English and American textile industries were the world's leading producers. By then, however, a number of other countries in Western Europe plus Canada became important textile producers. In most cases, the industries developed as a result of deliberate government encouragement. Western Europe and North America accounted for 85 percent of world cotton textile output by 1913 (Hanson, 1980; Taussig, 1914). In addition, Japan began to expand significantly during this period. Among these first countries to industrialize and develop important textile industries, only Great Britain and Japan expanded their textile sectors with exporting as a major goal.

The Early 1900s

In the early 1900s, world textile production grew impressively. Between 1900 and 1937, production increased by about 90 percent in real terms (Maizels, 1963). By this time, however, the developed countries started to see a decline in the relative share of the textile industry as a part of all manufacturing activity. A sharp drop in the developed countries' textile exports occurred between 1913 and 1929. Some of the loss in export markets resulted from increasing competition from Japan. Another factor may have been the import substitution policies in Central Europe and Latin America. This meant that as those countries began textile production, governments promoted use of their country's textile products rather than imports. As a result, countries that had been selling to those nations lost portions of the markets (GATT, 1984; Maizels, 1963; Paretti & Bloch, 1955).

From the start of the Great Depression in 1929 on, the developed countries began to experience a new era in textile trade. The industrialized countries perhaps would never again experience the luxury of dominating world markets in the same way they had earlier. First, textile trade slumped during the Depression. And second, although the Depression had hurt the industry in the industrialized countries, the strong competition that emerged had an even greater impact. By 1933, Japan had become the leading world exporter of cotton textile products

(Japan Spinners' Association, 1982; Juvet, 1967). Other developing Asian countries patterned themselves after Japan and soon made their presence known in world textile markets. These newcomers benefited from import substitution policies in their countries and from the comparative advantage they had in abundant, inexpensive labor (GATT, 1984).

Japan made impressive strides in industrial development and textile competitiveness in the period between World Wars I and II. Japan's active participation in world textile markets soon made it the target of restrictive measures from both Britain and the United States. Both these early leaders resented Japan's success in taking part of their markets.

In 1932 Britain reacted to the growing competition and loss of markets by passing protective measures to limit Japan's textile products. Other countries followed with similar policies designed to restrict Japanese products from their markets. Clearly, Japan was perceived as the major threat. By 1936, Japanese exports of cotton textiles were subject to restrictions on the amounts that could be shipped to 40 of 106 markets (GATT, 1984).

U.S. textile producers became concerned over Japan's textile shipments to the U.S. market. As a result, in 1935, the U.S. Tariff Commission investigated the increased shipments of Japanese cotton cloth. This led to the first known **voluntary export restraint (VER)** in textiles. The VER was an agreement by Japan to limit its textile shipments to the United States; however, the VER failed to reduce Japanese textile exports. By 1936, the United States imposed selective tariff increases on Japanese textiles, but these also failed to reduce imports. Finally, U.S. and Japanese trade associations negotiated a formal agreement to limit Japan's textile exports through 1940 (Brandis, 1982; Hunsberger, 1964).

In short, in the period between World War I and World War II, powerful newcomers—particularly Japan—challenged earlier patterns of textile trade. Developed countries responded

by passing tighter restrictions to keep textile imports from their markets. This era set the stage for an increasingly difficult textile trade climate that followed for the next half century.

The Early Years after World War II

Although the United States typically had a textile trade deficit before World War II, circumstances related to the war gave both U.S. and British textile and apparel industries an advantage in world markets. The textile industries in most other major textile-producing countries—and particularly in Japan—were seriously damaged during the war. While other countries were rebuilding their industries, the United States and Britain moved aggressively to capture world textile markets. By 1947, the United States experienced its largest textile trade surplus up to that time. American textile producers believed they would continue to enjoy those favorable market conditions. U.S. textile and apparel manufacturers were so confident that they provided technical advisement to assist Japan's industry in its rebuilding efforts. American government and industry leaders supplied technical as well as financial assistance to Japanese industries—including advice on export markets so that Japan might earn foreign exchange, which she desperately needed (Aggarwal, 1985; Destler, Fukui, & Sato, 1979; Hunsberger, 1964; Sato, 1976).

Japan's quick recovery in textile and apparel production soon caused concern among American manufacturers. By 1953, Japan exported textile and apparel products valued at $746 million, compared to $539 for the United States and $343 million for the United Kingdom (U.N. Statistical Office, 1953, cited in Aggarwal, 1985). In addition, Hong Kong, South Korea, India, and Pakistan were exporting growing amounts of cotton textile products. Although imports represented less than 1 percent of U.S. textile consumption in the United States, the American Cotton Manufacturers Institute[2] became quite concerned and started efforts to limit imports. In addition, textile producers became outspoken against U.S. foreign aid schemes that helped the developing countries (including Japan) in building their textile industries (Aggarwal, 1985; GATT, 1984).

Similarly, the British textile and apparel producers became concerned about imports from Japan and other developing countries. As a result, in 1950, Britain forced Japan to restrict textile shipments (Aggarwal, 1985). Although other European markets received an increase of textile imports, the impact of the war affected European industries so badly that imports were not one of their major concerns at that stage.

A review of overall trade policies during this era will be helpful at this point so that we may consider textile activities in relation to the broader picture for trade. In general, most of the developed countries—especially in Western Europe—had quite restrictive trade policies in place at the end of World War II. Complicated rules and high tariffs were common. **Bilateral agreements** (agreements between two countries) governed a good share of trade. A bilateral agreement limited the volume of products one country could ship to another. Although bilateral agreements helped to slow the growing tendency to place other restrictions on trade, many countries were unwilling to commit themselves to trade reductions when they were unsure of what other countries might do. Furthermore, bilaterals were time consuming to negotiate because they had to be established

on a country-by-country basis (Catudal, 1961; GATT, 1984).

Establishment of the General Agreement on Tariffs and Trade

The United States played a lead role in developing a multilateral approach (many countries) for trying to resolve international trade problems. These efforts led to the formation of the General Agreement on Tariffs and Trade (GATT) in 1947. The primary goal of GATT was to liberalize trade—that is, to free trade from the web of restraints that had evolved. GATT provided a forum for world trade problems and established several basic guidelines for more open trade.

From the time GATT was established and on through the 1950s, GATT and other organizations made remarkable progress toward liberalizing trade by reducing prior restrictions. First, the Organization for European Economic Cooperation (OEEC) was established in 1948 by 16 nations to analyze Europe's problems and to formulate a program of recovery, including use of aid from the Marshall Plan. The OEEC later evolved into the European Economic Community and the European Free Trade Association, both of which fostered freer trade. In general, the mood had shifted toward liberalized trade. Importantly, textile and apparel trade among developed countries in North America and Western Europe benefited from the general trend toward liberalization.

The same mood did *not* exist, however, for textile trade between the developed countries and their aspiring trading partners—Japan, the East European countries, and the developing countries. While restraints were being eased elsewhere, the developed countries' discriminatory restrictions on textile imports from Japan and the developing countries became more severe during the 1950s.

---

[2]The American Cotton Manufacturers Institute (ACMI) was the most important cotton textile producers organization. In the early 1950s, most textile and apparel products were made of cotton, since manufactured fibers were still relatively new and not produced in large amounts. This group was instrumental in achieving some of the earliest restrictions on imported textile and apparel products.

THE GENERAL AGREEMENT ON TARIFFS AND TRADE (GATT)[*]

The General Agreement on Tariffs and Trade (GATT) is a multilateral treaty, subscribed to by about 120 countries—officially called *Contracting Parties*. Nearly 30 additional countries subscribe to the rules of GATT but are not members. GATT is particularly important in textile and apparel trade (and, for that matter, *all trade*); the major global trade policies for the textile and apparel sectors come under GATT.

GATT's basic aim is "to liberalize world trade and place it on a secure basis, thereby contributing to economic growth and development and to the welfare of the world's peoples" (GATT, 1985b, p. 1). GATT membership accounts for more than 80 percent of world trade. About two-thirds of the Contracting Parties are in early stages of economic development; this is often a significant point in textile trade matters.

GATT is both a code of rules and a forum for world trade concerns. As a *code of rules*, the Agreement is the only multilateral instrument that establishes rules for international trade. As a *forum*, GATT is the main international body concerned with international trade relations and with negotiating the reduction of trade barriers and other measures that hinder trade. Member countries have voluntarily accepted the rights and obligations that the GATT endorses as being in their mutual interest. GATT oversees the application of these rules (GATT, 1985b).

Basic Aims of GATT

Although the General Agreement is a technical and complex document, because "the problems of international trade are technical and complex"

(Catudal, 1961, p. 1), the basic aims of GATT can be reduced to a few simple essentials. (The rules for implementing GATT principles are much more specific and complex, however.) Principles and aims of GATT are

1. *Trade without discrimination.* This basic rule results from the "most favored nation" clause that requires equal treatment of trading partners; this is known as **most favored nation treatment (MFN)**. Although this term seems awkward to the average person, it means that all trade must be conducted without discrimination. All Contracting Parties must extend the same treatment on trade matters to all members. No country is to give special trade advantages or to discriminate against another. (Textile trade has been a major departure from this rule.)

2. *Protection through tariffs.* Under this rule, if a country is going to protect a domestic industry, the country should impose tariffs on imports rather than through other means. (Textile trade is an exception here also.)

3. *A stable basis for trade.* If tariffs are agreed upon, they are binding and are published for each Contracting Party. This means that trading partners know what to expect.

4. *Consultation, conciliation, and settlement of differences.* Contracting members may call upon GATT if they feel their rights under the Agreement are being abused by other members.

5. *The "waiver" and possible emergency action.* When economic or trade circumstances warrant, a member may seek a derogation (departure) from a GATT obligation. (The textile sector has been a major user of these provisions.)

6. Quantitative restrictions on imports. Quantitative (quota) restrictions are prohibited; however, they are permitted under certain circumstances; e.g., for textile trade.

---

[*]The GATT will be replaced by the World Trade Organization (WTO), which is expected to embrace the principles of GATT. This will be discussed in Chapter 11.

THE GENERAL AGREEMENT ON TARIFFS AND TRADE (GATT)*
(continued)

7. *Regional trading arrangements.* When a group of countries, such as the EU member countries, agrees to abolish or reduce barriers against imports from one another, such arrangements are possible under the GATT if those countries do not raise barriers to trade with the outside world (GATT, 1985b; with parenthetical comments by author).

The developed countries were not alone in creating the unfriendly trade climate for textiles and apparel. The developing countries had their own policies restricting trade—but in different ways from the measures used by the developed countries. Developing countries used primarily the following two approaches to restrict textile and apparel products from their markets.

1. *Import substitution policies* promoted the use of the country's own products rather than imports.
2. A *balance of payments provision of GATT* (Article XVIII) permits a country to deviate from certain GATT rules to remedy serious balance of payments problems. Under this provision, a developing country might refuse to import textile products from other countries because it has balance-of-payments problems.

It is important to note, however, that the developing countries were applying these restrictions to a wide range of products, whereas textile and apparel products were the *only* nonagricultural areas for which the developed countries did not ease restraints (GATT, 1984). This difference reflects both the politicized aspects of textile/apparel trade plus the differing economic climates in the two types of countries.

Textile-Specific Restraints of the 1950s

Two important and contradictory events affecting textile trade occurred in 1955. First, Japan was admitted to the GATT. As we recall from the discussion of GATT's aims, this meant Japan became a partner in the liberalized trading climate fostered by GATT. Oddly, however, the second major event was a contradiction of what the GATT stood for. Growing pressure from American textile and apparel producers caused the U.S. government to encourage Japan to agree to the first post-World War II textile-specific restriction—a "voluntary" export restraint (VER) to limit certain cotton textile products. Hunsberger (1964) noted that, at this time, imports accounted for 2 percent of the U.S. market. American manufacturers were quite concerned, however, about the potential for import growth if the developing countries continued to develop their industries as rapidly as they had following the war.

One week after Japan agreed to the first VER, U.S. textile producers petitioned the U.S. State Department to consider stronger controls on Japanese textile products, asserting that the first VER placed too much of the responsibility for compliance on the Japanese (*Cotton Trade Journal*, 1955, cited in Aggarwal, 1985). After Japan's textile exports doubled in

1955, U.S. industry leaders doubted Japan's commitment to the VER. (We must also keep in mind that aggressive U.S. importers had an active hand in these developments [Destler et al., 1979].) In the new demands, industry representatives asked for U.S. government control of imports (Aggarwal, 1985; Destler et al., 1979; Lynch, 1968).

By this time, the U.S. textile and apparel industry had become quite skilled at "coalition-building and effective lobbying" (Aggarwal, 1985, p. 11). The industry's power had led to "encouraging" Japan to limit imports, and, because of its dependence on the U.S. market, Japan was forced to comply with the new limit in order to retain some of the market. Japan was hardly in a position to argue with American requests for textile export restraints. Japan's trade with the United States was eight times greater than with any other trading partner, and, in 1956, 20 percent of Japan's exports went to the United States (Aggarwal, 1985; Destler et al., 1979; Hunsberger, 1964).

As a result of U.S. industry pressure, a second VER with Japan went into effect in 1957, setting a five-year limitation on cotton textile products. Although Japan had "volunteered" more willingly for the first VER in 1955, the second one resulted more from U.S. industry pressure. Finding a way of forcing Japan to restrict textile shipments—without violating the GATT—had been a challenge to the United States. That is, forcing Japan to abide by quota limits would not have been permissible under GATT. Instead, pressuring Japan to sign a "voluntary" export restraint was discovered as a way to restrict shipments without breaking, at least technically, GATT rules (Aggarwal, 1985; Destler et al., 1979; Hunsberger, 1964).

After the second Japanese VER began to stem the tide of cotton textile and apparel products from Japan, a now-familiar pattern in textile trade emerged. That is, when exports from one country are controlled, then textile and apparel products become more abundant from *uncontrolled* countries. Aggarwal (1985) described this occurrence as being like "the little Dutch boy and the dike" (p. 43). That is, once an industry convinces the government to provide protection from imports, "as they plugged holes in the dike, new leaks sprang up" (p. 43). (Figure 10–1).

As Aggarwal noted, restricting imports from one country simply provided room for other countries to enter the competition for domestic markets. Table 10–1 illustrates the drop in Japanese textile exports after the 1956 VER, plus the increase that followed from other developing countries having no restraints. Hong Kong and other suppliers responded rapidly to fill the gap left by the restrictions on Japan's textile products. American textile producers attempted to limit Hong Kong imports in the same manner used to restrict Japanese imports; however, Hong Kong refused to restrain its imports to the United States. Several factors accounted for the U.S. failure in pressuring Hong Kong to set limits: Hong Kong was far less dependent on the United States than Japan had been; Hong Kong was shielded somewhat as a British colony; and, finally, negotiators for Hong Kong were experienced, sophisticated, and tough—they refused to give in (Aggarwal, 1985).

While the United States was concerning itself with the problem of imports from Japan and Hong Kong, Great Britain had similar problems. By the late 1950s, the country that launched the Industrial Revolution imported more cotton cloth than it exported. Britain had even greater problems than the United States, however, because of special relationships with countries under British rule. Under the Imperial Preference System, cotton textiles from India, Pakistan, and Hong Kong were imported free of duties. By the 1950s, all these countries had become important textile producers (GATT, 1984; Hunsberger, 1964). Britain, too, resorted to having these countries

FIGURE 10–1
The textile import control program provides protection from imports only until a new "leak" appears in the form of uncontrollable imports.

Source: Illustration by Dennis Murphy.

"voluntarily" restrict cotton textile products under an agreement called the Lancashire Pact (Aggarwal, 1985; Blokker, 1989; GATT, 1984).

Other European countries used a variety of measures to restrict textile and apparel products from the developing countries. First, the European countries used Article XII of GATT, which permitted imposing quotas on products from other countries for balance of payment reasons. Eventually, however, when the balance of payments provision was no longer appropriate, the European countries retained their quotas and were willing to be in open violation of GATT rules in order to restrict LDC textile imports. European countries used a variety of measures—both legal and illegal—to protect their industries from the textile imports from low-wage countries (Aggarwal, 1985; Blokker, 1989; GATT, 1984).

In summary, during the 1950s, governments of the developed countries initiated a variety of actions to restrict textile imports from the developing countries. These actions set the stage for other stringent measures that soon followed.

Early Development of Textile Trade Policies in the 1960s

U.S. leaders were opposed to the illegal actions taken by the European countries to protect their textile industries, believing the violations would undermine the GATT. Acting out of this concern, the United States began to press for a more comprehensive multilateral agreement to resolve textile trade difficulties. (The VERs with Japan and most other textile trade restrictions up to that point had been bilateral agreements.) The continued emer-

TABLE 10–1
U.S. imports of cotton manufacturers (in million dollars)

Countries	1956	1957	1958	1959	1960	1961
Total from all countries	154.3	136.2	150.0	201.3	248.3	203.3
Japan	84.1	65.8	71.7	76.7	74.1	69.4
Hong Kong	0.7	5.8	17.4	45.8	63.6	47.0
Other Asian countries	15.3	13.0	14.3	24.0	34.0	25.0
Egypt	0.4	0.5	0.3	0.3	5.9	1.0
Spain	0.3	0.3	0.4	1.6	7.2	3.2
Portugal	0.0	0.1	0.3	1.0	5.2	2.3

Source: From *Japan and the United States in World Trade* (p. 325) by W. Hunsberger, 1964, New York: Harper & Row. Reprinted by permission of the Council on Foreign Relations, Inc.

gence of important developing country exporters led to pressure for other approaches to controlling "low-wage imports" into the industrial countries.

Market Disruption

The concept of **market disruption** grew out of the desire to limit low-wage textile imports in the developed countries' markets. At the 1959 session of the GATT Contracting Parties, the U.S. delegate stated that "sharp increases in imports over a brief period of time and in a narrow range of products could have serious economic, political and social repercussions in the importing countries, and officially proposed that the GATT study the problem posed by 'the adverse effects of an abrupt invasion (by sharp increases in imports) of established markets'" (GATT, 1984, p. 64). A GATT study that followed found that many countries were already attempting to restrict imports they feared *might* disrupt their markets (GATT, 1960).

A GATT Working Party was established to consider the problem. In November 1960, the Working Party reported that a problem did exist and that it would be called *market disruption*. The report added that "there were political and psychological elements in the problem"

(GATT, 1984, p. 64) that suggested the tendency to use exceptional measures (outside GATT rules) to control textile imports would not stop until more comprehensive policies were in place to handle the problem (GATT, 1984).

As a result, in November 1960 the Contracting Parties adopted "Avoidance of Market Disruption" (GATT BISD 9th Supplement, pp. 26–28), which introduced three important changes into GATT fundamentals:

1. The injurious increases of imports need not have already occurred—*a potential increase could be sufficient* to justify added restrictions.

2. Imports of a product from *a particular country could be singled out* as the source of a problem rather than overall imports of the product. This provision meant restrictions could be applied on a country-specific (discriminatory) basis rather than according to the "most favored nation" rule. (The change in GATT rules applied primarily to exports from Japan and the developing countries.)

3. The existence of *a sizable price difference* between particular imports and comparable goods in a domestic market could be used to justify additional restrictions on imports. That is, the price difference for textile products made in the developing countries—compared to prices for similar product in a developed country—could justify added restrictions on the imports from developing countries. This provision was based on the notion that the developing countries had an unfair advantage because of the disparity in labor costs between the developing nations and the developed countries (discussion of 1960 document in GATT, 1984).

Establishing the concept of market disruption within GATT may seem like a minor occurrence. On the contrary, this change was tremendously important both in the history of the GATT and what GATT stood for—and for the future of international textile trade policy. As we reflect briefly on each of these points, we might consider the strength of textile interest groups in effecting such fundamental changes in global policies that applied to all trade.

A number of sources believe that accepting the concept of market disruption (which resulted from textile trade concerns) was the beginning of a weakening of GATT power (Aggarwal, 1985; Blokker, 1989; W. Cline, 1987). GATT had been established to create a climate of openness and equality in trading; it had prohibited discrimination from one country to another (all trading partners were to be treated equally), and quantitative restrictions (quotas) were forbidden. Legitimizing market disruption as a way of limiting imports violated these fundamental aims of GATT. And, finally, we should not forget that it was the textile complex that was instrumental in introducing these departures into the GATT framework.[3]

Next, we should keep in mind that the introduction of the market disruption concept was the beginning of implementation of a special set of trade rules to manage the problems of global textile trade. Although not originally intended to apply only to textiles and apparel, these are the only two industries to which the Contracting Parties have applied the concept (GATT, 1984). In short, the market disruption provision paved the way for what would follow soon in textile trade policies.

THE SHORT-TERM ARRANGEMENT (STA)

By 1960, U.S. government leaders found themselves in a dilemma with regard to the growing difficulties posed by textile trade. Representatives of the U.S. textile industry grew increasingly impatient with the growth of imports from low-wage countries in domestic markets. Both U.S. government and industry leaders were angered by the EC's[4] measures—many of which were "illegal" under GATT—to restrict LDC textile imports from the European markets. In other words, the Americans thought the Europeans were not taking "their share" of low-cost textile imports.

Faced with the growing pressure from industry to restrict imports, U.S. government officials found it difficult to respond to the textile industry's demands without violating the rules of GATT. After all, the United States had played a leading role in the establishment of GATT and wanted to preserve it. Moreover, U.S. government representatives were concerned by the growing restrictions that threatened to undermine the GATT.

---

[3]Although the market disruption feature was discussed and formulated by the Contracting Parties, it never became part of the GATT articles. This is why although all textile agreements have been negotiated in the GATT, the participation is on the one hand limited to those contracting parties who accept the textile rules and on the other hand is open to non-GATT countries (personal communication from M. Raffaelli and T. Jenkins, 1993).

[4]Although the European Union was called the European Economic Community at the time, we will refer to it as the European Union (or EU) for consistency.

U.S. politics entered the picture at this point as well. As a presidential candidate, Senator John F. Kennedy, who was from Massachusetts, a state with a seriously declining textile industry, sought and received the support of the U.S. textile industry. Senator Kennedy was keenly aware of the number of voters employed in the textile and apparel sectors. Prior to his election, Senator Kennedy sent a letter to South Carolina Governor Ernest F. Hollings[5] on August 31, 1960, which included the following statement:

> I agree . . . that sweeping changes in our foreign trade policies are not necessary. Nevertheless, we must recognize that the textile and apparel industries are of international scope and are particularly susceptible to competitive pressure from imports. Clearly the problems of the Industry will not disappear by neglect nor can we wait for a large scale unemployment and shutdown of the industry to inspire us to action. A comprehensive industry-wide remedy is necessary. (Brandis, 1982, p. 17)

Having pledged to support the textile industry in his campaign, President Kennedy proposed a seven-point program to assist the U.S. textile complex. One of Kennedy's points directed the State Department to convene an early conference of textile importing and exporting countries to develop an international agreement governing textile trade (Brandis, 1982). Subsequently, President Kennedy charged the undersecretary of state, George Ball, with responsibility for negotiating an international agreement on textile trade.

In an effort both to satisfy the domestic textile industry and yet maintain the integrity of GATT, U.S. officials proposed a multilateral arrangement to handle textile trade problems. U.S. negotiators denounced the unilateral approaches being used by the European

countries to limit textile imports, charging that quantitative restrictions (quotas) were expressly forbidden under GATT. The U.S. proposal also suggested that in developing an agreement, "Such a mechanism should permit the distribution of cotton textile trade over a larger number of importing countries" (GATT Document L/1592, p. 5, cited in Aggarwal, 1985). That is, the United States believed that European countries should take their "share" of textile exports from the LDCs.

The outcome of negotiations was the Short-Term Arrangement Regarding International Trade in Textiles (the STA), which was effective from October 1961 to September 1962. The STA authorized one-year restrictions on 64 categories of cotton textiles *to avoid market disruption*—until a more permanent mechanism could be developed. The STA covered only cotton textile products. Although U.S. industry sources pressed to have wool included, government officials resisted (Aggarwal, 1985).

U.S. government and industry sources believed they had found the "near-perfect" answer to textile trade problems. In referring to the STA, an article in *Daily News Record* (December 1961, cited in Aggarwal, 1985) noted: "The cotton textile pact is to be cited as an ideal example of how the U.S. can liberalize its trade policies while still protecting specialized industries from market disruption."

Not all countries involved in the STA negotiations viewed the agreement or the negotiations favorably. Some representatives resented the U.S. negotiators' subtle threat to close off their markets unless the **multilateral agreement** materialized:

> There were strong domestic political pressures urging the U.S. Government to take unilateral action and establish import quotas. As action of this type would be contrary to the generally liberal trade policies of the U.S. in recent years, this government has advanced its proposals for a multilaterally acceptable solution. (GATT Document L/1535, p. 3, cited in Aggarwal, 1985, p. 85)

---

[5]Governor Hollings later became a strong textile industry advocate in the U.S. Senate.

Although the STA was a stopgap measure, its establishment (and the Long-Term Arrangement that followed) represented a particularly significant occurrence in trade history. Textiles and apparel were the only products to be formally exempted from the provisions of GATT and given a special set of rules (a **regime**) of their own. Initially, two criteria were the justification for treating textile and apparel trade as a "special case" and for granting the special status.

1. "The challenge presented by 'low cost' imports was, with only minor exceptions, unique to textiles (and later to apparel), and
2. "The importance of employment and production in those industries to the country's overall economic activity" (GATT, 1984, p. 10).

In summary, beginning with the STA in 1961, a new set of trade rules for textiles and apparel was created alongside the existing rules of the General Agreement for Tariffs and Trade. Beginning with formalization of the STA, we might think of textile and apparel trade policies in the manner depicted in Figure 10–2. The STA—and the LTA which followed—were significant events in GATT's history. An important part of world trade was formally exempted from GATT rules—in particular the *nondiscrimination* rule and the general prohibition of *quantitative* restrictions (that is, *quotas* were legitimized under the STA).

THE LONG-TERM ARRANGEMENT (LTA)

In February 1962, 19 major trading nations agreed to the Long-Term Arrangement Regarding Cotton Textiles (LTA), which was effective for a period of five years. Like the STA, the LTA included provisions for govern-

FIGURE 10–2
Textile trade since 1961.

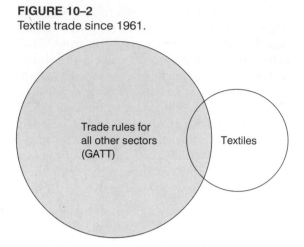

Trade rules for all other sectors (GATT)

Textiles

ments to follow if they claimed *market disruption* or *threat of market disruption* from imports. When market disruption (or the perceived threat of market disruption) occurred, importing countries were permitted to (1) negotiate bilateral agreements with exporting countries or (2) impose unilateral restraints if they and the exporters could not arrive at an agreement (certain provisions were required in taking unilateral restraints). Most importing countries chose to negotiate bilateral agreements with exporting countries, and, by 1966, the United States had bilateral agreements with 18 countries (Aggarwal, 1985; Dam, 1970).

At first glance, one might wonder how the bilateral agreements or **unilateral restraints** permitted under the LTA differed from the measures taken by European countries prior to the STA and LTA. The measures were similar. The difference was that the STA and LTA now provided a special provision—*outside normal GATT rules*—which *legitimized* the bilateral agreements (with quotas) and conditional unilateral restraints.

The LTA was an international regime that limited volume growth of imports to 5 percent per year for most cotton textile products. In some cases, other agreements might alter the 5 percent growth permitted. W. Cline (1987) and Keesing and Wolf (1980) noted that the allowed annual 5 percent growth rate seemed ironic since the U.S. textile and apparel trade deficit was only 4 percent of value added at that time and the EC had a surplus. See Tables 9–3 and 9–5 for U.S. import penetration levels at that time.

U.S. politics appeared to have played an important role in the establishment of the LTA. Political realities fostered early "protective" action for the textile and apparel industries. At that time, the textile and apparel industries in the developed countries employed 17 percent of all manufacturing workers in the industrial countries. This concentration of workers represented significant political power at the domestic level. By contrast, at the international level, the countries whose products were being restricted—Japan and the developing countries—had far less influence in GATT. Furthermore, President Kennedy wanted to launch a major global round of trade negotiations—known as the "Kennedy Round"—to reduce trade barriers. He knew that the powerful U.S. textile lobby would provide strong opposition to such an effort and might prevent it altogether. Therefore, the LTA provided President Kennedy an opportunity to deliver on his campaign promises to assist the industry in its concern over imports and, at the same time, permitted him to proceed with the Kennedy Round with little likelihood of protests from textile industry groups (Aggarwal, 1985; W. Cline, 1987; Destler, 1986; Keesing & Wolf, 1980).

Basically, the LTA permitted importing countries to restrain imports of cotton textiles from the more important low-wage countries. Imports were subject to a slow growth in quota rates from year to year, once a supplier was brought under restrictions (that is, once the supplier joined the "plan"). Another key point to remember is that the LTA was limited to *cotton* textiles—defined as textile products in which cotton was over 50 percent of the

fiber content. In some countries, the 50 percent was based on weight, but the system in use in the United States at the time was based on value (called the *chief value method*).

The LTA was renewed in 1967 and again in 1970. Although the LTA had its share of critics, its sponsors claimed it to be the lesser of two evils. That is, without the multilateral arrangement, the importing countries would have continued to increase their unilateral restraints on textile imports from Japan and the LDCs. Advocates of the LTA believed it provided "orderly growth."

THE MULTIFIBER ARRANGEMENT (MFA)

Development of the MFA

By 1973, 82 countries had signed the LTA and participated in textile trade under the cotton arrangement. U.S. textile and apparel imports had grown substantially despite the LTA, however. W. Cline (1987) noted (using 1982 prices) that U.S. textile imports grew from $1.02 billion in 1961 to $2.4 billion in 1972. Apparel imports increased from $648 million to $3.5 billion. Together, U.S. textile and apparel imports grew 11.5 percent annually during this decade. Adding to this growth was an increasingly overvalued dollar during this period.

The growth in imports entering the markets of the United States and other developed countries could be attributed to two evolutionary changes occurring during the 1960s in the global textile industry:

1. A major technological change occurred with the development and increased use of manufactured fibers.
2. An important economic change occurred as a growing number of newly developing countries began to produce and export textile products.

The fast growth of global trade of manufactured fibers merits special attention at this point. In the United States, for example, imports of manufactured fiber textiles grew tenfold between 1960 and 1970—from 31 million pounds in 1960 to 329 million pounds in 1970 (Davidson, Feigenoff, & Ghadar, 1986). Although the development of manufactured fibers would have affected the global textile industry at any rate, the existence of the LTA encouraged increased growth. In effect, the LTA had fostered another case of the "little Dutch boy and the dike" phenomenon. That is, because the LTA had placed controls on shipments of cotton textile products, many exporting countries shifted to the *uncontrolled* manufactured fiber product areas.

Earlier, American textile and apparel producers sought to have the LTA renewals include products of other fibers. Those efforts had not been successful, however. By the late 1960s, growth of imports of other fibers confirmed to U.S. industry leaders that the trade policy arrangements must be broadened to include other fibers (Destler et al., 1979). By the 1968 presidential elections, U.S. textile and apparel industry groups had secured the support of all presidential candidates (Richard Nixon, Hubert Humphrey, and George Wallace) to extend textile import restraints to include products made of manufactured fibers and wool. In his campaign, Nixon pledged:

> As President, my policy will be . . . to assure prompt action to effectively administer the existing Long-Term International Cotton Textile Arrangement. Also, I will promptly take the steps necessary to extend the concept of international trade agreements to all other textile articles involving wool, man-made fibers and blends. (Telegram to Republican members of Congress who supported textile import control legislation, August 21, 1968. Cited in Brandis, 1982, p. 39.)

Shortly after Nixon's inauguration, he appointed Secretary of Commerce Maurice Stans to follow through on the campaign textile commitment. Stans began his efforts to develop an arrangement to cover all fibers by going first to the EC countries. The Europeans were not interested in a multifiber arrangement for two reasons: (1) The EC Member States were controlling the influx of wool and manufactured fiber imports into their markets quite successfully with bilateral and unilateral measures. (2) The EC countries were exporting a substantial volume of textile products to U.S. markets; they naturally resisted an arrangement that might restrain their own products. Even when Secretary Stans tried to explain that the United States was most concerned about Asian imports, the Europeans resisted U.S. efforts to broaden the coverage of the LTA (Aggarwal, 1985; Brandis, 1982; Destler et al., 1979).

Secretary Stans proceeded with an alternative plan for enticing the EC countries to join a multifiber approach for controlling textile imports. Stans believed that by first concluding more restrictive U.S. agreements with major Asian suppliers, textile exports from those countries would be diverted from U.S. markets to the EC markets. He anticipated that this strategy would provide for EC countries an increased interest in a multifiber restraint program (Aggarwal, 1985; Destler et al., 1979).

Proceeding with his plan, Stans tried to secure multifiber textile export restraint agreements from Japan, but the Japanese were unwilling to respond to his requests. The textile and apparel industries were among the most vital sectors in Japan at that time, accounting for a substantial portion of Japan's total exports. Secondly, Japan was a member of GATT and a more established participant in world trade than in earlier years when she had agreed to voluntary export restraints on textile products. Just as the Europeans had refused a broad multifiber plan, the Japanese refused to participate in Stans's plan to enforce comprehensive controls on manufactured fiber and wool textile products exports (Aggarwal, 1985; Destler et al., 1979).

U.S.-Japanese negotiations over textile trade were intense during the 1969–1971 period, at times moving to the highest levels between President Nixon and Japanese Prime Minister Eisaku Sato. In an extensive study of the U.S.-Japanese textile trade dispute, Destler et al. (1979) noted that efforts included two summit conferences, two cabinet-level ministerial conferences, and at least nine other major negotiations. Textile trade difficulties dominated economic relations between the two countries for the better part of three years, straining relationships far beyond the textile issue. Destler reported that President Nixon's resentment of Prime Minister Sato's failure to deliver a textile quota agreement led to Nixon's eagerness to administer rebuffs to Japan on other policy issues.

In addition to the fact that a textile agreement was one of Nixon's high priorities, he became worried that negotiations would extend through the election. Therefore, Nixon increased pressure on the Japanese. First, he imposed a 10 percent across-the-board import surcharge and then threatened to invoke the "Trading with the Enemy Act"[6] to impose unilateral restraints on textile and apparel imports. Finally, on the day the Trading with the Enemy provision would have taken effect, the Japanese gave in to a textile and apparel bilateral agreement to limit wool and manu-factured fiber products (Aggarwal, 1985; Brandis, 1982; Destler et al., 1979).

During 1971 and 1972, both the United States and Canada resorted to several bilateral agreements that imposed quota restraints to limit shipments of textile goods of manufactured fibers and wool. These agreements were outside the auspices of both GATT and the LTA. In addition to the Japanese agreement, the United States concluded bilateral agreements with Hong Kong, South Korea, and Taiwan to limit products of these additional fiber categories (Aggarwal, 1985; GATT, 1984).

As a result of the additional U.S. restraints on textile products from the major Asian producers, growing quantities of Asian textile goods were diverted from the American market to European markets. Within EC Member States, the textile and apparel industries began pressuring for protection from exports originally destined for the United States. Soon, EC countries that had refused earlier to consider an expanded textile agreement were willing to negotiate. Stans's earlier prediction that bilaterals with major Far Eastern suppliers would encourage the Europeans to change their minds had proven true (Aggarwal, 1985; W. Cline, 1987; Destler et al., 1979).

Once the EC became a willing participant, a multifiber arrangement seemed inevitable. In 1972, a GATT Working Party began a study of world textile trade. Following completion of that study, the GATT Council asked the Working Party to seek alternative multilateral solutions to the problem of world textile trade. Negotiations followed under GATT sponsorship.

By the time negotiations for the arrangement occurred in 1973, Japan was beginning to experience the loss of comparative advantage to the LDCs as well as the effects of a currency realignment in 1971. Although the Japanese were not enthusiastic about the plan, they were amenable because they considered the arrangement inevitable (Destler et al., 1979).

---

[6]The U.S. Trading with the Enemy Act was considered (and used as a threat) by President Nixon in 1971 to force Japan to sign an agreement to limit her textile shipments to the United States. Invoking this act might be viewed as "bringing in the tanks" to pressure Japan. This act was originally signed in 1917, when the enemy was Germany, and amended 11 days after the Pearl Harbor attack to provide: "During the time of war of during any other period of national emergency declared by the President, the President may . . . regulate . . . any . . . importation or exportation of . . . any property in which any foreign country or a national thereof has any interest" (55 STAT, Chapter 593 [Public Law 77-354, December 18, 1941], cited in Destler et al., 1979, p. 293). The textile dispute was interpreted as a "state of emergency" in these 1971 deliberations on how to deal with the Japanese (Destler et al., 1979).

The LDCs participated in the early multifiber discussions in a way that has been characteristic of later textile negotiations. Under the UNCTAD, which provides a forum through which LDCs unite to counter GATT measures on trade, the Group of 77 issued a resolution to "demand abolition of all tariffs and quotas on textile imports from developing countries by a fixed target date" (*Textile Asia*, October, 1973, p. 11; cited in Aggarwal, 1985 p. 133).

The LDCs presented an outwardly unified position on textile trade, but in reality, maintaining a cohesive position among the group was difficult then and continues to be true. The division occurred because the countries varied in their competitive position in textile trade. Countries that had become proficient in production and trade (the major producers in the Far East) and already had large quotas for U.S. and EC markets based on "past performance" (Aggarwal, 1985, p. 130) would retain those, whereas newly developing countries would have little access to the major markets based on their prior exporting records. In a sense, earlier quotas provided *guaranteed market access* in an intensely competitive market with an overabundance of producers. This division among the LDCs has continued throughout the period in which the present textile restraint programs have existed. In general, however, the first multifiber arrangement offered adequate provisions to encourage the developing countries to join fairly readily (discussions with trade ministers from various countries, 1983–1989; GATT, 1984; Keesing & Wolf, 1980).

MFA I (1974–1977)

The new multilateral framework to resolve textile trade problems known as the **Arrangement Regarding International Trade in Textiles**, and more commonly known as the Multifiber Arrangement, or MFA, was concluded at the end of 1973 and became effective in January 1974 for a four-year period. Approximately 50 countries were in the original group that signed the agreement, which was developed and operates under the auspices of GATT. As the name implies, the new arrangement included products made of manufactured fibers and wool—extending beyond the provisions for cotton in the STA and LTA. In exchange for their willingness to negotiate a new agreement, Japan and the developing countries were able to have significant influence on the terms and conditions of the first MFA.

In working terms, the Arrangement was a general framework under which textile and apparel trade would occur—and could be controlled. The Arrangement would be imple-

---

 EARLY IDEALISM OF THE MFA

Authors of the MFA attempted to represent the needs of both the importing and exporting countries. Idealistic in its intent, the formal Arrangement read as follows: "The basic objectives shall be to achieve the expansion of trade, the reduction of barriers to such trade and the progressive liberalization of world trade in textile products, while at the same time ensuring the orderly and equitable development of this trade and avoidance of disruptive effects in individual markets and on individual lines in both importing and exporting countries" (GATT, 1974, p. 6).

mented through provisions in Article 4,[7] which provided guidelines for bilateral export-restraint agreements. The MFA is quite general; the bilateral agreements concluded under the MFA provide the specifics of "managing" textile and apparel trade. In other words, the *bilateral agreements are the vehicles through which the MFA is operationalized* for participating countries. We might think of the MFA as an umbrella arrangement, under which the bilateral agreements are concluded (Figure 10–3).

Although any country would be permitted to establish a bilateral agreement with another country, the realities of textile trade fostered a more predictable pattern. First of all, bilateral agreements exist only where textile trade problems have occurred or may occur. Since bilateral agreements are built upon the concept of market disruption, such agreements are not sought unless market disruption or the threat of market disruption is a concern. In reality, a bilateral agreement occurs because the importing country (a developed country) determines that specific textile and apparel imported products from a particular country are disrupting (or may disrupt) the importing country's market. The bilateral agreement

------

[7]The United States used Article 4, which permitted restraints agreed upon between two countries to deal with problems of *real risk of market disruption*. Other countries used Article 4 as well as Article 3; the latter allowed for one-year unilateral restraints or bilateral agreements to deal with problems of market disruption (personal communication with M. Raffaelli and T. Jenkins, 1993).

FIGURE 10–3
Under the multilateral agreement, the MFA, each signatory member has negotiated bilateral agreements with its trading partners with whom textile trade is a concern.

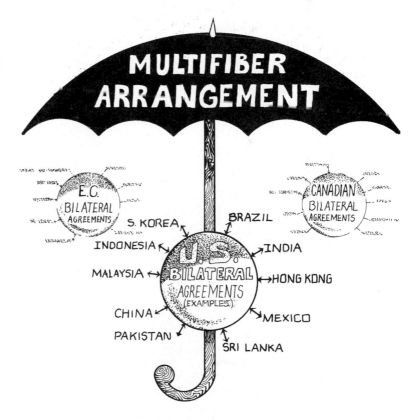

Source: Illustration by Dennis Murphy.

that results from negotiations between the two countries identifies the export levels agreed to by the exporting country. In other words, *the bilateral agreement establishes the quota restraints on some, or less frequently, most of the exporting country's products.* Quotas set limits on the quantity of goods to be exported—by some measure such as weight or number of items, according to the product description.

An example of how quotas are set and implemented may be helpful at this point. In a hypothetical example, let's assume that the United States negotiated a bilateral agreement with Hong Kong that permitted Hong Kong to send 300,000 women's cotton sweaters to U.S. markets within a year. In Hong Kong, the quota allowances are distributed among sweater manufacturers. If a manufacturer wants to increase production of cotton sweaters for U.S. markets beyond the firm's original allowance, that producer may buy more of a quota on the free market. However, all producers must work within Hong Kong's total allowance, which would have been spelled out in a bilateral agreement. (The exporting countries have various methods for

distributing quotas among their manufacturers.) Similar activities would occur for each product area covered by quotas in the bilateral agreement between the two countries. Quotas cover products of concern in the markets of the importing country. The products are identified by category numbers for defined product groupings.

The import control system established under the bilateral agreements is complex. In fact, operational details are more complex than we need to consider here. A few additional terms may be useful, however, for a general understanding of the type of limits set by the bilateral agreements:

- *Aggregate Ceiling*: The total amount of equivalent square meters a country can export to the United States in any year under the terms of its bilateral agreement.
- *Group Ceiling*: Within the aggregate ceiling, there is a breakdown into groupings, and each group has a ceiling. This provides greater restrictions on more sensitive categories.
- *Category Ceiling*: Upper base limits against which a country can export for a particular

---

  THE CATEGORY SYSTEM USED FOR IMPORT CONTROL PURPOSES

The category system used for import control purposes is a completely separate system from the SIC categories used to designate U.S. manufacturing sectors. In the category system for import control purposes, the numbering system designates both the fiber content and the product. All product categories in the 300 series are cotton; those in the 400 series are wool; products in the 600 series are manufactured fibers; and those in the 800 series are silk-blends or vegetable fibers other than cotton. The first digit

indicates fiber content and the second two digits, the product line. Category 635, for example, is women's and children's manufactured fiber coats. The fiber of chief weight in the garment generally determines its fiber classification (O'Donnell, 1988). In 1988, the United States changed its category structure to conform with the Harmonized System, which took effect in 1989 (personal communication with U.S. Department of Commerce staff, 1990).

product category (AAMA, 1980; U.S. Department of Commerce, 1990).

The Arrangement is a voluntary agreement, as Wurth (1981) noted: "The Arrangement is in effect a multilateral contract, freely entered by those countries wishing to participate in it" (p. 61). Only about half GATT's Contracting Parties have ever participated in the special arrangement for textiles. Only 17 members of GATT, even counting EU Member States individually, have ever used the special rules for textiles to impose import restrictions (GATT, 1984). As might be expected, the 17 are the leading textile-importing countries because those are the nations concerned about market disruption.

As part of the new Arrangement, several provisions were added that had not been part of the STA or LTA. Among the new features were the following:

- A Textile Surveillance Body (TSB) was created to serve as a "multilateral surveillance institution" (GATT, 1984, p. 75) to monitor implementation of the MFA.
- Stricter rules for determining market disruption were developed to discourage unwarranted claims of disruption.
- Quota allowances were permitted to grow by 6 percent annually rather than the 5 percent under the LTA.
- New provisions for **quota flexibility** were initiated (although various degrees of flexibility had been possible in earlier agreements); these were:
  - "Swing" permitted the transfer of a quota from one category to another. That is, if the quota for a product were not filled, another product could be shifted to take advantage of the unused quota.
  - "Carry forward" permitted the exporting country to borrow from the next year's quota.
  - "Carryover" permitted the exporting country to add unused quota to that for the sub-

sequent year. Sometimes this provision caused a **surge** in importing markets.

The new MFA posed certain challenges for the EC that the United States did not have to face. First, trade rules within the EC permitted free circulation of products among member countries. Some countries had a number of restraints against LDC textile imports; others had few. To get their products to countries with greater restraints, the LDCs simply shipped to an uncontrolled EC country and had them redirected to the countries with stricter controls. Therefore, the EC found it difficult to resolve these variations among its member countries to conform to the MFA. Then and now, the EC has had difficulty in resolving the differences among its member countries to arrive at a unified position on trade matters.

Second, EC countries were faced with the problem they called "**burden sharing**." This was the EC term for determining how member countries would share the "burden" of accepting LDC textile and apparel imports that came into the Community. A formula was determined to be certain that all countries took their "fair share."

In short, while the EC delayed negotiating bilaterals under the MFA because of the difficulty in coordinating internal differences, the United States quickly concluded bilateral agreements with the major exporting countries. The first EC bilateral agreements were concluded almost two years after the MFA was established. The U.S. and EC differences in the speed of establishing bilaterals accounted for a substantial contrast in trade patterns that occurred under MFA I.

The textile and apparel industries in both Canada and Australia[8] fared poorly during MFA I; consequently, both countries initiated

---

[8]Australia was a signatory to the original MFA but has not participated in later renewals.

unilateral measures along with their bilateral agreements to deal with their trade problems. For example, in late 1976, Canada imposed quotas on *all* apparel imports for 1977. Canada's approach was controversial within the GATT and was not well received in general at the international level (Anson & Simpson, 1988).

MFA II (1977–1981)

Although the MFA was concluded initially for a four-year period, it was renegotiated in 1977. The renewals of the MFA that followed were "Protocols of Extension"—that is, extensions of the original MFA to which changes were appended.

Although the United States had been the leader in pushing for the original multilateral agreement, the EC took the lead in pressing for an increasingly restrictive renewed MFA. The United States had fared much better than the EC under MFA I, due to a great extent to the quick conclusion of bilateral agreements with major exporting nations. The prompt U.S. bilaterals had two effects. First, they protected U.S. markets; and secondly, they diverted LDC textile products to the EC market where bilateral agreements had been negotiated slowly. Textile and apparel imports in Europe had increased 49 percent between 1973 and 1976. Although similar U.S. imports grew 40 percent, the increase was from a much smaller base (GATT, 1977). Furthermore, the EC had been affected much more severely than the United States by the post oil-shock recession. Consequently, U.S. textile and apparel employment declined only slightly between 1974 and 1977.

As a result of the general economic conditions plus the growth in imports, EC demands influenced significantly MFA II—resulting in a protocol that permitted more restrictive bilateral agreements. EC officials took a strong position in demanding greater restrictions because of the intense pressure being exerted by their industry groups. Additionally, certain EC member countries threatened to refuse to participate further in the MFA and to impose their own unilateral restraints, unless the renewed Arrangement permitted substantially tougher controls on imports.

Of particular concern to EC representatives was the 6 percent annual growth rate for quotas permitted in the first MFA. Although Annex B of the Arrangement permitted a departure from the 6 percent growth rate in "exceptional cases," the EC had found it tedious to have to prove market disruption in each case. Consequently, the EC wanted to free itself from the MFA's constraints of having to provide proof of market disruption in order to negotiate quota growth below 6 percent in its agreements with exporting nations (Keesing & Wolf, 1980).

U.S. textile and apparel industry sources were also concerned over the 6 percent annual growth rate—particularly during periods when domestic growth was low. Manufacturers argued that it was unfair for imports to increase 6 percent per year when their own share of the domestic market was increasing sometimes as slowly as 1 percent per year. Industry leaders sought to have import growth rate tied to the domestic growth rate.

The EC achieved its goal, and the MFA that was signed in December 1977 permitted *"jointly agreed reasonable departures"* from the terms of the MFA. That is, the "reasonable departures" clause permitted participating countries to negotiate bilateral agreements that no longer complied with the provisions of the original MFA that had been agreed upon by all members (GATT, 1984). These were intended to be only temporary. The developing countries opposed this highly controversial clause because it meant that "departures" worked to their detriment (for example, reduced quotas, denials or reductions in flexibility, and growth rates reduced below 6 percent). Nevertheless, the greater power of the importing countries prevailed.

Although MFA II became more restrictive on textile and apparel imports allowed in the developed countries, it is important to remember that the MFA provides only the general framework and basic mechanisms for textile trade. With each revision of the MFA, new bilateral agreements generally are negotiated. Within the MFA framework, negotiators for various countries determine the degree or level of restrictions by the bilateral agreements they sign.

As the EC set about to negotiate new bilateral agreements, the result was "a system of quotas so restrictive as to change everyone's perspective of what was possible. Its aim was 'to achieve a real stabilization of imports, particularly for products with a high penetration rate . . . on the Community market'" (Keesing & Wolf, 1980, p. 64). Many quota growth rates fell below 6 percent; some dropped to zero.

The EC established a complex system that divided products into 114 categories and 5 groups, from Group I through Group V. Group I consisted of the eight most sensitive product categories on which the most severe limits were imposed. Groups ranged through Group V, which were the least sensitive and had the least severe limits on the volume of imports that would be permitted. Over 60 percent of the LDC imports in the reference year 1976 were Group I products; nearly half the remainder were in Group II (Keesing & Wolf, 1980). The EC also developed a "**basket extractor**" or "basket exit" mechanism. If the exports of an unrestricted exporting country reached a certain threshold (for example, 1 percent) of EC imports, the EC would seek a consultation and apply restraints after the threshold levels had been greatly exceeded.

Although U.S. bilateral agreements under MFA II included increased protection for the domestic industry, the U.S. position was far less restrictive than that of the EC. As a result of special U.S. concern over imports from Hong Kong, South Korea, and Taiwan, bilat-eral agreements with those countries tightened swing and carryover provisions. The U.S. negotiated new bilateral agreements with the "Big Three" despite the fact that five-year agreements had been signed only a year earlier. For products where quotas had gone unused to a significant extent, some of those quotas were abolished and a new mechanism—the "**call**" **mechanism**—was instituted. Under the call mechanism, consultations between governments of the two trading countries on new quotas would be triggered if imports exceeded certain levels—or if the importing country established market disruption or serious threat of market disruption. In general, however, U.S. agreements froze imports from the "Big Three" suppliers but were more lenient on the new, smaller textile-exporting nations.

In summary, bilateral agreements under MFA II reduced textile and apparel imports in both U.S. and EC markets. The reasonable departures clause of MFA II changed the Arrangement fundamentally. Keesing and Wolf (1980) noted that the bilateral agreements negotiated as a result of this "reasonable departures" clause became the heart of the textile trade regime. Aggarwal (1985) asserted that the MFA served basically only as a cover for the EC's bilateral agreements. Keesing and Wolf referred to the "reasonable departures" clause as a sharp departure from the norms of the MFA. They concluded that this clause provided a "'departure from a departure'—a way of waiving the provisions of an agreement which was itself a derogation from GATT principles" (Keesing & Wolf, 1980, p. 70).

MFA III (1981–1986)

The 1981 negotiations for renewal of the MFA were particularly difficult. From the perspective of both the EC and U.S. textile and apparel industries, MFA II—despite its increasingly restrictive features—had not been effective in slowing the tide of imports.[9] Both the United States and the EC had growing textile and apparel trade deficits. Apparel trade deficits were particularly significant, since a growing portion of LDC exports were in the apparel area (Aggarwal, 1985; GATT, 1984).

More than ever, the development of textile trade policy was dominated by political pressures. Moreover, with each successive renewal of the MFA, the opposing players became increasingly organized and proficient in pressing for their special interests. The textile and apparel industry leaders in both the United States and the EC grew increasingly impatient and vocal in their desires for greater protection. At the same time, a group of the exporting countries (developing countries) became more organized with support from the UNCTAD and became increasingly vocal. The EC Commission (which handles "government" matters for the EC) and the U.S. government were pressed on the one hand by domestic industry sources who demanded increased protection and on the other hand by the LDCs who demanded a more liberal approach. U.S. and EC negotiators often found themselves in a no-win dilemma—if they pleased one side, they alienated the other.

Furthermore, the EC complained again that "burden sharing" was not fairly distributed. The EC claimed that its per capita share of LDC imports was much greater than that for the United States and Japan, which by this time had become an important *importing* nation.

As in previous instances in which "burden sharing" has been discussed, this refers to taking a "fair share" of the low-cost textile and apparel imports. Although trade shifts cause various sides to express this complaint from one time to another, concerns over burden sharing always come from importing countries who believe their peer countries are not absorbing their fair share of exports from the developing countries.

American industry sources demanded greater protection, using the argument that "low-cost imports undermined their production" (Aggarwal, 1985, p. 169). A leader from the Knitted Wear Association expressed concern for the growing number of new entrants, particularly in the *apparel* market: "[No] matter how hard we run, the gap in wage costs between the U.S. and these new developing countries is so great that there will always be vulnerability in certain sectors to devastating import competition from extra low cost countries" (Vargish, 1980). U.S. industry sources believed the *price differential* between imported products and comparable domestic goods provided justification for added protection from imports.

The coalition of developing countries was successful in having the "reasonable departures" clause withdrawn for MFA III. Instead, a less restrictive *"anti-surge" provision* provided for special restraints in the event of "sharp and substantial increases" in imports of the most sensitive products with previously underutilized quotas. MFA III tightened the definition of market disruption by requiring proof of a decline in the growth rate of per capita consumption. This Protocol provided more precision regarding favorable treatment of small country suppliers and new entrants. During MFA III, however, a growing number of countries came under restraints (Anson & Simpson, 1988; GATT, 1987).

With each MFA renewal, various groups threatened to pull out of the Arrangement by not signing the revised agreement. Usually,

---

[9]We must remember that the MFA provides only the framework for the textile import control program. Therefore, the negotiated bilaterals would have determined the level of import shipments. The growth of imports might have resulted also from the growing number of supplier nations not under restraint as well as inefficient monitoring programs to assure that shipments complied with agreements.

this was a ploy to bargain for certain provisions a group wanted in the renewal agreement. The EC threatened to leave the MFA and manage textile trade through its own bilateral and unilateral restraints. The LDCs threatened to avoid signing unless they received more liberal provisions. Although threats were made, many persons conceded that total chaos would occur in global textile and apparel trade if the MFA were suddenly dismantled. Although the MFA had few supporters, most sources acknowledged that it provided a certain *predictable climate* for textile and apparel trade.

Simply put, major players sought to develop trade policies that regulated others' behavior. The United States and the EC were particularly interested in each other's stance. If, for example, the EC took harsh measures to restrict imports, products would be diverted to U.S. markets, or vice versa. Both the United States and the EC wanted to control the LDCs' exporting activities and, hopefully, force them to open their markets to products from the developed countries. Although the developing countries lacked the power to make demands of the developed countries, they sought an MFA that would constrain the demands of the importing countries.

Restraints under MFA III were more extensive and more restrictive than before (GATT, 1987). Although MFA III became somewhat more protectionist as a result of growing domestic industry pressures in both the United States and the EC, the Arrangement was not as restrictive as the industries had hoped. Although the agreement provided far less protection than the American industry wanted, negotiations revealed that the U.S. government found it increasingly difficult to resist strong protectionist pressures from the domestic industry. In the U.S., textile industry decline, accompanied by a growing flood of imports, caused textile leaders to condemn MFA III as a failure (Anson & Simpson, 1988).

MFA IV (1986–1991)

While MFA III was in effect, U.S. market conditions took a turn for the worse. Between 1982 and 1984, textile and apparel imports from both high-cost and low-cost sources grew at unprecedented levels. Imports almost doubled in just over two years (Anson & Simpson, 1988). As a further result of a rapidly rising dollar, exports declined. Domestic textile output dropped by 10 percent. During the years of MFA III, the United States initiated several tightening measures to reduce imports:

- Additional claims for the "presumption of market disruption" resulted in over 100 **consultation calls** in late 1984 and early 1985. This meant quotas were being considered for products previously not covered.
- **Countervailing duties** (added duties) were imposed on textile goods from 20 countries that were shown to have subsidized their textile industries. GATT rules prohibit that governments subsidize their industries; this gives an unfair advantage in trade.
- New **"rules of origin"** were introduced to prevent transshipment (rerouting products through a country other than where they were produced in order to take advantage of unused quotas).
- Bilateral agreements were renegotiated, on tougher terms, with the Big Three two years before they were due to expire.
- A bill, known as the Jenkins bill, was introduced in Congress to set additional limits on textile and apparel products, because industry leaders believed the U.S. government was ineffective in negotiating workable trade policies. This bill will be discussed later.

The additional restrictive provisions initiated during MFA III indicate the type of U.S. textile/apparel trade climate that prevailed by the time MFA IV negotiations began. As these actions would suggest, U.S. officials went into the 1986 MFA renewal negotiations under heavy pressure from domestic textile and apparel industry sources to provide increased protection from low-wage imports. During this period, the EC industries had been affected less by imports, and most of the European industries enjoyed a relatively healthy period. The EC did, however, join the United States and Canada in presenting a joint statement of the major importing countries' desires for the 1986 renewal.

Although the **exporting countries**[10] (the NICs and the LDCs) were more organized than in the past, the diverse composition of the group continued to cause a lack of unity. In addition, the exporting group lacked the bargaining power to offset the strength of the developed countries. Because quotas were set on past performance, the small suppliers (usually the least developed countries) had little opportunity to obtain substantial quota increases. In an effort to improve the exporting nations' bargaining position, a new body,

the International Textiles and Clothing Bureau (ITCB), organized to represent the interests of the developing countries. (Additional information on ITCB is provided in Chapter 11.)

In general, the exporting countries considered MFA IV to be more restrictive than the previous extension. The most significant new provision of the renewed Arrangement was that it covered additional fibers beyond cotton, wool, and manufactured fibers. Additional fiber coverage resulted because the U.S. market had experienced another example of the "Dutch boy and the dike" phenomenon. As cotton, wool, and manufactured fiber products became increasingly restricted from the markets of developed countries, the exporting nations shifted production to goods made of uncontrolled fibers—ramie, silk, and flax. Consequently, the U.S. market in particular received huge percentage increases of fibers that were not covered by the MFA. For example, 1985 U.S. imports from China made of non-MFA fibers increased 346 percent over 1984. Although the United States was hard pressed to claim market disruption from ramie products because the country produces no ramie, domestic producers believed that these products replaced similar items of other

---

[10]GATT officials use the terms *exporting countries* (primarily the NICs and the less developed countries) and *importing countries* (primarily the more developed nations).

"RULES OF ORIGIN"

In 1984, "Rules of Origin" (also known as the *origin rules*) were passed to make significant changes in how country of origin is determined for textile/apparel imports headed for the United States. Prior to enactment of these rules, some of the major Asian exporting nations extended their quota by sending items to other Asian nations with *unused* quota (sometimes called *quota havens*) where final processing and packaging occurred. Shipments were counted against the

second country's quota. In other cases, transshipment occurred as countries that had exhausted their quota shipped through another country to take advantage of the second country's unused quota. The 1984 Rules of Origin required substantial transformation in the second country in order to consider that it "originated" in that country—and that it should be counted against the second country's quota, rather than the country from which it first came.

RAMIE STOPS THE CLOCK

Extended fiber coverage was of utmost importance to U.S. sources during the negotiations for MFA IV. The U.S. textile industry persuaded American negotiators that this provision must be included. At the same time, certain exporting countries were equally committed to avoiding coverage of additional fibers. Ramie became the stumbling block on which agreement could not be reached, particularly because it had become an important fiber area for China and India.

MFA III was scheduled to expire at midnight on July 31, 1986. Although negotiators had already debated ramie coverage for quite some time, discussions on the last day continued through the day and night in an effort to reach an agreement by midnight. Midnight arrived and no agreement had been reached. At midnight, trade officials stopped the clock at the GATT headquarters in Geneva, Switzerland. This tactic permitted negotiations to continue under

the illusion that MFA III had not expired. As talks continued through the night, negotiators found it difficult to proceed because of great time differences and the need to call home to consult their governments. That is, negotiators from China, India, the United States, and other countries needed to confirm their positions with their respective governments, but time differences created difficulties in reaching government officials during waking hours in the home countries.

At one point the United States threatened to withdraw from the MFA unless the renewal included the additional fibers. China withdrew temporarily to seek advice from Beijing.

Finally after many long, exhausting hours of discussions, weary negotiators concluded the renewal of the Arrangement—which included ramie products and other extended fiber coverage—and officials started the GATT clock again.

fibers. For the United States, the extended fiber coverage was the most important feature desired from this renewal. This point was, however, the most difficult one to resolve in the 1986 renewal.

The extended fiber coverage applied to products in which the previously uncontrolled fibers exceed 50 percent of the weight or value of the imported goods; pure silk was excluded. Coverage did not apply to "historically traded textiles in commercially significant quantities prior to 1982" in product areas such as sacks, carpet backing, cordage, and similar products made from fibers such as jute, coir, sisal, abaca, maguey, and henequen.

Briefly, some of the main provisions of MFA IV were:

- Unilateral restraints may be placed on uncontrolled products for up to 12 months

if market disruption is proven but a bilateral agreement has not been reached in 60 days.
- Some of the poorer, developing countries were to be given "significantly more favorable" treatment than the NICs.
- The Nordic countries' clause for preserving **minimum viable production** was retained. This is an MFA provision instituted by the Scandinavian countries that permits restriction of imports to maintain a healthy domestic industry—so that in wartime a country would be assured of having minimal viable production capacity. This meant the Nordic restraints were even more restrictive than MFA norms.
- The anti-surge clause remained; this permitted action to be taken if an underutilized quota was filled in a short time period.

- No cutbacks or tightening of quotas were permitted under MFA IV; that is, growth cannot be "negative." Instead exporting countries were required to accept lower rates of growth and flexibility.
- The EC decided to reduce the number of quotas negotiated under MFA III, particularly if the quotas were underutilized. The "basket extractor" mechanism was maintained, however, so action could be taken if imports grew enough to cause concern for market disruption.
- Cotton and wool production in developing countries continued to receive special consideration (Anson & Simpson, 1988; GATT, 1987; personal communication with M. Raffaelli & T. Jenkins, 1993).

The developed countries pressed to require that the developing countries open their markets to reciprocal trade in textiles and apparel. However, the developing countries maintained the right to close their market (if desired) under the **infant industry** provision permitted by GATT.

Extensions of MFA IV (1991, 1992, 1993)

By the time MFA IV was slated to expire in July 1991, global trade talks (the Uruguay Round, which will be discussed later in this chapter) had been underway for nearly five years. As we shall consider in the later section, the global trade talks included a provision that would affect the future of the MFA. Therefore, as MFA IV reached expiration in 1992 and the global trade talks were stalled, an extension of MFA IV was agreed upon rather than going to what might logically have been MFA V. In fact, two additional extensions of MFA IV were agreed upon in December 1992 and December 1993. In official terms, these extensions were called *Protocols* ("Global Textile Trade Policies" boxed insert).

For the 1991 and 1992 Protocols, the exporting members of the MFA were not in agreement about how long the extensions should be. They were unanimous, however, in asking that their bilateral agreements be more liberal (i.e., that they would be permitted to ship more into the developed countries' markets). On both occasions, the exporting members' requests were not accepted because of the short periods of the extension. The 1991 and 1992 Protocols did, however, include clauses to suggest that trading situations would be improved for the exporting countries. At the insistence of the developed importing countries, especially the United States, the 1992 Protocol included a statement to deal with the problems of **circumvention**, thus reflecting the growing concern over this problem (personal communication with M. Raffaelli & T. Jenkins, 1993).

Another point of interest during this time was Sweden's radical change of policy. Sweden left the MFA on July 31, 1991, thus dropping all MFA restraints.

Reflections on the MFA

The MFA has represented a compromise between the interests of the exporting and the importing countries. It is, however, an agreement with which few participants have been satisfied because, as a compromise, the MFA has provided none of the players all the provisions desired.

Further, the MFA has had many critics among trade experts and economists who are not affiliated with any of the special interest groups that have a stake in textile trade policies. Some of the concerns over the MFA include:

- *Removal of a sector of trade from GATT rules.* Providing special trade rules for textile and apparel products, especially after most fibers were included, effectively has removed a large portion of world trade

GLOBAL TEXTILE TRADE POLICIES

The following summary shows major developments in global textile trade policies from the 1950s to the present:

- **1955, December**
  Japan announced first VER on cotton textile products to the United States beginning January 1956.
- **1956, September**
  Japan announced five-year VER on cotton products to the United States beginning January 1957.
- **1959, February**
  The United States tries to get Hong Kong to agree to a VER on cotton products; Hong Kong refuses.
- **1958–1960**
  Europeans use various illegal measures to restrict cotton products from LDCs.
- **1960, November**
  GATT members agree on a definition of *market disruption*.
- **1961, July**
  STA agreed upon; commenced October 1, 1961.
- **1962, February**
  LTA agreed upon; commenced October 1, 1962.
- **1962–1967**
  Various bilateral and unilateral measures taken under LTA.
- **1963–1964**
  The United States tries to secure international agreement to cover wool products; efforts do not succeed.

- **1967, April**
  LTA renewed for three years; commenced October 1967.
- **1969, April**
  The United States tries to get EC to agree to multilateral arrangement to include wool and manufactured fiber trade.
- **1970, October**
  LTA renewed again.
- **1969–1971**
  The United States gets Far Eastern countries to restrain wool and manufactured fiber products sent to U.S. markets.
- **1973, December**
  MFA I agreed upon; commenced January 1, 1974.
- **1977, December**
  MFA II agreed upon; clause allows "jointly agreed reasonable departures."
- **1981, December**
  MFA III agreed upon; "anti-surge" provision included.
- **1986, July**
  MFA IV agreed upon; fiber coverage extended.
- **1991, July**
  MFA IV extended to December 1992.
- **1992, December**
  MFA IV extended to December 1993.
- **1993, December**
  MFA IV extended to December 1994.

Source: Adapted and updated from *Liberal Protectionism* (pp. 203–204) by V. Aggarwal, 1985, Berkeley, CA: University of California Press. © 1985 The Regents of the University of California. Used by permission.

from the jurisdiction of normal trade rules. The unique feature of the MFA is that it has involved a multilaterally and formally agreed upon departure from normal GATT rules for the benefit of a particular industry.

- *Discrimination is permitted.* The MFA violates GATT's most-favored-nation and nondiscrimination principles because it permits import controls that discriminate against particular countries. It permits countries to regulate trade on a country-by-country basis, primarily through negotiation of bilateral agreements.

- *Quotas are permitted.* Quota limitations—otherwise contrary to the GATT—may be negotiated on textile products.
- *No compensation is required.* Importing countries are not required to compensate the countries whose products are placed under restrictions (another principle of GATT).
- *The concept of "market disruption" introduced.* The concept of market disruption was developed for the textile sector, and although the provision might be used by other trade areas, only the textile sector has used it (W. Cline, 1987; Keesing & Wolf, 1980).

In short, the MFA has been a departure, often called a *derogation*, from GATT rules. Critics of the MFA believe it has gone against the basic principles of the GATT (Figure 10–4).

Other criticisms often leveled at the MFA are:

- *Opposition to the "gentlemen's agreement."* The MFA established a precedent of imposing quotas on products from the developing countries—but not the developed countries. This strategy was established by the informal "gentlemen's agreement" between the U.S. and EC textile negotiators

in 1977, in which representatives agreed to refrain from imposing restrictions on each other's products. This strategy was justified, officials believed, because of the similar costs of labor and other production costs in the two areas.

Another of the justifications usually offered for the gentlemen's agreement (which also applied to the EFTA countries and Canada) was that the markets for textile products in these countries were open, unlike the markets of many exporting countries, which had high tariffs or even excluded all imports. While this was the general case during the 1970s and part of the 1980s, the rationale is much less valid today, in view of the opening of the markets of many developing exporting countries (personal communication with M. Raffaelli & T. Jenkins, 1993).

Additionally, in the past, each of the EU countries had its own quota limits on imports. However, with the unification of the EU market, which became effective January 1, 1993, EU quotas are no longer divided into "country shares." Exporting nations considered this a liberalizing step, albeit involuntarily, on the part of the EU. This means that exporting countries can use more of their quotas.

- *Extended "temporary" protection.* And, finally, the original Arrangement was intended as a temporary measure to provide a "breathing space" for the industries in the developed countries to adjust to the increased competition in global markets. Critics believe the protection provided by the MFA became addictive, causing the industries in the developed countries to restructure or adjust more slowly than they might have without the added protection.

In sum, the special provisions of the MFA were based on the assumption that textile trade is "a special case." A central issue in 1986 discussions for the renewal of the MFA was

FIGURE 10–4

Many critics of the MFA have believed that it goes against everything the GATT represented.

whether textile trade should be brought back into the mainstream of GATT policy. The basic question has been: Is the textile sector a special case? *Advocates* argue that no other sector has the special problems that are characteristic of textile/apparel production and trade. *Critics* contend that the problems associated with textile trade are simply more exaggerated and politicized than similar problems in other sectors.

THE MFA IN OPERATION

At the conclusion of negotiations for MFA IV, 43 signatories agreed to the Arrangement, representing 54 countries (the 12 EC countries represented one signatory) (GATT, 1986). The United States had negotiated bilateral import-restraint agreements with about 40 countries as of January 1994 (personal communication with R. Levin, 1994).

Approximately 65 percent of U.S. textile and apparel imports were covered by restraints in 1994 (personal communication with R. Levin, 1994). Similarly, the MFA cov-

ers only a portion of world textile and apparel trade. Table 10–2 shows the portion of trade covered by the MFA as well as that covered by other nontariff restraints. As the table indicates, only about one-fourth of world textile and apparel trade in 1986 was subject to the MFA (39.9 percent for apparel and 14 percent for textiles). When the category of other restraints (bilateral agreements outside the MFA, and so on) was added to the MFA coverage, about 60 percent of global trade in textile and apparel products occurred under some type of restraints (see Table 10–2 subtotal, restrained). This means that approximately 43 percent of world trade in textiles and 35 percent of the trade in apparel were free from nontariff restraints (W. Cline, 1987).

Considering the attention given the MFA, why has so much textile and apparel trade been outside the Arrangement? Several explanations are relevant:

- *Restraints are for problem areas.* Restraints are applied only to specific products from specific countries perceived to be a threat to the markets of the importing countries. Products that do not represent a threat are

---

 PERSPECTIVES ON THE MFA

The following are a few of the comments on the MFA made to the author during visits with various trade officials in Geneva, Switzerland, during the 1980s. These comments perhaps foretold the eventual fate of the MFA:

- "The GATT is ashamed of the MFA. Yet, the Arrangement provides transparency to trade activities which would otherwise occur under the table." (In the latter statement, the individual explained that trading partners may now see what is happening, in contrast to the situation in pre-MFA periods.)

- "The balance is fragile. The MFA hangs by a thread."
- "The developing countries will not continue to accept the increasingly harsh restrictions imposed on their textile products through MFA measures."
- "The MFA is to the GATT as a brothel is to a cathedral."

(Comments to the author were confidential; sources cannot be shared.)

TABLE 10–2

Shares of world trade in textiles and apparel subject to MFA and other restraints (percentage)

Importing Area	Supplying Area	Textiles	Apparel	Total
1. Free of restraints	Industrial countries			
Industrial countries	except Japan	42.8	35.1	39.2
2. MFA restraints				
Industrial countries	Japan	3.0	1.4	2.3
	Developing countries	11.0	38.5	23.9
Subtotal		*14.0*	*39.9*	*26.2*
3. Bilateral or national restraints				
Industrial countries	Eastern area	3.6	5.0	4.3
Developing countries	All sources	30.8	12.8	22.4
Eastern area	All sources	8.7	7.2	8.0
Subtotal		*43.1*	*25.0*	*34.7*
Subtotal, restrained	(2 + 3)	57.1	64.9	60.8
Total		100.0	100.0	100.0
Memorandum: value (billion dollars)		*53.5*	*46.0*	*99.5*

Source: From *The Future of World Trade in Textiles and Apparel* (p. 157) by W. Cline, 1987, Washington, DC: Institute for International Economics. Reprinted by permission. (Updated data not available.)

not covered. The EU uses the basket extractor mechanism and the United States uses the consultation call mechanism to respond to concerns for products from countries that may suddenly pose a threat.

- *Exclusion for industrialized countries.* Textile and apparel exports flow between the industrialized countries free of restraints—accounting for the largest portion of trade not covered by the MFA. About one-fifth of non-MFA textile/apparel trade is intra-EU trade (among EU countries). In contrast, however, Japan is an exception as a developed country in having other developed countries (notably the United States) restrict her products because she is considered a *supplier* country.
- *Nonparticipation in MFA.* A few major developed countries do not participate in the MFA or may not do so fully. Three important industrialized countries—Australia, New Zealand, and Sweden—do not. Japan and Switzerland are members of the MFA

but do not maintain quotas under bilateral agreements as the MFA permits. Although importing countries have bilateral agreements with Taiwan and the East European countries, most of these are outside the MFA. Therefore, trade from these countries would be restrained but not counted in the MFA-covered trade.

- EU *preferential treatment agreements.* (1) As discussed in Chapter 6, the EU gives preferential treatment to Mediterranean basin countries such as Algeria, Egypt, Morocco, and Turkey. If those countries' textile and apparel products are limited, restrictions are more favorable than for most other supplier countries. (2) Furthermore, the EU has given preferential treatment to developing countries identified in the Lomé Convention. The Lomé Convention describes the European Union's financial and technical assistance programs to more than 60 Associated Countries of Africa, the Caribbean, and the Pacific—known as the

ACP countries. The agreement gave preferential treatment to the ACP countries' products in EU markets by permitting products to enter free of customs duties.

As noted earlier, only certain products from a country—those perceived to be a threat—are covered by restraints for an importing country. Therefore, as one might guess, a large portion (often 70 percent or more) of the products exported by the major Asian suppliers were under quota restraints. In general, during the years the MFA has been in effect, both the number of countries and the number of categories of products subject to restraints have increased. For example, U.S. quota restraints on China's textile and apparel products went from 13 categories under MFA II, to 59 under MFA III, and to 66 under MFA IV. In many instances, exporting countries do not fully utilize all the quotas permitted; however, most of the major Asian suppliers utilize their quotas fully or nearly so.

The impact of quota controls was demonstrated clearly by the results of the extended fiber coverage to include silk blends, linen, and ramie textiles in MFA IV in 1986. For example, in 1988, U.S. imports of products of these previously uncontrolled fibers declined about 25 percent over the previous year. Similarly, U.S. quotas have limited wool imports to a fairly constant level for many years.

Future Outlook of the MFA

For years, the exporting nations have demanded to have the MFA eliminated and have textile trade brought back under the normal rules of the GATT. This was, in fact, a significant feature considered in the Uruguay Round multilateral trade negotiations. As in previous instances, the political drama associated with those negotiations was staged by a broad cast of international players and directors—all of whom have a great deal at stake in worldwide textile trade. The Uruguay Round is discussed later in this chapter.

ATTEMPTS TO CONTROL IMPORTS THROUGH THE LEGISLATIVE PROCESS

At times in recent U.S. history, the domestic textile and apparel industries have become impatient with what they believe to be ineffective foreign policy approaches to controlling imported products. In several instances in the last 20 years, industry groups have shifted their energies away from international negotiations and have, instead, attempted to secure solutions through the U.S. legislative process. Believing the industry would not receive the **protection** from imports it wanted through negotiations with trading partners, producers sought legislation through Congress that would impose unilateral restrictions on imports. Discussions of the legislative approaches follow.

The Mills Bill

In 1970, when the textile and apparel industries were distressed by the failure to secure a bilateral agreement with Japan, U.S. producers turned to Congress. Wilbur Mills, chairman of the House Ways and Means Committee, introduced a bill (H.R. 16920) to restrict apparel, textile, and footwear imports through the use of quotas. The bill would have limited 1970 imports to the 1967–1968 average and would have tied quota growth to changes in domestic consumption. The fiber, textile, and apparel coalition grew even stronger with the addition of the footwear industry.

The Mills bill passed the House of Representatives, and, although it encountered difficulty in the Senate, the optimistic outlook for passage of the bill caused the Japanese to feel pressure to come to an agreement. Confident the bill would pass, U.S. negotiators offended the Japanese with their demands, and talks collapsed. The bill did not pass; however, Mills tried to pursue a unilateral agreement with the Japanese on his own. Although the

Japanese were receptive, President Nixon rejected the plan (Aggarwal, 1985; Destler, 1986; Destler et al., 1979).

The Textile and Apparel Trade Enforcement Act of 1985 (The Jenkins Bill)

The U.S. textile and apparel industries experienced a particularly difficult time during late 1984. Imports doubled, exports dropped, and the industry feared increased plant closings and job losses. Many of the countries that shipped textile and apparel products to U.S. markets were unwilling to open their markets to U.S. products. As a result of these circumstances, American manufacturers believed the U.S. government was giving little attention to domestic industry problems, and protectionist sentiment ran high, especially in textile-producing states.

Convinced that imports must be controlled through provisions stronger than those the MFA provided, industry supporters sought a legislative approach. In March 1985, Representative Edward Jenkins (a Democrat from Georgia) introduced H.R. 1562, the Textile and Apparel Trade Enforcement Act of 1985, which became known as the "Jenkins bill." The bill would have replaced the existing system based on bilateral agreements with a unilaterally controlled import license program. Through this plan, U.S. sources would have controlled the imports permitted from a country by granting a license to ship a certain volume. Under the bilateral agreements, supplier nations at least have had a voice in designing the restraints. Furthermore, the Jenkins bill would have negated more than 30 bilateral agreements—which were in effect—that the United States had negotiated in good faith with trading partners.

The Jenkins bill included rollbacks of import levels from the major Asian supplier nations of about 30 percent, with lesser cuts for other developing nations. Again, the restraints were to be applied only to the developing countries. Canada and the EU were exempted (except for Portugal and Spain, the two newest EU members, who still had relatively low wages and many other developing-country characteristics). Although exempting the EU and Canada from the bill was in keeping with the gentlemen's agreement," doing so seemed particularly ironic at that time because substantial import growth had come from these developed countries.

A new industry coalition, the **Fiber, Fabric and Apparel Coalition for Trade (FFACT)**, developed to promote passage of the Jenkins bill. The coalition was composed of fiber, textile, and apparel manufacturers plus labor groups. The industry provided widespread support—money, energy, and talent—to support the objective of FFACT: passage of the Jenkins bill.

FFACT's lobbying efforts were effective in garnering congressional support for the Jenkins bill. Going into the vote in October 1985, the industries had secured 292 cosponsors in the House of Representatives. That number of votes provided a credible threat to override the expected presidential veto.

By this time, however, retailers had become an active lobbying force as well. Retailers and importers had become increasingly angry and outspoken over the textile and apparel industry's efforts to restrict imported products— products they wanted to obtain for their stores or other businesses. Retailers and importers had formed their own coalition, the **Retail Industry Trade Action Coalition (RITAC)**, to oppose the bill. By the time the Jenkins bill came to a vote, RITAC had convinced a number of the bill's cosponsors of the bill's pitfalls. As a result, although the bill passed in the House, the final vote was 262 to 159 (Samolis & Emrich, 1986). Clearly, the bill had lost some of its earlier support.

The Senate version of the bill (S. 680) passed in November by a vote of 60 to 39. Although supporters added amendments to protect the shoe industry and the copper industry in an effort to garner additional support, votes were insufficient to override the expected veto. The House passed the amended bill on December 3, 1985 (255 to 161, representing an additional loss of support). As expected, President Reagan vetoed the bill on December 17, 1985.

Industry leaders vowed that the efforts to pass the bill were "a good fight that isn't over yet" ("Textile Trade," 1985, p. 2). The bill's supporters scheduled a veto override attempt for August 6, 1986—six days after MFA III would expire (Wightman, 1985a). The strategy would provide additional pressure on U.S. negotiators to secure a "tight" MFA in the renewal. That is, the threat of an override would encourage U.S. negotiators to obtain as much protection as possible for the domestic industry, or, if not, the industry believed it would succeed in having adequate votes (two-thirds of Congress) to override the veto of the bill. If the MFA renewal did not provide adequate protection to stem the import tide, supporters believed this would gather additional votes for the override. Negotiators were in a difficult plight. They knew they must come home with a tough package to satisfy the supporters of the Jenkins bill, yet had to maintain the credibility of the Reagan administration's free trade policy.

Although domestic textile and industry sources were dissatisfied with MFA IV, America's trading partners believed the United States had succeeded in getting its wishes on major points in the MFA renewal—particularly the extended fiber coverage. As promised, supporters introduced the Jenkins bill in Congress again on August 6 for an attempted vote to override the presidential veto. The House vote was 276 to override the veto and 149 to sustain the veto—only eight votes short of what supporters needed to overturn the veto (Schwartz, 1986a). The final House vote meant the bill was dead. Industry supporters lost—but barely (Figure 10–5).

FIGURE 10–5

Textile and apparel workers demonstrated both at the national and local levels in an effort to garner support for the Jenkins bill.

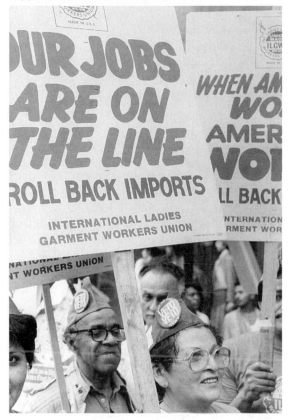

Source: Photo courtesy of International Ladies' Garment Workers' Union.

Support for the Jenkins bill attests to the political power of the U.S. textile and apparel industries at the time—that is, that the industry coalition could come close to having an act of Congress passed to protect it from foreign competition.

Needless to say, the Jenkins bill had few supporters abroad. The developing countries were angry over the heavy-handed approach it would represent if the bill passed. Not only would the United States be violating its GATT commitments, but the nation would also be abandoning trade agreements already signed and in operation to coordinate textile trade with more than 30 countries. Trading partners began to question U.S. integrity in following through on its commitments. Even the EU and Canada, who were to receive preferential treatment under the bill, did not want the bill to pass. The protection the bill would have provided to U.S. markets would have diverted the developing countries' textile and apparel products to EC and Canadian markets.

The Textile and Apparel Trade Act of 1987

Early in 1987, congressional representatives from South Carolina introduced the Textile and Apparel Trade Act of 1987 (H.R. 1154). Like the Jenkins bill, this was a legislative approach for limiting textile and apparel imports; however, the strategies proposed for limiting imports differed from the earlier bill. Having failed in securing passage of the Jenkins bill, sponsors attempted to make the Textile and Apparel Trade Act of 1987 more acceptable, and possibly more attractive, to members of Congress and the constituencies to whom the senators and representatives answered.

The 1987 bill provided for comprehensive **global quotas** on imported textiles, apparel, and footwear, based on actual 1986 volume. Global quotas set a limit on the total textile and apparel imports permitted into the country during a given period. Quota growth would be held to only 1 percent per year for textiles and apparel; footwear would be held at the 1986 level. This bill did not call for rollbacks in quotas, as the Jenkins bill had done; rather, it based growth rates on the 1986 import level.

The global quota approach would have included the EC and Canada, for the first time, in the import limits. This provision was included to overcome criticism that the Jenkins bill had discriminated against developing countries. Further, proponents of the bill believed provisions of the 1987 bill were more compatible with GATT and MFA commitments. Opponents of the bill believed it to be more restrictive than the 1985 bill because of its comprehensive (global) nature. The EC was expected to retaliate by introducing additional restrictions to prohibit the diversion of low-wage textile and apparel imports from the United States to EC markets.

The 1987 bill suffered the same fate as the 1985 bill. By the time the revised bill went to a vote in Congress in 1988, the mood in Congress was less supportive of sector-specific legislation than it had been earlier. By this time, the Omnibus Trade bill (see next section) had been signed, and some members of Congress saw little need for a bill to protect the textile/apparel sectors from imports. The bill passed the House in 1987 by a 263 to 156 vote, but the Senate vote was delayed because of the stock market crash in the fall of 1987. In September 1988, the Senate passed the bill by 59 to 36, with the Senate version of the bill containing provisions to secure the support of agriculture groups (who have typically opposed the textile bills because of fear of retaliation by foreign purchasers of U.S. farm products). The Senate bill would have tied a textile-exporting country's share of the domestic textile and apparel markets to the quantity of agricultural products it purchased from the United States (LaRussa, 1988a).

President Reagan vetoed the bill on September 28, labeling it "protectionist" and "unnecessary in light of the strong economic gains posted by the textile and apparel industries" (LaRussa, 1988a, pp. 1, 12). When the bill went back to the House, the veto was sustained by a vote of 272 to 152—this time, 11 votes short of the necessary two-thirds majority to override the veto.

The Textile, Apparel, and Footwear Act of 1990

The Textile, Apparel, and Footwear Act of 1990 was introduced in Congress in April 1990

(5.2411). The proposed bill, based on a global quota plan limiting textile and apparel import growth to 1 percent per year, resembled the 1987 textile bill. Additionally, this bill would have overturned textile bilateral accords the United States had negotiated in good faith with 38 exporting nations. To gain agriculture's support, a feature built into this bill from the beginning was that countries that increased their purchase of U.S. agricultural products would be given higher textile quotas (Barrett, 1990b, 1990d; Hackett, 1990a; Lachica, 1990; Jacobs, 1990).

Surprisingly, however, the American Apparel Manufacturers Association did not support this bill. This was the beginning of a significant division in the strong textile-apparel-labor coalition that had long stood united against imports.[11] For the first time, some apparel firms joined forces with retailers in opposing the measure.

The 1990 bill passed the House and the Senate (with a vote of 68–32 in the Senate—the most favorable of any of the Senate votes on the three textile bills). President George Bush vetoed the bill, however, as he had indicated he would, terming it as "highly protectionist" and added that it would devastate ongoing Uruguay Round trade talks (Barrett, 1990b, p 3). When the bill was brought back to the House in an attempt to override the veto, the vote was 275 to 152—only 10 votes shy of the two-thirds margin needed (Barrett, 1990b, 1990c, 1990d). Once again, the industry came amazingly close to succeeding in having a congressional bill in place to protect its interests. Although industry leaders and congressional supporters were disappointed by their defeat, they believed the show of support in Congress for the industry would send a strong message to the Administration to protect textile interests in the Uruguay Round talks, which were looming as an even larger concern. U.S. industry leaders feared that the textile industry would be "sold out" in the GATT talks.

The override vote on the 1990 textile bill came during the time when the United States had already begun to send troops to the Middle East for what became known as the Gulf War and Desert Storm in the Persian Gulf. The rapid troop deployment, along with the fact that previous camouflage uniforms were forest green rather than for a desert environment, meant that some troops had to be sent to the desert in forest-green uniforms. Although the industry had responded quickly to producing new fabrics and uniforms, the U.S. textile industry used this as an opportunity to sensitize the public—and policymakers—to the importance of the domestic industry in the nation's defense. One month prior to the override vote, the industry organized the largest rally in its history in Washington around the Capitol. Some 3,000 textile and apparel workers carried Desert Storm uniform fabrics plus banners containing 250,000 signatures in support of the bill (Figure 10–6).

COMPREHENSIVE TRADE LEGISLATION: THE OMNIBUS TRADE BILL

In August 1988, after four years of debate, defeat, and revision, the U.S. Congress passed a generic trade bill—the Omnibus Trade and Competitiveness Act of 1988—designed to open foreign markets and bolster domestic industries. The 1,000-page bill was designed

---

[11]In 1989, the American Apparel Manufacturers Association announced a new position on trade. As growing numbers of U.S. apparel firms engaged in offshore assembly operations, AAMA retreated from its strong anti-import position. The AAMA chairman at the time indicated that another reason AAMA withdrew from the anti-import coalition was that U.S. apparel producers were having to rely increasingly on foreign sources of fabrics and other supplies (Hackett, 1990b).

FIGURE 10–6

As the textile industry tried to secure congressional passage of the 1990 textile bill, industry leaders used this opportunity to sensitize the public and policymakers to the importance of the industry in the nation's defense.

Source: Reprinted courtesy of American Textile Manufacturers Institute.

to reduce the growing U.S. trade deficit, which was a record $170 billion the year prior to its passage. The overwhelming passage of the bill in the final vote (85 to 11 in the Senate, and 376 to 45 in the House) indicated the increased sensitivity of Congress to trade concerns—which had come to be described as "competitiveness" concerns.

The omnibus bill was described as the most extensive revision of U.S. trade laws in 25 years. Then-Texas Senator Lloyd Bentsen,

who later became Secretary of Treasury, considered the bill "the most important piece of legislation on competitiveness this country has ever considered, . . . a great victory for restoration of U.S. economic leadership" (Castro, 1988, p. 32).

Although many members of Congress considered the trade bill as a panacea, other observers believed the results remained to be seen. The legislation tightened the process of trade regulation in the United States in many ways. For example, the law gives the president power to counteract unfair trade practices by foreign countries—and would permit the president some discretion to decide whether to retaliate and how. For several provisions of the bill, the stance of the president would determine results.

The omnibus bill took a strong unilateral approach to controlling trade, in contrast to the more multilateral approach the United States had generally taken. Under this policy, the United States could tell trading partners how trade relationships would be defined rather than negotiating with other nations. The "muscle" of the omnibus bill was something called the *Super 301 provision*, which permitted the United States to identify countries for a "301 list" if they appeared to have unfairly restricted markets. The Super 301 provision was intended to achieve reciprocal access to what the United States defined as unfairly restricted markets. Countries were to be warned if their trade practices appeared unfair, and the United States could retaliate by restricting *all* the products from that specific country if the other country did not improve its practices (Dicken, 1992).[12]

---

[12]Dicken (1992) notes that the 1974 Trade Act contained a Section 301 clause that met GATT criteria for dealing with unfair trade practices in a specific industry. However, the 1988 omnibus bill adapted this to a strong *unilateral* measure. Dicken calls the 301 provision the "crowbar" of the omnibus bill (p. 170). Critical of the act, Bhagwati (1989) calls it the "'ominous' trade . . . act."

Under the broad trade bill, domestic industries that sought federal relief because of injury from imports were required to show they were prepared to make a "positive adjustment" to import competition. That is, a declining industry could not win relief unless it could demonstrate that it could become competitive again (Langley & Mossberg, 1988).

A number of foreign trading partners were concerned over the passage of the omnibus bill. Some saw the bill as fulfilling "mercantilist" goals that place a high premium on exports as a source of national wealth and power. A number of U.S. trading partners felt pressured to lower import barriers, as the United States attempted to reduce its trade deficit. And, not surprisingly, major exporting nations did not reduce willingly their shipments to U.S. markets. Many countries were concerned that the bill permited Washington to decide unilaterally what was fair and what was not (Farnsworth, 1988; Yates, 1988).

In fact, many of the United States's trading partners believed that completion of the GATT Uruguay Round (to be discussed in a later section of this chapter) represented an end to the "Super 301" protection. However, as this book goes to press, U.S. industry sources who wish to retain this powerful provision are not convinced that "Super 301" is dead (author's confidential discussions with industry sources, 1994).

A number of the provisions of the omnibus bill have implications for the U.S. textile and apparel industries and for global trade for the sector. The legislation did not, however, include specific provisions for textiles and apparel. In 1986, supporters of the Jenkins bill explored possibilities for attaching the bill to the omnibus legislation. A similar strategy was considered for the 1987 textile bill. The omnibus legislation supporters discouraged textile bill proponents; an effort was being made to avoid controversial, sector-specific provisions in the broader bill (LaRussa, 1986). Later, proponents of the 1987 textile bill were

assured they would be given an opportunity to introduce their textile proposal for congressional consideration if they did not persist in their efforts to attach the proposal to the omnibus bill.

MULTILATERAL TRADE NEGOTIATIONS (MTN)

Eight rounds of multilateral trade negotiations (MTNs) have been held since 1947 under the auspices of GATT. The goal of each negotiation has been to reduce or eliminate tariffs (and, in some cases, non-tariff barriers) in world trade among the Contracting Parties. The MTN negotiations focus on all trade areas; however, textile and apparel products have secured special treatment in these agreements. Some of the most widely known GATT MTN trade "rounds," as they are known, are discussed below.

The Kennedy Round

These multilateral trade negotiations, which occurred between 1964 and 1967 in Geneva, Switzerland, were named for U.S. President John Kennedy, who initiated the trade talks. The U.S. entered the Kennedy Round on the authority of the Trade Expansion Act of 1962, which Congress had passed with President Kennedy's encouragement. This act promoted freer trade. Ellsworth and Leith (1984) noted that passage of the Trade Expansion Act was the high point of public support for liberal trading policies in the United States. In the Kennedy Round, 37 nations joined in making tariff (duty) reductions that covered about 80 percent of world trade—mostly on manufactured goods (agricultural products posed difficulty in negotiating tariff reductions). The United States, for example, reduced tariffs by about 30 percent on nearly two-thirds of her imports subject to duties. Most other industrialized countries also made major tariff reductions (Ellsworth & Leith, 1984; Mansfield, 1983).

It is important to remember that tariffs represent a form of protection against imports—although domestic manufacturers would say tariffs do not provide effective protection. That is, tariffs add to the price of imports coming into a market, thus increasing prices and making the imported product somewhat less attractive in the importing market.

In general, textile and apparel products were given special treatment in the Kennedy Round. Although textile and apparel products carried some of the highest tariffs on any manufactured products entering OECD markets prior to the Kennedy Round, *tariff reductions* were among the lowest for these product areas. Although tariff structures varied within the different OECD countries, our discussion will focus on the average for all the OECD countries at the time.

Figure 10–7 displays average tariffs for the nine OECD countries before and after the Kennedy Round of cuts. The reader is encouraged to compare textile and apparel categories to other product areas. Figure 10–8 illustrates even more clearly the tariff concessions provided textiles and apparel in the Kennedy Round. Whereas the prior chart showed tariff *levels*, this chart shows the percentage tariff *cuts* for most manufactured product areas. As Figure 10–8 shows, fibers, other textiles, and clothing received the lowest tariff cuts of any product areas.

Following the Trade Expansion Act and the Kennedy Round, many types of manufactured imports began to rise rapidly. Domestic industries began to press for measures to limit imports, fueling a shift toward protectionism. The textile and apparel sectors were among those industries, and the Long-Term Arrangement was a response to those concerns.

FIGURE 10–7

Average tariffs for nine OECD countries (six EC countries, USA, UK, Japan) before and after the GATT Kennedy Round cuts. Tariff averages are weighted according to total OECD imports.

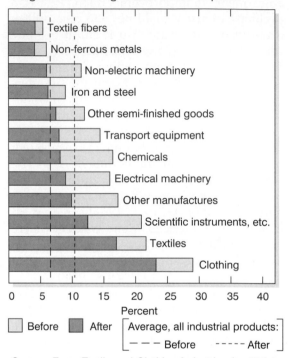

Source: From *Textile and Clothing Industries* (p. 107) by *Organization for Economic Cooperation and Development*, 1983, Paris: Author. Reprinted by permission.

The Tokyo Round

The official U.S. stance on trade remained comparatively liberal in the early 1970s. In 1974, Congress passed the Trade Reform Act of 1974, which contained many provisions of the 1962 act but permitted the president authority to make further tariff reductions under certain circumstances. The 1974 act provided for **trade adjustment assistance** to help workers, firms, and communities hurt by more liberal trade measures.

The 1974 act allowed the president to negotiate further tariff reductions; therefore, this

FIGURE 10–8

Percentage tariff cuts, Kennedy Round.

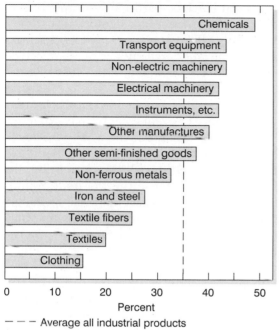

– – – Average all industrial products

Source: From *Textile and Clothing Industries* (p. 105) by Organization for Economic Cooperation and Development, 1983, Paris: Author. Reprinted by permission.

act authorized U.S. participation in the forthcoming GATT round of MTN negotiations. In 1973, more than 100 nations met in Tokyo to plan a new round of trade talks. The Tokyo Round occurred from 1973 to 1979 in Geneva. This round focused on negotiation of additional tariff cuts and developed a series of agreements governing the use of non-tariff measures. **Non-tariff barriers** include quotas, import licensing programs, technical standards (often contrived standards), and other measures to keep out foreign goods. The industrialized countries agreed to reduce tariffs below those in effect under the Kennedy Round (by about one-third over an eight-year period). However, organizers viewed as the major achievement of the Tokyo Round the steps taken to control the use of non-tariff barriers.

At the time of the Tokyo Round, as was true at the time of the Kennedy Round, textile and apparel tariff rates in the OECD countries (which had grown in number from 9 to 17 nations by this time) were among the highest for all manufactured goods. The textile fiber category was an exception. Figure 10–9 illustrates average tariffs in these countries before and after the Tokyo Round tariff cuts. As Figure 10–9 indicates, OECD countries reduced

FIGURE 10–9

Average tariffs for 17 OECD countries (all EC countries, USA, Canada, Japan, Switzerland, Austria, Nordics) before and after the GATT Tokyo Round cuts.

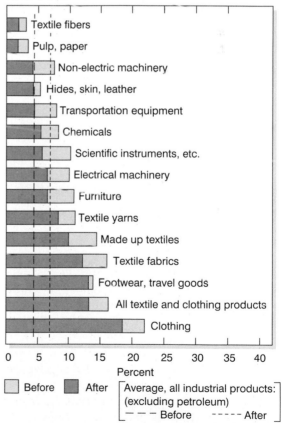

Source: From *Textile and Clothing Industries* (p. 102) by Organization for Economic Cooperation and Development, 1983, Paris: Author, Reprinted by permission.

FIGURE 10–10

Percentage tariff cuts, Tokyo Round. (This figure is not directly comparable to Figure 10–8.)

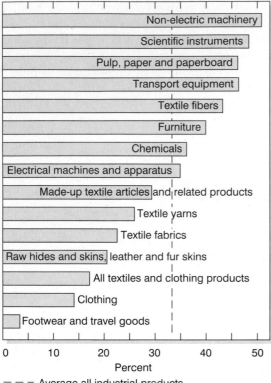

Percent

− − − Average all industrial products

Source: From *Textile and Clothing Industries* (p. 105) by Organization for Economic Cooperation and Development, 1983, Paris: Author. Reprinted by permission.

tariffs less on most textile and apparel products than on other manufactured goods. Tariff-reduction patterns for a majority of textile and apparel products were similar to those for the Kennedy Round. Furthermore, Figure 10–10 shows even more clearly the relative percentage tariff cuts for the Tokyo Round (but keep in mind that Figure 10–8 and Figure 10–10 are not directly comparable).

One must also keep in mind that the Tokyo Round negotiations occurred shortly after implementation of the Multifiber Arrangement. Although the Tokyo Round attempted to resolve the problems of non-tariff barriers,

it followed on the heels of a complex system—the MFA—that was designed to *permit* non-tariff barriers, particularly in the form of quotas. Moreover, it was significant that even with the MFA in place, most textile and apparel product areas nevertheless received quite favorable treatment in the Tokyo Round of tariff cuts that followed.

Let's reflect for a moment on the contradictory sequence of events that we have covered. That is, at the same time the GATT was developing a special regime to *restrict* trade in textiles and apparel (the LTA and the MFA), the GATT was also sponsoring the trade rounds to *liberalize* trade. Why would these seemingly contradictory events occur in this manner? The answer lies for the most part in the dilemma posed by world textile trade in most contexts. Because of the surplus global production capacity, the importance of the sectors to most nations, and the political aspects of textile and apparel trade, these sectors have continued to receive special attention. Often, the special provisions for textile and apparel trade have been developed to try to resolve the sector's trade problems and get those "out of the way" so that broader trade discussions will not be hampered by the difficulties posed by the textile and apparel sectors (author's discussions with global trade officials, 1983–1988).

The Uruguay Round

Trade ministers, meeting in Punta del Este, Uruguay, in September 1986, launched a new round of trade talks aimed at strengthening the GATT and expanding its coverage to new areas. Whereas the Kennedy and Tokyo Rounds focused especially on tariff reductions, planners sought to have the Uruguay Round rethink trade policy areas in general. Although most of the negotiations occurred in Geneva, this round of MTN talks was called the Uruguay Round.

Textile and apparel trade was involved in early controversy regarding whether or not a new round of trade talks would actually occur (see "Textiles: Early Stumbling Block in Uruguay Round" boxed insert). The developing countries pushed for having the MFA gradually dismantled so that textile and apparel trade might return to normal GATT rules. That is, the developing (exporting) countries chafed under the growing restrictions on textile and apparel products—a vitally important export area for most of the LDCs.

As GATT representatives met in Uruguay to launch the MTN talks, U.S. negotiators found themselves in a difficult position. If they gave the developing countries too much

encouragement on liberalizing textile and apparel trade, this would have increased chances for the Jenkins bill's passage. Had the Jenkins bill passed, most textile trade officials expected that the MFA would have ended then. The MFA has existed primarily as a structure to "manage" textile and apparel trade flow from the LDCs to the markets of the developed countries—particularly the major markets of the United States and the EU. If either of these major players had withdrawn (perhaps to impose its own unilateral restraints, as in the case of the Jenkins bill), the Arrangement would not likely have continued.

Without the MFA, textile trade problems would have escalated to such an extent that

 TEXTILES: EARLY STUMBLING BLOCK IN URUGUAY ROUND

At the 1984 annual GATT meeting in Geneva, as early discussions began for the proposed round of trade talks, the LDCs made it clear they would not participate unless the United States and other developed countries "live up to commitments under the MFA" ("3rd World," 1984, p. 10). The LDCs charged that both the United States and the EU were ignoring internationally negotiated rules on world textile trade, and "the situation in the field of textiles and clothing has deteriorated further" (Callcott, 1984c). To this charge, a U.S. official responded, "If recent U.S. import actions are as restrictive as alleged, how can it be explained that Hong Kong's exports of textiles and clothing to the U.S. have risen by 56% over the past 12 months?" (Callcott, 1984c).

U.S. negotiators entered the annual meeting asking that several areas not covered previously by GATT be included in the next round of trade talks: trade in services (for example, banking and communications), high technology, and the problem of counterfeit goods. The United States

also wanted rules against piracy of intellectual property. (This has been a source of contention in joint ventures and licensing programs in developing countries that have no rules to govern these activities.) The LDCs refused for the most part to include these areas unless industrial nations reduced restrictions on imports from developing countries. Formal sessions at the annual GATT meeting were canceled because of the deadlock between the United States and the developing countries. U.S. representatives implied that the United States might withhold its $3.4 million contribution to GATT's 1984 $22.6 million budget (Callcott, 1984a).

Finally, the Contracting Parties arrived at a compromise. Both U.S. and LDC demands were mentioned in the program of work that developed, with several "working parties" and "GATT studies" commissioned to examine the issues prior to the proposed round of trade talks (Callcott, 1984b; "Compromise," 1984).

the MTN talks would have been unlikely. As a way of handling the textile/apparel matter delicately, the ministers at the Uruguay talks made indefinite reference to "eventual integration of this sector into GATT" (W. Cline, 1987, p. 221). By the end of 1986, however, MFA IV was in effect, the Jenkins bill had failed, and the Uruguay Round was launched.

In December 1988, a ministerial meeting of the Uruguay Round (which was intended to mark the halfway point of the talks) was held in Montreal. Ministers from the 19 developing countries in the International Textiles and Clothing Bureau asserted they were unwilling to continue participating in the broader MTN talks—unless problems related to the MFA were addressed in the Uruguay Round. The Third-World representatives requested a clear timetable for the phase-out of the MFA restrictions and a reintegration of textiles back into the broader GATT rules. Representatives from the developed (importing) countries found it hard to agree to the demands. In fact, in a report made public at the beginning of the Montreal talks, a U.S. labor advisory committee recommended that the MFA not only be renewed when it expired in 1991 but that it also be more restrictive on imports. Textile discussions in the Montreal meeting ended in a stalemate (Dunn, 1988a, 1988b; Kryhul & Chute, 1988).

As the GATT talks dragged on, various countries offered different proposals for bringing textile trade back under mainstream GATT regulations (Chute, 1989c; "Further Trade Talks," 1989). Most trading nations agreed to eventually phase out the MFA; however, several years and a great deal of emotion were invested in various proposals and the debates that followed.

In 1990, for example, the United States officials offered a proposal for a global quota plan that would include quota allocations for each country (which would be eliminated gradually) and an overall global quota. This proposal was offered to end selective quotas,

which many consider **discriminatory restrictions** against certain supplier nations (Chute, 1990a, 1990f). The U.S. proposal encountered strong opposition from many quarters. Exporting nations considered the proposal unacceptable; most refused to even consider it (Parry, 1990). Even the U.S. textile industry was skeptical and interested only if import growth were kept to a minimum (Chute, 1990a). Retailers and importers believed the plan would be detrimental to their interests and termed it "the same wine, just a new bottle" (Chute, 1990b, p. 2). Similarly, proposals by the EU, Canada, and Japan were unpopular.

Deadline after deadline for completing the Uruguay Round passed with little progress. However, the Chairman of the Negotiating Group on Textiles and Clothing began to draft a text that attempted to deal with the stalemate on several unresolved issues. The Chairman's "Draft Text" of July 12, 1990, attempted to summarize various negotiating positions rather than resolve disagreements. The "Draft Text" identified four alternative options for integrating textiles into the normal rules of GATT. During 1990, the Textiles Negotiating Group made progress in resolving the disputed issues. By November 1990, the group had developed the "Chairman's Text" of the Negotiating Group on Textiles and Clothing, which identified an MFA-based transition system but did not develop complete details for phasing out the MFA (Hurewitz, 1993).

When GATT talks resumed in Brussels in December 1990, a new proposal was introduced to reduce worldwide subsidies and protective barriers for agriculture. U.S. textile producers were concerned that concessions would have to be made for textiles. U.S. textile makers were hoping the overall agreement would remain elusive, for fear the textile sector would be "sacrificed" to gain approval from other countries in other areas of negotiation, including services and Intellectual property rights (Chute, 1990d; Ostroff, 1990a). Textile leaders in the importing nations were relieved when the 1990 talks stalled over agricultural issues.

Despite the unsuccessful end to the 1990 meeting, the Negotiating Group on Textiles and Clothing had continued to make progress. Included in the document for the overall Brussels meeting was a revised version of the "Chairman's Text" entitled "Agreement on Textiles and Clothing," which became known as the Brussels Draft. This text clarified that textile products would be integrated into GATT (and, consequently, quota restrictions eliminated) in three stages but did not specify the time frame or growth rates for each stage (Hurewitz, 1993).

In October 1991, GATT talks resumed, working toward what was then termed as the *final* deadline for completion of the Uruguay Round. By December, however, talks were deadlocked again over European farm subsidies. The GATT Negotiating Group on Textiles and Clothing had made progress on textile trade but reached an impasse on certain issues related to phasing out the MFA, such as how much quota growth to allow during a phase-out period. Arthur Dunkel, Director General of GATT at the time, then released his own proposals on textile trade and other areas the negotiating groups could not resolve ("GATT Talks," 1991; Hurewitz, 1993; Ostroff, 1991a, 1991b).

The Director General's plan, known as the "Dunkel Draft" or "Dunkel plan," set forth a proposed "Agreement on Textiles and Clothing" (also known as the "Draft Final Act"). Dunkel recommended (1) a staged *phasing out of MFA import quotas*, with certain percentages of textile trade to be removed in stages from the quota system over a 10-year period and (2) *increases in growth rates on quotas* as well (GATT, 1992; Hurewitz, 1993). The Dunkel plan met with hostile response, however, from nearly all affected industry sectors (textiles, labor, and retailers/importers) in both the United States and the EU (Ostroff, 1992b).

In an effort to get GATT talks moving again, the EU trade ministers agreed they would again consider agricultural subsidies, and Dunkel set *another* deadline, April 15, to complete the talks. Like others, this deadline passed with goals unmet.

The global trade talks lumbered along. At various points, when it appeared that a MFA phase-out might occur, textile industry supporters in the U.S. Congress indicated that if a phase-out were proposed, they would modify the agreement when it came to a vote of approval in Congress. Realizing the prospects for influence from many industries when the trade agreement would be presented to Congress for approval, President Bush enlisted a cross section of industry leaders from many sectors to assist him by asking Congress to support his request for **fast track authority** for both the Uruguay Round as well as the efforts to secure a North American Free Trade Agreement. Bush was successful in getting this authorization. The fast track authority meant that Congress could only approve or disapprove the agreements and could not amend them. The expectation was that the textile industry supporters would otherwise modify the agreement if they were dissatisfied with the outcome of the GATT talks, and that prospect was very likely ("Bush Asks," 1991). Support for the three textile bills had shown the strength of the textile lobby.

In December 1993, the Uruguay Round talks resumed once again. With troublesome issues still unresolved, many questioned whether the talks could be completed by December 15, when President Clinton's fast track authority would expire. In early December, it was announced that U.S. tariffs on textiles would be reduced far less than had been proposed. (The negotiations had broken down two months earlier as the U.S. and EU teams reached a stalemate on tariff cuts.) The EU had demanded that U.S. tariffs on imported textiles be cut substantially. However, as a political payoff to the United States for granting the EU new concessions on farm subsidy levels, U.S. tariffs on textile imports were to be cut only about 50 percent of what had been proposed (Zaracostas, 1993). This concession reflected similarities to the Kennedy and Tokyo Rounds discussed previously. The reader is reminded that if tariff levels remain fairly high on imports, this adds to the price for importers, thus making imports less attractive.

By the December 15 deadline, a landmark GATT accord was agreed upon—after seven long years, and to the surprise of many observers. The long-term negotiations had caused some critics to refer to the GATT as the "General Agreement to Talk and Talk."

The December 1993 textile agreement portion of the Uruguay Round was in large measure a modification of earlier drafts, begun first by the Negotiating Group on Textiles and modified by Dunkel. Although many of the MFA participants were not satisfied with the agreement, a general feeling existed that if contracting parties began to tinker with the compromise as it stood, all the progress up to that point would have unraveled (author's conversations with trade officials in Geneva, 1994).

The Uruguay Round agreement called for a 10-year phase-out of the MFA. Under the GATT plan, each country's share of a textile-apparel import market, as represented by quotas, would increase once the GATT provisions took effect, slated at the time for July 1, 1995.[13] A staged phase-out will occur until all quotas are eliminated at the end of 10 years.

On the date the World Trade Organization (WTO) Agreement becomes effective, the MFA phase-out begins. (As a result of the Uruguay Round, the WTO will replace GATT; this is discussed further in Chapter 11.) At each stage, each importing country may choose the quota categories that will be **integrated** into the GATT. This means quotas will no longer exist on those product categories. Categories to be integrated must encompass products from *each* of the following groups (equal amounts from the groups is not required): tops and yarns, fabrics, made-up textile products, and apparel (GATT, 1994). The three-stage quota phase-out schedule for each importing country is based on the country's 1990 import volume and is to be carried out as follows:

Stage 1: (a) 1995.[13] Starting date for the phase-out. Quotas chosen for surrender must account for at least 16 percent of the country's total textile and apparel imports in 1990. (Some sources referred to this stage as the "down payment.")

(b) Remaining quotas will be allowed to grow at higher rates than the typical 6 percent quota growth rates that existed under the MFA. This added quota growth is known as the "**growth on growth**" provision. During Stage 1, remaining quotas must grow in each of the three years at rates no less than 16 percent higher than in 1994 if the WTO takes effect January 1, 1995 (or the preceding 12 months, if WTO takes effect later).

Stage 2: (a) 1998:[13] The importing country must choose for integration product categories whose imports account for at least 17 percent of the country's 1990 import volume.

(b) Remaining quotas will be permitted to grow in each of the four years at rates which are at least 25 percent higher than under Stage 1.

Stage 3: (a) 2002:[13] The importing country again chooses the categories to surrender to integration. The categories must account for at least 18 percent of the country's 1990 import volume.

(b) Remaining quotas will be allowed to grow in each of the three years at rates which are at least 27 percent higher than under Stage 2 (GATT, 1994; Khanna, 1994).

---

[13]Projected dates at the time this book goes to press.

No MFA: 2005:[13] Textile and apparel trade will be integrated fully into trade rules for all other sectors.

In addition to quota phase-outs, tarriffs will be reduced on an annual basis. After 2005, only tariffs will remain.

The Uruguay Round textile and apparel agreement included a **safeguard mechanism** to be used during the phase-out period. If an importing country determines that imports are causing injury or threat of injury to the domestic industry, that country will be permitted to impose restraints on the products *from a specific country* and *for a maximum of three years* or until those products are integrated into the GATT, whichever comes earlier. Manufacturers in the importing countries see this provision as a ray of hope against being inundated by imports, but representatives of the developing exporting nations fear this mechanism will be abused by the developed countries.

Although U.S. importers and retailers were pleased with the Uruguay Round Textile and apparel agreement, textile leaders and supporters were not. Only a short time before, in an effort to secure the necessary votes to approve NAFTA, President Clinton had promised textile supporters in Congress that he would seek a 15-year phase-out of the MFA. Therefore, the textile group felt betrayed and believed the industry had been "sold out"—that is, a "pawn" traded off for concessions in other areas by the U.S. Administration in its eagerness to conclude the Uruguay Round (Figure 10–11).

A number of informed individuals have noted, however, that the difference between the 15-year and 10-year phase-out is negligible because of the "**growth on growth**" provision. Compounded quota growth rates represent such dramatic increases in imports that by the end of 10 years, restraints will be minimal anyway (author's conversations with government sources and industry consultants in Washington, April 1994).

Additionally, U.S. textile leaders were angry that negotiators had not secured access to certain other markets for U.S. exports. EU textile leaders had been vocal much earlier

FIGURE 10–11
The U.S. textile industry has often believed that it is a "pawn" traded off for concessions in other areas by the Administration in efforts to secure trade agreements such as the Uruguay Round.

Source: Illustration by Dennis Murphy.

than U.S. leaders on the issue of **market access** (that is, reciprocity). U.S. industry sources joined their European peers in arguing that if they were required to open their markets more fully to imported products, other countries should reciprocate. Market access was a particular concern for trade with India and Pakistan; both had pressed for the 10-year phase-out but were reluctant to open their markets to U.S. and EU textile products (Ostroff, 1993b).

Between December 1993 and April 15, 1994, trade officials in various GATT member countries worked to resolve outstanding issues before the formal signing of the Uruguay Round. During this time, U.S. and EU officials persisted in efforts to secure market access for textile products in those Asian nations that resisted. In the end, however, the United States did not insist that these nations open their markets for fear the final signing of the Round would be disrupted (Ostroff, 1994d).

On April 15, 1994, the Uruguay Round was formally signed in Marrakech, Morocco, by trade ministers from 109 countries. The pact has been called "the most sweeping trade liberalization accord in modern history" ("Uruguay Round," 1994, p. 27).

The new trade pact requires ratification by the individual countries. In the United States, this requires approval by Congress. As this book goes to press, a number of issues have clouded the prospects for easy passage in Congress; the most significant is the debate over how to make up for the revenue shortfalls resulting from the Uruguay Round tariff cuts. U.S. tariff revenue losses are estimated at $13 billion to $16 billion for the first five years when trade barriers are reduced. As various proposals are considered, the groups that are potentially affected have become outspoken. The Office of Management and Budget proposed, for example, that nearly $6 billion could be raised by reducing subsidies to farmers. As a result, 18 agriculture groups opposed the GATT agreement. The agriculture coalition, combined with the textile forces that

oppose the pact, could represent a formidable force when the GATT accord comes before Congress (Barrett, 1994b; 1994d).

During this time, the textile and apparel sectors in each of the importing countries faced the prospects of how they were to be affected by the pact. In the United States, industry groups were busy trying to influence the implementing legislation. As one lobbyist described this to the author, "The implementing legislation isn't like putting ornaments on the tree by adding this or that provision. The basic guidelines are there and can't be changed. The implementing legislation means doing a little here and there to tidy up the shape of the tree" (confidential conversation with author, April 1994).

A significant aspect of the implementing legislation has to do with the *process* for determining the product categories to be surrendered during each stage of the phase-out. For example, the manufacturers want the one branch of government more supportive of their interests to be in charge; the retailers want a different agency they consider more objective to manage the phase-out. Industry groups have been involved in considerable gamesmanship in determining which product categories to surrender. For example, textile industry supporters were successful in having *non-quota products* count in the categories to be surrendered. A number of items containing textile materials that were not covered by the MFA were included, such as umbrellas, parachutes, safety belts, and garments for dolls. As Khanna noted, including non-MFA "junk" products "puts off the day of reckoning" (1994, p. 24).

By permitting the importing countries to count non-MFA and what Khanna terms as "junk" products, the importing countries—particularly the United States—will have to surrender very little to integration in the first three years. Similarly, during the next four-year stage, U.S. quotas will be only marginally reduced. In the short term, the effect of integration will be only modest because the product categories surrendered will be those that are not import-sensitive and not under quota control. By the seventh or eighth year, the impact of the MFA phase-out will be felt by many of the players involved. An even more substantial change will occur at the end of the tenth year, when the final 49 percent of textile and apparel trade will be quota-free. By using the strategies to postpone the "day of reckoning," the importing countries have, in fact, positioned themselves to experience an avalanche at the end of 10 years.

In short, the completion of the Uruguay Round—most particularly the plan to phase out the MFA—represented a historic moment in the history of textile and apparel trade. For many it was a supreme victory; for many it was an all-time low point. Global trade for the sector would surely change radically from this point on. The rules of textile trade had been rewritten.

GENERALIZED SYSTEM OF PREFERENCES (GSP)

The **generalized system of preferences (GSP)** is a system of tariff preferences, agreed to by the OECD countries, designed to encourage the expansion of manufactured and semi-manufactured exports from developing countries. In principle, the GSP allows products to enter developed country markets duty free or at reduced rates of duty to give LDCs an advantage over suppliers not granted these tariff advantages.

In 1968, GATT accepted a generalized system of preferences for developing countries as an exception to the nondiscrimination and most-favored-nation principles. The GSP was further legitimized by the Tokyo Round as a special provision to help the LDCs. In keeping with the global effort, the U.S. Congress authorized a 10-year GSP scheme under the Trade Act of 1974 (and later extended it under the Trade Act of 1984).

Under the GSP, the country granting the tariff preferences has the right to determine the scope of the special treatment given, with the understanding that recipient countries might be required to meet certain conditions. The GSP was intended to help developing countries in sectors where they are not already strong exporters. Consequently, it is not surprising that most of the GSP exceptions are in the textile and apparel sectors—because MFA products are not eligible for duty elimination under that program. Since most of the LDC exporters are quite competitive without the GSP benefits, this system has had little influence on the volume of textile and apparel exports from developing countries (OECD, 1983).

When the GSP was legitimized under the Tokyo Round, the agreement accepted the principle of **non-reciprocity** by the developing countries. That is, the developing countries were not required to reciprocate by making the same special concessions to the developed countries so the latter might have access to LDC markets. Under the GSP, the developing countries are permitted to use trade restrictions in order to achieve broader development objectives (Ellsworth & Leith, 1984).

In talks to promote more liberal trade, a source of contention in the Uruguay Round was the developed countries' desires to see developing country markets opened as well as their own. The industrialized countries have grown increasingly impatient with Third-World demands for greater access to the major importing markets while many LDCs are unwilling to reciprocate.

CANADA-U.S. FREE TRADE AGREEMENT (CFTA)

The textile and apparel industries of the United States and Canada were affected by the free trade agreement formalized between the two countries in January 1989. Prior to the agreement, nearly 80 percent of the trade between the two countries occurred with no duties or restrictive regulations. However, textile and apparel products were among the 20 percent of trade subject to tariffs, and tariffs were high on these products on both sides of the border. Even before the agreement, Canada and the United States were important trading partners in many sectors; trade in textiles and apparel had been significant in certain segments.

Initially, Canadian textile and apparel manufacturers were reasonably supportive of the free trade agreement; polls showed about half the producers in each segment favored it (Dafoe, 1986; Wall & Dickerson, 1989). Many wanted access to the U.S. market, which is approximately 10 times larger in terms of population. Canadian apparel manufacturers had been concerned, however, that items made of fabrics manufactured outside North America would not be duty exempt. Canadian apparel producers rely on a far greater amount of non-North American fabric than do U.S. apparel manufacturers.

Although the United States had a $70 million (U.S.) trade surplus in textiles and clothing with Canada at the time, U.S. textile and apparel producers were opposed to the agreement from the beginning. U.S. manufacturers were concerned over the potential transshipment of imports from low-wage countries through Canada, because of Canada's more liberal importation laws. U.S. producers offered suggestions for ways in which their concerns might be addressed.

During negotiations, U.S. manufacturers became increasingly alarmed by a proposed Canadian plan that would subsidize duties on imported fabric used by its apparel industry. This duty remission plan intensified the earlier negative views held by U.S. producers. As negotiations progressed, portions of the Canadian textile/apparel industries became less supportive of the pact as work-

ers feared potential negative impact on their jobs. Within the broader Canadian population, many persons feared loss of national identity.

The CFTA became effective January 1, 1989, and provided for gradual phasing out of all tariffs and quotas within 10 years. However, special controls were negotiated restricting Canadian apparel to limited amounts of third-country fabrics. As noted in Chapter 6, both the Canadian and U.S. textile complexes have benefited from the agreement. (For additional information on the development of the agreement, particularly in regard to the perspectives of both Canadian and U.S. manufacturers, retailers, consumers, and policymakers, see Wall and Dickerson [1989].)

From a broader perspective, many persons now consider the Canada-U.S. Free Trade Agreement as an important first step in developing more open markets in the Western Hemisphere. This agreement set the stage for the North American Free Trade Agreement that followed in 1994.

NORTH AMERICAN FREE TRADE AGREEMENT

Under President George Bush's Enterprise for the Americas Initiative (EAI), the next logical step after the Canada-U.S. Free Trade Agreement (CFTA) was the establishment of free trade among the three countries of North America—a North American Free Trade Agreement (NAFTA). President Salinas of Mexico had been the instigator of these talks, however. The much-debated NAFTA accord became effective on January 1, 1994, establishing one of the largest and richest markets in the world. As noted in Chapter 3, the three countries already had strong trade relationships before the agreement; NAFTA facilitated more trade—and trade with no (or few) restraints.

Although CFTA had been controversial at times, those discussions would have seemed placid compared to the political frenzy that surrounded the NAFTA debates. Pro-NAFTA and anti-NAFTA rallies were held at various sites around the United States.

In the United States, the potential problems of entering into a free trade agreement with a developing country (Mexico) caused the average citizen to be much more aware of these free trade discussions than had been true when only the United States and Canada were involved. Politicians who opposed NAFTA, particularly former presidential candidate Ross Perot, became quite visible and vocal about potential job losses to a country where wages are a fraction of those in the United States and Canada.

Because of the issues of wage differences and possible job losses along with environmental concerns, an unusual coalition of NAFTA opponents emerged that included labor, African Americans, and environmental activists. Some apparel manufacturers, along with leaders in other industries who wanted to retain production in the United States, were opposed to the agreement. Partisan politics were scrambled in a most unusual manner on the NAFTA debate. Many Democrats in Congress (including Democratic House Majority Leader Richard Gephardt) opposed President Clinton and voted against NAFTA, creating a deep division in the President's own party.

Supporters of NAFTA were equally diverse. The successful vote of 234 to 200 in the House[14] occurred *only* because of the support of Republican members. Republican Senate Minority Leader Robert Dole (usually a critic of Clinton) played a vital role in garnering support for NAFTA. Prior to the vote, all for-

mer presidents came out to show bipartisan solidarity for the trade accord. However, in the final days before the vote in the House, when NAFTA may not otherwise have passed, the President had to bargain hard to put together a majority vote. He did so "vote by vote—and interest group by interest group" until obtaining the necessary votes (Garland, Harbrecht, & Dunham, 1993, p. 35). In these bargaining rounds, congressional textile supporters were promised, in exchange for their votes for NAFTA, that the Administration would seek a 15-year phase-out of the MFA—rather than the proposed 10 years—in the GATT talks that soon would follow. (As we noted earlier in discussions on the Uruguay Round, textile supporters felt betrayed when the 15-year MFA phase-out was not achieved.)

The NAFTA agreement had to be voted on by the legislative bodies in all three participating countries. The Mexican Parliament readily supported the agreement. Although Canada's newly elected Prime Minister Chretien had opposed NAFTA in his campaign, he eventually supported the agreement, and the Canadian Parliament voted favorably. Although trade with Mexico was not particularly significant for Canada at the time, the agreement offered long-term potential. Moreover, the Canadians did not want to be left out of efforts that were expected to lead to far broader open market agreements in the Western Hemisphere.

U.S. textile industry leaders, generally *opposed* to freer trade, were out front campaigning for NAFTA. Except for executives in a few firms, the textile industry saw free trade with Mexico as the opening of a large market for their business. As we noted in Chapter 6, the textile mill products sector in Mexico was not well developed; therefore, Mexico represented a potential 25 percent market increase for U.S. textile producers. In an effort to offset concerns over possible U.S. job losses, board members of the American Textile Manufacturers Institute (ATMI) pledged that they would

---

[14]The Senate vote had appeared favorable for NAFTA, particularly with the support of Senator Dole and other Republicans. Therefore, the passage or defeat of NAFTA depended on the House vote.

not move their jobs, plants, or facilities to Mexico. The forceful support of textile leaders for NAFTA swayed some members of Congress from the major textile-producing states to vote in favor of the agreement (Barrett, 1993).

Of concern to textile and apparel leaders during the NAFTA debate was the potential for Far Eastern shipments to enter the U.S. market by way of Mexico. In early stages of the negotiations, U.S. textile leaders were successful in gaining a **yarn-forward provision** (also called the **triple transformation** provision) that would require yarn, fabric, and apparel to have been made in North America to be eligible for free trade. That is, apparel products must have gone through three substantial transformations to qualify as having been produced in North America (National Retail Federation, 1993). The Canadian apparel industry opposed this provision because that sector sources more than 60 percent of its fabrics from other counties. In the United States, in the last days of bidding for undecided votes on NAFTA, President Clinton responded to U.S. manufacturers' continued concerns about Far Eastern transshipment to the United States through Mexico by pledging to strengthen the Customs Service to guard against such violations (Ostroff, 1993a).

Retailers and importers, hearty advocates of free trade, had actively campaigned for NAFTA and were ecstatic over the completed agreement. For them, NAFTA meant added options for buying merchandise and, also for many major chains, the prospects of more easily establishing stores in the Mexican market. Moreover, the passage of NAFTA set a positive precedent for future free trade agreements ("Execs Cheer," 1993).

NAFTA provisions for textiles and apparel take effect in stages. All apparel made from North American yarn and fabric (meeting the "substantial transformation" rules) were immediately excluded from quota restraints, except for certain suits and shirts that are sub-ject to quotas in varying stages for 10 years. In addition, duties on these products were dropped immediately. In cases where market disruption occurs, quotas and duties may be reimposed on short notice. In addition to quota limitations on most apparel meeting NAFTA rules of origin, all garments made in Mexico under the U.S. 9802/807 and Special Regime programs can also enter the United States both duty- and quota-free. Limited imported products are permitted to qualify for free trade; these are generally goods not produced in North America. Once NAFTA was a reality, trade experts cautioned that it would take time for companies—and their partners in the other countries—to learn the intricacies of the rules. The U.S. Customs Service would monitor shipments coming into the United States, being lenient at first, but eventually imposing harsh penalties for offenders (Ostroff, 1993c).

In the end, trade policies such as NAFTA are implemented at the working level, and the impact varies. In all three NAFTA countries, the larger textile and apparel companies appear to be better prepared to face a **free trade** era than most smaller operations. Larger firms generally have better marketing networks, even within their respective countries, that can be expanded to include neighboring markets. Smaller companies are usually short-handed when it comes to marketing and management specialists who can access the differing economic, political, and cultural systems in other countries. Moreover, the smaller companies are more vulnerable to the competitive forces of business. In the free trade area, small operators compete with producers from three countries rather than one. Therefore, many "mom-and-pop" operations, particularly in Mexico, are being viewed as an "endangered species under free trade" (Fairchild News Service, 1993, p. 5).

In summary, NAFTA represents a new era in trade for the three nations. All segments of the softgoods industry will be affected in profound ways as executives and their companies venture into new partnerships and other business endeavors with their North American neighbors.

SUMMARY

From its earliest beginnings in England, the textile industry has garnered special attention in trade matters. In England, other European countries, and the United States, textile production was usually the first, or one of the first, areas to be afforded special protection from products made in other countries. The industry's vital role in a country's economic development encouraged governments to raise barriers to imported products that might threaten the health of the nation's own industry.

Although the English and American textile industries were the world's leading textile producers in the early 1900s, competitive conditions changed markedly during the Great Depression and thereafter. Japan became a major cotton exporter whose products posed a perceived threat to the more established industries in England and the United States. By the mid-1930s, the United States attempted to restrain Japanese cotton products, beginning a pattern that would continue. As additional textile supplier nations entered the global market, the growing competition fostered increasingly comprehensive and complex trade policies to deal with these trade problems.

Shortly after World War II, the General Agreement on Tariffs and Trade (GATT) became a force to liberalize overall world trade by reducing restrictive barriers that had evolved. The problems of textile and apparel trade, however, taxed the GATT system. Soon, GATT legitimized several exceptions to the agreement's normal rules to accommodate the problems of textile and apparel trade. First, the concept of "market disruption" altered the GATT ideals. Therefore, GATT developed a series of special multilateral trade agreements to accommodate textile and apparel trade: the STA, the LTA, the original MFA, MFA II, and MFA III, and MFA IV. Significantly, all of these arrangements removed an important segment of world trade from GATT rules applicable to other sectors and established provisions counter to GATT principles to cover textile and apparel trade.

The MFA represents a compromise to mediate the different positions of the exporting countries (developing countries) and the importing countries (developed countries). As a compromise solution, few actors are satisfied with the Arrangement. In recent years, the developing countries have been increasingly vocal about what they believe to be unduly harsh restrictions on their textile and apparel products.

On several occasions, as U.S. textile and apparel manufacturers have become impatient with what they perceived as the government's ineffectiveness in obtaining adequate measures to restrict LDC imports, producers have sought a legislative solution. That is, the industry's supporters in Congress have introduced bills to unilaterally control imports. These include the Mills bill in 1970, the Jenkins bill in 1985, the Textile and Apparel Trade Enforcement Act of 1987, and the Textile, Apparel, and Footwear Act of 1990. The three most recent of these bills passed both houses of Congress, but were vetoed by the president. All three narrowly missed receiving enough votes to override a presidential veto.

Finally, two major multilateral trade negotiations (MTNs), the Kennedy Round and the Tokyo Round, provided special concessions on most textile and apparel products. As tariffs were being reduced for most manufactured goods, those on most textile/apparel goods were reduced among the least of any product areas.

From the time the Uruguay Round was launched in 1986, textile trade was an issue, as the developing exporting countries expressed frustrations over growing restrictions on their textile and apparel products. One of their primary goals in this round of talks was to have textile trade brought back under normal GATT rules rather than "managed" under the MFA. For seven years, the Uruguay Round talks moved slowly; one deadline after another passed with no resolution. Finally, on December 15, 1993, the Contracting Parties of GATT concluded the Uruguay Round, including plans to phase out the MFA over a 10-year period. Agreeing to phase out the MFA meant, in effect, a re-writing of the rules of world textile trade, replacing a system of "managed" trade that had begun with the Short Term Agreement in 1961. Developed importing countries were disappointed that although they were expected to open their markets and provide greater market access, some exporting nations seemed unwilling to reciprocate.

Another landmark trade agreement, the North American Free Trade Agreement, was signed in late 1993. Effective January 1, 1994, Canada, Mexico, and the United States entered into a free trade agreement that was expected to have a profound impact on the softgoods industry in North America.

GLOSSARY

Arrangement Regarding International Trade in Textiles (also known as the *Multifiber Arrangement* or *MFA*) is a general trade framework, also called a regime, under which textile and apparel trade occurs.

Basket extractor mechanism is an EC provision whereby unrestricted textile and apparel products become subject to controls if imports reach a certain level.

Bilateral agreements are agreements between two ("bi-") countries. Under current global textile and apparel trade policies, bilateral agreements are the most common form of restriction on trade.

"Burden sharing" refers to the distribution of LDC textile and apparel imports among the developed countries. The industrialized countries are aware of the responsibility for assisting the LDCs in their development—which requires giving the LDCs access to their markets. Problems arise as developed countries concern themselves about whether peer nations are sharing equally in the "burden."

"Call" mechanism or *consultation call* has been a U.S. government provision to restrict imports from a country in a category not already under quota restraints.

Category is a textile/apparel product or aggregation of similar products for import control purposes. Examples include the following: women's cotton woven blouses, men's wool trousers, or boys' manufactured fiber knit shirts. Several thousand types of textile and apparel products are grouped into major categories. Limitations on imported textile and apparel products are usually placed on certain categories.

Circumvention refers to activities that bypass quota limits on shipments. The most common form occurs when a country with limited quota transships products through another country with available quota. According to technical GATT interpretation, this is the *only* activity considered *circumvention*. However, in common usage circumvention often has a broader meaning than just transshipment. It also includes misrepresentation of the product to avoid quota limitations. Examples include giving an inaccurate item count or mislabeling of the fiber content/product category of merchandise, which affects the quota category under which products are imported.

Countervailing duties are added duties levied on an imported good to offset subsidies to producers or exporters of that good in the exporting country. GATT rules permit these duties if material injury to the importing country's producers occurs.

Discriminatory restrictions are trade restraints that discriminate against some countries but not others. That is, limits are imposed on products from some countries and not from others.

Exporting countries are the supplier nations. Although most countries export certain goods, in textile and apparel trade the term *exporting countries* refers to the NICs and the low-wage developing nations whose textile/apparel industries are oriented largely toward exporting to the markets of the industrialized countries.

Fast track authority is a provision whereby trade agreements or other bills that come before Congress may be either approved or disapproved but cannot be amended.

Fiber, Fabric and Apparel Coalition for Trade (FFACT) is a textile and apparel industry and labor coalition formed in 1985 to fight for legislation to restrict imports.

Free trade or **liberalized trade** refers to trade without restrictions such as tariffs, quotas, and VERs.

Generalized system of preferences (GSP) is a system of tariff preferences designed to encourage the expansion of manufactured and semi-manufactured exports from developing countries.

Global quotas represent a limit on the total textile and apparel imports from all sources combined permitted into the country during a period of time.

"Growth on growth" refers to the provision of the Uruguay Round textile and apparel agreement which requires *additional growth* over and above the typical 6 percent quota growth rates that exist under the MFA.

Harmonized Tariff Schedule is a system of tariff classification that replaced the Tariff Sched-

ule of the United States (TSUS) in 1989. The new system, which applies to more than 5,000 overall categories of products, has a standardized six-digit international code used by all participating trading nations known as the **Harmonized System**.

Import substitution is an effort within a country to encourage substitution of domestic products for previously imported goods. This may be an effort promoted by a country's government, particularly if the country is encouraging development of its industry.

Importing countries are the recipients of textile and apparel products from the exporting countries. Although most countries import certain goods, in textile and apparel trade, the term *importing countries* refers to the more developed nations whose markets are attractive to supplier nations.

Infant industry protection refers to temporary protection (in the form of tariffs or non-tariff barriers) to help establish an industry and foster its competitiveness in world markets.

Integration refers to returning textile products to the rules of GATT that apply to all other trade. Under the MFA phase-out, importing nations must select a portion of textile imports (by Harmonized System product categories) to be "returned" to GATT rules, which applied to textile trade prior to the MFA and its predecessor agreements. Products that are integrated into GATT will no longer have quotas on imports.

Market access is the term used during the Uruguay Round negotiations to refer to the importing countries' desire for reciprocity. That is, the developed countries believed that if they are required to open their markets more freely to the developing exporting countries' textile and apparel products, the developed countries should also have an opportunity to ship to the developing countries. Market access was one of the most contentious issues in negotiations over the MFA phase-out.

Market disruption was a term embraced under GATT (originally in 1959–1960), specifically for textile problems, which fostered the following exceptions to GATT fundamentals: discrimination against a particular country, permitting a "potential" increase in imports to justify added restrictions, and allowing price differences to justify import restrictions when disruption of domestic markets was occurring or threatened.

Minimum viable production allows a country to restrict textile imports on the grounds that the nation must preserve a certain basic level of production capability for the potential defense needs of that country.

Most favored nation (MFN) treatment occurs when one country agrees to give one country the same trade concessions it grants to any other MFN recipients. For example, goods from a country accorded MFN status by the United States would be assessed lower tariffs in the U.S. tariff schedule. The concept may apply to non-tariff measures as well. GATT members have agreed to give each other MFN status. Preferential treatment accorded to developing countries, customs unions, and free trade areas all represent allowable exceptions to the MFN concept.

Multilateral agreements are agreements among many ("multi-") countries.

Nonreciprocity is an accepted principle under GATT whereby the developing countries are not required to offer fully reciprocal concessions. In general, under GATT, nations extend comparable concessions to each other, but the nonreciprocity principle permits the LDCs to impose trade restrictions on products from other countries.

Non-tariff barriers (NTBs) are measures other than tariffs imposed by governments that restrict imports with or without the intent to do so. Examples are quotas, import licensing, labeling requirements, or technical standards.

Protection or *protectionism* refers to a government's efforts to limit or exclude those imports that compete with the country's own production.

Quota flexibility refers to the degree of variation permitted under the MFA and bilateral agreements in the physical volume of products that can be shipped in the aggregate, in group ceilings, and categories with specific limits. Flexibility includes swing, carryover, and carry forward (AAMA, 1980).

Regime or *international regime* is a set of governing arrangements that affect relationships of interdependence among countries. The Multifiber Arrangement is considered an international regime.

Retail Industry Trade Action Coalition (RITAC) is a coalition of retailers and importers formed in 1985 to oppose trade restraints, particularly textile and apparel trade restraints.

Rules of origin are laws, regulations, and administrative practices that are applied to ascribe a country of origin to goods in international trade. The U.S. rules of origin for textile and apparel trade were modified to prevent transshipment.

Safeguard mechanism is a provision of the Uruguay Round textile and apparel agreement to be used during the phase-out or transition period. The safeguard mechanism permits an importing country to impose import restraints on products if that government believes imports are causing serious damage or the threat of serious damage to the domestic industry. The importing country is permitted to impose restraints on products *from a specific country* and *for a maximum of three years*, or until those products are integrated into GATT rules.

Surge is a sharp increase in imports from a country from one year to the next, usually in specific product areas. Domestic manufacturers consider surges disruptive to markets.

Tariffs are taxes on imported goods; tariffs are also known as import duties. Often, tariffs are designed to protect domestic producers from foreign competition.

Trade adjustment assistance is funding granted under the U.S. trade acts to those individuals and firms proven to have suffered injury as a result of the U.S. government's policies to promote freer trade. Firms that are "certified" as having suffered injury may obtain technical and financial assistance. Individuals who lose their jobs may obtain compensation, retraining, and, at times, relocation at government expense.

Triple transformation or *triple rule of origin* is another way of stating the yarn-forward provision of NAFTA. Apparel, for example, must have been through three substantial transformations (i.e., yarn processing, fabric formation, and apparel assembly) to qualify as having been produced in North America.

Unilateral restraints are restrictions imposed by one ("uni-") country against another.

Voluntary export restraints (VER), also known as voluntary restraint agreements (VRAs), voluntary export quotas, or sometimes export restraints, are agreements in which an exporting country agrees to limit exports so that the importing country will not formally impose quotas, tariffs, or other import controls. VERs are referred to euphemistically as "voluntary," but they are not truly voluntary; they are in fact quotas.

Yarn-forward provision is a facet of the NAFTA accord that requires that textile and apparel products must be made of North American components "from the yarn forward" to qualify for free trade. The intent of this provision is to require the use of North American intermediate inputs. Also see **triple transformation**.

SUGGESTED READINGS

Aggarwal, V. (1985). *Liberal protectionism: The international politics of organized textile trade.* Berkeley, CA: University of California Press.
A study of the evolution of the international regime for textile trade (through the 1981 MFA renewal), including the political and economic factors affecting regime development and change.

Blokker, N. (1989). *International regulation of world trade in textiles.* Dordrecht, The Netherlands: Martinus Nijhoff.
A study of international textile trade policies from a legal perspective.

Brandis, B. (1982). *The making of textile trade policy, 1935–1981.* Washington, DC: American Textile Manufacturers Institute.
An industry-sponsored review of the development of textile trade policies.

Catudal, H. (1961). *The General Agreement on Tariffs and Trade: An article-by-article analysis in layman's language.* (Publication No. 7235). Washington, DC: Department of State.
An interpretation of the GATT treaty in lay language.

Choi, Y., Chung, H., & Marian, N. (1985). *The Multi-Fiber Arrangement in theory and practice.* London: Frances Pinter Ltd.
A review of the MFA developed by representatives for the developing country exporters of textile and apparel products.

Cline, W. (1990). *The future of world trade in textiles and apparel* (revised edition). Washington, DC: Institute for International Economics.
This study, an update of Cline's earlier work, analyzes the costs and benefits of MFA phase-out plans for different countries and groups.

Dickerson, K. (1988). The textile sector as a special GATT case. *Clothing and Textile Research Journal, 6*(3), 17–25.
A review of special trade policies and structures under GATT to serve the textile and apparel industries.

Friman, H. R. (1990). *Patchwork protectionism: Textile trade policy in the United States, Japan, and West Germany.* Ithaca: NY: Cornell University Press.

This book is a study of protectionist policies using a comparative analysis of U.S., Japanese, and German textile trade policies.

General Agreement on Tariffs and Trade. (1984, July). *Textiles and clothing in the world economy.* Geneva, Switzerland: Author.
A GATT analysis of textile trade policies.

General Agreement on Tariffs and Trade. (1994). Agreement on textiles and clothing, MTN/FA/Corr. 8. *Final Act Embodying the Results of the Uruguay Round of Multilateral Trade Negotiations.* Geneva: Author.
The textile and apparel section of the Uruguay Round agreement spells out the terms of phase-out of the MFA and other matters pertaining to trade for the sector.

Hamilton, C. (Ed.). (1990). *The Uruguay Round: Textiles trade and the developing countries.* Washington, DC: World Bank.
A collection of papers from academic researchers, textile experts, and negotiators to address the effects of the MFA on the trade of developing countries as well as their suggestions on ways to phase out the MFA.

Hurewitz, L. (1993). *The GATT Uruguay Round: A negotiating history (1986–1992): Textiles.* Deventer, The Netherlands: Kluwer Law and Taxation Publishers.
A negotiating history of the textiles portion of the Uruguay Round through 1992.

Khanna, S. (1991). *International trade in textiles: MFA quotas and a developing exporting country.* New Delhi: SAGE.
A case study in India of the effects of the MFA on developing countries.

Khanna, S. (1994, March). The new GATT agreement: Implications for the world's textile and clothing industries. *Textile Outlook International,* pp. 10–37.
An overview of the implications of the Uruguay Round textile agreement.

Silbertson, Z., & Ledic, M. (1989). *The future of the Multi-fiber Arrangement: Implications for the UK economy.* London: Her Majesty's Stationery Office.
An evaluation of the effects of the MFA on the UK economy; however, the conclusions are helpful for textile and apparel trade more broadly.

Sweet, M. (1994, February). Recent trade treaties likely to stimulate continuing changes in global sourcing of apparel. *Industry, Trade, and Technology Review* (published by the U.S. International Trade Commission), pp. 1–8.
Implications of NAFTA and the Uruguay Round for apparel sourcing.

United States International Trade Commission. (1978). *The history and current status of the Multifiber Arrangement.* (USITC Publication 850) Washington, DC: Author.
A review of the historical development of U.S. textile trade policies and an overview of the implementation of the Multifiber Arrangement.

U.S. Senate, Committee on Finance. (1985). *Textile and Apparel Trade Enforcement Act: Hearing before the Subcommittee on International Trade* (1985, July 15). Washington, DC: U.S. Government Printing Office.
The testimony considered in hearings on the Jenkins bill provides a good summary of the perspectives of various interest groups concerned with textile trade and textile trade policy.

U.S. Senate, Committee on Finance (1985). *Textile and Apparel Trade Enforcement Act: Hearing Before the Subcommittee on International Trade* (1985, September 12, 23). Washington, DC: U.S. Government Printing Office.
The testimony considered in hearings on the Jenkins bill provides a good summary of the perspectives of various interest groups concerned with textile trade and textile trade policy.

INTRODUCTION

As global textile and apparel production and trade have become increasingly competitive and difficult, a number of unique trade policies and other provisions have evolved to provide special treatment for the problems of trade in these sectors. Chapter 10 provided an overview of the development of the major textile and apparel trade policies.

The complex system of textile and apparel trade policies requires an equally complex array of structures for the implementation of those policies. The term *structure* is being used as a generic term to include organizations, networks, and other systems associated with the development and implementation of textile and apparel trade policies. Most of these are structures devoted to operationalizing the existing textile trade policies at global and national levels; however, in a few cases the organizations we will consider are devoted to the dismantling of those trade policies.

In this chapter, we will examine various structures associated with textile and apparel trade policies (both those that develop and implement the policies as well as those that seek to dismantle them). We will consider these structures at both the international level and the national level, with primary emphasis on the United States. We will review both the "official" governmental structures and those of **special interest groups**. Although the return of textile and apparel to normal GATT rules will change or eliminate some of these, these structures are expected to remain in place for well past the turn of the century.

A discussion of all the organizations involved in textile and apparel trade would be too lengthy for purposes of this book; therefore, key organizations and structures are presented with the acknowledgment that many worthwhile efforts cannot be included.

11

Structures for Facilitating and "Managing" Textile and Apparel Trade

STRUCTURES AT THE INTERNATIONAL LEVEL

"Official" Governmental Structures

The World Trade Organization (WTO)*

When the Uruguay Round was signed in December 1993, the agreement included the establishment of the World Trade Organization (WTO) in 1995 to replace the GATT. The WTO provides a permanent forum to address new issues facing the international trading system. The change of GATT into the WTO will be gradual; they will exist in parallel for some time.

The WTO will implement the trade agreements reached in the Uruguay Round by bringing all agreements under one institutional umbrella. The WTO extends and refines the responsibilities that were under GATT by covering more areas of trade, and the WTO has greatly increased powers to set rules and resolve problems in international trade disputes. In the past, because the GATT operated

---

*As this book goes to press, this assumes that the WTO will become a reality.

on a consensus basis, it was often criticized for lacking real power to resolve trade disputes.

Two new areas are covered by the World Trade Organization that previously were not covered by GATT. In addition to covering traditional trade areas of agriculture and manufactured products, the WTO's responsibilities also include trade in (1) services and (2) trade-related intellectual property rights (TRIPS).

Until the establishment of the WTO, the GATT was the principal international body concerned with trade, which, of course, included textile and apparel trade. Although textile and apparel trade provisions were (and still are, during the phase-out of the MFA) atypical, they occurred as a GATT-sponsored exception to the General Agreement.

As we learned in the previous chapter, the trade policies that evolved for textiles and apparel under the auspices of GATT represent a significant departure from the rules that apply to other sectors. In effect, textile and apparel trade was singled out from the general principles of GATT and given a special regime of its own. Initially, special trade rules for textiles and apparel were justified for the

FIGURE 11–1
Headquarters of the World Trade Organization (WTO), formerly the General Agreement on Tariffs and Trade (GATT), Centre William Rappared, in Geneva, Switzerland.

Source: Photo courtesy of GATT.

following reasons: (1) the challenge presented by "low-cost" imports was unique to textiles, and later to apparel, and (2) the production and employment in those industries were seen as critical to the importing countries' overall economic activity (GATT, 1984).

Since 1961, multilateral arrangements negotiated under the auspices of GATT provided a framework for regulating textile and apparel trade. First came the Short-Term Arrangement Regarding International Trade in Cotton Textiles (STA) and the Long-Term Arrangement Regarding International Trade in Cotton Textiles. These were followed in 1974 by the Multifiber Arrangement (MFA), which was renewed six times (three of those were extensions of MFA IV). Under the MFA, textile trading nations negotiated bilateral agreements that regulated partially the flow of textile and apparel imports from exporting countries to the importing markets.

Logically, it follows that the special policies for textile and apparel trade required unique structures to implement those arrangements. Within the World Trade Organization, one division exists specifically to deal with textile and apparel trade issues: the Textiles Division. Another body, the Textiles Monitoring Body, is charged with supervising the implementation of the WTO textile agreement.

The Textiles Division. The Textiles Division, previously the Special Projects Division under GATT, is the only division that exists to handle trade matters *for a specific sector*, other than one for agriculture. The Textile Division manages a wide range of concerns related to textile and apparel trade. An important role of this division is to service the Textiles Monitoring Body (to be discussed in the following section). Additionally, the division services ad hoc committees concerned with textile trade matters.

Prior to the agreement to phase out the Multifiber Arrangement, this division also serviced the Textiles Committee, consisting of representatives of the more than 40 parties (the EU was considered as *one* party) of the Arrangement. Since the Textiles Committee was the MFA's political forum for evaluating its effectiveness and considering renewals, the committee was eliminated as the MFA phase-out began (author's personal communication with GATT sources, 1986, 1988, 1994).

Textiles Monitoring Body (TMB). In the Uruguay Round negotiations to bring textile trade back under GATT rules, the plan called for a Textiles Monitoring Body (TMB) to be established. The purpose of this body is to

FIGURE 11–2
Jan-Eirik Sorensen, Director of the Textile Division of WTO (GATT).

Source: Photo by Kitty Dickerson.

TMB

supervise the implementation of the agreements, to handle disputes, and to conduct a major review before the end of each stage of the phase-out of the MFA.

The TMB replaces the Textiles Surveillance Body (TSB), which was established by an article in the Multifiber Arrangement and operated until the Uruguay Round was completed. The TSB was a "multilateral surveillance institution to supervise the implementation" of the MFA (GATT, 1984, p. 75). The TSB was responsible for seeing that all bilateral agreements were consistent with the MFA and handled all routine problems and complaints related to textile and apparel trade under the MFA. In effect, the Textiles Monitoring Body assumes many of the same functions of the TSB.

If two or more trading nations have a dispute regarding textile trade, they may bring their problem before the Textiles Monitoring Body for dispute resolution. Although the TMB cannot force any party to comply with its recommendations, efforts are made to resolve problems. Findings of the TMB are not binding if a member country considers itself unable to conform to the recommendations of the TMB. After extended deliberations, if a matter is still not resolved, the member may bring the matter before the Council for Trade in Goods or the Dispute Settlement Body.

Because of the political nature of the Textile Monitoring Body's functions, the group is composed of 10 members—a carefully balanced number of members from both the developing countries (exporters) and developed countries (importers). Members shall rotate at appropriate intervals. Although TMB members come from the national delegations, individuals are expected to function as impartial participants rather than serving their own nation's interests. The group works in strict confidentiality, which encourages countries to share data and also makes it easier for members to move from a national position to one of consensus.

Although the exact structure or composition of the TMB has not been defined as this book goes to press, it is believed that the new body will draw heavily on the experience of the Textiles Surveillance Body. Although the 10 representatives are drawn from various national delegations, the chairman is an international diplomat attached to the GATT (WTO) who serves in an impartial role (GATT, 1992, 1993; personal communication with GATT staff and R. Shepherd, 1993, 1994; Sung, 1994).

Other Textile Bodies

- The Negotiating Group on Textiles and Clothing was the GATT body to carry out the program of negotiations for the Uruguay Round. The Uruguay Round text resulted in large part from the work of that body.
- In addition to the standing bodies designated to coordinate textile trade matters, special "working parties" or task forces have been assigned responsibilities for specific textile trade matters.

Other International Organizations

A number of international organizations may become involved in specific aspects of textile and apparel trade. Two examples are:

1. *The United Nations Conference on Trade and Development (UNCTAD)*, whose main offices are in Geneva, is part of the UN framework. Its aim is to further the interests of the developing countries in matters related to their economic development, including trade aspects. UNCTAD has followed the situation of international trade in textiles and has opposed the increasing restrictions on textile and apparel products. UNCTAD supported the establishment of a separate organization of developing exporting countries, the International Textiles and Clothing Bureau, which focuses specifically on textile/apparel trade concerns. UNCTAD remains, however, an important trade forum for the LDCs.

2. *The International Labor Office (ILO)*, also located in Geneva and under the United Nations, conducts research on global production and trade shifts for various sectors, including several related to textiles and apparel. Studies focus on international labor standards, working conditions, employment and development, shifts in comparative advantage, and other topics relevant to the global textile and apparel sectors. The ILO Textiles Committee focuses on timely issues related to textile and apparel employment, working conditions, training, worker rights, and similar issues related to work in the industry (personal communication with ILO staff, 1994).

3. *The International Trade Center (ITC)*, also located in Geneva, is part of the United Nations system. The primary role of ITC is to assist developing countries in their trade promotion efforts. This includes developing national trade promotion strategies, working with national governments to establish institutions and services within the country to facilitate exporting, and helping countries find export markets for their products (personal communication with ITC staff, various dates).

4. *The Organization for Economic Cooperation and Development (OECD)*, located in Paris, conducts research and publishes studies on various aspects of the textile and apparel sectors from time to time as part of the ongoing work programs cited in Chapter 3.

National Missions

Since GATT headquarters (as well as many other important international organizations) are in Geneva, most countries that are Contracting Parties to the agreement have diplomatic representations (typically called *missions*) in that city. Within each mission, the size and backgrounds of staff who represent trade interests vary a great deal. Usually the major industrialized nations have fairly large, specialized staffs, while many of the LDCs

have limited staff to represent all of the country's interests.

The U.S. trade ambassador to GATT (who is a deputy U.S. trade representative) is located in a separate office in Geneva. Several staff members handle specific trade issues. At press time, William Tagliani, U.S. Trade Attaché, handles textile trade matters along with trade for other sectors. Tagliani's predecessor, Robert Shepherd, served as U.S. Minister-Counselor of Textiles in Geneva for much of the life of the MFA, providing ongoing expertise which was helpful to the United States during the years in which the MFA was fully in effect (Figure 11–3). Like this predecessor, Tagliani receives policy guidance and technical support as necessary from U.S. government agencies in Washington, D.C.

Most other countries are less fortunate than the United States with respect to both the size of staff and the ongoing expertise for representing textile interests. Developing countries with limited resources may have one or two trade ministers or counselors to represent all sectors; therefore, attention to textile matters is far more limited.

Special Interest Groups

The International Textiles and Clothing Bureau (ITCB)

In the mid-1980s, the International Textiles and Clothing Bureau (ITCB) developed as a result of earlier efforts by exporting countries to form a coalition to oppose increasing restraints on their textile and apparel exports. Now a formal organization recognized by the Swiss government, the ITCB coordinates the interests of approximately 20 textile/apparel exporting nations. The organization is supported by member governments who contribute according to the percentage of import markets taken by that country (if Country X supplies 15 percent of the textile and apparel

FIGURE 11–3

U.S. officials who handle textile trade matters in Geneva work closely with government agencies in Washington. Robert Shepherd (left), who served as U.S. Minister-Counselor of Textiles for most of the life of the MFA, and William Tagliani (right), U.S. Trade Attaché in Geneva, whose responsibilities now include textile trade, confer on policy issues with Ambassador Jennifer Hillman in Washington (see Figure 11-6).

Source: Photo by USTR staff.

market in the importing countries [combined], then Country X provides 15 percent of ITCB's budget) (personal communication with S. Bagchi, 1988).

ITCB provides a forum in which member countries can become more fully informed on textile and apparel trade matters, particularly since a number of the members do not have specialized trade assistance. ITCB members share information and exchange views to become more informed individually and collectively. Skeptical of data provided by their developed-country trading partners, ITCB staff conduct a certain amount of research on their own. Finally, the ITCB provides members an opportunity to speak with a unified voice on trade matters (personal communication with S. Bagchi, 1988, 1994).

One of the ITCB's primary efforts was to work toward the elimination of the Multifiber Arrangement. Very early in the Uruguay Round discussions, the ITCB submitted a strong statement to the Negotiating Group for Textiles and Clothing, which, in effect, said the original intent of the MFA had been far exceeded. ITCB noted, "the Arrangement and subsidiary bilateral agreements have become increasingly restrictive in extent and intensity, accentuating the discriminatory character of the existing trade regime in textiles." The statement added, "exports of textiles and clothing of developing countries have been subject to discriminatory restrictions which have imposed intolerable burdens on their economies" (International Textiles and Clothing Bureau, 1988, pp. 1, 2).

International Industry Federations

The following are federations of industry associations from member countries. These federations include both importing nations and exporting nations as members; therefore, these groups do not take positions on trade. The federations provide an opportunity for industry leaders to establish international networks and to consider matters of common concern to the industries in member nations. In many respects, these federations provide opportunities to build relationships among representatives of countries that may otherwise be at odds over textile and apparel trade problems.

International Apparel Federation (IAF). The International Apparel Federation includes the national apparel associations in nearly 40 countries (counting the EU member countries separately). The American Apparel Manufacturers Association, for example, represents the United States in this federation. IAF headquarters are located in Berlin, Germany.

International Textile Manufacturers Federation (ITMF). Like IAF, the International Textile Manufacturers Federation includes national associations from member countries. For example, the American Textile Manufacturers Institute represents the United States in ITMF. This federation's headquarters are in Zurich, Switzerland.

Retailing. No international federation appears to exist for retailing. Rather, activities are coordinated through national and regional retail groups.

FIGURE 11–4
Sanjoy Bagchi, Executive Director of the International Textiles and Clothing Bureau (ITCB), was India's Chief Textile Negotiator earlier in his career. More recently, he served as a textile advisor to the Director-General of GATT.

Source: Photo by Kitty Dickerson.

STRUCTURES AT THE NATIONAL LEVEL: THE UNITED STATES

"Official" Governmental Structures

At this juncture, as we begin discussion on structures for facilitating and managing trade at the U.S. level, a review of the international structures and how United States policies and structures relate to those will be helpful. Figure 11–5 provides an overview of these relationships.

Figure 11–5 reviews for us the hierarchy of WTO bodies under which the Multifiber Arrangement is administered. At this point, it is appropriate to consider how the U.S. system meshes with functions at the international level. To begin, we shall consider the two portions of Figure 11–5 not covered previously.

Section 204 of the Agricultural Act

Although this provision may seem an oddity in present-day textile trade policies, it is quite significant to U.S. involvement in global textile policies. This provision is the cornerstone of U.S. participation in the MFA.

In the 1950s, when cotton was the primary fiber in both U.S. production and the growing volume of imports, U.S. textile industry advocates sought relief (or protection, depending upon one's perspective) from imports under Section 22 of the Agricultural Adjustment Act. That provision authorized the president to impose import fees or quotas to restrict imports of agricultural commodities (or the products thereof) if those imports interfered with U.S. agricultural programs. Although several textile industry efforts to secure special assistance under Section 22 failed, a provision in the Agricultural Act of 1956 (Section 204), which established cotton export subsidies, also *authorized textile import quotas*. This act *authorized the negotiation of bilateral agreements*; the first negotiated was the 1957 five-year agreement with Japan. Section 204 of the

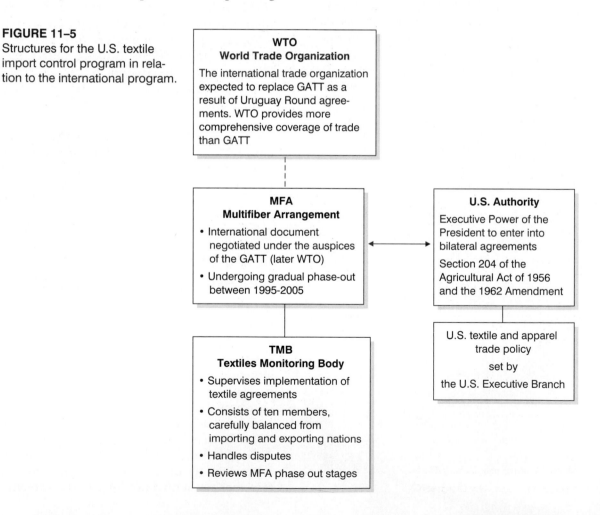

FIGURE 11–5
Structures for the U.S. textile import control program in relation to the international program.

SECTION 204 OF THE AGRICULTURAL ACT

U.S. authority for establishing textile quotas was extended when the Agricultural Act of 1956 was amended in June 1962, to provide:

> that the President may, whenever he determines such action appropriate, negotiate with representatives of foreign governments in an effort to obtain agreements limiting the export from such countries and the importation into the United States of any agricultural commodity or product manufactured therefrom or textiles or textile products, and the President is authorized to issue regulations governing the entry or withdrawal from warehouse

> of any such commodity, product, textiles, or textile products to carry out any such agreement. In addition, if a multi-lateral agreement has been or shall be concluded under the authority of this section among countries accounting for a significant part of world trade in the articles with respect to which the agreement was concluded, the President may also issue, in order to carry out such an agreement, regulations governing the entry or withdrawal from warehouse of the same articles which are the products of countries not parties to the agreement. (Brandis, 1982, pp. 22–23; original source: U.S. Code Annotated, Title 7, Sec. 1854.)

Agricultural Act of 1956 was amended in June 1962 to extend U.S. textile quota authority even further. (See "Section 204 of the Agricultural Act" box insert.)

Although the original focus was on cotton textiles, consistent with an agricultural policy, textile industry proponents were able to secure coverage for all textiles, regardless of fiber. Moreover, it is the 1962 amendment that permits the United States to apply *unilateral restraints* on imports from any country that is not a part of a multilateral agreement. In contrast to the MFA, which permits unilateral restraints against countries that are parties to the MFA, Section 204 of the Agricultural Act permits unilateral restraints by the United States against countries that are not parties to the MFA (AAMA, 1980).

In 1980, for example, the United States imposed unilateral restraints on seven apparel categories from China, under Section 204 of the Agricultural Act. At that time China was not a participant in the MFA. After China became a participant in the MFA, the United States negotiated bilateral agreements with the Chinese to limit textile and apparel shipments. In another instance, Section 204 of the Agricultural Act has provided the basis for the U.S.

bilateral agreements with Taiwan, since Taiwan is not a member of GATT and the MFA.

U.S. Executive Branch

U.S. textile and apparel trade policy is set by the executive branch. Although the president has the power to set trade policy, the United States Trade Representative (USTR) is the chief official—with cabinet-level and ambassadorial rank—responsible for representing the president in coordinating U.S. foreign trade matters. The U.S. Trade Representative coordinates and represents the U.S. position in international trade negotiations. The USTR designation also refers to the White House office, which the representative heads.

The Chief U.S. Textile Negotiator (and assistants) are located within the USTR complex. Significantly, the textile and apparel sector is the only one with its own institutionalized negotiator within USTR (Samolis & Emrich, 1986).

Three tiers of committees represent the principal mechanism for developing and coordinating U.S. government positions on international trade and trade-related investment issues. These are the highest level bod-

FIGURE 11–6
Ambassador Jennifer Hillman is Chief Textile Negotiator in the Office of the U.S. Trade Representative.

Source: Photo by Kitty Dickerson.

ies concerned with trade policies, and although these groups would not normally be involved in day-to-day textile trade issues, these are likely to be involved on trade matters that have serious implications for the nation's broad interests.

- *The Trade Policy Review Group (TPRG)*, chaired by USTR and composed of individuals at the under-secretary level, considers particularly significant policy issues, especially if they cannot be resolved at the TPSC (below). This is a subcabinet interagency group central to trade policy coordination.
- *Trade Policy Staff Committee (TPSC)*, also an interagency body chaired by USTR, is the working level first assigned responsibility for economic analysis of trade matters. Interagency committees are assigned the projects, and these groups attempt to reach a consensus. If agreement is not reached at this level, or if particularly significant policy matters are at stake, issues are then taken up by the TPRG.
- *National Economic Council (NEC)* is the final tier of the interagency trade policy mecha-

nism. Chaired by the president, the NEC includes appropriate cabinet members and several other top-level government officials. The NEC Deputies Committee considers decisions from the TPRG as well as particularly important or controversial trade-related issues. Once policy decisions are made, USTR is responsible for implementation of those decisions (United States Trade Representative, 1993).

We have discussed the linkage of the U.S. textile and apparel trade structures to those at the international level. At this point, we will focus more specifically on the structures and mechanisms within the United States devoted to managing textile and apparel trade interests. Figure 11–8 displays major U.S. structures that provide the liaison to international authority. A brief discussion follows.

Committee for the Implementation of Textile Agreements (CITA)

CITA carries out the day-to-day operations of the U.S. textile and apparel import control program. CITA is an interagency committee, chaired by the Deputy Assistant Secretary of

Commerce for Textiles, Apparel, and Consumer Goods, the top textile official at the U.S. Department of Commerce. Most of CITA's daily work is handled by Commerce personnel. CITA agencies are as follows:

- *The United States Trade Representative (USTR)* is responsible for trade policies. USTR is represented in CITA because the textile negotiations are handled by that agency's staff. Moreover, it is important to coordinate CITA's work with USTR's broader trade policy efforts.
- *The U.S. Department of State (DOS)* represents the broader diplomatic interests of the country. That is, if textile trade policies endanger political relationships, the Department of State provides a diplomatic perspective to balance the pressures that

may be exerted by domestic special interest groups.

- *The U.S. Department of Commerce (DOC)* represents U.S. commercial interests. The Department of Commerce, perhaps more than any other cabinet-level structure, is concerned about the economic health and international competitiveness of U.S. industries. Therefore, the DOC representative in CITA may have more of an "industry-advocacy" stance than others.
- *The U.S. Department of Treasury (DOT)* represents a free-trade perspective within the CITA group. The U.S. Customs Service is under the Department of Treasury.
- *The U.S. Department of Labor (DOL)* represents the interests of domestic labor. The DOL provides input on trade policies that may affect the U.S. workforce.

As Figure 11–8 illustrates, CITA receives information from a number of sources. The U.S. Customs Service controls the entry of products under quota agreements; therefore, Customs works closely with CITA. The Department of Commerce Office of Textiles and Apparel (OTEXA) is the central office within the government responsible for monitoring trade and tracking each category from each controlled country. Efforts of the U.S. Customs Service and OTEXA will be discussed in greater detail in sections that follow.

A study by the General Accounting Office reported that the CITA process was generally adequate but that actions were weighted somewhat toward protecting the domestic industry (Davidson et al., 1986). We must remember, however, that this was the purpose of the textile import control program, of which CITA is a key part.

U.S. Congress

The U.S. Congress plays an important role in influencing textile trade policy. This may occur through passage of trade legislation or in more informal ways. As Figure 11–8 indi-

FIGURE 11–7
Rita D. Hayes, Deputy Assistant Secretary, Textile, Apparel, and Consumer Goods Industries, U.S. Department of Commerce, serves as Chairman of CITA.

Source: Photo by Kitty Dickerson.

FIGURE 11–8

Structures for the U.S. textile import control program.

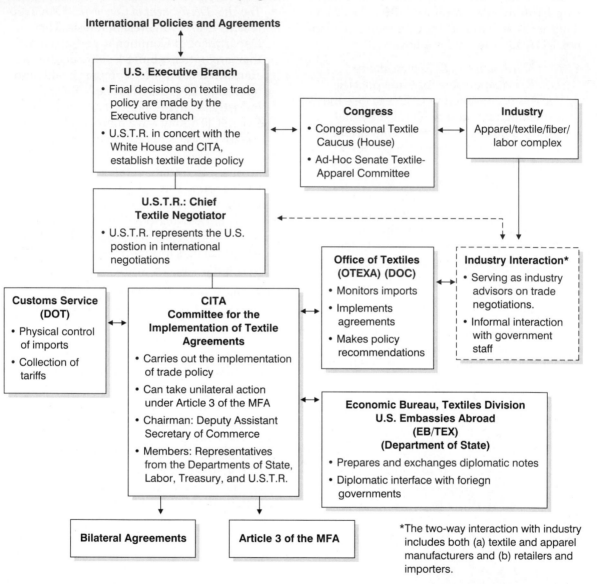

cates, the industry has input into congressional activities. This occurs primarily through the **Congressional Textile Caucus**, a group of nearly 90 members of Congress who are supportive of textile and apparel trade interests. As might be expected, most members of the Textile Caucus are from states in which textile and apparel production contributes significantly to the economy and to employment. Former Caucus Chairman Rep. Derrick Butler (R-SC) noted, "The mission of the Caucus is to promote the textile, apparel, and fiber industries across the country" (LaRussa, 1989b, p. 15).

The bipartisan Textile Caucus has been quite influential, boasting among its members many powerful leaders of both the Senate and the House. Members of the Textile Caucus were instrumental in introducing and promoting the Jenkins bill, the 1987 textile bill, and the 1990 textile bill in Congress. In addition, the caucus represents industry concerns on other matters that may affect U.S. textile and apparel interests; examples include the NAFTA accord and legislation pertaining to the Caribbean Basin Initiative.

The Office of Textiles and Apparel (OTEXA)

The Office of Textiles and Apparel (OTEXA) in the U.S. Department of Commerce has the largest concentration of government staff devoted to textile and apparel trade matters. As part of the DOC International Trade Administration, OTEXA has a specialized staff who coordinate a variety of functions related to trade in the sector. Figure 11–9 displays the major divisions within OTEXA. A brief discussion of the functions of each follows.

Industry Assessment Division (IAD). The IAD compiles and monitors data (originated elsewhere) on production and employment in the U.S. textile complex. This unit groups production data to conform to the import category system so that the two can be compared. One of the primary concerns is the impact of imports on the domestic industries. Data on domestic industry performance are reviewed to watch for the impact that imports may have on the U.S. industry. Another function of the IAD is to interpret movements within the industries and assess change in the competitive status of the U.S. textile and apparel industries.

International Agreements Division (AD). The AD not only provides preparation for negotiating bilateral agreements but also plays an important role in the actual negotiations. Within this division are country specialists who are intensely familiar with U.S. textile and apparel trade with various countries. During negotiations on a bilateral agreement with a particular country, the AD country specialists who know the status of quota categories and shipments help to determine

FIGURE 11–9

Organizational structure of the U.S. Department of Commerce Office of Textiles and Apparel (OTEXA).

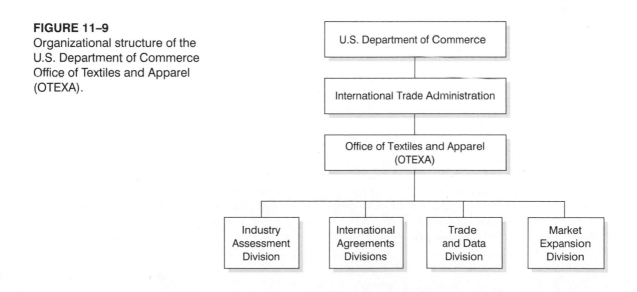

allowable levels of imports to be permitted under new agreements (personal communications with R. Levin, 1994).

Trade and Data Division (T&DD). The T&DD recommends and implements trade classification schemes to carry out the MFA and bilateral textile agreements, initiates and participates in fraud and transshipment investigations, participates in negotiations and consultations related to free trade agreements and GATT agreements, and brings investigation issues to CITA. This division assures import data quality by reviewing the data, identifying problems, and working with the Census Bueau and the U.S. Customs Service. T&DD conducts data investigations with foreign governments and helps those governments to resolve differences in data, handles visa matters, obtains descriptions and samples of imported textile and apparel products, and operates the Textile Information Management System (TIMS), a computer textile data system (personal communication with Martello, 1994).

Market Expansion Division. The Market Expansion Division is geared toward assisting U.S. textile and apparel manufacturers in expanding their markets to other countries.

This division organizes trade missions and international trade fairs for U.S. producers, develops market analysis studies to help U.S. manufacturers better understand specific foreign markets and their potential for success in those markets, and serves in a general advisory capacity to domestic producers who seek to export.

The U.S. International Trade Commission (USITC)

The U.S. International Trade Commission was established in 1916 as the U.S. Tariff Commission. It was created to monitor trade, provide economic analysis, and make recommendations to the president in cases of unfair trade practices. The ITC responds to the Congress—the Senate Finance Committee and the House Ways and Means Committee, in particular—and to the executive branch through the Office of the U.S. Trade Representative. The special status of USITC removes its activities, to some extent, from the political pressures of special interest groups. Interest groups such as trade associations, however, may petition to investigate the trade practices of other countries to determine whether "material harm" has resulted from imports or other trade concerns.

 EMBARGOED SHIPMENTS

In recent years, U.S. Customs has embargoed hundreds of shipments of apparel from China and other countries when shipments failed to comply with trade agreements. For example, at the end of a year when China had exhausted its quota in certain categories but continued to ship merchandise to the U.S. market, these shipments were not permitted to enter. Most importers chose to hold them in bonded warehouses until the start of a new year when quotas were again available. Embargoed shipments represent a potential risk to retailers and importers who expected merchandise for seasonal promotions.

THE HARMONIZED SYSTEM (HS)

The Harmonized Tariff Schedule is a system of tariff classification that went into effect in the United States in January 1989 as part of an international effort, the Harmonized System (HS), to have a similar system used by trading nations that choose to participate. The Harmonized System was implemented to facilitate foreign trade and to standardize, to a degree, the collection and use of trade data. In the United States, the HS replaces the Tariff Schedule of the United States (TSUS).

The new system, which applies to more than 5,000 overall categories of products, has a standardized six-digit international code used by all trading nations to designate the same merchandise classifications. Textile and apparel products account for the largest number of categories for any single trade area—a reflection of the sensitive nature of international trade in textiles and apparel. The HS categories have precise descriptions for products, which are used by customs officials to monitor product shipments.

The Harmonized System brought about several substantial changes in U.S. tariff treatment of imported textile and apparel products. Some changes were:

- Prior to HS, products were classified on the basis of *chief value* of the fibers in the article. The HS classification is determined on the basis of *chief weight* of the fibers. Under HS, a 60/40 cotton/linen blouse is classified as cotton although the linen component may be of more value.
- The metric system is used for all measurements—length, weight, etc.
- The concept of *ornamentation* is no longer considered under HS. Tariffs were higher for ornamented items under the prior system.
- Sizing classifications changed, particularly in certain infants' and children's categories (O'Donnell, 1988).

Both exporters in the producing country and U.S. importers were responsible for adapting shipments to the new system or risk having merchandise embargoed by the U.S. Customs Service.

Although USITC's responsibilities include wide product coverage, this agency's Textiles and Apparel Branch focuses specifically on trade issues pertaining to these product areas. When concern arises regarding the material harm (essentially "market disruption") caused by imports to certain segments of the domestic textile, apparel, or leather products industries, this division is responsible for investigation of those claims. In addition, this division conducts and publishes studies on the U.S. textile, apparel, and leather products industries as well as on the production in competing nations (particularly exporting nations).

The Office of Textiles and Apparel (OTEXA) does the work and may make recommenda-

tions; however, CITA makes determinations of market disruption for actions taken under the MFA and Section 204 of the Agricultural Act. Once CITA makes a decision, a cable is sent to the foreign government to notify the country of CITA's decision. That country is then given a period of time in which to respond before action is taken. (personal communication with R. Levin, 1994).

U.S. Customs Service

The U.S. Customs Service is responsible for processing imported goods coming into the U.S. market. The primary duties of Customs are making sure proper tariffs are paid on imports and that the proper goods are admit-

U.S. CUSTOMS' HEADACHE: CIRCUMVENTION

One of the most troublesome trends for the importing countries has been the efforts of firms in certain exporting nations to bypass the quota system by misrepresenting merchandise. In common usage of the term, circumvention includes (1) misrepresenting the *country of origin by transshipping* textile and apparel goods to the importing markets by way of a third country with available quota, or (2) misrepresenting *product identity in other ways (item count, fiber content, type of product)* to affect the quota category under which merchandise is imported. Technically, GATT sources consider only the first activity to be circumvention (conversation with GATT sources, 1994).

Widespread circumvention, particularly on the part of China, has angered many U.S. manufacturers and government officials involved in textile trade. Even the Congressional Textile Caucus planned to draft a bill to deal with transshipment. The U.S. Customs Service estimated that China illegally transshipped more than $2 billion worth of textiles and apparel to the United States annually in recent years through some 40 third-party countries or territories who disguise the country of origin. In response to the activities, in late 1993, the U.S. government enacted measures to strengthen enforcement of transhipping. These included (1) inspection of factories in other countries, and (2) inserting a circumvention provision in all bilateral agreements negotiated (Emert, 1993b; Jacobs, 1993a).

The U.S. Customs Service was authorized to force foreign countries to allow inspection teams to visit factories. The intent of this was to determine if production was occurring in countries from which products were being shipped. Although 1993 policies strengthened Customs' authority to make inspections, similar efforts had occurred, to a degree, earlier. In 1991, for example, inspection teams found that the tiny city-state of Macao had only a fraction of the capability to produce all the merchandise shipped from there, and virtually everything being shipped in certain categories was found to be of Chinese origin. The conclusion was that Macao did not produce enough products to require such extensive quota; therefore, Macao's U.S. quota was reduced. Pakistan's 1993 quota in two categories were reduced because of transshipping. Moreover, China's quotas had suffered chargebacks (i.e., reducing a year's quota by the amount overshipped) for 15 categories in 1991, 26 in 1992, and 23 in 1993 (Emert, 1993b).

The Chinese bilateral textile agreement with the United States expired on the last day of 1993, but Chinese negotiators were unwilling to include a provision in a new agreement to deal with transshipment. In the first days of 1994, U.S. Trade Representative Mickey Kantor announced that China faced 25 to 35 percent cuts in that country's textile and apparel quotas unless transshipment was controlled. On the last day before the cuts would have gone into effect, the two countries signed an agreement that froze silk shipments to 1993 levels (previously silk was not limited) and severely restricted quota growth rates on other textile/apparel imports from China. For cases in which transshipping can be proven, the agreement permits triple quota reductions in the category in which the violation occurred.

Beyond issues of transshipment, the 1994 agreement severely restricts China's U.S. imports through 2005, because when the Uruguay Round takes effect in 1995, growth rates will be based on bilateral textile agreements in force at that time. Some critics of the agreement saw it as a way for the Administration to make up for what the domestic manufacturers felt they lost in the Uruguay Round (Ostroff, 1994a, 1994b, 1994c).

ted in proper quantities. In other words, the U.S. Customs Service, on instructions from the head of CITA and through a visa system, is responsible for scrutinizing shipments of imports from around the world as they enter the United States and monitoring compliance with trade agreements and other regulations. The United States can determine whether its trading partners are complying with bilateral agreements only to the extent that shipments are monitored by the Customs Service. Customs may embargo products shipped to the United States.

Although the U.S. Customs Service processes imports of all products from around the world, officials have regarded textile and apparel imports to be among the most difficult. First, U.S. imports of textile and apparel products account for over 3 million Customs entries each year (Hartlein, 1988). More critically, however, the complex system of import restraints on textile and apparel products has taxed the Customs Service's capacity for monitoring shipments to the degree the domestic industry would like. To put this task in proper perspective, one must recall that more than 5,000 types of products are grouped into categories for import control purposes. And, nearly 200 countries produce textile products for the world markets. Of course, not all countries ship all product categories to the United States, and, further, many that are shipped do not pose a concern to the domestic industry. Therefore, only about 65 percent of all U.S. textile and apparel imports are under MFA or other restraints (personal communication with R. Levin, 1994). However, monitoring shipments at varying category levels from a large number of countries is a mammoth task.

Furthermore, the Customs Service is charged with monitoring fraudulent shipments (falsified paperwork), transshipments, mislabeled products (fiber content, care, country of origin), counterfeit trademarks and copyrights, and various other illegal practices.

In 1987, for example, the U.S. Customs Commissioner reported that more than half of the 1,000 **textile visas** shipped from China that had been checked by inspectors turned out to be counterfeit (Honigsbaum, 1987b).

Monitoring shipments of counterfeit luxury items is also a challenging task for the U.S. Customs Service. According to reports, the importing of phony designer goods into the United States has mushroomed in recent years. Counterfeit products include everything from fake Luis Vuitton handbags and luggagge, Cartier and Rolex watches, Gucci bags, Chanel fragrances and accessories, Tiffany products, and Hermes scarves to Ray Ban sunglasses. The International Chamber of Commerce, based in Paris, estimates that worldwide counterfeit trade in all types of goods is a $70-billion-dollar-a-year business. In just over two years in the early 1990s, the U.S. Customs Service caught more than $384 million in counterfeit accessories and apparel, leather goods, and watches coming into U.S. ports. The U.S. Customs Service and luxury goods firms have been aided by at least one state, New York, that has passed laws to deal seriously with the counterfeit trade. In November 1992, the sale and manufacturing of counterfeit products in New York state changed from a misdemeanor to a felony if the value of the confiscated goods exceeds $3,000. Very high fines and prison sentences accompany higher valued product confiscations (Meadus, 1992).

Similarly, the Customs Modernization and Informed Compliance Act (the so-called Mod Act), which became effective in December 1993, imposes harsh fines for misrepresented import shipments. The new act is the most extensive revision of the U.S. Customs regulations in decades. Attached to the implementing legislation for NAFTA, the Mod Act permits fining importing firms up to $100,000 for failure to give the Customs Service documents for post-entry audits. The intent is to prevent importers (or their **import brokers**) from misstating the value or origin of goods and then claiming that the incriminating documents were lost or accidentally destroyed. The Mod Act gives the Customs Service a stronger "enforcement weapon." The fines are part of a new system to make importers more accountable for complying with trade laws. At the same time, U.S. Customs is required to work with businesses closely and to be sure they understand the regulations (Emert, 1993a).

In addition, the U.S. Customs Service has established a sophisticated multimillion-dollar computer system with ties to all American ports and to a large number of import brokers. This system, known as the Automated Commercial System, permits tracking of import shipments and eliminates the painstaking documentation of cargo by hand. The system is able to select "high-risk" shipments for examination—based on stored data on the importer's reputation, the country of origin of the merchandise, the manufacturer of the products, and the type of merchandise being imported (Honigsbaum, 1987a).

In late 1993, the U.S. Customs Service began trial use of a new electronic visa information system (known as *ELVIS*) intended to facilitate faster processing of imported textile and apparel shipments through Customs. The electronic transmission of visa information from a foreign government to the U.S. Customs Service may replace paper visas from a number of countries if the system proves satisfactory and is accepted by industry sources. The ELVIS system has the potential to reduce the heavy paperwork burden that textile and apparel shipments represent for the U.S. Customs Service (Jacobs, 1993b).

Tariffs are levied on the imported products, with the importer responsible for payment of the tariffs. Tariffs on textile and apparel products vary by type of item, but most are relatively high compared to other products.

Figure 11–10 provides a simplified overview of the steps through which textile and apparel products under import restraint (1) originate in the exporting country, (2) are processed through the U.S. Customs Service, and (3) later reach U.S. consumer markets. Figure 11–11 provides an added explanation of the steps that occur as merchandise is processed through U.S. Customs; this diagram may be helpful in understanding the involvement of other government agencies.

Embassies for Other Countries Located in Washington

A number of the textile-exporting nations that have a great deal at stake in textile and apparel trade have trade counselors or other officials in their Washington embassies to attend to textile interests. In some cases, these individuals are quite familiar with textile trade and interact with U.S. officials themselves. In other cases, foreign embassy officials secure—with the support of their home governments—the services of Washington lobbyists to represent their textile trade interests in interacting with the U.S. government. In recent years, when a number of textile-exporting nations have been especially concerned over tightened restrictions in the U.S. market (for example, during debates over the three textile bills), a number of these countries worked together to fight against further restrictions. These representatives from textile-exporting nations employed U.S. lobbyists to represent their countries' textile/apparel interests.

Special Interest Groups

Although many other import groups are involved in representing various perspectives in the textile trade dilemma, space permits discussion of only those that are more comprehensive in membership and scope and are among the most influential in trade matters. Because of their roles in representing the

FIGURE 11–10
Simplified flow chart for textile and apparel products entering the United States under import restraints.

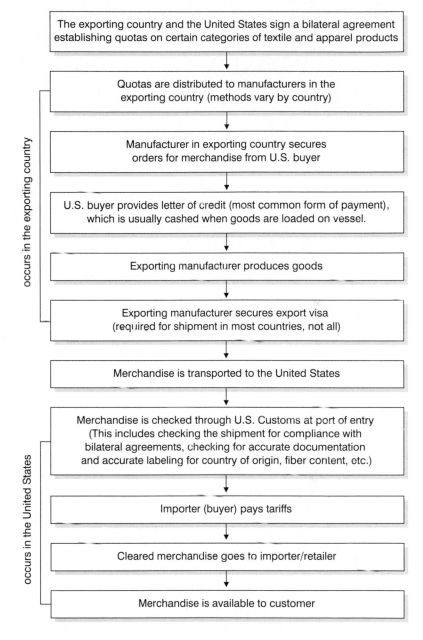

occurs in the exporting country

The exporting country and the United States sign a bilateral agreement establishing quotas on certain categories of textile and apparel products

Quotas are distributed to manufacturers in the exporting country (methods vary by country)

Manufacturer in exporting country secures orders for merchandise from U.S. buyer

U.S. buyer provides letter of credit (most common form of payment), which is usually cashed when goods are loaded on vessel.

Exporting manufacturer produces goods

Exporting manufacturer secures export visa (required for shipment in most countries, not all)

Merchandise is transported to the United States

occurs in the United States

Merchandise is checked through U.S. Customs at port of entry (This includes checking the shipment for compliance with bilateral agreements, checking for accurate documentation and accurate labeling for country of origin, fiber content, etc.)

Importer (buyer) pays tariffs

Cleared merchandise goes to importer/retailer

Merchandise is available to customer

interests of their constituencies in the policy-making arena, the following organizations either are located in Washington or have offices in Washington. These organizations serve members in a variety of roles—such as providing educational services to members, acting as spokespersons for members on a host of subjects, and coordinating other industry activities. In recent years, however, textile and apparel trade concerns have

FIGURE 11–11
The processing of merchandise through U.S. Customs.

When merchandise is processed through Customs

Customs collects shipment data and sends the data to the Department of Commerce. Data are used to monitor shipments on products from various countries against quota allowances.

Customs collects tariff (duties) on products. These are paid by the importers. Tariffs that are collected go to the U.S. Department of Treasury.

Importers and retailers pick up goods from Customs (at docks, airports, etc.)

demanded increasing time and energy from most of these groups.

American Textile Manufacturers Institute (ATMI)

The American Textile Manufacturers Institute represents manufacturers primarily in the textile mill products industry. Of the industry associations, ATMI is one of the strongest and most influential. With offices in Washington, the ATMI staff assists association members in establishing and maintaining a strong presence in Congress and in other areas in which textile trade policy is considered.

American Fiber Manufacturers Association, Inc. (AFMA)

American Fiber Manufacturers Association, Inc. (formerly Man-Made Fiber Producers Association, Inc.) represents the producers of manufactured fibers—both artificial and synthetic fibers. Representing nearly 20 major producers of fibers, this association's members constitute one of the textile complex's most competitive segments in global markets. A number of these fiber producers are part of large chemical conglomerates. Although this association represents a small number of firms, because of the member companies' size and competitiveness, AFMA is an influential group in the trade policy arena.

American Apparel Manufacturers Association (AAMA)

Of all segments of the textile complex, apparel manufacturing is the most fragmented and has the largest number of firms (23,515 in 1991)—many of which are quite small. The American Apparel Manufacturers Association represents this segment of the industry; however, many U.S. apparel producers are not members. Member firms are those that understand the collective advantages of membership, whereas many firms are so small that either they are unaware of these advantages or feel they cannot afford the luxury of participation. One must keep in mind that the average number of employees in apparel establishments is 43 persons, and 63 percent of the U.S. apparel establishments employ fewer than 20 workers. Although AAMA is one of the strongest associations, if all apparel manufacturers were members, it would be even stronger. AAMA is no longer active in the U.S. industry coalition that seeks trade restraints (personal conversation with C. Priestland, 1994).

U.S. Apparel Industry Council (USAIC)

USAIC is a coalition of apparel manufacturers who have 9802 (807) manufacturing operations. The group was formed in 1985 to represent the interests of these manufacturers who felt their interests were not being represented in policy matters pertaining to apparel trade. Although most members of this relatively small group are also members of AAMA, organizers established USAIC as a separate organization because AAMA's policies at the time did not consider or support 9802 (807) production. AAMA considered 807 products to be "imports." In addition to making sure their members' views are heard on policy matters, USAIC leaders keep members apprised of matters that affect their 9802 (807) operations: government legislation, customs interpretations, or foreign trade negotiations (Santora, 1989).

The International Ladies' Garment Workers' Union (ILGWU) and the Amalgamated Clothing and Textile Workers Union (ACTWU)

With lobbyists located in Washington, both ILGWU and ACTWU are active in matters pertaining to textile and apparel trade. Although the unions generally have little in common with industry management, they share similar concerns on many issues pertaining to trade for these sectors. If contributions for political action committees (PACs)

can be used as a gauge of political activity, these two unions rank high. In a report of spending for the 1992 elections, ILGWU and ACTWU spent more than $1.1 million to support their favorite candidates compared to slightly under $1 million for all the textile/apparel manufacturing and retailing associations plus individual major firms combined (Federal Election Commission, 1993).

Fiber, Fabric and Apparel Coalition for Trade (FFACT)

Although the fiber, textile, apparel, and labor groups have had a strong coalition for many years that worked together on trade concerns, FFACT was formed in 1985 specifically "to fight for textile–apparel import-curbing legislation being drafted on Capitol Hill" (Wightman, 1985b, pp. 1, 19).

FFACT was formed to promote passage of the Jenkins bill, the 1987 bill, and the 1990 bill. The group still exists on paper but is not active (personal discussion with ATMI source, 1994).

 ## U.S. TEXTILE AND APPAREL TRADE COALITION WEAKENS

For decades, the U.S. textile and apparel industries and unions had a solid and very powerful coalition that represented a unified front against imports. The American Apparel Manufacturers Association (AAMA) had been an important player. By the late 1980s, however, many AAMA member firms were actively involved in a range of offshore activities, particularly 9802 (807) production. Because of this, AAMA's traditional anti-import position was no longer tenable. Consequently, at the 1989 annual AAMA meeting, the group announced that it would not support legislation to further limit imports (Chute, 1989b).

This was the beginning of a crack in the coalition that had been steadfast on restricting imports (Figure 11–12). Additionally, the new AAMA position was not supported by all the group's own members; quite a number were still opposed to offshore activities. AAMA was reported to have lost one key member firm because the association had become *too liberal* on trade; at about the same time, the group lost another because it was *not liberal enough* (personal communication with industry sources, 1990). After a while, however, most AAMA members appeared to accept the new position on trade.

FIGURE 11–12

As a growing number of U.S. apparel firms engaged in offshore activities, the American Apparel Manufacturers Association (AAMA) left the strong textile and labor anti-import coalition. After the break from the anti-import group, the apparel manufacturers' position (especially the position of the largest firms) on trade sometimes resembles that of the retailer/importer/exporter coalition that does not want imports limited.

Source: Illustration by Dennis Murphy.

American Association of Exporters and Importers (AAEI)

AAEI is a coalition of exporters and importers of products in many sectors, organized to lobby against protectionist trade policies and legislation that limit foreign trade. Since the livelihood of members of this group depends upon trade, this group is vocal on behalf of free trade. The Textile and Apparel Group of AAEI has been especially critical of textile and apparel producers' efforts to secure increased protection for the domestic industry and was one of the first groups to pose organized resistance to manufacturers' strategies to influence trade policy.

In 1989, after losing a number of AAEI members to a new organization (USA-ITA, discussed next) formed to represent exclusively the interests of textile and apparel importers, AAEI moved to target funding from its 300 textile/apparel-related members more specifically for activities related to this sector, including lobbying (Orgel, 1989).

United States Association of Importers of Textiles and Apparel (USA-ITA)

In December 1988, a group of major importers and retailers of textiles and apparel announced formation of this group, devoted exclusively to the interests of textile and apparel importers, the USA-ITA. Most founders had been active in the AAEI, which represents all product areas. Members of the new group asserted, "U.S. imports of textile and apparel products are now over $26 billion annually and account for over three million Customs entries each year. . . . A strong and independent Association devoted exclusively to the protection of textile and apparel importing is essential to defend the interests of textile and apparel importers. We have established USA-ITA to meet this need" (Hartlein, 1988, p. 2). The new organization was formed primarily to represent textile and apparel importers on trade policy and U.S. Customs problems confronting the segment. In addition, the association provides a full range of member services to help textile and apparel importers in their daily business.

National Retail Federation (NRF)

In 1990, the National Retail Merchants Association (NRMA) and the American Retail Federation (ARF) merged to form the National Retail Federation. The new organization has two operating divisions: (1) the Retail Services Division, which provides advisory, educational, and research information, and (2) the Government and Public Affairs Division, which represents the interests of retailers on trade and other policy matters. This merger permits a stronger presence in Congress for the large U.S. retailing constituency. Prior to the merger, NRMA had over 4,000 members who operated more than 45,000 department and specialty stores in the general merchandise retail industry. Similarly, the American Retail Federation brought broad representation from its 50-state retail associations, 22 specialty retailing associations, and hundreds of corporate members (Ostroff, 1990b).

Retail Industry Trade Action Coalition (RITAC)

The Retail Industry Trade Action Coalition was composed of the major retail industry trade associations as well as a large number of leading retail firms. RITAC might be described as the retailers' answer to FFACT. Although

tensions had grown for quite some time between manufacturers who sought restrictions on textile/apparel imports and retailers who wanted unrestricted imports, these clashes heightened with the introduction of the Jenkins bill in Congress in 1985. As supporters of the bill gathered a startling number of cosponsors in Congress, retailers and importers formed RITAC as a defense to FFACT's efforts to pass the bill. RITAC's efforts were, no doubt, instrumental in the bill's defeat after the president vetoed the legislation. RITAC was also an active force in the defeat of the 1987 and 1990 textile bills and continued to fight textile and apparel trade restrictions. NRF now handles most of the activities previously handled through RITAC (Contact with RITAC board member, 1993).

Various Consulting and Lobbying Firms

There are a number of firms in Washington that represent trade interests. These are commercial operations available for hire to represent groups with various positions on textile trade. As one example, the International Business and Economic Research Corporation (IBERC) is a consulting and lobbying group representing the free trade interests of importers, retailers, and exporting countries. According to Roboz (1981), IBERC is registered under the Foreign Agents Act as an agent of a number of developing countries that seek to export textiles and apparel to the United States. IBERC conducts and publishes studies to show the problems associated with the U.S. textile and apparel industries' protectionist measures and provides other services for its clients concerned with reducing import restraints.

Attention has been focused in recent years on former high-level U.S. government officials who leave their positions and become lobbyists for foreign governments to influence U.S. policy. Choate (1990) calls these individuals *agents of influence*. A significant example occurred in the textile and apparel sector. Walter Lenahan, former Deputy Secretary of Commerce for Textiles and Apparel, left his government position, in which he was privvy to the highest levels of U.S. government information on textile trade, to become a lobbyist for foreign governments seeking to increase their access to the U.S. market (communication with government officials and industry leaders, various years).

Textile Trade Associations for Exporting Nations

The textile/apparel industries in certain nations, which have a great deal at stake in trade with the United States, have established U.S. offices to represent their interests. These offices represent industry, in contrast to trade ministers in embassies mentioned earlier. An example is the Korean Textile Federation, which has an office in Washington. In addition, certain countries have trade development or trade promotion offices in a number of major U.S. cities to promote products from the home country.

Brief View of Structures in the European Union (EU)

Although it is difficult to begin reviewing the structures in other countries because space does not permit an adequate presentation, a brief review of the EU may be useful. In addition to the United States, the EU is the other major importing power in the present textile and apparel trading scheme.

"Official" Government Structures

The 12 member countries in the EU have governed themselves quite independently of each other with only certain policies—particularly those pertaining to trade—determined at the community level.

Several levels of government are involved in the official business of the European Union. We shall consider each of these very briefly.

European Parliament. The European Parliament, one of the bodies involved in making EU policy, consists of 518 elected representatives from Member States (with a designated number of seats that vary from one member country to another). The Parliament has powers on matters such as the internal market, the EU budget, and the accession of new Member States. The Parliament's Secretariat is located in Luxembourg, with sessions generally held in Strasbourg and committee meetings in Brussels.

European Council. The European Council brings together the heads of state or government of Member States and the president of the Commission (discussion follows); this Council meets at least twice a year. The European Council has provided political impetus on issues related to direct elections of the European Parliament; accession of Greece, Spain, and Portugal; financial reform; changes in the common agricultural policy; and other strategic matters.

Council of Ministers. The Council of Ministers is the European Union's *decision-maker*. Laws—including textile policy—are actually formulated by this body after going through preliminary approval in other governmental bodies. The Council of Ministers is composed of the representatives of governments of Member States, generally the ministers for whatever subject area is on the agenda (for example, foreign, economic, financial affairs, agriculture, etc.). The Presidency of the Council of Ministers passes to each Member State in turn for a period of six months. Meetings of the Council of Ministers take place behind closed doors.

Commission of the European Union. The Commission of the European Union serves as the community's executive. The Commission initiates EU policy and acts in the general interests of the collective EU. The Commission is the guardian of the treaties that established the European Union by monitoring the application of EU law and has the responsibility for regulating competition. Members of the Commission must be independent beyond doubt and neither seek nor take instructions from any government or from any other body in carrying out their duties. Most international policymaking for the EU has been delegated to the Commission, whose headquarters are in Brussels, Belgium (Commission of the European Communities, 1992).

Within the Commission, primarily two divisions deal with the textile and apparel sectors:

- The Directorate-General for External Relations (known as DG I). This division deals with EU textile trade policy.
- The Directorate-General for Industrial Affairs (known as DG III). This division focuses on matters pertaining to the competitive status of EU sectors. As an example, DG III works closely with the following organization.

The European Observatory for Textiles and Clothing (L'Observatoire Européen du Textile et de L'Habillement or OETH). The European Commission established OETH as an inde-

FIGURE 11-13
Berlaymont Center, official headquarters of the Commission of the European Union.

Source: Photo courtesy of the EC Commission.

pendent organization in 1991 to increase objective knowledge of the economic conditions of the textile and clothing sectors, especially in EU countries. OETH conducts research by its own staff and in collaboration with the EU Commission. OETH works closely with textile/apparel and retail industry leaders.

In summary, policymaking is complex and slow in the European Union because of the layers of government, not only at the EU level, but also because governmental bodies in the Member States must weigh the impact of EU policies on their respective nations. Therefore, the process of formulating textile policy in the EU is much more complex than in the United States. Before EU diplomats go to the negotiating table in Geneva or elsewhere with a common policy to present on behalf of the Union, long and difficult debates often have already occurred within the EU.

Formulating common textile policies is particularly difficult for the EU because the industries vary greatly among Member States, ranging from sophisticated manufactured fiber production in some countries to simple apparel assembly (similar to that in developing countries) in others. To a great extent, this is a reflection of the stages of development of the different member countries, ranging from an advanced industrialized country such as Germany to Portugal, which has characteristics of a developing country. Moreover, a great deal of disparity exists among the Member States' stance on protecting the textile and apparel industries. Germany, with other highly competitive export industries, wants virtually no protection for the textile/apparel sectors for fear of retaliation by trading partners. Other Member States desire a strong protectionist policy and have subsidized their industries (which is illegal under both EU and GATT guidelines). These differences must be compromised within the Council of Ministers so one common policy or position goes forth from the Union as a whole.

Special Interest Groups

Until 1994, separate umbrella organizations existed for the textile industry and for the apparel industry in the EU. The two organizations were:

- *COMITEXTIL (Coordination Comittee for the Textile Industries of the European Community)*, which was the EU-wide association for the textile industries.
- *ECLA (European Clothing Association)*, which represented the interests of the European clothing industry.

EURATEX (European Apparel and Textiles Organization). The the two trade associations and ELTAC (European Largest Textile and Apparel Companies) formed EURATEX (effective January 1, 1996). This new mega-association has two types of members: (1) the textile and apparel associations for all member countries (plus associate members from EFTA countries and other countries that have applied for EU membership) and (2) the EU organizations representing specific segments of the industry. For illustrative purposes, this group is shown only for the textile sector in Table 11–1.

EURATEX represents and promotes the interests of the European textile and apparel industries to government bodies, institutions, or international associations. Camille Blum, who headed COMITEXTIL, assumed the role of Director General of EURATEX (Figure 11–14).

Foreign Trade Association (FTA). The FTA represents the trade policy interests of European retailers. The FTA leaders meet regularly with European government bodies and officials to discuss trade matters of concern to Europe's retailers. Members include 14 national and European trade organizations as well as a number of department stores and mail-order houses that hold direct membership.

The FTA advocates free international trade and opposes all efforts to impede or distort trade; they also seek reductions in tariffs. The Association represents the interests of its

TABLE 11-1
COMITEXTIL Member Associations.

Textile associations in member countries

Gesamttexil—Germany
Union des Industries Textiles—France
British Apparel and Textile Confederation—
  Great Britain
Consiglio Affari Internazionali Federtessile
  (C.A.I.F.)—Italy
Febeltex—Belgium
Fenetextiel—Netherlands
Consejo Intertextil Español—Spain
Union Intertextile Hellenique—Greece
Federaçao Intertextil Portuguesa—Portugal
Textil-og Beklædingsindustrien—Denmark
Irish Textiles Federation—Ireland

Associate members

Associations from EFTA and former EFTA
  countries; these are likely to become full
  members as their countries are admitted to
  the EU.
Fachverband der Textilindustrie Österreichs—
  Austria
Tekoindustrierna—Sweden
Tekstiiliteollisuusliitto—Finland
Tekstilfabrikkenes Forening—Norway
Schweizerischer Textilkammer—Switzerland

Apparel associations in member countries

Bundesverband Bekleidungsindustrie—Ger-
  many
Union Francaise des Industries de l'Habille-
  ment—France
British Apparel and Textile Confederation—
  Great Britain
Associazione Italiana Industriali Abbigliamen-
  to—Italy
Federation Belge des Industries de l'Habille-
  ment—Belgium
Fenecon—Netherlands
Federacion Espanola de Empresas de la Con-
  feccion (FEDEECON)—Spain
Association Hellénique du Prêt-à-Porter—
  Greece
Associacao Nacional das Industrias de Vestu-
  ario e Confeccao (NNIVEC)—Portugal
Federation of Danish Textile and Clothing
  Industries—Denmark
Apparel Industries Federation—Ireland

Associate apparel members

Associations from EFTA and former EFTA
  countries; these are likely to become full

members as their countries are admitted to
  the EU.
Fachverband der Bekleidungsindustrie Oster-
  reichs—Austria
Tekoindustrierna—Sweden
Vaatetusteollisuuden Keskusliitto (VATEVAO)—
  Finland
Teko Landsforening—Norway
Swissfashion—Switzerland

EU Textile associations for industry segments

Groupe "Marché Commun" du Comité Interna-
  tional de la Rayonne et des Fibres Synthé-
  tiques (CIRFS)—manufactured fibers
Comités réunis de l'Industrie de l'Ennoblisse-
  ment textiles dans les C.E. (CRIET)—dyeing
  and finishing
Comité des Industries du Coton et des fibres
  connexes de la C.E. (EUROCOTON)—cot-
  ton
Comité des Industries Lainières de la C.E.E.
  (INTERLAINE)—wool
Comité des Industries de la Maille de la C.E.E.
  (MAILLEUROP)—knitting
European Association of Textile Polyolefins
  (E.A.T.P.)—polyolefins
Comité de liaison des industries de corderie-
  ficellerie de la C.E.E. (EUROCORD)—
  cordage
Conféderation Internationale des Fabricants de
  Tapis, Velours et Tissus d'ameublement
  (CITTA)—carpets and home furnishings
Assocation International des utilisateurs de
  filés de fibres artificielles et synthétiques
  (AIUFFAS)—filament weavers
Federation International de la Filterie—sewing
  thread
Conféderation Internationale du Lin et Chan-
  vre—linen

Textile associate members

Association Européenne des rubans, tresses
  et tissus élastiques (AERTEL)—narrow fabrics (ribbon, elastic, trims)
Comité de liaison International des broderies,
  dentelles et rideaux (CELIBRIDE)—curtains,
  lace
Association Européenne du Moulinage—tex-
  turization

Source: COMITEXTIL (1994).

FIGURE 11–14
Camille Blum serves as Director General of ATEX, the combined textile and apparel trade association of the European Union. Previously, Blum served as director general of COMITEXTIL, the association for textiles only.

Source: Photo by Kitty Dickerson.

members in multinational trade negotiations. Additionally, FTA provides information to assist members transact business abroad in the consumer goods sector.

Brief View of Other Structures in North America

As member players of the North American Free Trade Area become more acquainted with one another and establish working relationships, it is likely that a number of NAFTA structures will form to coordinate textile and apparel trade interests within the continent. To date, the following has formed.

North American Textile Council

Heads of the major textile associations in the three nations (American Textile Manufacturers Institute, Canadian Textile Institute, and the Mexican Cámara Nacional de la Industria Textil) met in January 1994 to initiate the first steps toward forming the North American Textile Council.

Canada

Within Canada, we will examine briefly the structures involved in textile and apparel industry matters, particularly those related to trade.

Official Government Structures. In the 1960s, the Canadian textile and apparel industries began to feel the impact of low-cost imports. This led to the establishment of an official textile policy and the formation of the Textile and Clothing Board (TCB) in 1970 to monitor policies and to make recommendations to the Canadian government. Pestieau (1976) described the history of these developments in Canada.

Canadian International Trade Tribunal (CITT). On December 31, 1988, the Canadian International Trade Tribunal (CITT) became operational and replaced the Textile and Clothing Board, the Tariff Board, and the Canadian Import Tribunal, forming a body similar to the U.S. International Trade Commission.

Special Interest Groups. As in the United States and the EU, Canada has a variety of trade groups to represent specialized segments of the textiles complex.

Canadian Textiles Institute (CTI). The textile industry's association is the Canadian Textiles Institute (CTI), representing man-made fiber producers, yarn producers, fabric producers, plus manufacturers of household and industrial textile products. The carpet sector's association is the Canadian Carpet Institute (CCI). Both are located in Ottawa.

Textile Federation of Canada (TFC). The Textile Federation of Canada (TFC) is made up of a number of associations and societies offering membership to individuals, with scientific or technical qualifications, who are employed in the textile industry or who represent suppliers. The main purpose of these groups is professional development and the encouragement of technical education.

Canadian Apparel Federation. The clothing industry's association is the Canadian Apparel Federation (CAF), formed in 1993 to replace the Canadian Apparel Manufacturers Institute (CAMI). It is located in Ottawa. Its members are the various provincial and sectoral associations representing clothing manufacturers (personal communication with E. Barry, 1994).

Mexico

The textile and apparel industries in Mexico are represented by separate "national chambers" as instituted by the National Chamber of Commerce and Industries Law. Membership is compulsory. In addition to the national chambers, there are also subordinate "district" chambers.

Cámara Nacional de la Industria Textil (Textiles). This is the national chamber for the textile industry, which includes yarn production, weaving, and finishing. Mexico has nearly 2,250 textile mills spread throughout the country. The Cámara Nacional de la Industria Textil represents about 1,400 companies in 18 states. In addition to this national chamber, three major district chambers also represent the industry:

- Cámara de la Industria Textil de Puebla y Tlaxcala, representing about 460 companies located in states by the same names;
- Cámara Textil de Occidente, representing about 300 companies in the states of Colima, Guanjuato, Jalisco, Michoacán, Nayarit, and Sinaloa; and
- Cámara Textil del Norte, with about 25 companies in the states of Chihuahua, Coahuila, Durango, Nuevo León, and Tamaulipas.

Asociación National de la Industria Química (Chemical Industry). The manufactured fiber sector belongs to the chemical industry and is represented by this group.

Camara Nacional de la Industria del Vestido (Apparel). Organized in 1944, the chamber is a private organization that represents the interests of the apparel industry, promotes the development of the industry, and interacts with the government of behalf of the industry. The chamber represents all manufacturers, garment assemblers, and their affiliates. Elected officers provide the governance of the chamber. A staff provides assistance to manufacturers on trade matters, taxes, working conditions, and other matters of concern to the industry.

REFLECTIONS ON STRUCTURES FOR FACILITATING AND "MANAGING" TEXTILE AND APPAREL TRADE

After the development of GATT's first multilateral arrangement for international trade in cotton, the Short-Term Arrangement in 1961, the number of structures to "manage" textile trade increased. As textile trade policies grew in number and complexity, so did the organizations and mechanisms to implement and monitor those policies—both at the international and national levels.

Furthermore, the increased politicization of textile and apparel trade has fostered the development of a large number of organizations to represent the special interests of groups involved in this sector's trade. In fact, one might even say the politics of textile trade have spawned a form of trade drama: Certain organizations represent the interests of nations against other nations; others represent manufacturers against retailers and vice versa; some groups represent consumers against industry; others represent industrial sectors in adversarial relationships with their governments; and some groups represent the interests of governments and industries in other countries against those in their native countries (for example, the U.S. retailer-importer coalition works closely with lobbyists who represent textile exporting countries and the industries in those countries). Each interest group has the right to represent the concerns of its members, and, yet, many of these efforts cancel one another. Often, the special interest groups most successful in achieving their goals are those who have political or financial power to press hardest for their demands.

And finally, we might consider for a moment the combined global energies and expenditures invested in implementing and maintaining the present policies and supporting the structures that exist to "manage" or facilitate textile and apparel trade. The management of global textile and apparel trade has become a small international "sector," of sorts, of its own.

The existence of present-day textile and apparel trade policies and the plethora of organizations and structures to implement or influence those policies attest to the global importance of the textile complex. Because of the sectors' significant contributions, particularly to employment, in both the developed countries and the developing countries, a complex system has evolved to mediate the interests of the large numbers of individuals whose livelihood is at stake. Although there are those who would argue that the complex regime has resulted from the politics of protectionism, nevertheless, the policies and structures would not have evolved without the widespread support in the political systems of the importing countries.

Although changes in trade policies may alter the governmental structures to "manage" textile and apparel trade, and the political climate may alter the number of special interest groups involved, the prospects for reducing these structures in the near future appear slim.

SUMMARY

A complex system of structures has existed to facilitate and "manage" textile and apparel trade. From 1960 to 1994, textile trade was under the auspices of the GATT, with a trade policy, the MFA, that was unique because it was outside the normal GATT rules. Because it was unique, textile trade had its own structures to handle trade for this sector.

Upon completion of the Uruguay Round, which included a 10-year phase-out of the MFA, the structures were changed at the international level. The World Trade Organization began to replace GATT as a more comprehensive, more powerful body to handle world trade. The Textiles Division and the Textiles Monitoring Body became the major bodies concerned with textile trade. Additionally, representatives of national missions located in Geneva are involved in textile trade matters. An important special interest group at the international level is the International Textiles and Clothing Bureau (ITCB), a coalition of developing (exporting) countries that opposed the developed countries' trade restraints on their textile and apparel exports.

At the U.S. national level, trade policy is a responsibility of the president. The United States Trade Representative (USTR) is the cabinet-level official responsible for representing the president on trade issues; therefore, USTR plays an important role in textile trade policy matters. The Trade Policy Review Group (TPRG), the Trade Policy Staff Committee (TPSC), and the National Economic Council (NEC) are the highest level interagency groups under USTR involved in trade policy decisions. The Committee for the Implementation of Textile Agreements (CITA) carries out the implementation of the textile-apparel import control program, with most of CITA's daily work handled by the U.S. Department of Commerce Office of Textiles and Apparel. The U.S. Customs Service plays an important role in processing and monitoring import shipments. A significant array of special interest groups is involved in textile and apparel trade, representing various segments of the industry and different positions on trade.

European Union trade policy is handled by multiple layers of government both at the EU level and Member State level. Most international policymaking for the EU has been delegated to the Commission located in Brussels. One umbrella organization, EURATEX, represents manufacturers' interests for a broad range of industry segments and member-nation associations. The Foreign Trade Association represents the interests of European retailers on textile and apparel trade matters.

Completion of the NAFTA accord spawned the beginning of continent-wide North American trade groups. The first for textiles and apparel was the North American Textile Council, launched by the textile trade groups in the three partner nations.

In Canada, the government structure involved in textile trade is the Canadian International Trade Tribunal (CITT). Major trade groups are the Canadian Textiles Institute (CTI), the Textile Federation of Canada (TFC), and the Canadian Apparel Federation (CAF).

In Mexico, the industries are represented through national chambers; companies are required to be a member of a chamber. Separate national chambers exist for the textile, apparel, and chemical industries. Additionally, at least three major district chambers exist for the textile industry.

GLOSSARY

Congressional Textile Caucus is a bipartisan group of senators and representatives concerned about the economic well-being of the domestic textile and apparel sectors. The caucus has promoted legislation to limit imports.

Import brokers coordinate the details of importing foreign-made products for buyers in the United States.

Interest group or *special interest group* is an organized body of individuals who share some goals and who try to influence public policy (Berry, 1984).

Letter of credit is a financial document whereby the importer's bank extends credit to the importer and agrees to pay the exporter. When a U.S. buyer contracts with a manufacturer in another country to produce textile/apparel items, a letter of credit is cashed typically when goods are loaded on the vessel.

Textile visa (also called **export license**) is an endorsement in the form of a stamp on an invoice or export control license executed by a foreign government. Visas are used to control the export of textile and apparel products to the United States and to prohibit unauthorized entry of textile products into the country.

Visa System is a method of tracking and controlling the quantity of textile products exported to the United States. This system monitors compliance with restraint levels agreed upon in bilateral agreements or consultations.

SELECTED READINGS

American Apparel Manufacturers Association. (1980). *Apparel trade primer*. Arlington, VA: Author.

A summary of textile and apparel trade terms and an overview of the structures for implementing global trade policy for the sectors.

Berry, J. (1984). *The interest group society*. Boston: Little, Brown.

This book focuses on how interest groups operate within the context of a democratic society; discussion also relates interest group politics to broader developments in the American political system.

Brandis, B. (1982). *The making of textile trade policy, 1985–1981*. Washington, DC: American Textile Manufacturers Institute.

A review of the development of textile trade policy; written and published by textile industry sources.

Choate, P. (1990). *Agents of influence*. New York: Alfred A. Knopf.

This book focuses on the hiring of former U.S. government officials to lobby for foreign governments in Washington.

U.S. Department of Treasury, United States Customs Service. (1984, May). *Importing into the United States*. Washington DC: U.S. Government Printing Office.

An overview of procedures involved in importing into the United States; written for importers.

Textile and apparel trade issues are difficult to resolve because, in many cases, the interests of one set of players are directly contrary to those of another. If one group achieves its demands, its success is often at the expense of players with different needs.

Part VI provides an overview of the varying perspectives that must be considered in balancing the interests of various groups with a stake in global textile and apparel production and trade. This section focuses on the perspectives of specific groups in the United States whose interests must be considered in the formulation and implementation of textile trade policies. Space limitations necessitate a focused presentation of these perspectives; therefore, the following chapters relate primarily to the U.S. setting. Although the U.S. market and the country's governmental system are different from those in other industrialized countries, we would find that, in most of these countries, equally disparate objectives exist among groups with a stake in textile and apparel trade.

Chapter 12 focuses on the interests of U.S. textile and apparel industry and labor groups. Various adjustment and policy strategies are considered, with attention given to arguments that have been used to justify special policies of protection for the textile/apparel sector. Included in the chapter are the concerns of U.S. industry and labor groups for reciprocity, or a "level playing field." In addition, Chapter 12 considers some of the unexpected outcomes of protectionist measures that have produced undesirable consequences for the industry. Further discussion focuses on new marketing initiatives of the U.S. industry, as well as on a variety of international production and marketing arrangements now being employed to enhance global competitiveness.

VI

Balancing Conflicting Interests in Textile and Apparel Trade

Chapter 13 focuses on the interests of U.S. retailers and importers in textile and apparel trade. The opposing objectives of retailers and manufacturers, with respect to trade for the sector, are considered. A summary of retailers' advantages and disadvantages in foreign sourcing is presented. In addition, Chapter 13 focuses on changes in the softgoods industry, which have led to a more integrated softgoods chain and improved channel relationships. A brief review of global retailing is included.

Chapter 14 considers the consumer perspective in relation to textile and apparel trade. The chapter begins with an examination of consumer expenditures and the influence of foreign competition on those expenditures. Additional consideration is given to consumer gains from textile/apparel trade. Various types of trade restraints are evaluated from the consumer perspective. Estimates of the costs to consumers and the estimates of welfare, or "dead weight," costs are considered; summaries of these costs from several studies are included. The chapter ends with a discussion of consumers' lack of an organized voice on textile trade matters.

Chapter 15 examines the role of policymakers in textile and apparel trade. As textile/apparel trade matters have become politicized, policymakers are pressured to represent the views of various interest groups. In Chapter 15, we will consider ways in which policymakers have found themselves caught between the political demands of industry groups and the need to represent broader diplomatic concerns. Special attention is given to industry efforts to use the legislative approach to secure added protection against imports.

12

The Interests of Industry and Labor in Textile and Apparel Trade

INTRODUCTION

Previous chapters have provided an overview of the textile and apparel industries, and, throughout the book, the perspectives of these sectors in the United States and other developed countries have been considered. This chapter is intended to provide an overview of the interests of industry and labor, especially in relation to textile and apparel trade policies. Therefore, this chapter builds upon a prior understanding of the U.S. industry and its relative standing in global trade.

The U.S. textile and apparel industries have been among the first industrial sectors to experience severe international competition. A similar pattern has occurred in most other developed countries. The nature of the industries has made them forerunners in an era when many other sectors followed with similar problems. The limited capital and technology requirements, along with the high labor demands of certain segments of the textile and apparel industries, made these basic industries particularly attractive to developing countries. Many LDCs started textile and apparel production first for import substitution and, later, as a primary export area for earning foreign exchange. For those countries, textile and apparel production became a leading sector to gain earnings for each nation's broader economic and social development.

Therefore, as we consider the interests of manufacturers and labor on trade policy issues, it is important to remember that the textile and apparel industries have a longer history of facing severe international competition than most other U.S. sectors. Although many other sectors now face similar problems in global markets, textile and apparel's longer history (as well as unique characteristics of the global textile/apparel market) may account for some of the present system for responding to that competition. The textile and apparel sectors in most other OECD countries have experienced similar competition, and, within the context of differing political systems, the concerns and responses of industry and labor in those countries have been similar to those in the United States.

In this chapter, we will consider the positions of industry and labor in the United States and other industrialized countries as they have responded to changing international competition in the textile/apparel sector. We will consider **industry strategies** for adjustment, policy strategies, new marketing initiatives, and various types of international production and marketing arrangements being used by industry and labor in the developed countries.

BRIEF HISTORICAL PERSPECTIVE

Textile and apparel industries in most developed countries prospered during the 1950s and 1960s; however, by the late 1960s and early 1970s, market conditions changed dramatically. Particularly by the mid-1970s, as the impact of increased oil prices affected most of the world economy, industrialized market growth slowed dramatically.

At the same time that growth of domestic markets slowed in the industrialized countries, a growing number of developing countries chose the textile and apparel sectors as a primary means for economic development. By the 1970s, difficult global market conditions forced many U.S. manufacturers to change their strategies. Ghadar et al. (1987) noted that most OECD countries began to emphasize increased production and mass marketing, hoping that economies of scale would help them retain their competitiveness. The development of large firms, particularly in textiles, resulted in production that became less flexible. Firms were less able to respond to changing fashion demands. Furthermore, the economies of scale, particularly in some segments, still were inadequate to offset developing country wage rates. Employment in both the textile and apparel industries declined.

In the 1970s and 1980s, the textile and apparel sectors in the United States and most other OECD countries pursued two types of strategies in their quest to retain markets: (1) adjustment measures and (2) increased trade restraints to protect the domestic industries from imports. During these years, substantial adjustment occurred in the industry. In addition, textile and apparel trade policies grew increasingly complex and institutionalized. Also, during this time, a number of producers in the OECD countries began to establish various forms of global production-marketing arrangements. In some cases these arrangements provided access to local markets; in other cases, access to low-cost labor was the primary motivation.

ADJUSTMENT STRATEGIES

Adjustment, also called structural adjustment, is considered at both the national and international levels (Ghadar et al., 1987). At the *national* level, adjustment refers to restoring the competitiveness of an industry within the domestic economy. A **rationalization** process occurs, which results in fewer, larger, and more efficient firms, plus some specialized suppliers. As Ghadar notes, rationalization occurs as a result of government policy or market forces. Although public policy (that is, the government) has directed textile and apparel industry rationalization in some European countries, the U.S. approach is largely market-driven.[1] Under a market-

---

[1]Over the last 20 years, U.S. public policy has become increasingly important, however, as an influence on corporate behavior.

driven approach, the market forces firms to alter products, production methods, and company structures to remain competitive.

At the *international* level, adjustment refers to the relationship of the national economy to that of its trading partners. In this sense, adjustment occurs through changes in exchange rates and through the regulation of trade (Ghadar et al., 1987). Adjustment also considers the relationship of a sector to the international market. The national and international aspects of adjustment are interrelated. As Ghadar et al. note:

> Industrial sectors that increase productivity faster than the overall national economy should become more competitive in the international economy. However, exchange rate movements can dramatically affect the competitiveness and trade performance of national economies and individual industries within an economy. An overvalued dollar can cause intrinsically healthy sectors to register losses and can even lead to their elimination. During these periods, government policy may turn to trade regulation to give these industries time to cope with changes in the international economy. (p. 2)

The Goal of the Adjustment Process

Textile trade experts generally agree that the Multifiber Arrangement was intended originally to allow the older textile/apparel industries in the developed countries time to adjust to the growing low-wage competition. The industry in the industrialized countries was believed to have a competitive advantage in high-quality and/or capital-intensive goods, which would permit the developing countries to produce other goods in which they could be competitive. Most countries have been unwilling to vacate any part of the sector, however.

Further, the adjustment process was expected to include both firm and industry reorganization, which would promote more efficient operations. The U.S. and most other developed-country industries have made significant strides in adjustment through restructuring the industry and through investment in new technology (particularly textiles). Despite these shifts, the developing countries have asserted that the textile and apparel sectors in the industrialized countries became too comfortable with the protection provided by the MFA and have moved too slowly in the adjustment process.

Adjustment Progress

A number of changes have occurred in the U.S. textile and apparel industries; similar adaptations have been made in the European and Canadian industries. Although the firms involved would not think of these actions as part of an adjustment process, when viewed from a broader, objective perspective, these changes can be considered part of a restructuring of the industry. Among these are mergers, consolidations, acquisition of smaller firms by larger ones, shifts to vertical operations, investment in new production technology and processes, and shifts to a stronger marketing orientation. In addition, the textile and apparel industries are part of an important change in the softgoods industry—the rethinking and reorganization of the production and distribution processes to reduce response time for merchandise delivery.

European countries vary a great deal in their types of textile/apparel industry adjustment processes and the end results. Since the mid-1970s, nearly all EU countries, as well as the EU itself, have developed schemes to aid various textile and/or apparel sectors (Anson & Simpson, 1988; Arpan et al., 1982). For example, Germany provided little support for the industries in the adjustment process (however, regional governments have assisted the industry extensively). The German government's strategy was based on the belief that companies that responded effectively to existing market forces would remain competitive in global markets. As part of this strategy, a great deal of German apparel is produced through **outward processing**.

France, Britain, and Italy have given varying degrees of governmental guidance in their adjustment process, with differing end results. The British and French industries have lost a substantial number of textile/apparel jobs in spite of the government's supportive position. At times, Italy has provided extensive support for the industry (Anson & Simpson, 1988; Arpan et al., 1982), and the Italian industry remains one of the most competitive globally. Some of the European countries' schemes to subsidize the textile and apparel industries in the adjustment process have been declared illegal by the European Commission (for example, the Belgium program was ruled illegal in 1987). Certain EU treaty regulations prohibit trade restraints, subsidies, or other measures that would give one country unfair competitive advantages over other Member States.

In comparing adjustment strategies of European, Asia Pacific, and U.S. textile and apparel industries, Toyne et al. (1984) found that the following several common elements were evident:

1. All countries used protectionist measures (tariff and non-tariff restrictions) against imports;

2. All countries, industrialized and developing, sought to reduce the impact of wage increases with productivity increases and with strategies that minimized wage increases (for example, use of immigrant labor in the European Union and offshore investments by Japan—and increasingly by the Asian NICs);

3. All industrialized and maturing developing countries sought some degree of specialization at the company or national levels;

4. All countries sought to integrate (or link) their textile complexes vertically and/or hori-

FIGURE 12–1
Emptied of people and machines, a closed-down textile mill is a lonely place. Plant closings, which may be part of the adjustment process, take a toll on workers and their communities. Particularly when plants are located in small towns and rural areas, the impact of the closing is especially difficult.

Source: Photo by J. Maillard, courtesy of International Labour Office.

zontally (although Toyne et al. listed the United States and the Netherlands as exceptions, a great deal of integration has occurred in the U.S. industry since the writing of Toyne's book); and

5. All countries sought to upgrade their technologies and their manufacturing processes.

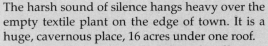

DEATH OF A TEXTILE PLANT

The harsh sound of silence hangs heavy over the empty textile plant on the edge of town. It is a huge, cavernous place, 16 acres under one roof.

Once 1,000 people worked there, handling up to 2 million yards of textile goods daily. Now, only 23 people remain on the payroll at the Old Fort Finishing Co.

They have one job—to close the place down.

"It's pretty lonely now," plant manager Thurmond Padgham sighs. "I'm going on 38 years here. It feels just like your family broke up. You get close to everyone. You know their families, their situations. It's very saddening."

The plant, owned by United Merchants and Manufacturers Co., halted production July 31, sending shock waves through this town of 752 along the Catawba River at the foot of Black Mountain in western North Carolina.

The same scene has been repeated in dozens of towns across the South in recent months. In 1984, 61 textile plants shut down in North and South Carolina alone. The industry as a whole shrank by 19,500 workers.

There is a certain irony in the closures, a painful lesson for an entire region.

The textile industry originally moved south seeking cheap labor. Now it is leaving for pretty much the same reason. Cheap labor in the form of foreign imports has undercut the market for American-produced textiles.

Now some southern towns are undergoing the same trauma that old textile centers in the North experienced decades ago. And an industry once viewed by some as the salvation of the region has come to be viewed as a curse in places like Old Fort, named after a frontier fort built in 1756.

There is little hope of improvement in the near future. Apparel imports have more than doubled during the last three years, and some textile spokesmen say the industry faces its most difficult days in a quarter century.

It is hard to exaggerate the upheaval caused by the closing of Old Fort Finishing Co., which dyed and finished cloth for apparel manufacturers.

The move eliminated 492 jobs. The average worker was paid about $7 an hour, considered a good wage here, and had 20 years of seniority, according to the company.

Since then, a supermarket, a general store, a tire distributorship, a florist and a cafe have closed in Old Fort, according to Mayor Robert Wilson, the former night superintendent at the plant.

The shutdown announcement last May caught almost everyone by surprise. People knew about problems in the textile industry, but United Merchants had embarked on a $17.5 million modernization program here and workers thought their jobs were secure.

"It hit us all like a lightning bolt, or a death in the family," said Jim Settles, 51, who was hired soon after he graduated from high school and never worked anywhere else. "It still hurts. There are times you get mad. You feel the company let you down because you gave them so many years of your life."

Wilson and others estimate that about 150 of the plant's former workers have found other jobs. The rest have retired or are living on unemployment benefits.

With three other textile plant closures in surrounding Marion County, "it has gotten to the place where nobody is hiring," said Wilson, who has joined other local leaders in an effort to find another industry to take over the Old Fort Finishing plant.

Several firms have visited the facility, and Wilson thinks that eventually someone will take it over. But, he said, "I'm afraid things are going to get worse before they get better."

Settles and his wife, Jan, a plant secretary, have applied for about 15 jobs in the surrounding area.

DEATH OF A TEXTILE PLANT *(continued)*

"The county has become too dependent on the textile and furniture industries," he said. "We didn't make much by national standards, but it was good money here. Every time you apply for another job they ask, 'What did you make at your last job?' You tell them and they laugh at you."

Settles has resisted applying for unemployment benefits, but now is resigned to doing so. "That's something I never wanted to do," he said, sitting on a living room sofa. "I really don't know what to do. It's like your whole life is in limbo. You're physically able to work, you want to work, but you can't find anything to do."

Settles, who has been living on severance benefits, is luckier than many here. Unemployment benefits for many are running out, and the Labor Department has rejected company claims that foreign imports caused the shutdown. If the department had accepted the claims, workers would have been eligible for extended unemployment benefits beyond 26 weeks.

Joe Allison, his wife and his daughter all lost their jobs when the plant closed. Another daughter is a freshman at North Carolina State University in Raleigh, a four-hour drive away.

Allison, 47, worries that his daughter may not be able to finish her education.

"My brothers and my sisters, all my nieces and nephews all worked at that plant. That's all we ever knew," he said, shaking his head. "I stayed there 28 years. The only thing I've ever done is finish cloth. All I know is textiles.

"To get out and hunt another job is hard, real hard," continued Allison, a wiry, energetic man. "When they slide the rollers under you like this, it's not a good feeling. They hurt us bad. They hurt the whole community when they closed that plant."

Source: BILL PETERSON Reprinted by permission of *The Washington Post*, January 31, 1985.

Toyne et al. (1984) added, "However, the results have been quite mixed when measured in terms of performance and international competitiveness" (p. 161). Although Toyne's group did not include the Canadian industry in their study, the industry adjustment in Canada has been roughly parallel to that in the United States.

Often industry investments associated with the adjustment process have resulted in both positive and negative outcomes. Employment declines usually follow adjustment measures. As firms merge to form more efficient operations and as more sophisticated machinery and processes are introduced, employment is usually reduced. In the EU, employment in the textile and apparel sectors declined by a third from the mid-1970s to the

mid-1980s; job losses were extensive but somewhat less in the United States compared to the EU (Anson & Simpson, 1988). To the frustration of industry leaders, most economists tend to view the shrinking labor force as a positive indication of adjustment for industries having difficulty remaining globally competitive. That is, economists consider that labor and other resources are shifting to more viable sectors. This theoretical perspective on adjustment does not take into account, however, the toll on workers, their families, and their communities.

As part of the adjustment process, **mechanization** resulting from advanced machinery has accounted for productivity increases that have reduced jobs. In most cases, it has been difficult to determine the extent to which job losses have resulted from competition from low-wage imports or from productivity increases accompanying the installation of advanced production machinery and processes. Nevertheless, as the textile and apparel sectors in most developed countries have participated in various forms of structural adjustment, job losses have resulted.

In the not-too-distant future, it appears that textile mills will become so highly automated that they may become what is known as **"lights-out" plants**. That is, weaving mills will be unattended, and workers will not have to be on hand to take care of repairs, creeling, or doffing. Even now, many mills are attended by very few individuals, who are directed to problems by a computer (Clune, 1993). Figure 12-2 shows the contrasts in the number of workers required in a modern high-technology plant, compared to an unautomated one in a less developed country. The advances in technology enhance productivity and lower manufacturing costs, but the contrasting photos clearly depict the impact on employment.

Investment in new production machinery has resulted in another peculiar outcome. As investments (**capital deepening**) have helped to reduce the unit labor content of textile and apparel goods, manufacturers assumed that this strategy would preserve markets threatened by low-cost imports. Ironically, the domestic industries that spent large sums to implement the latest production technologies began to feel an increased need for market protection in order to protect the large investments (Anson & Simpson, 1988).

POLICY STRATEGIES

In the 1960s, textile and apparel manufacturers in the United States and Europe became alarmed by the increasing entry of low-wage imports into their domestic markets. Although the volume of imports was modest at that time compared to the quantity that would later enter, manufacturers were successful in securing the groundwork for a multilateral system for controlling the entry of low-wage imports into their markets. Earlier chapters of this book provide a detailed discussion on the development of the Short-Term Arrangement, the Long-Term Arrangement, and later the Multifiber Arrangement with its subsequent renewals.

Several factors accounted for the increased emphasis on policy strategies as a means of aiding the textile and apparel industries in the developed countries. Among the influential factors are the following.

Substantial Import Growth

Among all the consumer-oriented manufacturing industries, textiles and apparel (especially apparel) have been among the most affected by low-cost imports. Although various sources give differing data for imports entering U.S. markets, all show substantial growth in recent decades. Frequently, rates of import growth exceeded growth in domestic output. Data from the U.S. Department of Commerce Office of Textiles and Apparel summarize the increase in imports in U.S. markets.

Data in Table 12–1 are given in dollars, which W. Cline (1987) believes to be more appropriate for reporting import penetration than volume data. In Cline's analysis of import penetration rates, reported in earlier chapters, he adjusted data by using the U.S. Department of Commerce domestic product shipment price index. Cline's adjusted data show less dramatic rates of import penetration than those displayed in Table 12–1.

Market conditions in most other developed country markets were similar, with periodic shifts between the United States and the EU in terms of which country accepted larger portions of low-cost imports.

FIGURE 12–2

Technology and automation improve productivity but *reduce employment*, as seen by contrasting these two textile mills. The less-modern weaving factory (a) requires many workers to tend the machines, but the modern spinning room (b) uses few workers to produce a large quantity of yarn. For a view of a modern *weaving* facility, see Figure 1–4.

(a) *Source*: Courtesy of International Labour Office.

A Growing Protectionist Mood

As the developed countries experienced growing trade deficits, and at times increased unemployment, public sentiment for erecting trade barriers intensified. As a result, the textile and apparel industries' interest in securing tighter import restraints was reinforced by the general mood that prevailed in the country. In the United States, numerous measures for protecting domestic industries were introduced in Congress, including the 1985, 1987, and 1990 textile bills. In fact, the 1985 textile bill was one of the first sector-specific bills introduced in

Congress that year; the bill was seen at times as a test case for other sector-specific legislation that followed.

Employment Losses

Textile and apparel job losses in most developed countries have been severe. The EU experienced dramatic loss of employment, dropping by approximately one-third within 10 years—from 4.5 million workers at the time the MFA was developed to under 3 million in 1992 (Comitextil, 1993c). In the United States,

FIGURE 12–2 *(continued)*

(b)   *Source*: Courtesy of American Textile Manufacturers Institute.

TABLE 12–1

U.S. Imports, Exports, and Trade Balance of Apparel and Textile Mill Products (millions of dollars, unadjusted)

| Year | Apparel | | | Textile Mill Products | | | Textile/ Apparel Trade Balance |
	Imports	Exports	Balance	Imports	Exports	Balance	Balance
1983	8,872	694	-8,179	3,320	2,327	-993	-9,173
1984	12,273	674	-11,599	4,593	2,358	-2,235	-13,834
1985	13,745	638	-13,107	4,973	2,302	-2,671	-15,778
1986	16,033	771	-15,262	5,760	2,517	-3,243	-18,505
1987	18,809	1,000	-17,809	6,466	2,846	-3,620	-21,429
1988	19,245	1,355	-17,890	6,253	3,528	-2,725	-20,615
1989	22,221	1,811	-20,410	6,607	3,602	-3,005	-23,415
1990	23,338	2,240	-21,099	6,878	4,565	-2,313	-23,412
1991	24,149	2,924	-21,225	7,463	5,157	-2,306	-23,531
1992	28,828	3,806	-25,022	8,353	5,543	-2,810	-27,832
1993	31,153	4,552	-26,601	8,878	5,746	-3,132	-29,733

Source: Textile & Apparel Trade Balance Report—computer printout (1990, 1991, 1994). U.S. Department of Commerce and personal communication with Department of Commerce staff, 1994.

textile employment was 980,000 and apparel employment was 1.4 million in 1973. However, by 1992, textile employment was 630,000 and apparel employment had declined to 986,000 (U.S. Department of Commerce 1993). Although the introduction of advanced machinery accounted for some of the job losses, nevertheless industry and labor groups in the developed countries understandably viewed the dramatic employment losses with alarm.

Protection of Investments

As noted earlier, the industries (particularly textiles, and apparel to some extent later) in the developed countries invested substantially in advanced equipment and processes to reduce unit labor content and thereby become more competitive with low-cost imports. As Anson and Simpson (1988) noted, manufacturers invested with the assumption that markets would be preserved; consequently, the industry became increasingly concerned that import restraints be put in place to protect these investments.

Competitive Disadvantages

U.S. textile and apparel manufacturers are at certain competitive disadvantages in competing in world markets, and a number of these "disadvantages" are imposed by government regulations that increase the cost of doing business. Among the governmental regulations are such measures as minimum wage requirements, social benefits such as Social Security programs, environmental protection measures, and health and safety regulations imposed by the Occupational Safety and Health Act (OSHA). For example, OSHA regulations on cotton dust and noise standards were estimated to cost the textile/apparel industry about $6 billion through the mid-1980s (Arpan et al., 1982).

Although most of these regulations have resulted from a broader social commitment to American workers, these programs or requirements add to a firm's cost of being in business. Although most U.S. citizens would not wish to return to an era in which these regulations were nonexistent, nevertheless these requirements for American industry do affect the international competitiveness of the domestic industry. Similarly, regulations peculiar to each of the other developed countries exist and affect global competitiveness of the textile and apparel industries. Additional costs of government regulations become an issue when developed country manufacturers are competing with products produced in low-wage developing countries that typically have no similar requirements.

In addition, U.S. industry and labor sources believe they have received far less government assistance than many of their counterparts in competitor nations. For example, the industries in a number of other countries have advantages such as closed domestic markets (that is, they accept little or no textile/apparel goods from other countries), government aid and subsidies in a number of forms, advantageous tax structures, and various assistance efforts such as government-supported export organizations to promote and sell products in other markets.

Concerns for "Burden Sharing"

Once early measures were established to "manage" textile and apparel trade, the industrialized countries soon realized that provisions were needed to assure that all developed countries "shared the burden" of low-wage imports. At times, the United States and the EU have each felt that the other was not accepting an adequate share of the low-cost imports, and, as a result, a disproportionate quantity was being diverted to the respective domestic market. Similarly, until the EU integration, burden sharing was an issue among the EU Member States. Therefore, as the global system for managing textile and apparel trade developed, an important aspect of the multilateral trade policies that evolved assured that major markets share fairly in "bearing the burden" of low-cost imports.

Political Prowess

Finally, policy strategies have been pursued by the U.S. textile and apparel sectors because industry and labor leaders have learned to be effective in securing policies to restrain imports. Leaders have been aware of the power inherent in the size and geographic dispersion of the industry. That is, nearly 2 million workers represent a large number of votes, and the industry is located in virtually every state. Therefore, few members of Congress can ignore the industry's concerns over trade. Similarly, the textile and apparel industry and labor groups in most other developed countries have been able to exert political pressure because they represent large numbers of workers relative to the total work force.

ARGUMENTS TO JUSTIFY POLICY STRATEGIES FOR SPECIAL PROTECTION

Industry and labor groups in the developed countries offer several arguments to justify import restraints to provide special protection for domestic industry. Among these arguments are the following (modified from World Bank, 1987, sources).

Maintaining Employment

If increased imports result in reduced sales for an industry, protecting that industry can help—at least, in the short run—to maintain employment. In view of job losses experi-enced by the textile and apparel sectors in most developed countries in recent decades, industry and labor leaders have been able to make persuasive arguments using this justification. Most developed countries have faced political problems in coping with job losses in textiles and apparel. Especially because of the geographical concentration of the industry in many of the industrialized nations, job losses can become a politically sensitive issue. Therefore, policymakers, who must respond to their constituencies, find job losses to be a compelling argument. Similarly, large employment declines capture readily the public's sympathy and support.

Providing protection to save jobs has inherent risks, however. Other industries may be affected. For example, if the protected industry provides intermediate inputs to other industries, then import restraints may raise costs and reduce employment in industries using the protected input materials. In addition, trading partners may **retaliate** against the protective measures by imposing their own trade barriers. A result of retaliation is that the protection to save jobs in one industry may reduce employment in another. Occasionally, the retaliation may affect another segment of the same industry. As an example, in the early 1980s, as the United States attempted to tighten restraints on Chinese textile and apparel imports, the Chinese cancelled orders for U.S. textile mill products that were being used to produce their goods for export.

Slowing the Pace of Adjustment

Industry and labor groups have argued that protection is needed to provide a cushion from the hardships resulting from adjustment that occurs too quickly. That is, if U.S. textile and apparel markets were opened suddenly to all imports, massive unemployment would occur in the domestic industry. Although this argument is a variation of the one to maintain employment, it is generally more acceptable to policymakers. This argument advocates temporary import restraints because resources cannot be shifted easily. That is, time is required to retain workers and to allow investment to effect changes.

The Multifiber Arrangement was established on this premise. The MFA was developed in part to provide temporary protection to the industries (and labor) in importing markets to allow more time for adjustment to occur without causing hardship to firms and workers. The GATT acknowledges this argument as valid; however, critics of the MFA believe the protection that was originally intended to be temporary was extended too long. Industry and labor leaders in the developed countries believe MFA protection is still warranted because global market conditions in textiles and apparel became far more difficult than envisioned at the time the MFA was drafted.

Preserving the Incomes of Certain Groups

This argument has been one of the primary justifications for protecting agriculture in industrial countries. Subsidies for producers of cotton, mohair, and other wool fall under this category. A variation of this argument is used also for maintaining U.S. textile and apparel jobs. A large number of persons with few other job alternatives are employed in textile and apparel production. These individuals include a large number of women (these industries employ more women than any other), minorities, new immigrants, persons of limited training for other employment, and individuals with little or no mobility. The argument that the textile and apparel industries play a special role in providing incomes for these groups is quite valid. For many of these workers, other employment alternatives are limited or nonexistent, particularly in certain regions.

Protecting Domestic Labor Against Cheap Foreign Labor

Although this argument is related to those concerned with maintaining employment and preserving the income of certain groups, it is often a separate justification for trade restrictions. Nearly all economists see this argument as unjustified because they believe that letting the principle of comparative advantage prevail gives mutually beneficial end results for all countries. At the same time, considering the perspective of the domestic producer in a developed country makes this concern understandable. Responsible textile and apparel leaders are concerned about the potential long-term impact on their workers when competing against wages in the LDCs, which are a small fraction of those in the United States or other developed countries.

Preserving Key Industries

A number of sectors have argued they need special protection because they have strategic importance. Typically, this argument focuses on the importance of maintaining a domestic industry for defense purposes. That is, the domestic industry argues that in case of war, the country should be self-sufficient in producing goods of strategic importance for defending itself. In the case of textiles and apparel, U.S. industry leaders argue that the country should not let its domestic industry erode to the point that the country would be dependent upon other nations for its military uniforms, shoes, and textile goods such as tents and parachutes.

Figure 12–3 is a *Washington Post* advertisement based on the argument for protecting strategic industries. The advertisement was sponsored by FFACT during the final days of congressional debate on H.R. 1562, the Textile and Apparel Trade Enforcement Act of 1985 (the Jenkins bill). Similar campaigns occurred for the 1987 and 1990 textile bills. Because of the Persian Gulf War in 1990, the campaign for that textile bill was tied closely to U.S. military reliance on the domestic textile industry.

Under the Berry amendment, the U.S. Department of Defense is required to purchase textile and apparel products from domestic manufacturers. Industry leaders voiced strong support for the amendment,

saying that it "preserves the defense industrial base for certain critical products that are vulnerable to foreign competition and essential to U.S. military preparedness" (Hackett, 1989). Although the Berry amendment was included in defense appropriations bills every year since World War II, the provision was an annual one. Because both the Reagan and

FIGURE 12–3

FFACT ran this advertisement in the *Washington Post* in the final days before the vote on the Jenkins bill. The purpose of the advertisement was to show the potential threat to the nation's defense system if the U.S. textile complex was decimated by imports.

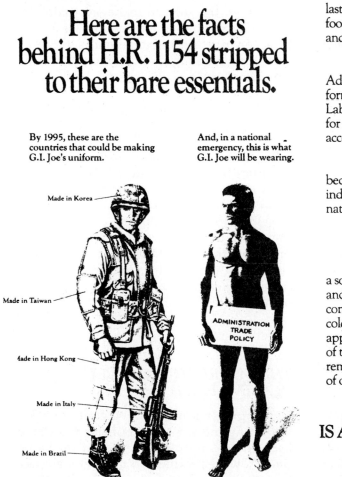

Source: Reprinted courtesy of the Fiber, Fabric and Apparel Coalition for Trade.

Bush administrations proposed to weaken or eliminate the amendment, textile supporters in Congress secured permanent passage of this provision in October 1992 (ATMI, 1993).

Using a similar rationale for preserving key industries, Sweden and some of the other Nordic countries decided, for strategic concerns, that it was unwise to be totally dependent on other supplier nations for textile and apparel products. These countries uphold the **minimum viable production** concept, which permits protection of the domestic industry on the grounds that the country needs a basic level of production for strategic reasons. The GATT has accepted this argument as one that may be used to justify import restraints.

Certain industries are claimed to be critical for economic reasons. Although economists generally question this argument, the World Bank (1987) noted that if allowing domestic producers to collapse led to creation of a global monopoly, this might result in much higher prices. World Bank writers conceded that these speculative circumstances might justify subsidies to preserve competition.

Supporting New (High-Technology) Industries

This is a variation of the "infant industry" argument used to secure protection for new industries to give them time to become established and competitive in global markets. Inherent in this argument is the need to assist new industries during a learning period, when the domestic firms cannot compete with foreign firms that have been operating for a longer period of time. Typically, this argument is used for high-technology industries in the developed countries.

In general, the textile and apparel industries in the developed countries have been established for so long that this argument is rarely used to secure protection. On the other hand, the textile and apparel industries in less developed countries often use the new indus-

try argument to justify restraints on products from other countries.

Using Protection as a Lever to Open Markets

Sometimes in recent years, certain industrialized nations have used the threat of protection as a means of securing access to markets in other countries. Particularly in cases in which a developing country may rely heavily on exporting to an industrialized market, a threat of this type can provide considerable leverage if pursued seriously. World Bank (1987) sources note that this is "yet another step down the road to managed trade" (p. 144). Each restraining measure invites a similar action in return and undermines the GATT rules for governing trade. Section 301 of the 1988 Omnibus Trade Bill is based on this rationale.

Combating Unfair Trade

Increasingly, industries in the developed countries have demanded "fair trade" rather than free trade. By this, industries have desired similar conditions and rules for trade in selling to the developing countries that they have been required or have chosen to provide to the LDCs. Developed country concerns for a reciprocal trade climate are presented in greater detail in subsequent sections of this chapter.

THE DESIRE FOR A "LEVEL PLAYING FIELD"

Developing countries have chafed under importing-market trade policies that have been increasingly restrictive. At the same time, however, textile and apparel manufacturers in the developed countries have become outspoken regarding what they believe to be "unfair" trade. These manufacturers advocate "fair trade" rather than free trade and have begun to demand that trade take place on "a level playing field." That is, manufacturers in the developed countries believe international textile trade policies have provided many generous concessions to the developing countries and that manufacturers in the industrialized countries are short-changed by nonreciprocal treatment (Figure 12–4). As evidence of EU concerns for this, the EU textile and apparel industries sponsored a 1990 conference on "Levelling the Playing Field in International Textile and Clothing Trade" (COMITEXTIL, 1990).

In short, manufacturers in the developed countries are starting to demand reciprocity. **Reciprocity** is a principle of GATT under which governments are expected to extend comparable concessions to each other. Many developed country producers have begun to tell the developing countries to open their markets if they wish to have greater access to markets in the industrialized countries. Textile and apparel markets, especially in the NICs,

have grown but have been relatively restricted to outside products; however, restrictions have eased somewhat in several countries in recent years. Although many newly developing countries may be able to justify closed markets on the basis of protecting infant industries and problems of indebtedness, many of the NICs and ASEAN members in the Far East have moved beyond the poorer stages in their economic development. Therefore, many industry and government sources in the developed countries believe reciprocity should be expected from the more developed Asian countries.

In their quest for fair trade, textile and apparel manufacturers in the developed countries have found a number of trade practices troublesome. Examples include the following.

Dumping

Dumping occurs when a product is exported at a price below fair market value. This may mean the product is sold for less than the cost

FIGURE 12–4

U.S. textile and apparel manufacturers believe they are losing a significant portion of the domestic market because trade practices give what is perceived as unfair advantages to the developing countries.

Source: Illustration by Dennis Murphy.

of production or it may mean the product is sold abroad for less than the price in domestic markets.

Dumping may be a means of disposing of a capacity surplus of products; it permits producers to recapture a portion of the costs of production while maintaining a position in export markets. Sometimes, "predatory dumping" (Salvatore, 1987, p. 223) occurs. In this form of dumping, products or commodities are sold at below cost or at a lower price to capture the business of producers in other countries. The intent of this form of dumping is to drive foreign competitors out of business to acquire a monopoly on the market, after which prices are raised.

"Diversionary dumping" occurs when foreign producers sell to a third-country market at less than fair value and the product is then further processed and shipped to another country. Wolf et al. (1984) noted that Hong Kong, Singapore, and Macao have little fiber or fabric production, but they secure these input products from China, Taiwan, and Korea (or from Europe or Japan for high-quality fabric). Wolf et al. asserted that much of the fiber and fabric produced in East Asia is subsidized or dumped, or that it must be priced to compete with subsidized or dumped products. Wolf and his coauthors believe this enables the garment producers in Hong Kong, Singapore, and Macao to obtain their inputs at a very lost cost. He believes that these low costs, along with low labor costs, have made these three city-states major producers in world markets.

COMITEXTIL, the European textile association, issued this statement:

> Open trading countries such as Hong Kong and Singapore can maintain low cost clothing industries despite rising labor costs, by using marginally priced, dumped fabric from neighboring, protected developing countries as their raw material. There is no defense for the developed countries against this kind of "second generation" dumping under GATT. (*COMITEXTIL*, 1986, p. 29)

Subsidies

A **subsidy** is a financial benefit conferred by a government on an industry or a firm. A significant number of countries make grants or low-interest loans to their textile and apparel industries to encourage expansion and/or modernization. In addition to the subsidies provided to firms in a number of developing countries, this form of assistance has been prevalent in several West European countries (France, Sweden, Belgium, and Italy) and a number of British Commonwealth and East Asian countries (Canada, Australia, Thailand, Indonesia, and China) (Wolf et al., 1984).

Subsidies may be granted to facilitate restructuring and to prevent unemployment and social unrest. **Export subsidies** are granted to foster an export strategy for an industry or a firm within a country. Export subsidies are any form of government payment or benefit to a manufacturer or exporter that is contingent upon exporting products. Export subsidies are in a sense a form of dumping and are seen as a strategy that distorts normal market conditions.

The Tokyo Round produced an agreement on subsidies and countervailing duties on manufactured and semimanufactured goods. **Countervailing duties** are duties levied on imports to offset subsidies to producers or exporters of those products in the exporting country. That is, if it can be proven that the government in Country X has subsidized producers (or that merchandise was dumped), the importing country may place an added duty on the products. The countervailing duty is intended to raise the cost of the exported goods closer to what a reasonable price might have been initially.

In addition to distorting market conditions, subsidies may foster the expansion of the textile and apparel industries where economic theory would suggest that expansion should not occur. Sometimes subsidies bolster inefficient firms, not only permitting them to survive but also to expand. Further, subsidies can

DUMPING CHARGES: ASIAN SWEATERS AND CAPS

Sweaters

In 1990, the U.S. National Knitwear and Sportswear Association (NKSA) filed charges against specific sweater firms in Taiwan, Hong Kong, and Korea for allegedly selling their sweaters in U.S. markets for less than their fair market value. In a highly publicized case, the Asian firms were fined **anti-dumping duties** as high as 24 percent on Taiwan sweaters, and lower levels for the Hong Kong and Korea firms involved. Two years later, the U.S. Court of International Trade ordered the International Trade Commission to reconsider its decision. In the end, the decision was reversed, and the Asian firms who had paid penalties were reimbursed (Farnsworth, 1992; Ostroff, 1992a; Taylor, 1990).

Caps

In 1988, the Headwear Institute of America filed an anti-dumping petition against Chinese exporters for dumping baseball caps in U.S. markets for one-fourth to two-thirds their true value—selling for half the price of other Asian caps and about one-fourth U.S. production costs for caps. Between 1982 and 1987, Chinese cap sales went from 579,000 to 5.9 million caps as a result of dumping, according to the Institute. Although this, too, is a typical anti-dumping petition, an investigation by the U.S. International Trade Commission resulted in a negative ruling (Honigsbaum, 1988; personal communication with R. Wallace, 1990).

provide cost advantages to less efficient firms compared to sometimes more efficient but unsubsidized competitors (Wolf et al., 1984). Although export subsidies are illegal by international agreement, "many nations provide them in disguised and not-so-disguised forms (such as the granting of tax relief and subsidized loans to potential exporters, and low-interest loans to foreign buyers of the nation's exports)" (Salvatore, 1987, p. 224).

Salvatore notes that all major industrial nations provide to foreign buyers of domestic products the "incentive" of low-interest loans to finance purchases through agencies such as the U.S. Export-Import Bank. Although these low-interest credits finance about 10 percent of U.S. exports, they account for as much as 40 percent of Japan's and France's exports. This practice represents a major complaint of the United States against other developed countries (Salvatore, 1987). On the other hand, other countries considered the U.S. Domestic International Sales Corporation (DISC) program to be a form of subsidy and a violation

of GATT. The DISC program was basically tax legislation to stimulate U.S. exports by reducing the effective rate of taxation on income from exports. In the Tax Reform Act of 1984, Congress replaced the DISC provision with three new entities (one of which is the interest-charge DISC, or IC DISC) to benefit exports sales activities, yet be within GATT guidelines (Protass, 1991).

Although United States industry leaders may be quick to look for instances of dumping and subsidies on the part of trading partners, a close look at U.S. production of natural fibers reveals that subsidies are prevalent in that sector. (In fact, subsidies are prevalent for many agricultural sectors in both developed and less-developed countries.) U.S. examples include:

- *Cotton.* In the 1991 crop year, the government funded $700 million in subsidies to growers and another $75 million to U.S. textile mills and exporters when the average cost of U.S. cotton was higher than the

SUBSIDIES IN TEXTILE AND APPAREL TRADE

China

The U.S. International Trade Commission reported that the rapid expansion of China's textile exports to the major developed country markets appeared to result primarily from government incentives. Because the textile complex is China's leading export industry, the government has provided tremendous support for the industry, including a system under which export enterprises were awarded bonuses on the basis of the value of exports. This incentive was in addition to a subsidy system that repays producers for losses they incur in filling export quotas assigned to them by the government. Apparently, the Chinese government has been so intent on building a strong export business that the textile complex has been given many special favors, including lowered taxes (USITC, 1987a).

Moreover, the entire Chinese textile bureaucracy appears to have been reorganized to avoid the appearance of providing subsidies. Because of China's interest in joining the GATT, the previous Ministry of Textiles that made all decisions pertaining to textiles has been changed. The government support of China's textile industry through the Ministry would have signaled textile exports were state-subsidized, and, therefore, should have been subject to countervailing duties. To avoid hurting chances of joining the GATT and also possibly having to pay countervailing duties, the Ministry became the China National Textile Council, and a number of large corporations have been established to handle various segments of the industry ("More Corporations," 1987).

average world price. The rationale is that the subsidies have maintained the quantity and quality of cotton, while lowering the price for mills, leading to increased consumption. The subsidy is said to help mills compete with imported cotton fabric from China and other countries that can tap into inexpensive cotton markets forbidden to U.S. mills. U.S. producers insist that without the subsidy, they could not exist (Ramey, 1993).

- *Wool.* In 1991, the U.S government paid $134 million in wool subsidies (Ramey, 1993).

- *Mohair.* Subsidies were $52.1 million in 1991, or more than $50,000 to each grower. Although 33 states have mohair producers, 86 percent comes from 4,000 ranchers in Texas. Ninety percent of U.S. mohair fiber is exported, much of which comes back to the United States in finished apparel. In the Clinton administration's budget-cutting

efforts, this highly publicized example of subsidies illustrated to many citizens the startling extent to which they were unknowingly supporting various sectors. As a result, mohair subsidies were phased out in stages and completely eliminated by 1996 (McNamara, 1993; Ramey, 1993).

Highly Restrictive Tariff Levels

Although the developed country producers resist the lowering of tariffs on textiles and apparel under the Generalized System of Preferences (GSP), many resent the highly restrictive tariffs placed on textile and apparel products by a number of developing countries; the high tariffs discourage exporting to those markets. Developed country manufacturers feel that the developing countries want special concessions on many aspects of trade but, in return, place high tariffs on products entering their markets. Figure 12–5 provides examples of average tariff levels[2] for textiles and apparel for a number of developing countries.

As in the developed countries, tariffs tend to be higher on apparel and fabrics than on other textile products. Figure 12–6[2] shows the tariffs for apparel for the same countries included in Figure 12–5. Hong Kong and Macao are not shown on the charts because they have no tariffs. Singapore is duty free except for a low tariff on apparel.

Closed or Partly Closed Markets

A number of countries have partly closed markets: Apparel is not permitted to enter, but textile goods are accepted. Apparel may be blocked but textiles permitted when the level of development in a country does not support the apparel industry's input needs. That is, the country may have an apparel industry dependent upon obtaining component parts for the garments from other countries because the nation has not developed textile production (or that for other components) to support it needs. Similarly, under import licensing systems, licenses may be issued for textile but seldom for apparel. Anson and Simpson (1988) reported that the British Joint Textile Committee (JTC) found Australia, Nigeria, and South Africa to be partly closed markets of this type.

Anson and Simpson (1988) reported that many other markets are virtually closed by techniques such as the following:

---

[2]Latest available information, developed for the 1984 GATT textiles study. Due to the methodological difficulties and scarcity of available data, these figures have not been updated; however, GATT sources suggest that although a number of countries have opened their markets substantially, there is no reason to presume there have been major changes in most tariff rates. We do know, for example, that Taiwan reduced tariffs in that country's bid for GATT membership. Additionally, GATT sources caution that because of difficulties in obtaining and processing these data, the information in the charts should be considered only as a rough guide indicating a general order of magnitude (GATT, 1987).

FIGURE 12–5

Average tariff levels for *textiles and apparel* in 19 developing markets in the early 1980s. (Percentages shown are unweighted averages of *ad valorem* duties.)

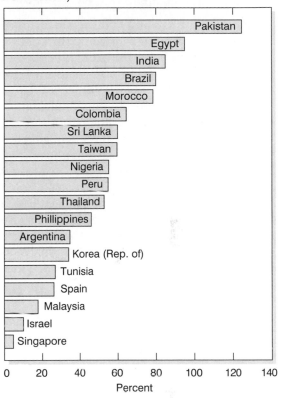

Source: From *Textiles and Clothing in the World Economy* (p. 122) by General Agreement on Tariffs and Trade, July 1984, Geneva, Switzerland: Author. Reprinted by permission.

- Comprehensive systems of import licenses, often awarded, according to the JTC report, "only after demonstration of non-availability of local substitutes and/or adequate bribes" (p. 153).
- Outright import bans.
- State monopoly purchasing bodies.
- Domestic content rules for downstream products.
- "Eccentric" labeling or other bureaucratic requirements.

- Administrative sabotage, such as losing license applications.
- Use of foreign exchange controls that discourage imports and create unpredictable changes in regulations (p. 153).

In recent years, many of the less-developed countries have moved toward much more open trading policies for accepting textiles and apparel produced in other countries. For example, at the December 1992 meeting of the GATT Textiles Committee, the Chairman of the Textiles Surveillance Body reported on findings from a survey of MFA member countries regarding their restrictive measures that limit imported textiles and apparel (this does not include tariffs). The TSB Chairman noted that of the 39 reporting countries, 22 indicated they applied no restrictive measures or else did so on only one or very few products. He concluded that "no one can deny that substantial liberalization of trade in textiles has occurred" (Raffaelli, 1992).

Foreign Aid

The United States provides generous support to aid developing countries, and this money is funneled through a wide range of organizations and projects. U.S. textile and apparel industry supporters have taken exception, however, to providing support to develop the textile/apparel industry in developing countries.

Members of Congress who represent regions where textile/apparel production is heavily concentrated have led the protests against loans and other aid being granted to develop or expand LDC textile and apparel industries. When these concerns began to surface, critics asked for an accounting of loans that went to develop textile manufacturing. The U.S. Treasury secretary supplied official figures, which showed that between January 1980 and December 1982, international lending institutions had loaned over $500 million

FIGURE 12–6

Average tariff levels for *apparel* in 19 developing markets in the early 1980s. (Percentages shown are unweighted averages of *ad valorem* duties.)

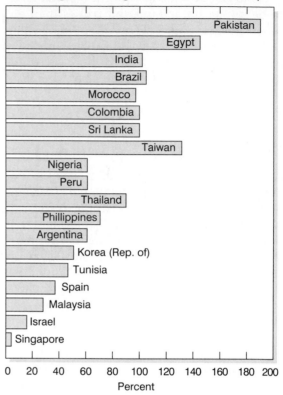

Source: From *Textiles and Clothing in the World Economy* (p. 124) by General Agreement in Tariffs and Trade, July 1984, Geneva, Switzerland: Author. Reprinted by permission.

to finance Third-World textile projects (Hosenball, 1984).

Loans were made by such institutions as the World Bank, the International Development Association, and the Asian Development Bank. Grants between 1980 and 1982 went to Bangladesh, Egypt, Turkey, Nigeria, Thailand, Sri Lanka, Zambia, Pakistan, the Philippines, China, and Malawi (Hosenball, 1984).

In 1984, the powerful U.S. House Appropriations Committee advised the Reagan administration to instruct U.S. delegates to interna-

FROM "60 MINUTES" TO "NIGHTLINE" TO CAPITOL HILL IN FOUR DAYS

U.S. funding of textile and apparel production in developing countries came to the attention of taxpayers and members of Congress when "60 Minutes" televised a segment on A.I.D. (U.S. Agency for International Development) funding of the apparel industry in the Caribbean and Central America. Two segments followed on "Nightline." Prompted by a group called the National Labor Committee, representing unions, the TV segments reported on the use of A.I.D. funds to establish garment assembly plants in developing countries to lure manufacturing to those nations, taking jobs from U.S. taxpayers. As the reporters presented it, U.S. citizens were being expected to pay millions of dollars to fund manufacturing in the Caribbean and Central America (to aid those economies) as well as pro-

motional efforts to encourage U.S. apparel firms to close domestic plants and move their manufacturing to those regions. Since 1981, an estimated $1 billion of U.S. tax monies had been spent for the programs critics termed as "luring U.S. jobs overseas" (most of which were in apparel).

Within four days, the controversy was considered in Congress. Legislation followed quickly that eliminated all A.I.D. money spent on providing incentives to U.S. industry to relocate out of the United States if the move costs U.S. jobs. Also, money for developing foreign export processing zones would be eliminated unless the president can certify that the zone would not cost U.S. jobs (Barrett, 1992a, 1992b; Ramey, 1992b; "Senate Nixes," 1992).

---

tional lending institutions such as the World Bank to "strongly oppose" loans to textile and apparel projects in the Third World. The committee reported that it was "extremely concerned" about the growth of U.S. imports of textile products and added that the "World Bank and other regional developmental institutions are contributing to this rate of growth by providing subsidized funds to developing countries to expand their textile imports" (Hosenball, 1984, p. 2).

Textile and apparel industry supporters in Congress were outraged to learn later that the U.S. delegation to the World Bank, under the Department of Treasury, had been instructed by an interagency group to vote to approve a $175 million loan to China—which included a commitment of $8.1 million to develop China's textile industry. ("Congressmen Seek," 1984).

Given the adaptability of the textile/apparel sector to the economic development strategies

of developing countries, our discussion in prior chapters helps us understand why the LDCs sought loans to develop or expand these industries. Ironically, however, many developing countries have entered textile and apparel production upon the recommendations of Western advisors from organizations such as the World Bank and others.

At the same time, one can easily understand the frustrations of U.S. textile and apparel manufacturers (and labor groups) when they learn their tax monies are helping to *finance their competition*. As taxpayers, U.S. citizens help to support a number of international organizations such as the World Bank. The World Bank is an apolitical international lending institution that makes loans to Third-World countries. Although the World Bank is supported by over 100 nations, the United States is a chief contributor, supplying about 20 percent of the bank's funds. The United

States influences World Bank disbursement decisions through weighted voting and has additional influence through congressional appropriations to the institution ("Congressmen Seek," 1984).

Encouraging increased Third-World production of textile/apparel products appears to be a questionable practice from the perspective of the developing country itself. That is, loans from the World Bank or other institutions prepare a nation with few resources to invest in a sector for which a global overcapacity already exists. Moreover, as the LDC producers attempted to sell their products, they have encountered an increasingly difficult system of trade restraints designed to "manage" the excessive supply of products in the international market. Although the quota system will be phased out, many developing countries will lack the marketing skills to compete.

UNEXPECTED OUTCOMES OF PROTECTION

As textile and apparel producers in the developed countries have secured additional protection from LDC imports, many of the restrictions have had unforeseen consequences. Many of the consequences were quite different from what industry leaders desired initially, and in fact some of these unexpected outcomes provided positive benefits for the *LDC producers*. In many respects, the import control system can be compared to the "Dutch boy and the dike" dilemma. As soon as one "leak" is stopped, another occurs. Among the unexpected consequences of the import control system for textiles and apparel are the following.

Development of New Suppliers

Ironically, the MFA quota system has fostered the development of textile and apparel pro-

duction in a number of LDCs. As controlled countries exhausted their quota availability, many of the Asian suppliers, Japan and the NICs in particular, established production facilities in less-developed countries to take advantage of lower (or nonexistent) quota restraints (and usually lower wages as well). In some cases, these were the first textile/apparel production facilities in the poorest LDCs; in other cases, the outside investment from NICs fostered the expansion of the industry in newly developing countries. As a result, the quota restraints on leading suppliers caused a *proliferation of producer nations*. Although the textile and apparel sectors would have been likely first industries for most of the developing countries, the quota system caused the spread to those LDCs to occur more quickly than it might have otherwise. Consequently, as the developed countries applied quotas to limit the imports from major Asian suppliers, the net result was a larger number of supplier nations.

As an example, Hualon Textiles, Taiwan's fifth largest producer of manufactured fibers, established a $75 million plant in Malaysia to manufacture polyester; additional downstream facilities followed. In 1988, Taiwanese firms invested more than $311 million in Malaysia to become the country's second largest investor after Japan (King, 1989).

Shifts in Product Lines

In addition, the "holes in the dike" phenomenon discussed previously occurred also for product lines. As importing countries placed restrictive limits on various product categories perceived to be a threat, the exporting nations simply shifted to uncontrolled or less controlled categories. These shifts continue to occur. For example, if import controls on men's dress shirts are tightened, the producers in an exporting country may shift to women's dresses or raincoats to avoid quota restrictions. In other words, quotas have

FIGURE 12–7
An unexpected outcome of the quota system has been a proliferation of exporting nations. When more advanced Asian nation's exports were blocked by increasingly restrictive quota limits in the major developed markets, firms in those countries relocated production in other nations—providing capital, manufacturing expertise, and marketing networks—creating a growing number of proficient producer nations in the global market.

Source: Illustration by Dennis Murphy.

encouraged diversification of product lines among the growing number of producers in the world market.

Diversification fostered by the quota system may create more difficulties for manufacturers in the importing countries than allowing a slow increase in already established lines. Under the latter circumstances, manufacturers in the importing countries are able to predict more realistically the categories in which import increases would occur. When an exporting country's producers quickly shift production from one category to another, competitive market conditions are much less predictable for producers in the developed countries. That is, if producers in Country Z suddenly shift from shirt production to coat production to avoid quota restraints, then the coat manufacturers in an importing country

suddenly face market uncertainties because of the new and unexpected competition from low-cost sources.

Shifts in Fiber Categories

In addition, quota restraints have affected import shipments by *fiber* categories. Prior to MFA IV, silk and the natural vegetable fibers other than cotton were not controlled. Consequently, a number of exporting countries began making and shipping large quantities of ramie, linen, and silk items because no quota limits had been imposed on product categories made of these fibers. Because of the widespread use of this strategy to circumvent quota restraints, the importing countries pressed to have the additional fiber categories covered under MFA IV (where previously uncontrolled fibers exceed 50 percent of the weight of the imported goods; pure silk was excluded).

Upgrading

Because quotas limit the volume, but not the value, of imported apparel, exporters have found it advantageous to upgrade products to maximize the value added per unit. Therefore, manufacturers in developing countries have continued to upgrade their products. In many respects, this was advantageous to the developing countries. In addition to maximizing profits, this shift permitted a country to compete in a more diversified market. Furthermore, it bolstered the development of a more sophisticated industry within that country. Rather than producing inexpensive, low-quality products, the quota system encouraged the industries in exporting countries to advance more rapidly than they might have otherwise.

Again, ironically, the consequences of the quota system were hurtful to certain producers in the developed countries. Earlier, as low-cost imports began penetrating the markets of the developed countries, a large portion of the products could be described as moderate quality and low price. Believing that they would have a competitive advantage in higher quality and price lines, many manufacturers in the industrialized countries shifted to upper-price markets. As the quota system encouraged upgrading on the part of the developing countries, this competitive advantage for the developed countries diminished.

Guaranteed Market Access

Although most textile/apparel exporting nations publicly protested quota restraints, officials in a number of countries actually considered quotas a form of *security* for market access. Many countries would like increased quotas but, at the same time, acknowledge that existing quotas have been a form of *guaranteed market access* up to the agreed limits. Surely, this perspective on quotas was not a predicted end result for industry leaders in developed countries who worked to secure quota restraints.

The security of access provided by quotas benefits two groups of exporting nations. First, the "Big Three" producer nations have large quotas as a result of history. These countries have large quota allotments due to growth on quotas established at a time when many fewer nations were involved in textile/apparel production and trade. When fewer nations competed for markets, quotas were more generous. Therefore, the Big Three countries with large quota allotments sought to retain the market access those quotas provide. A second group of countries, the newest global market entrants, also benefited from the security of access provided by quotas. Many of the newer producer nations would have found it extremely difficult to participate in today's intensely competitive global markets without the access provided by quota allotments. In other words, the quota system holds back the more experienced nations—thus, giving newcomers a chance to compete.

Establishment of Foreign-Owned Plants in the Importing Markets

Perhaps the most startling boomerang effect of import restraints has been the establishment of foreign-owned plants in the United States and other major importing countries. A number of Asian producers, in particular, who felt hampered in their export operations because of increasingly tight quota limits, established their own production operations in the importing countries to avoid those restraints and have immediate market access. Rather than protecting domestic markets, the tightened quota system encouraged foreign producers to invest and compete face-to-face in the developed country markets.

In effect, international competitors become back-yard neighbors and compete in the same market. A significant number of textile firms that are owned by parent firms in other countries have moved to the southeast United States. For example, during 1987 alone, a total of 51 companies from other countries, mostly in textiles and apparel, moved or expanded operations in South Carolina (Standard & Poor's, 1988). Among the countries that have made significant U.S. textile investments are Korea, France, Germany, Switzerland, and Japan. In apparel, for example, Hong Kong-based Odyssey International Pte. Ltd. (which produces sportswear, skiwear, and camping equipment for companies such as The North Face, Eddie Bauer, and Lands' End) acquired Cal Sport in Yuma, Arizona, as part of its plan to build or buy 10 to 12 manufacturing facilities in the United States ("Odyssey Begins," 1991). The EU has also experienced this trend; for example, Japan's textile giant, Toray, built a plant in England that is one of Europe's largest textile facilities.

NEW MARKETING INITIATIVES FOR U.S. TEXTILE/APPAREL PRODUCERS

In addition to adjustment strategies and policy strategies, the U.S. textile complex has undertaken new market initiatives in its continued efforts to compete against producers in other countries.

A Service Commitment to Retailers

In response to the growing concern that improved marketing and service functions were needed by the industry in the efforts to secure retailers' business, the textile and apparel manufacturers worked with Kurt Salmon Associates, a consulting firm, to develop the groundwork for the Quick Response program. Kurt Salmon made three basic recommendations to the textile/apparel industry:

1. Point-of-sale tracking and merchandise-control software, as well as close attention to what customers are buying rather than what retailers are offering, should provide better forecast information about consumer demand.
2. Shorter lead times for new products and improved timing of deliveries can be accomplished by using new technology, such as laser cutting, and through computer-to-computer linkage from retailer to apparel and textile manufacturers.
3. Finally, direct order systems and electronic data exchange would allow the industry to introduce a shorter reorder cycle. The one-year pipeline could be cut in half.... The relationship between retailer, manufacturer, and mills will have to become more focused and interrelated, and the industry will have to be more innovative and more responsive to retailer and consumer demand. (Pohlandt-McCormick, 1985, p. 14)

A growing number of U.S. textile and apparel companies adopted the Kurt Salmon charge. Following the lead of firms including Haggar Apparel Company, Levi, and Arrow, the industry began to move toward the Quick Response concept. Quick Response was based on service and improved communication between retailers and suppliers—a change that has revolutionized stock-keeping and distribution in the softgoods industry.

Promotional Campaign for Domestic Products

Building on results from consumer studies, which indicated that a majority of U.S. consumers preferred domestically produced apparel, the textile and apparel industry and labor groups joined forces to promote U.S.-

made textile and apparel products. Industry leaders initially launched the Crafted with Pride in U.S.A. campaign in 1983 and in 1984 formed the Crafted with Pride in U.S.A. Council. The multimillion dollar Council budget comes from member organizations and firms.

When the Crafted with Pride campaign began, its primary goal was to increase awareness of U.S.-made textile and apparel prod-

ucts and to motivate consumers, retailers, and apparel manufacturers to buy domestic rather than foreign-made products.

At various stages of the Crafted with Pride campaign, spending has been directed largely toward media efforts to reach consumers. In the early stages, a number of commercials featured well-known celebrities who promoted the quality and style of U.S.-made garments. Later, commercials began to publicize the

---

 ## REQUIRED COUNTRY-OF-ORIGIN LABELING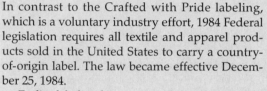

In contrast to the Crafted with Pride labeling, which is a voluntary industry effort, 1984 Federal legislation requires all textile and apparel products sold in the United States to carry a country-of-origin label. The law became effective December 25, 1984.

Earlier labeling laws required that the country of origin be identified for foreign-made items; however, labeling was not requried for U.S.-made items. Consumers who preferred domestic textile and apparel products were left to assume that if no country of origin was given, the product was American-made. The lack of domestic labeling left most consumers in doubt.

The 1984 legislation took the form of an amendment to the Textile Fiber Products Identification Act and the Wool Products Labeling Act. Although regulations pertaining to the labeling of consumer products are under the jurisdiction of the Federal Trade Commission (FTC), the FTC origin rules are compatible with the U.S. Customs country-of-origin regulations, which cover imports controlled under the MFA.

The 1984 labeling legislation stipulated that a product is considered misbranded unless it is prominently labeled or tagged as to country of origin. Labels must be placed on the neck of a garment or in another easy-to-find place. Manufacturers may label small items like stockings on the package rather than on the actual item. All mail order catalogs are required to provide coun-

try-of-origin information on the products offered for sale.

"Global products," or those that result from manufacturing operations in several different countries, pose the greatest difficulty in defining and labeling country of origin to meet U.S. labeling requirements. Labeling is particularly difficult when various steps in fabric production, for example, occur in different countries. If a garment is made of fabric from another country, or was assembled in another country, the label must say "made of imported fabric" (sometimes the country is named) or "assembled in Country X" (the country of assembly must be named).

Although the country-of-origin labeling requirements were enacted to aid consumers in their decision making, another goal of the legislation was to "exploit a supposed consumer preference for American-made merchandise" (Schwartz, 1984a, p. 11). To no one's surprise, sponsors of the legislation were members of the Congressional Textile Caucus.

Most other countries do not have requirements for country-of-origin labeling. In the past, certain EU countries have attempted similar measures to encourage preferences for domestically produced merchandise. These practices have been discouraged, however, as inconsistent with the more open trading climate sought within the EU.

"dying industry because of imports" theme that created a poor image of the industry in the minds of viewers.

Although manufacturers' participation in the Crafted with Pride effort was purely voluntary, many firms affixed labels bearing the Crafted with Pride logo or other forms of "Made in U.S.A." identification.

INTERNATIONAL PRODUCTION AND MARKETING ARRANGEMENTS

Increasingly, U.S. textile and apparel producers are realizing the importance of participating in global production and marketing activities as competitive strategies for survival. A number of U.S. firms have long, profitable histories of participation in the global economy, but these companies have been exceptions. The vast domestic market once offered seemingly unlimited opportunities for growth until foreign competition changed that outlook. Many manufacturers became so concerned by the influx of imports into domestic markets (and have directed their energies to controlling those imports) that they gave little attention to how they might participate in the markets beyond their borders.

Currently, however, a growing number of U.S. textile and apparel firms appear to be joining their European and Asian competitors in assuming a more international orientation in their operations. Although new skills are required for participating in the global arena, more enlightened producers are realizing the potential for gaining market share or other advantages from international links. A number of global initiatives are discussed.

International Sourcing

Perhaps more than any other form of global linkage, many U.S. manufacturers have uti-

lized various international sourcing strategies. Through these, apparel manufacturers, in particular, have taken advantage of the low-cost labor in developing countries. This strategy may include securing finished products or may involve assembly operations only (9802 [807] or, to Europeans, "outward processing"). Particularly as new legislation made production in the Caribbean basin attractive, these offshore assembly operations have been used increasingly by U.S. apparel manufacturers. Since sourcing strategies are discussed in greater detail in Chapter 9, the reader may refer to that discussion.

Multinational Enterprises (MNE)

Multinational enterprises or firms are those with an integrated global approach to production and marketing and those that have both domestic and overseas operations. (MNEs are also called transnational corporations; these were discussed briefly in Chapter 4 in relation to development.) Although multinationals are somewhat limited in the textile and apparel industries, a number of outstanding examples exist (see "Multinational Textile and Apparel Leaders" boxed insert). Some of the large chemical-based manufactured fiber firms have been leaders in assuming a global orientation. For example, Hoechst, a large German multinational chemical firm, has a global orientation for its fiber business. In 1986, Hoechst secured the U.S. fiber division of Celanese and became known as Hoechst-Celanese.

International Licensing

As discussed briefly in Chapter 9, international licensing involves an agreement between a U.S. firm (firms from other countries grant licensing arrangements as well) and foreign manufacturers to use the U.S. company's trademark. The U.S. firm receives agreed-upon royalties and provides technical,

MULTINATIONAL TEXTILE AND APPAREL LEADERS

- *Coats Viyella* is a large, broadly diversified textile and apparel firm based in the United Kingdom that produces yarns, threads, fabrics, trims, zippers, apparel, and textile home furnishings and has the Jaeger and Viyella retail chains. With 1992 sales of nearly $3.5 billion, Coats Viyella has operations in countries throughout Europe, North America, South America, Asia, Africa, and Australia. Operations vary by name; for example, in North America, Coats American is a leading supplier of industrial threads. North Americans would also recognize the Talon zipper and Jaeger apparel (Coats Viyella, 1992).

- *DuPont* is one of the world's largest chemical producers, with fiber sales of more than $6 billion in 1992. DuPont Fibers produces specialty fibers serving end uses that range from high-strength composites to protective apparel, active sportswear, and packaging. Included are high-volume fibers for fabrics, carpet, and industrial applications; products are sold to textile mills or other industries for processing into products for consumer and industrial markets. In addition to U.S. plants, DuPont Fibers has production facilities in Australia, Germany, Mexico, Canada, Brazil,

Japan, The Netherlands, Singapore, the United Kingdom, Turkey, Spain, and Luxembourg. Sales offices are located in additional countries (DuPont, 1993).

- *Levi Strauss & Co (LS&Co.)* is one of the world's most geographically dispersed firms in the textile complex, in part because of the "pull" of Levi® products. To consumers in many parts of the world, Levi jeans epitomize American popular culture and the American lifestyle that many wish to imitate. Complementing the appeal of the products, however, is one of the most culturally sensitive and socially conscious executive teams in the industry. Executives and employees have embarked on soul-searching sessions to consider the social responsibilities of being a global corporation. As a result of Levi's® product appeal and the company's forward thinking, Levi Strauss & Co. is the world's largest apparel firm with sales of more than $5 billion in 1992. Of LS& Co.'s 114 facilities (production, distribution, and sales offices), more than half were outside the United States (author's visit to LS& Co. headquarters, 1992; "Levi's Life," 1992).

---

merchandising, and promotional support to the licensing company to produce and market the brand in the licensing company's market.

Licensing is a way of market expansion abroad and may be the only practical means for doing so in certain countries in which regulations restrain imports or foreign investment. In other words, licensing is an alternative to exporting. In many countries (particularly Latin America and other LDCs), however, royalties are limited by the government (1–3 percent) and for only a short duration for an agreement (personal communication with E. Ott, 1989).

A number of apparel firms derive 3 to 10 percent of their earnings from licensing their trademark in other countries (AAMA, 1984; Ott, 1989). For the licensor, relatively limited investment is required. However, for the arrangement to be successful, the licensor must continue to give something new and innovative. Often, when a licensing arrangement provides a designer's name and little else, those efforts are not as successful as lines for which continued innovation is supplied (Ott, 1989).

Although Jockey International has an outstanding track record in its use of licensing,

FIGURE 12–8
Jockey products sell quite successfully in many Asian markets. These Korean advertisements indicate that consumers are accepting of Western models in the advertisements.

Source: Photo courtesy of Jockey International.

FIGURE 12–9
This billboard promotes Jockey International's products to Mexican motorists.

Source: Photo courtesy of Jockey International.

FIGURE 12–10
According to this sales associate, Vanity Fair products are very popular with shoppers in this Taipei department store, despite the fact that Taiwan's tariffs make them more expensive than domestic lingerie.

Source: Photo by Kitty Dickerson.

not all firms have been as successful. Problems have occurred in protection of trademarks and collection of payments for the use of those trademarks, particularly in developing countries. Producers in some developing countries believe they have a right to secure and use trademarks and technology with little cost to them. For example, some countries have laws that prohibit payment of royalties for the use of a trademark; in certain countries, the length of time in which trademarks are protected is shorter than in the United States.

Foreign licensing requires a long-term commitment from manufacturers to develop a market for their products in other countries. To be successful, licensors must provide design, merchandising, and other expertise over the lifetime of the contract (personal communication with E. Ott, 1989). Although licensing can expand markets and generate additional income, manufacturers must be aware that developing markets in other countries takes several years.

Direct Investment

Direct investment refers to ownership of a substantial interest in a foreign operation. Investing in a foreign operation in this man-

FIGURE 12–11

Levi Strauss & Co. sales representative (left) talks over Levi's® jeans with one of her clients at a store in Leipzig, Germany.

Source: Reprinted courtesy of Levi Strauss & Co.

her represents the highest level of commitment to operations in another country and usually includes transfer of significant technology and personnel by the firm. Direct investment and joint venture operations are used by apparel manufacturers for offshore production to take advantage of lower wages. Both types of ventures represent forms of "owned production overseas," which were discussed in more detail in an earlier chapter. Often direct investment occurs when a firm wants access to a market for the products the company produces. The establishment of manufactured fiber plants in regions beyond the home country has occurred often for this reason; for example, U.S. fiber producers and the German Hoechst firm have used this

strategy successfully. DuPont will spend $1 billion in the 1990s to build nylon plants in Asia to assure DuPont's place in a region where consumption is growing twice the rate of the world average ("DuPont Slates," 1990). Conversely, foreign-owned textile and apparel manufacturers are using this strategy as they establish operations in the United States to gain access to the U.S. markets.

Joint Ventures

A **joint venture** results when a firm seeks to join with a partner located in the overseas country. The local partner offers the advantage of understanding the market and how to function in it. Various forms of joint venture arrangements exist, often including more than two partners. The proportions of ownership are not necessarily equal, and, in some cases, the extent of foreign ownership is regulated by the local government. In some cases, local governments may be a partner in joint ventures. The advantages and disadvantages of owning overseas production operations were considered in Chapter 9.

Exporting

In many ways, direct exports are the simplest way of entering the markets of other countries. We have considered earlier, however, a number of restrictive measures that may pose difficulties for companies seeking to export to other markets. As a result, other production or marketing arrangements have provided alternative means of participating in the markets of those countries.

Exporting is an obvious means by which U.S. textile and apparel producers can expand markets. As we have noted earlier, the potential for exporting has not been adequately explored by most U.S. firms, particularly in view of the appeal of many U.S. products in other countries. Although exchange rates have at times posed serious difficulty in

SUCCESS STORIES: INTERNATIONAL TEXTILE AND APPAREL OPERATIONS

- *Jockey International*'s brand is known virtually all over the world. One may see this familiar brand advertised on the wall in an airport in Germany or on a billboard in Mexico. Jockey International markets its products in over 100 countries and has manufacturing in a number of countries. The company has used licensing as a means of selling more abroad, with some 1,000 registrations of its trademarks and patents in 135 countries. As a privately held firm, exact sales figures are not known; however, about 40 percent of its estimated $500 million in annual sales are overseas. Jockey International's commitment to global marketing is evident in the multilingual staff in offices in Europe, Hong Kong, Brazil, and the headquarters in Kenosha, Wisconsin; staff travel constantly. Jockey International's success negates the myth that U.S. producers cannot compete in lower-wage markets; the company sells more than $1 million in products annually in Hong Kong (anonymous industry source).

- *Kellwood Company* has evolved from a firm that once not only served just the U.S. market, but also mainly one customer—Sears, Roebuck and Company—to become a large multinational corporation. Kellwood is a marketer, merchandiser, and manufacturer of apparel, textile home furnishings, and recreational camping softgoods products. Composed of 15 separate companies—including one in Hong Kong—Kellwood's 1993 sales were over $1.2 billion. In addition to nearly 20 U.S. manufacturing plants, Kellwood has production in the Caribbean basin, Hong Kong, Sri Lanka, Canada, China, and Saipan. Sales offices outside the United States are located in Hong Kong, Canada, and Mexico. Serving every retail channel of distribution and more than 25,000 retail customers, Kellwood is recognized as one of a relatively limited number of major suppliers that can provide the volume of merchandise needed by today's mega-retailers. Kellwood's emphasis on value-oriented products has meshed well with interests of the new, value-conscious consumer of the 1990s—resulting in performance for the firm that exceeds that for many industry competitors. The company gives high priority to advanced technology and communications systems to coordinate its global network and to provide service to customers (author's visits with Kellwood executives; Kellwood Company, 1993).

- *Sara Lee Corporation*'s Personal Products division has pursued an aggressive strategy for international expansion. Sara Lee has purchased companies in other countries, such as the Mexican hosiery firm, Mallorea SA de CV (Mexico's second largest hosiery manufacturer); an Italian hosiery manufacturer, Filodoro; the French manufacturer of the *Dim* line; and many others. Through these acquisitions, Sara Lee not only sells the products of the acquired company but also is provided access to those markets for its brands better known in the United States, such as Hanes, Playtex, Bali, L'eggs, and so on. Additionally, the company has built its own production and distribution facilities in other countries as part of its worldwide expansion plan. As a result of the global expansion efforts, sales in other countries accounted for 30 percent of the division's more than $6 billion in sales in 1993 (Sara Lee Corporation, 1993).

exporting, looking beyond the U.S. borders offers the potential both to expand sales and to offset the growth of imports in domestic markets. Vigdor (1989) asserted that exporting may be the key to many firms' survival and prosperity in the future. Table 12–2 shows sample exports from U.S. apparel firms in 1993.

The apparel exports shown in Table 12–2 indicate that United States apparel manufacturers *can* sell their products in other markets. The reader should take note that Japan is the single largest apparel customer of the United States, accounting for $680 million in sales in 1993. This was a 49 percent increase over 1992. It is ironic to think of Japan as the United States' leading apparel *customer*—after having considered Japan the country's major *threat* as a textile and apparel exporter only 20 years earlier.

Most textile and apparel firms that have a serious commitment to exporting have foreign sales organizations. Sales operations may consist of a company's own sales force or may utilize sales agents who represent several companies. Obviously, direct representation has many advantages if a company is in a position to commit the required resources.

Successful export markets take time to build and require ethical business practices to establish a long-lasting export business. A number of U.S. textile/apparel firms have created poor images for the American industry by viewing overseas markets as a dumping ground for leftovers. Foreign representatives have reported practices known as *seeding the goods*, in which poor quality is included in shipments, and *dropping by container*, in which large shipments (containers for tractor trailers) worth $100,000 to $150,000 are exported with poor-quality merchandise intentionally mixed with that of more desirable quality (anonymous industry source).

U.S. textile and apparel firms have missed a number of opportunities when doors were opened to them, but industry executives passed them by. For example, when the author was in Hong Kong in the early 1990s and met with a number of industry and government leaders, person after person described an incident that had left each puzzled about the interests of U.S. textile producers in securing business.

Hong Kong produces very limited quantities of fabrics (because of space and environmental considerations), so Hong Kong apparel makers must purchase most of their fabrics from elsewhere. Now that Hong Kong produces primarily high-quality garments, its apparel firms need superior fabrics. Many apparel companies were much more dependent on Japanese textiles than they wished to be. Therefore, when a major trade fair for textiles and apparel was held, Hong Kong leaders issued personal invitations to textile manufacturers in the United States and Western Europe because they *wanted to purchase more fabrics from those countries*. The Hong Kong industry leaders who had issued the invitations were baffled by the fact that *not one* U.S. textile firm accepted the invitation. In con-

TABLE 12–2
U.S. Apparel Exports, 1993 ($US millions)

World	$4,552
Japan	680
Canada	369
Belgium/Luxembourg	101
Germany	78
United Kingdom	64
France	57
Saudi Arabia	37
Russia	37
Italy	32
Netherlands	30
Spain	25
EU (total)	407
ASEAN	44

Source: From *U.S. Export Markets (by Group)* (pp. B3,B4) by U.S. Department of Commerce, 1994 (unpublished print out).

ONE MANUFACTURER'S DETERMINATION TO EXPORT: FROM THE SUITCASE UP

Today Riverside Manufacturing Company, with headquarters in Moultrie, Georgia, is the largest privately owned uniform company in the world. The company manufactures uniforms for businesses that want to project a certain company image. Although Riverside Manufacturing now exports to 185 countries, this didn't just happen as a result of good luck. Riverside's stellar export record happened as a result of hard work and the willingness to take risks.

In 1975, Jerry Vereen, who is now president, treasurer, and chief executive officer, took a courageous step that launched Riverside's export efforts. The family-owned company already shipped to all 50 states and sold to several multinational customers—but only for those accounts in the U.S. markets.

In an effort to expand Riverside's international business, Mr. Vereen set out for Europe with four suitcases of samples. He started in Frankfurt, Germany, and started calling on accounts across the continent and on to England. Mr. Vereen proceeded to call on the London marketing director of a major multinational soft-drink bottling company, who was not enthusiastic about doing business with Riverside but did agree to have two employees test the uniforms. Later, Vereen went on to Dublin, Ireland, and, among others, called on an executive with a major security firm who was lukewarm about prospects of being able to get fast response from a U.S.-based firm.

Within a month of the time he returned to Georgia, Vereen had a call from the bottling company's British marketing director, saying he had "a real problem." He reported that workers in the company's 28 plants were demanding uniforms like those tested by their co-workers within 30 days or they were going out on strike. Riverside filled that order.

Shortly afterward, on a Thursday morning, the Dublin executive from the security firm called to say that his company had a new contract with a major automobile firm and needed uniforms for 200 guards *by the following Monday morning*. He had been unable to find a manufacturer in Europe who would help him. Vereen asked for each worker's name and size and told the executive to have a representative at the Dublin airport on Saturday morning to meet the plane. Guards were to try on their uniforms and, in the event some did not fit, another shipment would arrive the next day. The shipment arrived in Ireland on Saturday morning, and every uniform fit. Moreover, the Dublin security firm executive was a speaker at a European security conference shortly afterward and shared the story with conference attendees.

Riverside's international business was launched. Today, the company provides uniforms to firms around the world. Accounts include the major bottling companies (soft drinks and beer), transportation, security, and product and package delivery firms. According to one Department of Commerce source, Riverside exports American-made products to more countries than any other U.S. firm.

Riverside's export business began because one man had the courage to try.

trast, a number of European firms accepted and participated in the trade fair.

In sharing their concerns about the lack of interest on the part of U.S. firms, Hong Kong leaders related that, a few years earlier, one of the large U.S. textile firms established an office in Hong Kong but abandoned it after a relatively short time. They contrasted this to the Japanese determination to establish their sales offices *for the long term* (Hong Kong industry and government leaders' discussions with author, various times).

FIGURE 12–12
The U.S. athletic shirt worn by this employee in a Japanese apparel factory attests to the appeal of U.S. products in other markets.

Source: Photo J. Maillard, courtesy of International Labour Office

INTERNATIONAL MARKETING CONSIDERATIONS

Although the study of international marketing is an extensive subject on its own, we might identify a few basic considerations relevant to our study of the marketing of textile and apparel products globally.

International marketing is "the performance of business activities that direct the flow of a company's goods and services to consumers or users in more than one nation" (Cateora, 1987, p. 4). This definition is similar to any definition of marketing, except for the added focus on more than one country. Although the mechanics of marketing differ little for the global setting, it is the varied environments in which the marketing plan is implemented that makes international marketing a greater challenge than domestic marketing.

Cateora (1987) considers that "the task of marketing managers is to mold the *controllable* elements of their decisions in light of the *uncontrollable* elements of the environment in such a manner that marketing objectives are achieved" (p. 6). A number of elements in the marketing operation may be controlled within the company; these controllables include product, price, promotion, and channels of distribution. In Cateora's model, these elements are shown in the center (Figure 12–13).

Beyond the four elements identified as "controllables," most other influences are external to the firm and beyond the control of the firm's decision makers. Figure 12–13 illustrates the added challenge in international marketing because the marketer must deal with *two levels* of "uncontrollables" rather than one—the domestic environment uncontrollables.

The second circle represents the uncontrollable elements of the domestic environment that have an effect on foreign operations: the political forces, the competition, and the economic climate of the home country. For example, a U.S. (or any country's) foreign policy decision might alter drastically the marketing climate for a company's products in a particu-

FIGURE 12–13

In international marketing, the elements that cannot be controlled are present at two levels—in the domestic environment and in the foreign environment.

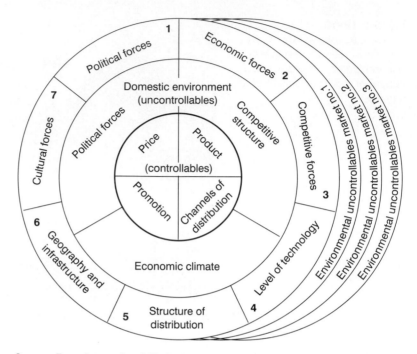

Source: From International Marketing, 6th ed. (p. 9) by P. Cateora, 1987, Homewood, IL: Richard Irwin. Reprinted by permission of Richard Irwin.

lar country. Or competition from another U.S. company may affect a firm's ability to perform successfully in a foreign market. Similarly, domestic economic conditions affect the ability to invest in efforts to pursue international markets.

The outer circles represent the foreign uncontrollables—the elements of the foreign environment in which the marketer operates; a different set of these elements exists for each foreign market. These elements include political forces, economic forces, competitive forces, level of technology, structure of distribution, geography and infrastructure, and cultural forces. Each of these elements represents uncertainty for firms entering a new market, and success will depend on the ability to interpret the influence and the impact of each of the uncontrollable elements on the marketing plan. A comprehensive study of international marketing considers these dimensions in greater detail.

Sensitivity to environmental differences is among the greatest challenges to textile and apparel manufacturers who attempt to enter other markets. J. Lee (1966) noted "the unconscious reference to one's own cultural values [is] the root cause of most international business problems overseas" (p. 106). Similarly, Cateora (1987) stated:

> In any study of the market systems of different peoples, their political and economic structures, religions, and other elements of culture, foreign marketers must constantly guard against measuring and assessing the markets against the fixed values and assumptions of their own cultures. They must take specific steps to make themselves aware of the home-cultural reference in their analyses and decision making. (p. 12)

As an example of cultural differences, in many parts of Asia, individual behavior is bound by constraints that force compliance with norms of various groups. The primacy of group identity over individual identity can have a powerful impact on one's dress. In some settings, uniforms or attire that nearly fulfills the role of a uniform (e.g., formal business suits for the managerial class) reflects the power of group norms compared to more individualistic dress in the West. For example, female dress that could be considered provocative or revealing is not allowed. Practical limitations of the setting come into play as well. In Japan, for example, women who travel to work on the trains where commuters are "packed like sardines" may feel compelled to choose conservative attire since they may involuntarily be pressed against an unknown male for the entire trip (anonymous industry source, 1993). Consequently, a manufacturer who intends to sell in certain Asian markets must keep in mind that low necklines and other features that might be considered provocative will severely affect garment sales.

Similarly, cultural differences may have been a factor in the story given in the last section about the lack of U.S. textile producers' participation in the Hong Kong trade fair. When the author related this story to a U.S. textile industry leader, he indicated that the Hong Kong trade fair organizers had "asked a lot of information about our companies that was none of their business." This is, in fact, how most U.S. citizens would react to having been asked what might appear to be privileged information about their businesses. To Asians, however, the inquiry about the textile firms may have been simply part of the honest openness many Asians have about matters that the typical U.S. individual would call "none of their business." In preparing for a trip to Asia, the author had been cautioned that one should not be offended, for example, if asked about personal matters such as one's income, age, and so on. This was wise counsel because the author was asked many times about her height (which, incidentally, is much above the U.S. average for women). On one occasion in Taipei, a group of Chinese girls

(who were probably looking for an opportunity to practice their English) asked the author's height; after receiving an answer, they burst into giggles and ran away. The Hong Kong request for information from U.S. textile firms may have been as innocent and harmless as the queries about the author's height. The key is to be accepting of practices that may be quite different from those in one's own culture. A good rule of thumb is to give others the benefit of the doubt.

International Marketing Philosophies

As firms consider participation in overseas markets, they may subscribe to one of several international marketing philosophies:

1. We sell what we make.
2. We make what we sell.
3. We adapt what we make to the needs of foreign consumers (Daniels & Radebaugh, 1986, p. 625).

A company's adoption of one of these marketing philosophies makes a great deal of difference in the decisions the company makes regarding its products for the international market.

- *We sell what we make.* This philosophy may exist when a country begins exporting in a passive manner when buyers learn about the product and order it. Under this approach, companies typically do not adapt products to foreign markets and often sell what is left over from the domestic market. In some cases, the foreign markets are considered too small or the expense may be too high for the return involved to justify product adaptation. This philosophy has a production orientation.
- *We make what we sell.* In this case, a country's market is identified but the product is varied (although some standardization of products for the global market may occur).

This philosophy may prevail when a firm wants to penetrate the market in a certain country because of the nation's size, growth potential, desirability of the market location, or for other reasons. This philosophy has a consumer marketing orientation.

• *We adapt what we make to the needs of foreign consumers.* This philosophy combines the other two. The company retains some standardization in which it has established expertise and efficiencies but adapts to the needs of foreign markets in order to retain long-term business (Daniels & Radebaugh, 1986).

In the future, as an increasing number of U.S. companies assume an international orientation in their business operations, success will depend upon the ability to develop multicultural sensitivities and skills.

SUMMARY

The textile and apparel industries in developed countries have been among the first sectors to experience severe international competition. The relative ease of entry by developing countries into textile and apparel production has created intense competition for the industries in the developed countries—both for retaining their own domestic markets and for competing in global markets. As industry and labor in the developed countries attempted to defend their interest and compete in the international market, these groups have used a number of strategies.

First, adjustment strategies have included both firm and industry reorganization to promote more efficient operations. The textile and apparel industries in most developed countries have made substantial progress in restructuring through mergers, consolidations, vertical integration, investment in new technology, and shifts to a stronger marketing orientation. Governments in these countries

have given varying degrees of support in the adjustment process, and results have been quite mixed in terms of performance and international competitiveness. Many adjustment strategies have resulted in job losses. Despite significant structural adjustment in the industries in the industrialized countries, manufacturers find it hard to compete with low-cost producers.

Policy strategies represent another common response to increased global competition. Initially, trade policies designed to restrain low-wage imports were justified to give the textile and apparel industries in the developed countries a "breathing space"— that is, time to adjust to the growing competition. The LDCs, many economists, and free traders have asserted that industry restructuring has occurred too slowly because producers have relied on trade restraints to protect the developed countries' markets.

Several factors led to increasingly complex and institutionalized policies to control imports from the developing countries. Among these factors were the following: substantial import growth, a growing protectionist mood, employment losses, a concern for protecting industry investments, competitive disadvantages, concerns for "burden sharing," and the industry's political prowess. Arguments to justify increased use of protective policy strategies included the need to maintain employment, slowing the pace of adjustment, preserving the incomes of certain groups, protecting domestic labor against cheap foreign labor, preserving key industries, supporting new industries, using protection as a lever to open markets, and combating unfair trade.

While the developing countries have protested against the restraints on their textile/apparel exports, producers in the developed countries have begun to demand reciprocity in trade matters—that is, "a level playing field." Manufacturers are troubled by practices such as the following: dumping, subsidies, high tariffs, closed or partly closed markets, and the granting of foreign aid to assist in the development of textile/apparel industries in developing countries.

Ironically, the policy strategies of the developed countries designed to restrain imports resulted in unexpected consequences. In many cases, restraints led to the development of new suppliers, shifts in product lines, product upgrading, guaranteed market access, establishment of foreign-owned plants in the importing markets, and circumvention of quotas.

Whereas restructuring and policy measures are responses to global changes, the U.S. textile and apparel producers launched *proactive* marketing efforts as an offensive approach in countering foreign competition. Manufacturers learned they must assume a stronger marketing and service orientation to regain and retain retailers' business. The Quick Response initiative began in an effort to fill this need and has resulted in a closer working relationship within the domestic softgoods chain.

In addition, a number of developed country textile and apparel producers have realized the importance of participating more actively in the international arena. Textile and apparel firms have become aware of the advantages of international linkages for both production and marketing operations. Among these global initiatives are the following: international sourcing, multinational enterprises, international licensing, direct investments, joint ventures, and exporting. A number of basic international marketing considerations must be taken into account to assure success in differing cultural environments.

In summary, industry and labor groups in the developed countries have used a number of strategies to defend their interests in an increasingly complex and demanding global market. A number of the strategies have helped increase global competitiveness, while other approaches have protected domestic markets.

GLOSSARY

Anti-dumping duties are duties that may be levied against dumped goods if dumping causes injury to the industry in the importing country. These duties may be equal to the difference between the export price of the products and their "fair value" in the export market.

Capital deepening refers to an increasing investment in a firm or in the industry in general.

Countervailing duties are duties levied on imported products to offset subsidies to producers or exporters of those products in the exporting country. GATT provisions permit the levy of countervailing duties if material injury to the importing country's producers occurs.

Direct investment refers to ownership of a substantial interest in a foreign operation.

Dumped products are those products exported at prices below fair market value. **Dumping** may refer to selling products abroad for less than they sell for domestically. Dumping is considered an unfair trade practice.

Export subsidies are government payments to a manufacturer or exporter contingent upon export of goods. Export subsidies are also a form of dumping and are illegal under international agreements.

Fair trade is a term used by the textile and apparel industries in developed countries as they seek reciprocal trade privileges with the LDCs. The developed country industries have argued that trade should take place on "a level playing field."

Industry strategy refers to the prevailing or dominant strategy adopted by an industry's larger and more "progressive" firms; it does not mean all firms within an industry have adopted identical strategies, and combinations are common (Toyne et al., 1984).

International marketing is composed of "business activities that direct the flow of a company's goods and services to consumers or users in more than one nation" (Cateora, 1987, p. 4).

Joint venture refers to the partnership between a foreign-owned firm with a partner in another country. More than two partners may be involved.

Mechanization refers to the replacement of human labor with machines.

Minimum viable production is a concept developed by the Nordic countries to justify protecting their textile and apparel industries for strategic reasons (usually defense reasons). This means the country may protect its domestic industry so the country can be self-sustaining—in other words, that it will have minimum viable production capabilities in a national crisis such as war.

Multinational enterprises (MNE) are firms with an integrated global approach to production and marketing and which have both domestic and overseas operations. Also see "transnational corporations" in Chapter 4.

Outward processing is the European term for shipping cut garment pieces to low-wage countries for labor-intensive assembly operations (comparable to 9802 [807] production).

Rationalization refers to the elimination of excess steps in the labor (production) process. In industrial terms, this also refers to eliminating the weak (or "irrational") components of a business or a sector.

Reciprocity is a principle of GATT under which governments are expected to extend comparable concessions to each other. However, the developing countries have not been required to offer fully reciprocal concessions; that is referred to as *nonreciprocity*.

Retaliation in trade occurs when one country responds to another's trade restraints by enacting measures intended to be detrimental to the country imposing restraints (for example, by refusing to buy certain products because restraints were imposed on other products or services).

Subsidies are financial benefits conferred on a firm or industry by the government. Providing subsidies is considered an unfair trade practice.

SUGGESTED READINGS

Anson, R., & Simpson, P. (1988). *World textile trade and production trends.* London: The Economist Intelligence Unit.
A review of global textile and apparel trade and trade policies.

Bernstein, A., Konrad, W., & Therrien, L. (1992, August 10). The global economy: Who gets hurt? *Business Week*, pp. 48–53.
This article discusses the impact of the global economy and global shifts of production on the U.S. workforce.

COMITEXTIL. (1986). The importance of reciprocity of access in textile markets. *COMITEXTIL Bulletin*, 86/1, 24–30.
A review of EU concerns for reciprocity in textile trade.

COMITEXTIL. (1990). *Levelling the playing field in international textile and clothing trade.* Brussels: Author.
Proceedings from an industry-government conference on unfair trade practices, sponsored by the European textile and apparel manufacturers' associations.

Congress of the United States, Congressional Budget Office (1991, December) *Trade restraints and the competitive status of the textile, apparel, and nonrubber-footwear industries.* Washington: Author.
An evaluation of the status of the industries, particularly in terms of the potential impact of the Uruguay Round and NAFTA agreements.

Ghadar, F., Davidson, W., & Feigenoff, C. (1987). *U.S. industrial competitiveness: The case of the textile and apparel industries.* Lexington, MA: Lexington Books.

This book reviews global and domestic forces that have affected the performance of the U.S. textile and apparel industries.

U.S. Department of Commerce. (published periodically). *A basic guide to exporting.* Washington, DC.: Author.
Basic information on how to start exporting and to have export efforts succeed.

Vargish, G. (1988). *What's made in the U.S.A.?* New Brunswick: Transaction Books.
A critical assessment of U.S. trade policy by a retired U.S. textile industry executive.

Vigdor, I. (1991). *Exporting: Get into it!—For the fashion industry* (2nd ed.). Merrick, NY: Redwood Associates.

A useful collection of articles, basic information, and examples of shipping documents to assist exporters and potential exporters.

Wolff, A., Howell, T., & Noellert, W. (1988). *The reality of world trade in textiles and apparel.* Washington, DC: Dewey, Ballantine, Bushby, Palmer & Wood.
This report summarizes the perceived disadvantages to U.S. textile and apparel producers in the present world trading scheme.

13

The Interests of Retailers and Importers in Textile and Apparel Trade

INTRODUCTION

Retailers and **importers**, like textile and apparel manufacturers, have a great deal at stake in textile and apparel trade matters. Representing positions on textile/apparel trade as seemingly incompatible as oil and water, the importing/retailing sector and the manufacturing sector[1] have been at odds in recent years and have taken their differences to the public and political arenas.

Although conflict between suppliers and retailers is not new, the complexity and the intensity of the conflict between the two sectors regarding textile/apparel imports have added an especially tense dimension to these relationships. U.S. textile/apparel manufacturers consider imported products as the primary reason for decline of the domestic industry; therefore, industry and labor leaders are strongly committed to restricting imported products. On the other hand, as retailers have experienced a difficult competitive period themselves, they have found imported products to be quite helpful to sales and profits. Consequently, most retailers and importers have favored imports as much as most manufacturers and labor have opposed them. Because of these conflicting positions, it is easy to see why manufacturers and retailers have become adversaries on textile and apparel trade.

U.S. textile and apparel industry leaders believe retailers have played a key role in creating the large trade deficit in this sector in recent years. Since retailers are the "gatekeepers" in determining the merchandise that ultimately reaches the consumer, most domestic

---

[1]We must keep in mind that many apparel manufacturers are also importers; therefore, those manufacturers are not included in the anti-import group.

manufacturers believe that imported products would not be available for consumers to buy if retailers did not offer them for sale.

Friction between the manufacturers' and the importer/retailers' groups might be expected. Each of these sectors employs large numbers of persons across the nation. Each provides lifeblood for communities—both large and small. Both are intensely competitive sectors in which an overcapacity exists: Overcapacity for production has occurred at the global level, and a U.S. overabundance of retail space—that is, "over-storing"—has developed at the national level. Both are highly competitive sectors in that profit margins (on certain measures) tend to be lower than for many other business and industry areas.

Global market conditions have affected each sector in important ways and have intensified the ill will between suppliers and retailers. In fact, imports have been the most important influence on the U.S. textile and apparel market since the early 1960s. In recent decades, as U.S. manufacturers experienced intermittently sluggish markets because of declines in the economy, they also felt the impact of a growing number of new global suppliers who took an increasing share of their markets, particularly for apparel. The global proliferation in the supply of textile and apparel products created a "buyer's market," in the truest sense of the word. Low-cost products and other favorable market conditions began to encourage retailers and importers to bring increasing amounts of textile and apparel imports into U.S. markets (Figure 13–1). As importers and retail buyers sought greater variety, exclusivity, and attractive prices in their merchandise selections, they soon considered global sourcing as a normal strategy. Buyers' proficiency in tapping into the international array of products has not enhanced their popularity within textile/apparel industry circles, however.

Many U.S. manufacturers see textile and apparel imports, unless controlled, as leading to the demise of the industry. Retailers and importers, on the other hand, find increased import restraints both frustrating and devastating to their business interests. In recent years, each side has devoted increasing time, energy, and funding to furthering its position on textile/apparel trade policies.

In this chapter, we will consider the special interests of retailers and importers on textile

FIGURE 13–1

Retailers and importers buy textile and apparel products from many countries to bring to the U.S. market. This practice has caused U.S. manufacturers to blame retailers, in particular, for the large increases in imported textile and apparel merchandise.

Source: Photo courtesy of World Bank.

and apparel trade and trade policies. In the softgoods industry, retailers account for a majority of the importing of textile and apparel products; therefore, most of this discussion will focus on retailers. One should remember, however, that there are also import firms that purchase large quantities of products and sell them in turn to retailers.

Discussion will consider retailers' reasons for buying imported textile and apparel goods and the types of problems associated with foreign buying. In addition, new strategies that are improving U.S. supplier-retailer relationships will be considered.

RETAIL SECTOR OVERVIEW

Retailing (all types combined) is a major industry in the United States, employing over 19 million persons, roughly 17 percent of the nation's work force. Annual retail sales are over $2 trillion (U.S. Department of Commerce, 1994; U.S. Department of Labor, 1993). Although these statistics refer to all types of retailing combined, apparel sales alone represent the *most important merchandise category* for department stores, mass merchandisers, and specialty stores (Ghadar et al., 1987).

Department stores and department chain stores (including J.C. Penney, Sears, and Montgomery Ward) have in the past been the largest source of retail apparel sales; however, other types of retail outlets are taking some of the apparel market. *Retail consolidations* are a fact of life that affect softgoods companies. In 1987, the five largest softgoods retailers accounted for 35 percent of all retail apparel sales. By 1991, the five largest retailers sold over 45 percent of all apparel (Mellen, 1993). Shifts have occurred in *types of stores* where apparel and other softgoods merchandise are sold as the major discount and other off-price retailers gradually taking market share from department and specialty stores.

The number of U.S. primary retail establishments selling apparel and accessories is as follows:

	National Population	
	N	%
General merchandise stores	35,434	19.2
Apparel and accessory specialty stores	149,435	80.8
Total	184,869	100.0

Sales by major types of stores (in billions of dollars) that sell softgoods products are as follows:

	1991	1992	1993	1994*
General merchandise group	228	247	280	320
Apparel group	97	105	108	112

*Estimate (U.S. Department of Commerce, 1994)

Despite consolidations in retailing, a substantial portion of retail firms carrying apparel/accessory lines are relatively small, using the number of employees as a measure. Data from the *Census of Retail Trade* indicate the distribution shown in Table 13–1 according to number of employees.

We must keep in mind that retailing—like apparel manufacturing—is quite fragmented and consists of a large number of small operations, along with firms that are quite large. Representatives of many of these small retail firms are not likely to be vocal or politically active in representing the interests of the retailing sector on trade matters.

A number of broad retailing trends have had an impact on apparel retailing. Discussion of a few particularly important trends follows.

TABLE 13–1
Retail firms carrying apparel/accessory lines, by number of employees

Number of Employees	General Merchandise Stores (%)	Apparel/Accessory Specialty Stores (%)
4 or fewer	23	37
5–9	16	30
10–19	11	15
20–49	11	5
50–99	11	0.9
100 or more	20	0.2

Source: U.S. Department of Commerce (1985).

Excess Selling Space

As a result of many retailers' aggressive expansion strategies, the U.S. market is "overstored," creating intensely competitive conditions for retailers. Ghadar et al. (1987) noted the 200 percent growth in shopping space square footage between 1972 and 1984. Expansion continued during the 1980s despite the saturation of many major markets. As retailers attempted to cope with excess selling space, they vacated marginal locations, consolidated, scrutinized investments carefully shifted resources to areas where they received the best returns, and enhanced their marketing efforts. A number of retailers tried repositioning strategies.

Low Profitability per Square Foot

In the 1980s, retailers' profitability per square foot remained the same or dropped lower than levels for the mid-1970s. The drop resulted from increased operating costs, overstoring, and a decline in consumer expenditures ("The State", 1993; Ghadar et al., 1987).

Restructuring

As a result of mergers, takeovers, and consolidations, apparel retailing has changed dramatically. Now, more and more power is concentrated in the hands of fewer retailing firms. Additionally, **mass merchandisers** have become increasingly powerful. The concentration of buying power means that an increasingly small pool of megamerchant buyers will be working with suppliers, both globally and domestically.

Emergence of Power Retailers

Power retailers are fast-growing chains that attract customers with superior merchandise, sharper pricing, or greater convenience (examples are Wal-Mart, Home Depot, and Toys "R" Us) than their competitors. They are revolutionizing the retailing industry with performances that far exceed the industry average. The collective share of the market being taken by the power retailers, plus the consolidations of other large retail firms, means that the gulf is widening between the large megamerchants and the smaller, less-competitive retailers.

Repositioning Strategies

The intense competition in retailing has caused many retailers to reposition their companies—either in the types of merchandise sold or, in some cases, in the markets sought. J.C. Penney, for example, used both these strategies. J.C. Penney shifted to softgoods lines and away from household durables and automotive products. Then, within softgoods lines, Penney traded up from the "mass merchandiser" image to higher-cost product lines to lure the traditional department store customer.

In contrast, in 1989, Sears assumed a discount store orientation and to an extent reduced its emphasis on apparel. Having difficulty in defining who and what it was, within three years Sears decided to become primarily a softgoods merchandiser, which included ending the catalog business and revamping stores to draw particularly the apparel customer.

Non-Store Retailing

Between 1988 and 1992, home shopping purchases (this includes catalog shopping and tv shopping) grew 30 percent (after inflation), compared to a 3 percent decline at shopping centers for the same period. However, Sears' abandonment of its catalog, which had become an American tradition, and the slump in television shopping via the Home Shopping Network appeared to spell a decline for non-store shopping. Suddenly, the QVC Network became one of the hottest topics in the softgoods industry, with sales that astounded manufacturers and retailers alike. QVC reported that apparel constituted 17 percent of total sales, compared to only 10 percent in 1990. Despite the fact that QVC is considered a major retail force, other retailers such as Saks Fifth Avenue contracted for blocks of time and had remarkable sales. Manufacturers began to see the tremendous potential for television shopping (Eldridge, 1993; conversations with industry sources).

Private Label Programs

Private label lines are merchandise lines manufactured for specific retailers and sold exclusively in their stores. Private labels have been used as merchandising tools, particularly in apparel merchandising. When private label lines originated, these goods were used to reflect a store's originality (or, in many cases, good value for the price). Soon, however, they became important sources for improved markups. Private label retailers have been major users of lower-cost imported products in many cases to provide the healthy **markups**. Imports for private label use will be discussed further later in this chapter.

Matrix Buying

As retailers have scrambled to survive the difficult economic environment in recent years, many have concentrated their purchasing power to a much more limited group of **vendors**, in a strategy called **matrix buying**. Called *"the matrix"* in the industry, this preferred vendor list consists of suppliers who can supply the products, service, and pricing that retailers need to execute their respective strategies. For example, Federated Stores centralized its former divisional men's tailored clothing and reduced the number of vendors from 52 to 11. A Kurt Salmon Associates study revealed that half the top retailers planned to reduce supplier lists in most categories. As a result of this trend, apparel manufacturers will find it increasingly important to work to develop close relationships with retail customers (Abend, 1993; "Doing Business," 1993; Mellen, 1993).

BACKGROUND ON CHANNEL RELATIONSHIPS

For several decades, scholars in the fields of marketing, management, and retailing have studied relationships among members within the supplier-retailer channels of distribution. Although many different definitions exist, Bucklin (1966), one of the early writers on channel relationships, defined **channels of distribution** as a set of institutions that performs all the functions required to move a product and its title from production to consumption.

Literature on channel relationships helps us to realize that the conflict between manufacturers and retailers is not new. Therefore, as we consider the difficulties between manufacturers and retailers pertaining to textile and apparel trade, we might think of these as late-twentieth-century global chapters in a saga that has persisted for decades. Admittedly, several changes in the global business environment have intensified the difficulties in supplier-retailer relationships.

Although channel relationships are basically economic in nature, social relationships underlie economic connections. Sturdivant and Granbois (1973) asserted that channel complexity and dynamism make economic and quantitative models inadequate. Therefore, a large part of the theoretical and empirical work in this field has focused on the behavioral aspects of channel relationships such as power and conflict. Conflict and struggles for leadership or power are natural in working relationships and are inevitable in distribution channels; therefore, power and conflict have been among the most commonly examined dimensions of channel relationships (Etgar, 1976; Frazier, 1983; Lusch & Brown, 1982). L. Stern (1969) considered a social systems approach for channel relationships, which had the following three major implications: (1) each member of a distribution channel is dependent upon the behavior of other channel members; (2) a behavior change at any point in the channel causes change throughout the channel; and (3) the whole channel must operate effectively if the desires of any one member are to be realized (p. 2).

Most experts have concluded that retailers have an inevitable degree of power in the channel relationship (that is, **channel control**) because merchants provide access to the consumer. Most consumer goods pass through a channel of distribution, through various suppliers early in the channel and retailers at the end (Mallen, 1963). Since merchants represent the means through which suppliers get their products to consumers, harmonious working relationships with retailers are critical to manufacturers. If retailers do not buy a manufacturer's products for their stores, the producer has limited opportunity to get the company's merchandise to end-use consumers. This power puts retailers in a position to make increasing demands on manufacturers if they choose to do so. Retailers may impose quality, price, or timing demands that are difficult for the supplier to meet—yet, manufacturers must comply to retain accounts. J. Brown (1981) found that in more formalized marketing channel relationships, retailers tended to make greater demands of their suppliers than is true for less formalized relationships. Shootshtari, Walker, and Jackson (1988) found that members of the three retail trade associations perceived their associations as a modest source of power in relation to their suppliers.

In short, as each segment of the channel pursues its own business strategies, often these are not in the best interests of that segment's traditional channel partners. Although this has been true traditionally, global market conditions have intensified the difficulty in apparel supplier-retailer relationships. As retailers turned increasingly to low-cost imports for their apparel lines, U.S. manufacturers felt the impact of lost sales. Traditionally, retailers have had greater power in the supplier-retailer relationship; however, the added options of being able to turn to foreign producers for lower-cost products or for other reasons has increased retailers' power in channel relationships.

RETAILERS AND IMPORTS

In recent years, most retailers have been attracted increasingly to the purchase of textile and apparel products, particularly apparel, made in low-wage countries as part of their **sourcing** strategies. Data from the American Apparel Manufacturers Association (1984) indicate that as recently as 1975, only 12 percent of the apparel sold by U.S. retailers was imported. By 1984, stores had doubled their use of imported apparel. In earlier years, retailers bought and sold imported apparel in a relatively limited number of product lines, including inexpensive shirts, blouses, sportswear, and decorative infants' wear. More recently, however, retailers expanded both (1) the *new garment lines* in which imports became an important part of inventories (imports are found now in virtually all lines), and (2) the *number of countries* from which they sourced apparel. Now retailers carry in varying degrees imported apparel in most product lines and from a wide range of countries around the world. Moreover, a majority of retailers consider "foreign sourcing" or "international sourcing" a fact of life in today's competitive retailing environment. As a result, a typical U.S. clothing store (or department) now resembles an international apparel shop when one considers the array of countries in which the garments were produced (Dickerson, 1988a).

Textile and apparel retailers became part of a larger economic shift away from self-sufficient national economies to an integrated system of worldwide production. As we considered in earlier discussions on trade theories, the critical question was: Where can products be produced most efficiently in terms of resource availability and relative cost of resources compared to production in other countries? For apparel production, labor costs involved in assembling garments were at the heart of the issue.

In today's international division of labor, labor receiving higher wages has been replaced increasingly by unskilled or semi-skilled labor receiving lower wages. For apparel production, this meant that more and more of the manufacturing has taken place in developing countries where wages are lower. As active participants in the global economy, retailers have taken advantage of the choices and prices available to them in this international market. As a growing number of countries began to produce apparel for the world markets, retailers found foreign suppliers increasingly eager to cater to merchants' needs. Producers in developing countries

offered garments produced by workers earning as little as 25 cents per hour, in contrast to those produced at much higher wages in U.S. (or other developed country) factories.

Eager to attract business, foreign textile and apparel producers were willing to produce according to retail buyers' wishes—which might include special design features, smaller production runs than many U.S. firms would consider, or other special requests. And, significantly, retailers' foreign sourcing options increased dramatically during an era when U.S. retail competition became more intense. Therefore, as over-storing and more difficult retail competition occurred, foreign sourcing provided merchants with alternatives for variety, exclusivity, and attractive prices. In short, retailers secured foreign-made textile and apparel products because these served their interests well. Conditions of a market economy attracted retailers to foreign suppliers—with no intent to cause injury to the U.S. textile and apparel industries.

Types of Foreign Sourcing

Retailers secure foreign-made textile and apparel products through a variety of arrangements. Business relationships range from those in which the retailer is involved minimally in the production of the merchandise to those in which retailers have assumed more and more of the production responsibilities, essentially becoming manufacturers of sorts themselves. When retailers take on manufacturing responsibilities, this is known as **vertical retailing**. Until fairly recently, retailers imported apparel that was adapted from U.S.-produced garments. Now, however, retailers may initiate their own styling and designing, develop garment specifications, hire contractors, and arrange for the packaging and shipping of merchandise to their stores. In general, sourcing options for retailers (which also include domestic sourcing options) are as plentiful and varied as they are

FIGURE 13–2
Retail buyers negotiate to purchase hand-woven textile items at an outlet in the Middle East. (Photo courtesy of the International Labour Office.)

for manufacturers. A review of apparel manufacturers' sourcing options in Chapter 9 may be helpful at this point.

A number of major U.S. retail firms have established **foreign buying offices** in the Far East, in particular, to monitor production and other aspects of sourcing in those regions. Retailers' representatives have worked closely with foreign manufacturers in assuring that garments meet certain standards required by the retail firm. In some instances, U.S. retail firms have trained foreign producers to be more competitive by helping them to be sensitive to American expectations of style and quality. Often, this has included technical assistance in producing garments to meet these expectations. In these arrangements, retail agents have played a role in transferring

expertise (and sometimes accompanying technology) to foreign producers. In particular, technical assistance has been required by producers in countries first entering apparel production; however, as a nation and its industry become more advanced in technological and other skills, the outside advisement is required less and less. For example, countries that have advanced to the level of the Big Three, the NICs, have sophisticated industries and require little technical assistance; however, some retail firms have offices in the region to coordinate details related to design, production, shipping, and trade regulations.

Regardless of the types of business relationships U.S. retail firms have established with manufacturers in other countries, these foreign suppliers have benefited from production, marketing, and other expertise provided them. As might be expected, U.S. textile and apparel manufacturers have resented having U.S. retail firms "train" foreign competitors. (On the other hand, manufacturing firms often do the same thing when they contract for offshore production.)

Retailers' Reasons for Buying Imports

Most retailers have bought and sold imported textile and apparel products (most of our discussion will focus on apparel) for a variety of reasons. Some of the more common reasons are presented and discussed.

Lower Costs—and Possibly Higher Markups

As noted earlier, the lower costs of imported apparel have been an asset to retailers during difficult competitive periods in retailing. In the 1970s, retailers in most developed countries turned to imports for a growing portion of their apparel inventories. Maas (1980), a member of the Board of Management of Herma BV of Amsterdam (one of Holland's larger chain stores) and also past-president of the European Foreign Trade Association in Brussels and Cologne, defended retailers' heavy purchases of imported items by saying: "The trade is forced to supply the best possible value at the lowest possible prices. Such supplies must increasingly be purchased in those Third [-World] countries which provide good quality products at reasonable prices because of the advantages they have over others" (p. 179). Maas reflected the sentiment of a large number of retailers in most developed countries.

A U.S. study by Pregelj ("When Free Trade," 1977) was the first to call attention to retailers' markup practices on lower-cost imported apparel. Pregelj's "Library of Congress Study on Imports and Consumer Prices" concluded that many retailers, not consumers, benefit financially from apparel produced in low-wage countries. Pregelj's findings triggered many questions regarding retailers' higher markups on low-cost imports from developing countries.

The National Retail Merchants Association (NRMA, 1977) replied to the Pregelj Study, detailing added costs involved in importing, which necessitate higher markups. Cited were (1) higher buying expense; (2) longer lead time; (3) absence of recourse to return defective shipments; (4) uncertainty of costs due to currency fluctuations and freight rate changes; (5) absence of cooperative advertising funds and promotional packages; and (6) difficulties associated with sensitive timing for fashion items in relation to the unpredictable nature of importing. The report also emphasized the competitive nature of the department store business, which resulted in a 3 percent average net profit on sales during the 10 years prior to the report. Some of these points will be discussed further in considering the disadvantages of importing; however, NRMA offered these points as justification for higher markups on imports.

A fact of life in today's retail climate is that most merchants feel the need to find ways to offset downward pressure on margins. As Van Fossan (1985), a consultant to the softgoods industry, noted to manufacturers: "The search for higher initial mark-on, followed (in theory) by higher **gross margin**, is a critical factor in any sourcing decision. . . . Remember the buyer's perspective; he can land merchandise at 60% to 70% mark-on[2] and still play the promotional game with better than average gross margin results. There is a real benefit in being able to plan off-price events without giving away the store" (p. 1). Some retailers also

---

[2]Markup or mark-on figures used in this chapter are based on retail, unless stated otherwise.

believe that the higher markups on imports helps to offset the greater risks of importing.

Attractive Prices to Customers

If the savings associated with production in low-wage countries are passed on to customers—rather than absorbed in higher retail markups—imported products may be offered at attractive prices. Many mass merchandisers (and other retailers as well) whose reputations are based on good quality at affordable prices do, in fact, pass the lower costs on to consumers. In addition, imported apparel products offered for sale in these stores may feature tedious, complex production details possible only where labor costs are quite low; examples are smocking, hand embroidery, piping, and intricate tucks and pleats. Labor costs in developed countries such as the United States would make garments with labor-intensive details of this type exceedingly costly and perhaps not within the price range of mass market customers.

In short, many retailers believe imported apparel has been a good buy for their stores and for their customers. Sternquist and Tolbert (1986) found that a majority of retail buyers believed imported merchandise "provided better quality for the price than domestic apparel" (p. 8). Department store buyers, in particular, acknowledged higher markups on imported apparel. In many cases, retailers assert the higher markups are used for **price averaging**.

Variety and Exclusivity

Retailers argue that foreign-made products provide important variety and exclusivity for their inventories. Fashion retailing thrives on variety. Furthermore, the demand for uniqueness is critical so retailers can distinguish their merchandise and their stores from their competition. Because apparel retailers require a steady flow of new and distinctive products, sourcing global markets yields more variety than a national market can provide.

Often retailers have gone offshore for their apparel lines because they have been unable to get the design and fabrication they wanted from U.S. manufacturers. As we discussed earlier in chapters pertaining to the domestic textile and apparel industries, this sector of U.S. manufacturing has been geared toward volume production. Moreover, the large, captive domestic market of earlier decades had not required the U.S. industry to pursue a serious marketing orientation. Manufacturers produced what they believed they should produce, and, in the days before increased foreign competition, the U.S. market generally absorbed the merchandise. As a result of this earlier lack of a marketing orientation, retailers have claimed that American manufacturers have not been receptive to merchants' requests for special styling, fabrication, or other features that provide variety and exclusivity. In short, retailers have felt that the high-volume orientation of U.S. suppliers has provided too much "sameness" and that U.S. suppliers are not close enough (i.e., sensitive enough) to the consumer.

Imports for Private Label Lines

As competitive conditions of retailing fostered development of private label lines to provide distinctive merchandise, apparel retailers have been primary users of this strategy. Both department stores and specialty stores have made increasing use of private label programs. Private label apparel represents a major retailing trend that has permitted stores to develop their own lines—that is, the apparel line is created according to the retailer's request and bears a label adopted by that retail firm for its private label or "branded" lines. Examples of private label lines are: J.C. Penney's Silk Avenue, Gentry, Hunt Club, and Fox; Macy's Charter Club and Aéropostale; and The Limited's Outback Red.

Strong private label programs permit retailers to differentiate themselves from their competition. Private label merchandise is manufactured (contracted) by retailers and sold exclusively in their own department stores or specialty shops. Private label lines create new brand names in a customer's mind, providing a measure of exclusivity to the retailer. Although department stores have long produced a number of house brands, most were staple merchandise. Now, however, updated private label lines are taking business away from well-known designer lines. According to Kurt Salmon Associates (a consulting firm that works with both manufacturers and retailers in the softgoods industry), private label goods constituted about 25 percent of the total market in 1993, and that share is expected to increase (Perman, 1993). Products typically provide good value for the cost, which is often about 20 percent less than brand-name counterparts (Rudolph, 1988).

Most off-price retailers prefer to carry well-known (national) brands for the bulk of their lines and do not consider private label merchandise. In contrast, department and specialty stores use private label lines to an increasing degree. Kurt Salmon Associates (1988; 1993) noted that several major department store groups have revealed that private label merchandise will soon account for 30–50 percent of the apparel they sell. At J.C. Penney, private label makes up 60 percent of the women's apparel volume and is the fastest growing portion of the chain's merchandise mix. At Saks Fifth Avenue, 30 percent of the women's sportswear, excluding designer goods, is private label (Perman, 1993).

Although private label lines can be produced for retailers by U.S. manufacturers, more often than not, goods are produced in low-wage developing countries. In fact, private label programs have accounted for a substantial portion of retailers' increased purchase of foreign-made goods. In most private label programs, the retailer goes directly to the foreign manufacturer and bypasses the U.S. producer. Retailers often feel they have more "ownership"—that is, they can be more creative and exercise greater control—over their private label programs that use imports, compared to buying their merchandise from domestic resources.

 ## WHO IS A RETAILER AND WHO IS A MANUFACTURER?

Kurt Salmon Associates (1988) noted that private label production has spawned new sights in the softgoods industry:

- Among the crowded lofts of New York's garment district, a large department store group has its own design studio, fully equipped with CAD terminals that are the envy of its apparel manufacturer neighbors.
- On the classified pages of industry publications, retailers' large help-wanted ads compete with manufacturers for the same designers, production coordinators, and quality assurance people.
- At apparel industry trade shows, retailers now inspect garment components and production equipment alongside apparel manufacturers.
- In Asia, a U.S. retailer takes a position in cashmere futures to assure that the firm will have enough yarn for its private label sweater program in the year ahead.

Although it is a sensitive subject, experts generally agree that private label merchandise carries higher than usual markups—another reason for the healthy growth of private label programs. Examples of sources that indicated that private label merchandise carries higher markups follow.

- Fendel (1984) reviewed private label programs and noted, "Markup values were, predictably, cited as an important factor behind stores' desire to use private label" (p. 131).
- Bruna Sumberao, an executive with Associated Dry Goods Marketing at the time, noted: "As competition among retailers increases, private label provides stores with the added advantages of higher markups, exclusivity, and a more flexible promotional calendar, plus the opportunity to offer consumers a lower price for quality merchandise by cutting out the middleman" ("Markup Benefit," 1984, p. 24).
- Brick (1983) reported: "Independent men's wear retailers are developing private label clothing packages that provide them with 60 to 75% markups to improve their profit margins" (p. 1). He cited examples of men's wear specialty stores that obtained markups in this range, quoting one as saying, "But, later in the season, we can reduce those retail prices by about 30% and still realize markups of 40%" (p. 15).

The move toward private label lines represents a significant shift in merchandise procurement that appears to be permanent in the softgoods industry. Retailers have already shifted millions of dollars toward private label lines and are expected to continue the trend. Consumers are said to like private label merchandise because it gives them more choices. Many resent seeing so many other copies of their clothing when they buy brand names.

Certain Products Are Not Available From Domestic Producers

Retailers say that certain products either are not available or have been increasingly difficult to secure domestically. Here, retailers are referring to products other than those for which they are seeking variety or exclusivity. In some cases, these are product areas in which domestic firms have abandoned production because of difficulties in competing with foreign competition. The following products are examples.

- Shoes are a prime example. As the labor-intensive U.S. shoe industry finds it increasingly difficult to compete with lower-cost imports, American shoe factories continue to close their doors. Currently, about 80 percent of all shoes sold in the United States are imported. Retailers can no longer secure an adequate domestic inventory of shoes for their customers, even if prices were comparable and they chose to do so.
- Gloves have become increasingly difficult to buy from U.S. suppliers. Again, the labor-intensive aspects of glovemaking pose difficulties for manufacturers in higher-wage developed countries. Consequently, few U.S. glove suppliers remain in business.
- Standard-quality dress shirts (and some other shirts as well) are becoming increasingly difficult to buy from U.S. suppliers. The labor-intensive nature of dress shirts—with the characteristic banded collars, placket cuffs, yokes, and placket fronts—has caused a great deal of this production to shift to low-wage countries. In fact, retailers might have some degree of difficulty in securing domestically produced shirts from U.S. apparel firms—because they, too, have taken advantage of lower wages and have their own lines produced in other countries.
- In most developed countries, a supply gap has occurred in domestically produced

children's wear, particularly at lower prices. Because wages represent a high proportion of production costs in children's wear (this is also true for adult clothing, but it is more so for children's clothing), manufacturers in high-wage countries have found it difficult to produce inexpensive children's clothing. In recent years, however, retailers such as Wal-Mart, who are committed to working with domestic suppliers, have found that U.S. manufacturers can incorporate production efficiencies that permit them to compete effectively in the children's wear market.

Foreign Producers' Service, Willingness to Please

Eager to secure and maintain the business of U.S. and other developed-country retailers, manufacturers in the textile and apparel exporting nations make a special effort to serve retail customers. Many foreign producers are keenly aware of the global oversaturation of textile and apparel products and know that if they are to succeed within that climate, they must not only offer good prices but be willing also to accommodate the wishes of the customer. Therefore, foreign manufacturers often have been more receptive to retailers' styling and other requests than domestic producers have been. Similarly, retailers have reported that overseas producers have been willing to provide short production runs and exclusivity, whereas most American manufacturers turned their backs on these orders.

Inertia

Van Fossan (1985) speculated that "inertia" counts for some of retailers' direct importing. As he noted, it is last season's or last year's performance, good or bad, that provides a direction or course of action for many retailers. Inertia refers to the established way of looking at things or doing things. Van Fossan asserted that inertia is usually present in retail

organizations, especially in those companies characterized by rapid turnover at the buyer and divisional merchandise manager levels. Van Fossan's point was that if buyers secured their apparel lines overseas in the previous year, they probably continued doing so without a thorough review of long-term costs and benefits available through a wide array of sourcing options.

A Survey of Retailers' Reasons for Buying Imported Apparel

In a study of 191 U.S. retailers' practices in buying and carrying imported apparel, merchants were asked to identify their reasons for buying imported clothing. Retailers' answers, which were generated in response to open-ended questions (in other words, options for answers were not presented), are summarized in Figure 13–3.

FIGURE 13–3
Retailers' reasons for buying imported apparel.

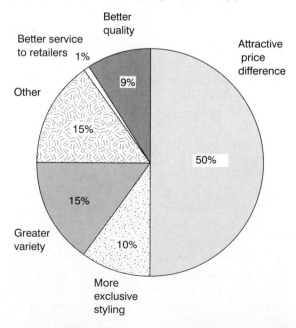

Findings from the study supported assumptions that retailers carry imports primarily because of attractive price differences; however, results also show that greater variety, exclusivity, and providing better quality were important reasons.

On another question in this study, retailers were asked to share their views on the quality of imported apparel compared to U.S.-made clothing. Of the respondents, 10 percent saw imported apparel as better quality; 31 percent saw quality as the same; 51 percent believed imports to be of lesser quality; and 7 percent were undecided (Dickerson, 1989).

Problems for Retailers in Buying Imported Apparel

Although retailers have found a number of advantages in overseas sourcing, they have encountered a substantial number of problems and disadvantages. For many retailers, imported products have been a mixed blessing. Some of the more common problems are presented and discussed.

Poor or Unpredictable Quality

Particularly when Third-World countries are in the earlier stages of development and when the country has first entered production in the industry (generally in apparel assembly operations), often products have been of poor or unpredictable quality. Also, garment design often has been lacking in sophistication and inconsistent with current style trends. Although quality generally improves as the country's industry develops, large quantities of products are shipped to the importing markets of the United States and Europe before production skills and other expertise reach the level to produce merchandise consistently acceptable to discriminating consumers in developed countries.

Workers in developing countries who have never owned—or perhaps even seen—quality garments according to Western standards may have difficulty in understanding expectations for straight stitching and other perfected details. Even plant supervisors who are natives of the exporting country may fail to recognize the types of flaws in a garment that will cause it to be considered "poor quality" in the markets of industrialized countries.

As a result, many retailers and many consumers have experienced poor quality in imported apparel. Particularly in earlier years, many Asian imports were poorly sized; sizes seemed more appropriate for smaller stature Asians than for Western customers. Major shortcomings were prevalent in garments—for example, children's knit shirts often had crew necks that would not go over a child's head without hurting the child. Stitching has continued to be a major problem, especially for new producers. Puckered stitching and crooked stitching are telltale signs of a beginning country's level of production skills. Shirts with two front pockets may have asymmetrical placement on the two sides. Or, at times, stitching will be executed well but poor quality thread is used—which shrinks dramatically in laundering or breaks easily in wear. Similarly, poor quality interfacings and other component parts yield poor end products. At times, the component parts are acceptable until the garment is worn or cleaned; then interfacings shrink and buttons crack.

Negative experiences with imported products may leave a disproportionately unpleasant memory in the mind of the consumer or the retailer. When this happens, one may have a tendency to consider imports in general as being of poor quality. For retailers, the disappointing products may lead to **markdowns** (Figure 13–4).

Adept retailers learn how to guard against risks. Proficient buyers establish and maintain relationships with foreign producers who provide consistently acceptable merchandise. Moreover, retailers have provided training to

FIGURE 13–4

In a well-known vacation area where T-shirts are popular souvenirs, a merchant plays on the customers' recollections of unsatisfactory experiences with imported garments. (We should note that in recent years Pakistani producers have made a concerted effort to upgrade the country's textile products. Often, however, negative impressions remain with the consumer.)

Source: Photo by Kitty Dickerson.

foreign producers to aid them in making garments of acceptable quality. Or, at times retailers believe the attractive pricing in a developing country makes the gamble on obtaining acceptable products worthwhile. Staff in the inspection department of a major retailing firm recently remarked that they experienced many quality problems in their merchandise from Bangladesh. This country fits the description of a poor, developing country struggling to establish a viable apparel sector—consequently, buying products made in Bangladesh carries with it the risks we have discussed. Retailers may, however, find the attractive price differential (for example, hourly wages for workers in Hong Kong are several times as much as those for workers in Bangladesh) makes it worthwhile—even with the risks and headaches involved—to secure products from Bangladesh rather than a more proficient country.

Up to now, we have discussed the circumstances that tend to produce poor-quality imported merchandise. Although retailers list poor quality as the major problem in buying imports (Figure 13–5), this does not mean that a majority of imports are poor quality. In particular, Hong Kong, Taiwan, and South Korea have developed sophisticated apparel industries that generally produce very good quality products. This does not mean every manufacturer in those countries produces first-class products—just as all U.S. manufacturers do not produce top-quality merchandise. In general, these countries and many others have perfected production skills so that quality is not a problem.

In fact, the *quota system has led to improved quality levels*. Since quotas limit the volume (equivalent square meters)—but not the value—of products shipped from a country, exporting nations have found it to their advantage to "trade up" to higher value-added garments. When quota limits are tight, a country finds it advantageous to produce $50 garments rather than $5 items. Given competitive market conditions, quality increases must accompany this trading up in price; therefore, imported products—particularly from the NICs—have improved significantly in styling and quality features to get maximum value under the quota. This upgrading has been common among NIC and other more advanced developing countries,

FIGURE 13–5

Problems encountered by retailers in buying imported apparel.

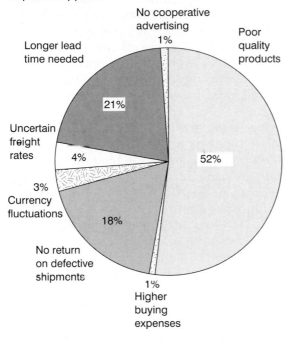

make commitments for apparel long before a selling season, buyers risk ordering merchandise that fails to mesh with fashion trends by the time it arrives months later. Or, the opposite may occur when buyers fail to sense an important trend and, because of their reliance on imports, can get neither imported nor domestic merchandise in time to take advantage of the trend. Because of the difficulties associated with synchronizing imports with current fashion trends, some retailers have limited their use of imports to more staple or more classic product lines rather than trendy lines.

Financial Concerns. Long lead times for imported merchandise place serious constraints on buyers' financial operations for an extended period. When a buyer places an order with a domestic supplier, payment does not occur until after merchandise is delivered. In contrast, letters of credit (which represent payment) are required from retailers at the time an order is placed for overseas sourcing. The letter of credit is a document from the importer's bank that extends credit to the importer and agrees to pay the exporter. Consequently, retailers' funds are committed for long periods of time when imports are purchased. For buyers, the limitation on **open-to-buy** funds for a long period of time poses a serious handicap. Retailers profit from frequent stock turns; with each turn, funds are freed to buy new merchandise to sell. When funds are tied to long-lead-time commitments for imported merchandise, buyers have reduced or eliminated their opportunities for more frequent stock turns. Even though the services of **factors** may be used in international sourcing, retailers' funds are committed for long periods of time.

but it is less common among the most underdeveloped countries.

Longer Lead Times Are Required

When retailers buy merchandise from overseas suppliers, long lead times are common. **Lead time** refers to the time between ordering the merchandise and having it arrive in the store. Although producers in some countries are striving to shorten lead times, a six- to nine-month wait has been common.[3] The following disadvantages are associated with the long lead times.

Fashion Concerns. Given the fickle, unpredictable nature of fashion, a number of risks accompany the long lead times required for imported merchandise. Since retailers must

Slow, Unpredictable Deliveries

Many factors account for slow, unpredictable deliveries of imported textile and apparel goods. Among the reasons are the following.

---

[3]The Limited is said to charter its own 747 airliner to bring merchandise from Asia to its Columbus, Ohio, distribution center as a way of avoiding the long lead times.

A Differing Sense of Urgency. Because of cultural differences, business life in many developing countries may not function with the same sense of urgency for meeting deadlines and being on time—characteristics that are both valued and expected in business dealings in the United States and most other importing (developed) countries. In some cases, lack of familiarity with the timing demands of fashion in the importing countries may mean that the manager of a local garment plant in a remote developing country (where clothing has mostly functional value) has difficulty in comprehending why garments are needed by a certain time to meet the whims of fashion.

Lack of an Adequate Infrastructure. To assure prompt, predictable deliveries, manufacturers must have a sound infrastructure to support those deliveries. This means that roads, transportation systems, and communication systems must be developed to a level that provides dependable service. In many developing countries, even if the apparel producer completes production on time, the nation's infrastructure may not be developed to a level that supports the supplier by assuring safe, predictable delivery of products to major ports for shipping to importing countries.

Political Instability. A number of Third-World countries have an unstable political climate, which makes both production and delivery of merchandise uncertain. Orders have been delayed or permanently lost when factories were burned, when workers were afraid to report for work because of military takeovers in a country, or when transportation systems were taken over in political riots. In these circumstances, representatives from the importing firms in the developed countries are reluctant to visit production sites to check on quality or other progress. Consequently, most firms in the developed coun-

tries soon lose patience in trying to deal with political upheaval and find other production sites. In these cases, domestic political battles take an economic toll on countries who can least afford to lose business opportunities. Sometimes political uncertainty or threats of terrorism may even make foreign buying trips risky. For example, during the Persian Gulf war many business trips were curtailed.

Other Unpredictable Events. Just as many other types of unpredictable events may affect prompt shipment of domestic merchandise, the same is true for import shipments. A flood in Bangladesh or a typhoon in the Philippines can play havoc with delivery dates. The loss or delay of import shipments may seem more dramatic, however, because of the long lead time and distances involved. A classic case for this point is the story told by a divisional merchandise manager with a leading department store chain. A large portion of this divisional manager's business was in the sweater area. Her division had committed a majority of its sweater open-to-buy for the forthcoming season to imports from an Asian country (and the orders had been placed six to nine months earlier). Sweaters were completed and shipped on time by boat. Then, the ultimate disaster occurred—the boat sank! The division's sweaters for the season were gone. Timing did not permit reorders from another overseas supplier, and U.S. manufacturers already had commitments to retailers who ordered from them initially. Moreover, domestic suppliers had little sympathy for a divisional manager and buyers who lost their imports in a sinking boat. As a result, this major retailer had difficulty finding sweaters for the season.

Uncertainties Related to Trade Regulations
As U.S. textile and apparel industry representatives have pressed for increased protection from imports, retailers have experienced a

number of additional barriers in securing imported merchandise. Examples follow.

Lack of Quota. Under the quota system established by the MFA, if a category of products is under quota limits from an exporting country, a manufacturer in that country must have access to quota to ship products to a retailer in the importing country. To illustrate, a Korean dress shirt supplier may take orders from a U.S. retailer and produce the garments, but if the manufacturer has not secured quota to cover the shipment, products cannot enter the United States. Experienced Korean suppliers, who wish to retain the retailer's account, will have taken precautions to have adequate quota to cover shipments; however, less experienced or less ethical producers may try to take their chances on shipping merchandise anyway.

Previously, the U.S. Customs' workload prevented close monitoring of **overshipping** (exceeding the country's quota limit for certain categories). Therefore, in the past, foreign producers who lacked quota sometimes succeeded in shipping merchandise anyway. More recently, however, tightened U.S. Customs controls would likely **embargo** the merchandise. This means the merchandise must then be reexported or placed in a bonded warehouse until the quota for that period expires or a new quota allowance is in effect.

In recent years, merchandise from China has been embargoed in December because Chinese suppliers had used all the quota in certain categories for the year. While distraught retailers waited for their shipments for the holiday season, the merchandise from China was embargoed in a U.S. Customs warehouse. At the beginning of January, a new quota year began; Chinese shipments were released but not in time for the holiday season for which retailers had ordered them. Retailers who had planned their seasonal

---

CHINA TURMOIL AFFECTS BUSINESS

In June 1989, the Chinese government initiated a military crackdown on Chinese students and workers who were protesting for democracy. The events at Beijing's Tiananmen Square will long be remembered for shaking the political structure in China. As might be expected, politics affected business quite seriously.

In the weeks and months that followed the upheaval, textile and apparel trade was affected in a number of ways. Workers in some regions were afraid to report to factories; some shipments were delayed; and in some instances, U.S. importers had their goods shipped without proper visas and other documentation—for fear they would be unable to get their goods out of China. A number of the U.S. staff in retailing/importing offices in China fled to Hong Kong for safety; thus, U.S. firms were unable to determine the status of their goods for several days.

Other Asian countries were affected by the impact of the problems in China. Within days of the Beijing crackdown, foreign buyers were shifting back to the relative stability of other Asian suppliers, particularly the NICs (until the turmoil, foreign buyers had sought merchandise from China because of far cheaper labor costs). Other Asian countries were experiencing uncertainties themselves because many rely on China for raw materials. For example, Korea relies on China for about 90 percent of its raw silk imports.

Although retailers and importers shifted their business back to China after tensions eased, this example illustrates how quickly political upheaval can affect business.

lines around these products lost valuable sales and later received merchandise they no longer wanted.

Embargoes Because of Failure to Comply with Other Regulations. The U.S. Customs Service monitors imported products for fraudulent shipments (those with falsified paperwork), transshipments, products mislabeled according to fiber content or country of origin, and counterfeited trademarks or copyrights (fake Gucci bags, fraudulent Rolex watches, etc.). Merchandise in violation of any of these regulations may be embargoed, leaving retailers without the merchandise they ordered. The massive problems with circumvention in the early 1990s and the U.S. government's resolve to deal with these violations means that retailers and importers must be certain they are dealing with reliable foreign suppliers. Shipments in violation of circumvention regulations may be embargoed and the importer or retailer fined.

Escalating Quota Costs. As quotas tightened, particularly for major Asian suppliers, the scarcity of quota made this authorization to export a valuable commodity. Access to quota is critical in nations with a large apparel industry dependent on exporting. Since quota is required for a firm to ship products, apparel producers are eager to obtain this authorization. Quota is distributed in different ways by foreign governments, but in Hong Kong, for example, quota is freely traded—at a price— among manufacturers. At times in the past when quota became more scarce and demand increased, the price of quota escalated. In fact, the buying and selling of quota has become a profitable business on its own in Hong Kong. At times when quota prices have been high, some manufacturers have been reported to be earning as much from selling their quota rights as from manufacturing and selling apparel. Although garment manufacturers in

Hong Kong may be willing to pay a high price for quota, this does not mean they are willing to absorb that cost personally. Therefore, escalating quota costs add to the cost of apparel shipped under those quota rights.

Uncertainties of Cost

A number of other factors lead to uncertainties on the cost of imported products. Some retailers have reported that currency fluctuations can make a great deal of difference in what the retailer pays for shipments. In addition, freight rates may be unpredictable. Because of these unpredictable cost aspects of buying imported merchandise, retailers may not know the status of these expenses until the time when goods are shipped. Retailers with extensive importing experience may be able to avoid these uncertainties.

Lack of Recourse to Poor Service

Unless retailers have established successful working relationships with overseas suppliers who value their business, buyers run the risk of having a lack of recourse to poor service—particularly when products and their delivery do not meet expectations. The privilege of returning unsatisfactory merchandise, which is an expected "right" in dealing with domestic manufacturers, is not common in doing business with foreign suppliers. To put it more bluntly, usually the retailer is stuck with import shipments, even if they are unsatisfactory.

Similarly, retailers have found service lacking on problems such as incomplete orders or delayed shipping. Language and cultural differences often account for miscommunication. Distances and time differences pose problems in resolving difficulties.

In addition, retailers miss the special services or concessions they receive in dealing with domestic suppliers. As an example, advertising rebates are out of the question when buying apparel from foreign suppliers.

THE HIGH COST OF A "BARGAIN"

The men's shirt buyer for a major department store chain purchased a large quantity of imported men's casual shirts. He found the shirts at an exceedingly attractive price and felt he had secured a true bargain. Shortly after the shirts arrived in the store, he began to question his good buy. Within a short period of time, as customers picked up the shirts to examine them, the buttons cracked and fell off. He found himself the proud owner of a large shipment of shirts with defective buttons. Returning the defective shipment to the overseas supplier was out of the question. Few customers seemed interested in shirts that lacked buttons. The buyer took massive markdowns to sell some of the shirts and later sold most of the remaining supply to a rag dealer. The buyer's bargain was an expensive lesson on the lack of return privileges for imported merchandise (story told to author by confidential source, 1985).

Buying and Shipping Expenses

As retailers have begun to look more seriously at the total costs of sourcing overseas, many have found importing to be less cost effective than first believed. That is, the **first cost** is only a part of the total cost of securing the products. Although the initial costs of direct imports are considerably less than the prices for domestic merchandise, additional expenses reduce some of the advantage. Among these additional costs are the following.

Costs of Buying Trips. Several trips per year for buying staff members, particularly to destinations in the Far East, can add substantially to the costs of merchandise secured.

Shipping Charges. Composite industry data on shipping charges are hard to obtain. The top apparel executive for a major mass merchandising chain stated that shipping costs for importing are roughly three times that for domestic purchases. For that company, domestic shipping charges are 0.7 percent (based on retail sales) compared to 2.0 percent for imports (confidential retail source, 1989). While this may seem a relatively small difference, it would be quite significant for retailers who purchase millions of dollars of merchandise.

Tariffs and Other Importing Fees. One must recall at this point the earlier discussions pertaining to tariffs or duties on textile and apparel merchandise. Furthermore, it is important to remember that the tariffs on apparel (more than other textile products) are among the highest on imported manufactured goods. U.S. apparel imports carry an average tariff of nearly 23 percent. Retailers must concern themselves with tariff charges because, as the importing agent, the retail firm is responsible for payment of tariffs on imported merchandise as it enters the United States. Although retailers pay the tariffs initially, they cannot absorb these added expenses—therefore, tariffs are passed on to consumers in the prices they pay for imported products. Retailers must be concerned, however, with the amount by which tariffs inflate the selling price of imported merchandise. Added tariff charges should be a consideration in weighing the costs of imported versus domestic merchandise.

Negative Customer Reaction

During the 1980s, as concern mounted over the U.S. trade deficit, a certain number of consumers became quite negative toward the proliferation of imports in U.S. stores. Pro-

American views of the 1980s sometimes transferred to preferential sentiment toward U.S.-made merchandise. Several studies indicated that consumers believed U.S.-made apparel is of better quality than imports and that consumers preferred domestic garments.

A number of retailers have reported hostile comments from shoppers who were concerned that apparel lines, particularly in certain product areas, were composed of predominantly imported garments. For example, a manager of a specialty store told of a woman shopping for a blazer who walked out, expressing displeasure that all the store's blazers were imported. A number of retailers have had consumers express similar disapproval.

A Survey of Retailers' Problems in Buying Imported Apparel

In the study reported earlier on retailers' buying and stocking of imported apparel, the 191 retail participants in the study were asked if they had experienced difficulties in buying imported garments for their stores; 48 percent reported having had problems, while 42 percent had not (Dickerson, 1989). Respondents who had experienced problems were asked to identify the types of difficulties they had encountered in buying imported clothing. A summary of retailers' responses is shown in Figure 13–5.

In the retailer study, in most cases, merchants who viewed importing of apparel less positively reported that imports represented a limited proportion of the store's inventory. Although 58 percent of the retail respondents had experienced difficulties in buying foreign-made products, all but 13 of the sample of 182 (out of the total sample of 191) carried varying levels of imported apparel in their lines. Apparently, the attractive price differences of imports offset the disadvantages many had experienced (Dickerson, 1989).

RETHINKING IMPORTED VERSUS DOMESTIC BUYING

In recent years, retailers have begun to look more carefully at the long-term costs and benefits of their sourcing options. Instead of basing buying decisions on the simple initial cost differences of imported merchandise compared to domestic, retailers are looking at a broader range of variables.

Retailers have found it increasingly necessary to consider important factors other than cost of the merchandise. As mergers, buyouts, and other restructuring in the retailing sector have increased competitive pressures, merchants are finding *speed of delivery* for merchandise to be increasingly critical. As retailers find they need to respond quickly to customer demands, the long lead times required for production in the Far East have become a handicap, despite cost differences. Many stores have come to view operations as too costly when they tie up funding in long lead times and large inventories and result in large markdowns. Because retailers need to respond quickly to customer demands, they must in turn rely on apparel manufacturers who can deliver merchandise quickly.

Consequently, shifts in the retail climate have created a receptive environment for the U.S. textile and apparel industry's Quick Response (QR) initiative. Retailers and suppliers have become increasingly aware that the end-use customer is the same for both these segments of the softgoods industry. Although Quick Response is based on computerized systems of data interchange, the QR effort represents a much more important change in the working relationships within the softgoods industry. More importantly, QR represents a marketing orientation on the part of U.S. producers who are committed to serving their customers, the retailers, more effectively.

As U.S. manufacturers continue to reduce lead times on domestic merchandise, this gives domestic suppliers an added advantage in meeting retailers' needs. Retailers can order much closer to the time merchandise is needed and can order a much smaller quantity. Then, reorders can be placed as needed. This strategy cuts inventory, reduces the investment in inventory at a given time, and results in fewer markdowns. Under the QR system, markdowns are reduced because retailers follow customer demands closely rather than ordering massive quantities of merchandise six to nine months ahead of the season.

Representatives of Kurt Salmon Associates, Inc., evaluated retail profit margins on imported and domestic merchandise when all the cost variables were considered. Because of tariffs, shipping costs, increasing quota charges, and other buying/shipping expenses, Kurt Salmon consultants estimated that the overall benefits from purchase of imported merchandise were not what the initial cost of goods would indicate.

As a growing number of retailers considered the broader aspects of domestic versus overseas sourcing, more and more buyers are looking at domestic sources (Tombaugh, 1988; Weiner, Foust, & Yang, 1988). (And, for many of the same reasons, a number of manufacturers are moving their production back to the United States.)

A MORE INTEGRATED SOFTGOODS CHAIN

Competitive forces of today's economy have fostered a much closer working relationship between manufacturers and retailers, creating a more integrated softgoods chain—a chain that has little room for the animosity that has existed between these two industry segments in the past. Much of this integration goes back to serving a changing consumer, the higher costs of doing business today, and the intensity of competition.

Consumers have become more conservative in their spending. Lacking both economic security (at least as measured by consumer confidence, even if individuals have not suffered income loss) and time for shopping, the consumers of the 1990s are value-oriented and want products to be available when they are ready to make purchases.

Retailers, including some American stalwarts such as Macy's, have experienced bankruptcies, take-overs, consolidations, buyouts, mergers, and closings. More than an estimated 19,000 retailers went bankrupt in 1992 up about 45 percent from 1990 (The Trade Partnership, 1993). Many have suffered heavy debt loads as they recovered from their respective traumas. As they have attempted to reduce overhead, many have consolidated buying staffs. As we noted earlier, many have gone to matrix lists of suppliers, who become their preferred vendors.

Retailers have moved increasingly toward working with apparel manufacturers who can provide the quality, service, and price they desire for their respective strategies. This is particularly true if the retailer uses a matrix system; some use it but do not wish to discuss it publicly.

Consequently, developing close working relationships between manufacturers and retailers has become a priority of the 1990s. Retailers need suppliers who know and understand the retailers' needs. For example, the retailer needs vendors that can respond with fast **inventory replenishment** as needed. That is, the retailer needs to be able to have the right merchandise available when the time-impoverished customer wants it. Therefore, a new era of relationship-building has occurred in the industry, often with top-level vendor executives working directly with retail CEOs. Although the relationship may later be implemented between a vendor's sales representative and the retail buyer, the relationships are forged at the highest levels of the partner firms. In essence, this is the background of a matrix system. The retailers know they have the commitment of the vendors, from the highest levels down, to work with that retailer in providing what the retail firm needs.

The integrated relationships are actually implemented through modern technology. Vendors respond rapidly on deliveries of merchandise by using electronic data interchange (EDI) or Quick Response (QR) systems. That is, through these electronic interfaces, as consumers purchase merchandise, retailers can notify suppliers that they need replenishment, and the vendor can provide "at-once" deliveries. Not only does this prevent stockouts of certain basic merchandise the customer may always expect to find at a certain store, this rapid replenishment system reduces the inventory and, consequently, the investments that accompany large inventories on the part of the retailer.

These partnerships have led to a new openness and sharing among many retailers and vendors. That is, both segments of the softgoods chain benefit from being able to share customer and sales data. Both segments win when the customer makes purchases and is satisfied.

The new relationships are perhaps the most important agenda item of the day for the softgoods industry. Often, these relationships are the difference between the winners and the losers in both segments of the industry. However, it is costly for companies in each segment to participate. Retailers must be prepared to capture the consumer data through bar code merchandise marking. Firms in both segments must invest in technology that facilitates the retailer-vendor communication. And manufacturers must invest in EDI systems that permit the rapid replenishment of their retail customers' demands. Firms that are too small to afford the investment will be seriously disadvantaged (Holding, 1990).

RETAILERS WHO HAVE ACTIVELY SOUGHT DOMESTIC MERCHANDISE

Marks and Spencer, Britain's largest and most successful retailing firm with over 260 stores in the UK plus stores in other parts of Europe and Canada (with controlling interests in over 200 Canadian stores), was one of the first major retailers to establish a policy for buying domestic merchandise. Marks and Spencer has garnered about 15 percent of the United Kingdom's clothing market, where it sells about one-fourth of all sales of women's trousers; one-third of the sales of underwear, pajamas, bras, and nightgowns; and one-half of ladies' slips.

Marks and Spencer has a policy of importing merchandise only if they cannot find the quality and value the company seeks from British manufacturers. Under this policy, about 90 percent of the company's merchandise is made in Britain. Marks and Spencer buys approximately 20 percent of all the clothing produced in Britain. Concerned for the broader economy, Marks and Spencer chairman, Lord Sieff noted: "There is more scope for the development of good quality and high value production at home than many people believe. The more produced in the United Kingdom the better it is for employment, our economy in general, and the well-being of the British people" (1984, (p. 37).

In the United States, Wal-Mart Stores, Inc. has made a commitment to buying U.S.-made merchandise whenever possible. Under the leadership of its late chairman, Sam Walton, Wal-Mart's "Buy American" program developed out of concern for local economies in its trading area. The company's phenomenal success resulted from a strategy of locating stores in towns too small to attract other major retailing chains. Concern for the employment and other aspects of the economy in those small towns was an important stimulus to the Wal-Mart "Buy American" policy. Mr. Walton and other company executives were acutely aware of the importance of local manufacturing plants in those regions. Often, one or two factories are the only major sources of nonfarm employment in rural areas, and much of the economy in the town or region is supported by that employment. Too often, when a factory closes, it closes permanently. Wal-Mart executives understood

the scenario clearly—if people are not working, they can buy little or nothing.

Wal-Mart's "Buy American" program is based somewhat on patriotism and to some extent on concern for American workers who buy and make Wal-Mart's merchandise. More importantly, Mr. Walton and his colleagues saw their program as an opportunity to help suppliers make fundamental changes in the way they operate. That is, concern for Ameri-

---

 ## THE BIRTH OF WAL-MART'S "BUY AMERICAN" PROGRAM

The near-closing of a Brinkley, Arkansas, shirt factory helped to launch Wal-Mart's "Buy American" program. Already troubled by the overall U.S. trade deficit, Mr. Walton was receptive to a contact from then-Arkansas governor, Bill Clinton, who asked for help in saving Farris Fashion, Inc. The struggling apparel factory was ready to close because the company for whom the plant had produced shirts decided to have its merchandise produced in East Asia. In a decision that launched Wal-Mart's "Buy American" strategy, the major retailer contracted with Farris Fashions to produce printed flannel shirts—an item Wal-Mart had been buying from Far East suppliers.

Wal-Mart's efforts to work with domestic suppliers include making commitments to manufacturers far in advance and paying quickly. Wal-Mart executives decided that it was only fair to treat domestic producers on the same favorable terms given foreign suppliers. For overseas orders, the retailer had been required to place orders far in advance (sometimes as much as a year) and to provide payment before merchandise was shipped. Giving similar treatment to domestic suppliers meant that manufacturers could do a better job of their own production planning and could get better prices on piece goods or other component parts. Similarly,

prompt payment (compared to the typical retail practice of paying domestic manufacturers 30 days after merchandise is shipped) kept U.S. suppliers from being at a competitive disadvantage with offshore firms.

Following the 1985 effort to work with Farris Fashion, Mr. Walton sent a letter to the company's major U.S. suppliers, inviting them to take part in Wal-Mart's "Buy American" program. Mr. Walton offered to work with manufacturers to produce goods that were competitive in price and quality with imports. Mr. Walton wrote:

Our American suppliers must commit to improving their facilities and machinery, remain financially conservative and work to fill our requirements, and most importantly, strive to improve employee productivity. Wal-Mart believes our American workers can make the difference, if management provides the leadership." (Barrier, 1988, pp. 21,24)

After four years as a Wal-Mart supplier, Farris Fashion, Inc., produced an annual 1.5 million garments—mostly men's and women's flannel shirts—for the retail firm. The manufacturer's annual payroll more than tripled, and the company employed 325 workers (compared to 90 in 1985) in the two Arkansas towns of Brinkley and Hazen. Farris Fashion and one other U.S. supplier produce about 75 percent of Wal-Mart's flannel shirts.

can industry's competitiveness is at the heart of the program. Wal-Mart refuses to subsidize inefficient American manufacturers by paying higher prices for goods that might be bought more cheaply overseas. And the retailer continues to buy imported merchandise that provides greater value for the price than can be found in the United States.

Wal-Mart's "Buy American" program encountered negative publicity when NBC's "Dateline" broadcast a scathing report on Wal-Mart's foreign sourcing efforts. The National Labor Committee, the same group that appeared to spur the "60 Minutes" segment on use of A.I.D. funding to start garment factories in Central America and the Caribbean, was involved in the effort to expose Wal-Mart's sourcing program. For the "Dateline" program, reporters went to a Wal-Mart store where clothing racks with "Buy American" signs held clothing made entirely in underdeveloped Asian countries. Dismissing the fact that the ironic signage could have been a mistake of the local store, reporters berated the Wal-Mart Stores corporation for misrepresenting the company's intentions to the American public. Reporters visited Asian factories that were allegedly producing merchandise for Wal-Mart Stores and emphasized the number of children employed in the factories. Moreover, reporters intimated that Wal-Mart Stores also knowingly purchased transshipped merchandise from China ("SA Sees Little," 1992).

Like many stories, this one appeared to be part truth and part fiction. Wal-Mart has never said the company buys no imported merchandise. They would be a very rare retailer if that were true. One textile-apparel industry leader noted in defense of Wal-Mart that, throughout the mid- to late-1980s, the company had the lowest percentage of imports in dollars and units of all the major retailers.

Additionally, the "Dateline" exposé raised a new consciousness among U.S. consumers regarding the the issue of child labor and other labor conditions in the developing countries from which growing quantities of imported softgoods products are originating. This concern caused several companies in both manufacturing and retailing to establish policies and to issue public statements to assure the buying public they would not do business with foreign firms guilty of these labor infractions. Firms such as Levi Strauss & Co. have terminated business relationships with firms in other countries where similar violations occurred.

In late 1993, perhaps responding in part to the "Dateline" story, the U.S. Labor Department issued a study of child labor practices in other countries. This study was required by the powerful Senate Appropriations Committee as a condition of the Labor Department's funding appropriations for 1994. If passed, pending bills in Congress will crack down on firms importing merchandise made by firms that use child labor.

RETAILERS AND TEXTILE TRADE POLICIES

In recent years, many retailers and importers, favoring unrestricted trade so that they will be less hampered in buying imports, have become vocal in campaigning for greater representation in the U.S. government's textile and apparel trade policy, charging they have been "virtually ignored" when crucial decisions are made by the government (Wightman, 1981b).

In a report prepared for the National Retail Merchants Association (now NRF) (Rosen, Turnbull, & Bialos, 1985), retailers charged that they play only a tangential role in developing textile and apparel trade policy while the textile and apparel manufacturers represent "favored interests." The following excerpts from that report express the frustration of retailers and importers.

For the most part, the process for the formulation of U.S. policies on textiles and apparel has been closed and one-sided. While the domestic textile and apparel industries are consulted, other affected domestic industries are *not*. Restrictions are imposed on imports without notice, an opportunity to comment and other appropriate forms of due process. Further, while representatives of textile and apparel industries are invited to attend U.S. multilateral and bilateral negotiations, representatives of other industries traditionally have been excluded. NRMA

believes that the U.S. policy process should be opened to all affected parties, including the retail community. (Rosen et al., 1985, p. vii)

Authors of the NRMA report cited examples of the lack of due process afforded retailers and others on textile and apparel trade matters. These included the imposition of new trade regulations on imports without notice or an opportunity for retailers and importers to comment. The report added:

 ## RETAILERS STARTLED BY NEW ORIGIN RULES

In August 1984, retailers and importers were startled by the sudden announcement of new country-of-origin regulations designed to prevent circumvention of certain quota rules. As a result of the U.S. textile/apparel sector's concern over transshipment of goods (discussed in Chapter 9) to take advantage of some countries' unused quota, the revised Country of Origin Rules, known as the "Origin Rules," were hastily imposed on import shipments (Daria, 1984b).

Under the earlier rules, as an example, sweaters made of panels knit in China but sewn together in Hong Kong counted as part of Hong Kong's quota (which in relative terms is much more generous than China's quota). Under the new Origin Rules, the sweaters were counted against China's much smaller allotment. Hong Kong officials and U.S. importers and retailers estimated very high potential losses (Resnick, 1984).

Retailers and importers were irate over the Origin Rules. Not only had this sector not been given advance warning that the rules were about to be implemented, but even worse, the new regulations were scheduled to go into effect within one month of the announcement (Kidd & Ehrlich, 1984). Retailers and importers with outstanding overseas orders were gravely concerned over the implications for their merchan-

dise. After all, various types of multiple-country processing had been accepted business practices up to that point. Suddenly, foreign suppliers who relied on transshipments were unable to use this strategy and be assured that their merchandise would be permitted to pass through the U.S. Customs Service.

Although the enforcement deadline was extended as a result of protest from retailers, importers, and the governments of exporting nations, the affected retailers and importers experienced delays and losses of shipments. Moreover, in retaliation against the Origin Rules, China cancelled an order for 273,700 metric tons of wheat ordered from U.S. farmers ("China Cancels," 1984).

Despite retailer/importer protests that the new quota rules were "unconstitutional, arbitrary, capricious and contrary to previous rulings" (Resnick, 1984, p. 1), the Court of International Trade ruled that the U.S. Customs Service was not required to provide any prior notice or comment period before issuing the regulations (Resnick, 1984).

The Origin Rules provided perhaps the primary early stimulus for the mounting retailer/importer campaign to organize and to become a stronger political force to oppose textile and apparel protectionist measures.

There are virtually no limitations on the discretion of the Executive Branch to impose restrictions on textile and apparel products under domestic law and virtually no procedural protections for parties affected by such U.S. actions. Thus, ironically enough, while the U.S. cannot impose the lesser sanctions authorized under other trade remedy laws unless such sanctions are truly justified and all parties' views are considered, it can nevertheless impose the severe trade sanctions under the MFA (e.g., embargoes) on an *ad hoc* basis without any process whatsoever. The absence of such safeguards lends itself to substantial errors by CITA and gives the Executive Branch unfettered discretion to control textile imports with no check whatsoever from other branches of government. (Rosen et al., 1985, p. 49)

The NRMA report added that the same lack of due process had prevailed also in the *formulation of major textile trade policies.* Authors noted that for the first time in the history of textile trade policy, the U.S. Trade Representative's Office invited a retail representative to serve as an advisor during the 1986 MFA renewal negotiations. Prior to that, only textile and apparel manufacturers were invited to attend in an advisory capacity. On that point, the report added: "The previous exclusionary policy has given the domestic textile and apparel industries unprecedented input into such negotiations while other affected industries, namely importers, retailers, and consumers, played no role whatsoever in the negotiations and have little opportunity to comment on the decisions being reached therein as they occur" (Rosen et al., 1985, p. 50).

Retailers have generally opposed the MFA and asserted that it is a protectionist measure that favors U.S. manufacturers (Lanier, 1986; Wightman, 1981b).

- Retailers believe the quota levels imposed under the MFA restrict flexibility in responding to changing fashions and trends (Lanier, 1981).

- Merchants believe that restrictions on textile and apparel imports seriously limit their ability to secure the best variety and price for their customers.
- Furthermore, retailers are keenly aware of the added costs imposed by the import control system; they note the added costs both to them and to consumers that result from tariffs, quota costs, etc.
- Merchants believe the trade restraints add to their burden of doing business, requiring them to become familiar with the complex MFA quota system.
- And finally, retailers resent the risks they experience because of the import control system; in particular, the risks of having their merchandise embargoed when they need it in their stores (interaction with retail sources, 1985–1994).

Frustrated by consultation calls, embargoes, and other restrictions that create what retail leaders believe to be "an unreasonable rate of uncertainty" (Lockwood, 1984), retailers and importers launched several initiatives to counteract industry and government policies. Retailers and importers decided to become more active politically to have their interests represented on textile trade policy matters. Thus, if we consider the textile and apparel industry as a "pressure group" (i.e., organized to influence policymakers), we might think of retailers and importers as a **counterpressure group**.

Retailers Become Politically Active on Trade Matters

As retailers grew increasingly frustrated with tightened restraints on imported textile and apparel merchandise, the Retail Industry Trade Coalition (RITAC) was formed in 1984 to lead the counterattack. RITAC was formed specifically to fight for freer trade in apparel, footwear, and possibly other consumer product areas. A basic tenet of the group was "Free trade means economic expansion and that economic growth means greater prosperity for the American consumer, translating to greater prosperity for the retailer" (Colgate, 1987, p. 90).

Composed of seven retailing industry associations and 50 large and small retail companies, coalition members asserted that they intended "to do everything within our power to oppose protectionism, whether legislative or administrative" (Wightman, 1984). Similar to the manufacturers' efforts, RITAC collected substantial funding from members to make its presence felt in Washington and to influence public opinion.

RITAC was formed at the time when the Fiber, Fabric and Apparel Coalition for Trade (FFACT) was organized by the textile and apparel industry to promote the passage of the Textile and Apparel Trade Enforcement Act of 1985 (the Jenkins bill). In fact, RITAC might be considered a counteroffensive to FFACT and the Jenkins bill.

Soon after the Jenkins bill was introduced in Congress, the increased political prowess of retailers became apparent. The bill, which retailers believed would roll back textile/apparel imports by about 30 percent, soon gained far more congressional support than most observers had expected. The Jenkins bill was at first thought to be a pressure point to aid the textile and apparel sector in securing desired changes in the forthcoming MFA renewal negotiations. According to Hughes (1987), at other times in the past MFA renewal negotiations had been preceded by some type of congressional activity. The mood in Congress had changed in 1985, however, largely due to the trade deficit, Japanese trade restrictions, and job losses. Even textile/apparel industry backers were surprised by the speed with which the bill gained co-sponsors. At one point the bill had enough backers in Congress to override a presidential veto.

RITAC members heavily lobbied members of Congress and formed a coalition with agricultural and financial services industries, sectors that stood to lose from retaliation by countries affected by the proposed U.S. textile restraints (Arlen, 1985; Greene, 1985a; Mullin, 1985; Spalding, 1985). Retailers' and importers' efforts were successful. Although the bill passed in both the House and the Senate, the counterpressure coalition had managed to shift critical votes that the textile/apparel coalition needed to override the presidential veto that followed. Supporters introduced the bill again in August 1986. Although more House members voted for the bill than previously, the count was eight votes short of the needed number to override the Reagan veto. Defeat of this bill was seen as a major victory by retailers; they had played a significant role in its defeat ("House Fails," 1986).

From the time the Jenkins bill was introduced in Congress until its defeat in August 1986, this potential legislation caused retailers to reevaluate their position on the MFA. Fearing passage by Congress of far more restrictive textile trade measures, the NRMA endorsed the 1986 renewal of the MFA, with provisions for a phaseout by 1991 (Rosen et al., 1985). Hughes (1987) asserted that in the end, even though the Jenkins bill was defeated, the U.S. textile complex secured most of its demands through MFA IV and bilateral agreements worked out with the major exporting nations before MFA IV was signed. Retailers and importers considered these combined measures more restrictive than conditions under MFA III.

When the second bill, the Textile and Apparel Trade Act of 1987, was introduced in Congress, retailers and importers were as opposed to it as to the earlier bill. RITAC lobbied against this second textile bill, as they had earlier to oppose the Jenkins bill. In this case, however, RITAC lost some of its support from agriculture groups because the Senate version of the 1987 bill would have tied a textile-exporting country's share of the domestic textile and apparel markets to the quantity of agricultural products it purchased from the United States (LaRussa, 1988b). The bill was defeated (see Chapter 10 for additional information). For a second time, RITAC felt successful in deterring passage of a bill it considered quite detrimental to retailers' interests. Similarly, RITAC was actively involved in the defeat of the 1990 congressional textile bill.

Although RITAC was officially disbanded in 1993, this does not mean that retailers will assume any less-active political role on trade policy matters in the future. Now, retailers' political activism is coordinated through the National Retail Federation. Retailers carry many products other than textile and apparel products and might logically be active on trade issues for other industries. However, retailers and importers acknowledge that most of their efforts related to trade have been tied to the textile and apparel sectors because of the complex MFA quota system and other measures the domestic textile and apparel manufacturers have managed to erect to protect their industries.

In short, retailers and importers have learned that lobbying Congress can pay off. In the past, perhaps retailers were not very active politically because they were unaware of the potential power they held. Retailers are a lobbyist's dream because they employ more than 19 million Americans, or almost *one-fifth* of the nation's workforce. Of this number, more than 5 million are employed in retailing segments that sell textile and apparel products (Trade Partnership, 1993; U.S. Department of Commerce, 1994). Retailers are located in every congressional district. Having discovered its lobbying potential, the National Retail Federation hopes to harness the political force of its members to help "educate" members of Congress on other key issues of concern to the retailing community, such as labor issues and tax measures (Ostroff, 1993c).

Retailers mounted a strong offensive on the trade front during the early 1990s. In 1993, for example, the National Retail Federation announced that it would triple its lobbying efforts in that year alone. More than 150 meetings were scheduled between retail executives nationwide and their congressional representatives in Washington and in their home districts. Just as the textile industry leaders had done for years, key retail executives went in small groups to pay visits to members of Congress, particularly those serving on committees related to trade. Even before Bill Clinton was nominated as the Democratic presidential candidate, the National Retail Federation made plans to host a reception at the Democratic national convention for party leaders. Not wishing to show any party favoritism, a similar reception was held at the Republican convention.

The early 1990s gave retailers many opportunities to flex their new political muscles—always in the corner of freer trade. In addition to helping defeat the third congressional textile bill, retailers became actively involved in talks to conclude the Uruguay Round. As textile manufacturers lobbied for a 15-year phase-out of the MFA, retailers and importers lobbied equally hard for a shorter phase-out. Retailers and importers also lobbied strongly for NAFTA and against the yarn-forward provision of NAFTA.

Similarly, retailers and importers were strongly opposed to any efforts to restrict China's "most favored nation" trade status with the United States. Although many in the United States believed that China's MFN status should be tied to improvement in human rights issues (stemming from the time Chinese officials executed leaders in the democratic movement), retailers and importers lobbied for China to retain MFN status. The reader is reminded that if an exporting country has MFN status, that country's products are subject to much lower tariffs than would be true without the MFN status. Therefore, retailers and importers who are buying products from China would have to pay considerably more for merchandise if higher tariffs were required because of a lack of MFN status. For example, an executive at one major retailing chain shared with the author that, for his company, the difference in whether China had MFN status accounted for well over $1 million dollars *on shoes alone.*

Now that retailers have discovered their power in the political arena, chances are slight that they will choose to abandon their new skills. Retailers have learned that they must educate and influence policymakers to understand their perspective on textile and apparel trade matters.

A MOVE TOWARD IMPROVED CHANNEL RELATIONSHIPS

Although suppliers and retailers have experienced frequent conflict in their relationships, difficulties related to textile and apparel trade pitted the two sectors against each other as never before. In a sense, the trade problems were unfortunate for both sectors. Both manufacturers and retailers operated in intensely competitive markets. Overall, both industries are quite fragmented. Both sectors have undergone dramatic restructuring as a result of changing competitive conditions. Both sectors are major U.S. employers, vital to the country's economy. And although there are stellar performers in each sector, in general, earnings over a five- or ten-year period have been relatively lean for both sectors. Therefore, the battle over imports has been unfortunate both to retailers and to suppliers. The diversion of both energy and funds for each sector's battle against the other might have been used more productively in strengthening each industry's competitive status—in ways other than in political skills.

The tide has begun to shift, however. As the key participants in a shared broader industry—the softgoods industry—manufacturers and retailers have a great deal in common. Although each sector has a different objective in the channel relationship, the end goals of each are the same: supplying the right merchandise to the customer at the right time and at the right price and, in the process, earning a profit to sustain the firms involved.

Restructuring in both textile/apparel manufacturing and retailing has created a new business environment for each sector. Each is faced with increasingly competitive conditions for survival and success. Ironically, as we noted earlier, the difficult climate faced by each sector has led to improved working relationships between softgoods suppliers and retailers. U.S. textile/apparel producers have learned that they must assume a more serious marketing and service orientation with their customers, the retailers. Domestic manufacturers have learned that retailers can bypass them and have their needs met by willing suppliers in other countries. Therefore, growing numbers of U.S. textile/apparel producers have become sensitive to retailers' needs and are willing to assist retailers in their business activities. Quick Response initiatives on the part of manufacturers help retailers work closer to their markets (in timing), reduce inventories (and therefore investments), and permit merchants to have merchandise when they need it without the burden of excessive markdowns.

Similarly, **restructuring** within the retailing sector has made working with domestic suppliers more attractive to U.S. retail firms. Mergers, buyouts, and other retail restructuring have intensified competition. Over-storing is a serious underlying problem for retailing in general. The proliferation of off-price and discount retailers has tightened markets for both department and specialty stores.

In general, the changes in the U.S. retailing sector require that firms be exceedingly sensitive to customers' needs and that retail firms be managed with ultimate efficiency in order to survive. More than ever before, this efficiency and sensitivity to customers' needs depend on *faster turnarounds and deliveries* in responding to the whims of fashion. Retailers who can respond quickly to changes in consumer demands will be more successful. (An interesting question to ponder is whether consumers need this fast turnaround or whether retailers are more competitive and proficient at stimulating "needs.") Therefore, U.S. retailers have developed a new appreciation for domestic producers who can provide merchandise quickly and who can shift product lines as consumer demands change. Retailers have learned that working with domestic producers requires not only less lead time but also less investment at a given time. In addition to responding more effectively to the customer, working with U.S. suppliers may be beneficial to earnings through more frequent stock turns, fewer stock-outs, and fewer markdowns.

In short, the increasingly difficult business conditions in both retailing and textile/apparel manufacturing have helped each sector to have a growing appreciation for the other. Perhaps, as the two sectors continue in their efforts to work together more effectively toward common goals, retailers and producers can continue to nurture a partnership interaction rather than perpetuating the adversarial relationship that heightened over trade issues.

Mutually advantageous supplier-retailer relationships are now seen as the means by which both segments of the industry will move successfully into the next millennium. Firms in either segment that lack the foresight to develop and nurture relationships may be added to the growing list of casualties (Bartlett & Peterson, 1992).

GLOBAL RETAILING

Although most of our discussion has focused on the retailer's position with regard to global aspects of *production*, today's global economy brings with it another phenomenon—**global retailing**, the expansion of retailing operations on an international scale. Also a result of improved transportation and communication systems, retailing—like manufacturing—has entered the global age. Considering the global expansion of most other industrial and service industries, retailing has been relatively slow to expand globally, however. The growing number of retailers that have launched plans to expand into new regions of the world suggests this trend is going to change rapidly.

Global retailing may be considered from two perspectives:

- First, we may consider it as the international flow of retailing concepts or know-how. This means that new retailing concepts or expertise become diffused as a result of travel or through exchange at international meetings. Kacker (1988) noted that the concepts of self-service and the supermarket moved to several countries as a result of interchange at international meetings on food distribution. Transfer to the United States of the West European hypermarket concept by Wal-Mart and Kmart is another example. In his 1985 book, *Transatlantic Trends in Retailing*, Kacker discussed in detail the global shifts of retailing concepts and know-how.
- The conscious development of a *global retailing strategy* is the second way of considering this change in the international marketplace. This planned globalization of retailing results from a company's intent to establish its operations in several countries, or it may result from a business agreement between two companies (or sometimes

governments) for a management contract or joint venture.

Our discussion will focus primarily on this latter way of viewing global retailing.

Management Horizons[4] writers have suggested that one of the reasons retailing has expanded slowly on a global basis has been retailers' focus on the "local" nature of business in order to know and understand customers and their needs. These retailing experts suggest that new technology will now permit **micro-marketing** on a global scale. According to Management Horizons, we are likely to see retailers that are large and well equipped with technology that facilitates micro-marketing, cost reduction, and efficiencies in the distribution pipeline apply these strategies to *global* operations (Management Horizons, 1993).

Until recently, most retailing beyond national borders has been in the form of investment by a limited number of retail firms who are seeking to expand in other markets, and doing so on a fairly conservative scale. The U.S. market has attracted retailers from other countries for many of the same reasons that foreign manufacturers want to ship their products to American markets. The U.S. market is large, both in geographic size and the size of the population, and consumers have an exceptionally high level of disposable income (relative to the rest of the world), along with a hearty appetite for consumer goods. Because many retailers from other countries have outgrown their domestic markets, and particularly when the currency exchange rate has been favorable, the U.S. market has become attractive as a site for expansion.

Similarly, as the U.S. market has become saturated by over-storing and as U.S. consumers have become more conservative in their spending, U.S. retailers have begun to look at the markets of other countries as offering potential for growth and expansion. Table 13–2 illustrates market potential in various regions. Sears and Wal-Mart's successful expansion into Mexico was on the forefront of a much broader trend for U.S. retailers to set their sights aggressively on markets in other countries. Wal-Mart's Mexican operations are a joint venture with Mexico's Cifra SA stores. Wal-Mart purchased Woolworth stores in Canada and converted them to Wal-Mart stores. Wal-Mart has explored further expansion in China. Kmart has launched its global efforts with stores in Singapore, the Czech Republic, and Mexico. L.L. Bean has a store in Japan. The Gap has franchised stores in the

TABLE 13–2
Retail market potential in select countries

Country/ Region	*Average Annual Growth of Real Consumer Spending 1980–91*
United States	2.4%
Canada	3.4
Germany	2.2
France	2.4
United Kingdom	3.8
Japan	3.7
China	7.3
Korea	8.3
Czechoslovakia	1.7
Mexico	1.8

Source: From *Retail World: Window of Opportunity* (p. 2) by Price Waterhouse/Management Horizons, 1994, Columbus, OH: Author. Reprinted by permission.

---

[4]Management Horizons, a retail consulting firm, became part of Price Waterhouse. Becoming part of Price Waterhouse's global network permits the company to have greater access to retail markets around the world.

United Kingdom, and Woolworth has a successful business in Germany. J.C. Penney has embarked on an ambitious plan for global growth that includes new stores, catalog outlets, and licensing arrangements to sell Penney's private-label merchandise. Through various approaches, Penney already sells in Aruba, Bermuda, Japan, Malaysia, Mexico, the Mideast, Portugal, Puerto Rico, Russia, Singapore, and Spain. Plans include Chile, as a potential springboard to South America; China is another possibility (J. Black, 1992; Haber, 1993; Hirano, 1992; "K-Mart Going," 1992).

Various sources have analyzed what it takes to succeed in retail multicountry or global expansions. Kacker (1988) noted that retailers who have succeeded have been those with unique concepts or techniques that enable them to find a specific market niche and win the clientele without much waiting. As examples, Kacker gives IKEA (contemporary home furnishings from Sweden) and Bennetton (an Italian apparel firm). Loeb Associates, a retail consulting firm, has emphasized the importance of knowing the customer and adapting to the local market (J. Black, 1992). Management Horizons staff believe that successful global retailers must create a strong franchise with customers through image and service, develop loyal shoppers, use technology to reduce costs and engage in micro-marketing, develop strong networks with global suppliers, and have a flexible management style (1993). Barry and Warfield (1988) have identified a successful trend they label **dispersion retailing**, in which both the manufacturing and retailing functions are orchestrated by the retailer, who carefully identifies target markets and pursues niches in foreign markets after careful research. Merchandise is carefully planned for the specialized market niche, and customers come to expect a certain type of merchandise, a characteristic atmosphere, and a consistent retail philosophy in all the firm's stores. They identified Italy's Benetton, Britain's Laura Ashley, and Sweden's IKEA as successful examples.

A Profile of Global Retailers

Through its network of international offices and contacts, Price Waterhouse/Management Horizons conducted a study of the top 100 retailers of the world ranked by 1992 sales (1994). U.S.-based Wal-Mart and Kmart are the *first and third* largest retailers worldwide. The Price Waterhouse/Management Horizons study included all retailers, of which supermarkets are an important category. Table 13–3 identifies the world's top 10 retailers and their respective shares of worldwide sales in 1992.

The regional distribution of companies and sales of the top 100 retailers globally is shown in Figure 13–6 on page 484. In 1992, the Americas ranked behind Europe, losing market share of the sales volume of companies in the top 100. Both Europe and the Far East gained in market share.

The Price Waterhouse/Management Horizons study found that 65 percent of the top 100 global retailers had expanded retail operations outside their base country. For the study, Management Horizons distinguished between **global retailers, international retailers**, and single-country retailers. Table 13–4 on page 485 gives a summary of geographic concentration of the top 100 retailers.

European retailers have the highest concentration of firms that operate outside their base country. An important factor to keep in mind, however, is that many European countries are relatively small. That is, a retailer selling in several other European countries can be compared to a U.S. retailer that sells in several states. Nevertheless, retailers in the Americas are significantly behind their counterparts in the other two regions of the world: Only 41 percent of American "top 100" firms are active outside their own respective countries, and fewer than 18 percent are global.

TABLE 13–3

Top 100 retailers worldwide: economic concentration of leading companies

Company, Country	Sales (US$8)	Percent of Top 100 Sales	Cumulative Percent of Top 100 Sales
Wal-Mart Stores, Inc.			
United States	$56.0	5.1%	5.1%
Metro/Asko,			
Switzerland	48.0	4.3	9.4
Kmart Corporation,			
United States	37.7	3.4	12.8
Sears, Roebuck and Co.,			
United States	32.0	2.9	15.7
Tengelmann,			
Germany	31.4	2.8	18.6
Rewe Zentral AG,			
Germany	27.4	2.5	21.0
Ito-Yokado Co., LTD.,			
Japan	23.9	2.2	23.2
The Kroger Company,			
United States	22.1	2.0	25.2
Carrefour SA,			
France	22.1	2.0	27.2
Intermarche,			
France	21.5	1.9	29.2
Total Top 10	$322.2	29.2%	29.2%
Total Top 25	$562.9	50.9%	50.9%
Total Top 100	$1,105.1	100.0%	100.0%

Source: From *Retail World: Window of Opportunity* (p. 11) by Price Waterhouse/Management Horizons, 1994, Columbus, OH: Author. Reprinted by permission.

The Price Waterhouse/Management Horizons study makes a compelling case for the advantages to retailers in expanding operations well beyond the home base country. As Figure 13–7 on page 485 indicates, between 1987 and 1992, retailers with global operations had a higher average annual growth rate in sales (13.4 percent) compared to the international retailers (10.8 percent) or single-country retailers (9.1 percent).

In summary, global retailing represents a phenomenal new and growing dimension to the globally interdependent softgoods chain,

offering additional challenges and opportunities to both manufacturers and retailers. The expansion of global retailing holds the potential for reshaping conventional patterns of business relationships in the softgoods industry on a worldwide scale.

The technology of communications and transportation has brought the world closer together. Similarly, many geographic borders and global trade barriers are fading away. This would appear to be a time in which opportunities for global retailing will expand exponentially. Price Waterhouse/Management

FIGURE 13–6

Top 100 retailers worldwide shift in sales among trilateral regions

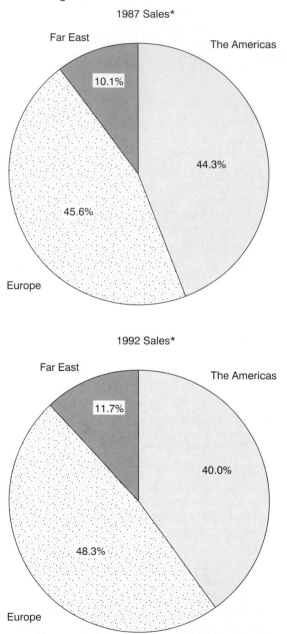

*Includes 92 of the top 100 Retailers whose sales were available for both 1987 and 1992.

Source: From *Retail World: Window of Opportunity* (p. 12) by Price Waterhouse/Management Horizons, 1994, Columbus, OH: Author. Reprinted by permission.

Horizons staff believe that a narrow window of opportunity exists for moves into international retail expansion. Globally oriented firms are likely to move quickly in market expansion; those that hesitate are likely to be left behind.

SUMMARY

Although conflict between retailers and suppliers is not new, the increased entry of textile and apparel imports into U.S. markets has heightened the conflict greatly in the last decade. Retailers have been attracted increasingly to apparel and other textile products produced in low-wage countries, using imports from many additional countries and in a wider range of products than in the past. Many retail buyers found foreign producers eager to respond to their needs. Moreover, as retail conditions became increasingly difficult, merchants found that foreign sourcing provided alternatives for variety, exclusivity, and attractive prices. In addition, private-label programs have relied heavily on products made in low-wage countries.

As retailers contracted directly with foreign manufacturers to produce their merchandise, merchants began to assume more of the manufacturing responsibilities. Particularly for private-label lines, retailers assumed nearly all the responsibilities for creating and controlling production of the apparel. In sum, retailers increasingly bypassed domestic textile/apparel producers to secure merchandise.

Although many retailers found foreign sourcing to be a helpful strategy, problems have been common. Among the common problems are poor or unpredictable quality, long lead times, slow and unpredictable deliveries, uncertainties related to trade regulations, and poor service or lack of recourse on defective shipments.

TABLE 13–4
Top 100 retailers worldwide: geographic concentration

Economic Bloc	Number of Top 100 Companies	Percent Single Country Operators[1]	Percent With Operations Outside Base Country[2]	Percent With Global Operations[3]
Europe	53	22.6%	77.4%	39.6%
Far East	13	23.1	76.9	30.9
The Americas	34	58.8	41.2	17.6
Total Top 100	100	35.0%	65.0%	31.0%

[1]Within home country only
[2]Outside home country (includes global retailers)
[3]Outside own economic trade bloc

Source: From *Retail World: Window of Opportunity* (p. 13), 1994, by Price Waterhouse/Management Horizons, 1994, Columbus, OH: Author. Reprinted by permission.

FIGURE 13–7
Top 100 retailers' worldwide sales distribution and growth by level of foreign activity

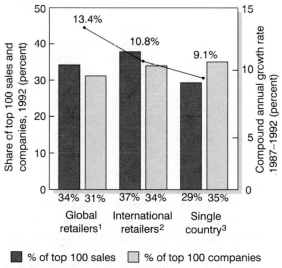

[1]Operating outside own trade bloc.
[2]Operating outside base country but within trade bloc.
[3]Operating only within base country.

Source: From *Retail World: Window of Opportunity* by Price Waterhouse/Management Horizons, 1994, Columbus, OH: Author. Reprinted by permission.

For some time, U.S. textile/apparel manufacturers have considered retailers and importers responsible for the large growth of textile and apparel imports in domestic markets (often failing to mention manufacturers' own offshore production). After all, retail operations represent the conduit through which merchandise passes to the consumer. In other words, manufacturers reasoned that imports would not be taking substantial portions of the domestic market if retailers were not bringing the foreign-made products to consumers. As retailers assumed manufacturing functions and bypassed domestic producers, U.S. textile/apparel industry leaders became aware increasingly of the power held by retailers.

Two important shifts in the softgoods industry have meshed to foster an improved working relationship between retailers and domestic textile/apparel producers. First, U.S. manufacturers saw that retailers were becoming increasingly self-sufficient in contracting manufacturing overseas and bypassing them altogether. As a result, a growing number of domestic manufacturers realized the importance of assuming a stronger marketing orientation and making a special effort to assist their retail customers. Thus, the Quick Response initiative resulted, and suppliers and retailers are working together more closely in their efforts to serve the same consumer.

Second, retailers have found it increasingly necessary to consider factors other than the initial cost of the merchandise in their buying decisions. Growing competitive pressures resulting from the mergers, buyouts, and other restructuring in the retailing sector have necessitated fast deliveries on merchandise. Some U.S. retailers have determined that overseas buying can be costly because it ties up capital and requires long lead times, it results in large inventories, and the resulting markdowns can be devastating to profits. By working with domestic producers who can deliver merchandise quickly, rapid replenishment programs help retailers give improved service to customers and, at the same time, permits a reduction of inventory and markdown costs.

A few retailers have developed merchandising programs that focus especially on domestically produced merchandise. British firm Marks and Spencer and Wal-Mart stores have used this strategy.

In general, retailers and importers believe they have been given unequal representation in textile and apparel trade policy matters, compared to the attention given to domestic textile/apparel manufacturers' concerns. Retailers and importers have witnessed the effectiveness of the industry/labor pressure groups (lobbies) in persuading policymakers to provide increased protection against textile and apparel imports. Consequently, retailers have also become politically active to oppose trade restraints.

Global retailing is another reflection of today's global economy. In some cases, this involves an international flow of retailing concepts from one region of the world to another. In other instances, global retailing refers to the conscious development of worldwide retailing strategies; that is, a firm establishes operations in several countries. Global retailing appears to represent a new area for growth potential for firms with the capital to support the expansion and the courage to try it.

GLOSSARY

Channel control occurs when one member of a channel is able to impose its will on other independent channel members through economic, political, or legal power, superior knowledge, or promotional tactics (Berman & Evans, 1986).

Channels of distribution refer to a set of institutions that performs all the functions required to move a product and its title (legal right to the possession of goods) from production to consumption (Bucklin, 1966).

Counterpressure group is a term that might be used to describe retailers and importers in their relatively recent political efforts to limit restraints on imported textile and apparel products encouraged by manufacturers and labor (who were the earlier "pressure group" and who possessed greater experience in the political arena).

Dispersion retailing is a term for vertical retailing and market segmentation on a global scale, with direct marketing by the manufacturer to the consumer. Barry and Warfield (1988) use this term for an export strategy by vertically integrated overseas firms.

Embargoes, as we shall consider them in our discussions, occur when more goods are presented for entry into the United States than the quota level allows, and the U.S. Customs Service denies entry of the merchandise. In addition, products may be embargoed because of improper documentation or for lack of compliance with labeling or other regulations.

Factors are intermediary credit agents who finance goods while they are in various stages of manufacture, remanufacture, or assembly. Factors usually relieve the selling company, and often the buying company, of credit risks. Factors perform these functions at both the domestic and international levels; however, because of the complexity of international credit, factors may play a particularly important role in global transactions.

First cost is the price a retailer pays to the foreign vendor for the products the retail firm purchases; first cost is the cost before freight, insurance, and tariffs.

Foreign buying offices are offices maintained by large retail firms in a region from which merchandise is sourced. Staff in the buying office work closely with exporting manufacturers in the region to secure and/or track merchandise to assure that quality and delivery meet the expectations of the retail firm back in the importing country.

Global retailers, as defined by Price Waterhouse/Management Horizons (1994), are those firms that operate outside the company's own regional trade bloc.

Global retailing is the expansion of retailing operations on a global scale.

Gross margin is the resultant gross profit *after* original markups have been reduced by subsequent markdowns and other elements such as inventory shortages and alternative costs (Samolis & Emrich, 1986).

Importers are individuals or firms who secure products from other countries to sell in the domestic market either to other businesses (for example, retailers) or sometimes directly to consumers.

International retailers, as defined Price Waterhouse/Management Horizons (1994), are those firms that operate outside the base country, but within the company's own regional trade bloc.

Inventory replenishment refers to using Quick Response (QR) or other programs based on EDI systems through which manufacturers can quickly respond to retailers' needs to have inventory replenished as it sells.

Lead time refers to the difference between the time the retailer places an order for merchandise and the time it is delivered to the store.

Markdown is the amount by which a retailer decreases the price of merchandise if it is not sold at the initial retail price. Markdowns occur because of competition, overstocking, leftover or incomplete lines, or, in some cases, as a promotional tool to increase store traffic.

Markup is the difference between the cost of an item to a retailer and the retail price for which it is sold. The markup covers both business (overhead) expenses and profit for the retailer. The term **markon** is used in a variety of ways; often "markon" is used interchangeably with "markup." Lewison and DeLozier (1989) consider a markon to be an additional markup and upward adjustment in the initial selling price made to either (1) cover increased wholesale prices or operating expenses or (2) correct consumers' quality perceptions of merchandise. That is, if consumers believe the quality of a product is questionable because of its low price, retailers may correct the misconception by increasing the price.

Mass merchandisers are retailers with large numbers of stores and powerful buying potential. Typically, they sell a large quantity of any one item. As the name suggests, these retailers aim toward mass markets— consumers in the middle- and low-income ranges.

Matrix buying is a strategy used by retailers, in which they develop a list of preferred vendors who can supply the products, service, and pricing that retailers need to execute their respective strategies.

Micro-marketing is a marketing approach in which a company focuses on meeting the needs of very narrow or specialized target market groups.

Open-to-buy is the retail buyer's "account," or available funds, to buy merchandise for a season. The term refers to the buyer's balance of the account *open to buy merchandise* at a given time; that is, it is the amount left to spend during any point in a season (or month). Open-to-buy is the difference between planned purchases and purchase commitments made by a buyer during the period and is reduced each time a purchase is made.

Overshipping is the term often used when exporting firms (or countries) knowingly ship in excess of quota limits. Although overshipping may result from honest mistakes, when the U.S. Customs Service was staffed less adequately to monitor shipments, a number of foreign exporters knew they could overship and probably not be caught. Tightened Customs enforcement has reduced overshipping.

Power retailers are fast-growing chains that attract customers with superior merchandise, sharper pricing, or greater convenience than their competitors and are revolutionizing the retailing industry with performances that far exceed the industry average.

Price averaging occurs when retailers mix merchandise from multiple sources. The costs are different for merchandise from different sources, but the selling price is the same for all. For example, retailers assert they save on costs of foreign-made products which, when averaged with costs on domestic goods, yield savings that are passed on to the consumer.

Private label lines are merchandise lines (most commonly apparel) manufactured for specific retailers and sold exclusively in their own stores.

Restructuring in retailing refers to the changes in the industry resulting from mergers, buyouts, and other consolidations that have reshaped the U.S. retail sector. One of the most significant aspects of restructuring has been the concentration of retail power in the hands of fewer, but larger, retail conglomerates.

Retailers are businesses that secure merchandise for the purpose of reselling it to consumers at a profit. If a merchant secures merchandise from other countries, this makes the retailer an importer as well.

Sourcing, for retailers as well as manufacturers, refers to the process of determining how and where manufactured goods will be procured (obtained).

Vendor is an industry term for the manufacturer or supplier.

Vertical retailing, like vertical production, means that a firm takes on an additional stage or stages of operations in the production-marketing chain. Retailers use the vertical retailing term when retailers also assume the role of manufacturer.

SUGGESTED READINGS

Barry, M., & Warfield, C. (1988, January). The globalization of retailing. *Textile Outlook International, 15*, 62–76.
This paper describes the global retailing development that the authors call dispersion retailing.

Berman, B., & Evans, J. (1992). *Retail Management: A strategic approach*, 5th Edition. New York: Macmillan.
An excellent basic retailing textbook.

Dickerson, K. (1989). Retailers and apparel imports: Variables associated with relative proportions of imports carried. *Journal of Consumer Studies and Home Economics, 13*, 129–149.

A study of retailers' buying of imported apparel and variables that appear to be related to the volume of imports carried.

Holding, H. (1990, August). Selling to the U.S. retailer. *Textile Asia*, pp. 148–151.
An excellent article on new U.S. vendor-retailer relationships.

Hughes, J. (1987). A retail industry view of the Multifiber Arrangement: How congressional politics influence international negotiations. *Law and Policy in International Business, 19*(1), 257–261.
A retail perspective on the textile and apparel industry strategy of linking the Jenkins bill with 1986 MFA negotiations.

Kacker, M. (1985). *Transatlantic trends in retailing.* Westport, CT: Greenwood Press.
A study of international transfer of retailing concepts and expertise.

Kacker, M. (1988). International flow of retailing know-how: Bridging the technology gap in distribution. *Journal of Retailing, 64*(1), 41–67.
A review of the transfer of retailing concepts across nations; a conceptual framework is presented.

Kurt Salmon Associates. (annual). *Financial profile for (annual): The KSA retail 100.* New York: Author.
A performance review for the top 100 largest public retailers.

Lack, H. (1987, August). How important is the retailer? *Textile Asia*, pp. 200–201.
This article emphasizes that manufacturers who succeed will be those that remain in close touch with their retail customers.

Management Horizons. (1993). *Global retailing 2000.* Columbus, OH: Author (A Division of Price Waterhouse).
An overview of global retailing that features a Management Horizons study of the top 100 retailers worldwide.

Peterson, R. (Ed.). (1992). *The future of U.S. retailing: An agenda for the 21st century.* New York: Quorum Books.
A book of edited papers from a conference by the same name. Authors are leading retail academicians and retailing executives who consider a variety of perspectives on the future of U.S. retailing.

Price Waterhouse/Management Horizons. (1994) *Retail world: Window of opportunity.* Columbus, OH: Author.
An excellent overview of global retailing developments.

Retail Industry Trade Action Coalition. (1987, July 30). Prepared statement of the Retail Industry Trade Action Coalition (RITAC) in Opposition to S. 549, The Textile and Apparel Trade Act of 1987. Unpublished statement presented before the Committee on Finance, U.S. Senate.
A summary of RITAC's view of the 1987 textile bill and retailers' reasons for opposing the bill.

Rosen, S., Turnbull, B., & Bialos, J. (1985). *The renewal of the Multi-Fiber Agreement: An assessment of the policy alternatives for future global trade in textiles and apparel.* Washington, DC: National Retail Merchants Association.
Retailers' and importers' views on the MFA.

Standard & Poor's (annual). *Standard & Poor's industry surveys* (retailing basic analysis). New York: McGraw-Hill.
An annual retail industry overview.

14

The Interests of Consumers in Textile and Apparel Trade

INTRODUCTION

The U.S. softgoods industry is consumer driven. In market economies, such as that in the United States, the consumer determines ultimately what sells and what does not. As one may recall from the train analogy presented in earlier chapters, the interrelated segments of the softgoods industry must respond effectively to consumer needs for the overall complex to function efficiently and profitably.

Similarly, the consumer perspective in international textile and apparel trade is a vitally important one. As we consider various consumer perspectives on textile and apparel trade, the reader will see that a number of consumer concerns parallel those discussed earlier for retailers. Yet, the interests of consumers are distinctive and exceedingly important to consider as textile and apparel trade matters are debated. First, consumers represent by far the largest U.S. group of individuals affected by textile/apparel trade and trade policies for the sector. Second, consumers are affected as much or more than any other group by whether textile/apparel trade occurs and what that trade costs. If imports are restricted, consumers are affected by limited choices and potentially higher domestic product costs. If imports are permitted to enter the United States under the present system of controls, consumers are affected by tariffs and other costs.

Although consumers are affected as much or more than any group with a stake in textile and apparel trade, the consumer perspective is perhaps the least represented in policy matters. Consumers are not organized with effective organizations and spokespersons to present their case.

Most economists believe that free trade assures that consumers get the best quality goods at the lowest prices. Similarly, most economists would argue that consumers, like retailers and importers, benefit from trade and are disadvantaged by trade restraints.

In this chapter, we will examine some of the consumer gains from textile and apparel trade and will consider some of the costs to consumers associated with various aspects of trade for the sector. Although most of our discussion will focus on U.S. consumers, similar points could be made for consumers in a majority of developed countries.

CONSUMER TEXTILE/APPAREL EXPENDITURES

Trends in consumer apparel expenditures can be followed more easily than similar trends in consumer textile expenditures. Textile products may be either components or finished goods in apparel, interior furnishings, and other product areas—for which total consumer end-use consumption is difficult to track consistently. Apparel, on the other hand, represents a more easily defined product area, which permits examination of expenditure trends over a period of time. Similar comparisons may be made for textiles if specific areas such as interior furnishings are defined as to the products included.

Apparel Prices

Since the early 1960s, apparel has been a good buy for consumers. Apparel prices have risen more slowly than overall producer or consumer prices. Figure 14–1 depicts the consumer price index for apparel during the late 1980s and early 1990s and shows the comparison for apparel in relation to all items. The comparisons are based on an index that puts 1982–1984 prices at 100, with changes shown in relation to that. In addition, the accompanying table provides specific price indexes for various consumer expenditure categories.

Overall, the consumer price index for apparel and textile interior furnishings rose less than that for most other expenditure categories. We note in the table in Figure 14–1 that prices for women's and girls' apparel fluctuated more than prices for men's and boys' clothing.

In many respects, the competitive global and national market conditions, which have made business difficult for U.S. manufacturers and retailers, have resulted in apparel prices (and those for some categories of textile interior furnishings) that might be considered bargains for consumers compared to price changes for other consumer goods and services. Although the typical consumer is unlikely to think of apparel or textile interior furnishings prices as bargains, government statistics support this assertion when changes in prices of these products are compared to those for most other consumer expenditures.

Apparel Expenditures

Measured in dollars of purchases, personal spending on apparel has increased rapidly, as shown in Figure 14–2. Figure 14–2 depicts another equally important trend. Although apparel expenditures increased, the percentage of disposable personal income used to buy apparel decreased.[1] A number of factors are believed to have influenced the decline in apparel expenditures as a percentage of disposable income. Among the factors are the following:

- Other consumer expenditures rose rapidly, as shown in the table portion of Figure 14–1. In particular, housing expenditures, energy costs, and medical expenses increased rapidly, leaving less disposable

---

[1]The reader may recall higher percentages given for apparel expenditures in Chapter 7 (see Figure 7–7). The percentages in Figure 7–7 are a portion of total consumer expenditure, whereas the percentages in Figure 14–2 are a portion of disposable personal income.

FIGURE 14–1

Consumer price index for apparel and textile interior furnishings compared to all other items.

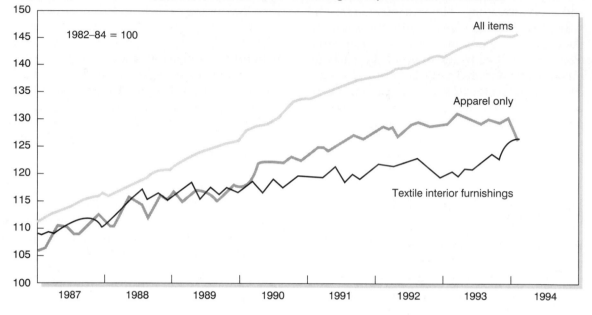

Commodities and/or Services						
Index: 1962-84 = 100	**1988**	**1989**	**1990**	**1991**	**1992**	**1993**
All items[1]	118.3	124.0	130.7	136.2	140.3	144.5
Food	118.2	125.0	132.4	136.3	137.9	140.9
Housing	118.5	123.0	128.5	133.6	137.5	141.2
Transportation	108.7	114.1	120.5	123.8	126.5	130.4
Medical Care	138.6	149.2	162.8	177.0	190.1	201.4
Apparel & Upkeep	115.4	118.6	124.1	128.7	131.9	133.7
Miscellaneous Textile Categories (seasonally adjusted)						
Apparel less footwear[2]	113.8	116.1	121.7	125.9	128.9	130.4
Men's and boys' apparel	112.8	116.2	119.3	123.3	125.7	126.8
Women's and girls' apparel	114.3	115.4	121.8	126.4	129.2	130.7
Textile interior furnishings[3]	114.9	116.6	118.0	119.7	121.5	122.4

[1] All urban consumers.
[2] Included in apparel and upkeep.
[3] Included in interior furnishings and operations: linens, curtains, drapes, slipcovers, sewing materials.
Note: New seasonal adjustment factors have been applied to CPI data from 1989 through 1993.

Source: American Textile Manufacturers Institute (1994, March). *Textile HiLights*, p. 22, and personal communication with D. Link. Based on U.S. Department of Labor data.

FIGURE 14–2

Consumer apparel expenditures, 1975–93.

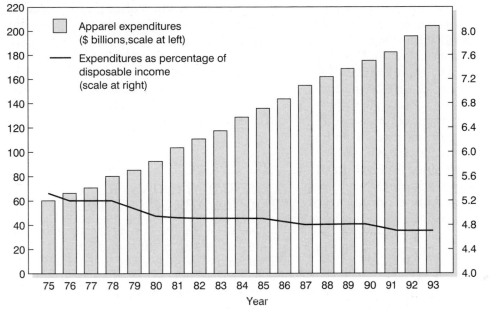

Source: 1975–1989 graph reprinted by permission, Standard and Poor's *Industry Surveys* (1994). Updated with data from U.S. Department of Commerce, Bureau of Economic Analysis 1994.

income for personal expenditures. consider, for example the consumer price index for medical costs in 1993 compared to textile and apparel areas.

- Many new consumer products that were not readily available in the 1960s (for example, microwave ovens, home video equipment, and so on), along with increased personal travel compete for disposable income.

- Apparel prices have declined in relative terms since the 1960s as a result of the following:

  Lower costs for imported apparel. Evidence suggests that consumers have benefited, at least to some extent, from less-costly imports produced in low-wage countries.

  Competitive pressure from imports has led to reduced prices for U.S.-made apparel. Domestic producers have been forced to keep prices competitive to be able to

retain markets. In addition, pressure from foreign competition has encouraged restructuring within the American industry. This restructuring has fostered efficiencies that have been passed on to consumers in the form of attractive apparel prices.

In addition, sharp domestic competition has kept U.S. apparel prices low. Competition among a large number of U.S. apparel producers, even without the added threat of imports, would keep prices at attractive levels compared to price increases in other product and service areas.

Textile Prices and Expenditures

Although consumer textile expenditures are harder to track because of the difficulty in identifying clear categories of "consumer" textiles, data are available on prices and expenditures for select categories of interior furnishings textiles. The table with Figure 14–1 provides a summary of the consumer price index for textile interior furnishings. Often the price index for textile interior furnishings from the early 1990s on has been below that for categories and even lower than apparel. U.S. Department of Commerce data on personal expenditures for textile interior furnishings goods show a healthy increase for a period of more than three decades. Figure 14–3 illustrates these expenditures since 1980.

Textile home furnishings expenditures in the first 15 years after World War II were relatively limited as the U.S. economy went through a recovery period. Although large numbers of households were formed during that era, funds for expenditures beyond the basic necessities were quite limited for many individuals and families. By the 1960s, however, the overall U.S. economic prosperity was reflected in the rapid rise of per capita expenditures for textile household goods. Although

FIGURE 14–3

Personal consumption expenditures on semidurable home furnishings, per capita (1982 dollars)

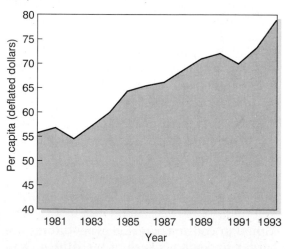

Source: Personal conversations with ATMI Staff and D. Link, 1994, based on U.S. Department of Commerce data.

expenditures have fluctuated, in general the higher spending levels have continued. Consumers are expected to place greater emphasis on spending for the home in the 1990s compared to the 1980s.

Until relatively recently, most interior furnishings textiles were domestically produced. In recent years, however, certain portions of this market have been increasingly attractive to foreign producers.

CONSUMER GAINS FROM TEXTILE/APPAREL TRADE

As we examine the consumer's position on issues related to textiles and apparel in the international economy, we will consider consumer **gains from global trade** in textile and apparel products.

An Increased Range of Products Available

The apparel industry and, to a lesser extent, the home furnishings industry thrive on variety. For many of these products, consumers make choices that promote self-expression through distinctiveness or uniqueness. Similarly, retailers attempt to attract customers to their stores rather than their competitors' by offering lines that provide variety and distinctiveness. Domestic manufacturers also try to offer lines different from other producers to attract business. Thus, in developed country markets, the softgoods industry is based on a constant flow of new and distinctive merchandise to respond to consumers' appetites for these goods.

International trade offers a far greater range of products to consumers. Logically, purchasing from a global market offers a far greater variety than is possible from a domestic market. Examples of products available as a result of trade follow.

Goods Not Available in One's Home Market

In the United States, for example, certain natural fibers are not produced at all. The silk industry is virtually nonexistent in the United States today. The kind of highly specialized hand production that silk manufacture requires does not exist in the United States; only limited processing of silk produced in other countries occurs here. Yet, many U.S. consumers are attracted to silk as a luxury fiber for a variety of uses. Other examples of fibers available only through trade are linen, ramie, angora, and a number of less-common natural fibers.

Products with Distinctive Design Features

Buying foreign-made goods in order to obtain items with distinctive design qualities is not a new idea. In fact, for many decades, affluent U.S. consumers have bought foreign-made apparel as they sought to be among the fashion-elite. The purchase of European high-fashion apparel has been a way of life for a small segment of the population.

Increased global trade in textile and apparel products has brought distinctive foreign-made products within the range of a much larger segment of the U.S. population. Looking to imported products for variety may result from several factors. Consumers (and retailers) have welcomed the relief from the high-volume, mass production runs characteristic of certain segments of the U.S. industry. A number of foreign suppliers have been willing to produce smaller runs that offer more assurance of uniqueness than American producers have wanted to provide in the past.

In addition, certain types of products with distinct style qualities are both available and affordable to U.S. consumers of average means only because they are made by individuals in low-wage developing countries (Figure 14–4). Among products of that type are

- *Hand-woven items.* Many hand-woven textile products are valued for their distinctive qualities. An example is hand-woven Indian madras (plaid) fabric. These attractive multicolored, handloomed fabrics, which have been popular in U.S. markets periodically, would be prohibitively expensive if produced by workers earning U.S. wages.
- *Hand-knitted sweaters and other items.* U.S. consumers have purchased large numbers of hand-knitted sweaters, often encompassing complex color and stitch variations. Hand-knitted sweaters offering the design complexity of many of these popular styles would carry exorbitant price tags if produced at U.S. wage rates.
- *Distinctive hand-decorated items.* Hand-embroidered and hand-printed products offer variety to today's consumer. These products may be native designs from a particular country or they may be produced according to the specifications of a U.S. buyer. At any rate, various techniques result in products that are unique, distinctive, and affordable when produced in low-wage countries.
- *Hand-crafted rugs.* Hand-woven or hand-tied rugs from certain parts of the world are highly valued. Particularly the hand-tied rugs are exceedingly labor intensive to produce because each yarn is handknotted. Because of the labor involved, it is unlikely that these rugs would exist if production occurred other than in the low-wage developing countries (Figure 14–5).

(Although these imported products add variety in our selections, these examples also offer potential for reflecting on the development theory we covered briefly in Chapter 4. The reader might reflect on the relationships between the core and the periphery countries for the production and sale of these items and also ponder on the extent to which the workers profit from production of these items.)

FIGURE 14–4
This Andean Indian woman in Cota Cota Baja Altaplana, Bolivia, folds and packs a hand-knitted sweater she has made in her home to sell in the export market.

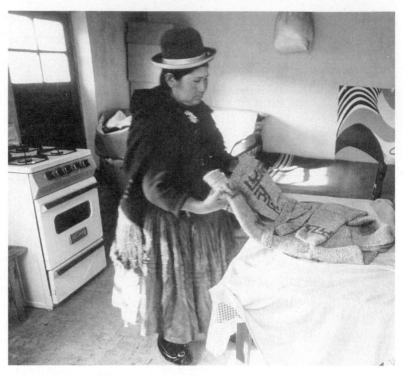

Source: Photo by J. Foxx, courtesy of United Nations.

Products No Longer Produced Domestically

Certain products may be available only from foreign suppliers. In some cases, these products once were produced by domestic firms who abandoned the markets; in some cases, this was because of intense foreign competition that the U.S. firms felt they could not match. Shoes are a prime example, with fewer and fewer domestic shoe producers in operation. Similarly, a number of labor-intensive apparel lines (for example, dress shirts and men's trousers), including many sold under familiar American brand names, are being produced elsewhere in growing proportions. In many cases, shoe firms and apparel companies import for distribution under their brand names. In short, a limited domestic supply exists in certain product areas.

Over the years, consumers have grown increasingly dependent on suppliers from around the world to produce the variety of products they desire. Today's consumer in most industrialized countries has come to expect the array of products that is currently available only through global sourcing. Careful scrutiny of a typical U.S. consumer's apparel, shoe, and accessory possessions might uncover an international consumer such as the one depicted in Figure 14–6.

Potentially Lower Prices

As we noted in Chapter 13, certain sources have questioned the extent to which retailers pass the savings of low-cost imports on to their customers. Arriving at a conclusion on this point is difficult because retail practices

FIGURE 14–5

In this scene, Afghanistan men and boys in a refugee camp in Pakistan are learning how to make complex hand-tied rugs for consumer markets in more developed countries.

Source: Photo by A. Hollman, courtesy of U.N. High Commissioner for Refugees.

vary greatly from one company to another. Dardis (1988) noted that although some retailers may take higher markups on imported products in the short run, this practice is unlikely to continue in the long run because of the competitive conditions of retailing.

Evidence suggests that consumers *have* benefited. For example, W. Cline (1978) found imported products to be an average of 10.8 percent cheaper than comparable domestic products. Moreover, the affordable prices on imported merchandise in certain stores, particularly the discount and mass merchandise chains, are an indication that customers are

benefiting from the low initial costs of the merchandise.

Increased Global Production and Consumption

All nations—and the consumers in each nation—have a higher standard of living as a result of international trade. International trade allows greater specialization, and all countries reap the benefits of this specialization. A nation produces goods and services for which it has a comparative advantage and trades with other nations for the things it

FIGURE 14–6
Today's "man of the world."

TODAY'S "MAN OF THE WORLD"

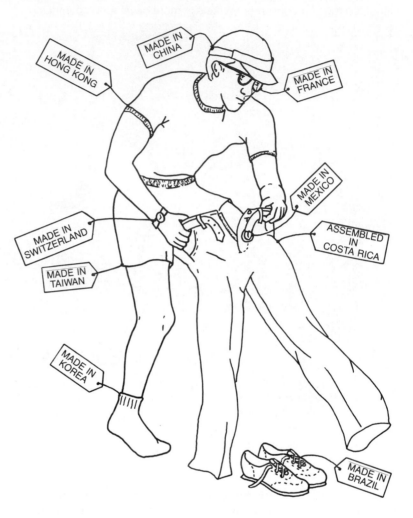

needs. Thus, the gains of trade permit all countries to have more goods and services than they could if they tried to be self-sufficient.

Consumers buy imported textile and apparel goods when they find inherent benefits in doing so. The most common benefits for purchasing imports in these product areas are price differences and variety. Seldom are choices among products so limited that consumers are *forced* to buy imports.

International trade accounts for the presence of foreign-made products and services in a domestic market—brought into that market because of some apparent benefit or advantage over domestic products or services. And the consumer has purchased the good or service because of those apparent advantages. However, the presence of the foreign-made product—especially when it has displaced a domestically made product—is generally viewed as a threat by the domestic producer.

Domestic producers can respond to the foreign competition in a variety of ways. Some firms may be determined to improve their product, the production efficiencies, or whatever it takes to compete effectively against the foreign-made product. When this happens, not only has the consumer gained from an improved domestic firm (or industry), but also the firm (or industry) has strengthened itself to be more competitive in global markets. Moreover, the competitive threat that accompanies trade fosters a climate in which manufacturers are more responsive to consumer needs. On the other hand, another common response from textile (and, some apparel), manufacturers in the developed countries has been to influence domestic trade policies to provide protection for the domestic industry. Most economists and consumer advocates consider that this approach is not in consumers' best interests.

THE CONSUMER PERSPECTIVE RELATED TO TEXTILE/APPAREL TRADE RESTRAINTS

As we have discussed in earlier chapters, the United States and most other developed countries have extensive and complex mechanisms in place for controlling the flow of low-cost imports into their markets. As the number and proficiency of developing country producers have increased dramatically, so, too, have the measures to control entry of imports into the markets of developed countries.

Although consumer advocates may decry the "evils" of pressure-group power in influencing textile and apparel policies, we must keep in mind that this phenomenon is not unique to the textile and apparel industries. Political science scholars have observed the growth of interest groups in recent years. In a

respected study on foreign trade legislation between 1953 and 1962, Bauer, Pool, & Dexter (1963) wrote:

> We note . . . how few were the congressmen who had heard anything from the major pressure groups and how many there were who were genuinely puzzled as to how they should vote and who would have appreciated clear indications of where their constituencies stood and what the issues were. (p. 351)

In contrast, in Berry's (1984) study of interest groups, he noted:

> Two decades later it is inconceivable that anyone doing research on any important public policy issue would find many congressmen who had heard nothing from interest group lobbyists or the constituents they represent back home. By any standard, the amount of lobbying in Washington has expanded significantly. Many previously unrepresented interests are now represented before the government by recently formed organizations. Interests that were already represented in Washington tend to be even better represented today. (p. 44)

Berry (1984) concluded that the growing strength of interest groups represents both an expression of freedom and a threat. In a statement that critics of the present system of textile/apparel import controls would consider particularly relevant to the consumer perspective on trade, Berry wrote: "In a system such as ours, interest groups constantly push government to enact policies that benefit small constituencies at the expense of the general public" (p. 1).

Textile industry leaders in the United States and most other developed countries have been successful in pressuring governments to enact policies to protect the domestic sectors from imports. Several sources (W. Cline, 1987; Toyne et al., 1984) consider the U.S. textile/apparel sector to be one of the most protected in the country. Later in this chapter, we will consider how these protective measures affect consumers.

U.S. textile and apparel trade restraints consist primarily of tariffs and quotas. Although tariffs on certain categories of apparel products are among the highest for any U.S. imports, tariffs are seldom a barrier to shipping goods to U.S. markets. Quotas (established under the MFA)[2], on the other hand, are far more restrictive.

Although the United States was not perceived to have high overall import restrictions in the past, the protectionist mood in the country fostered by concerns over the trade deficit has given rise to tightened restraints. Prior to completion of the Uruguay Round, pressure had increased both to deepen and to widen restraints—to cover additional product and services areas and to intensify restraints. Pressure for additional protection came from virtually all sectors—with textiles as one of the most vocal and most politically active sectors.

A number of different types of import restraints are applied. Each type has a distinctive impact on trade with different effects on the availability of products and on consumer prices. First, we will identify the common types of import restraints and their impact on trade. Second, we will review research findings on consumer costs related to U.S. trade restraints.

Restraints that Involve Costs to Consumers

Tariffs (Duties)

U.S. tariff rates average only 4.4 percent (some sources give 4.3 percent) for all industrial products—a rate comparable to the average rates for other industrialized countries. The relatively low average rates have resulted from the multilateral trade negotiations (MTN)—in particular, the Kennedy Round

and the Tokyo Round—sponsored by GATT since the 1950s (Hickock, 1985; Wolf et al., 1984). Although tariffs for most product areas were lowered substantially as a result of the MTNs, tariffs on most textile and apparel products were reduced only to a limited extent. In the Uruguay Round, tariffs on all U.S. industrial products, except textile, were reduced by 34 percent. However, textile and apparel tariffs were reduced only 12 percent. In addition, the preferential tariff treatment—the Generalized System of Preferences (GSP)—normally given to developing countries is widely excluded for textile and apparel products.

Table 14–1 displays the tariffs for textile and apparel categories for most of the OECD countries. Weighted percentages are appropriate to use for comparisons. The average tariff rates for all industrial products (excluding petroleum) are provided to permit comparisons.

For mot countries, clothing is subject to considerably higher tariff rates than textile categories. Higher tariff levels indicate that imports are a greater threat for those product categories; the higher tariffs are levied in hope of discouraging imports. Furthermore, the U.S. clothing tariffs are third highest among the OECD countries shown in the chart. Fabrics have considerably higher tariffs than fibers; however, the United States has the highest fiber (weighted) tariffs of any country shown. For fabrics, U.S. tariffs are fifth highest. Comparative data following the Uruguay Round are not available as this book goes to press. Because the United States was required to reduce textile and apparel tariffs less than some other countries, U.S. tariff rates on these products are even high relative to those for other OECD countries.

Tariffs are "taxes" levied on imports. As such, they add to the final cost of consumer products. In addition, as a tax, tariffs produce revenue for the U.S. government. Tariffs may be of two types:

---

[2]Although quota restraints are not *legislated*, the import control program under the MFA has resulted from interest-group pressures.

TABLE 14–1
Post-Tokyo Round Tariffs on Textile Products and All Industrial Products (in percent)

Countries	Fibers		Fabrics		Clothing		All Textile Products[a]		All Industrial Products (excl. petroleum)	
	Simple	Weighted	Simple	Weighted	Simple	Weighted	Simple	Weighted	Simple	Weighted
United States	2.9	3.4	11.7	11.5	12.6	22.7	9.8	18.2	6.3	4.3
Japan	3.2	0.5	9.6	9.4	13.2	13.8	9.8	5.4	6.0	2.7
EC	2.8	0.6	9.7	10.6	12.5	13.3	10.2	8.5	6.4	4.6
Austria	2.7	0.1	21.6	23.4	30.4	37.1	16.3	20.2	8.1	7.7
Finland	1.7	0.3	30.1	28.5	39.5	39.2	28.7	22.1	11.4	5.5
Norway	2.5	0.0	16.1	15.7	20.1	21.6	15.6	17.9	6.7	3.1
Sweden	1.5	0.3	12.9	12.9	13.9	14.0	11.0	12.1	4.8	4.0
Switzerland	2.0	0.2	6.6	8.4	8.9	10.8	6.0	5.7	2.9	2.2

[a]Including fibers, yarns, fabrics, made-up articles, and clothing.

Note: Weighting is according to imports of MFN origin. Tariff reductions were staged during an eight-year period, and the rates shown in the table normally applied as from 1 January 1987.

Source: From *Textile and Clothing Industries* (p. 103) by Organization for Economic Cooperation and Development, 1983, Paris: Author. Reprinted by permission.

- SPECIFIC TARIFFS are determined by levying a certain amount of charge per unit of the product; these are levied primarily to raise *revenue* for the government.
- AD VALOREM TARIFFS are a percentage of the price of the product; these are levied to provide *protection*. Our discussion focuses primarily on tariffs of this type.

Although textile and apparel tariffs are relatively high for most OECD countries and GSP concessions are often withheld for these product areas, tariffss have not been a significant deterrent to imports.

Figure 14.7 shows average tariff rates on imports.

Quotas

Although tariffs are intended to make imports more costly and therefore less appealing to purchase, tariffs provide minimal detriment to entering developed country markets. Quotas, on the other hand, block imports. To compare these two types of restraints, we might first think of tariffs as funnels. The flow may be slowed somewhat, but the products still go through. By contrast, quotas are like doors. When the door is open, the flow occurs, but when the door is closed, the flow ceases. Quotas establish limits on the *volume* of products that may be shipped; when the limit if filled, the door is closed.

Using a quota system of import restraints, rather than tariffs, represents a revenue loss to the U.S. government. Hickock (1985) estimated that, in 1984, the United States lost potential tariff revenue of $1.8 billion to foreign apparel producers by using quantitative restraints rather than tariffs. Similarly, the International Business and Economic Research Corporation (IBERC)[4] estimated that the government would lose nearly $800 mil-

lion through reduced tariff revenues if the Jenkins bill had passed (Hays, 1985).

Although the principles of the General Agreement on Tariffs and Trade (GATT) prohibited the use of quantitative restraints—quotas—to limit trade, the MFA has legitimized quotas for textile and apparel products. Furthermore, the MFA has permitted a violation of the most favored nation provision of GATT and has allowed importing countries to establish varying quota limits from one country to another.

Although quota limits are negotiated through bilateral agreements between trading partners, the umbrella framework of the MFA establishes maximum annual growth rates for import shipments. In the early years of the MFA, exporting countries were permitted annual quota growth rates of around 6 percent. As global market conditions became more competitive, the later renewals of the MFA included provisions that permitted lowering the annual growth rates. Textile and apparel producers, particularly in the United States and the EC, felt that import growths of 6 percent per year were inappropriate because domestic output grew at much lower rates. Growth rates for the major Far Eastern exporters were reduced to 2 percent or less at times; some categories were permitted no growth. Because quotas place limits on the amount (volume) of textile and apparel products shipped, this form of restraint produces side effects that will be discussed in the next section.

Other Non-Tariff Barriers (NTBs)

In addition to quotas, other non-tariff barriers (NTBs) may impede the flow of imported products available to consumers in a country. These barriers occur in many forms. In the United States, certain labeling or other regulations (in some cases, not developed with the intention of being barriers to imports) may restrict foreign goods or require compliance

---

[4]The reader is reminded that this consulting firm represents free trade interests.

FIGURE 14-7
Average Tariff Rates on Imports

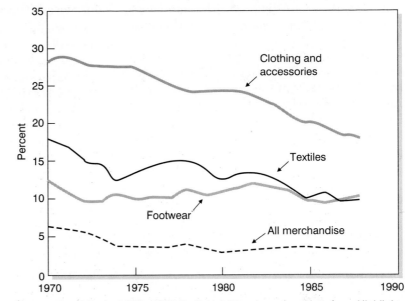

Congressional Budget Office (1991). Calculations based on data from *Highlights of U.S. Export and Import Trade*, Report No. FT990, U.S. Bureau of the Census, various issues. *Note*: Average rates were calculated by dividing total tariff revenue collected by customs value of imports. Products are classified according to Schedule A, SITC-Based Statistical Classification of Commodities Imported into the United States.

with regulations. Examples are the following: U.S. fiber content, care, and country-of-origin labeling requirements, U.S. anticounterfeiting regulations, and U.S. flammability requirements for children's sleepwear.

Consumers in other countries also experience the limiting effects from their countries' non-tariff barriers. For example, in the past Japanese consumers may not have had a chance to consider the fullest possible range of potential product choices because Japan's market was difficult to enter (although this has begun to ease).[5] A few organizations con-

trolled the Japanese trade channels; the resulting distribution system was complex for producers in other countries to enter. In other cases, countries may have **domestic content laws**, which require that a certain percentage of the component parts for products be made in the country where the product is sold. In Chapter 12, as we discussed non-reciprocity, we considered a number of other obstructive measures that function as non-tariff barriers. Consumer choice is limited by these obstructive measures (which of course is the reason the measures are imposed).

Costs Associated with Trade Restrictions

Trade restraints that provide protection to domestic textile and apparel industries are typically supported by the following two arguments: (1) it is necessary to ensure

---

[5]Some of Japan's trading partners, including the United States, have pressed Japan to make its market more accessible to products from other countries. Progress has occurred. In recent years, Japan has been the U.S. textile and apparel industry's leading export market, after Canada/Mexico and the EU. When considering apparel only, Japan has been the leading export market.

fair competition in the face of foreign subsidies, and (2) it is necessary to save domestic jobs.

Many opponents of textile and apparel trade restraints—including most economists—consider that the array of costs resulting from trade restrictions are quite high for the aid provided to the domestic industry. Moreover, the costs of protection are complex. World Bank sources (1987) asserted that most analysts have measured only the simplest costs of protection, and those are difficult enough. The World Bank writers noted that estimates generally ignore the effects of competition in influencing management efficiencies; in addition, trade encourages acquisition of new techniques, economies of scale, and investments to improve performance. In that sense, the World Bank authors consider that most of the estimates are probably too low. Further, the authors noted that most studies do not include the adjustment costs incurred when protection is removed—unemployment, worker displacement, and so on.

Dardis (1987) used the following categories as a way of distinguishing between the more immediate costs of textile and apparel trade restraints and those that have broader, long-term consequences:

- *Static effects.* **Static costs** and benefits refer to the short-term impact on consumer prices and choices. Static effects also include the output and employment gains in the protected industries.
- *Dynamic effects.* The **dynamic costs** of trade restrictions refer to the reduced incentives for producers in the importing countries to become more efficient and competitive. In this sense, protection does more than protect; it also insulates the industry to some extent from international competition.

The following are among the consumer costs of protection.

Increased Prices

The **consumer cost of protection** can be considered the extra amount consumers pay for goods because of protection-induced price increases. According to a report published by the Federal Reserve Bank of New York (Hickock, 1985), there are three aspects to the change in a protected good's average consumer price: (1) the increase in import prices that accompanies trade restrictions; (2) the price differential consumers may pay when trade restraints force them to shift to buy domestic goods, which may be higher in price, rather than buying imports; and (3) a possible rise in the price of domestically produced goods if import competition is reduced. Increased prices may result from the following.

Increases from Tariffs.   Price increases from tariffs are relatively easy to discern, since tariff rates are public information (see Table 14–1). Consumer prices are raised by the amount (percentage) of the tariff. Although retailers and importers are the initial agents who pay tariffs on imported merchandise, those costs are passed on to consumers in the price of garments or other textile products.

Increases from Quota Premia.   A **quota premium** (plural is *premia*) is the price exporting manufacturers must pay to secure quota rights in some countries to be able to export. Under the MFA quota system, alloted quotas have grown scarce for some nations, particularly the major Asian suppliers. As quota has grown more scarce—because of tightened import controls—generally it has become more valuable. Required of manufacturers in an exporting country in order to ship products to importing markets (for those product categories under control), quota has become a valuable commodity on its own. In the exporting nations in which quota may be sold—and Hong Kong is the most notable—manufacturers may pay relatively high prices for the quota. (This is called the *quota premium*). Producers pay the quota premia because they know they cannot ship their products without the appropriate quota authorization.

Jenkins (1980) found that the value of the quota license (that is, the premium paid to obtain the license) was sometimes as much as three to four times as great as the profits to be earned by the firm purchasing the quota and producing the garments. Sometimes the quota premium was as much as 50 percent of the value of the goods exported. Depending on how the quota is administered abroad, quota premia go to the foreign government, quota brokers, or foreign suppliers. At any rate, for goods produced where quota premia are part of the system, the consumer pays a price that incorporates these costs.

Increases from Quota "Rent" (Scarcity Rent). **Scarcity rent** is equivalent to a tariff revenue, with the exception that it may be obtained by either the exporting or importing country. Quota premia are an example of a scarcity rent that is obtained by the exporting country (personal communication with R. Dardis, 1989). See the "Welfare Loss from Tariffs or Quotas" boxed insert and Figure 14–8.

Reduced Selection Available to Consumers Due to Quotas

Variety tends to be more limited when trade restraints reduce the products that may be imported into a market. Retailers have charged that controls on textile and apparel goods prohibit them from providing the best possible array of products for consumers.

Children's clothing is an area in which import controls have reduced the choices available to consumers. The quota system encourages foreign producers to obtain maximum value from items produced to export; therefore, many overseas manufacturers are unwilling to use their quota for children's garments when they might, instead, ship higher-value adult apparel. (As we noted in Chapter

---

 THE COST OF BUYING QUOTAS

When the United States renegotiated bilateral agreements with the Asian Big Three in 1986, import restraints were tightened. As quotas became scarce, exporting manufacturers faced unprecedented costs to secure quotas to ship to the U.S. market. The high 1987 costs reflected the scarcity. By January 1993, however, the future of the quota system was uncertain, and quota prices were relatively low compared to the 1987 prices. However, in January 1994—after the conclusion of the Uruguay Round one month earlier and the decision to end the MFA after 10 years—the quota prices were even lower, as shown (although quota prices had dropped, it is important to keep in mind that these must be added to the cost of the garments):

	1987	January 1993	January 1994
Women's cotton jackets	211.54	40.16	27.20
Men's cotton jackets	83.33	41.45	29.15
Women's cotton skirts	141.03	19.43	9.72
Women's cotton sweaters	54.49	37.56	29.79
Women's wool skirts	262.82	51.81	36.27

Note: All prices are US$ per dozen.

Source: 1987 prices: Ehrlich, 1988c; 1993 and 1994 prices: personal communication W. Fung in Hong Kong, 1994

13, some manufacturers in high-wage countries have shifted away from children's lines because wages represent such a high proportion of production costs compared to adult apparel. What might be the potential combined effect of these two shifts? Or, why is it unlikely that the cumulative effect of these two shifts will cause a diminished availability of children's clothing?)

Product Upgrading. The quota system affects the availability of products for consumers in another way. The present system imposes limits on the quantity—but not the value—of products that may be shipped to the importing country. Therefore, exporters find it advantageous to increase the value of the goods exported to increase the return per unit. As a consequence of the quota system, foreign manufacturers have produced more and more high-value goods to maximize sales and profits from shipments to the importing markets. Smallbone (1986) reported that the Hong Kong and Taiwan governments actively encouraged exporting producers to shift to higher-value lines to maximize profits under the quota available. This practice leaves a gap in the low end of the market, particularly since new entrants (new developing country producers), which typically produce less expensive products, are locked into the smallest quota limits (Keesing & Wolf, 1980; Wolf et al., 1984).

Trading up to maximize quota values hurts lower income consumers most. This group of consumers spends a larger portion of their income on low-cost imported goods than those in higher income brackets. Consequently, when the quota system reduces the supply of products in the lower price range, those who can afford it least are affected most.

Other Ways in Which Consumers Are Affected

Regressive Effects of Costs of Protection. Costs of protection tend to be regressive (the tax rate

decreases proportionately as the tax base increases). In one of the most extensive studies on the costs to consumers (in this case, Canadian consumers) resulting from the textile and apparel import restraint system, Professor Glenn Jenkins of Harvard University found that poorer families were affected most (Jenkins, 1980). Import restrictions cost lower-income families over three times as much relative to their income as they cost high income households (Table 14–2).

Jenkins also found that poor families purchased a greater than average proportion of their clothing from the categories covered by quotas.

Costs of Operating the Textile/Apparel Import Control System. The present import control system under the MFA has been complex and costly to operate. The costs of staffing at both national and international levels have been substantial; however, total costs are difficult to estimate. The tariff system is far less costly to administer than the quota system. As examples of costs of operating the quota system under the MFA, representatives of governments require time, travel costs, and varying degrees of backup staff assistance to negotiate

TABLE 14–2

What Import Restrictions Cost the Canadian Consumer[a]

| Household Earnings | Higher Clothing Costs: | | |
	Due to Quotas	Due to Tariffs	Total
Under $10,000	$36.51	$49.55	$86.06
$20,000 to $30,000	$51.82	$70.39	$122.21
Over $30,000	$83.81	$99.30	$182.61

[a]Data are in Canadian dollars.

Source: From *Cost and Consequences of the New Protectionism: The Case of Canada's Clothing Sector* (2nd ed., revised) by G. Jenkins, 1980, Ottawa: North-South Institute.

WELFARE LOSS FROM TARIFFS OR QUOTAS

Dardis (1988; personal communication, 1989) has provided the following model to show consumer losses from tariffs or quotas; the model also illustrates scarcity rent.

A comparison of the impact of tariffs and quotas is shown in Figure 14–8. The domestic demand and supply curves are given by DD and SS respectively. The world supply curve, P_1P_1 is horizontal, indicating that the world supply is perfectly elastic as far as imports for this particular country are concerned. In the initial situation the domestic price is P_1, with imports accounting for Q_E–Q_A units and domestic production accounting for Q_A units. Imposition of a tariff shifts the world supply price from P_1 to P_2 with a resulting decline in imports to Q_F–Q_B. The loss in consumer surplus from the price increase is equal to the area P_1P_2FE. Part of the loss, however, is returned to the government in the form of tariff revenue—area CBFG. In addition there is a gain in producer surplus from the higher prices which is equal to the area P_1P_2BA. The welfare loss from the tariff is equal to the two areas, ABC and EFG. The first area represents a production efficiency loss when domestic production replaces lower cost imports. The second area represents a consumption efficiency loss as some consumers who are willing to buy low-cost imports are forced out of the market due to higher prices. These areas are often called the deadweight production and consumption losses.

Imposition of a quota limiting imports to Q_F–Q_B could achieve the same price increase from P_1 to P_2 and entail similar gains and losses to producers and consumers respectively. However, the area CBFG, which is called the scarcity rent, may go to either the importing or exporting country. If the importing country auctions quotas, then the scarcity rent will accrue to the government in the same manner as tariff revenue. If the importer is free to select his source of supply among exporters, then the importer, as opposed to the government, will gain the scarcity rent. Mintz comments, however, that both these developments are unlikely and notes that "when quotas are assigned to specific countries, the exporters in these countries typically control the allocation of the quota and pocket the profit. This is always true of voluntary quotas which means high profits for selected foreign exporters—profits which are, of course, a pure burden on the importer's economy" (Mintz, 1972). Voluntary quotas will thus result in a higher welfare loss than tariffs due to the loss of scarcity rent.

(Dardis, 1988, pp. 340–42)

(For additional information, including economic models, on consumer losses from tariffs and quotas, see Dardis, 1988, and Morton and Dardis, 1989.)

quotas in the bilateral agreements. Then, importing countries require complex monitoring and compliance systems to follow the shipment of goods to check for conformity to the agreements. In addition, staff are required at the international level as well to coordinate trade policies for the sector and to resolve difficulties.

Lobbying Costs. As textile and apparel trade has grown increasingly politicized, various interest groups have spent substantial sums in making certain that members of Congress have heard their views. As one example, textile/apparel firms, retail firms, trade associa-

tions, and industry unions spent more than $2 million to support their favorite candidates in 1992 elections (Federal Election Commission, 1994). (See Table 15–1.) Other lobbying costs include employment of consultants such as law firms, public relations agencies, and firms that develop publications to document trade statistics and other relevant information. Travel and other expenses associated with calling upon policymakers or presenting testimony before congressional committees must be considered also.

Lobbying is costly. These expenses must be covered by businesses participating in political activities. Although political action committees

FIGURE 14–8

Welfare loss from tariffs or quotas: homogeneous product. Shaded area represents scarcity rent. This quantity is similar to a tariff revenue and it may go to the exporting country (as, e.g., quota premia) or to the importing country. Welfare loss = (ABC) + (EFG) + scarcity rent (if retained by the exporting country).

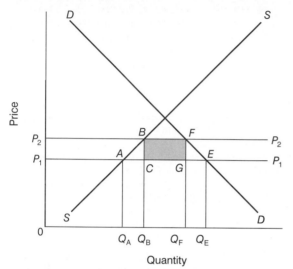

Quantity

Source: From "International Trade: The Consumer's Stake" by R. Dardis, in *The Frontier of Research in the Consumer Interest* (p. 341) by E. S. Maynes and ACCI Research Committee (Eds.) 1988, Columbia, MO: American Council on Consumer Interests. Reprinted by permission

(PACs) and other political contributions may be tax deductible, firms must cover these expenses in some manner. Data are not available on the extent to which these costs are passed on to consumers in higher prices for products; however, the likelihood is great that consumers involuntarily support these activities to an extent. An irony of these costs is that the consumer may be supporting (through higher costs on consumer products) lobbying efforts that are at cross-purposes— manufacturers' efforts and retailers'/importers' efforts, each of which offset activities of the

other. Unwittingly, the consumer is providing financial support for both sides in the textile/apparel political tug of war.

Costs of Retaliation. Policies that impose restraints on imports to protect domestic industries create potential risks of **retaliation** by other nations that purchase U.S. products. And, since U.S. consumers employed in other sectors stand to lose from retaliatory trade efforts, this is another potential concern. For example, in 1983–1984 the Chinese retaliated for textile trade restraints by boycotting U.S. wheat, substantially injuring the wheat growers through loss of trade (an estimated $500 million in sales), jobs, and farm income (RITAC, 1987; Rosen et al., 1985).

Loss of International Goodwill with Other Nations. Protectionist restraints always pose the potential risk of injuring broader political relationships with trading partners. U.S. consumers—in this case as citizens—have a stake in maintaining harmonious global relationships in a world that has grown increasingly interdependent.

U.S. textile and apparel industry advocates would add, however, that maintaining international goodwill is a two-way street. Domestic manufacturers have resented the protests against U.S. trade restraints when they have come from nations whose markets are closed against U.S. textile/apparel goods.

Estimates of the Costs of Protection

A number of scholars have analyzed protective measures in textile and apparel trade to determine the costs to consumers and to the economy more broadly (the welfare effects). Numerous studies have focused on various aspects of the costs of protection, and researchers have employed an array of methodologies to analyze costs; therefore, results from one study to another may not be comparable. The following tables, based originally on World Bank information, summarize results from several studies (taken from a more comprehensive listing that included other industries; newer studies have also been added). Among the studies are several published since 1980; the list is not intended to be exhaustive. Fewer researchers appear to have focused on this topic in the early 1990s (perhaps because findings from prior studies were so similar).

Estimates of the Costs to Consumers

Studies cited in Table 14–3 focused on the costs to consumers. As a review, these consumer costs of protection refer to the extra amount consumers pay for goods because protection has increased prices.

In a similar effort, Wolf et al. (1984) compared a number of analyses from the 1970s, which included studies by the Council on Wage and Price Stability (COWPS) (1978), Morkre and Tarr (1980), Bayard (1980), and

TABLE 14–3
Some Estimates of the Costs to Consumers of Protection (in millions of dollars)

Sector and Country	Year and Source	Cost
Clothing		
United States	1984 (Hickock, 1985)	8,500–12,000
United States	1984 (Hufbauer, Berliner, & Elliott, 1986)	18,000
United States	1980 (Dardis, 1988)	13,113 (low estimate) 13,527 (high estimate)
Canada	1984 (Morton & Dardis, 1989)	(C)$923 (low estimate) (C)$1,462 (high estimate)
Australia	1980 (Australian Industries Assistance Commission, 1980)	(A) $235 per household*
Textiles		
United States	1980 (Munger, 1984)	3,160[a]
United States	1981 (Wolf, 1982)	2,000–4,000[b]
Textiles and clothing		
United States	1980 (Consumers for World Trade, 1984)	18,400
United States	1991 (Congressional Budget Office, 1991)	39,000–74,000* for each job saved

[a]Tariffs only.
[b]Quotas only.
*Not in millions, but in dollars as shown
Source: Assembled by author. Some information from World Bank, 1988.

Pelzman and Bradberry (1980). In particular, the COWPS study showed that in 1975 high protection costs were passed on to consumers—approximately $175 a year per household. In Pelzman's (1983) review of studies on the costs of textile and apparel trade restraints, he concluded that the protective measures are costly to consumers. Spinanger and Zietz (1985) arrived at a similar conclusion in their case study for West Germany. Results of a study by Silbertson and Ledic (1989) showed the same was true for UK consumers.

Estimates of Welfare ("Deadweight") Costs

While the studies identified in the previous section focused on consumers' cost burden of protection, another group of studies have addressed the **welfare costs of protection**. Welfare costs refer to the extra cost to the economy as a whole of producing more of the goods domestically rather than importing them. Some sources refer to this as the *deadweight losses*—that is, the amount of income that is lost in the process of increasing domestic production and reducing domestic consumption of the protected items. These are the aggregate national costs of protection—that is, the losses in a nation's welfare because of inefficiencies in production and distortions in consumption. Table 14–4 identifies several analyses that examined the welfare costs of textile and apparel trade restraints.

In a study by the U.S. International Trade Commission (1993a) that was unveiled just prior to the completion of the Uruguay

TABLE 14–4
Some Estimates of the Welfare Costs of Protection (in millions of dollars)

Sector and Country	Year and Source	Cost
Clothing		
Canada	1979 (Jenkins, 1980)	(C)$92
Canada	1984 (Morton & Dardis, 1989)	(C)$73 (low estimate) (C)$356 (high estimate)
EU	1980 (Kalantzopoulos, 1986)	1,409
United States	1980 (Kalantzopoulos, 1986)	1,509
United States	1980 (Dardis)	736 (low estimate) 1,150 (high estimate)
Textiles and clothing		
United States	1984 (Hufbauer, Berliner & Elliott, 1986)	6,650
United States	1991 (Congressional Budget Office, 1991)	9,000–38,000* for each job saved
United States	1991 (U.S. International Trade Commission, 1993)	15,300–16,400

*Not in millions, but thousands as shown.

Source: Assembled by author. Some information from World Bank, 1988.

Round talks, ITC staff evaluated the economic effects of significant U.S. import restraints on the domestic economy. The study considered several manufacturing sectors, agriculture, and services and was based on 1991 data. For each sector analyzed, ITC staff analyzed the welfare gains to the economy if restraints were removed, as well as estimates of the effect on employment, output, and trade. Results showed that if restraints were dropped for all the sectors, the economy would have a $19 billion gain. Of the total estimated gain, *a major portion* would come from the textile and apparel sector if that trade were liberalized—an estimated $15.3 to $16.4 billion. The apparel sector was projected as the sector most affected by eliminating import restraints, resulting in a 24.5 percent increase in imports and a loss of nearly 47,000 jobs.

After analyzing earlier studies, Wolf et al. (1984) observed that "the costs of protection, especially of clothing, are considerable and the transfers from consumers even larger" (p. 112). This observation seems applicable to most of the studies considered in Tables 14–3 and 14–4. In fact, two conclusions may be drawn. First, the costs of protection are generally more significant for apparel than for textiles. Second, the total costs to consumers generally far exceed the welfare costs (deadweight losses). A study by Dardis and Cooke (1984), which focused on the costs of trade restrictions on apparel in 1980, reinforced the notion that costs to consumers far exceed the welfare losses.

Estimates of the Costs of the Congressional Textile Bills

Several studies evaluated the consequences of the 1985 Jenkins bill and the 1987 Textile and Apparel Trade Act. Those are not included in the tables because they focus on the potential impact of specific bills that did not pass. In addition, some of the studies were commis-

sioned by special interest groups. Two analyses of the potential impact of the 1987 bill received considerable attention. The IBERC group prepared an analysis for the Retail Industry Trade Action Coalition, which estimated that U.S. consumers would pay an additional $8.1 billion annually on textile and apparel purchases and another $2.3 billion on footwear (Baughman, 1987). The IBERC study estimated that costs of protecting each textile and apparel job under the bill would be $262,000. In an ICF Incorporated study, commissioned by the Fiber, Fabric and Apparel Coalition for Trade, analysts concluded that the bill would add $1 billion to the GNP in 1987 and another $1.7 billion in 1988 (ICF Incorporated, 1987).[6]

W. Cline (1987), an economist at the Institute for International Economics, developed estimates on the costs of the 1987 bill and also evaluated the IBERC and ICF analyses. Cline noted methodological shortcomings in the two earlier studies, particularly the ICF study. Cline's estimates plotted the costs of protection that would result from the bill against jobs saved for a 10-year period. He estimated that consumer costs per job saved in 1987 would have been $48,403, increasing to $62,887 by 1996. Similar studies also occurred for the 1990 textile bill.

Weighing the Costs of Protection Against the Alternatives

Although this subject is treated in more depth in Chapter 12, we must keep in mind a fundamental question regarding the consumer position on textile and apparel trade. That is, are the costs of preserving jobs for the textile and apparel sector—through various import restraint measures—justified in terms of the

---

[6]Contrasting findings of the two studies are not surprising. IBERC represented the interests of retailers and importers; ICF represented the interests of U.S. textile and apparel producers.

costs borne by consumers for these restraints? Findings from most of the studies on the costs of protection have indicated that consumers have paid high prices to protect textile/apparel jobs.

For example, Hickock (1985) concluded that the increase in tariff and quota costs have caused imported apparel prices to be 17 percent to 25 percent higher than would have been the case without restraints. Jenkins (1980) estimated that Canadian consumers paid (C)$32,959 to protect each job in that country's industry. A U.S. Federal Trade Commission study concluded that each American job protected by quotas on textile/apparel products from Hong Kong costs $40,000 (*Daily News Record*, 1985). In short, most empirical studies have concluded that the costs of protecting textile/apparel jobs are high.

Textile and apparel industry leaders object, however, to the results of these analyses of the alleged costs to consumers, charging that estimates have been exaggerated. Industry objections to estimates of consumer costs related to trade restraints center on these concerns:

- The assumption that quota rent is passed on in its entirety to consumers
- The belief that, if quotas or tariffs were removed, prices would drop
- The idea that the number of jobs saved by present restraints is inconsequential. (Ghadar et al., 1987, p. 68)

Similarly, Wolff, Howell, and Noellert (1988) asserted in a publication developed for the textile industry that the studies on consumer costs are questionable, charging that the models "apply a simplistic approach and assume that all quotas will restrict U.S. imports and drive up domestic prices" (p. 31). Wolff et al. noted that these conclusions are inconsistent with actual trade patterns. That is, U.S. "quotas are applied on a product-specific basis by country rather than in the aggregate;" therefore, many of the "quotas are actually nonbinding and have no consumer costs associated with them" (p. 31). Wolff et al.

(1988) suggested that the rapid growth of imports from controlled countries is evidence of this. As a result, he concluded that by failing to account for the nonrestrictive effects of the U.S. import control system, most of the studies have overestimated consumer costs. Examples of the "nonrestrictive effects" of the system include the following: not all countries or products are under quota restraints and many exporting countries do not fully utilize their quota.

Although one might expect a textile industry-sponsored publication to question results of studies showing high costs to consumers, a government study also challenged claims that import restraints add to consumer costs. A 1985 study by the House Government Operations Committee found no evidence that import restraints resulted in higher apparel prices. Moreover, the committee found little evidence that consumers benefited from lower apparel prices as a result of the import surge. The committee concluded that in several instances where domestic producers were forced out of business because of cheaper imports, prices subsequently increased to previous levels after the domestic competition was eliminated ("House Committee," 1985). In Sweden, the quota system was eliminated in 1991. At least initially, clothing prices did not drop as expected (personal communication with Swedish apparel executive, 1992).

In addition to industry critics, other sources have suggested that the United States must evaluate other long-term considerations in establishing trade policies. In general, many of these sources are less critical (than those just presented) of the costs of protecting the U.S. industry. Professor John Culbertson, an economist who views free trade quite differently from most of his economist peers, asserted:

Today the evidence should be clear to anyone who wants to look at it: our blind allegiance to free trade threatens our national standard of living and our economic future. By sacrificing our home market on the altar of free trade, we are condemning ourselves and our children to a future of fewer competitive businesses, fewer good jobs, less opportunity, and a lower standard of living. (Culbertson, 1986a, p. 122)

In another instance, Culbertson noted:

When imports from low-wage nations undersell our manufacturing production, they necessarily undercut our domestic wage level and the productivity of the American worker. Thus, eventually, the shift of our industries and jobs to other countries (to produce goods for our market) reduces American incomes and productivity just as would the migration of workers from low-wage countries to take jobs in the United States. (Culbertson, 1986b, p. 1)

Although Culbertson's views emphasize national interests, he is not alone in his concern over the status of American industry and the resulting **adjustment costs**. Similarly, business analysts and writers have become concerned over the decline of manufacturing in the United States and the impact on the U.S. economy. Jonas (1986) noted that in industry after industry, manufacturers are closing or curtailing their operations and becoming marketing organizations for other producers, mostly foreign. As U.S. manufacturers lose their market dominance, a new form of a company has evolved—manufacturers that do no manufacturing. Termed *hollow corporations* because they lack a production base, these new companies perform design, marketing, and service functions only. Invariably, hollow corporations have production done in low-wage countries. Some worry that the deindustrialization will leave the U.S. economy with an empty manufacturing shell, that America's valuable technology and engineering skills crucial to innovation will be transferred overseas, and that the shift to service-sector jobs will reduce the country's standard of living (Dreyfack, 1986; Jonas, 1986).

Many business writers have considered the impact of the global economy on manufacturing workers in the developed countries. As a majority of the world's population, located in the developing regions, strives to advance economically, many less-educated, lower-skilled workers in the industrialized nations have found they are losing jobs to overseas rivals. In a feature issue on "The Global Economy: Who Gets Hurt," *Business Week* writers note that global competition results in lower pay for lower-skilled workers, widening the gulf between rich and poor (Bernstein, Konrad, & Therrien, 1992; Farrell et al., 1993). Generally, these concerns are not taken into account as economists calculate the costs of protection. The U.S. International Trade Commission (1993a) study on the costs of import restraints to the U.S. economy did include estimates of the job losses if restraints were removed. Although the apparel industry was projected as the sector to lose the most jobs, when estimated job losses were combined for all segments of the textile and apparel industries, a total of 71,723 jobs may be lost if all trade restraints were removed. Most of these are likely to be production jobs. If workers in industry after industry are affected in this manner, this, too, changes the potential that consumers have to purchase other goods and services. Consumer spending in the early 1990s has indeed been affected by the economic uncertainties felt by consumers.

In short, although protecting jobs is costly to consumers, a number of sources are beginning to question the long-term consequences of losing the domestic manufacturing base. Like most other issues related to textile and apparel trade, no easy answer exists for this aspect of the dilemma.

CONSUMERS' LACK OF AN ORGANIZED VOICE

Although consumers are the largest group with a stake in textile and apparel trade, they generally lack the organization of other interest groups. To a great extent, consumers are not aware of the various issues affecting them on matters related to trade. Since most consumers are not sensitive to the issues at stake, naturally they express little concern for having their interests represented when trade policies and trade legislation are debated. In the U.S. political system, in particular, in which interest groups have grown increasingly vocal in order to have their positions represented, the "quiet" consumer perspective is underrepresented on trade matters.

When McRobert and Smallbone (1980) were invited to represent consumers' interests in a Brussels Conference on International Trade in Textiles and Clothing, they noted the rare opportunity to represent a consumer perspective on textile trade concerns. The authors, who were employed by the Consumers' Association of the United Kingdom, noted:

> Consumers in industrialized countries are the subjects of international textile arrangements, since it is these arrangements which seek to influence their pattern of behavior. The ostensible aim of any protectionist policy such as the Multifiber Arrangement and the bilateral agreements permitted by it is to force consumers to buy home-produced goods. This results in restrictions on consumer choice, more expensive goods, inflation and a decline in living standards; or increased pressure for higher wages to maintain living standards, and hence inflation. That is why consumer organizations in Europe and Australia campaign against the international trend towards greater restrictions on trade.
>
> On the other hand, consumer organizations in America have not made their views on protectionism known so forcefully. The association of sections of the consumer movement with the labor movement may be part of the reason for this. (p. 170)[7]

---

[7]For example, labor unions are actively involved in the Consumer Federation of America. Since many unions [and certainly those for the textile and apparel industries] are actively involved in seeking protectionist measures for their respective industries, union members of consumer groups are quite unlikely to take a stance against trade barriers.

The International Organization of Consumers Unions

The International Organization of Consumers Unions (IOCU) took a public position to oppose the MFA in the early 1990s. With offices in Europe, Asia, and South America, the IOCU links the activities of some 180 groups that serve consumer interests in 64 countries worldwide, representing consumer interests at the global level. At the group's world congress in 1991, IOCU called for eliminating the MFA. IOCU's position was based on the grounds that (1) the agreement hurts low-income consumers in the developed countries who cannot fully benefit from imports from low-wage countries, and (2) many impoverished workers in Third-World countries desperately need the income from exports that are restrained by the quota system (IOCU, 1991). In general, however, consumer groups such as those that follow have not been aware of the issues involved in textile and apparel trade, nor have they taken a position on this trade.

Examples of consumer organizations in the industrialized countries include:

- *The Bureau Europén de Unions des Consommateurs.* This umbrella consumer organization for the EU included growing protectionism among its five most important areas of concern.
- *The Consumers' Association in the United Kingdom.* This group is one example of a consumer group within a specific EU country. This is an independent organization financed by the sale of its research-based consumer magazine, which has over 700,000 subscribers. The group campaigns for consumer rights and responsibilities on various issues.
- *Consumer Federation of America.* The Consumer Federation of America is a nonprofit umbrella organization for 240 member organizations that include grass-roots con-

sumer groups, senior citizens' groups, labor, cooperatives, and state and local consumer groups.

- *Consumers for World Trade (CWT)*. CWT is a nonprofit organization established in 1978, which

  supports expanded foreign trade to help promote healthy economic growth; provide choices in the marketplace for consumers; and counteract inflationary price increases. CWT believes in the importance of increasing productivity and competitiveness through the efficient utilization of human and capital resources and the expansion of international trade. CWT conducts its educational programs to keep American consumers informed of their stake in international trade policy and speaks out for the interests of consumers when trade policy is being formulated. (D. Brown, 1987, p. 1)

- *Citizens for a Sound Economy (CSE)*. CSE is a U.S. "public interest advocacy group dedicated to returning economic decision-making to citizens. With an active membership of 250,000 citizens, CSE promotes initiatives which reduce government interference in people's economic affairs" (Alexander, 1987, p. 13).

- *Consumers' Association of Canada (CAC)*. The CAC is a "non-profit, voluntary organization with a national membership as of April 1985 of approximately 150,000 Canadians. The Association's objectives include bringing to the attention of federal tribunals the consumer perspective on various issues" ("Consumers' Association," 1985, p. 62).

These consumer organizations represent a range of commitment to consumers' perspectives on trade. And, although the organizations report large memberships, the numbers may be an overstatement in terms of active participation. Most of these consumer organizations have small staffs and limited resources for representing their constituents effectively, particularly against the broad-based, well-funded efforts of manufacturers and retailers.

SUMMARY

Although consumer apparel expenditures have increased in recent decades, apparel has been a "good buy." Consumer textile expenditures are more difficult to track because of the diverse range of products under the "textiles" term. Apparel prices and textile interior furnishings have risen more slowly than other consumer prices. Apparel has taken a smaller proportion of disposable personal income over a period of 20 years. Low-cost imports and pressure on domestic producers to be competitive account for some of these expenditure patterns.

Consumers gain from textile/apparel trade by having greater variety and, if savings are passed on to consumers, low-cost imports usually represent a good buy. Most economists believe, however, that the present system of textile and apparel trade restraints reduces the potential benefits of trade for consumers.

Trade restraints, primarily tariffs and the MFA quota system, are designed to encourage consumers to purchase domestic goods rather than foreign-made products. The intent of trade restraints is to save jobs and to protect the domestic industry from what is perceived as unfair foreign competition. Economists generally believe, however, that these measures to protect the domestic industry are costly to consumers. Most economists believe the import control systems seriously limit consumer choices and add to prices. A number of studies have estimated the dollar costs to consumers and to the economy more broadly. Nearly all the estimates have shown high costs to consumers. Most of these studies, however, have not considered the adjustment costs to workers and to the economy if the protection were removed. Moreover, a number of concerned individuals, including several business writers, have begun to question the long-term impact on the U.S. economy if manufacturing continues to shift to low-wage countries.

Although consumers have a great deal at stake in textile and apparel trade matters, this group's interests are generally represented minimally in decisions on trade policies or trade-related legislation. Several consumer organizations exist in the industrialized countries; however, these are relatively weak in terms of resources and grass roots participation (particularly on matters related to trade) compared to the more powerful organizations representing manufacturers and retailers.

GLOSSARY

Adjustment costs are the costs to a country and to individuals when competitive global market conditions force a sector to "adjust" to the competition. Adjustment costs might include the demise of inefficient firms or job losses for workers.

Consumer cost of protection is the extra amount consumers pay for goods because of protection-induced price rises.

Domestic content laws require that a certain percentage of the component parts for products be made in the country where the product is sold.

Dynamic costs of trade restraints include the impact of decreased competition on firms in the importing country.

Gains from trade refers to a country's advantages, through trade, in obtaining goods in which that nation does not have a comparative advantage—compared to what it would have if the country tried to produce all its own goods.

Quota premium is the price manufacturers pay to secure quotas in those exporting countries in which quota allocations are openly bought and sold. Where a nation's exports are limited by MFA bilateral agreements or other measures, manufacturers must have access to quotas to ship goods to the importing market. Thus, where quotas are bought and sold, exporting firms pay quota premia to secure a portion of the quota allowance.

Retaliation occurs when one nation responds to restraints imposed on its products in an importing country by refusing to buy products from the country enacting the restraints.

Scarcity rent is the higher price paid by consumers due to the quantity restrictions on imports (quotas). It may accrue to the exporting or importing country (personal communication with R. Dardis, 1989).

Static costs of trade restraints refer to short-term effects on consumer prices and choices as well as output and employment gains in the protected industries.

Welfare costs of protection are the costs to the economy as a whole of producing more goods domestically rather than importing them. These "deadweight losses" represent production inefficiencies, reduced consumption due to higher prices, and may also include transfers to foreign manufacturers due to quotas if the scarcity rent from quotas is retained by foreign manufacturers (personal communications with R. Dardis, 1989).

SUGGESTED READINGS

Blackhurst, R. (1986). The economic effects of different types of trade measures and their impact on consumers. In *International trade and the consumer*. Paris: Organization for Economic Cooperation and Development.

This paper identifies the effects of trade policies on consumers.

Cline, W. (1978). *Imports and consumer prices: A survey analysis.* Unpublished report. Washington, DC: Brookings Institution.

A market study that indicates that prices were lower on imported products than on comparable domestic products.

Cline, W. (1987). *The future of world trade in textiles and apparel.* Washington, DC: Institute for International Economics.

This book considers the consumer costs of the Textile and Apparel Trade Enforcement Act of 1987; in addition, it evaluates studies conducted for RITAC and FFACT.

Congressional Budget Office. (1991). *Trade restraints and the competitive status of the textile, apparel and nonrubber-footwear industries.* Washington, DC: Author.

Results of a study requested by the House Subcommittee on Trade.

Dardis, R. (1987). International textile trade: The consumer's stake. *Family Economics Review, 2,* 14–18.

A concise review of the impact of textile trade restraints on consumers.

Dardis, R. (1988). International trade: The consumer's stake. In E. S. Maynes & ACCI Research Committee (Eds.), *The frontier of research in the consumer interest* (pp. 329–359). Columbia, MO: American Council on Consumer Interests.

A study of the impact of trade restrictions on consumer welfare; this paper includes economic models for estimating consumer losses.

Dardis, R., & Cooke, K. (1984). The impact of trade restrictions on U.S. apparel consumers. *Journal of Consumer Policy, 7,* 1–12.

An estimation of the costs of U.S. trade restrictions.

Hickock, S. (1985). The consumer cost of U.S. trade restraints. *Federal Reserve Bank of New York Quarterly Review, 10*(2), 1–12.

A study of consumer costs associated with trade protection; includes clothing.

Jenkins, G. (1980). *Costs and consequences of the new protectionism: The case of Canada's clothing sector.* Ottawa: North-South Institute.

A study of costs to consumers resulting from protectionist measures.

Morton, M., & Dardis, R. (1989). Consumer and welfare losses associated with Canadian trade restrictions for apparel. *Canadian Home Economics Journal, 39*(1), 25–32.

A study of the economic losses associated with Canadian textile trade restraints.

Organization for Economic Cooperation and Development. (1986). *International trade and the consumer.* Paris: OECD.

A collection of papers on consumers and trade.

Pelzman, J. (1983). Economic costs of tariffs and quotas on textile and apparel products imported into the United States: A survey of the literature and implications for policies. *Weltwirtschaftliches Archiv, 119*(3), 523–542.

This article provides a review of a number of studies that have examined the costs of trade restraints for consumers.

Silbertson, Z., & Ledic, M. (1989). *The future of the Multi-Fiber Arrangement: Implications for the UK economy.* London: Her Majesty's Stationery Office.

This study includes a section on the impact of textile and apparel trade restrictions (the MFA in particular) on UK consumers.

United States International Trade Commission. (1993, November). *The economic effects of significant U.S. import restraints.* Investigation No. 332-325. (Publication 2699). Washington, DC: Author.

A study analyzing the economic effects of U.S. import restraints on the U.S. economy; the study considers several sectors. Textile and apparel restraints were found to be the most costly.

Wolf, M., Glismann, H., Pelzman, J., & Spinanger, D. (1984). *Costs of protecting jobs in textiles and clothing.* London: Trade Policy Research Center.

A study of the costs of protection to the importing countries, weighed against jobs saved.

World Bank. (1987). The threat of protectionism. In *World Development Report 1987* (Chapter 8). New York: Oxford University Press.

A review of the increase in protectionist policies and costs associated with those policies.

15

Policymakers and Textile/Apparel Trade

INTRODUCTION

Especially in the last three decades, textile and apparel trade has posed a particular challenge to policymakers both at the national and international levels. Although these problems have intensified in recent decades, the difficulties are not new. As noted in historical reviews in various chapters, textile/apparel trade posed problems more than a century ago. In this century, as early as the mid-1930s, producers in the developed countries were concerned over textile and apparel imports.

Although trade in many sectors has been a problem for policymakers in recent years, resolving global trade problems associated with the textile/apparel sector has been a special challenge. Establishment of the Multifiber Arrangement as a departure from GATT rules is evidence of the special treatment given textiles and apparel in trade. Controversy surrounds the question of whether textile/apparel trade is a "special case" meriting departure from GATT rules as well as other exceptions to general trade rules. Regardless of whether textile trade *should* be a special case, the fact remains that, as a result of political activity, textile trade *has* been treated as a special case. Textile trade has been a "separate province . . . of trade policy with its specialized governmental agencies, international agreements, and industry-oriented participation" (Olson, 1987a, p. 16).

Many experts have come to view textile/apparel trade as a *political* problem rather than an economic one. Giesse and Lewin[1] (1987) asserted, "It is not the economic condition of this industry that determines its level of protection. Rather, politics dictate policy choices in the realm of U.S. textile and apparel trade" (p. 81).

Textile and apparel trade problems have long represented a dilemma for many policymakers (Figure 15–1). Frequently, policymak-

ers have found themselves caught between textile interest groups pressing for added protection against imports and the need to uphold broader economic and foreign policy concerns for the sake of international goodwill for the country. Not all policymakers have been faced with this dilemma, however; some who represent textile/apparel interests are strongly committed to support restrictions against low-cost imports.

In this chapter, we will consider the special dilemma that textile and apparel trade has represented for policymakers at both the international and national (United States) levels. After examining some of the reasons why policymakers give special attention to the industry, we will consider specific ways in which U.S. policymakers have been influenced by industry pressures. Additional dis-

---

[1]Although Giesse and Lewin (1987) are cited in this chapter, the reader should be aware that these author-attorneys are affiliated with the firm Mudge, Rose, Gutherie, Alexander & Ferdon, a lobby group known for representing free trade textile and apparel interests. The Giesse-Lewin paper is carefully written and documented, but, as might be expected, represents a critical perspective regarding the textile/apparel industry's political activities.

FIGURE 15–1
Resolving the problems associated with the textile trade has posed a dilemma for many policymakers.

Source: Illustration by Dennis Murphy.

cussion will focus on the conflict policymakers experience in being expected to represent both sectoral and diplomatic interests. Because of space limitations, this discussion is not intended to be an exhaustive analysis of policymakers and textile/apparel trade.

A REVIEW OF TEXTILE/APPAREL TRADE AS A SPECIAL PROBLEM

Textile and apparel production is among a number of established industries in the developed countries that have experienced difficulty in remaining competitive in global markets. Among the others are the shipbuilding, steel, and shoe industries. Often these established industries are called the **smokestack** or **sunset industries** because of their long existence and the belief (by some sources) that these are declining industries in the developed countries.

The textile and apparel industries have faced a variety of problems for several decades. Some of these difficulties are a result of changes in the international arena; other problems are domestic in origin.

Particularly after a worldwide recession in the mid-1970s, competitive difficulties in the international arena have been exacerbated by increased competition from low-wage developing countries. Producers in the industrialized countries experienced difficulty in retaining domestic markets that they had taken for granted up to that time. Despite increased trade restraints in the developed countries, the volume of low-cost imports continued to grow substantially.

Considered from the domestic perspective, the U.S. textile/apparel industry (along with similar industries in most developed countries) has been suffering from what Anson and Simpson (1988) term "long term structural decline" (p. 107). **Structural decline** is a term used to describe the decline of an indus-

trial sector, particularly in terms of global competitiveness. **Structural unemployment** is often a by-product. Textile and apparel industries in the developed countries that are successful today have undergone substantial restructuring and updating with modernized equipment and production processes. In some cases, this restructuring has occurred with government assistance. Or, as Anson and Simpson noted, the industries in some developed countries are successful because they have been more heavily protected by trade barriers against imports than their industrialized competitors.

Political Problems Related to Employment

Concern over employment losses related to imports is the most common way that a troubled industry secures the attention of policymakers. Unemployment is a political problem that policymakers cannot dismiss lightly. Although employment declines may be related to improved productivity resulting from the introduction of advanced technology, the competition from low-cost imports is generally seen as the reason why the industry needs special protection. **Special protection** refers to exceptional restraints on imports, implemented through high tariffs, quotas, or other limitations. Arguments for special protection are not unique to the U.S. textile and apparel sectors. Similar arguments have been used by a number of other domestic industries experiencing problems in international competitiveness. And, furthermore, the approaches for securing added protection are amazingly similar from one industrialized country to another, despite the differences in political systems.

In a large number of the developed countries, textile/apparel employment is a sensitive issue. Often, employment is geographically concentrated, frequently in areas of already high unemployment. (Although the U.S. industry is located in every state, manufacturing is concentrated in certain areas.) Moreover, social concerns add to the arguments that the textile/apparel sector is a "special case," in need of protection. Examples of *social arguments* follow.

- As one of the oldest established industries, textiles and clothing are often an established part of a country's infrastructure, employing large numbers of people, many, typically, from ethnic minorities.
- Employment is often geographically concentrated and in locations where no alternative employment is available.
- Textiles and clothing employ relatively more females than males and any reduction affects females disproportionately. (Anson & Simpson, 1988, p. 159)

In addition to the social arguments for maintaining employment in textiles and apparel, *economic reasons* add to the arguments for special treatment for this sector. In most developed countries, the textile and apparel industries remain major contributors to the economies. In addition to the sector's significant contribution to employment, these industries typically contribute in terms of exports and value-added manufacturing. Moreover, a number of other related industries are affected by the conditions within this sector.

As Anson and Simpson (1988) noted, governments have tended to write off these industries as "sunset" industries and to place expectations on newer "sunrise" industries, such as microelectronics and biotechnology. Even together, these newer industries employ far fewer persons than textiles and apparel. Furthermore, the microelectronics industry has been another field in which the international division of labor occurred rapidly. Therefore, this newer industry has experienced many of the same problems in global competitiveness that occurred earlier in the textile/apparel sector. Other mainstay industries have experienced similar problems that led to reductions in domestic output and employment.

And although developed countries such as the United States may shift increasingly to becoming *service* economies, that shift is not without its problems. A number of experts believe this change will result in a lower standard of living for U.S. citizens, since many of the service industries are the low-paying industries in general (Culbertson, 1986b; Dreyfack, 1986; Jonas, 1986). Moreover, the question remains as to whether service industries can absorb workers from all the manufacturing sectors experiencing structural decline.

In short, arguments on the importance of maintaining a viable textile/apparel industry—particularly in view of the numbers of workers (voters) represented and other contributions to the economy—have not been lost on policymakers. Consequently, policymakers from the areas where the industry is concentrated have been the sector's strongest advocates in securing advantageous trade and other policies. At the same time, the geographic dispersion of the industry, particularly apparel, has accounted for widespread support for textile and apparel trade concerns. In most cases, supporters of protectionist policies have argued for protection as a means of sustaining employment.

TEXTILE TRADE AND THE U.S. POLITICAL PROCESS

Hufbauer and Rosen (1986) noted that American presidents since Franklin D. Roosevelt have proclaimed the virtues of free trade. Most have promoted international initiatives (for example, the establishment of GATT and MTN trade rounds) to promote free trade through reduction of tariff and nontariff barriers. However, at the same time, while they have promoted bold international programs to reduce trade barriers, these same presidents have been granting special concessions to protect troubled industries. Resulting trade policies reflect these contradictory approaches. While tariff barriers are greatly reduced from the Smoot–Hawley tariffs of 1930 (from 53.5 percent in 1933 to 4.4 percent in the 1980s), a number of special protection regimes have been developed to protect problem sectors from foreign competition.

Although the United States was a leader in efforts after World War II to develop the GATT to facilitate global trade, ironically, during this same time, special protection grew to protect industries facing severe import competition. We recall from earlier discussion that textile trade accounted for landmark departures from general trade rules. As special protection for a number of sectors grew more common, it also became more accepted in trade policy circles.

How Policymakers Become Involved in Originating Special Protection

Constitutional responsibilities as defined for the president and for the Congress indicate why both these branches of government become involved in setting international trade policy. The regulation of *foreign commerce* is entrusted to the Congress; the conduct of *foreign affairs* is entrusted to the president (Tribe, 1978). Since trade incorporates both these elements in international relationships, both the president and Congress may seek to participate in trade matters—or in some cases, both try to avoid the problems. Often the drama is intriguing, as policymakers alternately avoid and take credit for trade-related actions.

Although this section focuses on policymakers within the U.S. political system, similar scenarios may be found in other industrialized countries. The scenery, the language, and the faces may differ, but strategies of both the industrialists and the policy-makers are quite similar to those that occur in the United States.

Hufbauer and Rosen (1986) suggest that common scenes unfold as the U.S. executive and legislative branches of government are confronted by industries seeking special protection.

- In the first scene, the president generally resists protectionist solutions. He points to the costs of protection, America's international commitments, and the virtues of self-help. If the industry is politically ineffective or recovers its economic health, that usually ends the drama. However, if the industry is politically strong, yet continues to feel the competition from imports, congressional pressure for relief often builds.
- In the second scene, key senators and members of Congress urge the industry's case. To emphasize their interest, the lawmakers may attach riders to legislation needed by the administration.
- In the third scene, the president sees his political goals endangered and grudgingly comes to accept the case for the trade restraint. But the president tries to build maximum flexibility into the regime so that restrictions may be liberalized as economic and political winds change.
- The fourth scene is an apologia, in which the president defends his program as less protective than the solution threatened by Congress. (pp. 5–6)

The Executive Branch and Textile/Apparel Protection

Giesse and Lewin (1987) asserted that the special protection afforded the textile/apparel sector is primarily a result of the executive branch's eagerness "to satisfy the demands of a powerful, special interest group" (p. 82). Similarly, Hufbauer and Rosen (1986) attribute major policy concessions for the textile/apparel sector to presidential desires to please the large constituency represented by the industry. After all, the industry, because of its size and its concentration in key regions, has provided critical support in presidential elections. Thus, as Giesse and Lewin noted, the industry has been able to obtain commitments from presidential candidates in exchange for political support.

Perhaps the most significant example of a political trade was John F. Kennedy's establishment of special protection through the Short-Term and Long-Term Arrangements Regarding Cotton Textiles—the first official trade policies that removed a major portion of world trade in manufactured goods from general provisions of the GATT (GATT, 1984). In pursuing the STA and the LTA, President Kennedy fulfilled campaign promises that secured for him the political support of the textile-producing states (Destler, 1986).

Similarly, President Richard Nixon fostered development of the Multifiber Arrangement (see Chapter 10), and, later, President Jimmy Carter further tightened restraints on textiles and apparel. During the 1980 presidential campaign, candidate Ronald Reagan gave the industry personal assurances that he would work to protect it from imports. Aware that the industry was dissatisfied with his progress, as an election year approached, the Reagan administration attempted to be more supportive of tightening textile/apparel trade restraints (Destler, 1986; Pine, 1984).

Although the textile/apparel industry continued to believe that President Ronald Reagan defaulted on campaign promises to assist the industry (Schwartz, 1984b; "Textile Trade Bill," 1985), retailers and importers considered that MFA IV favored the domestic industry by allowing further restraints on imports (Wightman, 1986a). In addition, under the Reagan administration, renegotiation of U.S. bilateral agreements with the "Big Three" resulted in significantly tighter restraints. In short, most recent presidents have been quite helpful to

the U.S. textile/apparel industry. As the volume of uncontrolled imports continued to grow, however, sector leaders often felt the assistance was inadequate.

Congress and Textile/Apparel Production

A Large Constituency

The size of the textile/apparel workforce is a major influence in the sector's record of securing special trade protection. The U.S. fiber, textile, and apparel complex is the single largest manufacturing employer in the country. In addition to the approximately 2 million workers directly employed by the industry, including workers in every state, additional large numbers are employed in supporting industries. For example, farmers are involved in cotton and wool production for the industry. Employment in the textile/apparel sector represents approximately 10 percent of the U.S. industrial workforce—more than the U.S. automobile and the U.S. steel industries combined. Thus, large numbers of workers are dispersed throughout several hundred congressional districts. As Giesse and Lewin (1987) noted, "Few legislators in these districts, therefore, can be totally indifferent to the political demands of this industry" (p. 83).

Geographic Location

Historically, the textile/apparel industry has been concentrated in politically strategic geographic regions of the United States. Heaviest concentrations are in the Southeast and the Mid-Atlantic regions of the country. In several Southeastern states (North Carolina, South Carolina, Georgia, Alabama, Tennessee, and Virginia), the textile and apparel industries are the leading manufacturing employer. In South Carolina, as an extreme case, this sector accounts for nearly 50 percent of all manufacturing employment and 40 percent of all industrial output (author's conversation with congressional aide, 1986; Giesse & Lewin, 1987).

The South has the greatest concentration of apparel employment, with plants often located in rural areas where little or no other nonfarm employment exists. The Mid-Atlantic region (New York, New Jersey, and Pennsylvania) accounts for approximately one-third of the country's apparel workers, with apparel manufacturing located both in rural areas and in cities, especially New York City and Philadelphia.

Conditions That Facilitate Political Activity

The size and distribution of the U.S. textile and apparel industry have made it possible for manufacturers and labor groups to orga-nize effective political strategies. (Figure 15–2). Moreover, the industry has been among those with a long tradition of political activity. In the early nineteenth century—perhaps before the word *lobbying* was popular—the industry sought congressional protection from imports. Thus, when the industry's history of political activity is added to its size and distribution, this combination makes the textile and apparel sector, in Giesse and Lewin's (1987) words, "perhaps the U.S. industry most effec-tively organized for political action" (p. 86). Similarly, Goldstein (1983) noted, "Benefiting both from an historic precedent and regional concentration, the textile lobby had long been a formidable political force in American poli-tics" (p. 175). And, finally, R. Cline (1984) con-cluded that the textile and apparel sectors would receive special protection—even if the

FIGURE 15–2
Prior to the vote on a textile bill, textile and apparel workers marched on the Capitol with petitions containing thousands of signatures.

Source: Photo courtesy International Ladies' Garment Workers' Union.

import penetration were nil—because of the large share of the country's manufacturing employment in these industries.

Active Industry and Labor Organizations

Textile and apparel industry trade associations and labor unions have provided the leadership and coordination arms for the industry's political activities. Key groups have been the American Textile Manufacturers Institute (ATMI), the American Fiber Manufacturers Association (AFMA), the National Cotton Council, the Amalgamated Clothing and Textile Workers' Union (ACTWU), and the International Ladies' Garment Workers' Union (ILGWU).[2]

In 1985, a broad industry coalition, the Fiber, Fabric and Apparel Coalition for Trade (FFACT), was formed specifically to help win approval for the Textile and Apparel Trade Enforcement Act of 1985 (the Jenkins bill). Similarly, FFACT was a major force during consideration of the Textile and Apparel Trade Act of 1987 and the 1990 textile bill. FFACT has not been active since defeat of the 1990 bill.

Minimal Opposition

In contrast to the long record of political activity of the textile and apparel industry and labor organizations, until the mid-1980s no group(s) had developed strategies that had an impact in providing opposing views. That is, no group was organized or had similar strength to provide counter views to the textile/apparel sector's position that greater protection against imports was needed. Consumers have never been well organized on

trade matters. Although retailers had potential strength through the widespread distribution of stores throughout the country, they had not given high priority to trade issues. Retail political activity up to the 1980s had focused primarily on safety, wage, and other labor issues. Consequently, policymakers heard mostly the textile/apparel industry-labor views on trade matters.

Opposing Groups Emerge

In the 1980s, other groups whose interests are affected by textile/apparel trade became more organized, more vocal, and quite active in presenting their concerns on trade to the executive branch and to members of Congress. Among the vocal groups have been the Retail Industry Trade Action Coalition (RITAC), the National Retail Federation (NRF now handles. RITAC work), and the American Association of Exporters and Importers' Textile and Apparel Group (AAEI-TAG). The Consumers for World Trade group is a U.S. group that argues for consumers' stake in trade.

Together, the retailer, importer-exporter, and consumer groups have asserted their presence in the textile/apparel trade arena. Policymakers no longer hear only the industry-labor views. Influence of these newer counterpressure groups was readily apparent during debate over the 1985, 1987, and 1990 congressional textile bills.

VARIOUS TEXTILE POLICIES AND BILLS—POLITICAL "TUGS OF WAR"

Since the mid-1980s, many trade policies and legislative bills pertaining to textile and apparel trade have come before policymakers at the national level. The primary ones include the 1985, 1987, and 1990 congressional textile bills, approval of the Canada-U.S. Free Trade Agreement, renewal of China's most

---

[2]Until 1989, the American Apparel Manufacturers Association (AAMA) was part of this coalition. However, in 1989, AAMA announced a change in its position of trade. As a result of increasing member usage of various offshore sourcing arrangements, AAMA departed from its earlier anti-import position.

favored nation (MFN) status, approval of the North American Free Trade Agreement, and approval of the Uruguay Round agreement. For virtually all of these, the stakes have been very high for the players involved. In most cases, industry and labor groups have maintained one position while retailers and importers held another. Consequently, for nearly all these policy or legislative issues, harsh political battles ensued. For most of these trade matters, both sides expended enormous amounts of funding and energy.

To illustrate the political "tugs of war" (Figure 15–3), we shall focus on the 1985 Jenkins bill. This is a good example to illustrate the kinds of political activity involved in most of the decade's trade issues noted above. In a sense, the Jenkins bill sounded the rallying cry for the special interest groups involved to organize and play "hardball" politics. It was during the efforts for this bill that each faction learned to develop, orchestrate, and refine lobbying to try to sway policy in its favor. Keep in mind that portions and modifications of these activities would have been used throughout the decade. The specific techniques used and the intensity of the battle depended upon the specific issues at stake.

Although the textile bills were discussed earlier, our focus here is on the *political strategies* associated with the bills. A study of efforts surrounding attempted passage of these bills provides insight into the political activity associated with special trade protection for the U.S. textile/apparel sector. Moreover, a review of political activity related to these bills helps us to understand the positions of policymakers in the tug of war over textile/apparel trade. The battles over the congressional textile bills were among the most intense and most concentrated efforts up to that point to sway policymakers on trade matters for the sector.

Taking the Legislative Approach

As noted earlier, the textile and apparel industry had been successful in securing special trade protection through the *executive* branch of government. For nearly two decades, the rallying of industry votes for U.S. presidential candidates had paid off in special trade provisions for the sector (Destler, 1986; Giesse & Lewin, 1987; Hufbauer & Rosen, 1986).

By late 1984, textile and apparel industry and labor groups became disenchanted with

FIGURE 15–3

At times, textile trade issues have caused policymakers to feel pulled between the demands of opposing interest groups.

Source: Illustration by Dennis Murphy.

SUPPORTING POLITICAL SUPPORTERS

The textile, apparel, and retail industries and trade unions raised more than $2.7 million for the 1992 elections and spent it on their favorite candidates in a variety of congressional and state offices (Federal Elections Commission Printout, 1993). These expenditures reflect the various sectors' emphases on supporting candidates who will represent their respective interests in legislative and policy matters. Table 15–1 provides a summary of funds raised and campaign expenditures by the various groups.

Receipts and contributions for the retail group were slightly higher than those for the manufacturing group. Industry labor groups collected and gave about the same amount as both retailers and manufacturers combined. A lobbyist for ILGWU noted, "We contribute to candidates and incumbents who have a good record on our program.... We don't give excessive amounts, but we give to a lot of members or candidates" (Pullen, 1988, p. 7). Receipts and contributions in the table do not include individual contributions from industry executives, designers, or other leaders who may be donors.

---

the executive route as a means of securing special protection for several reasons and decided to intensify their already active congressional lobbying. First, the industry felt President Reagan had failed to deliver the industry assistance pledged during his campaign. Second, the domestic industry felt the impact of imports as never before. Still, despite strong campaign promises and a dramatic slump in the domestic industry, President Reagan did not respond. Thus, in the fall of 1984, industry leaders decided to develop legislation to be introduced in Congress to further restrict textile imports, and efforts were launched to build widespread support for the bill.

A Growing Climate of Concern Over Trade Matters

The industry's timing was advantageous because the country's growing concerns over trade created a receptive climate in Congress for introduction of a textile trade bill. Increasing media attention on America's economic decline in the global economy sensitized citizens to trade problems; unemployment rose;

consumers became aware of their growing purchase of imports; and policymakers began to focus on trade concerns.

Redefinition of Foreign Trade

According to Olson (1987b), another significant shift occurred. Foreign trade was redefined. As Olson stated, "The already broad issue was transformed from trade to the capacity of the American economy to compete internationally" (p. 11). Furthermore, Destler (1986) observed that issues of trade and competitiveness took on a partisan character, which increased the stakes and elevated the issue to the highest levels of Congress and the executive branch. Trade had become a high priority both among various constituencies and among policymakers.

Coalition-Building: FFACT

Prior to introduction of the first congressional textile bill, industry sponsors went through 20 or more drafts to develop a bill that would appeal to a broader coalition than had existed previously. For example, the National Cotton

TABLE 15–1
Business and Labor PAC Monies

	Receipts	*Contributions*
Labor		
ILGWU	$ 973,286	$ 673,398
ACTWU	344,273	340,368
Total	$1,317,559	$1,013,766
Retail		
National Retail Federation	$ 7,624	$ 5,477
Carter Hawley Hale	988	2,741
Dayton Hudson Corporation	90,434	69,650
J. C. Penney	237,456	219,888
Kmart	88,615	92,378
May Department Stores	144,526	143,913
Montgomery Ward	115,080	105,141
Sears, Roebuck and Co.	54,065	60,867
Spiegel	142,982	81,484
Wal-Mart Stores, Inc.	139,342	147,023
Total	$1,021,112	$ 928,562
Manufacturing		
Atlantic Apparel Co. Assn.	$ 3,925	$ 3,900
American Apparel Mfrs. Assn.	0	0
American Textile Mfrs. Inst.	127,610	142,087
Avondale Mills	21,824	23,103
Blue Bell, Inc.	6,193	9,966
Burlington Industries, Inc.	137,569	152,531
Cherokee Textile Mills	1,449	0
Clinton Mills, Inc.	5,284	13,523
Cone Mills	11,594	14,411
Greenwood Mills, Inc.	0	4,000
Hoechst-Celanese	171,809	186,773
Inman Mills	16,154	21,491
Milliken & Company	0	0
Pendleton Woolen Mills, Inc.	3,852	4,200
Russell Corporation	695	2,445
Springs Industries, Inc.	44,988	29,724
Total	$ 552,946	$ 608,154
Other		
National Cotton Council	157,281	205,778
Textile Machinery Good Govt. Comm.	4,935	5,137

Source: Federal Election Commission printouts, 1993, 1994.

Council had to be convinced that cotton producers were losing cotton markets because of imported cotton apparel (Olson, 1987a). As the FFACT coalition developed, key executives in the industry became highly visible as leaders. The FFACT coalition emerged with a singular purpose in mind: the successful passage of the Textile and Apparel Trade Enforcement Act of 1985 (called the Jenkins bill after its sponsor, Representative Edward Jenkins, D-GA).

Coalition-Building: RITAC

Exasperated by the success of the textile and apparel industry in securing special trade protection, retailers and importers assumed a new determination to counter the industry's political efforts. Retailers and importers believed they had suffered already from textile and apparel trade restraints and that future prospects looked even more bleak.

The introduction of the Jenkins bill and the apparent power of the broader industry coalition in the newly formed FFACT stirred retailers and importers to mount a similar campaign to represent their interests. Although retailers had potential political strength because of their broad representation throughout the country, particularly through retail associations, they had neither given priority to trade issues nor had they been very active politically. However, the potential effects of the Jenkins bill, if it passed, provided the impetus for retailers and importers to fight this bill.

As in the case of FFACT, coordinators of RITAC sought to develop a broad coalition to represent the interests of retailers and importers on trade matters. RITAC began to demand that its members' interests be represented on trade advisory committees and in other forums in which textile/apparel producers had been permitted to have input but retailers/importers had not.

Like FFACT, RITAC sought to incorporate a wider range of participants than might be associated typically with the respective groups. Thus, RITAC formed alliances with consumer groups and others believed to benefit from less-restrictive trade. Similarly, RITAC sought support of agriculture groups that feared retaliation if textile restraints were tightened further (that is, the U.S. agricultural sales would be affected). In addition, RITAC included other exporters in its coalition. While FFACT's coalition consisted primarily of trade associations, RITAC's membership consisted of more corporations than associations, perhaps because fewer trade-oriented associations existed in the latter sector. Top management in many of the country's leading retail firms became leaders and spokespersons for RITAC's concerns.

The Battle Began

Although the textile and apparel industry announced the March 1985 introduction of the textile bill and the formation of FFACT at a major media event, few observers expected the bill to amass the support it quickly gained. As a result of early effective efforts by FFACT to inform members of Congress of the industry's trade dilemma—in concert with the general congressional concerns over competitiveness, the balance of trade, and unemployment—the textile bill quickly gained a remarkable and unexpected number of co-sponsors. In the early stages of the bill's introduction, more than enough members of the House of Representatives had pledged to support the bill than would have been required to override the presidential veto that followed its later passage.

As retailers and importers reeled from the shock of the textile bill's early success, leaders of these sectors saw the immediate need for a counteroffensive. RITAC mobilized quickly to present the retailers' and importers' views to members of Congress. The number of cosponsors for the bill dropped, and although the number of supporters varied from time to time during consideration of the bill, the textile/apparel proponents never fully regained the original number of cosponsors. RITAC, as a countercoalition, had a decided impact on the congressional vote and, therefore, on the outcome of the textile bill.

The development of the two coalitions to influence policymakers' vote on the textile bill, and the activities associated with each side's approach, provided a near-classic case in the study of interest group politics. Furthermore, the development of an active and powerful counterlobby group representing free trade interests changed decidedly the relative ease with which U.S. textile/apparel interest groups could influence policymakers to provide special protection against imports.

Although the manufacturers and retailers are less formally organized into coalitions now, these efforts illustrate lobbying

---

NAFTA: THE POLITICAL FRAY

One of the most highly politicized battles facing U.S. policymakers in recent years involved the congressional passage of the NAFTA pact. Although the NAFTA agreement covered free trade in all sectors (after a phase-in period for some products) among Canada, Mexico, and the United States, the textile and apparel industries were important players in that debate.

Many of the tactics for influencing policymakers were similar to those used to attempt to secure passage of the three textile bills; however, the team alliances were different. Oddly enough, the textile manufacturers were on the same side with retailers and importers; in this case, manufacturers had an eye toward expanding markets in Mexico. Many textile and apparel labor groups, like virtually all organized labor, opposed NAFTA. The alliances were even more unique in that many Republicans supported President Clinton, and many members of his own party opposed him on NAFTA.

In the last few months before the NAFTA bill would go to Congress for a vote, trade was the drama: NAFTA was the leading act; and the United States was the stage. The level of grass-roots involvement was unique for a trade policy because the issue had been politicized as costing U.S. jobs. Alliances worked hard to influence members of Congress to vote in a certain way for the agreement. Early on, a close vote was expected. Therefore, all factions went the extra

mile in an effort to "wring out" as many votes as possible.

The National Retail Federation launched a letter-writing drive to have retailers around the country send letters to members of Congress. On Labor Day, several weeks prior to the vote, the AFL-CIO staged "NAFTA No" marches in about 75 cities around the country. Pro-NAFTA rallies were held, often featuring key leaders in the administration who traveled to various regions of the country to try to build support for the agreement. Banners, posters, t-shirts, caps, and buttons told the message of each side through these efforts staged around the country. The media were involved: Some groups ran advertisements, and persons representing every possible position were interviewed.

In the final days before the vote on NAFTA, when the House vote was still uncertain, President Clinton engaged in "horse trading" to secure the votes needed for passage. At this point, textile industry leaders were promised that Uruguay Round negotiators would seek a 15-year phase-out of the MFA rather than the proposed 10-year phase-out—if textile leaders could help assure passage of NAFTA.

In the end, grass-roots efforts, campaigning, rallies, and "horse trading" paid off; NAFTA passed with a House vote of 234 to 200. As expected, the agreement passed comfortably in the Senate.

approaches still in use by the different factions.

Tactics for Influencing Policymakers

A review of tactics used to influence votes on the textile bill gives insight into the strategies used by interest groups to attempt to influence policymakers. In the case of the textile bill, as each coalition attempted to influence policymakers to see its respective positions on textile/apparel trade—and to vote for that position—both sides used basically the same set of tactics. As Olson (1987a) made the following observations on common tactics (which have been condensed and modified somewhat for our purposes), he noted that these efforts are consistent with findings of Schlotzman and Tierney (1983), who asserted that interest groups use any and all strategies available to them.

Work with Government Officials

The bill's supporters possessed special skills and knowledge of the political actors in Congress and the strategies required to maneuver the bill through (in the Senate, around) hostile committees. Shepherding the bill through the "legislative labyrinth" required that proponents have a network of skillful, well-placed contacts who were able to negotiate with both congressional and executive branch officials at critical times. Although the countercoalition used this tactic as well, because of their shorter history, this latter group lacked the extensive network cultivated over time by the textile proponents.

Provide Numbers and Talking Points

Each coalition worked hard to provide data and other documentation to support its side of the argument. Both sides commissioned elaborate research booklets to provide trade statistics and other documentation. Data on import penetration, employment patterns, the trade balance for the sector, and other measures of the sector's performance were cited as proof by congressmen, representatives of the administration, and witnesses appearing before committees that their position on the textile bill was the "right" one.

Employment of Consultants

Because full-scale lobbying requires many types of skills, each coalition employed a law firm and a public relations firm. Both sides relied heavily on these commercial public relations and campaign management services; some of the consulting firms further "subcontracted" specific tasks such as economic studies and mass mailings.

Go Public

Although trade issues have not been taken to the public generally, Americans were sensitive to trade concerns at the time the first textile bill was introduced. Both coalitions launched public advertising campaigns at the national and local levels. Local textile/apparel industry efforts were especially strong in regions where production is concentrated. Through a related effort, the "Crafted with Pride in U.S.A." campaign, the textile/apparel coalition sought to sensitize consumers to the country of origin of garments they purchased.

Lobby Other Private Groups

Each coalition tried to find allies to strengthen its own base and, hopefully, weaken the other coalition. RITAC gained support from certain agricultural groups who feared retaliation if the bill passed. On the other hand, the National Cotton Council provided a textile industry tie to agricultural groups. In addition, RITAC sought support from consumer groups and from lobbyists representing the interests of textile-exporting countries. Later textile bills included incentives to draw agriculture into the manufacturers' camp.

FIGURE 15–4
Guilford Mills, in Greensboro, North Carolina, hosted a pro-NAFTA rally shortly before the Congressional vote on NAFTA. In the top photo, Secretary of the Interior Bruce Babbitt tells the crowd of textile executives and operators to encourage their friends to vote for NAFTA because of the advantages it will bring to the economy. In the lower photo, textile workers from a number of companies in the region demonstrate their support for the agreement.

Source: Guilford Mills, Inc. Used by permission.

Intensification of Lobbying by Group Members

In addition to the concentrated efforts of the trade associations within each coalition, a number of corporations on each side gave extensively of their executives' time and other resources to influence policymakers' votes. Individual firms opened offices in Washington; some assigned executives or their own lobbyists to give extensive effort to the textile bill.

For one of the textile bills, a leading textile "chieftain" rented a Washington hotel ball-

FIGURE 15–5
Garment workers demonstrated in New York City's Herald Square. The barrels symbolized unemployment due to imports.

Source: Photo courtesy International Ladies' Garment Workers' Union.

room and converted it into a telephone calling center. Dozens of telephones were installed, and textile executives were expected to work for a time in the "telephone ballroom." Textile executives focused on calling individuals who could influence members of Congress to vote in favor of the textile bill. Large display boards in the ballroom tracked the congressional supporters, opponents, and those who were undecided.

Coordination of Lobbying

Each coalition coordinated its respective members' lobbying efforts and, in addition, coordinated the roll call vote, lobbying with each side's governmental allies. Textile lobbyists worked in concert with the Congressional Textile Caucus, watching closely the status of anticipated votes. Similarly, RITAC was the coordinating point in working with the administration to seek the bill's defeat. (President Reagan had publicly opposed the bill from the beginning.)

Lobby Locally

Each coalition was active in having members of Congress approached by firms and employees within policymakers' home districts. Although members of Congress may not have known about a national coalition and its objectives, politicians were far more receptive to a case presented by voters in their home districts. Each coalition orchestrated carefully the personal visits to policymakers to be sure each member of Congress had been "properly informed."

On one occasion, the textile industry coalition even decided to try to use professors in their efforts to "bring around" the members of Congress who appeared to be unsupportive of the textile bill. The author was called and asked to contact select members of Congress from her state, particularly one well-known senator who appeared to oppose the bill. When the author indicated that her university would not wish to see her involved in lobbying, the caller suggested that the request "wouldn't be lobbying." After several attempts on the part of the author to decline graciously, the caller suggested that she (the author) would regret it "because when the textile industry goes down the drain, if we don't get this bill passed, your program will go down the drain, too" (conversation with anonymous industry caller). (Incidentally, the bill did not pass, yet the textile industry and the author's department are very much alive and well!)

Election Finance

In addition to the substantial funding raised by each coalition for general lobbying efforts, a number of participating companies and member associations had their own Political Action Committees (PACs). The intent of PAC financing was to tie support for the textile bill to campaign support for political candidates. Olson (1987a) reported that lobbyists conceded that votes on the textile bill would be key elements in the decision of whom to support in the 1986 elections.

Bill Drafting

The textile industry's drafting of the bill spurred the development of the two coalitions and the entire lobbying effort from both sides. Development of the bill by the textile sector and the skillful maneuvering through committees, which moved the bill on its way, provided the action to which the counter-coalition reacted.

Committee Testimony

Although interest groups generally testify for relevant congressional committee hearings, Olson (1987a) found that the textile bill coalitions were selective in their participation in hearings. Groups participated in testimony on the textile bill when it was relevant to their goals to do so. Moreover, each coalition understood the timing on the routing of the bill and knew when testimony would be most useful. A larger number of representatives of interest groups testified at the Senate Finance Committee hearing (the relevant Senate committee) than had been true at the House committee hearings. House passage appeared certain; however, the outcome in the Senate was unclear. Therefore, both groups believed testimony might influence the outcome of the Senate vote.

Outcome of Attempting the Legislative Approach

As discussed in an earlier chapter, the 1985 textile bill passed both the House and Senate but was vetoed by President Reagan. When the bill was introduced in the House a second time to attempt to override the veto, textile supporters lacked only eight votes in succeeding. In the meantime, however, textile strategists had delayed the override vote until after the signing of MFA IV, using the threat of an override to secure more restrictive measures in the global pact.

Olson (1987b) asserted that FFACT's main objective was not the passage of the textile bill, but rather to secure executive branch action to reduce textile/apparel imports. He noted, "Whether the bill passed was secondary to achieving desired action by the Administration. The Administration was the target, the Congress the means. The bill was another means by which industries and Congress send signals to the Administration seeking aid against trade problems as the price of continuation of the broader open trade policy" (p. 3).

When another textile bill was introduced in Congress in 1987, the two coalitions waged a similar battle to influence policymakers. Both groups used similar strategies to those employed for the 1985 bill, but each coalition had become more proficient in its use of various tactics. The 1987 bill shared the same fate as the Jenkins bill; however, the override vote was 11 votes short of the necessary two-thirds majority required to override a veto. Similarly, the 1990 bill lacked only a few votes to override the veto.

Although the three textile bills failed to pass, the support in both the House and Senate and the narrow loss on the veto override vote attest to the political strength of the textile and apparel group. And, although the RITAC coalition had not developed its full potential political strength, this counterpressure group had fulfilled its immediate mission in all three cases: to avoid passage of the textile bills.

As Olson (1987b) observed, passage of the textile bills may have been only one of the ultimate goals desired by the textile/apparel sector. As textile and apparel leaders considered the introduction of a third textile bill, they acknowledged that "the pressure they applied in Congress over the past few years has paid dividends in tighter bilateral agreements" (LaRussa, 1989a, p. 29). At approximately the same time that a third bill was being considered, textile leaders, accompanied by four Republican senators, met with the newly inaugurated President Bush to share concerns over industry import figures for the past decade. Not surprisingly, the retailer/importer coalition was poised to respond to efforts to secure added protection.

Multiple Pressures on Policymakers—An Example

As congressional policymakers assume their responsibilities for the regulation of foreign commerce, trade problems in sectors such as textiles and apparel engender multiple pressures. Trade issues are sensitive and complex. Most actors have persuasive cases. And, no easy answers exist.

Figure 15–6 illustrates the types of pressures placed on congressional policymakers during debate on the textile bills and other trade-related issues such as NAFTA. A similar figure could be developed to show pressure on the executive branch. Moreover, similar scenarios exist for efforts to secure protection for other sectors. The types of pressures are intended to be illustrative and not exhaustive. In this scheme, we might think of the pressures in two categories: the groups representing sectoral interests and the individuals and groups representing broader diplomatic and economic interests of the country.

- *Sectoral interests* refer to the interests of various industries or other sectors such as agriculture. Each of these groups is concerned with the well-being of its own sector.
- *Broader diplomatic and economic interests* refer to the interests associated with representing the nation more broadly as a member of the global community. Persons or groups representing diplomatic interests want to maintain favorable international relationships. This group would consider the issues beyond the immediate trade concerns of sectoral groups.

As we have seen for textile/apparel trade issues, there may be intense conflict among the sectoral interest groups. Nevertheless, in the broader picture, each of these represents a sector that stands to gain or lose by the outcome of policymakers' actions. Therefore, interest groups place a great deal of pressure on policymakers. In some cases, sectors may develop alliances with each other; the retailer/importer alliance with agriculture is an example. Typically, pressure on policymakers is greater as alliances are formed.

In these days of increased global participation by a number of U.S. firms, it is not unusual to find a conflict over trade policies within a single segment of the industry. For example, the American Apparel Manufacturers Association has a division between the group of large internationally focused firms favoring free trade and the majority of their members who represent small, U.S.-based firms favoring protectionism. A similar departure on trade matters has occurred within the American Textile Manufacturers Institute. At the April 1994 ATMI board of directors meeting, the textile industry's "father of protectionism" and a few other members of similar persuasion tried to encourage other CEO board members to attempt to derail the Uruguay Round/World Trade Organization legislation when it was presented to Congress. Although most of the industry

FIGURE 15–6
Here we see how the legislative branch, as an example, might receive multiple pressures from various sectoral interest groups as well as pressure from sources representing broader diplomatic and economic interests.

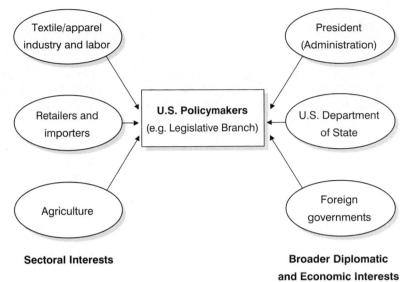

appeared to have been disappointed over the terms of the Uruguay Round, the majority of the ATMI board voted not to follow the protectionist faction's suggestions (author's conversations with various industry leaders, 1994).

Among the individuals or groups representing broader diplomatic and economic interests, alliances are natural, particularly since most of these represent a free trade position. For example, on the textile trade issue, the president and the U.S. Department of State would likely have similar foreign affairs interests in that both are concerned with representing the nation on all foreign affairs matters—not simply trade for one sector. In addition, representatives of foreign governments (often through the embassies located in this country)—the exporting nations—may become involved. As an example, these representatives of other countries may advise U.S. policymakers of the damage textile trade restraints will pose to the political relationship between their country and the United States.

Alliances may exist also between certain sectoral interest groups and those representing diplomatic interests. In the case of the tex-

tile bills, the retailer/importer coalition worked with the administration to attempt to defeat the measures. Similarly, the retailer/importer group worked with representatives of textile-exporting countries. In fact, the same lobbyist law firm that represented the retailer/importer coalition was retained also by a number of textile-exporting countries.

Alliances often change, depending on the issue at hand. For the heated battle over NAFTA, textile manufacturers, retailers, and importers worked with the Clinton Administration to secure passage. In this instance, labor groups were adamantly opposed to the bill for fear of losing jobs to Mexico. Apparel manufacturers varied in their positions, depending on whether they had or planned to have production in Mexico.

Support for NAFTA was a new position for the domestic textile industry. Up to that point, the textile manufacturers generally had not favored free trade on *any* issue that involved textiles. In the case of NAFTA, however, the U.S. textile industry leaders saw excellent market potential for the sector in Mexico and were strong advocates for passage of the

A NOTE ON LOBBYING

Earlier in this chapter, as well as in other chapters, we have referred to the political power of the textile/apparel lobby. As our discussions have indicated, the lobby has used its strength to secure increasingly restrictive measures against low-cost textile and apparel imports.

We must remember that the political actions of the textile/apparel lobby have occurred within the U.S. democratic system in which an industry or other group has a right to represent and defend its interests. Lobbying is certainly not unique to the textile/apparel sector. In fact, Berry (1984) has reported on the growing number and strength of groups representing a wide array of commercial as well as noncommercial special interests. Today, the industry would be unique if it had *not* cultivated its own special interest network. We must remember that the sector has felt abused by the influx of low-cost imports and the nonreciprocity in global markets. Therefore, the textile/apparel industries have become proficient in using the political system to their advantage to respond to these concerns.

Perhaps the crux of the concern is that, in the eyes of retailers and importers, the textile/apparel coalition has been *too* effective at using the political system to its advantage. Present trends suggest that rival special interest groups will continue to strengthen their own political expertise and power to attempt to match that of the textile/apparel lobby.

---

agreement. Favoring more open trade was such a new posture for the industry that some of the long-time strong congressional supporters of the industry appeared a bit confused at first. Finally, persuasive textile leaders helped their congressional supporters understand the positive side of NAFTA. In fact, textile leaders were instrumental in bringing in congressional votes for NAFTA from delegates that may not have voted for the bill otherwise.

TEXTILE TRADE AND THE GLOBAL POLITICAL PROCESS

We know from prior chapters that global textile trade has been "managed" under the GATT for more than three decades and is in a transition toward being under the World Trade Organization. We know that the MFA has provided the structure under which participating countries negotiated bilateral agreements that established quota limits and other terms of textile/apparel trade. Despite (or some would say, *because of*) the special mechanisms for textile/apparel trade, global commerce in this sector has been one of the most difficult for GATT and WTO officials.

Policymakers at the global level, like those at national levels, receive pressure from nations and factions seeking to influence policies to their advantage. The politics associated with global trade policies are complex and have been the subject of extensive studies.[3] For our purposes, we will focus on two simplified perspectives on the roles of policymakers as they coordinate and mediate textile trade policies at the global level: (1) the conflicting demands of exporting and importing countries and (2) the demands from within a nation participating in the global agreements

---

[3]See References for Ansari (1986); Avery and Rapkin (1982); Blake and Walters (1983); and Destler (1986, 1992).

(focusing in this case on the United States) to influence global policy.

Conflicting Demands of Exporting and Importing Countries

As we have discussed earlier, the textile/apparel trade dilemma is basically a division between the developed countries and the developing nations—in other words, a North-South dispute. This division among nations and the resulting efforts to influence textile/apparel trade policies represent a continuing source of conflict to come before global policymakers.

For the last three decades, textile/apparel trade problems at the global level have become increasingly difficult to resolve. As a growing number of producer nations have entered the global market, and as other exporting nations have become more proficient in their production and marketing efforts, the developed countries have pressed for additional restraints to limit the exporting countries' products in their markets. In fact, the MFA is a monument to the developed countries' abilities to press for special policies—policies contrary to the fundamentals of GATT.

Global pressure regarding textile and apparel trade can be reduced to two simple sets of demands. The exporting countries press for increasing opportunities to sell their products to the developed countries. And, conversely, the domestic sectors in importing countries press for increasing restraints to limit the flow of low-cost products from the developing countries. The obvious incompatibility of these two sets of demands accounts for the difficulties in developing trade policies acceptable to all the players.

As we recall, the textile/apparel sector is the leading global manufacturing employer. Because of the importance of the textile and apparel sectors in both the developed countries and the developing nations, officials at

the global level cannot dismiss lightly the political pressures related to international trade of these products. From any perspective, as global policymakers attempt to resolve textile/apparel trade problems, political pressures occur at that level as well.

Since many nations have a great deal at stake in textile/apparel trade, conflicts in this sector often have spilled over to broader trade concerns. For example, when the 1985 textile bill was being considered in Congress, Hong Kong's senior trade official warned a group of U.S. congressmen touring Asia in August 1985 that passage of the bill would create "rapid and damaging retaliation" (Ehrlich, 1985b, p. 2) against U.S. exports and would injure U.S. trade relations with developing countries throughout the world. The congressional delegation had gone to the Orient to discuss numerous trade issues; however, the protest to the pending textile bill dominated most trade conversations in Asian host countries (Ehrlich, 1985b, 1985c).

In fact, for many global trade initiatives, progress on a broader agenda has been possible only after textile trade problems are "disposed of" prior to a general trade initiative. W. Cline (1987) and Destler (1986) speculated that the Kennedy Round of trade talks materialized *only* because textile trade problems had been resolved beforehand through establishment of the Short-Term Arrangement. Similarly, Cline, Destler, and others have noted that participating nations were able to move ahead with the Tokyo Round *only* because the Multifiber Arrangement had been established to handle textile trade problems.

On matters related to textile trade, officials find themselves juggling both the demands of the developed countries and the demands of the developing countries. As officials attempt to juggle the opposing demands, each group of nations makes a compelling case. The developed countries wield far more power in global commercial policy although there are far fewer nations in this group. Of considerable significance, too, is the fact that the developed countries contribute a substantial portion of the funding for WTO (GATT) operations. On at least one occasion, the United States threatened to withhold its contribution if other contracting parties were unwilling to consider American demands (see the "Pressure Where It Hurts Most" boxed insert).

Although the developing nations have had far less power in global economic and policy matters, this group represents a much larger number of countries. Moreover, the LDCs have grown increasingly vocal in their demands for a new international economic order (NIEO), which would allow for an increased share of the world's industrial production to occur in developing countries.

Demands from within a Participating Nation

Another form of pressure on policymakers at the global level is that generated from within each nation participating in the MFA. That is, as various groups in a country—including those representing state interests (the nation itself)—seek to gain certain advantages for the nation and its industry, pressure is applied at the global level.

Pressure from within a participating nation may vary considerably according to the type of government and the freedom of various groups to influence policy; however, in most market economy countries, at least some of this activity appears to occur in relation to textile trade. In discussing national pressure on global policymakers, we will focus on the United States as an example.

In the United States the democratic political system permits this activity to influence policy. Moreover, the strength of special interest groups concerned over textile/apparel trade accounts for a great deal of political

pressure for policy concessions at the global level. Destler (1986) asserted that the U.S. textile/apparel coalition has had "sufficient political power to threaten the general trade policymaking system unless its specific interests were accommodated" (p. 23). Figure 15–7 provides a simplified representation of pressures on policymakers at the global level. Figure 15–7 is intended to illustrate the national pressures applied to policymakers who function at the international levels. For this discussion, global policymakers have been limited to two groups.

1. Trade Negotiators

A special staff of trade negotiators, within the U.S. Trade Representative's (U.S.T.R.) office, negotiate textile trade agreements at the global level. Although these negotiators represent national interests, they function in a global capacity. Since the U.S.T.R. is under the Executive Office of the President, these negotiators must try to represent the broader interests of the country on issues related to textile trade.

2. WTO (formerly GATT) Officials

The officials associated with the WTO (GATT) are global facilitators of policymaking and implementation, attempting to represent fairly the interests of all the member countries in textile trade. Our reference to WTO "officials" refers to those individuals affiliated with the WTO Secretariat who oversee WTO operations. In addition, at times we may use this term for delegates to the WTO who are functioning in policymaking roles.

Among the officials we will consider in our discussion are the individuals within the overall WTO Secretariat, as well as those identified specifically with textile trade: the Textiles Division and the Textiles Monitoring Body. For our discussion, we will consider first the pressure on international-level officials, which comes from two types of sources at the national level.

FIGURE 15–7
Policymakers at the global level may receive pressure from groups at the national level, representing both sectoral interests and state interests, to attempt to influence textile trade policies.

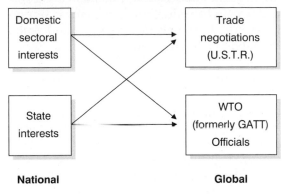

Domestic sectoral interests	Trade negotiations (U.S.T.R.)
State interests	WTO (formerly GATT) Officials

National   **Global**

A. Domestic Sectoral Interests. As one might guess from prior discussion, these are the special interest groups representing the sectors with a great deal at stake in the setting of global trade policy for the textile sector. These groups include, in particular, the U.S. textile industry-labor coalition and the retailer/importer groups. At times, if relevant interests are at stake, agriculture or other sectors may contribute to textile industry efforts to sway global policymakers.

B. State Interests. Various U.S. groups or individuals attempt to influence policymakers on textile trade policy issues when these national representatives believe broad interests of the state (country) are at stake. Persons concerned over state interests may include the president, members of Congress, representatives from various U.S. agencies, or even public interest groups dedicated to monitoring and influencing policy matters.

In the following sections, we will follow Figure 15–7 as we consider briefly how each of these groups at the national level may attempt to influence policymakers (both groups) at the international level. This discussion is intended to be illustrative rather than comprehensive.

How National Pressure Is Applied to Global Policymakers

Pressure from U.S. textile industry and labor groups represents the most common and most powerful example of the use of political strength within the country to influence global policy—and, hence, global policymakers. The retailer/importer coalition appears to be developing similar influence; currently, they are refining their political strategies.

Pressure on Global Textile Trade Negotiators

First, although the U.S. textile negotiator represents the executive branch of government at the global level and is expected to represent broad diplomatic interests of the nation as he or she negotiates policies, in reality this is difficult to achieve. The influence of the textile lobby has been readily apparent in negotiators' efforts at the global level.

Pressure from Sectoral Sources. Regardless of negotiators' intent to represent broader diplomatic interests of the country, they must worry about appeasing the domestic textile lobby and the retailer/importer lobby. Industry pressure results in part from the U.S. textile coalition's fears that the industry's concerns will be put aside in favor of other interests in broader diplomatic negotiations. That is, textile industry leaders worry that governmental concern for maintaining harmonious relationships with other nations will cause negotiators to ignore the sector's concerns for healthy survival (and their belief that import restraints are needed to achieve that survival).

The textile lobby influences the negotiators' roles in a number of ways. First of all, an individual's initial appointment to the negotiator position is influenced by lobbying inherent in the political process of the appointment. Since the chief textile negotiator is appointed through the executive branch but must be approved by Senate confirmation, the domestic lobby has numerous opportunities to influence this process via the Textile Caucus. Moreover, once a negotiator is appointed, the lobby's demands are not subtle. The negotiator is expected to maintain a position helpful to the domestic industry. In addition, U.S. industry advisors have accompanied the U.S.T.R. staff on negotiating missions and have been available to influence decisions whenever possible.

In recent years, as retailers and importers have been permitted to send advisors to textile negotiations, this group has attempted likewise to influence policymakers. Often, retailers and importers have combined forces with representatives of foreign textile-exporting interests in opposing trade restraints. This joining of interests has occurred rather easily because the same lobbyist and consulting organization (International Business and Economic Research Corporation, IBERC) has worked for a number of these free trade groups.

Pressure from State Sources. Second, because the textile negotiators must represent broad diplomatic interests of the state, they receive pressure also from individuals or groups representing those interests. For example, the president or State Department officials may be concerned over the damage of textile restraints on diplomatic relationships with another country. Concerns expressed to textile negotiators may dictate actions contrary to those desired by the textile lobby. In a few cases, negotiators have been required to consider defense concerns. For example, if the United States has military bases in a country with growing textile exports, state interests must be juggled against sectoral interests. Turkey was awarded substantial increases in

quota for being an ally in the Persian Gulf war. At times ideological concerns enter into the negotiating process. As an example, the executive branch of government (representing the state) may believe that allowing textile and apparel production to expand is important to the economic development and political stability of certain regions.

Conflicting Pressures on Negotiators. In short, U.S. textile negotiators must cope with many powerful advocates. Both the sectoral interest groups and the representatives of state interests wield tremendous political power. Negotiators are caught between two conflicting sets of demands: The industry lobby wants greater protection, while those persons representing state interests typically want freer trade. Even the most skillful negotiators find it impossible to meet the two sets of demands; consequently, few textile negotiators remain in the position for more than two or three years.

Pressures on Global Officials

For our discussion, the WTO (WTO) officials will include those with duties specifically identified with textile trade: the Textiles Division and the Textiles Monitoring Body (TMB).

Global officials experience many of the same pressures as U.S. textile negotiators. A major difference, however, is that global officials are individuals from all regions of the world. Although individuals sometimes represent "home" interests, these individuals typically assume a diplomatic perspective that permits them to look at issues from a global vantage point. Assuming a global perspective does not, however, shield these individuals from similar types of sectoral and state pressures discussed earlier.

Pressure from Sectoral Sources. The existence of a complex set of controls on textile and apparel imports is evidence that the textile/apparel sectors in the developed countries have been successful in exerting pressure on the global trading system. Often, however, pressure on global officials from the industry sector occurs indirectly. Although industry representatives from a country may make direct contact with global officials, industry pressures are applied more commonly to the home country's trade representatives or other diplomats who are expected to seek the provisions the industry wants. Generally, protocol does not permit industry representatives to be present and visible for negotiations or other policymaking sessions; however, the textile/apparel industries in the industrialized nations have been successful in applying pressure through existing diplomatic channels.

Since the 1960s, textile and apparel industries in the developed countries have applied pressure within the global framework to achieve special policy concessions to control imports. A review from our discussion in an earlier chapter includes these notable historic examples:

- Establishment of the concept of "market disruption"—a first-time departure from GATT rules (GATT, 1984).
- Establishment of the STA, LTA, and MFA—which removed textile trade from GATT rules that applied to all other trade (GATT, 1984).
- In GATT-sponsored MTN "trade rounds," textile/apparel tariffs have been permitted to remain much higher than tariffs in general (OECD, 1983 GATT sources, 1994).

At times, the policies developed for the textile/apparel sector were contrary to broader initiatives being undertaken. For example, the MFA (which permitted use of non-tariff barriers) became effective at about the same time that GATT sponsored the Tokyo Round negotiations to reduce non-tariff barriers.

We recall that GATT was established in the late 1940s to foster *more liberal trade* among the countries of the world. Almost since its beginning, however, GATT provided under its auspices special policies that *restricted* trade in textiles and apparel. How and why did this occur? These exceptions to GATT rules resulted from textile and apparel sectoral pressures from the developed countries, exerted through an understanding of and access to appropriate diplomatic channels.

Pressures from State Sources. Despite the idealistic aims of GATT for liberalizing world trade and "placing it on a secure basis, thereby contributing to economic growth and development and to the welfare of the world's peoples" (GATT, 1985b, p. 1), the demands of various countries or groups of countries often altered the idealism. A changing global economy and increasingly difficult international competition in many sectors eroded much of the original idealism intended for the GATT. Only time will tell whether the WTO can resist similar pressures that are inevitable.

Earlier, we discussed the conflict between sectoral interests and diplomatic interests in attempting to sway policymakers within the United States. Not surprisingly, these conflicting agendas are extended to the global level. At the national level, we recall that textile/apparel industry groups exerted pressures for special trade protection, which was frequently inconsistent with the wishes of those representing state interests. With regularity, these inconsistent demands were sought under the GATT.

In using the United States as a case, we may observe that "state interests" can assume varied forms when brought to the global level. First, we recall that the textile sector uses established diplomatic channels to exert pressure for greater trade protection; therefore, some representatives of the state may reflect a strong pro-industry position. Or, on the other hand, another representative of the state may dismiss industry pressures and seek

TEXTILE PRESSURES AT THE GLOBAL LEVEL

The following are examples of efforts to exert pressure at the global level to influence textile/apparel trade policies.

- *At the Textiles Monitoring Body Level.* As the unit that handles all routine problems and complaints related to textile trade, this group receives documentation and other persuasive assistance from countries whose disputes are being considered. Typical problems occur between an importing country and an exporting country. In these cases, the textile/apparel sectors in each of the two countries may attempt to provide evidence to persuade the TMB to see its respective side in the dispute. Although TMB members come from national delegations, these officials endeavor to function as impartial diplomats rather than simply serving their own nation's interests. Nevertheless, pressures are directed toward this "surveillance" group. The pressure may come from an industry within a country involved in a dispute, or may come from coalitions representing North or South interests.

- *During negotiations.* In July 1990, as the Negotiating Group on Textiles prepared to develop a proposal on how to integrate textiles into GATT rules, representatives of various sectors descended on Geneva. Concerned over the potential plan, the Retail Industry Trade Action Coalition (RITAC) delegation was one of the largest this group had sent to trade talks. During their stay, RITAC, along with the Foreign Trade Association, a group of European retailers, jointly sponsored a reception and dinner for about 100 people. Guests include GATT negotiators and representatives of developing countries (Chute, 1990b).

- *During Uruguay Round negotiations.* In the final days of Uruguay Round negotiations in Geneva, industry advisors for the textile sector as well as those representing the retailer/importer group assembled to advise U.S. negotiators on concerns affecting their respective sectors as the final agreement was concluded. Similarly, industry advisors from other sectors and other countries were on hand to advise their negotiators.

---

only broader diplomatic interests on behalf of the country. The president and the U.S. Department of State typically represent this latter category.

To illustrate these two variations of pressure from "state interests," we might consider the demands of select members of Congress with quite different agendas for U.S. interaction with WTO.

Although each congressional faction might consider its agenda to be in the best interests of the state, the perspectives on how textile trade policies should be handled at the global level would be quite different. Since Senator Strom Thurmond (R-SC) and Senator Ernest Hollings (R-SC) are from an important textile-

producing region and are active members of the group of U.S. congressional advocates, they would seek to have global textile trade policies provide increasingly tight restraints on textile imports directed toward the markets of the developed countries. In contrast, Senator Robert Packwood (R-OR) and Representative Robert Matsui (D-CA) would attempt to effect a trade system at the global level with as few restraints as possible. Senator Packwood represents a region with many importers and exporters. Nike, which imports many of its products, has headquarters in Oregon. Representative Matsui has a free trade orientation, and, additionally, The Gap—a major importer—is in a nearby district. In short, these powerful factions, the protectionists and the free-traders, each attempt to influence global trade policies according to what is believed to be in the best interests of the country. The only problem is the the two factions have directly opposing views on what will represent "state interests" best.

One might also envision similar conflicts of state interests within textile-exporting countries. For example, certain sources representing the state might demand more open markets for textile products because of the importance of the sector to the country's economic development. In contrast, other national officials might be more concerned with maintaining international political goodwill. In short, in the politicized arena of textile trade, the demands from state interests may or may not be those representing broad diplomatic concerns.

REFLECTIONS ON POLICYMAKING AND TEXTILE TRADE

The 1990s appear to be ushering in a new era of more open trade in the global arena. Although support for these changes is by no means universal within the United States, the executive branch, under the leadership of President Clinton, has taken a strong, proactive position in leading the nation in these initiatives—often at considerable political risk. First, the passage of the NAFTA pact was a milestone in opening markets, even when this required opposing organized labor groups to secure passage of the agreement in Congress. The NAFTA accord was followed soon afterward by the successful completion of the Uruguay Round—after the GATT negotiations had labored along for seven years. In short, these two landmark agreements appeared to signal a dramatic shift in the U.S

 PRESSURE WHERE IT HURTS MOST

As the 1984 annual meeting of the GATT Contracting Parties convened, initial planning was expected to begin for a new round of trade talks (which eventually became the Uruguay Round). The United States wanted to have trade in services (such as banking and insurance), high technology, protection of intellectual properties, and the counterfeiting of goods included in discussions in the new round of trade talks.

Textile-exporting countries took this opportunity to oppose growing textile trade restraints in the major importing markets. Third-World nations vowed to resist a new round of trade talks "until and unless" the United States and other countries reduced restraints on LDC textile and apparel goods.

Subsequently, the head of the U.S. trade delegation hinted that Congress might withhold the U.S. contribution to the GATT budget, nearly 15 percent of its total budget, if the additional trade concerns were not included in the new round of talks. Formal sessions of the annual GATT meeting were canceled until the deadlock was resolved. Finally, delegates reached a compromise, and the United States contributed its share to the GATT budget (Callcott, 1984a, 1984b, 1984c).

We now know that both U.S. demands and Third-World demands were included in the Uruguay Round agreement. Services and intellectual properties are now under WTO rules, and the MFA is being phased out.

position on trade. Reducing and eliminating subsidies on products such as mohair further indicated that U.S. sectors must learn to compete on their own merit in a global market economy. Figure 15–8 illustrates the crumbling of protectionist measures that have characterized the U.S. economy in the past.

Even if these two agreements do represent a significant departure from more typically protectionist positions, in which policymakers have often succumbed to special interest group pressures, we can benefit from considering patterns that have been more typical in influencing U.S. trade policy. As we reflect on the role of policymakers and textile trade, a number of observations may be useful to consider. Although some of these observations apply to trade in general, the points are especially relevant to textile and apparel trade. A common thread among these observations has been the political aspect of trade for the textile/apparel sector.

Goldstein (1983) concluded that political ideology—not social forces or international

shifts in power—has dictated American commercial policy. She noted that the U.S. political system does not foster decision making that may be in the best long-term interests of the nation. According to Goldstein, our system's limited power for economic intervention and the demands of pleasing voters make it "impossible for central decision-makers to use rational decision-making criteria to create policy" (p. 427).

In the absence of a national umbrella policy for trade, Goldstein (1983) concluded that "certain industries for anomalous and different reasons have been excepted from liberal policy and certain industries who are in decline but who employ large numbers of workers may get more aid than would be expected" (p. 427).

Similarly, Hufbauer and Rosen (1986) noted that special protection is inequitable among industries. Large industries with political clout—like textiles and apparel—"are able to shake the U.S. political system for massive benefits" (p. 27). In contrast, small industries

FIGURE 15–8
A business executive surveys the new landscape in which many of the past barriers and special forms of support are beginning to crumble.

Source: Illustration by Dennis Murphy.

with only regional influence—like footwear—get far less protection.

In addition to concerns about pleasing the electorate, Aggarwal (1985) asserted that the fragmentation of power among the legislative, executive, and judicial branches has provided the state limited opportunities to influence policymaking. Furthermore, he noted that the most unified branch, the executive branch, has numerous divisions with distinct constituencies. Aggarwal suggested the fragmented state is no match for the strong and previously cohesive political organization of the textile and apparel industry. Therefore, according to Aggarwal, the U.S. state has been too organizationally fragmented to establish a national policy or to resist industry and labor demands.

Similarly, Destler (1986) noted that the American trade policymaking system had eroded seriously. He observed that Congress has received more and more pressure from industries affected by imports, has been less protected than in the past from such pressure, and, therefore, has been less able to resist proposals for trade-restrictive measures.

In Aggarwal's (1985) extensive study on the politics of organized textile trade, he concluded that the global regime (the MFA) had "weakened" with each successive renewal because it permitted *individual nations* to impose additional textile trade restrictions. Aggarwal, a political scientist who examined MFA renewals using a theoretical framework for regime change, considered earlier versions of the MFA to be "stronger" as a *multilateral instrument*. In Aggarwal's view, earlier versions of the Arrangement provided greater restraint on national actions. As a result of the weakening of the multilateral agreement, Aggarwal concluded that participating countries took greater liberties in tightening restraints.

Policymakers who are not textile/apparel proponents at times feared that the model of "managed trade" that evolved for textiles might be copied by other sectors. When the first exceptions to the GATT were established through the STA, LTA, and MFA, certain aspects of the trade dilemma for this sector were unique. Later, a number of other sectors experienced similar difficulties. Policymakers feared that other sectors might secure similar institutionalized regimes that would have been additional exceptions to GATT rules. Other cases might have included, for example, a "Multi-Steel Arrangement" or a "Multi-Automobile Arrangement."

Overall, we may conclude that world trade in textiles and apparel has been regulated extensively through means other than simple market forces. Governmental intervention has been common, and the actions of national governments often reflected the political pressures from sectoral interest groups. In the United States, embattled officials found themselves expected to demand more of foreign trading partners and to offer less in return (Destler, 1986). In short, textile and apparel trade has posed a long-term and persistent challenge to policymakers.

SUMMARY

Although in recent years trade in general has been a problem for policymakers, both at the international and national levels, textile trade has been a special challenge. The importance of textile/apparel production to most nations and the growing competitive market conditions have led to intense political activity related to global trade for the sector. Policymakers have found themselves caught between the political demands of industry groups pressing for added protection and the need to represent broader diplomatic and economic concerns.

Textile/apparel trade issues have become highly politicized in the developed countries. This results in part from the concerns over job losses in a sector that is the major manufacturing employer in most industrialized countries; therefore, large constituency groups cannot be ignored. In addition, groups representing textile/apparel interests have become quite proficient in securing the sympathy and support of policymakers to gain increasing restrains on low-cost imports.

In the United States, the textile lobby has been successful in securing, in most cases, presidential support in their concern over imports. Most recent presidents have provided important trade concessions for the textile/apparel sector in exchange for the industry's support in elections. Moreover, nearly 2 million industry workers are dispersed throughout several hundred congressional districts, giving many members of Congress reason to take notice of the industry's trade and employment concerns.

In 1985, 1987, and 1990 the textile industry worked with members of the Congressional Textile Caucus in introducing bills in Congress to further limit imported products. Industry and labor leaders established an even broader coalition than they had maintained previously, in hopes of assuring widespread support for the textile bills. The political skills of the lobby-caucus group, along with the growing congressional concerns over trade and competitiveness, resulted in astonishing early success for the 1985 bill.

Previously, the textile/apparel lobby encountered minimal opposition in its efforts to secure protection. However, the early success of the 1985 textile bill stimulated rapid emergence of a broad retailer/importer coalition, whose primary motive was to defeat the textile bill. Each of the two coalitions engaged in extensive and costly lobbying efforts to influence the vote of members of Congress. In all three cases, bills passed Congress, were vetoed by the president, and in each case narrowly missed getting the two-thirds House vote to override the veto. Outcome of the bills illustrated the power of the textile lobby in securing a large number of supporters; however, the defeat of the bill also reflected the growing power of the countercoalition of retailers and importers. Olson (1987b) asserted that the textile industry's main goal was not the passage of the bill (referring to the 1985 bill); rather it was pressuring the administration to tighten textile restraints. Significantly, MFA IV had broader product coverage than earlier arrangements. In addition, the United States concluded more restrictive bilateral agreements with the "Big Three."

Similar strategies were used by various special-interest groups for more recent trade issues; however, the alliances sometimes took different forms depending on the issues. For NAFTA, textile manufacturers and retailers found themselves on the same side for a change. Nevertheless, the NAFTA debate resulted in a political flurry of protests, rallies, and letter-writing campaigns.

At the global level, pressures on policymakers result from the conflicting demands of exporting and importing countries and from within the nations participating in global agreements. The exporting countries demand greater access to markets; the importing nations demand more restrictions to protect home markets. The incompatability of these two sets of demands results in trade policies that fall short of each group's expectations.

In addition, policymakers at the global level are subject to demands from various factions within a specific nation. This was the case during negotiations to conclude the Uruguay Round. In the case of the United States, domestic sectoral interest groups seek special concessions in trade policies, which often are contrary to the demands of groups or individuals pursuing the interests of the state. The MFA is a monument to the success of sectoral groups in the developed countries being able to secure their demands.

A number of scholars have questioned the manner in which political pressures have influenced trade policies, especially for textile and apparel trade. Certain scholars believe that political ideology dictates commercial policy, making it impossible for decision makers to use rational decision-making criteria to create policy. Strong import-sensitive industries such as textiles and apparel have tended to receive favorable trade concessions. Some scholars believe the fragmentation of power in the U.S. system of government has not permitted the establishment of unified trade policies that would resist sectoral demands. More recently, however, conclusion of NAFTA and Uruguay Round pacts have signaled the beginning of a new era for more open trade.

GLOSSARY

Smokestack or *sunset industries* are the long-established, mature industries in the developed countries; often, these terms are applied to industries that some persons consider to be declining.

Special protection refers to exceptional restraints on imports, implemented through high tariffs, quotas, or other limitations.

Structural decline is a term used to describe the decline of an industrial sector, particularly in terms of global competitiveness.

Structural unemployment refers to job losses resulting from an industry's inability to respond to competitive market conditions; the inability to compete may result from changing technological developments or a change in the demand for products. Structural unemployment differs from widespread general unemployment.

SUGGESTED READINGS

Aggarwal, V. (1985). *Liberal protectionism: The international politics of organized textile trade.* Berkeley, CA: University of California Press.
This book provides useful insight into the role of policymakers in the development of textile trade policies.

Berry, J. (1984). *The interest group society.* Boston: Little, Brown.
A study of how interest groups operate and how they relate to broader developments in the American political system.

Blackhurst, R., Marian, N., & Tumlir, J. (1977). *Trade liberalization, protectionism and interdependence.* Geneva, Switzerland: General Agreement on Tariffs and Trade.
An analysis of trade policies in an interdependent world.

Choate, P. (1990). *Agents of influence.* New York: Alfred A. Knopf.
This book examines the influence of foreign governments, especially through hired U.S. lobbyists, in shaping U.S. economic policy.

Destler, I. (1986). *American trade politics: System under stress.* Washington, DC: Institute for International Economics.
An examination of the political pressures on American trade policies.

Destler, I. (1992). *American trade politics.* Washington, DC: Institute for International Economics.
This is an updated edition of Destler's book with somewhat different conclusions on the status of U.S. trade politics.

Friman, H. (1990). *Patchwork protectionism: Textile trade policy in the United States, Japan, and West Germany.* Ithaca, NY: Cornell University Press.
An analysis of the pressures and constraints that influenced policymakers in placing growing restrictions on trade in the 1980s.

Giesse, C., & Lewin, M. (1987). The Multifiber Arrangement: "Temporary" protection run amuck. *Law and Policy in International Business, 19*(1), 51–170.
A critical assessment of current textile trade policies; this includes discussion on the influ-

ence of textile/apparel interest groups on policies.

Hufbauer, G., & Rosen, H. (1986). *Trade policy for troubled industries*. Washington, DC: Institute for International Economics.
A review of existing trade policies with respect to troubled industries; recommendations for policy changes are included.

Wolf, M., Glismann, H., Pelzman, J., & Spinanger, D. (1984). *Costs of protecting jobs in textiles and clothing*. London: Trade Policy Research Center.
This book includes a discussion of the political aspects of protection.

VII

Conclusion

Chapter 16 provides a brief reflection on the difficulties associated with global production and trade of textiles and apparel. We are reminded of the difficulty in arriving at the right answer for the problems associated with this sensitive area of trade.

The chapter includes observations on the future outlook for the developed countries in textile/apparel trade; similar observations are considered for the developing countries. One section focuses on the future prospects for textile/apparel trade policies. The chapter concludes with an emphasis on the importance of a global perspective for persons involved in all segments of the softgoods industry.

16

Conclusions: A Problem with No Answer

INTRODUCTION

In many academic courses in which students are enrolled, the course concludes with a resolution of the questions or issues considered. The content may be summarized and/or issues resolved in such a manner that the student leaves the course with a sense of resolution. Often, however, toward the end of a course on textiles and apparel in the international economy, students ask, "But, what is '*the* answer' to problems related to global textile and apparel production and trade?" Typically, students are seeking the professor's stance on that rocky continuum between free trade and protectionism. Unfortunately, neither a "right" answer nor an easy answer exists. And, the more one studies the complexities associated with economic, political, and social concerns for trade in the sector, the more one becomes aware that easy answers are not likely to occur in the near future.

An inherent difficulty in finding an appropriate answer to textile trade problems is that the "right" answer is defined differently by each group with an interest at stake. As we have determined up to this point, many individuals and groups have a great deal at stake in the textile trade dilemma. Often, the concerns and demands of one group are directly contrary to the concerns and demands of another. In these cases, positions are often irreconcilable. For example, the LDC demands for greater access to the major importing markets directly contradict the demands of most manufacturers in the developed countries to reduce imports. Similarly, manufacturers' efforts to restrict imports are directly opposed to the interests of retailers and importers. Therefore, an attempt to provide a right answer may provide one that is "right" only for those representing a particular perspective.

In this chapter, we will reflect on the difficulties associated with global production and trade of textiles and apparel, which we have considered in earlier chapters. In addition, we will summarize a number of relevant considerations regarding the present status and future prospects for production and trade for the sector. The chapter is intended to highlight major issues and to encourage reflection on the content rather than to provide a comprehensive summary of the book.

THE DILEMMA: A BROAD VIEW
Shifts in Global Production

Profound structural changes in the world economy are causing a reorganization of production on a global scale, with increased production in the developing countries. Economies are in a state of constant flux because structural forces—technological advances, accumulation of capital, growth of skilled labor, changes in taste—alter international patterns of comparative advantage. A country's earlier ability to carry out various industrial activities can change over time. Developing countries acquire new capabilities, and the developed countries' abilities to compete efficiently in global markets may change.

As developing countries strive for economic development, the textile sector is often the first industry targeted for growth. As a labor-intensive industry that requires limited capital and technology (particularly the apparel industry), developing countries enter this sector when they could enter few others. Moreover, manufacturers and importers in the industrialized countries have sought the abundant, low-wage labor in the developing countries for the labor-intensive portions of textile and apparel production. As evidence of this trend, a substantial portion of U.S.

apparel imports are targeted for domestic manufacturers.

Thus, the structural movement known as the "international division of labor" has been both an advantage and a disadvantage to the textile and apparel industries in the developed countries. Although many manufacturers and importers in the industrialized countries have taken advantage of the low-cost labor, the dramatic shifts in production to the developing countries have created political friction both at national and international levels. Often the shift has engendered a political ripple effect, which has extended far beyond the textile/apparel sector. For example, foreign governments may retaliate against textile trade policies in ways that hurt sectors unrelated to textiles and apparel.

Use of Policy Measures

In general, theories of comparative advantage, accompanied by the system of free trade that blossomed after World War II, are now being refuted by many industrial sectors experiencing difficult global competition. International shifts in comparative advantage would entail the contraction of some industrial sectors, and, as a consequence, these shifts are being resisted through policy measures.

Perhaps more than any sector, trade in textiles epitomizes the conflicts that arise from a shifting international division of labor (de la Torre, 1984; Fröbel et al., 1980; Keesing & Wolf, 1980). Consequently, many of the players have looked to policy measures to resolve resulting difficulties. The outcome has been one of history's most intricate and complex set of trade rules devised to "manage" world trade in a specific sector.[1] As authors of the

---

[1]One critic of the MFA has termed it "the Mount Everest of protectionism."

FIGURE 16–1
No easy answer exists for the question: Who should produce textile products for the world market?

Source: Photo *a* courtesy of International Labour Office. Photo *b* courtesy of American Textile Manufacturers Institute.

FIGURE 16–2
Adjustment takes its toll. This photo captures the last working moments of an outdated British textile mill just before it closed permanently, leaving former workers unemployed.

Source: Photo by Jacques Maillard, courtesy International Labour Office.

GATT study *Textiles and Clothing in the World Economy* (1984) noted:

> More so than any other industries, trade in textiles and clothing—and thus the pattern of production and employment of those industries around the globe—has been influenced by government intervention. This holds whether we view it in terms of length of time that restrictions have been widely used . . . or in terms of the level of restrictions in force at any point in time . . . or in the number of different policies simultaneously influencing the level of imports. (p. 53)

In sum, no other world merchandise trade has been as comprehensively regulated as that in textiles and apparel (Anson & Simpson, 1988). Moreover, textile trade regulations have been an aberration, or "oddity," among global trade rules.

Although a primary principle of the GATT was the elimination of discriminatory restraints on trade from certain countries, the Multifiber Arrangement has permitted discrimination through quota limits. At the time the MFA was developed, policymakers acknowledged that the MFA violated the principles of GATT; however, the special circumstances of textile and apparel trade were believed to merit exemption. The belief prevailed that the longer-term interests of both exporting and importing countries could be served best through temporary mutual agreements to limit imports in the developed countries.

Problems Intensified Over Time

Problems associated with textile trade at the time the STA, LTA, and MFA were developed have not diminished. In fact, they have grown *more* difficult. As increasing numbers of new producer nations have begun to compete for world markets and as the already established LDCs have become more proficient producers, competition has intensified.

As a result, the importing countries enacted increasingly restrictive measures to limit LDC textile and apparel products. In response, the exporting nations became increasingly agitated and vocal, demanding that restrictions be reduced. In particular, the LDC exporting countries (along with many economists and other scholars who believe in free trade) called for dismantling the MFA.

Textile and apparel producers in the developed countries have their complaints, too. As these producers watched products from the LDCs and NICs take significant portions of their domestic markets, they believe that a majority of textile trade has been a one-way flow. Consequently, both producers and government officials in a number of developed countries are demanding reciprocity; that is, they believe that the producers in the industrialized countries should have greater access to LDC and NIC markets. At times, the issue of reciprocity becomes a matter of how different groups perceive the rules of trade, as the boxed insert, "Restricting Textile Trade 'Legally' versus 'Illegally,'" suggests.

The MFA—The Gradual Demise of an Imperfect Compromise

The MFA—which began as a compromise and a means of resolving textile trade problems—became an agreement considered effective by almost none of the global players. Producers in the developing countries believed the MFA has been used as a tool to strangle their textile/apparel exports. Conversely, producers in the developed countries viewed the MFA as an ineffective mechanism for regulating the entry of imports into their markets.

As the Multifiber Arrangement is eventually phased out and textile trade is brought under trade rules for all other sectors, this will represent major adjustments for the textile complex in many countries. Returning textile trade to normal GATT rules will not resolve the difficulties associated with a global overcapacity for production in these industries.

 RESTRICTING TEXTILE TRADE "LEGALLY" VERSUS "ILLEGALLY"

An impartial GATT official observed:

> The developing countries believe that restricting textile imports from their own markets—by use of the GATT balance of payments provision—is *legal.* On the other hand, these same countries believe

that when the developed countries use provisions of the MFA to restrict imports, those are *illegal* (i.e., that MFA provisions violate the rules of GATT).

(Confidential comment to author)

As we have noted numerous times throughout the book, persons in nearly all regions of the world rely on textile production to fulfill clothing and home furnishings needs—some of the most basic needs of humanity. Of equal importance, the economic remuneration from the production of textile goods provides a livelihood for the masses around the globe. The stakes are high.

FUTURE OUTLOOK FOR THE DEVELOPED COUNTRIES IN TEXTILE/APPAREL TRADE

The global economy has spawned a global system of manufacturing that has transformed production worldwide. Broad shifts in global production have occurred in most manufacturing sectors, and the textile and apparel industries are on the forefront of this broader global change. Over the last four decades, the developed countries' share of world manufacturing output (all sectors) has declined, while that for the developing countries has increased. This trend, which is fostered in part by multinational firms based in the developed countries, is expected to continue. The other side of this shift is that the developed countries have imported a growing share of labor-intensive manufactures from the developing countries. Figure 16–3 shows the growing share of these manufactures imported by the developed countries.

The figure shows imports for all sectors; the trend would be much more pronounced if similar data were available for textiles and apparel alone. In Table 16–1, we can see, for example, that the developed countries have imported more than 87 percent of all apparel imports in the early 1990s.

If we look at United Nations projections for the changing structure of all manufacturing, we can see certain trends. Figure 16–4 illus-

FIGURE 16–3
Developing countries' share of labor-intensive manufactures imported by industrial countries.

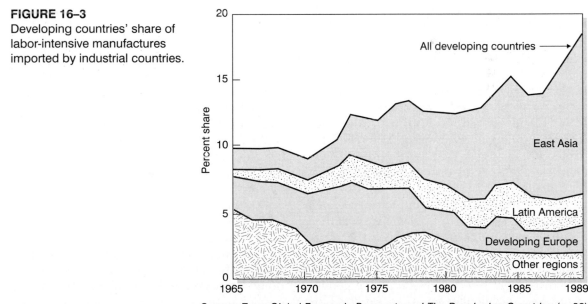

Source: From *Global Economic Prospects and The Developing Countries* (p. 32) by World Bank, 1993, Washington, DC: Author. Reprinted by permission. Staff estimates from COMTRADE.

TABLE 16–1
Shares of World Trade: A Brief Overview[a,b]

	Textiles		Apparel	
	1990	*1992*	*1990*	*1992*
Exports				
Developed countries[c]	62.6	58.9	40.0	39.4
Developing countries	36.1	40.0	55.2	57.6
Economies in transition	n.a.	n.a.	n.a.	n.a.
Imports				
Developed countries[c]	62.8	58.0	87.4	87.1
Developing countries	32.5	38.3	9.0	10.7
Economies in transition	4.0	3.4	3.3	2.2

[a]A comparison over a longer period is not possible because of GATT's change to a new system of country groupings.
[b]Figures may not add up to 100 due to rounding.
[c]Includes EU intra-trade.
n.a. = not available.
Source: Personal Communication with GATT staff, 1993, 1994.

trates the structure of manufacturing value added by industrial categories. We might think of textiles and apparel within the context of all industries shown. The *consumer goods* industries produce mostly traditional labor-intensive items; *intermediate goods* include the materials required to make finished products; and *capital goods* contain a high percentage of high-tech items. According to this UN projection, the structure of manufacturing value added is expected to change in both the developed countries and the developing nations by the year 2000. The UN projections suggest that for the developed countries, the proportion of manufacturing for consumer goods will decline, and the capital goods category will account for a growing share. This does not necessarily mean that the absolute amount of production in the consumer goods industries will decrease, but rather as the economy grows, more of the growth is likely to occur in the capital goods industries. Intermediate goods are expected to maintain the average pace of manufacturing output; their share will remain constant.

The position of the developed countries in textile and apparel trade will depend increasingly on the ability of the industries in those countries to be competitive in the world market. As we learned in Chapter 7 and may review in Table 16–1, the developed countries continue to dominate world *textile* production and trade (i.e., exports); however, their relative importance has continued to decrease. Developed countries are behind the developing nations in world *apparel* production and trade (GATT, 1993). The shield of protection, in the form of the MFA and its complex quota system, will gradually fade away. Therefore, the ability of the textile and apparel industries to compete will depend on the extent to which these industries can excel at producing and marketing their products. Globalization means that any given firm is competing with all the other firms in the world that produce and sell the same product lines. Just as in any domestic market, those companies that do the best job of responding to customer needs, and do so competitively, will be those that survive and prosper.

FIGURE 16–4

Structure of Manufacturing Value-Added by Industrial Category 1966–2000.

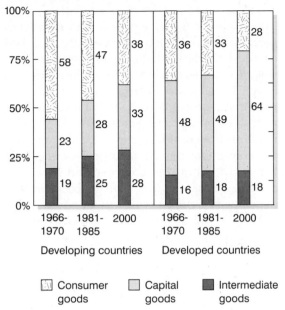

Developing countries   Developed countries

◻ Consumer goods   ◻ Capital goods   ■ Intermediate goods

Source: From *Global Outlook 2000* (p. 183) by the United Nations, 1990, New York: Author. Adapted by permission.

UN writers note that industrial transformation in the developed countries is occurring through information technologies. Only through use of these technologies, in many cases, can sectors continue to survive in the developed countries. Flexible manufacturing systems based on computerization of all stages of production (design, control, and manufacturing) are expected to continue to bring about profound changes in production processes. However, the more high technology (i.e. automation) is incorporated into the manufacturing process to compete in the global arena, the more employment is affected.

The textile and apparel industries in the industrialized countries have had varying degrees of success in facing structural adjustment. Most have attempted adjustment strategies; the sectors in some countries have improved their competitive positions while others have not. Anson and Simpson (1988) noted that the textile and apparel industries in many industrialized countries have "come back from the grave" as new technology, development of high-performance industrial textiles, and the necessity of responding quickly to fashion changes have begun to shift comparative advantage back to the developed countries (p. 159).

Similarly, the UN Centre on Transnational Corporations (1987) observed that technological changes have altered the competitive environment in which textile firms, in particular, operate. These changes have provided opportunities for the rejuvenation of the textile industries in the developed countries through use of labor-saving technology. The UN authors noted that the technological advancements have given the industrialized countries an advantage difficult for many developing countries to match. On the other hand, although technological changes were notable in recent years in the apparel industry, these advancements have not yet offset the low-cost labor advantage found in the developing countries. The low-cost labor advantage appears to be diminishing somewhat, however, as the demand for faster delivery of merchandise favors domestic producers in the developed countries.

Technological changes, and the productivity gains that accompany these developments, will continue to account for job losses in the textile and apparel industries in the developed countries. In addition, competition among domestic producers is a fact of life in a market economy. Therefore, competition is not just from imports—but also from other domestic producers. And, job losses will result from productivity gains, not from imports alone.

When structural changes affect the way in which people acquire their livelihood, profound social changes often occur in tandem. Regardless of whether economic changes are perceived as positive (in this case, gaining jobs) or negative (that is, losing jobs), the resulting social change may be disruptive. For example, change causes strain on the family unit and how individuals' roles are defined. In the case of job losses, the strains are tremendous. The developed countries must grapple with ways of solving unemployment problems that result from the global shifts in manufacturing and manufacturing jobs. In 1993, for example, unemployment in the OECD countries was about 30 million persons; however, all of these countries are not affected equally (OECD, 1994).

When global structural changes cause production to be transferred elsewhere, workers in the developed countries are often the ones to bear the brunt of this shift. For the textile complex, women workers are affected more adversely than men (Glenday, Jenkins, & Evans, 1980). Grunwald and Flamm (1985) concluded, "While in theory a system of transfers can be worked out to guarantee labor that its standard of living will not decline as a result of socially desirable changes in trade arrangements, these transfers have, in practice, not generally been made" (p. 220).

Although the general level of unemployment is very high in the developed countries,

the actual incidence is extremely uneven. Job loss is a selective process, as Dicken (1992) notes. Different social groups experience different levels of unemployment, with women, young people, older workers, and minorities most vulnerable to job loss; most are unskilled or semi-skilled workers. The geographic spread is uneven, with some regions affected much more than others. All of these are potential repercussions of global restructuring in textile and apparel production. The reader must keep in mind, however, that a substantial amount of this transfer of production in the textile complex has resulted from the activities of transnational firms based in the developed countries, some of which may not have survived or remained competitive without taking the steps to have some or all of the production occur elsewhere.

A decline in the textile and apparel workforce in the industrialized countries is expected to occur for yet another reason. Some experts believe that social-anthropological influences may foster a decline in industry employment, which, in a sense, adds to the momentum for structural adjustment. That is, many production workers in the textile and apparel industry want their children to aspire to employment other than working in this

 THE GOAL: ADJUSTMENT WITHOUT SUFFERING

We are looking through a magnifying glass at a problem that is characteristic of our type of society at the stage of economic development through which the world is now passing.

The problem, in principle, is not new. It is the old one of adapting to changing times. From the beginning of the Industrial Revolution, in particular, the challenge of adjusting to new inventions, new production methods, new markets, new competitors, and changing population patterns has

never been absent. The pressures may have abated at times, but they have never ceased. In the past, adjustment problems have been overcome many times, but too often at a cost of deep human suffering. Without a planned approach, the suffering today, the dislocation of men's lives, could be even greater, precisely because the pace of change is greater. To effect the adjustment without the suffering is indeed the essence of the matter. (Plant, 1981, p. 5) sector. Because textile/apparel (particularly apparel) production jobs are among the lowest paid in all sectors, workers aspire to a more economically rewarding future for their children. In addition, the repetition of tasks and the pressure to reach certain production goals result in work that is demanding and exhausting. In short, many textile/apparel workers who have had few other employment alternatives tend to encourage their children to prepare for other jobs. As a result of these changes, manufacturers in certain more developed nations have already experienced a labor shortage and anticipate an even greater shortage in the future.

FUTURE OUTLOOK FOR THE DEVELOPING COUNTRIES IN TEXTILE/APPAREL TRADE

The developing countries are expected to increase their share of world industrial output (all sectors), mostly at the expense of the developed market economies. Shifts in textiles and apparel are far more pronounced, however, because of the reliance of so many developing economies on these industries. When we consider *all* sectors, a very limited number of countries are expected to account for the major proportion of industrial activities among the developing group: Brazil, China, Hong Kong, India, South Korea, Singapore, and Taiwan. Only 10 developing countries produce more than two-thirds of the manufacturing output for the developing nations.

As we know by now, however, the textile and apparel production in developing countries is spread over a far greater pool of producer nations. Although the "Big Four" account for a very significant share of textile and apparel production for the world market, we also know that virtually every developing country has a textile/apparel sector and that for most developing countries, the sector is a

vital first step in the nation's efforts to manufacture for export. Therefore, if we consider Figure 16–3, the pattern for textile and apparel manufactures imported from developing nations into the developed-country markets, the total trend line would be far more exaggerated, with East Asia having an even greater share than is shown for all manufactures.

The more advanced developing countries, particularly the NICs, will undergo structural changes that resemble those for the developed countries. In Figure 16–4 we see that UN experts predict that although the consumer goods category will still be the largest portion (38 percent) of industrial output for the developing countries, that category will account for a *decreasing share* of manufacturing value added. Growing shares will occur particularly in the capital goods area, and to some extent, in the intermediate goods category.

As we ponder the shifts noted in Figure 16–4, it is important to keep in mind the extent to which a small number (10 or fewer) of the developing countries skew the trend for developing countries as a whole. That is, the advances of the NICs and other more advanced nations in the group will account for this shift from consumer goods toward capital and intermediate goods.

UN writers expect the industrial structures of the least-developed countries to change little during the 1990s. Yet, we know from our earlier discussions that these will be many of the countries in which significant growth in textile and apparel production will occur. (The reader may wish to reflect on the "flying geese" pattern.)

We must also consider the importance of textile and apparel manufacturing jobs in the developing countries. The NICs are rare in the broader group of developing nations to be experiencing labor shortages; this is not true in a majority of the developing world. The Third World's single greatest problem is poverty, together with a lack of adequate employment opportunities. Having a way to earn a livelihood is at least as critical in the developing world as in the industrialized countries; in most of the developing world, there are no social programs to provide a safety net for times of unemployment. Unemployment is a way of life—not by choice—in much of the Third World.

As Table 16–1 indicates, the developing countries increased their textile imports in the early 1990s. Much of this increase may have been used in producing garments and other finished goods that were then exported to the developed countries. The developing countries imported only about 10 percent of the world's apparel in 1992. The limited importation of apparel may be explained by a number of factors:

1. Much of the developing world cannot afford to buy any imported product; families must produce for themselves whatever they have.
2. Import-substitution policies in many countries encouraged the population to buy apparel from newly established domestic industries rather than from foreign producers.
3. Many countries have had a variety of policies that restricted imports.

As we know, these latter two points have been of serious concern to manufacturers in the developed countries, who expect the developing countries to provide greater access to their markets if the developed countries are expected to do so. Provisions of the Uruguay Round are intended to assure that the opening of markets be reciprocated by the developing countries; however, a few nations are still resistant.

Population Changes and Demand

The world's population of approximately 5.5 billion persons increases by about 93 million per year. Between 1995 and 2000, growth is expected to peak at about 98 million annually (United Nations Population Fund, 1993). As we have noted earlier, the growth is far greater in the developing world than in the developed countries. To help us grasp the differences, consider that in the time it takes to read this paragraph, roughly 100 children will be born—6 in the developed countries and 94 in the developing nations (World Bank, 1991). The reader should refer back to Figure 4–8 for a review of the United Nations population projections by areas.

The continued population growth in the developing areas is expected to affect both demand and the availability of workers in future decades. Population growth represents only one indication of potential demand for clothing and other textile products, however. Of more importance is the per capita expenditure on these products. And, of course, expenditures are determined to a great extent by the patterns of per capita income.

During the past 40 years, many developing countries achieved progress at an impressive pace. Some have seen their average incomes rise more than fivefold—a rate of progress that is extraordinary by historical standards. Many countries have fared poorly, however, and for some, living standards have *declined* during the past 30 years. Millions of people have yet to experience economic progress. The real income gap between the industrial countries and some developing economies, notably the Asian NICs, has narrowed dramatically since World War II. However, the gap between the industrialized countries and other developing countries has widened. The 1980s were a difficult decade for most developing countries (World Bank, 1992).

Although most of the developing world will be unable to increase consumption appreciably in the near future, an interesting phenomenon has occurred in many of the Asian NICs. Countries such as Taiwan, Hong Kong, and South Korea—countries that were on the leading edge as *producer nations* in textiles and apparel—have now become increasingly important *consumer nations*. Moreover, at the stages in which the NICs have become more important consumer nations, textile and apparel production has declined in relative importance. As in most other more-developed nations, production has been sent to less-developed regions through various foreign investment and outward processing arrangements in other Asian countries.

General Observations about the Outlook for the Developing Countries

Textile and apparel production and trade will continue to be important in the economic development of most developing nations. Except for primary commodities, textiles and apparel are the only product areas in which the developing countries have managed to achieve a surplus (Anson & Simpson, 1988).

Although the availability of low-cost labor will continue to be a major competitive advantage for the developing areas, certain global changes occurring in both manufacturing and marketing will have a potential impact on the industry in these countries. First, as technological innovations are used increasingly in production in the industrialized countries, the LDCs whose competitiveness is based on low labor costs may find their cost advantage reduced.

Second, as retail customers in the developed countries demand increasingly fast response time on deliveries, manufacturers in those countries will have an obvious advantage in being able to respond quickly. Retailers and importers in the major importing markets have begun to weigh broader costs and benefits against the earlier attraction to low-wage production. Together, the technological improvements and the demand for fast deliveries in the industrialized countries are likely to continue to reduce to an extent the competitive advantage possessed earlier by the developing countries.

In many ways, the plight of the textile/apparel exporting countries is unfortunate for all players in the sector's global trade picture. Perhaps too many developing countries have been encouraged to enter the textile and apparel sector—often upon the recommendation of Western advisers from interna-

LOW WAGES ALONE ARE NOT ENOUGH

- The following observation by management expert Peter Drucker reinforces the notion that the LDCs may lose some of their competitive advantage based on low wages:

  Lower wage levels alone won't make offshore manufacturing profitable. Blue-collar wages now account for only 18% of the total domestic manufacturing costs [for apparel production, the percentage is higher], so it takes a 50% wage differential to make up for increased transportation, communication, insurance and other costs. Competitiveness depends less and less on labor costs, more and more on productivity, quality, procurement, design, product innovation, customer service and marketing (Drucker, 1989).

- Ormerod, a British textile management consultant, also noted that despite a 30-year trend to consider *textile* manufacturing as a labor-intensive activity, he believes wage rates are of declining significance in determining the location of new plants (keep in mind that he refers to textiles, not apparel). He cited Italy and Switzerland as two successful high-wage countries (1993).

tional development agencies. Although the characteristics of the sector deem it an appropriate first industry for newly developing nations, producers are being encouraged to enter a global market already characterized by an oversupply.

When Third-World countries embark upon production for global markets, they are pitted against formidable competition. A vast portion of the products are aimed toward mass markets—the segment experiencing the greatest oversupply. In addition, some imports from the least-developed countries suffer from a poor quality image in foreign markets. And, in the past, as the newest entrants became proficient at producing for the glutted global market, importing nations imposed restraints to protect domestic markets.

Consequently, fostering the development of a textile and apparel sector as a means of economic development in a developing country often dooms the nation's producers and policymakers to disappointment and frustration. Economic development aspirations have been thwarted by import restraints and other problems. Further, many persons in developing nations perceive the developed country markets to be composed of affluent consumers with insatiable appetites for goods. Thus, the LDC representatives find it difficult to understand why an affluent country such as the United States has been unwilling to take all of their country's textile/apparel exports. Many seem unaware that a significant number of other countries are focusing on the same markets.

Leaders in most of the major industrialized countries have a genuine benevolent concern for the development of Third-World nations. Moreover, most of the developed nations have directed substantial financial aid to the developing regions. Altruism is dampened by politics, however, as policymakers in the industrialized nations are caught between the Third-World development goals of their governments and the

pressure from domestic industries that fear excessive import competition.

FUTURE OUTLOOK FOR TEXTILE/APPAREL TRADE POLICIES

The Multifiber Arrangement, originally developed as a temporary measure, had its shortcomings; however, a more acceptable system for moderating the difficult problems in textile and apparel trade did not emerge for the many years of its "reign." We must remember that the MFA has been a compromise agreement, and, as such, it satisfied few, if any, of the signatory nations. Typically, compromises are unpopular because players are unable to obtain their full demands.

Although the Multifiber Arrangement had many critics who were eager to see the agreement's demise, certain features of the MFA encouraged its longevity. Wolf (1983) asserted that the political aspects of the MFA assure that

> most of the significant producers are directly satisfied or indirectly bought off: domestic producers by protection; exporters from powerful countries by exemption from protection and by the protection against some of their competitors; and exporters from competitive restricted suppliers by the ability to enjoy the fruits of the cartelization that export restraints permit. (p. 482)

Although representatives of many developing countries publicly decried the evils of the Multifiber Arrangement, many of the major suppliers enjoyed the guaranteed market access it has provided. Similarly, the Arrangement provided market access to newly exporting countries, which may have difficulty penetrating global markets at all because of the intensely competitive conditions.

In the past, the representatives of the developing countries formed coalitions to protest formally against the continuation of the MFA. At critical points (such as the renewal of the MFA), the diverse positions of the developing countries became apparent. That is, as representatives of each country pursued national interests, the coalition became fragmented. Consequently, when these sources—the most vocal opponents of the MFA—failed to maintain a united position, the prospects for the group's plan for the Arrangement's demise often appeared slim.

Exporter opponents of the MFA forget that the Arrangement replaced a system that was even less desirable for them. Under the previous system, major importing nations had far greater liberty to impose harsh unilateral restraints than has been possible under the MFA. Moreover, as trade officials have conceded, the Multifiber Arrangement has provided a "transparency" to textile trade restraints. According to these officials, prior to the MFA, textile and apparel import restraints were often handled "under the table." In addition, the Arrangement has provided a relatively predictable climate for textile and apparel trade. Although many individuals may take exception to this statement, predictability is far greater than would have been true without the MFA. Consequently, in spite of its shortcomings, the MFA provided certain advantages to the exporting nations.

Increasingly, however, the exporting nations believed their products were unduly restrained, and, as a result, they presented a unified front for a gradual dismantling of the Multifiber Arrangement. Pressing collectively through the International Textiles and Clothing Bureau (ITCB), these nations demanded that textile and apparel trade be brought back under regulations that apply to trade in all other sectors. Many economists and trade experts have advocated a similar strategy. The exporting nations demanded that a gradual elimination of the MFA be included in the Uruguay Round trade talks. They were successful in achieving their goal.

Although a number of groups and individuals advocated the elimination of the Multifiber Arrangement, most informed sources did not favor an abrupt end to the Arrangement. Experts conceded that an abrupt elimination of the MFA system would cause global chaos in textile and apparel trade.

Public policy initiatives represent one approach to dealing with trade problems for textile and apparel, as well as for other industries. Protectionist trade regulations grew in popularity in the 1980s—with the textile/apparel sector as a leading user of protectionist strategies. As the first industry to feel serious effects from international competition, this sector was the first to benefit from U.S. trade policies to protect its interests. The Multifiber Arrangement has been a partial buffer against foreign competition, and other industries suffering from similar competition often viewed the MFA as a prototype to consider. In addition, the textile/apparel sector has been given other special assistance discussed in earlier sections of the book. Although many experts consider the U.S. textile/apparel sector to be protected substantially from imports, three efforts to acquire additional protection through legislation barely failed passage in Congress.

Although the textile and apparel industries have looked increasingly to protectionism as the answer to trade problems, policy measures should not be considered as the long-term solution. As many scholars, including Ghadar et al. (1987), have noted, "Long-term protectionism reduces overall industrial efficiency, isolates industry from the forces of progress, and increases costs to consumers" (p. 102). *Short-term* regulation of trade can be useful in "offsetting the artificial effects of currency misalignment and foreign subsidies and can buffer cyclical volatility in trade activities" (p. 102).

If the textile and apparel industries in the developed countries are to remain viable sectors in global markets, the ultimate response must come from within the industries themselves. The United States, the EU, and other developed country textile and apparel industries have made a number of significant strides in adjusting to foreign competition. More specifically, a number of forward-thinking firms have launched strategies to assure their continued success not only in domestic markets but in global markets as well. A few of these firms were discussed earlier in the book.

Although special policies have evolved to mediate textile trade problems, we must remember that trade for this sector occurs within the much broader context of economic shifts and policies. The textile and apparel sector may be a leader in some of these changes, but the interests of many other sectors and groups must be considered as well. That is, textile and apparel trade is part of a much larger picture. Policy decisions made for a particular industry must consider also the impact on other sectors, national interests, and the consuming population.

In sum, the MFA system for regulating world textile trade was a *political* approach for dealing with an *economic* issue. As a result of the completion of the Uruguay Round, the MFA will be phased out in stages, to remove quotas on all products by the year 2005 (projected). If we reflect on our symbolism in Figure 10–3 and think of the MFA as an umbrella, we may begin to think of it as an umbrella that will slowly close over a period of 10 years. At the end of 10 years, we shall have a completely closed umbrella, ready to retire out of sight. To supporters, the MFA should be buried with dignity as the crown jewel of protectionism. To MFA critics, the end would perhaps mean going to what they would consider to be the long-overdue rubbish bin.

Although the textile and apparel industries were already rapidly restructuring on a global scale, the end of the MFA will escalate this restructuring. Phenomenal changes in textile and apparel production and trade will occur

FIGURE 16–5
Globalization of the textile and apparel industries will occur at an increasingly rapid pace in the years ahead.

Source: Illustration by Dennis Murphy.

in the years ahead—and with greater speed than in the past—as we have attempted to portray in Figure 16–5. The manufacturers who had already faced the reality of globalization and who have taken steps to be a participant in the global economy will have an advantage during the eventful transition years ahead—as well as for "life after the MFA."

GLOBALIZATION OF RETAILING

As we noted in Chapter 15, the same forces that have propelled the manufacturing segment of the softgoods industry into a global era have also fostered an expansion of global and international retailing. However, retailers in the Americas lag behind those in Europe and Asia in expanding beyond their own borders or hemisphere. Retailers may have been slow to expand globally for the same reason manufacturers have thought little about exporting until recently. A large captive market had not required looking beyond the borders.

As consumer spending rates increase more rapidly in Asia and other parts of the world, retailers have an opportunity to expand into new markets. Technology is available to facilitate the expansion. Trade barriers are fading away, making it easier to sell in other markets. Although some retailers have expanded into the global arena, this is an area of global commerce that has been relatively unexploited to date. Staff at Price Waterhouse/Management Horizons (1994) have encouraged retailers to consider global expansion in the near term while opportunities are open. These retailing experts also advise that companies should be prepared to establish their firms for the long term. That is, it will take a substantial investment of capital, energy, and time to become established in new markets and build relationships before the payoffs accrue. Patience and an eye on the *long term* will be critical.

As we see an increased globalization of manufacturing—and of retailing—these two changes will perhaps be complementary in the years ahead. As a result of these changes in both manufacturing and retailing, we may soon see much more integrated channels of distribution, not just on a national level, but also at the global level.

HOW TIME CAN CHANGE THE GAME

We must keep in mind that dynamic changes in textile/apparel production and trade patterns occur over time. Neither nations nor firms can presume that the present status will be lasting. The future for the sector in a particular country depends upon changes not only within that respective country, but also the changes in other countries as well. A country may be a global leader in the sector at one point in time but later lose its competitive advantage. For example, England's textile industry led the Industrial Revolution, but more recently, the British industry has had difficulty remaining globally competitive. Similarly, France has a long history as the fashion capital of the world; yet, the French textile/apparel sector has struggled to remain prosperous in recent years.

Perhaps no country can equal Japan, however, in terms of dynamic changes in the sector within this century. We will review a few highlights of the dramatic changes in Japan's status over time to illustrate how the ebb and flow of global trade for the sector can change markedly over time.

Although Japan was a developing country in 1900, the nation's presence was felt in the global textile and apparel market. Even then, Japan was perceived as responsible for a slight drop in the industrialized countries' textile/apparel production as a share of total manufacturing activity. During the early

1900s, Japan concentrated on building a strong textile industry, using the sector as a primary foundation for the nation's economic development. By the 1930s, Japan became the world's primary exporter of cotton textile products. Japan's success made the country a major threat to other textile-producing nations, and, by the mid 1930s, Japanese textile products were limited in 40 of 106 markets (GATT, 1984; *Monthly Record*, 1936).

Although more than three-fourths of Japan's textile industry was destroyed during World War II, the nation's textile producers made a rapid recovery and soon became a threat once again to the industrialized countries. During the 1950s, Japan's proficiency in textile production garnered for the nation's producers many new measures to restrict her products from the markets of the developed countries. Many of these restrictive measures paved the way for trade policies that would be applied more broadly to textile and apparel products from all developing countries.

Within a few decades of Japan's defeat and destruction in World War II, Japan changed from being a developing country to a sophisticated leader of the industrialized world. During this time, the importance of the textile and apparel industries as a key sector in the country's economy diminished markedly. The following statistics show textile and apparel production as a percentage of all Japanese production (i.e., shipments) and illustrate the declining importance of this sector in the country:

Year	Textiles/Apparel as a Percentage of All Production
1955	19.1
1965	11.7
1975	7.4
1985	5.0

Source: Provided to author by Japanese trade counselor, T. Koda; Geneva (1988).

As the Japanese textile and apparel industries matured, many characteristics have become ironically similar to those of the industries in the developed countries after which the Japanese sector once modeled itself. The Japanese sector that once threatened the industries in the industrialized countries now experiences similar threats from less advanced nations. According to T. Koda (personal communication, 1988), Japan's textile and apparel sector is challenged by soaring competition in key NICs: South Korea, Taiwan, and Hong Kong. Other Asian nations are perceived as a serious threat, particularly by fiber and other textile producers.

In 1993, it was reported that high-quality imports had forced Japanese textile manufacturers to close plants, cut down working hours, and lay off workers. According to the Japan Spinners Association, 25 of 53 members closed their cotton spinning plants. The flood of imports from other Asian countries causes concern, especially as far as cotton is concerned—70 percent of total Japanese cotton consumption is covered by imports, and 40 percent of all cotton textiles comes from China. The Japanese textile industry demanded increased protection, but the government called on the industry to continue the structural changes (IAF, 1993).

In a scenario that is repeated in all the developed countries, as part of the textile complex bemoans the influx of imports, other sectors are rapidly investing in production in other Asian countries and establishing operations there to export back to the Japanese market. For example, a wave of Japanese investment has poured into China to establish apparel production, partly to ship to the Japanese market and partly to have access to the Chinese market (Furukawa, 1993).

And, finally, in the greatest ironic twist of all, Japan is buying a substantial quantity of imports from the traditional developed countries. Because of the value of the yen and very high wages in Japan, products from the traditional high-wage countries (Western Europe, the United States, and Canada) are in demand in the Japanese market. For example, Japan is the leading export market for U.S. apparel. That is, the textile complex in the country that was such a threat that it led to the origination of textile policies to protect the industries in developed countries now *buys* from the countries that considered Japan a major threat.

THE SOCIAL DIMENSIONS OF GLOBALIZATION

As responsible global citizens, we must always keep in mind the *social* dimensions of globalization. Perhaps economic forces have moved us toward global interdependence more quickly than we were ready for it socially. As global citizens, we must appreciate, not just tolerate, diversity. We must acknowledge that there are many "right" ways of doing things, and that we can learn other "right" ways from those whose lives have been spent in other parts of the world.

Acknowledging the interdependence that exists in the world means that we are dependent on one another, and our actions affect one another. Our economic decisions are not made in a vacuum; what individuals in one part of the world do affects those in other regions. For example, U.S. mohair growers have received government subsidies of over $50,000 per grower annually, and these growers are distraught because the U.S. government is phasing out the subsidies. The U.S. mohair growers perhaps gave little thought to the effect of these subsidies on mohair growers in other parts of the world, other than having an advantage over the competition. In this case, as in others, "the competition" represents humans whose families' lives are affected seriously by distorted market conditions. South Africa ranks first in world mohair production[2] (although a British writer notes that one would not be able to determine that

---

[2]The story of how angora goats were introduced into South Africa is an amusing tale of thwarted protection-

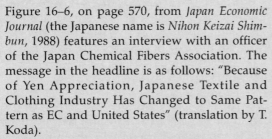

   FOLLOWING EARLIER "ROLE MODELS"

Figure 16–6, on page 570, from *Japan Economic Journal* (the Japanese name is *Nihon Keizai Shimbun*, 1988) features an interview with an officer of the Japan Chemical Fibers Association. The message in the headline is as follows: "Because of Yen Appreciation, Japanese Textile and Clothing Industry Has Changed to Same Pattern as EC and United States" (translation by T. Koda).

The chart insert on the left illustrates the import penetration for certain product categories in the mid-1980s. This chart and its message resemble those used frequently in the United States to show the increase in imports in domestic markets; only the language is different.

In sum, the nation that followed the United States and certain European countries in building a proficient textile and apparel sector has similar patterns of structural adjustment. In many ways, the Japanese industry has even greater difficulties. Textile wages in 1993 were the highest in the world (US$23.65), more than twice that of the United States ($11.61) (Werner International, 1993). Although considered a competitive threat for decades, the Japanese industry that played a critical role in the country's early industrialization and economic development— just as it did in the United States and Europe— has problems that parallel those of its earlier "role models."

FIGURE 16–6
This Nihon Keizai Shimbun article on the plight of the Japanese textile industry bears a message remarkably similar to that one might read about the U.S. textile sector.

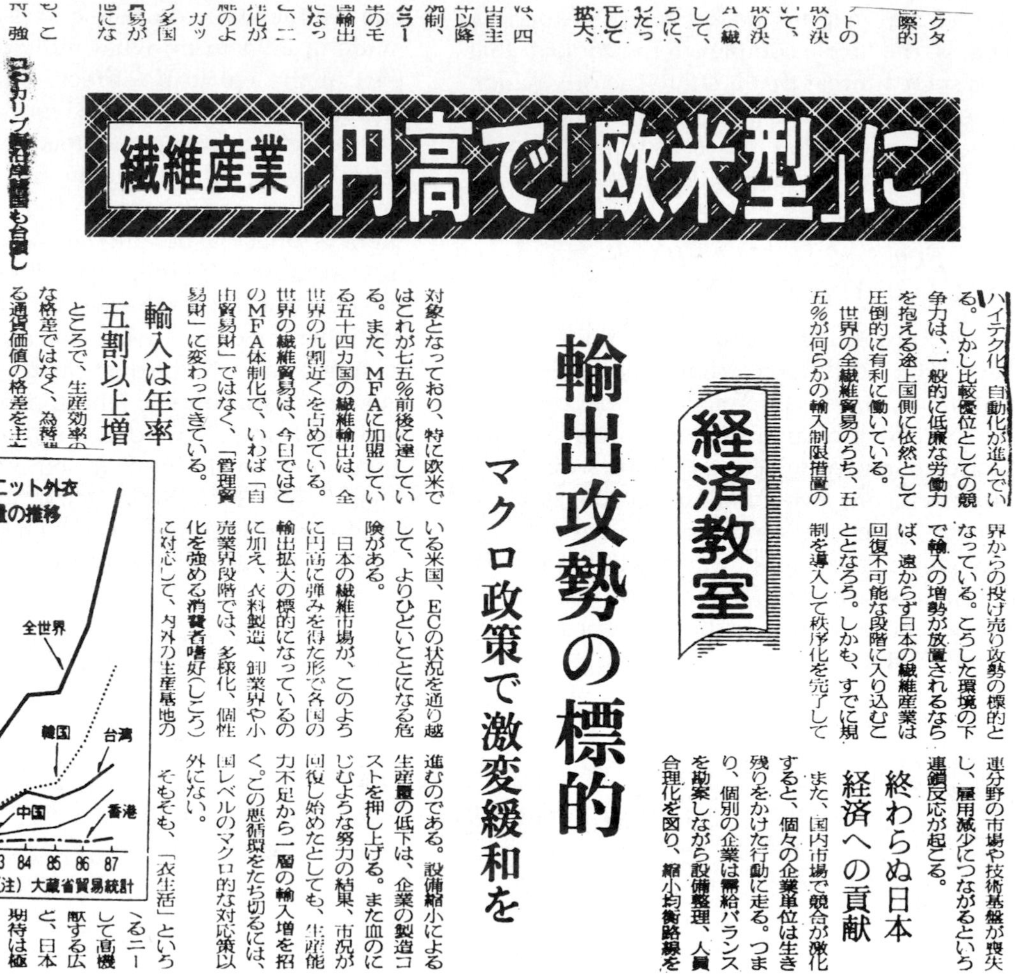

繊維産業 円高で「欧米型」に

経済教室

輸出攻勢の標的

マクロ政策で激変緩和を

ハイテク化、自動化が進んでいる。しかし比較優位としての競争力は、一般的に低廉な労働力を抱える途上国側に依然として圧倒的に有利に働いている。

世界の全繊維貿易のうち、五五%が何らかの輸入制限措置の対象となっており、特に欧米ではこれが七五%前後に達している。また、MFAに加盟している五十四カ国の繊維輸出は、全世界の九割近くを占めている。世界の繊維貿易は、今日ではこのMFA体制化で、いわば「自由貿易財」ではなく、「管理貿易財」に変わってきている。

輸入は年率五割以上増

ところで、生産効率の…な格差ではなく、為替…る通貨価値の格差を主…

…界からの投げ売り攻勢の標的となっている。こうした環境の下で輸入の増勢が放置されるならば、遠からず日本の繊維産業は回復不可能な段階に入り込むこととなろう。しかも、すでに規制を導入して秩序化を完了している米国、ECの状況を通り越して、よりひどいことになる危険がある。

日本の繊維市場が、このように円高に弾みを得た形で各国の輸出拡大の標的になっているのに加え、衣料製造、卸業界や小売業界段階では、多様化、個性化を強める消費者嗜好(しこう)に対応して、内外の生産基地の…

…連分野の市場や技術基盤が喪失し、雇用減少につながるという連鎖反応が起こる。

終わらぬ日本経済への貢献

また、国内市場で競合が激化すると、個々の企業単位は生き残りをかけた行動に走る。つまり、個別の企業は需給バランスを勘案しながら設備整理、人員合理化を図り、縮小均衡路線を進むのである。設備縮小による生産量の低下は、企業の製造コストを押し上げる。また血のにじむような努力の結果、市況が回復し始めたとしても、生産能力不足から一層の輸入増を招く。この悪循環をたち切るには、国レベルのマクロ的な対応策以外にない。

そもそも、「衣生活」という…くるニー…して高機…献する広…と、日本…期待は極…

日本のニット外衣
輸入数量の推移
全世界
韓国
台湾
中国
香港
千万枚
25
20
15
10
5
0
1980年
82
83
84
85
86
87
(注) 大蔵省貿易統計

Source: Reprinted courtesy of Nihon Keizai Shimbun.

from a Texas producer). For South African (and also neighboring Lesotho) mohair farmers, the U.S. mohair subsidies are bad news for those trying to make a living. They know that no matter how low the world price falls, their American competitors can undercut them . . . and still make a handsome profit ("Support Program," 1993).

Globalization has social responsibilities that businesses may not have been required to consider in the past when they worked within their own borders. Consumers, now sensi-

ism. In 1838, the South Africans imported 12 rams and one ewe from Turkey, but the Turks attempted to foil the effort and had sterilized the rams before shipping them (they didn't want competition from South Africa). However, they had forgotten about Mother Nature, and the ewe gave birth to a ram kid during the journey. This fertile ewe and her kid were crossbred with the indigenous goats—and thus began South Africa's mohair industry ("Support Program," 1993).

tized by various television exposés, are beginning to question the working conditions under which products are made. Perhaps some manufacturers and retailers in the past had scrutinized the working conditions of firms in the developing nations with which they did business, but for many, it may have been easier to turn their heads when seeing child laborers or learning that prison laborers produce goods to be exported to U.S. markets. Now, however, activist groups, television reports, socially conscious investors, and consumers have helped businesses to enforce their global consciences. Even before the media attention, many companies had written policy statements on their firms' ethical, environmental, and human-rights codes. Many are refusing to do business with firms that use child labor or prison labor or participate in unethical business practices. Additionally, the U.S. Congress has taken an interest in the child labor issue and may pass legislation to prohibit merchandise produced by children from entering U.S. markets ("Child-Labor," 1993).

Wages are often a controversial issue, because worker pay in many of the developing countries seems so low that some critics label the wages as exploitative. Nike received poor publicity when *Harper's* magazine ran a feature that dissected the pay stub of an Indonesian woman who netted the equivalent of $37.46 per month. Later, an article in *Far Eastern Economic Review* reported that Indonesians who make Nikes earn far more than most workers lucky enough to get factory jobs in the impoverished country (McCormick & Levinson, 1993). The wage question is another of those for which there appears to be no easy answer. Judging wages in developing countries by the standards in the developed countries may lead to erroneous conclusions. In many cases, workers would have no other jobs. The parent firm probably would not be there at all except for the competitive wages; therefore, the country

would not have the jobs. Nevertheless, the parent firm has a responsibility to the workers it employs in other countries to treat them as well relative to their setting as it does its domestic workforce relative to the home country setting. And many do. Many U.S. apparel firms, for example, with production in developing countries provide benefits not available to the U.S. workforce; examples are free meals and free transportation to and from work. Dormitories also are often provided.

Separating economic issues from social and political issues is often impossible to do. For example, the U.S. renewal of China's most favored nation (MFN) status has been uncertain in light of China's human-rights policies. Whether China has MFN status has a serious economic impact on business in China as well as on U.S. firms buying Chinese goods—because countries with MFN rights have much lower tariffs on their products shipped to U.S. markets. Many in the United States have not favored renewing China's MFN status because of China's slaughter of pro-democracy leaders, the persecution of citizens for political differences, and the use of forced prison labor in producing export goods. Congress attempted unsuccessfully to tie the renewal of China's MFN provision to requirements for a change in human-rights policies. So far, MFN status has been extended by U.S. officials—but with warnings that human rights violations must improve to retain MFN status.

The privileges of globalization include opportunities to extend businesses around the world and to enjoy the fruits of trade that bring us products from around the world. However, nearly all privileges have accompanying responsibilities, and this is true in globalization. The social dimension of globalization includes being sensitive to the needs of our neighbors in remote lands. Modern transportation and communication systems have made it possible to travel, communicate, and do business around the world. Our human spirit must rise to the challenge of trying to keep pace with what technology has facilitated for us so that we might understand, appreciate, and care about our global neighbors.

DEVELOPING A GLOBAL PERSPECTIVE

Concerns for Competitiveness

In recent years, many U.S. policymakers and industry leaders have been absorbed by concerns over international competitiveness. Trade deficits in nearly all major U.S. manufacturing sectors have provided a foundation for this concern. As a result, a number of prestigious national task forces have addressed various aspects of this national dilemma. Furthermore, Congress passed a comprehensive trade bill that sought to address, in part, the country's poor international economic performance.

Internationalization

While "competitiveness" has become a priority in the United States, Japan and Europe have become increasingly concerned with "internationalization." Holzner (1988) suggested that *internationalization* implies "the interpretation of domestic and international economic issues, the increase of international competition in domestic economies, and the growth of international opportunities" (p. 11). In addition to a global perspective, internationalization requires competencies for interacting with persons in other parts of the world.

Internationalization requires that we rethink how we function in global business matters. For example, growing internationalization has spawned a new breed of world corporation known as the "stateless" corporation. Unlike multinational corporations, whose foreign operations were treated as

"distant appendages for producing products designed and engineered back home . . . with the chain of command and nationality . . . clear," these world corporations are "making decisions with little regard for national boundaries" (Borrus, Zeller, & Holstein, 1990, p. 98). These global companies juggle multiple identities and multiple loyalties, making an effort to be localized wherever they operate—often turning out products simultaneously in several countries rather than treating foreign markets as afterthoughts. Increased flexibility and skills will be required of managers for these stateless corporations.

A Need for International Competence

In the latter part of the 1980s, a number of groups began to address the serious concerns over Americans' lack of international competence. Tests to assess knowledge and perceptions of global issues and relationships among individuals at all levels have yielded alarming results. In an article titled "America . . . Globally Blind, Deaf and Dumb," Lurie (1982) reported on America's "scandalous incompetence" (p. 413) in foreign languages and other global skills and knowledge. A number of other persons (Christiansen, 1988; DiBiaggio, 1988; Holzner, 1988) have addressed the country's shortcomings on global understanding and ways in which these shortcomings seriously compromise the U.S. position in the world.

Various U.S. policymakers and educators' groups have begun to address America's lack of global competencies. Among these groups, one of the most significant has been the National Governors' Association—a group that has addressed the concern for an increased international focus on education. The governors' group concluded: "The lack of individuals with international expertise seriously hampers the successful performance of

American business, sectors of government, and technologically oriented industries" (National Governors' Association, 1987).

Another group, the Task Force of the Association of International Education Administrators on International and Economic Competitiveness, has suggested that international competence should focus on three main areas:

- A generally educated public
- Internationally competent managers, professionals, and scientists and their organizations
- Specialized international research and expertise (Holzner, 1988, p. 12).

A Fading Away of Borders and Barriers

Recent years have seen the fading away of a remarkable array of borders and barriers in our world. All of these have moved us by degrees from more isolated entities toward increased globalization and interdependence. A new sense of openness and cooperation has surfaced. First, we witnessed the fall of the Iron Curtain, as the chipping away of the concrete barrier both literally and figuratively liberated millions of people who had been isolated from the rest of the world. We saw the former European Community drop barriers among member nations to become the European Union, with plans to encompass additional countries. We saw the North American Free Trade Agreement become a reality, linking three major countries into a single market, with plans to extend the free trade concept to other parts of the Western Hemisphere. We saw Asian nations form the Asia Pacific Economic Cooperation Conference. Regional and sub-regional trading arrangements sprang up around the world. The successful completion of the Uruguay Round ushered in a new era of more open trading relationships.

A growing number of nations of the world have moved to a stage in which they are thinking beyond their borders. Businesses were considerably ahead of nation-states in thinking beyond national borders, and the new open trade arrangements will help to facilitate even more what businesses were doing anyway.

Modern communications and transportation systems have removed barriers of distance. Through satellite television transmission, a citizen may virtually observe an earthquake tremor at the moment it happens half way around the world, see shots actually fired in a Persian Gulf war, watch minute-by-minute changes in the Shanghai stock market, or feel the pain of starvation in Somalia via poignant televised images.

Reducing distance barriers and the rapid flow of information has also spawned a new breed of *global consumer*. These are consumers around the world who see on television the latest fashions unveiled in the leading fashion centers of the world and want the garments available in local markets within the season. Lifestyles observed on television may be imitated in many countries quite far apart but carried out with similar clothing, hair styles, and accessories on persons of very different racial and ethnic origins. Young professionals in Turkey, Taiwan, and Tunisia may dress and behave very much alike. Teenagers in dozens of disparate countries are listening to the same music and watching the same movies. These global consumers will shape worldwide commerce in profound ways.

In short, this is a time—more than ever—to think globally.

Increased Interdependence

Individuals and companies will be required to have increased international competencies if firms are to be active participants in an increasingly interdependent world. Technological advances of the twentieth century have brought us closer to other nations and

"CHARGE IT TO MY VISA CARD, AND SEND IT BY FEDERAL EXPRESS"

Even the process of writing this book has been very much affected by the globalization of business and the rapid flow of information. Several textile and apparel industry executives in other countries learned about the first edition and wanted to order a copy. On several occasions, these executives in other countries (e.g., Japan and Italy) asked the author to have the publisher send them a copy. They requested that the publisher "charge it to my Visa card and send it by Federal Express." The transaction was almost as simple as it would have been to do business within the United States. Additionally, in efforts to update information for the book, the author has sought the assistance of contacts in various countries. In the last week of finishing the revised manuscript, faxes came from Switzerland, Belgium, Hong Kong, England, Canada, and Bangladesh, as well as from several offices in Washington and New York. In the three years since the first edition, the availability of fax machines changed the minimum time required to get international information from two to three weeks to sometimes less than an hour.

other peoples. Today, citizens of many countries are more closely linked to distant nations than neighboring states or provinces were to one another at the turn of the century. Economic and political changes have transformed widely divergent economic and marketing systems into an interdependent global marketplace. Our global trading partners are our global neighbors, and together we share a world that will require greater understanding and appreciation of one another.

If representatives of any nation think of our global trading partners as our neighbors and as persons with whom we shall share a long-time existence, this perspective requires that we interact with other nations as our neighbors. This goes beyond understanding other languages and cultural differences. Our trade relationships must reflect also the honor and integrity with which we treat our next-door neighbors. Even as we deal with the difficult area of textile trade, we must not lose sight of the larger concern for global relationships.

In the past, the United States has been known globally for its unsurpassed generosity in foreign aid and for sharing its abundance of resources with many other regions of the world in other ways. Americans, as well as citizens of all nations, must not let the political difficulties of trade obliterate our broader global concerns. Although we may have to establish guidelines to moderate trade problems, we must also remember the broader issues at stake. Even if continued regulations on textile trade are necessary for a time, we should be prepared to enforce these in ways that maintain our global integrity.

IMPLICATIONS FOR INDUSTRY PROFESSIONALS

The fading away of borders and barriers that we have observed in recent years propels us even more rapidly than ever before into a global economy. *We must think globally!*

Individuals employed in the softgoods industry must have an understanding of the breadth and complexity of issues related to textiles and apparel in the global economy in order to function effectively in the future. Most professionals in the softgoods industry will not be expected to resolve policy issues related to textile trade. On the other hand, individuals' positions and their work are likely to be affected by trade activities. Textile and apparel professionals must be able to look at the larger picture—the global view—of production and trade for the sector. One must be able to follow global trade activities as critical determinants of market activities at the immediate working level.

We are no longer functioning in a national economy; we are operating in a global economy. We must think in terms of an international market rather than a national market. In addition, we are citizens of a global community. We must be aware of and concerned about international issues that affect our economic well-being, our social interactions with neighbors on the other side of the world, and the political issues that affect our relationships with global neighbors.

Virtually all aspects of the softgoods industry are affected by this globalization. The future of one's company and the competitiveness of the industry segment of which that firm is a part are affected, often profoundly, by global activities. For example:

- A professional in the softgoods industry must understand the impact of textile activity in China (or any country) on a retail department store's merchandising efforts.
- Similarly, one should understand how the provisions of the MFA phaseout may affect the volume and cost of textile/apparel goods available to the retailer and the consumer.

- Executives at a firm in almost any country should be asking, What is the potential for exporting our company's products?
- What are the advantages of establishing close working partnerships within the domestic industry? Or the global industry?
- What factors should my company consider in weighing domestic versus offshore sourcing?
- How does a free trade agreement affect my company's business?
- How does my retail company become more global?
- What are my company's options for securing a broad range of fabrics to use in producing apparel?
- How much will tariffs add to the price of merchandise?
- What are the potential problems to be encountered in bringing merchandise through U.S. Customs? What are the possible penalties?
- What would be important considerations to keep in mind if one's firm decided to establish a joint venture operation in another country?
- Or, if the survival of the firm by which one is employed seemed in jeopardy due to high levels of import penetration, what might be appropriate responses?

An informed global perspective will be required of professionals entering the softgoods industry. This global perspective will be imperative both for the success of the individual and for the firms in which those individuals are employed.

APPENDIX

Participants in the Multifiber Arrangement

	MFA				1991 protocol	1992 protocol	1993[c] protocol
	I	*II*	*III*	*IV*			
Argentina	X	X	X	X	X	X	
Australia	X						
Austria	X	X	X	X	X	X	X[d]
Bangladesh	X	X	X	X	X	X	X
Bolivia[a]		X					
Brazil	X	X	X	X	X	X	X[d]
Canada	X	X	X	X	X	X	X
China (PRC)[a]			X	X	X	X	X
Colombia[a]	X	X	X	X	X	X	X
Costa Rica				X	X	X	X
Czechoslovakia	X	X	X	X			
Czech Republic						X	
Dominican Republic	X	X	X	X	X	X	
Egypt	X	X	X	X	X	X	X[d]
El Salvador[a]	X	X	X		X	X	X
EU	X	X	X	X	X	X	X[d]
Finland	X	X	X	X	X	X	X[d]
Ghana	X	X					
Guatemala[a]	X	X	X	X	X	X	
Haiti	X	X	X				
Hong Kong (until 1986: the UK for Hong Kong)[b]	X	X	X	X	X	X	X
Honduras							X
Hungary	X	X	X	X	X	X	X
India	X	X	X	X	X	X	X
Indonesia	X	X	X	X	X	X	X
Israel	X	X	X				
Jamaica	X	X	X	X	X	X	X

[a]Accession ex Article 13.2.

[b]Since 1986 Hong Kong, having full autonomy in the conduct of its external commercial relations and the other matters provided for in the General Agreement, is deemed to be a contracting party to the GATT in accordance with Article XXVI.5(c) of the General Agreement. Hong Kong communicated to the Chairman of the Textiles Committee that it continued to participate in the MFA (see COM.TEX/46). *Note:* A number of participants acceded after entry into force of MFA-I/II/III or IV and therefore only participated for a limited period of the respective MFA.

[c]Signatories of the 1993 Protocol as of May 27, 1994.

[d]Provisional

	MFA				1991 protocol	1992 protocol	1993[c] protocol
	I	II	III	IV			
Japan	X	X	X	X	X	X	X
Kenya							X
Korea (Rep. of)	X	X	X	X	X	X	X
Malaysia	X	X	X	X	X	X	
Maldives			X				
Mexico[a]	X	X	X	X	X	X	
Nicaragua	X						
Norway	X		X	X	X	X	X
Pakistan	X	X	X	X	X	X	X
Panama			X				X
Paraguay[a]	X						
Peru	X	X	X	X	X	X	X
Philippines	X	X	X	X	X	X	X
Poland	X	X	X	X	X	X	
Portugal (for Macao)	X	X	X	X	X	X	X
Romania	X	X	X	X	X	X	
Singapore	X	X	X	X	X	X	X
Slovak Republic						X	X
Spain	X						
Sri Lanka	X	X	X	X	X	X	X
Sweden	X	X	X	X			
Switzerland	X	X	X	X	X	X	X[d]
Thailand[a]		X	X	X	X	X	X
Trinidad and Tobago	X	X					
Turkey	X	X	X	X	X	X	X
United States	X	X	X	X	X	X	X
Uruguay	X	X	X	X	X	X	X
Yugoslavia	X	X	X	X	X		

Source: From *International Regulation of World Trade in Textiles* (p. 160) by N. Blokker, 1989, Dordrecht, The Netherlands: Martinus Nijhoff; personal communication with T. Jenkins of GATT (1993); personal communication with M. Raffaelli of GATT (May 27, 1994).

BIBLIOGRAPHY

A new way to look at the U.S. economy. (1990, December 17). *Business Week*, p. 70.

Abend, J. (1992, May). Canada's plight and plan. *Bobbin*, pp. 62–70.

Abend, J. (1993, February). Vendor lists getting pared, chopped, sliced and diced. *Bobbin*, pp. 58–62.

Addy, J. (1976). *The textile revolution*. London: Longman.

Agarwala, P. (1983). *The new international economic order*. New York: Pergamon Press.

Aggarwal, V. (1983). The unraveling of the Multi-Fiber Arrangement, 1981: An examination of international regime change. *International Organization*, 37.

Aggarwal, V. (1985). *Liberal protectionism: The international politics of organized textile trade*. Berkeley, CA: University of California Press.

Albright, J., & Kunstel, M. (1987). *Stolen childhood*. Cox Newspapers.

Alexander, M. (1987, August 14). Textile legislation socks it to consumers. *Citizens for a Sound Economy Issue Alert* (Report No 16). Unpublished report.

American Apparel Manufacturers Association. (Annual). *Focus: An economic profile of the apparel industry*. Arlington, VA: Author.

American Apparel Manufacturers Association. (1980). *Apparel trade primer*. Arlington, VA: Author.

American Apparel Manufacturers Association. (1982). *Fashion apparel manufacturing:*

Coping with style variation. Arlington, VA: Author.

American Apparel Manufacturers Association. (1984). *Apparel manufacturing strategies*. Arlington, VA: Author.

American Apparel Manufacturers Association, Apparel Political Education Committee. (1982). *The MFA and the American apparel industry*. Arlington, VA: Author.

American Apparel Manufacturers Association, Apparel Research Committee. (1985). *Apparel technology—Today's use and tomorrow's needs*. Arlington, VA: Author.

American Apparel Manufacturers Association, Apparel Research Committee. (1987). *Managing an industry in transition*. Arlington, VA: Author.

American Apparel Manufacturers Association, Technical Advisory Committee. (1987). *Getting started in Quick Response*. Arlington, VA: Author.

American Association of Exporters and Importers, Textile and Apparel Group. (1987, July 30). *Summary of statement of the textile and apparel group of the American Association of Exporters and Importers (AAEI-TAG) before the Senate Finance Committee in opposition to S. 549*. Unpublished summary. New York: Author.

American Fiber Manufacturers Association, Inc. (1988). *Manufactured fiber fact book*. Washington, DC: Author.

American Textile Machinery Association. (1984, October). *Development of National*

Approaches to the Application of High Technology to the Textile and Apparel Machinery Industries, for the U.S. Department of Commerce (Cooperative Grant No. 99-26-07170-10). Washington, DC: U.S. Department of Commerce.

American Textile Manufacturers Institute. (Quarterly). *Textile Hi-Lights*.

American Textile Manufacturers Institute. (1986, September 19). *Statement of the American Textile Manufacturers Institute, Inc., filed with the United States International Trade Commission in re the probable economic effects on U.S. industries and consumers of a free trade area between the United States and Canada.* Washington, DC: Author.

American Textile Manufacturers Institute. (1987, January 23). *Statements of the American Textile Manufacturers Institute, Inc., before the United States International Trade Commission in re origin rules for proposed U.S.-Canada Free Trade Area* (Commission Investigation # 332-243). Washington, DC: Author.

American Textile Manufacturers Institute. (March, 1993). Berry Amendment. *Textile Hi-Lights*.

Ankrim, E. (1988). Understanding world trade—An economic perspective. In D. Wentworth & K. Leonard (Eds.), *International trade teaching strategies* (pp. 3–7). New York: Joint Council on Economic Education.

Ansari, J. (1986). *The political economy of international economic organization.* Boulder, CO: Rienner.

Anson, R., & Simpson, P. (1988). *World textile trade and production trends.* London: The Economist Intelligence Unit.

Apparel Russia looking at new prospects for business. (1993, February). *Apparel International*, pp. 8–10.

Arlen, J. (1985, January 17). Retailers to seek allies in free trade battle. *Daily News Record*, pp. 1, 4.

Arpan, J., de la Torre, J., Toyne, B., Bacchetta, M., Jedel, M., Stephan, P., & Halliburton, J. (1982). *The U.S. apparel industry: International challenge, domestic response.* Atlanta: Georgia State University Press.

Asia's wealth. (1993, November 29). *Business Week*, pp. 100–112.

Au, K. (1992, August). Has Hong Kong peaked? *Textile Asia*, pp. 93–96.

Australian growers withhold wool from auctions for several weeks. (1993, March 3). *Daily News Record*, pp. 2, 9.

Australian Industries Assistance Commission. (1980). *Report on textiles, clothing, and footwear.* Canberra: Author.

Avery, W., & Rapkin, D. (1982). *America in a changing world political economy.* New York: Longman.

Axell, R. (Ed.). (1990). *Do's and taboos around the world.* New York: John Wiley & Sons.

Axell, R. (Ed.). (1991). *Gestures: The do's and taboos of body language around the world.* New York: John Wiley & Sons.

Axline, W. A. (1979). *Caribbean integration: The politics of regionalism.* London: Frances Pinter Ltd.

Bagchi, S. (1989, June 20–21). *Textiles in the Uruguay Round: Alternative modalities for integration into GATT.* Paper presented at the conference of International Textile Trade, the MFA, and the Uruguay Round, Stockholm.

Bagot, B. (1988, June 27). Pricing-structure changes aimed to make US cotton more competitive. *Daily News Record*, p. 2.

Bai, C. (1992, December). High-tech fiber & textile development in Taiwan. *J.S.N. International*, pp. 28–29.

Balkwell, C., & Dickerson, K. (1994). Apparel production in the Caribbean: A classic case of the new international division of labor. *Clothing and Textiles Research Journal, 12*(3), pp. 6–15.

Baker, S., Smith, G., & Weiner, E. (1993, April 19). The Mexican worker. *Business Week*, pp. 84–92.

Bane, M. (1989, December). No sweat. *Business Month*, pp. 34–35.

Bark, T., & de Melo, J. (1988, September). Export quota allocations, export earnings, and market diversification. *The World Bank Economic Review,* 2(3), 341–348.

Barnathan, J., Curry, L., Einhorn, B., & Engardio, P. (1993, May 17). China: The emerging economic powerhouse of the 21st century. *Business Week,* pp. 54–68.

Barnathan, J., McKinnon, A., & Harbrecht, D. (1994, February 14). Destination, Vietnam. *Business Week,* pp. 26–27.

Barnes, M. (1987, June). Quick Response helps ignite "The Information Revolution." *Bobbin Magazine,* pp. 138–140.

Barrett, J. (1988, September 28). Textile bill backers won't gain enough votes to nix veto: Experts. *Daily News Record,* p. 3.

Barrett, J. (1990a, October 24). Hollings will revive textile bill in 1991. *Women's Wear Daily,* p. 18.

Barrett, J. (1990b, October 11). House sustains textile bill veto. *Women's Wear Daily,* p. 3.

Barrett, J. (1990c, October 12). In wake of textile bill defeat, GATT talks emerge as bigger battleground. *DNR,* p. 2.

Barrett, J. (1990d, July 18). Textile bill clears Senate: 68–32. *DNR,* p. 11.

Barrett, J. (1992a, September 29). House moves to block U.S. aid for exporting jobs. *Women's Wear Daily,* p. 18.

Barrett, J. (1992b, October 5). House voting on AID programs siphoning U.S. jobs. *Women's Wear Daily,* p. 19.

Barrett, J. (1993, November 18). NAFTA wins in House. *Women's Wear Daily,* pp. 4–5.

Barrier, M. (1988, April). Walton's mountain. *Nation's Business,* pp. 18–26.

Barry, E. (1992, August). NAFTA: A Canadian perspective. *America's Textiles International,* pp. 44–46.

Barry, M., & Dickerson, K. (1987). Developmental patterns of Asia's apparel industry. In W. Kim & P. Young (Eds.), *The Pacific challenge in international business* (pp. 195–206). Ann Arbor, MI: UMI Research Press.

Barry, M., & Warfield, C. (1988, January). The globalization of retailing. *Textile Outlook International,* pp. 62–76.

Barry, M., Warfield, C., & Galbraith, R. (1987, May 4–7). Dispersion retailing: A global export strategy. In *Textiles: Product Design and Marketing.* Papers presented at the Annual World Conference. Como, Italy: The Textile Institute.

Bartlett, R., & Peterson, R. (1992). A retailing agenda for the year 2000. In R. Peterson (Ed.), *The future of U.S. retailing: An agenda for the 21st century* (pp. 243–292). New York: Quorum Books.

Bauer, R., Pool, I., & Dexter, L. (1963). *American business and public policy.* New York: Atherton.

Baughman, L. (1987). *Analysis of the impact of the Textile and Apparel Trade Act of 1987.* Washington, DC: International Business and Economic Research Corporation.

Bayard, T. (1980). *Comments on the Federal Trade Commission staff report on effects of restrictions on United States imports: Five case studies and theory.* (Available from the Office of Foreign Economic Research, U.S. Department of Labor, Washington, D.C.).

Belaud, J. (1985). Textiles: EEC policies and international competition. *European News Agency,* p. 37.

van Benthem van den Bergh, G. (1972). Science and the development of society. In *Science and the world tomorrow.* Discussion paper at the 20th anniversary conference, NUFFIC.

Bergsten, F. (1975, April 8). *The opportunity for U.S. consumers in the multilateral trade negotiations.* Statement before the International Trade Commission on behalf of Consumers Union, Washington, DC.

Berman, B., & Evans, J. (1984). *Retail management* (2nd ed.). New York: Macmillan.

Bernstein, A., Konrad, W., & Therrien, L. (1992, August 10). The global economy: Who gets hurt? *Business Week,* pp. 48–53.

Bernstein, H. (Ed.). (1973). *Underdevelopment and development.* Harmondsworth, England: Penguin Books.

Berry, J. (1984). *The interest group society.* Boston: Little, Brown.

Bertrand Frank Associates. (1985). *Profitable merchandising of apparel* (2nd ed.). New York: National Knitwear & Sportswear Association.

Bhagwati, J. (1989). United States trade policy at the crossroads. *The World Economy, 12,* 439–479.

Black, J. (1992, April 10). Discounters poised for global growth. *DNR,* p. 10.

Black, S. (1993, March). TALC/SAFLINC merger official. *Bobbin,* p. 14.

Blackhurst, R. (1986). The economic effects of different types of trade measures and their impact on consumers. In *International trade and the consumer.* Paris: Organization for Economic Cooperation and Development.

Blackhurst, R. (1988). Strengthening GATT surveillance of trade-related policies. In M. Hilf & E. Petersmann (Eds.), *The new GATT round of multilateral trade negotiations: Legal and economic aspects.* Deventer, The Netherlands: Kluwer Law and Taxation Publishers.

Blackhurst, R., Marian, N., & Tumlir, J. (1977). *Trade liberalization protectionism and interdependence.* Geneva: General Agreement on Tariffs and Trade.

Blake, D., & Walters, R. (1983). *The politics of global economic relations.* Englewood Cliffs, NJ: Prentice-Hall.

Blokker, N. (1989). *International regulation of world trade in textiles.* Dordrecht, The Netherlands: Martinus Nijhoff.

Blomström, M., & Hettne, B. (1984). *Development theory in transition.* London: Zed Books Ltd.

Blueweiss, H. (1989, July 10). Globalization of the textile industry. *DNR,* p. 44.

Bogert, C. (1989, December 4). Why there is no soap. *Newsweek,* pp. 46–47.

Borris, A., & Engardio, P. (1993, February 22). Will Congress Shanghai China policy? *Business Week,* p. 59.

Borrus, A., Zeller, W., & Holstein, W. (1990, May 14). The stateless corporation. *Business Week,* pp. 98–106.

Bow, J. (1993a, January 8). Good morning, Vietnam. *Daily News Record,* pp. 6, 7.

Bow, J. (1993b, July 1). Their own market going high-tech, China machinery firms look abroad. *Daily News Record,* p. 9.

Braithwaite, A. (1991). *Developments in the Asia Pacific apparel industry.* Paper presented at the International Apparel Federation convention, Taipei.

Brandis, B. (1982). *The making of textile trade policy 1935–1981.* Washington, DC: American Textile Manufacturers Institute.

Brick, B. (1983, February 1). 'Good' retailers learning to deal with the '80s, stores beefing up markups with private label clothing. *Daily News Record,* pp. 1, 15.

Brody, M. (1983, July 25). Naked protectionism: Quotas on clothing imports chill producers, consumers alike. *Barron's,* p. 11.

Brown, D. (1987, July 30). Statement before the U.S. Senate Committee on Finance re: the Textile and Apparel Trade Act of 1987. Unpublished report from Consumers for World Trade, Washington, DC.

Brown, J. (1981). A cross-channel comparison of supplier-retailer relations. *Journal of Retailing, 57* (4), 3–18.

Brown, P. (1989, February/March). Fashion's quickening pulse. *Retailing Technology and Operations: Quickening the Fashion Calendar* (supplement to Women's Wear Daily/Daily News Record), pp. 16, 20.

Bucklin, L. (1966). *A Theory of distribution channel structure.* Berkeley, CA: Institute of Business and Economic Research, University of California.

Buirski, D. (1992). South Africa—A matter of identity, a matter of urgency. *Textile Horizons International, 12*(11), pp. 20–29.

Bureau of Census. (various years). *County business patterns.* Washington, DC: U.S. Government Printing Office.

Bush asks business aid on fast-track authority. (1991, March 6). *Women's Wear Daily,* p. 24.

Business America. (monthly). Washington, DC: U.S. Department of Commerce.

Business Week. (weekly). New York: McGraw Hill.

Cable, V. (1987, September). Textiles and clothing in a new round of trade negotiations. *The World Bank Economic Review*, pp. 1, 619.

Callcott, J. (1984a, November 27). GATT meeting split on textile protectionism. *Daily News Record*, pp. 3, 8.

Callcott, J. (1984b, November 29). U.S.–Third World dispute puts GATT on hold. *Women's Wear Daily*.

Callcott, J. (1984c, November 28). U.S.–Third World trade aims collide at GATT annual parley. *Daily News Record*.

Can America compete? (1987, April 20). *Business Week*, pp. 44–69.

Canadian group established to promote fashion industry. (1993, March 3). *Daily News Record*, p. 8.

Canadian International Trade Tribunal Act. (1988, September 13). 35-36-37 Elizabeth II, Chapter 56. Ottawa: Queen's Printer for Canada.

Canadian Textile Institute. (1993). *Canadian textile and apparel industry data*. Unpublished materials.

Caporaso, J. (Ed.). (1987). *A changing international division of labor*. Boulder, CO: Lynne Rienner.

Carey, P. (1993, January). A United Europe hits rough seas. *International Business*, pp. 54–60.

Caribbean/Latin American Action. (1993). *Caribbean Basin databook*. Washington, DC: Author.

Carr, B. (1987). Development education in an ethical/humanistic framework. In C. Joy & W. Kniep (Eds.), *The international development crisis & American education* (pp. 59–76). New York: Global Perspectives in Education.

Castro, J. (1988, August 15). Going after the trade gap. *Time*, p. 32.

Cateora, P. (1987). *International marketing*. Homewood, IL: Richard Irwin.

Cates, M. (1992, August). NAFTA could enhance competitiveness of U.S. textile industry. *America's Textiles International*, pp. 36–38.

Catudal, H. (1961). *The General Agreement on Tariffs and Trade: An article-by-article analysis in layman's language*. (Publication No. 7235). Washington, DC: Department of State.

Cedrone, L. (1993). Sourcing the Caribbean & Latin America: 20th annual 807/CBI comparative analysis. *Bobbin, 35*(3), 62–63.

Chadwick, S., & Dardis, R. (1993). Demand for apparel imports in the United States, *Home Economics Research Journal, 22*(2), 156–179.

Chaikin, S. (1982). Trade, investment, and deindustrialization: Myth and reality. *Foreign Affairs, 60*(40), 836–851.

Chapkis, W., & Enlow, C. (1983). *Of common cloth*. Amsterdam: Transnational Institute.

Child-labor law bills introduced in Congress. (1993, March 19). *Women's Wear Daily*, p. 15.

China cancels contract for U.S. wheat. (1984, August 23). *Women's Wear Daily*, p. 18.

Chipps, E. (1987). Marketing management: Expanding market horizons. In *Managing an Industry in Transition*. Arlington, VA: American Apparel Manufacturers Association.

Chirot, D. (1977). *Social change in the twentieth century*. New York: Harcourt Brace Jovanovich.

Choate, P. (1990). *Agents of influence*. New York: Alfred A. Knopf.

Christiansen, G. (1988). International curriculum for the professions. *National Forum, LXVIII*(4), 27–30.

Church, G. (1985, October 7). The battle over barriers. *Time*, pp. 22–31.

Chute, E. (1989a, May 9). AAMA not looking to do battle with ATMI. *DNR*, p. 3.

Chute, E. (1989b, May 8). AAMA will not back any bills to curb imports. *Women's Wear Daily*, p. 7.

Chute, E. (1989c, April 11). Textile, apparel groups seek more data on GATT pact. *Women's Wear Daily*, p. 18.

Chute, E. (1990a, February 23). ATMI cautious on plan to phase out the MFA. *Women's Wear Daily*, p. 19.

Chute, E. (1990d, October 16). U.S. offers new proposal at GATT. *Women's Wear Daily*, p. 20.

Chute, E. (1990c, April 18). RITAC pushes own MFA phaseout plan. *Women's Wear Daily*, p. 31.

Chute, E. (1990b, July 5). Jittery retailers await outcome of GATT talks. *Women's Wear Daily*, p. 2.

Chute, E. (1990f, March 7). U.S. unveils details of MFA phaseout plan. *DNR*, p. 3.

Chute, E. (1990e, May 16). U.S. proposal for GATT on global quotas draws derision from importers. *Women's Wear Daily*, p. 20.

CIRFS (Comité International de la Rayonne et des Fibres Synthétiques). (1987). *Information on man-made fibers, 24*. Paris.

Clairmonte, F., & Cavanagh, J. (1981). *The world in their web*. London: Zed Press.

Clark, J. (1986). *For richer, for poorer*. London: Oxfam.

Cleghorn, S. (no date). *Signature of 450,000*. New York: International Ladies Garment Workers Union.

Cline, R. (1984). *Exports of manufacturers from developing countries*. Washington, DC: Brookings Institution.

Cline, W. (1978). *Imports and consumer prices: A survey analysis*. Unpublished report. Washington, DC: Brookings Institution.

Cline, W. (1983). "Reciprocity": A new approach to world trade policy? In W. Cline (Ed.), *Trade Policy in the 1980s* (pp. 121–158). Washington, DC: Institute for International Economics.

Cline, W. (1987). *The future of world trade in textiles and apparel*. Washington, DC: Institute for International Economics.

Clothing assembly: Automation versus flexibility. (1987, May). *Textile Outlook International*.

Clune, R. (1986, March 12). Do more than just talk 'USA,' give us goods we can sell. *Daily News Record*.

Clune, R. (1993, September 2). Making the switch to lights-out manufacturing. *Daily News Record*, p. 8.

Coats Viyella. (1993). *Coats Viyella report and accounts 1992*. London: Author.

Coker, J. (1993, November). World textile and clothing consumption: Forecasts to 2002. *Textile Outlook International*, pp. 10–41.

Coleman, J. (1989). *The Canadian International Trade Tribunal: What is it and what does it do?* Ottawa.

Colgate, A. (1987, October). The other side of the story. *Bobbin*, pp. 88–95.

COMITEXTIL. (1986). The importance of reciprocity of access in textile markets. *COMITEXTIL Bulletin*, 86/1, 24–30.

COMITEXTIL. (1988). Internal communication, p. 2.

COMITEXTIL. (1990). *Levelling the playing field in international textile and clothing trade*. Brussels: Author.

COMITEXTIL (1992a). The South Korea market study. *COMITEXTIL Bulletin*, 92/4, pp. 15–55.

COMITEXTIL. (1992b). The world trade of textile and clothing products. *COMITEXTIL Bulletin*, 92/6.

COMITEXTIL. (1993a). The E.E.C.'s external trade in 1992. *COMITEXTIL Bulletin*, 93/3.

COMITEXTIL. (1993b). Structure of the textile-clothing industry in Europe. *COMITEXTIL Bulletin*, 93/4.

COMITEXTIL. (1993c). *Textiles: An industry for Europe*. Brussels: Author.

Commission of the European Communities. (1992, April). *From single market to European Union*. Brussels: Author.

Compromise plan adopted by GATT. (1984, December 3). *Women's Wear Daily*.

Congressional Budget Office. (1991). *Trade restraints and the competitive status of the textile, apparel and nonrubber-footwear industries*. Washington, DC: Author.

Congressmen seek to block loan to China. (1984, July). *Textile World*, pp. 24, 27.

Consumers' Association gives brief to Textile & Clothing Board. (1985). *Canadian Apparel Manufacturer*, pp. 62–70.

Consumers for World Trade. (1984). How much do consumers pay for U.S. trade barriers? In *CWT Information Paper*. Washington, DC: Author.

Cotton Trade Journal. (1955, December 30). p. 1.

Cotton: Vital asset. (1992, April). *Textile Asia*, p. 140.

Council on International Educational Exchange. (1988, August). *Educating for global competence: The report of the Advisory Council for International Educational Exchange*. New York: Author.

Council on Wage and Price Stability (COWPS). (1978). *A study of the textile and apparel industries, including prices, wages, employment, foreign trade capacity*. Washington, DC: Executive Office of the President.

Crawford, M. (1959). The textile industry. In J. G. Glover & R. L. Lagai (Eds.), *The development of American industries*. New York: Simmons Boardman.

Culbertson, J. (1986a, September–October). The folly of free trade. *Harvard Business Review*, pp. 122–128.

Culbertson, J. (1986b, August 17). Importing a lower standard of living. *New York Times*, p. 1.

Curzon, G., de la Torre, J., Donges, J., MacBean, A., Waelbroeck, J., & Wolf, M. (1981). *MFA forever?* London: Trade Policy Research Center.

Czechoslovak constraints. (1992, November). *Textile Asia*, pp. 109–112.

Dafoe, F. (1986, September). A cautious "go for it" from the apparel/textile sectors. *The Canadian Apparel Manufacturer, 10*, 8–13.

Daily News Record (1961, December 13). Cited in Aggarwal, 1985.

Dam, K. (1970). *The GATT: Law and international economic organization*. Chicago: University of Chicago Press.

Daniels, J., & Radebaugh, L. (1986). *International business*. Reading, MA: Addison-Wesley.

Dardis, R. (1987). International textile trade: The consumer's stake. *Family Economics Review, 2*, 14–18.

Dardis, R. (1988). International trade: The consumer's stake. In E. S. Maynes & ACCI Research Committee (Eds.), *The frontier of research in the consumer interest* (pp. 329–359). Columbia, MO: American Council on Consumer Interests.

Dardis, R., & Cooke, K. (1984). The impact of trade restrictions on U.S. apparel consumers. *Journal of Consumer Policy, 7*, 1–12.

Daria, I. (1984a, September 19). Batus singing the praises of imported goods for U.S. *Women's Wear Daily*, p. 63.

Daria, I. (1984b, August 10). Importers go to court over rules. *Women's Wear Daily*, pp. 1, 11.

Das, B. (1983). The GATT Multi-Fibre Arrangement. *Journal of World Trade Law, 17*(2), 95–105.

David, P. (1970, September). Learning by doing and tariff protection: A reconsideration of the case of the antebellum United States textile industry. *Journal of Economic History*, pp. 521–602.

Davidson, W., Feigenoff, C., & Ghadar, F. (1986). *International competition in textiles and apparel: The US experience*. Washington, DC: National Chamber Foundation.

de la Torre, J. (1975, September–October). Product life cycle as a determinant of global marketing strategies. *Atlantic Economics Review*, pp. 9–14.

de la Torre, J. (1984). *Clothing-industry adjustment in developed countries*. London: Trade Policy Research Center.

de la Torre, J., Jedel, M., Arpan, J., Ogram, E., & Toyne, B. (1978). *Corporate responses to import competition in the U.S. apparel industry*. Atlanta: Georgia State University.

de Llosa, M. (1984). Threatened legacy. *American Fabrics and Fashions, 131*, 7–12.

Defining quick response. (1986, September). *Earnshaw's Review*, M26–M31.

De Vorsey, L. (1992). Western Europe. In J. Fisher (Ed.), *Geography and development: A world regional approach* (pp. 189–261). New York: Macmillan.

Destler, I. (1986). *American trade politics: System under stress*. Washington, DC: Institute for International Economics.

Destler, I. (1992). *American trade politics* (2 ed.). Washington, DC: Institute for International Economics.

Destler, I., Fukui, H., & Sato, H. (1979). *The textile wrangle: Conflict in Japanese-American relations, 1969–1971*. Ithaca, NY: Cornell University Press.

DiBiaggio, J. (1988). A case for internationalizing the curriculum: Higher education institutions in the United States. *National Forum, LXVIII*(4), 2–4.

Dicken, P. (1992). *Global shift: The internationalization of economic activity* (2nd ed.). New York: Guilford Press.

Dickerson, K. (1983a, May). Consumers prefer U.S. apparel. *Bobbin*, pp. 49–52.

Dickerson, K. (1983b, September). U.S. industry pridefully promotes domestic products. *Apparel Industry Magazine*, pp. 37–42.

Dickerson, K. (1986). *Managing textiles in the global marketplace*. Association of College Professors of Textiles and Clothing Proceedings: Combined Central, Eastern, and Western Region Meetings, 18–21.

Dickerson, K. (1988a). Meshing of the wheel of retailing and international trade theory to examine current apparel retailing procurement practices: A working model. In R. Kean & J. Laughlin (Eds.), *Theory building in apparel merchandising*. Lincoln, NE: University of Nebraska Press.

Dickerson, K. (1988b). The textile sector as a special GATT case. *Clothing and Textiles Research Journal, 6*(3), 17–25.

Dickerson, K. (1989). Retailers and apparel imports: Variables associated with relative proportions of imports carried. *Journal of Consumer Studies and Home Economics, 13*, 129–149.

Dickerson, K. (1994, April). *Textile CEO survey*. Presentation at the annual meeting of the American Textile Manufacturers Association, Orlando, FL.

Dickerson, K., Dalecki, M., & Meyer, M. (1989, July). Apparel manufacturing in the rural heartland: Its contributions to local economies. *Bobbin*, pp. 104–110.

Doing business in the '90s. (1993, March 29). *DNR*, pp. 14, 24.

Douglas, S. (1986). *Labor's new voice*. Norwood, NJ: Ablex.

Douglas, S. (1989). The textile industry in Malaysia: Coping with protectionism. *Asian Survey, 29* (4), 416–438.

Douglas, S. (1992). The administration of textile and apparel quotas: A case study of Malaysian policy and its implications for the U.S. *Clothing and Textile Research Journal, 11*(1), 1–9.

Douglas, S., Douglas, S., & Finn, T. (1994). The garment industry in Singapore: Clothes for the emperor. In E. Bonacich (Ed.), *Globalization of the garment industry*. Philadelphia: Temple University Press.

Dreyfack, K. (1986, March 3). Even American knowhow is headed abroad. *Business Week*, pp. 60–63.

Drucker, P. (1977, March 15). The rise of production sharing. *Wall Street Journal*, p. 22.

Drucker, P. (1989, February 1). *Boardroom Report*.

Dublin, T. (Ed.). (1981). *Farm to factory*. New York: Columbia University Press.

DuMont, S. (1994). *The textile industry: Back to the future . . . as soon as possible*. Paper presented at World Economic Forum. Davos, Switzerland: Author.

Dunn, B. (1988a, December 6). Third World ministers seek end to MFA. *DNR*, pp. 2, 11.

Dunn, B. (1988b, December 7). Third World nations in tougher stance at GATT talks on MFA elimination. *DNR*, pp. 2, 5.

Dunwell, S. (1978). *The run of the mill*. Boston: David R. Godine.

DuPont. (1993). *DuPont data book 1992*. Wilmington, DE: Author.

DuPont slates $1 billion for nylon plants in Asia. (1990, January 15). *Women's Wear Daily*, p. 15.

Earnshaw's Review. (various issues).

The East Asian miracle. (1993). Washington, DC: World Bank.

EC sees strides in combating import fraud. (1994, January 7). *DNR*, p. 9.

ECHO. (1991). *Textiles and clothing in Eastern Europe.* London: The Economist Intelligence Unit.

Economic Policy Institute. (1993). *Employment multipliers in the U.S. economy.* Washington, DC: Author.

Edwards, C. (1985). *The fragmented world.* London: Methuen.

Edwards, C. (1988). Textiles. *U.S. industrial outlook 1988.* Washington, DC: U.S. Department of Commerce.

Ehrenreich, B., & Fuentes, A. (1981, January). Life on the global assembly line. *Ms.*, pp. 54–71.

Ehrlich, P. (1984, August 23). Trade moves in Far East aim at U.S. origin regs. *DNR*, p. 11.

Ehrlich, P. (1985a, August 13). China warns US on textile import cuts. *Daily News Record*, p. 6.

Ehrlich, P. (1985b, August 22). Hong Kong warns of trade war. *Women's Wear Daily*, p. 2.

Ehrlich, P. (1985c, August 26). US delegation hears Asia trade bill threats. *Women's Wear Daily.*

Ehrlich, P. (1987, March 10). China striving to establish self-sufficiency in M-MF. *Daily News Record*, p. 3.

Ehrlich, P. (1988a, March 10). China raising acrylic fiber output with technology imported from US. *Daily News Record*, p. 8.

Ehrlich, P. (1988b, June 7). Chinese fiber plants diminish need for imports. *Daily News Record*, p. 12.

Ehrlich, P. (1989a, October 23). Cashmere, linen shortage from China hike rtw prices. *Women's Wear Daily*, p. 23.

Ehrlich, P. (1989b, August 2). Singapore firms mull $50 million complex for textile trade. *Women's Wear Daily*, p. 24.

Ehrlich, P. (1988c, July 18). West African nation woos Hong Kong apparel makers. *DNR.*

Ehrlich, P. (1988d, October 12). Hong Kong quota prices still falling. *Women's Wear Daily*, p. 31.

Ehrlich, P. (1988e, December 22). Thai benefits draw US textile firms. *DNR.*

Ehrlich, P. (1993, September 8). No new talks scheduled on U.S.–China textile agreement. *Daily News Record*, p. 12.

Eldridge, J. (1993, August). Non-store retailing: Planning for a big future. *Chain Store Age Executive*, pp. 34A–35A.

Ellsworth, P. T., & Leith, J. C. (1984). *The international economy.* New York: Macmillan.

Emert, C. (1993a, December 8). Customs Modernization Act will provide hefty fines for infractions of import rules. *Women's Wear Daily*, p. 4.

Emert, C. (1993b, August 24). Customs plans to get tough on anti-transshipment efforts. *Daily News Record*, p. 12.

Enderlyn, A., & Dziggel, O. (1992). *Cracking Eastern Europe.* Chicago: Probus.

Engardio, P., Barnathan, J., & Glasgall, W. (1993, November 29). Asia's wealth. *Business Week*, pp. 100–108.

Engel, J., & Blackwell, R. (1982). *Consumer behavior.* New York: Dryden Press.

Etgar, M. (1976, August). Channel domination and countervailing power in distributive channels. *Journal of Marketing Research, 13,* 254–262.

EU Commission. (1993, October 26). *Report on the competitiveness of the European textile and clothing industry.* Unpublished report.

The European Community and the textile industry (1985, December). Brussels: Commission of the European Communities.

European Economic Area. (1994). *Eur-Op News, 3*(1), 2.

European Union. (1992). Luxembourg: Office for Official Publications of the European Communities.

Execs cheer for NAFTA. (1993, November 18). *Women's Wear Daily*, pp. 6–7.

Fairchild News Service. (1993, November 18). Mexico breathes easy. *Women's Wear Daily*, p. 5.

Farley, L. (1993). *Canada and Mexico.* Unpublished paper, University of Missouri, Department of Textile and Apparel Management.

Farnsworth, C. (1988, August 8). U.S. trade bill increases import of mercantilism. *International Herald Tribune*, p. 11.

Farnsworth, S. (1992, June 2). NKSA blasts Customs on anti-dumping rule. *DNR*, p. 2.

Farrell, C., Mandel, M., Javetski, B., & Baker, S. (1993, August 2). What's wrong? Why the industrialized nations are stalled. *Business Week*, pp. 54–59.

Fayle, P. (1993, May). *The East Asian region—Power-house of growth.* Paper presented at the meeting of the Textile Institute, Hong Kong.

Fearon, F. (1993, April). Vietnam: Preparing for a global role. *Textile Horizons International, 13*(2), 42–43.

Federal Election Commission. (1993). *Business and PAC contributions.* Unpublished.

Federal Election Commission. (1994). *Business and PAC contributions.* Unpublished.

Feinberg, S. (1989a, June 23). Walton advocate of buy American. *Women's Wear Daily*, p. 11.

Feldman, A., & Levine, J. (1993, January 4). Sprucing up the cocoon. *Forbes*, pp. 64–65.

Fendel, A. (1984). The retail wave that's happening now. *1983 Knitting Times Yearbook*, pp. 131–132.

Fiber Economics Bureau. (various dates). *Fiber Organon.*

Fibers, Textiles, and Apparel Industry Panel, Committee on Technology and International Economic and Trade Issues. (1983). *The competitive status of the U.S. fibers, textiles, and apparel complex: A study of the influences of technology in determining international industrial competitive advantage.* Washington, DC: National Academy Press.

Fieleke, N. (1971, September–October). The cost of tariffs to consumers. *New England Economic Review*, pp. 13–18.

Finnerty, A. (1991). *Textiles and clothing in Southeast Asia.* London: The Economist Intelligence Unit.

Fisher, J. (Ed.). (1992). *Geography and development: A world regional approach* (4th ed.). New York: Macmillan.

Fishlow, A., Diaz-Alejandro, C., Fagen, R., & Hansen, R. (1978). *Rich and poor nations in the world economy.* New York: McGraw-Hill.

Fitzpatrick Associates. (1991). *The clothing industry and the single European market.* London: The Economist Intelligence Unit.

Fixing America's economy. (1992, October 19). *Fortune*, special feature issue.

Foner, P. (Ed.). (1977). *The factory girls.* Urbana, IL: University of Illinois Press.

Food and Agriculture Organization of the United Nations. (1992). *World apparel fibre consumption survey: 1992.* Rome: Author.

Food and Agriculture Organization of the United Nations & the Secretariat of the International Cotton Advisory Committee. (1993). *The world cotton market: Prospects for the nineties.* Rome and Washington, DC: Authors.

Ford, J. (1986). World trade in textiles. *Textiles, 15*(3), 72–77.

Foreign Policy Association. (1988). *Great decisions 1988: Foreign issues facing the nation.* New York: Foreign Policy Association.

Forman, E. (1988, August 18). Restructurings latest method to shore up sagging firms' health. *Daily News Record*, pp. 1, 11.

Forney, J. (1987). Recognizing the global significance of our field—fact or folly? *ACPTC Newsletter, 30*(2), 6.

Frank, B. (1985). *Profitable merchandising of apparel* (2nd ed.). New York: National Knitwear & Sportswear Association.

Frank, C. (1977). *Foreign trade and domestic aid.* Washington, DC: The Brookings Institution.

Frazier, G. (1983, May). On the measurement of interfirm power in distributive channels. *Journal of Marketing Research, 20*, 150–166.

Frazier, T. (1993). *A close look at the countries of Eastern Europe.* Unpublished paper. University of Missouri, Department of Textile and Apparel Management.

Friman, H. (1990). *Patchwork protectionism: Textile trade policy in the United States, Japan, and West Germany*. Ithaca, NY: Cornell University Press.

Fröbel, F., Heinrichs, J., & Kreye, O. (1980). *The new international division of labour*. Cambridge, England: Cambridge University Press.

Froyen, R. (1986). *Macroeconomics: Theories and policies*. New York: Macmillan.

Further trade talks cleared. (1989, April 10). *Women's Wear Daily*, p. 11.

Furukawa, T. (1989a, July 19). Japan looks back to when it led Asia in m-m fibers. *DNR*, p. 12.

Furukawa, T. (1989b, August 3). Soaring competition alarms Japan's textile industry. *DNR*, p. 8.

Furukawa, T. (1993, March 2). Japanese apparel manufacturers invade China. *Women's Wear Daily*, p. 16.

Gälli, A. (1992a, August). Baltics in distress. *Textile Asia*, pp. 109–111.

Gälli, A. (1992b, November). East European prospects. *Textile Asia*, pp. 113–121.

Gälli, A. (1993, September). Europe, how far the decline? *Textile Asia*, pp. 137–140.

Garland, S., Harbrecht, D., & Dunham, R. (1993, November 29). Sweet victory. *Business Week*, pp. 33–35.

GATT talks stalled, but hope seen for textile, apparel issues. (1991, December 23). *Women's Wear Daily*, p. 7.

Gelber, N. (1989, July). Deciphering the CBI and tariff nomenclature. *Bobbin*, pp. 20–24.

General Agreement on Tariffs and Trade. (annual). *International Trade*. Geneva, Switzerland: Author.

General Agreement on Tariffs and Trade. (1960, May 17). *GATT Document L/1164*. Geneva, Switzerland: Author.

General Agreement on Tariffs and Trade. (1966). *A study on cotton textiles*. Geneva, Switzerland: Author.

General Agreement on Tariffs and Trade. (1974). *Arrangement regarding international trade in textiles*. Geneva, Switzerland: Author.

General Agreement on Tariffs and Trade. (1977). *International Trade, 1976/77*. Geneva, Switzerland: Author.

General Agreement on Tariffs and Trade. (1984, July). *Textiles and clothing in the world economy*. Geneva, Switzerland: Author.

General Agreement on Tariffs and Trade. (1985a). *GATT activities, 1984*. Geneva: Author.

General Agreement on Tariffs and Trade. (1985b). *General Agreement on Tariffs and Trade: What it is, what it does*. Geneva, Switzerland: Author.

General Agreement on Tariffs and Trade. (1986, August 5). *Extension of the Multifiber Arrangement agreed*. (Press release 1390). Geneva, Switzerland: Author.

General Agreement on Tariffs and Trade. (1987a). *Protocol extending the arrangement regarding international trade in textiles*. Geneva, Switzerland: Author.

General Agreement on Tariffs and Trade. (1987, November 30). *Updating the 1984 GATT Secretariat study: Textiles and clothing in the world economy*. (Special distribution). Geneva, Switzerland: Author.

General Agreement on Tariffs and Trade. (1988). *GATT international trade 87–88*. Geneva, Switzerland: Author.

General Agreement on Tariffs and Trade. (1992). Textiles and clothing. *GATT activities 1991*. Geneva, Switzerland: Author.

General Agreement on Tariffs and Trade. (1993). *GATT international trade 91–92*. Geneva, Switzerland: Author.

General Agreement on Tariffs and Trade. (1994). Agreement on textiles and clothing, MTN/FA/Corr. 8. *Final Act Embodying the Results of the Uruguay Round of Multilateral Trade Negotiations*. Geneva: Author.

George, S. (1984, November–December). Scholarship, power and hunger. *Food Monitor*, pp. 23–26.

Georgia Institute of Technology for U.S. Department of Commerce, Economic Development Administration (1980). *Marketing strategies for U.S. apparel producers to compete more effectively with imports.* Vol. I. Washington, DC.

Ghadar, F., Davidson, W., & Feigenoff, C. (1987). *U.S. industrial competitiveness: The case of the textile and apparel industries.* Lexington, MA: Lexington Books.

Giddy, I. (1978). The demise of the product life cycle in international business theory. *Columbia Journal of World Business*, Spring, 90–97.

Giesse, C., & Lewin, U. (1987). The Multifiber Arrangement: "Temporary" protection run amuck. *Law and Policy in International Business, 19*(1), 51–170.

Gilbert, L. (1986, June 9). Sam Walton: Selling America. *HID*, pp. 1, 10.

Gilman, H. (1984, August 8). Apparel-import curbs force retailers in U.S. to shift their tactics. *Wall Street Journal*, pp. 1, 27.

Glasse, J. (1993, March). CIS report. *Textile Outlook International*, pp. 42–61.

Glenday, G., Jenkins, G., & Evans, J. (1980). *Worker adjustment to liberalized trade: Costs and assistance policies.* Staff working paper 426. Washington, DC: World Bank.

Goh, S. (1980, September). Canada counts the cost: How the consumer pays to protect Canada's clothing industry. *Textile Asia*, pp. 19–20.

Goldstein, J. (1983). *A re-examination of American trade policy: An inquiry into the causes of protectionism.* Unpublished doctoral dissertation, University of California, Los Angeles.

Greenberger, R. (1993, February 9). U.S. firms gear up for Vietnam business once trade ban ends. *Wall Street Journal*, pp. A1, A4.

Greene, J. (1985a, May 17). Retailers to lobby harder vs. trade bill. *Daily News Record*, p. 11.

Greene, J. (1985b, November 15). Yeutter sees: Phasing out of weaker industries. *Daily News Record*, pp. 1, 12.

Greenhaw, W. (1982). *Elephants in the cottonfields: Ronald Reagan and the new Republican South.* New York: Macmillan.

Grossman, G. (1982, December). *The employment and wage effects of import competition in the United States.* (Working Paper No. 1041). Cambridge, MA: National Bureau of Economic Research.

Grunwald, J., & Flamm, K. (1985). *The global factory.* Washington, DC: The Brookings Institution.

Guillaumin, C. (1979). Culture and cultures. *Cultures, 6*(1).

Gunawardena, D. (1993). *Focus on investment—Sri Lanka.* Paper presented at Textile Institute World Conference, Hong Kong.

Guobiao, J. (1993, May). *The development of China's textile industry and its reform and opening.* Paper presented at Textile Institute Conference, Hong Kong.

Haber, H. (1993, September 13). Penney's sets global growth plan in motion. *Women's Wear Daily*, pp. 1, 26.

Hackett, D. (1990a, July 13). Textile bill debate opens; veto is urged. *Women's Wear Daily*, p. 15.

Hackett, D. (1990b, April 19). Textile bill drama: Cracks in the coalition. *DNR*, pp. 3, 11.

Hackett, D. (1990c, April 5). Trade bill won't get AAMA vote. *DNR*, pp. 2, 9.

Hamilton, C. (1981). A new approach to estimation of the effects of non-tariff barriers to trade: An application to the Swedish textile and clothing industry. *Weltwirtschaftliches Archiv*, Band 117, Heft 2, 298–325.

Hamilton, D. (Ed.). (1990). *The Uruguay Round, textiles trade and the developing countries.* Washington, DC: World Bank.

Hamilton, J. (1989). Worlds apart: The high price of ethnocentricity for clothing and textiles and the cultivation of a global perspective. *Critical linkages monograph.* Monument, CO: Association of College Professors of Textiles and Clothing.

Hamilton, J., & Dickerson, K. (1990). The social and economic costs and payoffs of industrialization in international textile/apparel trade. *Clothing and Textiles Research Journal, 8*(4), 14–21.

Hammes, S. (1991, December). Europe's growing market. *Fortune*, pp. 132–133.

Hanson, J. (1980). *Trade in transition: Exports from the Third World, 1840–1900*. New York: Academic Press.

Harding, C., & Slater, K. (1986, March). The future of the textile and clothing industries in Canada. *Canadian Apparel Manufacturer*, pp. 60–64.

Harding, P. (1985, February). Is the apparel industry the weak link in the soft goods chain? *Textile Chemist and Colorist, 17*(2), 13–17.

Harding, P. (1988, September). New response for Quick Response. *WWD/DNR Retailing Technology and Operations*, pp. 30, 52.

Harris, C., Foust, D., & Rothman, M. (1987, August 3). The electronic pipeline that's changing the way America does business. *Business Week*, pp. 80–82.

Hartlein, R. (1988, December 22). Textile, apparel importers form USA-ITA trade group. *Women's Wear Daily*, p. 2.

Hays, T. (1985, July 15). *Testimony before the Subcommittee on International Trade, Textile and Apparel Trade Enforcement Act: Hearing before the Subcommittee on International Trade of the Committee on Finance, United States Senate, Ninety-ninth Congress, Part 1 of 2*, pp. 261–276. Washington, DC: U.S. Government Printing Office.

Heiland, R. (1980). Progress report: Georgia Institute of Technology study of market strategies. *Domestic apparel program: Technical review*. Washington, DC: U.S. Department of Commerce, International Trade Administration.

Herskovits, M. (1952). *Man and his works*. New York: Alfred A. Knopf.

Hess, A. (1986, February 7). Says trade bill nixed to protect consumers. *Daily News Record*, p. 19.

Hester, S. (1987). The impact of international textile trade agreements. *International Marketing Review, 4*, 31–41.

Hickock, S. (1985). The consumer cost of U.S. trade restraints. *Federal Reserve Bank of New York Quarterly Review, 10*(2), 1–12.

Hirano, K. (1992, November 13). L. L. Bean's first Japan store. *DNR*, p. 7.

HK quotas cost U.S. $40,000 a job saved. *Daily News Record*, p. 9.

Hodgson, J., & Herander, M. (1983). *International economic relations*. Englewood Cliffs, NJ: Prentice-Hall.

Hoffman, K. (1985). Clothing, chips, and competitive advantage: The impact of microelectronics on trade and protection in the garment industry. *World Development, 13*(3), 371–392.

Holding, H. (1990, August). Selling to the US retailer. *Textile Asia*, pp. 148–151.

Holzner, B. (1988). Economic competitiveness and international education. *National Forum, LXVIII*(4), 11–13.

Hong Kong Government Industry Department (prepared by Kurt Salmon Associates). (1992, March). *Techno-economic and market research study of Hong Kong's textiles and clothing industries 1991–1992*. Hong Kong: Author.

Honigsbaum, M. (1984, December 10). $30M in textile imports 'hit' by agents in month. *Daily News Record*, pp. 2, 8.

Honigsbaum, M. (1986, October 16). Study finds foreign competition shaped up textile industry in SE. *Daily News Record*, p. 2.

Honigsbaum, M. (1987a, March). Custom-ized computing. *Women's Wear Daily/T&O*, pp. 18–19.

Honigsbaum, M. (1987b, May 27). Customs chief faults global quotas plan. *Women's Wear Daily*, p. 31.

Honigsbaum, M. (1987c, December 2). Marianas sweatshops draw fire. *Women's Wear Daily*, p. 20.

Honigsbaum, M. (1988, July 7). ITC to probe alleged dumping of baseball caps by China. *DNR*, p. 11.

Hooper, C., Dickerson, K., & Boyle, R. (1994). A new course in world trade. *America's Textiles International, 23*(4), 52–56.

Horwitz, T. (1993, May 18). Europe's borders fade, and people and goods can move more freely. *Wall Street Journal*, pp. A1, A10.

Hosenball, M. (1984, June 27). House unit: 'Strongly oppose' int'l textile loans. *Daily News Record*, pp. 2, 8.

Hosenball, M. (1986, October 3). Override vote bans S. African textiles, *Women's Wear Daily*, p. 12.

Hossain, M. (1991, November). Bangladesh: Success story. *Textile Asia*.

House committee faults warning that restraints will hike consumer costs. (1985, October 9). *Women's Wear Daily*, p. 16.

House fails to override veto by 8 votes, but . . . (1986, August 7). *Daily News Record*, pp. 1, 11.

Hu, Q. (1993). *Attitudes of Chinese consumers toward foreign-brand apparel: A Shanghai study.* Unpublished paper. University of Missouri, Department of Textile and Apparel Management, Columbia.

Hufbauer, G., Berliner, D., & Elliott, K. (1986). *Trade protection in the U.S.: 31 case studies.* Washington, DC: Institute for International Economics.

Hufbauer, G., & Rosen, H. (1986). *Trade policy for troubled industries.* Washington, DC: Institute for International Economics.

Hughes, F. (1988, April). Japan's R&D yields results. *Apparel Industry Magazine*, pp. 36–42.

Hughes, J. (1987). A retail industry view of the Multifiber Arrangement: How congressional politics influence international negotiations. *Law and Policy in International Business, 19*(1), 257–261.

Hunsberger, W. (1964). *Japan and the United States in world trade.* New York: Harper & Row.

Hurewitz, L. (1993). *The GATT Uruguay Round: A negotiating history (1986–1992): Textiles.* Deventer, The Netherlands: Kluwer Law and Taxation Publishers.

IAF conference. (1991, June). Taipai, Taiwan.

IAF Newsletter. (1992, December). Berlin: International Apparel Federation.

ICF Incorporated. (1987). *Analysis of the employment and economic welfare effects of the Textile and Apparel Trade Act of 1987.* Washington, DC: Author.

Ilyasoglu, E., & Duruiz, L. (1991). *Turkish clothing industry.* Istanbul: Turkish Clothing Manufacturers' Association.

Imports: Apres le déluge, what? (1978, April). *Clothes, etc.*, pp. 55–59.

In the know. (1994, April 4). *Time* (European edition), p. 9.

India defends child labor. (1993, May 18). *Wall Street Journal*, p. A13.

Institut Francais de la Mode (IFM). (1993, May). Garment sourcing options for EC markets. *Textile Outlook International*, pp. 91–123.

International Apparel Federation. (1992, May). Slide show presented by Mexican government officials at presentation, Mexico City.

International Apparel Federation. (1993). *Yearbook 1993.* Berlin: Author.

International Business and Economic Research Corporation. (no date). *The MFA and protectionism in textiles and apparel.* Washington, DC: Author.

International Labour Office. (1991a). *Textiles Committee general report.* Geneva, Switzerland: Author.

International Labour Office. (1991b). *Vocational training and retraining in the textile industry.* Geneva, Switzerland: Author (Textiles Committee).

International Labour Office. (1991c). *Working conditions in the textiles industry in the light of technological changes.* Geneva, Switzerland: Author (Textiles Committee).

International Labour Office. (1992a). *Sources and methods: Volume 1 (3rd edition), consumer price indices.* Geneva, Switzerland: Author.

International Labour Office. (1992b). *Yearbook of labour statistics*. Geneva, Switzerland: Author.

International Labour Office. (1993). *Yearbook of labour statistics*. Geneva, Switzerland: Author.

International Organization of Consumers Unions. (1991). IOCU urges end to Multi-Fibre Arrangement (press release). The Hague: Author.

International Standing Working Group of Textile Geography (GEOTEX). (1989). *The role of the textile and clothing industries in national development*. Torin, Italy: Dipartimento Interateneo Territorio, Universita e Politecnico di Torino.

International Textiles and Clothing Bureau. (1988, April 27). Document for special distribution to GATT Negotiating Group on Textiles and Clothing for the Uruguay Round, MTN. Geneva, Switzerland: Author.

Isard, P. (1973). Employment impacts of textile imports and investment: A vintage-capital model. *American Economic Review, 63*(3), 402–416.

It's not just 'English spoken here': World economy has Americans learning languages. (1988, August 8). *International Herald Tribune*, pp. 1, 5.

Jacobs, B. (1989, May). New CBI legislation proposes duty-free GALs. *Bobbin*, pp. 26–32.

Jacobs, B. (1990, September). The textile bill's repeat performance. *Bobbin*, pp. 28, 30.

Jacobs, B. (1993a, September). Anti-transshipment initiatives at center stage. *Bobbin*, pp. 24–30.

Jacobs, B. (1993b, December). Elvis sighted at Customs. *Bobbin*, pp. 12–14.

Jacobs, B. (1994, January). New Customs law enacted—Finally. *Bobbin*, pp. 10–14.

Jacobson, H., Feldbaum, M., Sidjanski, D., Hougassian-Rudovich, A., & Somerville, C. (1986). *International economic negotiations: The views of participants in GATT, UNCTAD, and the UN*. Paper presented at the 1986 annual meeting of the American Political Science Association, Washington, DC.

Janardhan, R. (1993). *Bangladesh, India, Pakistan, Sri Lanka—Country reports*. Unpublished paper, University of Missouri, Department of Textile and Apparel Management.

Japan Spinners' Association. (1982, October 18–22). *The spinning industry in Japan: 100 years of progress to the present day*. Paper presented at the ITMF annual conference, Osaka.

Japan Spinners' Association. (1989). *Cotton & allied textile industry: Annual statistical review*. (No. 25). Osaka.

Jenkins, G. (1980). *Cost and consequences of the new protectionism: The case of Canada's clothing sector*. Ottawa: North-South Institute.

Jenkins, G. (1982). *Cost and consequences of the new protectionism*. Cambridge, MA: Harvard Institute for International Development.

Jenkins, G. (1985). *Costs and consequences of the new protectionism: The case of Canada's clothing sector* (2nd ed. rev.). Ottawa: North-South Institute.

Jeremy, D. (1981). *Transatlantic industrial revolution: The diffusion of textile technologies between Britain and America, 1790–1830s*. Cambridge, MA: MIT Press.

Jonas, N. (1986, March 3). The hollow corporation. *Business Week*, pp. 57–59.

Juvet, J. (1967, September/October). The cotton industry and world trade. *Journal of World Trade Law*, pp. 540–563.

Kabala, S. (1992, April). Global communications. *Apparel Industry Magazine*, pp. 40–46.

Kacker, M. (1985). *Transatlantic trends in retailing*. Westport, CT: Greenwood Press.

Kacker, M. (1986, Spring). Coming to terms with global retailing. *International Marketing Review*, pp. 7–20.

Kacker, M. (1988). International flow of retailing know-how: Bridging the technology gap in distribution. *Journal of Retailing, 64*(1), 41–67.

Kalantzopoulos, O. (1986). *The cost of voluntary export restraints for selected industries*. Washington, DC: Industry Department, Industrial Policy and Strategy Division, World Bank.

Keesing, D., & Wolf, M. (1980). *Textile quotas against developing countries*. London: Trade Policy Research Center.

Keller, R. (1987, November 1). King cotton is back. *Columbia Daily Tribune*, pp. 33–34.

Kellwood Company. (1993). *Kellwood Company 1993 Annual report*. St. Louis: Author.

Keohane, R., & Nye, J. (1977). *Power and interdependence: World politics in transition*. (Harvard Center for International Affairs). Boston: Little, Brown.

Khanna, S. (1991). *International trade in textiles: MFA quotas and a developing exporting country*. New Delhi: SAGE.

Khanna, S. (1994, March). The new GATT agreement: Implications for the world's textile and clothing industries. *Textile Outlook International*, pp. 10–37.

Kidd, J. (1983, March 8). Newly industrialized nations work long hours at low pay. *Daily News Record*, p. 24.

Kidd, J., & Ehrlich, P. (1984, August 6). New Customs rules set off alarm in Asia. *Women's Wear Daily*, pp. 1, 11.

Kidwell, C., & Christman, M. (1974). *Suiting everyone: The democratization of clothing in America*. Washington, DC: Smithsonian Institution Press.

Kim, K. (1992, December). The quest for efficiency (Korea). *Textile Asia*, p. 115.

Kim, W., & Young, P. (Eds.). (1987). *The Pacific challenge in international business*. Ann Arbor, MI: UMI Research Press.

King, R. (1988, May 16). Made in the U.S.A. *Forbes*, pp. 108–112.

Kissel, W., & Spevack, R. (1989, June 13). T's, jeans bridge Atlantic. *DNR*, pp. 1, 16.

Kleinfield, N. (1987, June 28). Patrolling the border at J.F.K. *The New York Times*.

Klopman, W. (1980, September). Call for protection. *Textile Asia*, pp. 184–196.

K-Mart going to Europe. (1992, May 8). *DNR*, p. 3.

Kniep, W. (1987). Development education: Essential to a global perspective. In C. Joy & W. Kniep (Eds.), *The international development crisis and American education* (pp. 145–158). New York: The American Forum.

Knight, F. W. (1990). *The Caribbean: The genesis of a fragmented nationalism*. New York: Oxford University Press.

Knobel, B., & Carey, P. (1993, February). Why Russia? *International Business*, pp. 53–56, 60–63.

Koekkoek, K., & Mennes, L. (1986). Liberalizing the Multi-Fibre Arrangement: Some aspects for the Netherlands, the EC, and the LDCs. *Journal of World Trade Law, 20*(2), 142–167.

Kolbeck, W. (1983, July). The meaning of retail price, or why the retailer doubles my price. *Bobbin*, pp. 81–86.

Koshy, D. (1993, April). Changing sourcing strategy of Indian importers: Are we in quick sand?, *Clothesline* (India), pp. 71–74.

Kotabe, M. (1992). *Global sourcing strategy*. New York: Quorum Books.

Krueger, A. (1980). Protectionist pressures, imports and employment in the United States. *Scandinavian Journal of Economics, 82*(2), 133–146.

Kry, S. (1985, March). The Canadian apparel industry: A global context. *Canadian Apparel Manufacturer*, pp. 26–34, 52.

Kry, S. (1989, October). Marketing apparel overseas. *The KSA Perspective*. pp. 1–4.

Kryhul, A., & Chute, E. (1988, December 12). Textile talks stalled as GATT meeting ends. *Women's Wear Daily*, p. 11.

Kurt Salmon Associates. (annual). *Textile profile, apparel profile—The KTA Perspective*.

Kurt Salmon Associates. (1988, January). *Private label development for retailers*, pp. 1–4.

Kurt Salmon Associates. (1993). *The textile and clothing industry in the EC until 2001*. Düsseldorf: Author.

Lachica, E. (1990, July 18). Restrictive quotas on textile imports cleared by Senate. *Wall Street Journal*, p. A10.

Lacitis, E. (1986, January 9). The social fabric: Hong Kong gives world the clothes on its back. *The Seattle Times*, p. C-1.

Lack, H. (1987, August). How important is the retailer? *Textile Asia*, pp. 200–201.

Lancaster, G., & Wesenlund, I. (1984). A product life cycle theory for international trade: An empirical investigation. *European Journal of Marketing, 18*(6–7), 72–89.

Langley, M., & Mossberg, W. (1988, August 4). Senate approves major trade measure by vote of 85–11 and sends it to Reagan. *Wall Street Journal*, pp. 3, 6.

Lanier, R. (1981, October). A major priority: The MFA. *Stores*, pp. 68, 70.

Lanier, R. (1986, April). From Washington: On the import issue. *Stores*, pp. 66.

LaRussa, R. (1986, December 1). Bentsen against attaching textiles to main trade bill. *Daily News Record*, pp. 3, 5.

LaRussa, R. (1987, June 25). Consumer-industry coalition warns Congress of trade bill dangers. *Daily News Record*, pp. 15.

LaRussa, R. (1988a, October 5). Override bill falls short on textile bill. *Daily News Record*, pp. 1, 12.

LaRussa, R. (1988b, September 13). Textile bill entering end game. *Women's Wear Daily*, p. 31.

LaRussa, R. (1989a, February 8). Free-traders gear up for quota bill battle. *Women's Wear Daily*, p. 29.

LaRussa, R. (1989b, February 2). Lloyd of Tenn. named to chair Textile Caucus. *Women's Wear Daily*, p. 15.

LaRussa, R. (1989c, February 23). Textile-steel alliance explored as way of restricting imports. *DNR*, p. 3.

LaRussa, R. (1989d, October 25). Textile trade lobby may be splintering. *Women's Wear Daily*, p. 27.

Lee, C. (1987). *Foreign lobbying in American politics*. Unpublished doctoral dissertation, University of Missouri-Columbia, Columbia, MO.

Lee, G. (1993a, March 29). 807 gets key to the city. *Women's Wear Daily*, p. 12.

Lee, G. (1993b, October 4). 807 keeps airports and harbors humming. *Women's Wear Daily*, p. 18.

Lee, J. (1966, March/April). Cultural analysis in overseas operations. *Harvard Business Review*, pp. 106, 111.

Lee, J. (1993, May). *Perspective of Korean textile industry*. Paper presented at the Textile Institute meeting, Hong Kong.

Leiter, J. (1986). Reactions to subordination: Attitudes of Southern textile workers. *Social Forces, 64*(4), 948–974.

Lerner, G. (1969). The lady and the mill girl: Changes in the status of women in the age of Jackson. *American Studies Journal, X*, 2–10.

Leung, P. (1992, December). Foreign funding perils. *Textile Asia*, pp. 72–74.

Levi Strauss & Co. (no date). *Levi Strauss & Co. business partner terms of engagement and guidelines for country selection*. San Francisco: Author.

Levi's life. (1992). San Francisco: Levi Strauss & Co.

Levitt, T. (1983, May–June). The globalization of markets. *Harvard Business Review*, pp. 92–102.

Lewinson, D., & DeLozier, M. (1989). *Retailing* (3rd ed.). Columbus, OH: Merrill.

Lockwood, L. (1984, April 13). 150 importers pledge $1M to fight quotas. *Daily News Record*, pp. 2, 11.

Lockwood, L. (1986, April 2). Poll says stores plan to get more US private-label goods. *Women's Wear Daily*, p. 16.

Lurie, J. (1982). America . . . Globally blind, deaf and dumb. *Foreign Language Annuals, 15*(6), 413–420.

Lusch, R., & Brown, J. (1982). A modified model of power in the marketing channel. *Journal of Marketing Research, 19*, 312–323.

Lynch, J. (1968). *Towards an orderly market: An intensive study of Japan's voluntary quota in cotton textile exports*. Tokyo: Sophia University Press.

Maas, A. (1980, September). Retailers' view. *Textile Asia*, pp. 176–180.

Mackie, G. (1993, August). Jute—Can it survive the battle with polypropylene? *Textile Horizons International*, 13(4), 51–55.

Magnusson, P. (1992, May 25). Building free trade bloc by bloc. *Business Week*, pp. 26–27.

Maizels, A. (1963). *Industrial growth and world trade*. Cambridge, England: Cambridge University Press.

Mallen, B. (1963, summer). A theory of retailer-supplier conflict, control, and cooperation. *Journal of Retailing*, pp. 24–33, 51.

Management Horizons. (1993). *Global retailing 2000*. Columbus, OH: Author (A Division of Price Waterhouse).

Mansfield, E. (1983). *Economics*. New York: W. W. Norton.

Mantoux, P. (1927). *The Industrial Revolution in the eighteenth century*. New York: Harcourt Brace Jovanovich.

Markup benefit of private label is cited. (1984, July 23). *Women's Wear Daily*, p. 24.

Marshall, S. (1992, August 6). Vietnam's slow road to apparel growth. *DNR*.

Marszal, T. (1985). Tendencies of the spatial development of textile industry in the world. *Folia Geographica, 6*, 33–48.

Martin, J., & Evans, J. (1981, March). Notes on measuring the employment displacement effects of trade by the accounting procedure. *Oxford Economic Papers, 33*(1), 154–164.

Mastering the new Europe. (1992, August). *International Business*, pp. 44–58.

Matsusaki, H. (1979). Marketing, culture, and social framework: The need for theory development at the macro marketing level. In O. Ferrell, S. Brown, & C. Lamb (Eds.), *Conceptual and theoretical development in marketing*. Chicago: American Marketing Association.

McCabe, J. (1989, January). Overseas business is vital for survival. *Apparel Industry Magazine*, p. 108.

McCormick, H. (1985, September 18). Crafted with Pride: The $11 million offensive. *Women's Wear Daily*, pp. 12–14.

McCormick, J., & Levinson, M. (1993, February 15). The supply police. *Business Week*, pp. 48–49.

McGarvey, R. (1992, June). Foreign exchange, *U.S. Air Magazine*, pp. 58–65.

McGowan, P. (1987). Key concepts for development studies. In C. Joy & W. Kniep (Eds.), *The international development crisis & American education* (pp 37–58). New York: Global Perspectives in Education.

McHale, J. (1969). *The future of the future*. New York: George Braziller.

McMurray, S., & McGregor, J. (1993, August 4). New battleground: Asia targets chemicals for the next assault on Western industry. *Wall Street Journal*, pp. A1, A4.

McNamara, M. (1993, December 21). No subsidies, less use cloud mohair's future. *Women's Wear Daily*, p. 11.

McNeill, W. (1965). *The rise of the West: A history of the human community*. New York: Mentor.

McNeill, W. (1986). Organizing concepts for world history. *Review, X*(2), 220–235.

McRobert, R., & Smallbone, T. (1980, September). Consumers' interests. *Textile Asia*, pp. 170–176.

Meadus, A. (1992, October 30). Counterfeiters beware: This law's for real. *Women's Wear Daily*, pp. 1, 14, 15.

Mellen, C. (1993, June 15). *Putting together the softgoods puzzle: How consumer change and consolidation will change retailing and softgoods*. Speech delivered at Kurt Salmon Associates Softgoods Breakfast, New York, NY.

Mexican Investment Board. (1993a, first quarter). *Mexico: Mexico investment update*.

Mexican Investment Board. (1993b, third quarter). *Mexico: Mexico investment update*.

The MFA is too costly a joke. (1984, December 22). *The Economist*, p. 73.

Mintz, I. (1972). *U.S. import quotas: Costs and consequences*. Washington, DC: American Enterprise Institute for Public Policy Research.

Moffett, M. (1993, March 8). U.S. firms yell olé to future in Mexico. *Wall Street Journal*, pp. B1, B5.

Moin, D. (1985, June 17). The retailers: Defending their sources. *Women's Wear Daily*, p. 8.

Monthly Record. (1936, September 30). The Manchester Chamber of Commerce.

Moran, C. (1988, September). A structural model for developing countries' manufactured exports. *The World Bank Economic Review*, 2(3), 321–340.

Morawetz, D. (1980). *Why the Emperor's new clothes are not made in Colombia*. World Bank staff working paper no. 368. Washington, DC: The World Bank.

More corporations, less bureaucracy. (1987, December). *Textile Asia*.

More poly plants being built in China. (1994, February 17). *DNR*, p. 10.

Morkre, M., & Tarr, D. (1980). *Staff report on effects of restrictions on United States imports: Five case studies and theory*. Washington, DC: Federal Trade Commission, Bureau of Economics.

Morris, D. (1986). *The fiber and textile industries of the U.S.S.R., Eastern Europe, and Yugoslavia to 1990*. Brussels: International Wool Secretariat.

Morton, M., & Dardis, R. (1989). Consumer and welfare losses associated with Canadian trade restrictions for apparel. *Canadian Home Economics Journal*, 39(1), 25–32.

Mowen, J. (1987). *Consumer behavior*. New York: Macmillan.

Mullin, T. (1985, September). New threats to imports. *Stores*, p. 82.

Multicultural correctness. (1993, January). *World Trade*, p. 28.

Munck, R. (1984). *Politics and dependency in the Third World*. London: Zed Books Ltd.

Munger, M. (1984). *The costs of protectionism: Estimates of the hidden tax of trade restraint*. Working paper 80. St. Louis, MO: Center for the Study of American Business, Washington University.

Nash, J., & Fernández-Kelly, M. (Eds.). (1983). *Women, men, and the international division of labor*. Albany, NY: State University of New York Press.

National Cotton Council of America. (annual). *Cotton counts its customers: The quantity of cotton consumed in final uses in the United States*. Memphis: National Cotton Council of America.

National Governors' Association. (1987). *Educating Americans for tomorrow's world: State initiatives in international education*. Washington, DC: Author.

National Governors' Association. (1989). *America in transition: The international frontier*. Washington, DC: Author.

National Retail Federation. (1993, August). *NAFTA textile and apparel provisions: A summary*. Washington, DC: Author by The Trade Partnership.

National Retail Merchants Association. (1977). *How consumers benefit from imports*. Unpublished report.

Navarro, P. (1984). *The policy game*. New York: John Wiley & Sons.

Nehmer, S. (1983). Comments. In W. Cline (Ed.), *Trade Policy in the 1980s* (pp. 568–573). Washington, DC: Institute for International Economics.

Neundörfer, K. (1987). *The fourth Multi-Fibre Arrangement: Protocol of extension and bilateral agreements of the EEC text and commentary*. Frankfurt: Gesamttextil.

New Wal-Mart in Mexico pulls 12,000 people. (1993, December 8). *Women's Wear Daily*, p. 16.

A new way to look at the U.S. economy. (1990, December 7). *Business Week*, p. 70.

Nihon Keizai Shimbun. (1988, March 4).

No gain without pain. (1992, August 15). *The Economist*, p. 54.

Noland, M. (1990). *Pacific Basin developing countries*. Washington, DC: Institute for International Economics.

Nordquist, B. (1985). International trade in textiles and clothing: Impressions for the future. *Clothing and Textiles Research Journal,* 3(2), 35–38.

Nurkse, R. (1961). *Patterns of trade and development.* Oxford, England: Basil Blackwell.

L'Observatoire Europeen du Textile et de L'Habillement. (1993, April). *The EC textile and clothing industry 1991/1992.* Brussels: Author.

O'Day, P. (1994, May). *The U.S. perspective on manufactured fibers: Issues and trends.* Paper presented at the 5th Beijing International Conference on Man-Made Fibers, May 10–14, Beijing: Author.

O'Donnell, T. (1988, July). Customs and imports. *Textile Asia,* pp. 98–110.

Odyssey begins major U.S. expansion plan. (1991, January). *Apparel Industry Magazine,* p. 10.

Office for Official Publications of the European Communities. (1992). *From single market to European Union.* Luxembourg: Author.

Ohmae, K. (1985). *Triad power.* New York: Free Press.

Ohmae, K. (1990). *The borderless world.* New York: Harper Business.

Olsen, R. (1978). *The textile industry: An industry analysis approach to operations management.* Lexington, MA: Lexington Books.

Olson, D. (1987a, April). *Interest groups and the politics of industrial policy and textile trade legislation.* Paper presented at annual meeting of Midwest Political Science Association, Chicago, IL.

Olson, D. (1987b, September). *U.S. trade policy: The conditions for congressional participation.* Paper presented at 1987 annual meeting of the American Political Science Association, Chicago, IL.

Onkvisit, S., & Shaw, J. (1993). *International marketing: Analysis and strategy.* New York: Macmillan.

O'Reilly, B. (1992, December). Your new global work force. *Fortune,* pp. 52–66.

Organization for Economic Cooperation and Development. (1983). *Textile and clothing industries.* Paris: Author.

Organization for Economic Cooperation and Development. (1994). *Quarterly labor force statistics* (No. 1). Paris: Author.

Orgel, D. (1989, January 10). Associations heat up own 'trade war.' *DNR,* pp. 2, 13.

Ormerod, A. (1993, May). *Why new textile mill projects fail.* Paper presented at Textile Institute meeting, Hong Kong.

Ostroff, J. (1988, September 1). USDA's cotton action could spur lower retail prices for textiles. *Daily News Record,* p. 8.

Ostroff, J. (1990a, December 27). New GATT accord expected at talks. *DNR,* p. 11.

Ostroff, J. (1990b, January 4). See merger adding muscle in Congress. *DNR,* p. 6.

Ostroff, J. (1991a, December 19). GATT Textile Committee completes plan to end MFA within ten years. *Women's Wear Daily,* p. 10.

Ostroff, J. (1991b, October 25). See new trade talks getting under way. *DNR,* p. 8.

Ostroff, J. (1992a, July 30, 1992). ITC is ordered to reconsider decision on sweater dumping. *DNR,* p. 4.

Ostroff, J. (1992b, January 8). Textile, apparel makers blast GATT plan on MFA. *Women's Wear Daily,* p. 20.

Ostroff, J. (1993a, November 10). Clinton pledges Customs aid in bid for undecided. *Women's Wear Daily,* p. 10.

Ostroff, J. (1993b, December 16). GATT gets it done. *Women's Wear Daily,* p. 8.

Ostroff, J. (1993c, December 29). Getting set for NAFTA. *Women's Wear Daily,* pp. 6–7.

Ostroff, J. (1994c, January 7). U.S. to China: If no progress, quotas get slashed Jan. 17. *Women's Wear Daily,* p. 2.

Ostroff, J. (1994a, January 12). Study shows textile, apparel duties took big bite out of U.S. consumers. *Women's Wear Daily,* p. 28.

Ostroff, J. (1994b, January 19). U.S. textile, apparel firms commend new China pact. *DNR,* pp. 2, 14.

Ostroff, J. (1994d, April 5). U.S. appears backing down on pressuring Asian nations to open markets to textiles. *DNR,* p. 2, 5.

The Pacific Basin: Alliances, trade, and bases. (1987). *Great Decisions 1987*. New York: Foreign Policy Association.

Pannell, C. (1992). Monsoon Asia. In J. Fisher (Ed.), *Geography and development: A world regional approach* (pp. 555–670). New York: Macmillan.

Pantojas-Garcia, E. (1990). *Development strategies as ideology*. Boulder, CO: Lynne Rienner.

Paretti, V., & Bloch, G. (1955). Industrial production in Western Europe and the United States, 1901 to 1955. *Banca Nazionale del Lavoro, Quarterly Review*.

Parry, J. (1990, April). *Time is running short . . .* Textile Asia, pp. 26–27.

Pechter, K. (1992, August). In Europe's epicenter. *International Business*, pp. 44–49.

Pelzman, J. (1983). Economic costs of tariffs and quotas on textile and apparel products imported into the United States: A survey of the literature and implications for policies. *Weltwirtschaftliches Archiv, 119*(3), 523–542.

Pelzman, J. (1984). The Multifiber Arrangement and its effect on the profit performance of the US textile industry. In R. Baldwin & A. Kreuger (Eds.), *The structure and evolution of recent US trade policy* (pp. 111–149). Chicago: University of Chicago Press.

Pelzman, J., & Bradberry, C. (1980). The welfare effects of reduced U.S. tariff restrictions on imported textile products. *Applied Economics, 12*, 455–465.

Pelzman, J., & Martin, R. (1987). *Direct employment effect of imports on the U.S. textile industry*. (Economic Discussion Paper 6). Office of Foreign Economic Research, Bureau of International Labor Affairs. Washington, DC: U.S. Department of Labor.

Pennar, K. (1992, July 27). In Russia, a journey back to the future. *Business Week*, pp. 48–49, 52–53.

Perlow, G. (1981, January). The multilateral supervision of international trade: Has the textiles experiment worked? *American Journal of International Law, 75*(1), 93–133.

Perman, S. (1993, December 8). Department stores to focus more on own brands. *Women's Wear Daily*, p. 24.

Pestieau, C. (1976). *The Canadian textile policy: A sectoral trade adjustment strategy*. Montreal, Canada: C.D. Howe Research Institute.

Peterson, B. (1985, January 31). Death of a textile plant. *The Washington Post*.

Pine, A. (1984, January 6). How president came to favor concessions for U.S. textile makers. *Wall Street Journal*, pp. 1, 13.

Plant, R. (1981). *Industries in trouble*. Geneva, Switzerland: International Labour Office.

Pohlandt-McCormick, H. (1985, September 18). Crafted with Pride: The $11 million offensive. *Women's Wear Daily*, pp. 12–14.

Pollard, S. (Ed.). (1990). *Wealth & poverty*. Oxford, England: Oxford University Press.

Population Reference Bureau, Inc. (1993). *1993 world population data sheet*. Washington, DC: Author.

Porter, M. (1980). *Competitive strategy: Techniques for analyzing industries and competitors*. New York: Free Press.

Porter, M. (1985). *Competitive advantage: Creating and sustaining superior performance*. New York: Free Press.

Porter, M. (Ed.). (1986). *Competition in global industries*. Boston: Harvard Business School Press.

Porter, M. (1990). *The competitive advantage of nations*. New York: Free Press.

Poulson, B. W. (1981). *Economic history of the United States*. New York: Macmillan.

Price Waterhouse. (1991). *Doing business in Germany*. Germany: Author.

Price Waterhouse/Management Horizons. (1994). *Retail world: Window of opportunity*. Columbus, OH: Author.

Pullen, R. (1988, November 2). Apparel, textile, retail PACs backing candidates to tune of $2M. *Daily News Record*, p. 7.

The quilts that struck a nerve. (1992, March 19). *The Washington Post: Washington Home*, pp. 1, 8–27.

Raffaelli, M. (1989, March 21–22). *Some considerations on the Multi-Fibre Arrangement: Past, present and future*. Preliminary manuscript sent to author. Paper presented at workshop on International Textile Trade, the Multi-Fibre Arrangement and the Uruguay Round, Stockholm.

Raffaelli, M. (1992). Unpublished report presented to GATT Textiles Committee.

Raghavan, A. (1993, June 1). Searching for overseas stock plays? Consider U.S. multinationals, some say. *Wall Street Journal*, section C, p. 1.

Ramey, J. (1992a, August 19). Mexican women want U.S. brands. *Women's Wear Daily*, p. 16.

Ramey, J. (1992b, September 30). U.S. funding of offshore apparel factories fuels spirited debate. *Women's Wear Daily*, p. 24.

Ramey, J. (1993, March 16). Cotton moves to protect its subsidies. *Women's Wear Daily*, p. 22.

Raper, S. (1992, September 4). Moscow's GUM: Gearing for growth. *Women's Wear Daily*, pp. 24–25.

Rapoport, C. (1992, December). Europe looks ahead to hard choices. *Fortune*, pp. 144–153.

Reed, W., & Montero, M. (1993, February). Will NAFTA-Mexico be a plus or minus for you? *Textile World*, pp. 33–39.

Resnick, R. (1984, October 8). Importers-stores lose bid to kill new origin rules. *Daily News Record*, pp. 1, 15.

Retail Industry Trade Action Coalition. (1987, July 30). *Prepared statement of the Retail Industry Trade Action Coaltion (RITAC) in opposition to S. 549, The Textile and Apparel Trade Act of 1987*. Unpublished statement presented before the Committee on Finance, U.S. Senate.

Rhee, K. (1992, December). Industrial textiles in Korea. *J.S.N. International*, p. 30.

Ricardo, D. (1960). *Principles of political economy and taxation*. New York: E. P. Dutton. (Original work published in 1817)

Ricks, D., Fu, M., & Arpan, J. (1974). *International business blunders*. Columbus, OH: Grid.

Roberts, S. (1988, September 29). President vetoes bill that limits imported textiles. *The New York Times*, pp. 1, 16.

Robertson, D. (1938, March). The future of international trade, *Economic Journal*, p. 48.

Roboz, T. (1981, September). In response . . . *Bobbin*, pp. 28–32.

Rosen, S., Turnbull, B., & Bialos, J. (1985). *The renewal of the Multi-Fiber Agreement: An assessment of the policy alternatives for future global trade in textiles and apparel*. Washington, DC: National Retail Merchants Association.

Rostow, W. (1960). *The stages of economic growth*. Cambridge: Cambridge University Press.

Rubenstein, J. (1992). *The cultural landscape: An introduction to human geography* (3rd ed.). New York: Macmillan.

Rudolph, B. (1988, November 21). Invasion of the cachet snatchers. *Time*, p. 114.

Rutberg, S. (1984, July 16). Less developed countries bank on: Always a borrower be. *Daily News Record*, p. 24.

SA sees little lasting harm for Wal-Mart in NBC show. (1992, December 28). *Women's Wear Daily*, pp. 2, 9.

Sakong, I. (1993). *Korea in the world economy*. Washington, DC: Institute for International Economics.

Salvatore, D. (1987). *International economics*. New York: Macmillan.

Samolis, F., & Emrich, T. (1986). *The politics of U.S. textile trade policy: Two centuries of temporary protection*. Washington, DC: Retail Industry Trade Action Coalition.

Santora, J. (1986, April). Retailers reassess domestic sourcing. *Bobbin*, p. 63.

Santora, J. (1989, May). USAIC addresses real-world 807. *Bobbin*, pp. 94–100.

Sara Lee Corporation. (1993). *Annual report 1993*. Chicago: Author

Sato, H. (1976). *The crisis of an alliance: The politics of US-Japanese textile trade, 1969–71*.

Unpublished doctoral dissertation, University of Chicago.

Schiavo-Campo, S., & Singer, H. (1970). *Perspectives of economic development*. Boston: Houghton Mifflin.

Schiller, B. (1983). *The economy today*. New York: Random House.

Schlotzman, K., & Tierney, J. (1983). More of the same: Washington pressure group activity in a decade of change. *Journal of Politics, 45,* 351–377.

Schraeder, T. (1989, February). The graying of the U.S. work force. *Apparel Industry Magazine*, p. 88.

Schwartz, L. (1984a, August 28). House unit approves anti-counterfeiting bill [also country of origin labeling legislation]. *Daily News Record*, p. 11.

Schwartz, L. (1984b, September 27). Mfrs., importers again slug it out in Capitol. *Daily News Record*, p. 7.

Schwartz, L. (1986a, August 7). Import bill dead: House sustains veto. *Women's Wear Daily*, pp. 1, 20.

Schwartz, L. (1986b, July 30). South Africa textile pact blasted. *Women's Wear Daily*, p. 18.

Scott, A. (1989, October 10). Peru gets OK to market vicuna. *Women's Wear Daily*, p. 38.

Senate nixes funds as Carib debate heats. (1992, October 1). *Women's Wear Daily*, pp. 1, 10.

Shelton, L. (1988). *Summary report on status of U.S. leather and leather products industries*. Unpublished report.

Shelton, L. (1993, September). Vietnam: Potentially competitive. *Textile Asia*, pp. 124–126.

Shelton, L., & Dickerson, K. (1989). Government textile trade: Implications for industry, government, and education. *Journal of Home Economics, 81*(4), 46–52.

Shin, S. (1993). *Textile and apparel investment opportunities in East Asian countries*. Unpublished paper. University of Missouri, Department of Textile and Apparel Management, Columbia.

Shooshtari, N., Walker, B., & Jackson, D. (1988). Retail trade associations: Enhancing members' power in relationships with suppliers. *Journal of Retailing, 64*(2), 199–214.

Sieff, L. (1984). Buying British-made goods. *American Fabrics and Fashions*, pp. 37–39.

Silbertson, Z., & Ledic, M. (1989). *The future of the Multi-fiber Arrangements: Implications for the UK economy*. London: Her Majesty's Stationery Office.

Silva, F. (1993, August). Mexico: The making of a new market. *Bobbin*, pp. 38–46.

Simai, M. (1981). *Interdependence and conflicts in the world economy*. Rockville, MD: Sijthoff & Noordhoff.

Skartvedt, D. (1979, February 2). Productivity gains keep textile, apparel prices low. *Daily News Record*, p. 2.

Sklair, L. (1989). *Assembling for development*. Boston: Unwin Hyman.

Smallbone, T. (1986). Consumer interest in textile and clothing policy. In *International Trade and the Consumer*. Paris: Organization for Economic Cooperation and Development.

Smarr, S. (1988, September). Thoroughbred takes Jockey to the winner's circle. *Bobbin*, pp. 170–176.

Smith, A. (1930). *The wealth of nations* (5th ed.). London: Methuen. (Original work published in 1776).

Solomon, B. (1987, June 6). Our facts, their facts. *National Journal*, 1460–1461.

Some lesser known aspects of the European textiles and clothing market. (1993, February). *Textile Horizons International*, pp. 40–42.

Spalding, L. (1985, September). Block those quotas. *Stores*, pp. 45–51.

Spinanger, D., & Zietz, J. (1985). *Managing trade but mangling the consumer: Reflections on the EEC's and West Germany's experience with the MFA*. Kiel Working Paper No. 245. Kiel, Federal Republic of Germany: Institut für Weltwirtschaft.

Spitalnick, I. (1985, May). Coming home. *Apparel Industry Magazine*, pp. 48–54.

Stabler, C. (1986, December 22). What is cuture's role in economic policy? *Wall Street Journal*, p. 1.

Standard & Poor's (Annual). *Textiles, apparel and home furnishings—Basic analysis and textiles*, and *Apparel and home furnishings—Current analysis*.

Standard & Poor's. (1984). *Standard & Poor's industry surveys*. New York: Standard & Poor's.

Standard & Poor's. (1987). *Standard & Poor's industry surveys*. New York: Standard & Poor's.

Standard & Poor's. (1988). *Standard & Poor's industry surveys*. New York: Standard & Poor's.

Standard & Poor's. (1989). *Standard & Poor's industry surveys*. New York: Standard & Poor's.

Standard & Poor's. (1992). *Standard & Poor's industry surveys*. New York: Standard & Poor's.

Standard & Poor's. (1993). *Standard & Poor's industry surveys*. New York: Standard & Poor's.

Standard & Poor's. (1994). *Standard & Poor's industry surveys*. New York: Standard & Poor's.

Stanton, B. (1987, October 9). Retailers finding out that lobbying Congress can pay off. *Daily News Record*, p. 33.

The state of the industry. (1993, August). *Chain Store Age Executive*, pp. 1A–40A.

Statistics Canada. (1993). Ottawa: Government of Canada.

Steele, P. (1988). *The Caribbean clothing industry: The U.S. and far east connections*. London: The Economist Intelligence Unit.

Steele, P. (1990). *Hong Kong clothing: Waiting for China*. London: The Economist Intelligence Unit.

Stein, L. (Ed.). (1977). *Out of the sweatshop*. New York: Quadrangle.

Stern, L. (1969). *Distribution channels: Behavioral dimensions*. Boston: Houghton Mifflin.

Stern, N. (1989, August). Industrial fabrics: The U.S. market. *Textile Asia*, pp. 162–164.

Sternquist, B., & Tolbert, S. (1986, May 23). Survey: Retailers shun industry's Buy American program. *Marketing News*, p. 8.

Stogdon, R. (1993, March). European fashion in recession. *Textile Outlook International*, pp. 93–108.

Stokes, R. (1984). *Introduction to sociology*. Dubuque, IA: W.C. Brown.

Streeten, P. (1972). Technology gaps between rich and poor countries. *Scottish Journal of Political Economy, XIX*(3), 213–230.

Strida, M. (1985). Early location of textile industry in central Europe. *Folia Geographica, 6,* 71–79.

Strugatch, W. (1993, February). Make way for the Euroconsumer. *World Trade*, pp. 46–50.

Sturdivant, F., & Granbois, D. (1973). Channel interaction: An institutional-behavioral view. In B. Walker & J. Haynes (Eds.), *Marketing channels and institutions: Readings on distribution concepts and practices*. Columbus: Grid.

Subhan, M. (1993, September). Not yet at sunset. *Textile Asia*, p. 21.

Sung, K. (1980, September). Protectionism and premia. *Textile Asia*, p. 18.

Sung, K. (1993). *Asian textiles 2000*. Paper presented at Textile Institute Conference, Hong Kong.

Support program the SA mohair industry could do without, A. (1992, December). *Textile Horizons*, p. 25.

Sweet, M. (1994, February). Recent trade treaties likely to stimulate continuing changes in global sourcing of apparel. *Industry, Trade, and Technology Review* (published by the U.S. International Trade Commission), pp. 1–8.

Tahmincioglu, E. (1989, December 11). VICS has a new mission—education. *Women's Wear Daily*, p. 15.

Taiwan Textile Federation. (1992). *Country statement*. Taipei: Author.

Taiwanese firm to construct cotton yarn plant in Malaysia. (1988, June 6). *Daily News Record*, p. 16.

Tanzer, A. (1992, September 28). The Chinese way. *Forbes*, pp. 42–43.

Taussig, F. (1914). *The tariff history of the United States* (6th ed.). New York: G. P. Putnam's Sons.

Taylor, H. (1984, November 9). FTC ready to unveil its new origin label rules. *Daily News Record*, p. 3.

Taylor, H. (1990, August 20). I.T.A. dumping margins on Taiwan sweaters set as high as 24.02%. *Women's Wear Daily*, p. 15.

Taylor, W. (1912). *Factory system and factory acts*. London: no publisher given.

TDA told retailers' problems make importing a necessity. (1985, June 6). *Daily News Record*, pp. 2, 15.

Textile and Clothing Board. (1985, October). *Textile and clothing inquiry: Report to the minister of regional industrial expansion* (Volumes I and II). Ottawa, Canada.

Textile Asia. (October 1973), cited in Aggarwal, 1985.

Textile Institute. (1993). *Asia and world textiles*. Textile Institute Conference Proceedings (Hong Kong). Manchester, England: Author.

Textile professionalism in India (1993, December). *Textile Horizons*, pp. 25–26.

Textile Organon. (monthly). Published by the Textile Economics Bureau.

Textile trade bill: A good fight that isn't over yet. (1985, December 19). *Daily News Record*, pp. 2, 10.

Textiles Committee (GATT). (1992, December 9). *Textiles Committee Meeting: Item A (II): Annual report of the Textiles Surveillance Body, Statement by the Chairman of the TSB*. Report given to the GATT Textiles Committee, Geneva, Switzerland.

Thall, N. & Sibley, W. (1989, April/May). New math for retailers. *Retail Technology and Operations* (WWD/DNR), p. 6.

Thiede, R. (1992). Eastern Europe, the Commonwealth of Independent States, and the Baltic States. In J. Fisher (Ed.), *Geography and development* (pp. 263–331). New York: Macmillan.

Third world countries to remain atop apparel market: UN study. (1987, November 3). *Daily News Record*, p. 7.

Thompson, W. (Ed.). (1978). *The Third World: Premises of U.S. policy*. New Brunswick: Institute for Contemporary Studies.

Tombaugh, P. (1988, January). Retailers boost domestic sources, commit to 'Made in U.S.A.' program. *America's Textiles International*, pp. 90–92.

Toyne, B., Arpan, J., Barnett, A., Ricks, D., & Shimp, T. (1984). *The global textile industry*. London: George Allen & Unwin.

The Trade Partnership. (1993, April). *Retail industry indicators*. Washington, DC: National Retail Institute.

Trela, I., & Whalley, J. (1991). *Internal quota allocation schemes and the costs of the MFA*. Working paper No. 3627. Cambridge, MA: National Bureau of Economic Research.

Tribe, L. (1978). *American constitutional law*. Mineola, NY: Foundation Press.

Truell, P. (1989, August 14). The outlook: Trading places in global commerce. *Wall Street Journal*, p. 1.

Tucker, B. (1984). *Samuel Slater and the origins of the American textile industry, 1790–1860*. Ithaca, NY: Cornell University Press.

Tugman, J. (1989, December). *MRCA Soft Goods Information Service Reports*. Stamford CT: Author.

Tully, S. (1991, December). Now the new new Europe. *Fortune*, pp. 136–142.

U.S. trade facts (1991, May 6). *Business America*, p. 10.

United Nations. (monthly). *Monthly bulletin of statistics*.

United Nations. (1982). Demographic indicators of countries.

United Nations. (1990). *Global outlook 2000*. New York: Author.

United Nations. (1992, December). *NGLS Go-between*, special insert No. 24. New York: Author.

United Nations. (1992). *World economic survey*. New York: Author.

United Nations Centre on Transnational Corporations. (1987). *Transnational corporations in the man-made fibre, textile and clothing industries.* New York: Author.

United Nations Conference on Trade and Development. (1984). *International trade in textiles, with special reference to the problems faced by developing countries.* New York: Author

United Nations Industrial Development Organization. (1982). *Changing patterns of trade in world industry: An empirical study on revealed comparative advantage.* New York: Author.

United Nations Population Fund. (1993). *The state of world population 1993.* New York: Author.

United Nations Statistical Office, various sources.

United States Chamber of Commerce (International Division). (1989). *Europe 1992: A practical guide for American business.* Washington, DC: Author.

United States Chamber of Commerce (International Division). (1992). *A guide to the North American Free Trade Agreement.* Washington, DC: Author.

United States Congress, Office of Technology Assessment. (1987). *The U.S. textile and apparel industry: A revolution in progress.* Washington, DC: U.S. Government Printing Office.

United States Department of Agriculture. (1987). *1987 economic census.* Washington, DC: Author.

United States Department of Agriculture. (1989). *1988–89 U.S. cotton crop.* Washington, DC: Author.

United States Department of Commerce. (annual). *Foreign Regulations Affecting U.S. Textile/Apparel Exports.* Washington: Author.

United States Department of Commerce. (annual). *U.S. Foreign Trade Highlights.* Washington, DC: Author.

United States Department of Commerce. (1985, October). *Highlights of U.S. export and import trade,* FT 990. Washington, DC: Author.

United States Department of Commerce. (1987). *A competitive assessment of the U.S. textile machinery industry.* Washington: U.S. Government Printing Office.

United States Department of Commerce. (1993). Chapters on textiles, apparel, and leather. *U.S. industrial outlook 1993.* Washington, DC: Author.

United States Department of Commerce. (1993, monthly). *United States national trade data bank [CD-ROM].* Washington, DC: Author.

United States Department of Commerce. (1994). *U.S. exports markets (by group).* Unpublished printout.

United States Department of Commerce. (1994). Chapters on textiles, apparel, and leather. *U.S. Industrial Outlook (1994).* Washington, DC: Author.

United States Department of Commerce report. (1994). *Major shippers report by category, 12/93 data.* Printout available from author.

United States Department of Commerce, Bureau of Census. (1985, October). *1982 census of retail trade: Establishment and firms size.* Washington, DC: U.S. Government Printing Office.

United States Department of Commerce, Bureau of Census (1986). *County business patterns (1986), United States.* Washington, DC: U.S. Government Printing Office.

United States Department of Commerce, Bureau of Census (1994). *County business patterns 1994, United States.* Washington, DC: U.S. Government Printing Office.

United States Department of Labor, Bureau of Labor Statistics. (1993, January). *Employment and earnings.* Washington, DC: Author.

United States Department of Labor, Bureau of Labor Statistics. (1993, March). *Employment and wages,* Bulletin 2419. Washington, DC: Author.

United States Department of the Treasury, U.S. Customs Service. (1986, June). *Importing into the United States*. Washington, DC: U.S. Government Printing Office.

United States Department of the Treasury, U.S. Customs Service. (1987, June). *ACS (Automated Commercial System Operations) Overview*. Washington: U.S. Government Printing Office.

United States Executive Office of the President, Office of Management and Budget. (1987). *Standard Industrial Classification Manual*. Washington, DC: Author.

United States International Trade Commission. (annual). *U.S. imports of textiles and apparel under the Multifiber Arrangement: Statistical report through 1987*. Washington, DC: Author.

United States International Trade Commission. (1982, August). *Emerging textile-exporting countries*. (USITC Publication 1273). Washington, DC: Author.

United States International Trade Commission. (1983, September). *The effect of changes in the value of the U.S. dollar on trade in selected commodities*. Washington, DC: Author.

United States International Trade Commission. (1985a, July). *Emerging textile-exporting countries*. (USITC Publication 1716). Washington, DC: Author.

United States International Trade Commission. (1985b, May). *The Multifiber Arrangement, 1980–84*. (USITC Publication 1693). Washington, DC: Author

United States International Trade Commission. (1987a, October). *International Economic Review*.

United States International Trade Commission. (1987b, December). *U.S. global competitiveness: The U.S. textile mill industry*. (USITC publication 2048). Washington, DC: Author.

United States International Trade Commission. (1989). *The effects of greater economic integration within the European Community on the United States*. USITC Publication 2204. Washington, DC: Author.

United States International Trade Commission. (1993a, November). *The economic effects of significant U.S. import restraints*. Investigation No. 332–325. (Publication 2699). Washington, DC: Author.

United States International Trade Commission. (1993b). *Potential impact on the U.S. economy and selected industries of the North American Free-Trade Agreement*. Washington, DC: Author.

United States International Trade Commission. (1994). *Harmonized Tariff Schedule of the United States, 1994*. USITC Publication 2690. Washington, DC: U.S. Government Printing Office.

United States Office of Management and Budget. (1972). *Standard Industrial Classification Manual*. Washington, DC: U.S. Government Printing Office.

United States Senate, Committee on Finance. (1985, July 15). *Textile and Apparel Trade Enforcement Act: Hearing before the Subcommittee on International Trade*. Washington, DC: U.S. Government Printing Office.

United States Senate, Committee on Finance. (1986). *Textile and Apparel Trade Enforcement Act: Hearing before the Subcommittee on International Trade*. (September 12 & 23, 1985). Washington, DC: U.S. Government Printing Office.

United States Trade Representative. (1993). *USTR annual report 1993*. Washington, DC: Author.

Uruguay Round comes to end as 109 trade ministers sign pact. (1994, April 18). *Women's Wear Daily*, p. 27.

U.S. consumers seen gaining by lifting of apparel quotas. (1980, July 25). *Women's Wear Daily*, p. 2.

U.S. ruling rejects mill bid on import subsidies. (1985, March 6). *Women's Wear Daily*, p. 20.

U.S. textile pact with Myanmar is not renewed. (1991, August 1). *Women's Wear Daily*, p. 10.

U.S. trade facts. (1991, May 6). *Business America*, p. 10.

Uzbekistan: Cotton, vital asset. (1992, April). *Textile Asia*, p. 140.

Van Fossan, C. (1985, March 14). *Retail decision-making and direct importing*. Unpublished excerpts from a speech delivered at Kurt Salmon Associates Third Annual Sourcing Breakfast, New York City.

Vernon, R. (1966, May). International investment and international trade in the product life cycle. *Quarterly Journal of Economics*, pp. 190–207.

Vernon, R. (1971). *Sovereignty at bay: The multinational spread of U.S. enterprises*. New York: Basic Books.

Verret, R. (1989, May 25). *The dynamics of competitiveness in the textile industry*. Paper presented at the annual meeting of COMITEXTIL, Brussels, Belgium.

Vietnam hopes and projects. (1992, November). *Textile Asia*, p. 106.

Vigdor, I. (1989, May). The global facts. *Apparel Industry Magazine*, pp. 58–59.

Vigdor, I. (1992a, February). Exporting to South Africa—Part 1. *Bobbin*, pp. 62–66.

Vigdor, I. (1992b, March). Exporting to South Africa—Part 2. *Bobbin*, pp. 128–133.

A voice for free trade. (1987, April). *Textile Asia*, pp. 156–157.

Voice of Industry. (1847, March 26).

Wall, M., & Dickerson, K. (1989). Free trade between Canada and the United States: Implications for clothing and textiles. *Clothing and Textile Research Journal*, 7(2), 1–10.

Wallerstein, I. (1974). *The modern world-system: Capitalist agriculture and the origins of the European world economy in the sixteenth century*. New York: Academic Press.

Wall Street Journal (daily, weekdays). New York: Dow Jones & Company.

Wal-Mart to buy more U.S.-made goods. (1988, November). *Apparel Industry Magazine*, p. 104.

Ward, K. (Ed.). (1990). *Women workers and global restructuring*. Ithaca, NY: ILR Press.

Ware, C. F. (1931). *The early New England cotton manufacture*. Boston: Houghton Mifflin.

Watanabe, M. (1992). *Development of chemical fiber and tendency of new products*. Osaka, Japan: Shikisen Co. Ltd.

Watters, S. (1992, August 19). U.S. to Canada apparel exports triple. *Women's Wear Daily*, p. 17.

Weinberg, S. (1985, September 12). Statement for Jack Shamash, Director, International Silk Association of the United States. In *Hearings before the Subcommittee on Finance, United States Senate*, part 2 of 2, 851–854.

Weiner, E., Foust, D., & Yang, D. (1988, November 7). Why made-in-America is back in style. *Business Week*, pp. 116–120.

Werbeloff, A. (1987). *Textiles in Africa: A trade and investment guide*. London: Alain Charles Publishing Ltd.

Werner International. (1993). *Spinning and weaving labour cost comparisons, summer 1993*. New York: Author.

Wertheimer, B. (1977). *We were there: The story of working women in America*. New York: Pantheon.

Westbrook, J. (1992, September). Taiwan: Setting up abroad. *Textile Asia*, p. 9.

What is culture's role in economic policy? (1986, December 22). *Wall Street Journal*, p. 1.

Wheeler, D., & Mody, A. (1987). Towards a vanishing middle: Competition in the world garment industry. *World Development*, 15(10/11), 1269–1284.

When free trade means higher consumer prices. (1977, September 5). *Business Week*, pp. 61–62.

Whittier, J. (1845). *Stranger in Lowell*. Boston: Waite, Peirce, & Co.

Wightman, R. (1977, October 19). Retailers told to educate consumer on free trade. *Women's Wear Daily*, p. 50.

Wightman, R. (1978, December 15). Consumers save $2 billion by buying imports. *Daily News Record*, p. 1.

Wightman, R. (1981a, February 20). Retailers gird for battle over MFA renewal. *Women's Wear Daily*, p. 1, 27.

Wightman, R. (1981b, March 18). Stores, importers ask for punch on trade policy. *Women's Wear Daily*, p. 10.

Wightman, R. (1984, June 28). Retailers rally for quota cuts. *Women's Wear Daily*, pp. 1, 15.

Wightman, R. (1985a, December 19). House won't attempt to override veto until August 6. *Daily News Record*.

Wightman, R. (1985b, February 5). New coalition forms to battle for import curbs. *Women's Wear Daily*, pp. 1, 19.

Wightman, R. (1985c, March 11). RITAC chief: Quotas costing consumers billions. *Daily News Record*, p. 5.

Wightman, R. (1986a, August 4). Affected industries here call pact a total disaster. *Daily News Record*, pp. 1, 6.

Wightman, R. (1986b, March 20). Study says '84 protection cost US consumers $27 B. *Women's Wear Daily*, p. 14.

Wightman, R. (1986c, September 11). U.S. warns it will exit GATT talks if priority issues omitted. *Daily News Record*, p. 21.

Wightman, R. (1987, January 13). Retail group begins battle against quota bill. *Women's Wear Daily*, p. 10.

Wilner, R. (1987, December 3). Importers need to bone up on Harmonized System regs. *Daily News Record*, pp. 3, 11.

Witchuroj, K. (1993, September). Thailand: Growth slows down. *Textile Asia*, pp. 122–124.

Wolf, M. (1982, January 12). Textile pact: The outlook. *The New York Times*.

Wolf, M. (1983). Managed trade in practice: Implications of the textile arrangements. In W. Cline (Ed.), *Trade policy in the 1980s* (pp. 455–482). Washington, DC: Institute for International Economics.

Wolf, M., Glismann, H., Pelzman, J., & Spinanger, D. (1984). *Costs of protecting jobs in textiles and clothing*. London: Trade Policy Research Center.

Wolff, A., Howell, T., & Noellert, W. (1988). *The reality of world trade in textiles and apparel*. Washington, DC: Fiber, Fabric and Apparel Coalition for Trade.

Woodruff, J., & McDonald, J. (Eds.). (1982). *Handbook of textile marketing*. New York: Fairchild Publications.

World Bank. (annual). *The World Bank atlas*. Washington, DC: Author.

World Bank. (1987). *World development report 1987*. Washington, DC: Author.

World Bank. (1991). *World development report 1991*. Washington, DC: Author.

World Bank. (1992a). *Global economic prospects and the developing countries*. Washington, DC: Author.

World Bank. (1992b). *World development report 1992*. Washington, DC: Author.

World Bank. (1993). *World development report 1993*. Washington, DC: Author.

World Bank. (1993). *The East Asian miracle: Economic growth and public policy*. Washington, DC: Author.

World Bank. (1994). *World development report 1994*. Washington, DC: Author.

Wurth, P. (1981). The arrangement regarding international trade in textiles. *Aussenwirtschaft, 36*(1), 57–69.

Yates, R. (1988, August 7). Trade bill bitter pill for Asian Partners. *Chicago Tribune*, pp. 7–12.

Yeung, K., & Li, S. (1993, May). *Education for a changing world*. Paper presented at the meeting of the Textile Institute, Hong Kong.

Yilmaz, T. (1991, November). *The Turkish clothing industry*. International Apparel Symposium, Istanbul.

Zaracostas, J. (1993, December 8). U.S. works out deal with EC to make smaller cuts in textile, clothing tariffs. *Women's Wear Daily*, p. 4.

Zaracostas, J. (1993, December 10). MFA extended for 1 year. *Daily News Record*, p. 2.

Zwirn, B. (1992, February). Indonesia's burgeoning apparel and textile industries. *Bobbin*, p. 86.

Note: *Daily News Record* changed its official name to *DNR* in 1988. Citations reflect the name used at the time articles were published.

INDEX